Voices from Early China

The *Odes* Demystified

Voices from Early China

The *Odes* Demystified

Geoffrey Sampson

Cambridge
Scholars
Publishing

Voices from Early China: The *Odes* Demystified

By Geoffrey Sampson

This book first published 2020

Cambridge Scholars Publishing

Lady Stephenson Library, Newcastle upon Tyne, NE6 2PA, UK

British Library Cataloguing in Publication Data
A catalogue record for this book is available from the British Library

Copyright © 2020 by Geoffrey Sampson

All rights for this book reserved. No part of this book may be reproduced, stored in a retrieval system, or transmitted, in any form or by any means, electronic, mechanical, photocopying, recording or otherwise, without the prior permission of the copyright owner.

ISBN (10): 1-5275-5212-8
ISBN (13): 978-1-5275-5212-8

The symbol on the title page is the Chinese title of this book—*Shi*, "Poetry"—in the hand of the Tang dynasty monk Huai Su, who called his greatly admired calligraphy "the handwriting of a drunken immortal".

VOICES FROM EARLY CHINA

VOICES FROM EARLY CHINA

Contents

Map of the *Tiw* Kingdom	xvi
Introduction	1
List of Works Consulted	43
A Timeline of Early Chinese History and Myth	46

THE POEMS

   Airs of the States

      State of *Tiw* and Southwards

1	The Fish-Hawk 關雎	47
2	The Spreading Lablab Vine 葛覃	48
3	The Mouse-Ears 卷耳	49
4	Sagging Branches 樛木	50
5	Locusts 螽斯	50
6	The Delicate Peach-Tree 桃夭	51
7	The Rabbit Net 兔罝	52
8	Gathering Plantains 芣苢	52
9	The Wide River Han 漢廣	53
10	On the Embankment of the *Nac* 汝墳	54
11	A Unicorn's Hooves 麟之趾	54

      State of *Daws* and Southwards

12	Magpie and Dove 鵲巢	56
13	Gathering Mugwort 采蘩	57
14	Insects in the Grass 草蟲	57
15	Gathering Water Clover 采蘋	58
16	The Birchleaf Pear 甘棠	59
17	Dew on the Road 行露	60
18	Braids of White Silk 羔羊	61
19	The Sound of Thunder 殷其靁	61
20	The Plum Tree is Shedding 摽有梅	62
21	Little Stars 小星	62
22	Sidestreams of the Yangtze 江有汜	63
23	A Dead Deer in the Fields 野有死麕	64
24	How Rich the Cherry Blossom 何彼襛矣	65
25	Tally-ho! 騶虞	65

      State of *Bùks*

26	Drifting With the Current 柏舟	66
27	The Green Jacket 綠衣	67
28	Swallows 燕燕	68

vii

State of *Bùks*, continued

29	Oh Sun, oh Moon! 日月	69
30	Ceaseless Wind 終風	70
31	The Drumbeat 擊鼓	71
32	The Gentle Breeze 凱風	72
33	Cock Pheasants 雄雉	72
34	The Gourds have their Bitter Leaves 匏有苦葉	73
35	Grey Skies and Rain 谷風	74
36	It's No Use 式微	76
37	The Lablab Beans 旄丘	76
38	The Scorpion Dance 簡兮	77
39	Spring Water 泉水	78
40	The North Gate 北門	79
41	The North Wind 北風	80
42	The Red Flute 靜女	80
43	The New Tower 新臺	81
44	Two Young Men Board Boats 二子乘舟	82

State of *Long*

45	This was Going to be the Right One 柏舟	83
46	The Creeper-Encrusted Wall 牆有茨	83
47	Utterly Submissive 君子偕老	84
48	Among the Mulberry Trees 桑中	85
49	Quails are Fiercely Uxorious 鶉之奔奔	86
50	Building a Palace 定之方中	87
51	Rainbows 蝃蝀	88
52	Look at the Rat 相鼠	89
53	The Ox-Tail Pennon 干旄	90
54	Canter, Horses 載馳	90

State of *Wets*

55	The Inlet in the River 淇奧	92
56	We Attained Ecstasy 考槃	93
57	A Stately Lady 碩人	94
58	A Jolly Man of the People 氓	95
59	Bamboo Rods 竹竿	97
60	The Rough-Potato Plant 芄蘭	98
61	The Wide Yellow River 河廣	99
62	My Warlike Lord 伯兮	99
63	A Fox 有狐	100
64	The Quince 木瓜	101

The Royal Domain

65	The Hanging Millet Ears 黍離	102
66	My Man Has Been Called Up 君子于役	103
67	My Lord is Elated 君子陽陽	103
68	Rising Water 揚之水	104
69	Parched Motherwort 中谷有蓷	105

70	The Slow-Moving Rabbit 兔爰	105
71	Creepers 葛藟	106
72	Gathering Beans 采葛	107
73	The Big Carriage 大車	107
74	Hemp on the Hill 丘中有麻	108

State of *Drengs*

75	The Black Robe 緇衣	109
76	Please, Second-Son 將仲子	109
77	Nobody Left 叔于田	110
78	Driving his Team 大叔于田	111
79	Men of *Tseng* 清人	112
80	Glistening Lamb Fur 羔裘	113
81	Heading for the High Road 遵大路	114
82	The Girl Says "The Cock is Crowing" 女曰雞鳴	114
83	A Girl in my Carriage 有女同車	115
84	Rose-Mallows 山有扶蘇	115
85	Dead Leaves 蘀兮	116
86	The Sly Boy 狡童	116
87	Tucking Up My Skirt 褰裳	117
88	If Only 丰	117
89	By the Sacrifice-Ground 東門之墠	118
90	Wind and Rain 風雨	119
91	The Green Collar 子衿	119
92	Just Me and You 揚之水	120
93	As I Go Out by the East Gate 出其東門	120
94	Dew on the Creepers 野有蔓草	121
95	Two Rivers 溱洧	121

State of *Dzì*

96	Cock-Crow 雞鳴	123
97	Athletic 還	123
98	Within the Gate-Screen 著	124
99	The Sun in the East 東方之日	125
100	Before Dawn 東方未明	126
101	Mount Tai 南山	126
102	Too Large a Field 甫田	127
103	The Hounds' Bells 盧令	128
104	Broken Fish-Traps 敝笱	129
105	Bowling Along 載驅	129
106	*Ay-tzay!* 猗嗟	130

State of *Ngwuy*

107	Delicate Hands 葛屨	132
108	In the *Bun* Marshes 汾沮洳	133
109	Peach Trees in my Garden 園有桃	134
110	On the Wooded Hill 陟岵	135
111	Within the Ten-Acre 十畝之閒	136

State of *Ngwuy*, continued

- **112** Felling Trees 伐檀 — 136
- **113** Sir Rat 碩鼠 — 138

State of *Glang*

- **114** The Cricket 蟋蟀 — 139
- **115** Thorn-Elms 山有樞 — 140
- **116** The Wild River 揚之水 — 141
- **117** The Peppers 椒聊 — 141
- **118** Tied Together 綢繆 — 142
- **119** Solitary 杕杜 — 143
- **120** Lambskin Coat with Leopard Sleeves 羔裘 — 143
- **121** The Bustards' Wings 鴇羽 — 144
- **122** How Could I Say I Had Nothing to Wear 無衣 — 145
- **123** The Pear Tree by the Road 有杕之杜 — 145
- **124** Overgrown Bushes 葛生 — 146
- **125** Gathering Cocklebur 采苓 — 147

State of *Dzin*

- **126** Rumbling Carriages 車鄰 — 148
- **127** Hunting Deer 駟驖 — 149
- **128** The Short War-Chariot 小戎 — 149
- **129** Reeds 蒹葭 — 151
- **130** The *Toung-nùm* Mountains 終南 — 152
- **131** Orioles on the Jujube Trees 黃鳥 — 152
- **132** The Falcon 晨風 — 153
- **133** I'll Share With You 無衣 — 154
- **134** Escorting my Cousin 渭陽 — 155
- **135** What I Was Used To 權輿 — 156

State of *Drin*

- **136** *Ont* Hill 宛丘 — 157
- **137** The Elms of the East Gate 東門之枌 — 157
- **138** Beneath My Rustic Lintel 衡門 — 158
- **139** The Pond by the East Gate 東門之池 — 159
- **140** The Poplars by the East Gate 東門之楊 — 159
- **141** By the Graveyard Gate 墓門 — 160
- **142** Magpies' Nests 防有鵲巢 — 160
- **143** The Moon Comes Out 月出 — 161
- **144** Stump Wood 株林 — 162
- **145** On the Edge of the Marsh 澤陂 — 162

State of *Kòt*

- **146** Lambskin and Fox Fur 羔裘 — 164
- **147** His White Cap 素冠 — 164
- **148** Starfruit Trees 隰有萇楚 — 165
- **149** It Isn't the Wind 匪風 — 166

State of Dzòu

150	The Mayfly 蜉蝣	167
151	Halberds and Clubs 候人	167
152	The Cuckoo 鳲鳩	168
153	Cold Spring Water 下泉	169

State of *Prun*

154	The Seventh Moon 七月	171
155	Tu-whoo! 鴟鴞	175
156	The Eastern Mountains 東山	176
157	Broken Axes 破斧	178
158	Shaping an Axe-Handle 伐柯	179
159	The Netted Fish 九罭	179
160	The Wolf 狼跋	180

Lesser Clarions

161	The Deer Bark 鹿鳴	181
162	The Four Stallions 四牡	182
163	Brilliant Flowers 皇皇者華	183
164	Cherry Trees 常棣	184
165	Trees are Felled 伐木	185
166	Sky Protects You 天保	186
167	Gathering Fiddleheads 采薇	188
168	Bringing Out Our Carriages 出車	190
169	Glossy Pears 杕杜	192
170	Fish in the Traps 魚麗	193
171	Barbel in the South Country 南有嘉魚	194
172	Sedge in the Southern Hills 南山有臺	194
173	Lad's-Love 蓼蕭	196
174	Soaked in Dew 湛露	197
175	The Red Bow 彤弓	197
176	Flourishing Mugwort 菁菁者莪	198
177	The Sixth Moon 六月	199
178	Harvesting White Millet 采芑	201
179	Well-Built Carriages 車攻	203
180	Auspicious Days 吉日	205
181	Wild Geese 鴻雁	206
182	Torches in the Courtyard 庭燎	207
183	The River in Spate 沔水	208
184	A Crane is Calling 鶴鳴	208
185	War Minister 祈父	209
186	The White Colt 白駒	210
187	Don't Peck at My Grain 黃鳥	211
188	Walking in the Countryside 我行其野	212
189	Bright Waters 斯干	212
190	No Sheep 無羊	215
191	The Southern Mountain Crests 節南山	216
192	The First Moon 正月	218

Lesser Clarions, continued

193	Eclipse 十月之交		222
194	Destruction 雨無正		225
195	Sky is Fearsome 小旻		227
196	The Turtle-Dove 小宛		229
197	The Ravens 小弁		230
198	Artful Words 巧言		233
199	What Kind of Man? 何人斯		235
200	The Eunuch's Song 巷伯		236
201	The East Wind 谷風		238
202	Tall Mugwort 蓼莪		238
203	East and West 大東		240
204	The Fourth Moon 四月		242
205	The North Hill 北山		244
206	Don't Try to Shift the Big Waggon 無將大車		245
207	On Campaign 小明		245
208	They Sound the Bells 鼓鍾		247
209	The Vigorous Puncture-Vine 楚茨		248
210	The Extensive Southern Uplands 信南山		252
211	Broad Fields 甫田		253
212	Seed-Time and Harvest 大田		255
213	See the River *Ràk* 瞻彼洛矣		256
214	Glorious Flowers 裳裳者華		257
215	The Grosbeaks 桑扈		258
216	Mandarin Ducks 鴛鴦		259
217	Split Bands 頍弁		259
218	The Linchpin 車舝		261
219	Bluebottles 青蠅		262
220	When the Guests First Take their Places 賓之初筵		263
221	The Fish in the Water-Weed 魚藻		265
222	Picking Beans 采菽		265
223	The Inlaid Bow 角弓		267
224	Willows in Leaf 菀柳		269
225	Gentlemen from the Capital 都人士		270
226	Gathering Lentils 采綠		271
227	Sprouting Millet 黍苗		271
228	Mulberries in the Wetland 隰桑		272
229	White Flowers 白華		273
230	Delicate Orioles 綿蠻		274
231	Melon Leaves 瓠葉		275
232	Lofty Crags 漸漸之石		276
233	The Bloom of the Trumpet Vine 苕之華		277
234	What Grass is not Withered? 何草不黃		277

Greater Clarions

235	*Mun* Dwells on High 文王		279
236	Illuminating the World 大明		281
237	Sinuous 緜		283

VOICES FROM EARLY CHINA

238	Stands of Oaks 棫樸		285
239	The Wooded Slopes of *Gànt* 旱麓		286
240	The Pure Lady *Num* 思齊		287
241	Almighty was God 皇矣		288
242	The Magic Tower 靈臺		292
243	Following in their Footsteps 下武		293
244	King *Mun* is Renowned 文王有聲		295
245	Giving Birth to the People 生民		296
246	Plants by the Roadside 行葦		299
247	We are Drunk 既醉		301
248	Wild Ducks 鳧鷖		302
249	Great Happiness 假樂		303
250	Lord *Rou* 公劉		304
251	Far Away We Dip Water 泂酌		307
252	A Sheltered Slope 卷阿		308
253	The People are Exhausted 民勞		310
254	A Rebuke 板		312
255	Woe to *Un* 蕩		314
256	Dignified Demeanour 抑		317
257	Mulberry Leaves 桑柔		320
258	The Milky Way 雲漢		324
259	The Foundation of *Lhin* and *Pac* 崧高		327
260	*Droungs Shàn* 烝民		330
261	The Greatness of *Gàn* 韓奕		332
262	The Yangtze and the Han 江漢		335
263	Unrest in *Sla* 常武		337
264	We Raise Our Eyes 瞻卬		339
265	Raining Down Death 召旻		342

The Eulogies
  Eulogies of *Tiw*

266	The Pure Temple 清廟		344
267	Sky's Mandate 維天之命		344
268	Clear 維清		345
269	Brilliant and Accomplished 烈文		345
270	Sky Made a Hill 天作		346
271	The First Three Kings 昊天有成命		346
272	We Present Our Offerings 我將		347
273	The Tour of Inspection 時邁		347
274	Awesome and Mighty 執競		348
275	The Millet Lord 思文		349
276	Ministers and Officials 臣工		349
277	Woo-hoo! 噫嘻		350
278	A Flock of Herons 振鷺		350
279	A Bumper Harvest 豐年		351
280	Blind Musicians 有瞽		351
281	In the Depths 潛		352
282	My Godlike Father 雝		352

Eulogies of *Tiw*, continued

283	Appearing Before the Rulers 載見	353
284	I Have a Guest 有客	354
285	King *Mac* 武	355
286	Have Pity for Me, a Small Boy 閔予小子	355
287	My Late Father 訪落	356
288	Be Reverent 敬之	356
289	Nobody Made Me Do It 小毖	357
290	When We Come to Plough 載芟	358
291	Sharp are our Ploughshares 良耜	359
292	His Silken Robe 絲衣	360
293	Your Majesty's Army 酌	360
294	Every Inch a Warrior 桓	361
295	Abundance 賚	361
296	The Destiny of *Tiw* 般	362

Eulogies of *Ràc*

297	Sturdy are the Stallions 駉	363
298	Solid and Strong 有駜	364
299	The Half Moon Pool 泮水	365
300	The Temple of the Mysteries 閟宮	367

Eulogies of *Un*

301	Splendid 那	373
302	Illustrious Ancestors 烈祖	374
303	The Dark Bird 玄鳥	375
304	The Roots of *Un* 長發	376
305	*Mac Tèng* of *Un* 殷武	379

Glossary   381

VOICES FROM EARLY CHINA

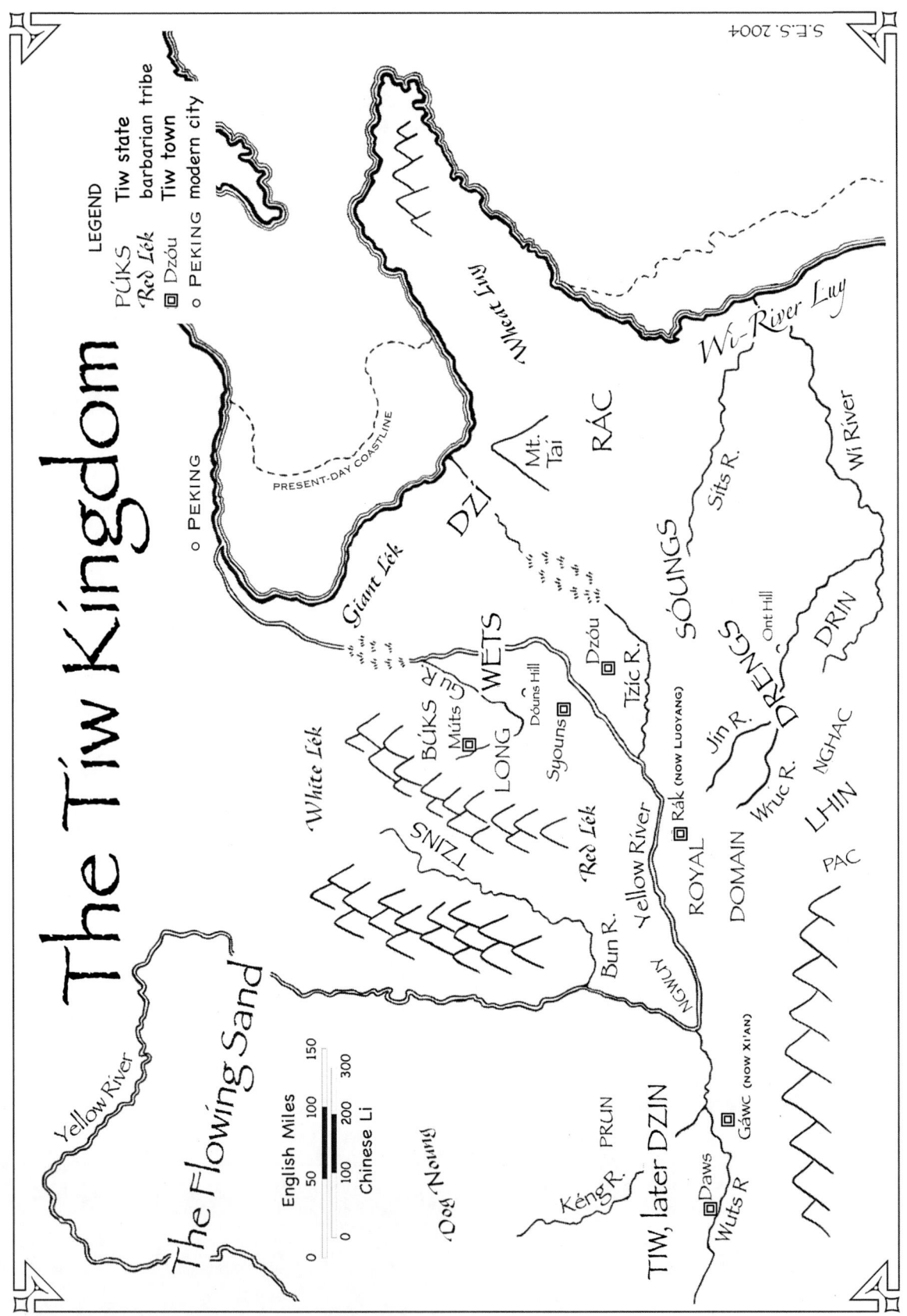

Introduction

This book offers a translation of the Chinese *Book of Odes*, a collection of 305 poems written over roughly the period 1000–600 B.C. It is one of the two earliest monuments of Chinese literature, and one of the oldest literary works in any still-living language—the earlier Odes may perhaps be the oldest such literature of all. The poems provide fascinating vignettes of life in a society almost unimaginably remote from us in time, and many are charming expressions of universal human experience, for instance by women about love problems. (For such early literature it is remarkable how many of the Odes are written by women.) In some cases we have good grounds for identifying the author of an Ode with some individual known to history, but in most cases the authors are unknown.

We also do not know who collected the poems into an anthology. Traditionally this was said to be Confucius (who lived from 551 to 479 B.C.), but that may merely reflect a tendency to attribute anything old to some famous figure. The tradition seems to be based on a brief and inexplicit allusion to two sections of the Odes in the *Analects*, the record of Confucius's sayings by his pupils; but there is evidence that the anthology already existed, in something like its eventual format, when Confucius was a child.

In everyday English, "ode" is usually a jocular synonym for "poem" in general. But technically it means a particular kind of poem—lyrical and personal rather than, say, the kind of long narrative poem called "epic"; and odes are commonly intended to be sung to music. The poems in the *Book of Odes* are not all identical in genre, and we cannot hope to find perfect matches between Chinese literary genres and those of Western literature, but that said, "ode" is a reasonable word for these poems or songs. (I shall use "Odes" with a capital O to refer to the poems in this anthology, as well as to the anthology as a whole.)

Unfortunately, the appeal of the poems has been concealed from a modern readership in many different ways. The aim of this book is to cut through these problems and make the Odes as transparent as they have ever been made, for Western readers and, if it is not presumptuous, also for East Asian readers.

Making the opaque transparent

The language of the *Book of Odes* is recognizably continuous with modern Chinese—any educated Chinese can read many brief passages with understanding. But over almost three millennia the language has changed so much, with many words becoming obsolete, that reading an entire poem is a challenge requiring specialist help. The book has been translated into Western languages several times, but usually by scholars who are more interested in the philological conundrums it poses than in producing straightforward wording that can be read for pleasure. Furthermore the meaning of many Odes has been systematically distorted by contributors to the Chinese commentary tradition and by Western translators.

The world of the Odes was a rather down-to-earth society concerned, much of the time, with very ordinary human predicaments. But, as China later grew into what for much of human history was the richest and most powerful society in the world, it developed a degree of pomposity, and one consequence was that it seemed intolerable for such ancient and revered literature to deal with topics that were less than august. Poems were reinterpreted to be about high politics. Ode 41, read for the plain meaning of its words, is about a poor girl trying to offer her body to a shy young man in exchange for shelter on a bitter winter night; but one commentator decided that it was really about the queen of a defeated nation seeking asylum with the ruler of a neighbouring country. Sometimes editors would modify the text to suit their ideas of morality: Ode 88 has a man waiting for his girlfriend *ghà dàng*, "in the hall", but one editor "corrected" this to *ghà dràng*, "by the gatepost", because it was not proper for him to be in the girl's house. As the centuries passed and theories like these acquired the authority of age, they were accepted as received truths which students of the Odes did not question. Early manuscripts unearthed by archaeologists over the past fifty years make it clear that, in their own time, the Odes were understood in a down-to-earth fashion; the "pompous" or "political" reinterpretations arose later—but, having done so, they became dominant.

I don't mean to suggest that Chinese interpreters of the Odes have regularly distorted their meanings while Western translators get them right. Sometimes it is the other way round. Odes 187 and 188 both appear to be by women who have married men living far from their homes and then found themselves rejected by their husbands, so that their only solution is to go back to their parents. James Legge, who in 1871 first translated the Odes into English (and who became Oxford University's first professor of Chinese), pointed out that the ancient Mao commentary on the Odes, seen as authoritative by many Chinese, explained the poems in just those terms; but according to Legge this interpretation is "too absurd to be dwelt on". For Legge both Odes are about officials who have had to leave the royal court to settle in outlying regions, and find the locals there difficult to deal with. But Legge offers no reason why the Mao interpretation is "absurd". I take it to be correct, and translate accordingly.

(This is not to say that "political" interpretations are always wrong. Ode 44, read for the surface meaning of its words alone, would make little sense, but when one hears the piece of history that lies behind it the poem becomes meaningful and poignant. Where traditional interpretations in terms of historical events are plausible, my translations reflect them—I only reject them when they seem redundant and forced.)

Much of the aesthetic impact which these poems must have had on their original readers or hearers stems from the "speech music" they incorporate. Most obviously, they rhyme—the *Book of Odes* is the earliest known rhyming poetry in any language. But the sounds of Chinese have changed over the millennia, as happens with all languages, and one consequence is that if an Ode is read in modern Chinese pronunciation the rhyming is largely destroyed. And even when rhyme-words in the Odes continue to rhyme today, their effect has been dissipated by the sound-changes just mentioned. The effect of rhyme depends on rhyming words not being too frequent, so that when lines do end with words that match in this way, they command attention and create a feeling of rightness. Unlike the Old Chinese of the Odes, modern Chinese has so few different sounds that any word rhymes with an enormous number of others, and the impact of rhyme is lost. (Only two consonants can end a modern Chinese syllable, *n* and *-ng*; all other syllables end in vowels, but there are effectively only four different vowels, though some of them can combine as diphthongs. The sound system of Old Chinese was much richer.) Rhyme apart, the Odes as they originally sounded contained a great deal of assonance and alliteration which were an important ingredient of their poetic value—and which, again, has been lost in the modern language. This book shows the Old Chinese sounds alongside the English translations, so readers can appreciate the poems for their speech-music as well as their meaning.

For present-day Western readers, these poems are far more accessible than the Chinese poetry which is commonly translated. Westerners who know anything of Chinese poetry are most likely to have encountered the lyric poets of the Tang and Song dynasties (seventh to thirteenth centuries A.D.)—writers such as Li Bo (sometimes spelled Li Bai) and Bo Juyi. That literature is subtle and beautiful, for those who understand it, but understanding it is difficult. China under the Tang had been a mighty and complex civilization for a very long time. (The Tang capital was easily the richest and most technologically advanced city anywhere in the world; the West only caught up far later, through our Industrial Revolution.) Poets and their audiences took for granted a large shared stock of historical and literary knowledge, and writers drew on this freely to achieve their own literary effects; as a result, many of these effects are lost on us. The China of the Odes by contrast was a young civilization that had had little time to build up a resource of cultural references. The poems in this book speak to us directly about human beings and the natural world. Their wording perhaps sometimes borders on the naive—this is not poetry with the intellectual subtlety of a Shakespeare or a Donne. But the directness makes it clear; and how many opportunities do we have to see directly into the hearts of men and women who lived almost three millennia ago, naive or not?

Furthermore, poetry of the Tang and Song used metrical effects which depended on the "tones" or pitch-patterns of words which are a distinctive feature of modern Chinese, but which Westerners find it hard to hear. The Old Chinese of the Odes was not a tone language, and its sounds are easier for Western ears to grasp.

One large barrier to Westerners wanting to engage with these poems is the nature of Chinese script, which assigns an individual written graph or "character" to each word, rather than spelling words out alphabetically. A Western reader may glimpse a little of the visual beauty of Chinese writing, but in all other respects it is entirely opaque. Even when two lines of poetry do rhyme, a Western reader would have no way of knowing it. And the script of the Odes is problematic for Chinese readers. Many words, and hence the graphs used to write them, are now long-obsolete; and the poems were written centuries before Chinese script was standardized, so words which do survive in the modern language are often written with graphs which are still used, but not for the words intended in the poem.

In this book, each Ode is rendered into straightforward, modern, and I hope readable English, representing what the poet actually seems to have been saying while ignoring political "reinterpretations". And below each translated verse I spell out alphabetically how the poems originally sounded. Chinese and Western scholars have put a great deal of effort over recent centuries into working out how Old Chinese was pronounced, and in the 21st century there is sufficient scholarly consensus to make this a meaningful exercise. I discuss my spelling system for Old Chinese later in this Introduction, for readers interested in the details. But many readers who care about poetry, or about the origins of Chinese culture, while having little special interest in phonetic matters may be content to assume that whatever precise sounds my Old Chinese spellings stood for, they were something roughly like what the spellings suggest at first sight. That will actually work quite well.

Old Chinese was an extremely simple language, with none of the apparatus of inflected word-endings, regular and irregular verbs, and so forth, which bedevils the study of European languages. Chinese was essentially a grammar-free language: an Odes line is a sequence of lumps of meaning, and the hearer or reader fills in the relationships between the lumps using common sense and hints from context. Thus a Western reader who is struck by some line or verse and wants to grasp how it works can look up the meanings of the words in the Glossary beginning on p. 381, and then has just about all the information needed to see how the passage means what my translation says it means.

For Chinese readers the essence of the poems lies in their written form, so alongside the alphabetically-transcribed Old Chinese I show the lines in Chinese script. But where it is clear that the usual editions of the Odes represent a word by a graph which is not the one which later became standard for that word, I give the standard graph rather than the graph found in commonly-available editions of the poems. (This is one justification for my presumptuous suggestion that the book makes the Odes more accessible than before even to Chinese-speakers.)

To achieve these various things I have of course had to soak myself in the relevant scholarly literature. But I have studied this material in order for my readers to have no need to do so.

Deeper roots than ours

It is worth taking a moment to reflect on how very old these poems are, in terms of history with which most of us are more familiar. The youngest Odes were written some 2,600 years ago. England was not yet England then: it would be a thousand years before the Angles and Saxons came to Britain. For that matter, Britain was probably not yet Britain; it is unclear when the Celts or "Ancient Britons" arrived, but the scholarly consensus seems to place it rather later than the Odes. We know little about the people who lived in Britain before the Celts; they appear to have been nomadic herdsmen. We have no idea what language or languages they spoke, or whether these were related to any languages known to history—they certainly had no idea of writing. The classical civilizations of Europe were only just getting off the ground. This was when the Greeks first learned to use the alphabet; the legendary date of the foundation of Rome by Romulus and Remus was 753 B.C.

In China, matters were different. The Chinese led settled lives; many lived in walled towns. Those who could afford it got about in carriages. Their culture was already sophisticated, politically, technically, and artistically. They spoke an earlier version of the language which their descendants in the same territory speak today: Chinese. And we know these things because they have told us. Before the time of the earliest Odes, Chinese was already a written language. The script used to write Chinese at that period looks superficially unlike modern Chinese writing—later changes in writing materials caused curves to give way to straight lines and angles, leading to a more abstractly stylized appearance; but a brief examination quickly reveals how one is a direct evolution from the other.

We must not exaggerate how far China had moved from barbarism towards civilization. Henri Maspero warns us that "we should not imagine the [ruling dynasty's] royal court, even at the height of its power in the late ninth and early eighth centuries, to be how it was depicted in literature composed many centuries later: a place of refined civilization, philosophy, and hierarchical ritualism. On the contrary, the early texts show it as still half-savage." This mixture of advanced culture with real barbarity (see Ode 131, for instance) is one aspect of the fascination of the Odes. At times the English of my translations may strike readers as too colloquial to suit ancient poetry, but at the Odes period blunt colloquial language was probably the only language available for most topics.

While the *Book of Odes* is among the world's oldest literary productions, it is far from being the oldest of all. The poetry of Sumer (in what is now Iraq), for instance the epic tales of Gilgamesh, date to the third millennium B.C. But the Sumerians and their language vanished from the historical record many centuries before the earliest Odes. China is the oldest civilization in the world which continues to flourish in essentially unbroken continuity today.

The Odes in roman script

Some scholars see spelling these poems out in their original pronunciation as a pointless waste of effort. I have known this view to be expressed by one of the same linguists who have devoted a great deal of their own effort to working out what that pronunciation was, without themselves doing anything with this knowledge. To me it seems misguided.

Already a thousand years ago (by which time the sounds of Chinese had already changed greatly), we find a scholar publishing a book, *The Rhyme-Mender*, which tried to reconstruct the original pronunciation of the Odes—in an unsophisticated fashion by modern standards, but a creditable first attempt; and another scholar commented that "only since the completion of the *Rhyme-Mender* can the Odes be seen as poetry". For anyone interested in poetry as a genre of literature, there is no way to get a feeling for the nature of these very early examples without saying some of them over to oneself in the jingly rhythms and sounds, or at least an approximation to the sounds, that the poets who composed them heard. One hears how central rhyme and assonance are to many of them—but also how tentative these early poets often were in their use of these effects. Sometimes an Ode will begin with a regular rhyme-scheme, but then after a verse or two it will be abandoned in favour of a different scheme, or no scheme at all. Metre is sometimes very regular, but sometimes it is violated for no immediately-obvious reason. In some cases there are reasons which are not obvious, and I return to that later. But in other cases the reason may have been simply that there were not yet any established conventions—these poets were feeling their way towards creating conventions, and had no fixed ideas about what might be permissible and what not. Some Odes use many "rhymers and chimers"—two-syllable compounds which gain expressiveness through alliteration or assonance, like *trent-tront* "toss and turn", or *dzòuy-ngòuy* "craggy". In present-day Mandarin Chinese it is not just that these particular compounds no longer alliterate: the language scarcely has such expressions at all. (Some other East Asian languages, for instance Vietnamese, use many such compounds today, but in Mandarin they have vanished.)

In the case of the Odes, the original pronunciation is all the more important because the sounds of Chinese are arguably not naturally suited to poetry: few would describe it as a mellifluous language. Consonants in European languages often bridge between one syllable and the next; in a word like *analogy*, there is no saying whether the consonants belong to the syllables which precede them or to those which follow—they belong equally to both. Chinese is and probably always has been different: syllables are sharply separated with no bridging consonants, giving the language a staccato character—a machine-gun rather than a violin. A poet must work with the material available to him, but it would be particularly regrettable in the case of this language if we could not hear even those phonetic effects that were available to the poets.

To my mind, in order to appreciate the Odes as literature rather than merely a set of philological puzzles, it is crucial to hear how they originally sounded. In the 21st century we are fortunate that this is now possible, not perfectly of course, but adequately for the purpose. Only this way can we get a feeling for what the poems were for their original audience.

And in any case, there is something magical in hearing people speaking to us across the millennia in something close to their own voices.

Names

A difficult decision I had to make was how to write names which occur in the Odes. Figures from Chinese history or Chinese mythology crop up in other English-language books and documents, where they will be spelled in terms of their modern pronunciation. For instance, the dynasty which ruled China over the Odes period (and which is frequently named within the poems) was, in terms of the language which its inhabitants spoke, the *Tiw* dynasty. But we in the 21st century know it as the 'Zhou' dynasty, using the modern pronunciation of the same word (it means something like "encircle"). Readers with an interest in Chinese matters will have read about it as the Zhou dynasty elsewhere.

When names occur within the poems, which are here spelled out in their Old Chinese pronunciation, they must be shown in their Old Chinese form along with all other words: the Zhou dynasty must be spelled "*Tiw*". But what about the English translations which appear above them? Should *Tiw* in a verse of Chinese be shown as 'Zhou' in the English translation?

If we were dealing with only a handful of names, all as famous and therefore likely to be encountered elsewhere as *Tiw*/Zhou, that might be the best solution. But there are many names in the Odes, mostly far less well known than that one. And Western readers often find Chinese names confusing even when they appear in a consistent alphabetic form. They contain no links to familiar names which might help them to stick in a Western mind. To display Odes names in alternative forms would risk readers drowning in a sea of confusion.

Indeed this understates the problem. There have been many alternative systems for spelling modern Chinese sounds using our alphabet, and the system treated as standard has changed during my working life. Many readers will remember that the (in)famous Chairman Mao, who now appears in newspapers and magazines as 'Mao Zedong', used to be 'Mao Tsê-tung'—this is the same name, pronounced the same way, but spelled using a different romanization system. The Zhou dynasty used to be spelled 'Chou', and plenty of books using the 'Chou' spelling are still in print.

Consequently I have adopted a policy which might seem questionable, but which I believe is the most satisfactory solution. Everything in the body of this book, both in the Old Chinese versions of the Odes and in the English translations, is spelled as Old Chinese. The *Tiw* dynasty is always and only the *Tiw* dynasty. The reader will inhabit a wholly Old Chinese world containing exclusively Old Chinese names, minimizing the risks of confusion.

For readers who are themselves Chinese this might seem a poor solution. They know most of the names, in their modern form, and they are no more likely than Western readers to know how they sounded in Old Chinese. But for a Chinese the essence of a name lies in its written form. When a Chinese reader encounters the name *Tiw*, he will probably not know what it stands for, but he can glance across to the line in Chinese script and see that *Tiw* stands for 周. Few Western readers can read Chinese script, but they are catered for in another way. My Glossary lists names as well as ordinary words, so when a Western reader wants to check how some personal or place name appears in other publications, he can look the name up in its Old Chinese form and see its modern spelling. That way, the information is available to those who want it, without being routinely obtruded on readers to their likely confusion.

I make just a few exceptions to this policy for major and enduring geographical names. Within a passage of English it would be silly to call the Yellow River and the Yangtze by their Old Chinese names, *Gày* and *Kròng*, and I use the modern names also for the rivers Han (Old Chinese *Hàns*), which gave the Chinese race its name, and Wei (Old Chinese *Wuts*), whose valley was the heartland of Chinese culture at this period. (Three different rivers mentioned in the Odes all have names pronounced 'Wei' in the modern language, but in my translations 'Wei' will always represent the *Wuts*.) Because the Yellow River was the chief river of the Odes world, rather than spelling its name out in full I often render it as just "River" with a capital R. Also, I use the modern name Mount Tai for the great 5000-foot mountain of eastern China, Old Chinese *Thàts*.

(The Yangtze is larger than the Yellow River, but at the beginning of the *Tiw* dynasty the Yangtze was at the extreme southern edge of the Chinese cultural area, if it had reached that far—modern authorities differ. Some geographical references, in Ode 262 for instance, would be easier to understand if *Kròng* at that early period referred to some river other than the Yangtze, but I have not pursued this idea.)

Another potential source of confusion is that Chinese people often used different names at different stages of their lives or for different purposes; major figures are often known to history by names bestowed on them after their death. So far as possible, in this book I use just one consistent name for any individual, even if it was not the name he used at the relevant time.

Old Chinese spellings will always appear in italics, even when they occur as names within a passage of English, while modern Chinese spellings will always be in roman, distinguished from surrounding wording where necessary by single inverted commas. Names from times later than the *Tiw* period will always be written as modern Chinese.

A sketch of early Chinese history

To understand what is happening in the Odes, we need to know just a little about the time when they were written. (Readers may find the timeline on p. 46 helpful.)

The *Tiw* dynasty, the longest-lasting of the many Chinese dynasties, probably began in 1040 B.C. I have to say "probably", because there are question marks about Chinese dates earlier than the ninth century B.C. There is conflicting evidence about the correlation between Chinese and Western dating systems, and dates differing by as much as a century have been proposed for the battle of Herdsman's Heath (*Muk Lac*, in modern Chinese 'Muye'), when the leader of the *Tiw* people conquered the preceding *Un* dynasty. In this book I follow the dating scheme proposed by David Nivison, who appears to have gone further than any before him towards reconciling the historical sources. I shall quote Nivison's dates on the assumption that they are correct, without complicating things by mentioning alternative theories.

(Since almost every date in this book will be a date B.C. rather than A.D., I shall omit "B.C." except where confusion might be possible.)

The *Un* dynasty was founded in 1554 by a man called *Lhàng*. That dynasty had alternative names: the name *Un* was taken from the place in Henan province where the dynastic capital was located in its later years, but it was sited earlier at a place called *Lhang*, and this name is also used for the dynasty. Sometimes the combinations *Lhang-Un* or *Un-Lhang* are used. For Western readers one name is enough to deal with, and since the name *Lhang* invites confusion with its founder *Lhàng*, I shall always call the dynasty *Un*.

Quite a number of Odes relate, centrally or indirectly, to the conquest of the *Un* dynasty by *Mac*, who ruled the fief of *Tiw*. Through this conquest *Mac* and his descendants became kings of China, and their new dynasty was named *Tiw* after *Mac*'s people.

Mac's father *Mun* is also standardly called "king". *Mun* never ruled all China, only the fief called *Tiw*, but as *Mac*'s father he is regarded as the founder of the *Tiw* royal dynasty. Some Odes, particularly 241 and 244, are worded as though *Mun* was king—not, I believe, because the poet was ignorant of history, but because *Mun* was seen as in some sense the rightful though not *de facto* king. (*Mun* had been leading an expedition which might have become an attack on *Un* at the time of his death.) To reduce confusion, my translations usually omit "king" with names such as *Mun*'s where historically it can only be seen as a courtesy title.

The tribe or nation who called themselves *Tiw* originated (according to their own account, at least—there is controversy among archaeologists) to the west of the Chinese cultural area. After wanderings which I shall discuss with Ode 250, by the time of *Mun*'s grandfather, *Tànt*, the *Tiw* were living at a place called *Prun*—a name which in its modern pronunciation, Bin, lives on today in the place-name Binxian (changed in 2018 to Binzhou), near the Shaanxi–Gansu border about seventy miles north-west of modern Xi'an. (The original *Prun* may have been further north-west, in eastern Gansu.) *Tànt* is often referred to in the Odes as *Thàts wang*, "Great king" (like *Mun*, "king" by posthumous courtesy); again to reduce confusion, my translations always call him *Tànt*.

Some time in the twelfth century, *Tànt* led his people southwards to resettle in the area of Mount *Ge* (modern Qishan), upstream from Xi'an; and when *Mun* eventually came to rule the *Tiw*, he moved their base again, east to *Phoung* in the Xi'an area, which became the nucleus of the *Tiw* state. (After *Mac* conquered *Un*, he would shift the *Tiw* capital yet again to *Gàwc*, just on the other side of the *Phoung* river.) By the time they were living in the Xi'an area if not before, the *Tiw* were a vassal state subordinate to the rule of *Un* further east.

The last *Un* king, *Drouc*, was by all accounts a supremely wicked man—like Milton's Satan, all the worse because a corrupted version of a ruler who had originally been particularly able. (*Drouc* was not the name the king used in life: it was given him by his conquerors. It means "crupper", the part of a horse's harness that gets filthy because it passes by the horse's anus.) The tales of *Drouc*'s wickedness that circulated after the *Tiw* conquest are of course victors' history, but whether exaggerated or not they became, and remained ever after, the accepted account. For instance, *Drouc* and his principal wife are said to have got off on watching prisoners tortured to death in imaginative ways.

For vassals like *Mac*'s father *Mun*, *Drouc* made life difficult by ignoring his responsibilities as sovereign. *Mun* tried, but failed, to persuade *Drouc* to change his ways. After *Mac* succeeded him, he led a successful rebellion, defeating the *Un* forces at Herdsman's Heath near the *Un* capital—now a district within Xinxiang in northern Henan province. When Herdsman's Heath was lost, *Drouc* set fire to his palace and died in the flames. (His corpse was found, and *Mac* dedicated *Drouc*'s head and the heads of his wives as a sacrifice in the *Tiw* ancestral temple.)

Only two years later in 1038, with the new dynasty far from firmly established, *Mac* died, leaving as heir a boy, *Deng*. *Mac*'s younger brother, known to history as the Duke of *Tiw*, took over as regent. (I normally use lower case for titles like "king", "duke", but I shall capitalize "Duke of *Tiw*" to make clear that this particular individual is meant.) It was really the Duke of *Tiw* who put the new régime on a firm footing, mopping up holdout *Un* loyalists, and dealing with opposition from other brothers who felt that one of them had a better claim to the regency. (Even the need for a regent may have been "victor's history". The standard account describes *Deng* as still a baby when his father died, but recent research argues that he was in his early twenties. Be that as it may, the Duke of *Tiw* succeeded in establishing his rule, before retiring in *Deng*'s favour in 1031.)

The names of "king" *Mun* and king *Mac* echo and re-echo through the later, more political sections of the Odes, and they have continued to do so in Chinese discourse ever since. (In modern pronunciation, king *Mun* and king *Mac* become respectively 'Wen wang' and 'Wu wang'.)

Un was not the earliest dynasty recognized by Chinese historians. Before *Un* there was the *Ghàc* dynasty, founded by a man called *Wac* in 1934. (And even before *Wac* there are lists of rulers reaching back into the third millennium, though these are legendary rather than historical—the "Yellow Emperor" is claimed to have reigned for a hundred years.) *Wac*, whose name occurs frequently in the Odes, is seen as the founder not just of a dynasty but of Chinese civilization in general, by virtue of taming the Yellow River floodwaters which have always created large problems for life in North China. *Wac*, and the *Ghàc* dynasty, are commonly regarded today as purely legendary—but then, one of the men who taught me Chinese history in the 1960s pointed out that when he was a student, the *Un* dynasty was equally seen as legendary, until archaeology demonstrated that it had been real enough. Whether *Wac* was mythical, or a real person whose achievements have been embroidered down the millennia, who can say?

(All this early history or legend is set out in a book called 'Shu Jing', the *Book of Documents*, one of the two earliest monuments of Chinese literature—the Odes being the other. Whatever the truth of the matter, much of the Shu Jing reads like factual—indeed often rather tedious—historical reportage, rather than like the legends about Theseus, Odysseus, and the Greek gods.)

The *Tiw* kings ruled a large area, perhaps 600 by 600 miles at the start of the dynasty, of what we now know as North China. Like the *Un* kings before them, and like the kings of the European Middle Ages, they could not administer such a large territory centrally. They directly ruled a much smaller "royal domain" surrounding their capital *Gàwc*, and divided the rest into fiefs which they granted to relatives and henchmen to rule as their vassals. As in the European Middle Ages, this vassal status was maintained for instance by succession to a fief not being automatic: when a ruler died, his son had to apply to the king to be confirmed as heir (we see a case in Ode 261). Vassal rulers were expected to attend the royal court regularly to demonstrate their loyalty.

What inevitably happens under a feudal system like this is that the subordinate rulers strive to assert increasing independence from their overlord. That is certainly what happened in *Tiw* history. Also in Ode 261, we find the king of the time appealing to a newly-confirmed vassal to help him deal with other vassals who were failing to show up at the *Tiw* court as they should.

Eventually, a vassal ruler in alliance with a non-Chinese tribe deposed and killed king *Iw*, who had come to the throne in 783. (Here and elsewhere, I aim to date reigns from the year the respective king actually succeeded, rather than from the official beginning of his reign, which was normally two or three years later to allow for a period of mourning the dead king.) *Tiw* society was polygamous, but a king's principal wife, whose son would normally be heir, was in a separate, superior position to his other wives and concubines. The story goes that *Iw* became so infatuated with one of his concubines, the outstandingly lovely *Bòu Sluc*, that he put aside his queen, and deprived her son of the succession in favour of *Bòu Sluc*'s son. This of course infuriated the queen's father, ruler of the fief of *Lhin*, who made an alliance with the "Dog *Noung*" tribe, longstanding thorns in the side of *Tiw*. Their chance came when *Iw*'s infatuation led him into another folly. *Bòu Sluc* was depressive, but on one occasion she delighted *Iw* by bursting into laughter when a false alarm led vassal rulers to rush to defend the king, only to find that they had arrived on a fool's errand. *Iw* then repeatedly had alarm beacons fired in hope of amusing *Bòu Sluc* further, so the vassals began ignoring them; in 771 this enabled *Iw*'s father-in-law and allies to attack an undefended capital and kill *Iw*.

The *Tiw* dynasty still had half a millennium to run. An early *Tiw* king had established a subsidiary capital at *Ràk*, near modern Luoyang, 200 miles to the east of Xi'an; now *Iw*'s original heir *Breng* was established as king ruling from *Ràk*, further and therefore safer from potentially threatening tribes. (The *Tiw* dynasty is known as "Western *Tiw*" up to 771 and "Eastern *Tiw*" thereafter.) But Eastern *Tiw* kings never recovered the degree of authority that Western *Tiw* kings possessed. Kingship faded into a religious more than political concept, and the fiefs of Western *Tiw* became more like independent countries. (In discussing Chinese history the term "state" is commonly used as a neutral word covering both the vassal fiefdoms and countries only nominally under *Tiw* suzerainty.)

From a cultural point of view, on the other hand, China went from strength to strength. The "classic" age of Chinese civilization fell within the Eastern *Tiw* period.

Fealty to Eastern *Tiw* did not even mean that nominally-subordinate rulers respected one another's independence. As the Eastern *Tiw* continued, states became increasingly inclined to make war on each other, to enlarge their territory or to annex neighbouring states. Eventually one semi-tribal state in the far west, *Dzin*, succeeded in conquering one Chinese state after another; it took the *Tiw* royal domain in 256, and by 221 *Dzin* (in modern Chinese, Qin) controlled the entire Chinese cultural territory, from a capital which had returned to the Xi'an area. The *Dzin* king set out to centralize Chinese rule, constructing a massive new road system and standardizing things like weights and measures China-wide; and he aimed to make the beginning of his new dynasty a "Year 1" of Chinese history, ordering all existing books to be burned except for those concerning useful practical information about agriculture and the like, and books about the *Dzin* royal family. Hundreds of scholars were put to death. (Modern scholarship claims that individual copies of books were preserved in the royal library, but adds that these were largely destroyed in fighting when the new dynasty fell.) The Odes were a particular target for destruction, because the *Dzin* ruler feared comparisons with the ideal rulers of the past described in some of the poems.

Not satisfied with the title "king", the new ruler invented a novel, godlike title, declaring himself 'Qin Shi Huangdi', First Emperor of Qin. Qin sounds like English "chin": it is the word from which we derive the name China.

As it turned out, the Qin dynasty was one of the shortest in Chinese history—it survived just a few years after the First Emperor's death in 210. The leader of one rebellious group subdued all rivals for the throne by 202 and established a new dynasty called Han, which lasted, with one brief interruption, for more than four centuries. The Qin cultural holocaust was reversed; many significant texts were rescued from the Burning of the Books, either because scholars had hidden their copies (at great personal risk), or because individuals had memorized texts. (The Odes are said to have been reconstructed in the latter way. Modern scholarship questions this, though we shall see occasional hints that it was so and that memories were not always perfect.) But the Qin imperial system was retained. With only occasional periods when it was split into two or three separate polities, China continued to be a centralized state ruled by an emperor until A.D. 1911.

A fluid geography

Each Ode in the first half of the book is associated with a particular place, and place-names are frequent within the Odes. The map on p. xvi is included to lend concrete reality to the landscape of the poems (I thank Sophia Sampson for drawing it). But even if I had spelled the names in their modern form rather than as Old Chinese, it would be useless to look for them in a modern atlas. Few are still used.

The map shows rough locations for the principal places mentioned, but it would be meaningless to plot exact boundaries of the states. Some were large territories, others were just one town and the countryside around it. As the decades passed, one state would expand its territory at the expense of a neighbour; a powerful state might swallow up a weak one, or new states might be carved out of an existing state's territory. In recent centuries, China has been divided into "provinces" with two-syllable names—even if a modern province roughly coincides in territory with a *Tiw*-dynasty state, its name will be unrelated to the single-syllable name of the latter. When I describe a place mentioned in the Odes as "in X", where X is a two-syllable province name, this is shorthand for "within the territory nowadays called X province".

(This may be the place to mention two confusing features of modern Chinese geography. Two adjacent modern provinces, which between them cover much of the territory of *Tiw* China, have names which differ only in the tones of their first syllables; this is reflected arbitrarily in romanized spelling by doubling the vowel in one case: Shanxi lies to the east of Shaanxi. And Chinese provinces, or most of them, are divided into "cities"—'shi'—which in turn are subdivided into 'xian', standardly translated as "counties"; so the relationship between these latter terms is the reverse of what it is in English. The smallest labelled points on a general map of China, by reference to which I aim to locate settlements mentioned in the Odes, are normally "counties", which contain towns and villages as well as countryside.)

In Europe, Athens and Rome are modern capitals on ancient sites, and classical buildings can still be seen there; but Chinese towns were not built to last. There were no cathedrals. A "palace" was not an imposing stone building visible to any passer-by; it was a walled park or compound, containing various wooden halls which were certainly more spacious and better-appointed than the homes of subjects, but were not built on a monumental scale. (There was little need for them to impress, because only the élite and their servants would ever see them.) We know where some towns mentioned in the poems were, but often they do not coincide with present-day settlements.

Even the principal geographical feature of the Chinese homeland, the Yellow River, shares this character of impermanence. This river is very different from any river of Europe. It is called Yellow because of the heavy burden of loess soil its waters carry, on their way southwards from what we call the Gobi Desert and in Old Chinese was called *Riw Shày*, the "Flowing Sand". As the river reaches the plains, the soil settles out so that the bed of the river is constantly rising, and the banks have to be built up artificially to contain it. (At present, in what was the Eastern *Tiw* royal domain, the river bed is more than fifty feet higher than the surrounding land.) Sooner or later, in times of storm and high water, the river has repeatedly broken out, destroying many lives and livelihoods and finding some new way to the sea. Currently, the mouth of the river is on the Gulf of Bohai. Before A.D. 1852 it was three hundred miles further south, on the other side of the hilly Shandong peninsula. There have been times in Chinese history when the Yellow River was a tributary of the Yangtze, far to the south. At the time of the Odes, conversely, it formed a vast delta whose main branch reached the sea well to the north of its present-day course, somewhere near modern Peking. (A secondary branch, called the *Tzìc*, was then one of the great rivers of China; it no longer exists.) The coastline itself has moved: the North China plain is the product of these continuing river-borne deposits, and in the *Tiw* dynasty the coast ran a hundred miles or more inland from its present position.

The fact that Chinese society was organized in a centralized fashion from an early period may not have been a matter of chance or individual rulers' preferences: it is often seen as a consequence of this property of the Yellow River. Civilized life could only develop in the North China plain if society was capable of requiring its members to co-operate in large-scale flood control efforts, so Chinese society had to be quite authoritarian. There is good reason why the culture-hero *Wac* is known principally for having tamed the floods.

The historical continuity of China is a continuity of culture. Physically, the country is a palimpsest on which Nature and successive dynasties have written, erased, and rewritten, again and again.

China's neighbours

On all sides of the collection of culturally-Chinese states lived various tribal societies. (At the beginning of the *Tiw* dynasty even the east coast was mainly inhabited by tribesmen; only in one small area did a Chinese state reach the sea.) The situation was very different from the corresponding stage of Western civilization. We think of our civilization as stemming from the Greeks and the Romans. The Greeks coined the word "barbarian" for members of alien societies (people who babbled "bar-bar" rather than uttering proper Greek words); but they knew that the Egyptians had a high civilization before themselves, and they had to confront the equally developed civilization of Persia. Educated Romans were soaked in Greek culture as well as their own; and the Roman Empire eventually adopted the worship of a Palestinian Jew, from a culture whose holy books dated back earlier than anything in Latin. At the other end of the Eurasian landmass there was nothing like this cultural diversity. Chinese civilization really was the only game in town. Today we think of Japan as an advanced society, technologically ahead of China until quite recently. But there was not even any writing in Japan before about A.D. 400, a time when China had been a literate society for almost two thousand years (perhaps a full two thousand—the beginnings of Chinese writing are lost from the historical record). Furthermore, that first writing in Japan was in Chinese, by Korean scribes recruited by the Japanese court to keep records. Korea was more advanced than Japan, but its culture was almost entirely derived from China, and it used Chinese as its written language. Korea maintained political independence, but culturally it aimed to be a "Sohwa", "Little China". On the Chinese mainland, the tribes surrounding China had scarcely emerged into history at all.

While their tribal neighbours remained unassimilated to Chinese ways, there was nothing "politically correct" about the Chinese attitude to them. Many names of tribes are written with Chinese graphs containing a "dog" or an "insect" element—we have seen that the name of one tribe actually included the Chinese word for "dog". But if they did assimilate and acknowledge Chinese suzerainty, the Chinese were happy to accept them as part of the family and treat their rulers as leaders of new Chinese states. While the *Tiw* dynasty proceeded, the Chinese cultural area expanded, particularly southwards where there were few natural barriers. Sometimes there were elements of compulsion in this expansion (see Ode 263 for instance), but often tribal leaders will have found it a good bargain to gain the benefits of Chinese civilization in exchange for a duty to make occasional visits to the Chinese court, taking products of the tribal society as tribute, but receiving presents from the emperor as rewards for loyalty (presents which may often have been more valuable than the tribute).

Thus the overall pattern at any time was a group of thoroughly Chinese states round the royal, or later imperial, capital, surrounded by a penumbra of states which were still semi-tribal, and beyond them areas untouched by Chinese civilization. The central area, and the penumbra round it, both expanded steadily. The thoroughly-Chinese area was called *Troung Kwùk*, "the Central States", and in its modern pronunciation this is now the Chinese name for China: 'Zhongguo'. (Westerners commonly translate it as "Middle Kingdom"; but Chinese makes no distinction between singular and plural, and the phrase was originally understood as plural—and never had any reference to kings.) My translations use the term "Home States", on the analogy of the Home Counties in England. By the Qin dynasty, "China proper" extended to the east coast everywhere, and even as far as the south coast in the Hong Kong area.

This continued to be the pattern throughout almost all the long sweep of Chinese history. More than once, China was conquered by less-advanced societies—Mongols in the thirteenth century A.D., Manchus in the seventeenth; but the conquerors proceeded to become Chinese, and their own cultures had little influence on their new subjects. Not until the eighteenth century A.D.—in Chinese terms, the day before yesterday—was China ever confronted by an alien civilization on a level with its own. (In consequence, when the Chinese did encounter the West, they did not even understand the situation, let alone know how to handle it. Both sides handled it badly, resulting in a couple of rather miserable centuries from which China is just emerging in our own time.)

The *Tiw* universe

The *Tiw* Chinese had no inkling that, thousands of miles to the west, there were cultures on a comparable level to their own, in Egypt and Mesopotamia. In Europe there was nothing at that level. During most of the Odes period, the Greeks were in their dark age following the collapse of Mycenaean civilization, when for centuries they were entirely illiterate. Rome was the name of a town, not a nation-sized and certainly not an empire-sized polity, and the Romans too could not yet read or write.

So how did the Chinese conceptualize the world? They did not know it was a sphere. According to the *Book of Documents*, the earth was a flat square, each side about 1500 miles long, surrounded by seas, and centred on the eastern Chinese capital. The sky was a flat disc, covering all but the corners of the earth and supported tens of thousands of miles above it on eight pillars; when the Odes talk of birds flying "right up to the sky", this would doubtless have been seen as hyperbole, but not as a meaningless idea as it is for us. (The north-west pillar had collapsed so that neither earth nor sky was perfectly level; this explained why the stars flow westwards while Chinese rivers flow east and southwards.)

Who was in charge of it all? For most of the historical period, China has been a strikingly irreligious society, at least at the level of the educated élite. Confucius discouraged his followers from thinking about supernatural phenomena. When Buddhist thought reached China from India, early in the Christian era, it made considerable headway among the common people, in a crude form that I imagine would have been disowned by Gautama Buddha himself, but educated Chinese never had much time for it. There was a famous occasion in A.D. 819 when the then emperor, himself attracted to Buddhism, proposed to import a holy relic, Buddha's finger bone, and a shocked intellectual wrote a memorial arguing that this was a terrible idea: "Buddha was a man of the barbarians who did not speak the language of China and wore clothes of a different fashion ... If he were still alive today and came to our court by order of his ruler, Your Majesty might condescend to receive him, but ... he would then be escorted to the borders of the state, dismissed, and not allowed to deceive the masses. How then ... could his rotten bones, the foul and inauspicious remains of his body, be rightly admitted to the palace?"

Back in the *Tiw* period, though, Chinese society did share a range of what we would see as religious concepts. There were a host of spirits who exerted influence over human affairs, and whose goodwill was cultivated through regular sacrificial rites; many spirits had been the human ancestors of the people taking part in the rituals. The Chinese have always (until some of them read Marx, at least) seen the present as a falling-away from an ideal past state of affairs —they did not traditionally have a concept of progress towards a better future. It followed that ancestors had a special claim to respect and obedience. In the Christian world the supreme virtue with respect to one's fellow man is to "love thy neighbour as thyself", but for the Chinese that idea was alien; the supreme Chinese virtue was *hràws*—usually translated "filial piety", but that is a bloodless rendering for the weighty duty of a Chinese to honour and obey his forebears, dead and living. (Some scholars claim that in the *Tiw* dynasty, unlike today, the word referred *exclusively* to one's duty to the dead, but this is hard to reconcile with various Odes passages.) The head of a family, which might comprise several generations living in separate quarters within a shared compound, would report significant family developments to the tablets representing his ancestors, and he would control the lives even of adult offspring. When a baby was born, it was the family head rather than the child's own father who decided whether to let it live or die.

Over all this, human beings and ancestral spirits, presided a supreme being: *Thìn*, "Sky", sometimes called *Gòuc Thìn*, "Bright Sky". The king or emperor was commonly called *Thìn Tzuc*, "Sky's Son", indicating that one of his chief roles was to mediate between the people and the divine realm.

An obvious question is how far the Sky idea resembled Jewish, Christian, and Islamic monotheism. But the question is not really answerable, because individuals had different ideas about Sky. There was nothing like a systematic theology with equivalents of the Nicene Creed or Thirty-Nine Articles. *Thìn* was sometimes envisaged as a stretch of blue over our heads, but sometimes as a giant living in a palace in the constellation Ursa Major. Another name was *Tès* or *Dyangs Tès*, "God, God on High"; this does not seem to have referred to something different from *Thìn* (they appear interchangeable in Odes 254 and 255, for instance), but the terms were not clearly synonymous either. It seems that identifying the sky as the supreme power was originally an idea of the *Tiw* people; after the *Tiw* conquest, the "Sky" concept was merged with the *Un* dynasty's *Tès*. (*Tès* became in modern Chinese the 'di' of 'huangdi', "emperor", the godlike title which the Qin ruler invented for himself.)

Some saw Sky as an impersonal force of nature, like gravity, which impinged on human life but with which no meaningful relationship was available. Ode 194 says "Bright Sky ... doesn't act by reason or calculation". But in other poems Sky is presented as a personal entity who took an interest in human affairs and whose anger needed to be placated (and it was an important task for rulers to offer regular sacrifices to Sky as well as to lesser spirits). When the Duke of *Tiw* became regent for his nephew, he used this idea to create an ideology legitimizing the change of dynasty: he invented the concept of *Thìn Mreng*, Sky's Mandate, according to which Sky decided who was fit to rule and conferred on him a mandate for him and his heirs to do so—a mandate which Sky might withdraw if the current holder proved unworthy. Some Odes poets felt it appropriate to appeal to Sky as a Christian prays to God for help in time of trouble; in Ode 65 a woman begs Sky for reassurance about a possible future husband. And *thìn* was also the ordinary word for the blue expanse overhead. Many translators use "Heaven" for *Thìn* when referring to a divinity, but I find it better to use the same word Sky: when a *Tiw* Chinese looked at the blue above, he believed he was looking directly at the Almighty. Chinese script has no contrast between upper and lower case; my translations necessarily distinguish "Sky" as a godlike force from "sky" as a stretch of blue, but for Chinese this is a distinction without a difference. Likewise, the English language forces me to choose between "he" and "it" in referring to Sky as a power, but this distinction has no basis in the Chinese language (Chinese does not use separate words for "he" and "she", let alone for "it").

Rather than choosing some way to resolve these ideas as the centuries went by, after the Odes period educated Chinese simply lost interest in them. Worshipping one's family ancestors continued to be central to Chinese life, but worship of a Creator or Supreme Being, the essence of Western religion, was not (though the political idea of Sky's Mandate remained current into modern times).

Social classes and "princely men"

Tiw China was essentially a two-class society of patricians and plebeians—I shall use the homelier terms "gentry" and "peasants". The gentry ran their own lives; the peasants were serfs. Peasants worked on the land, but they did not own it: they cultivated the plots allocated to them, planting the crops they were told to plant, and were monitored by a *tzyouns*, "field inspector", sent by their landlord to check their work. Members of the gentry class belonged to named clans, giving them a relationship with the spirits of known ancestors, whom they worshipped and from whom they derived social standing. Peasants had no surnames, and no known ancestors.

This is not to say that peasants invariably had harsher lives than gentry. Peasants did not own land, but they had the right to be allocated a set quantity, and only a fraction of their harvest was owed to their master. (The ideal pattern was that squares of territory were divided into nine smaller squares like a noughts-and-crosses diagram, with eight peasant households cultivating the outer squares for their own consumption and the central square cultivated communally for the overlord's benefit. Reality was surely often less neat than this, but if it is roughly right it implies an "income tax rate" of 11 per cent—modest by 21st-century Western standards.) The usual gentry career was some form of service to state ruler or to king, but this clearly depended on retaining the ruler's goodwill. Some gentry made their living in other ways, for instance as priests, doctors, or schoolmasters—Henri Maspero lists numerous careers known to have been followed by gentry members, including even chefs and butchers. But, if things went wrong, the gentry had no safety-net. The fourth–third century sage Mencius has a story about one nobleman who was reduced to seeking out funerals for the sake of the free food provided at the wakes.

Among the gentry there were differences of rank. The king was superior to everyone else, each state had a ruler who outranked others in his state, and some gentry who were not rulers had titles of nobility. Later in Chinese history there was a hierarchy of five noble titles, which for translation purposes are equated with the five European noble ranks from duke down to baron; but in the Odes period there seem to have been fewer different titles, and—as in early mediaeval Europe—a title might be a job description rather than an inherited status, so that the idea of titles of nobility occupying rungs on a scale of honour was less established. Rather than using the conventional translations for noble titles, I shall often use general words like "ruler" or "lord" to avoid unrealistic precision about the implications of particular titles.

A question on which people have disagreed is how far the Odes portray the lives of peasants rather than exclusively gentry. Anyone who could read and write must have had gentry status, but some have suggested that many Odes emerged orally from the peasantry before being written down. (It used to be believed that, like the Homeric epics, the Odes were transmitted orally for a long period before they were written, though the American Sinologist Edward Shaughnessy has recently argued against that.)

A key term is *kwun-tzuc*, literally "prince's son"—the conventional translation is "princely man". This is used with a systematic ambiguity analogous to the ambiguity of "gentleman" in recent centuries—either a man of property who did not need to earn a living, or a man whose behaviour was urbane and respectful towards others. In some contexts *kwun-tzuc* clearly means that someone is a nobleman, or at least belongs to the gentry class; but in other cases it seems to describe character rather than social status. In Ode 1 the poet describes himself as a *kwun-tzuc*, yet he belongs to a work gang foraging for food, so it seems likely that this poet sees himself as princely in character rather than descent. Admittedly we cannot be sure that he was not literally noble. Emmanuel Le Roy Ladurie has commented that in the French Pyrenees only seven centuries ago "there was no absolute distinction between artisan and peasant ... or even between artisan and noble. In this part of the world, everybody worked with his hands". In *Tiw* China, four times further into the past, noblemen may have been even less removed from the sphere of mundane physical labour. But consider Ode 66, where a woman describes how her *kwun-tzuc* is on *wek* (compulsory military or similar service), leaving her among the cattle and hens: here it is difficult to suppose that the man could have belonged to the gentry. In 21st-century English a wife could call her husband "my prince" or "my lord" only with tongue in cheek, which is no part of the intention here: I render this *kwun-tzuc* simply as "my man".

(Chinese is not a language in which sex is grammatically central, as it is in European languages—we have seen that it does not distinguish "he" and "she", for instance—and occasionally *kwun-tzuc* can refer to a woman, though the *kwun-tzuc* of Ode 66 was certainly a man.)

The most judicious answer may be that both gentry and peasant life are covered in various Odes, but that in terms of day-to-day physical texture (as opposed to intangible status) there was less difference between them than terms like "nobleman" and "serf" suggest.

Cultural contrasts

In its religious outlook *Tiw* China was more like the West (at least, the West as it was until recently) than China later became. And other fundamental aspects of *Tiw* culture can be compared to Western counterparts. The political structure, with vassal rulers subordinate to a king and related to him and to each other through a network of kinship, seems very like the feudal system which emerged in Europe two thousand years later; words which Sir Frank Stenton used to describe English feudalism, "the fabric of feudal history is composed of genealogical detail", apply equally to *Tiw* China. Some aspects of *Tiw* culture are alien to the present-day West, for instance the way that women were entirely dependent on their husbands or other male relatives—but one does not have to look far back in Western history for similar scenarios.

Other aspects of *Tiw* culture are less recognizable. Pre-modern Europe may have been a patriarchal society, but at least formally it was a monogamous one, whereas for China monogamy was not even an ideal. Economic necessity (and simple arithmetic) ensured that most men could have only one wife, but a wealthy man could and would take multiple wives. When a powerful man married, it was usual for him to take along with his principal wife a number of her junior relatives (*dìs*, "younger sisters") as secondary wives. And a man who could afford it might buy concubines from a merchant.

Perhaps as a corollary, there was little concept of romantic love. Young men were acutely attracted to good-looking girls—biology guarantees that in any society; on the other hand the idea of finding a "soulmate", of "falling in love" with a "one and only one", the theme of ten thousand pop songs as well as more elevated Western literature, was effectively unknown. (But then, the idea scarcely existed in Europe before about A.D. 1100, when the troubadours of the Languedoc began singing about "courtly love"; and the concept was not entirely alien to the Odes—see Ode 120.)

Some features of *Tiw* society have puzzled later Chinese commentators. They asked how it could be that in Ode 42 a respectable girl was meeting a man in public, unchaperoned. Under later dynasties, she might not have been able to; but a complex social machinery for keeping young women secluded depends on a society having sufficient resources to maintain the machinery, and to forgo the women's economic contributions. *Tiw* society was simpler and poorer. On the evidence of these poems, relationships between unmarried men and girls were relaxed, more like what we have known in the West in recent times than like later Chinese norms. We know that, outside the ranks of the aristocracy, a girl did not usually marry before she was pregnant.

Some cultural differences between *Tiw* China and ourselves are natural responses to different circumstances. We might see the way in which many poems are devoted to praise of current rulers as distastefully slavish. (This category of Odes can feel tedious to modern readers, and I was tempted to omit some of them; but while it is reasonable to offer the public a complete translation of a famous book, an almost-complete translation would be an odd offering.) In the safe, stable 21st-century West we take for granted so many layers of security that we can afford to poke fun at our rulers. But, in a young society where it was apparent that king and vassal rulers were the sole frail defence against a brutal "war of all against all", effort put into repeatedly reinforcing the legitimacy and authority of those rulers must have been well worthwhile.

Possibly the most unexpected feature of Odes culture is a propensity to wallow in self-pity. The expressive word *ou*, "grief", pronounced "ooh", recurs again and again, in phrases like *ngàyc ou sum*, "my grieving heart", and many other words for "sadness", "misery", are frequent. Western poetry is often about situations that are tragic for the poet, but more often than in the Odes the resulting misery is left to be inferred, rather than explicitly spelled out. A British reader of the Odes is sometimes tempted to say "pull yourself together, man". But poetry may have been a safety-valve. Misery may have been expressed in verse precisely because it was unacceptable to display emotion in public. (When the Odes are personal rather than liturgical in nature, we don't know who their intended audience would have been—though they can hardly have been solely for the poets' own private use, or how did they come down to us?)

Structure of the anthology

Both the division of China into feudal states, and the nature of religious practice in the period, are relevant to the structure of the *Book of Odes*.

Rather than printing the Odes as one continuous sequence of 305 poems, Chinese editions divide the anthology into four sections. For modern readers the most interesting aspect of this division is the contrast between the first section and the other three. The first 160 poems, more than half the total, are called *Kwùk Pum*, "Airs of the States". (*Pum* means "wind", but in this phrase it is used in an extended sense as "song" or "tune", so "Airs" is as close as one can get in English.) To a large extent the Airs of the States are about the everyday lives of the people, including their emotional lives, while the later sections are about life at the courts of kings and vassal rulers.

The Airs of the States are in turn divided into fifteen subsections attributed to individual feudal states (not all of even the large states are represented). Although the topics are not mainly political, we can sometimes link the contents of a poem to known historical facts about the relevant state (though in one or two cases the content of an Ode seems to link it to a state other than the one to which it is attributed).

Turning to the other end of the anthology: the last section is called *Slongs*, "Eulogies". These are praise-songs celebrating various rulers and their ancestors, which were probably sung during sacrificial rites at the relevant courts. The Eulogies section is in turn divided into subsections, labelled *Tiw*, *Ràc*, and *Un*. This looks illogical, since *Tiw* and *Un* were royal dynasties while *Ràc* was one vassal state among others. The explanation is that, exceptionally, the *Ràc* ruling family was allowed (for historical reasons recounted in Ode 300) to practise rites which were otherwise the king's prerogative.

The fact that one subsection relates to a previous dynasty, *Un*, might suggest that those songs have survived from as early as the second millennium, but modern scholarship regards that as very unlikely. The current scholarly consensus seems to be that almost all the Odes were probably written closer to 600 than to 1000 B.C. There is a possible alternative explanation of the subsection name: the rulers of the *Tiw*-dynasty state of *Sòungs* counted as representatives of the *Un* royal line. (It was only the last few *Un* kings who were reviled under *Tiw*. After the dynasty change, it was an early priority for the *Tiw* régime to set up a relative of

Drouc in a fief where the cult of the *Un* ancestors could be maintained—*Sòungs* was the original *Un* homeland.) The "*Un* Eulogies" perhaps came from the court of *Sòungs*.

Even if none of the poems pre-date the *Tiw* dynasty, it is probably true that the Eulogies are some of the oldest pieces in the anthology as a whole (and the Airs of the States are relatively young). It is noticeable that the poetic structure of the Eulogies is less developed than in other sections, with some Eulogies entirely unrhymed, others having only sporadic rhyming, and there are many metrical irregularities. The language of the *Un* eulogies, in particular, is seen by Chinese scholars as particularly difficult to understand; one scholar of the twelfth century A.D. suggested that with that group of Odes a student should not expect to do more than grasp the poet's general gist. The correspondence between vocabulary items and written graphs seems possibly looser in the Eulogies than elsewhere.

There remain the second and third sections of the anthology, whose titles are respectively "Lesser *Ngràc*" and "Greater *Ngràc*". The word *ngràc* has several meanings—it was some kind of musical instrument, and it can also mean "refined", "correct", "proper"; it is hard to say what it meant in this context. Traditionally these Odes, also, were said to have been used in court rituals, with "Lesser" and "Greater" referring not to the poems themselves but to the importance of the rituals to which they belonged; but many of these Odes are too personal to make such a use plausible. Whoever wrote the various poems did not know that they were destined to be collected into an anthology, still less how the collection would be divided into sections; the anthologist evidently saw these two sections as natural groupings, but we are not obliged to agree. Nevertheless, I must translate *ngràc* somehow, so I arbitrarily render it in this context as "clarion", a word for a musical instrument associated with ritual and heraldry. Apart from that I leave these two groups of poems to speak for themselves.

Meanings of words

We have seen that much Odes vocabulary is thoroughly obsolete, so something needs to be said about how we know what these words meant.

We have rather comprehensive statements about word-meanings by people living a few centuries after the Odes were composed, both in commentaries specifically on the Odes, including the second-century B.C. Mao commentary, and in general dictionaries—Chinese dictionary-making began in the third century B.C. However, the precision of the information we are given is quite variable. For concrete terms, such as plant or tree names, we are often given detailed descriptions, enabling species to be identified with reasonable confidence. Many of these are species that are unfamiliar to most Western readers, but English names for them usually exist, and my translations use these, as more suitable in a poetic context than the Latin botanical names (the Latin names are included in the notes or Glossary). On the other hand, for abstract terms, such as words for emotions, the definitions in the sources are commonly just single-word synonyms. This is adequate for a rough idea of word meanings, but useless for pinning down subtle nuances. We can get a little further by deducing shades of meaning from the contexts in which a word appears—that, after all, is normally how a child learns to understand the words of his mother tongue. But we have to accept that, for many abstract words, we cannot be sure about fine details of meaning. Any translator has to do some guessing.

Possibly for this reason, there are areas of vocabulary where Old Chinese appears to have more different words than any language ought reasonably to need. Some languages do seem to specialize in unusually rich vocabulary in particular areas (though the example which everyone thinks he knows, Eskimo words for kinds of snow, is a myth—the linguist Geoffrey Pullum looked into it and found that the Eskimo language does not have many words for snow, no more than English has). In Old Chinese the most striking case may be that dictionaries list very many words all meaning "luxuriant"—that is, for plants to grow vigorously and profusely. Perhaps, for Old Chinese speakers, there were subtle differences between the qualities of plant growth indicated by these words, but if so they are hidden from us (and it is hard to imagine how there could be so many distinct qualities). And we have seen that there are many Old Chinese words all roughly meaning "sad"—here it is easier to think of a range of emotional nuances to which these distinctions could correspond, but we cannot be sure which Chinese word refers to which nuance.

Translation problems can stem from differences between the social structures of *Tiw* China and the English-speaking world. In a constitutional monarchy like Britain, there is a sharp distinction between what Bagehot called the "efficient" and the "dignified" elements of the constitution: the royal court is one thing, the government and civil service another. The word "courtier" has an aristocratic and slightly foppish sound, whereas an "official", "functionary", or "civil servant" is someone doing a perhaps important but usually unglamorous job. When soldiering is a career specialization, a (military) "officer" is very different from a (civil) "official". In *Tiw* China these distinctions did not apply: courts, of the king and of vassal rulers, were the places where the down-to-earth work of government and administration went on, so that a *shuc* or official was both a courtier and a civil servant, and commanding a military unit was just one of the tasks that might be assigned to a functionary. We have no convenient English word which is neutral between these alternatives, so I use whichever word fits a context best; but readers should bear in mind that a "courtier" may be doing a demanding and humdrum job, an "official" may find himself leading an army into battle, and so forth. Likewise, Martin Kern notes that there was "no strict division between the religious and the political". The word *koung* is conventionally glossed as "palace", but in some contexts "temple" may be a better translation, and in others "office".

Another problem for any translation from the language of a distant culture is that cultures have different ideas, so some words have no neat translation because the ideas behind them are unknown to English speakers.

One word that occurs often in the Odes is *tùk*, standardly glossed in dictionaries as "virtue". But in modern English "virtue" is a rather namby-pamby concept, which is not what *tùk* meant. Dictionaries translate the word as "virtue" because *tùk* aligns rather well with the Latin word *virtus*, from which English "virtue" derives; but *virtus*, from *vir* "a man", originally meant something like "manliness", "courage"—a character which is the reverse of namby-pamby. And "virtue" also had a use, more or less obsolete today, to refer to the inward nature or hidden power of something: a drug might be said to have a "dormitive virtue", meaning that it sends people to sleep. *Tùk* could cover all this range of meanings. Often it meant a man's "character", as when we say that someone has character to mean that he has a mind of his own, and isn't a weathercock to go along with whoever shouts loudest. Constance Cook defines *tùk* in the ancestry-based *Tiw* society as "a person's 'merit' as it was accumulated through generations of related individuals". Usually it is a good thing to have *tùk*; a tutor to young royals begins Ode 256 with the aphorism *Uk-uk ouy-ngay wi tùk tu ngòc*, "A dignified demeanour is the counterpart of inner *tùk*". But sometimes it is neutral, referring to a person's nature without evaluation, and there are cases where someone's *tùk* is explicitly described as bad. In Ode 255, *Mun* condemns the last rulers of *Un* by saying *Nec tùk pu mrang*, "Your *tùk* is not enlightened".

Present-day English has no one word to do duty for the various facets of *tùk*. Sometimes it works well to render *tùk* as "character". In Ode 201, where a neglected wife complains "You forget the great *tùk* you had from me", I translate it as "kindness". In Ode 173 I render it as "strength". But in many cases I find no satisfactory alternative to translating *tùk* as "virtue". Normally I aim to make the English of my translations modern rather than quaint, but in this case I have to ask readers to bear in mind that "virtue" has different connotations from those we are used to. Sometimes I make this explicit by putting inverted commas round the English word.

This is a translation problem relating to a particular word. Another kind of problem can apply to a whole cluster of words in some semantic area. Old Chinese has a range of words for ideas like "bright", "shining", "brilliant", and these are unproblematic when they are applied to the sky, water, metal, or the like. But a Westerner finds it surprising when they are applied to people, as when Ode 299 says that a nobleman is *mrang-mrang*, "bright". In Ode 55 a ruler's looks are likened admiringly to tin—this sounds particularly odd because tin is a cheap metal today. I imagine it was not cheap in the *Tiw* dynasty, but we would not praise a man by comparing his face to shiny metal, even precious metal. If in English we call a man "bright" or "brilliant", we mean that he has a high I.Q., but in the Odes these terms don't seem to be about cleverness in particular. They are clearly used in an approving sense, and intelligence may be part of what is meant but it is only part. As I read the poems, a man is said to "shine" if he has what it takes to be successful and admired—a powerful, fair ruler, for instance. And I suspect that, for *Tiw* Chinese, this usage was not figurative. We today know that the skin of a Winston Churchill or a Margaret Thatcher reflected no more of the light falling on it than anyone else's skin. But our perceptions are determined only partly by physical reality, and partly by what our culture leads us to expect. I surmise that a *Tiw* Chinese thought that more light really did come off king *Mac*'s face, for instance, than off the faces of others.

Here, reaching back to older English usage, or to Latin, offers a translator no help. So far as I know, European cultures have never had an idea like this. In some cases one can finesse the translation by rendering *mrang* as "enlightened" rather than "bright", but this does not always work—it is not only people that are sometimes praised in the Odes as "bright" where this cannot be taken literally. In Ode 209 a ritual is called "bright"; in Ode 260 the king issues "bright commands". Often one can only translate literally, and readers must interpret words like "shine" or "bright" in the context of this explanation.

Again, several words, for instance *yuk*, each meant both "orderly, neat" and "respectful, reverent"—ideas which for us are scarcely aspects of a single concept, but for *Tiw* Chinese they were. I render *yuk* by an English word for whichever idea seems uppermost in a given context.

There is also the issue of grammar words. We have seen that Old Chinese had no inflected word-endings, but it did have a range of separate words with grammatical functions, comparable to "of" or "as" in English. There are two problems about offering explanations of these words. One is that sometimes the experts do not understand just what grammatical functions were performed by a given word; but also, even when we do have a good idea of this, such things are often hard to explain in non-technical language. (Imagine trying to spell out the difference between, say, "he did it" and "he has done it" to someone whose language contains no equivalent distinction—which would include many Americans.) Hence a number of words in this category are listed in the Glossary simply as "particles" or "grammar words", without further explanation; and even when a grammar word is explicitly glossed, for instance *kuts* is defined as "marker of perfect tense", we must accept that there will be cases which the definition fails to fit. (One might try to define the meaning of English "of" in terms of possession—but where is the possession in "He knew *of* a good hotel"?)

We can rarely expect Old Chinese grammar words to map neatly onto English grammatical categories. The language has several words which translate as "this" or "that"; but there is no specific word for "the", and in consequence Old Chinese often says the equivalent of "this X" or "that X" in context where we would just say "the X". There are words for "very", but in Chinese these tend to be inserted before adjectives almost automatically, so that something is described as "very X" where we would just say it is X.

Metre

Old Chinese words are monosyllabic (unless one counts rhymers and chimers like *trent-tront* for "toss and turn" as single words). The predominant metre of the Odes is groups of four beats, and the telegraphic quality of Old Chinese grammar means that few words were wholly unstressed; so four-beat groups are commonly four-word groups (with rhymers and chimers counted as two words each).

An issue for Odes translation is how to arrange the words into lines of print. Traditionally, a Chinese edition of this or other poetry will not set it out as "lines" on the page. A poem will be printed continuously, usually with a word-sized space between verses, and at most an undifferentiated, comma-like punctuation mark between the groups of words which act as units for metre and rhyming. An English translation needs to be divided into lines, and four-word units are too short to translate as separate lines in English—if one does, the result reads oddly, perhaps childishly.

The obvious solution is to group the Chinese units into longer lines for translation purposes. Often, treating pairs of four-word units as single lines works well, particularly when the rhyme words end every other four-syllable group, giving the pattern:

x x x x, x x x A
x x x x, x x x A

Frequently the eight-word couplets belong together as units of sense, reinforcing the rightness of this grouping. Sometimes each short Chinese word-group rhymes, giving a pattern like:

x x x A, x x x A
x x x A, x x x A

or

x x x A, x x x A
x x x B, x x x B

but one soon gets used to hearing internal rhymes within the translated lines.

When the rhyming or the metre is less regular, this system cannot always be maintained. Most obviously, if a verse has an odd number of four-word groups they cannot all be paired into couplets. Sometimes one word-grouping is much longer than others, and this can happen in a pattern that repeats between verses, so that the longer groups demand to be treated as complete lines. And there are cases where the best solution is quite unclear. Both metre and rhyme schemes can be much less regular than is usual in Western poetry, so that there is no one right way to arrange lines in translation. I pick whatever arrangement seems to work best, in these irregular cases.

To be able to discuss individual Odes passages, we need terminology which makes clear whether we are referring to the short Chinese word-groups, or the longer lines of my translation. I shall use *stich* for the former (which is a word of English, though not a common one—pronounced "stick", plural *stichs*), and reserve *line* for the lines of the English translation.

In some Odes, the four-word-stich pattern is maintained without deviation. But often there are divergences—these are particularly noticeable where the Odes are shown in Chinese script, because the rule of that script is that each word occupies an equal-sized square, so that a stich or line with an extra word will be visibly longer than those surrounding it.

Some stichs of more or fewer than four words are clearly intended to achieve poetic effects. For instance, each verse of Ode 129 consists of seven four-word stichs followed by a five-word stich, giving a sense of closure. In other cases, a stich has a word that does not count metrically. Although the great majority of words counted as beats, little grammar words will naturally have been less stressed, and are sometimes ignored for metrical purposes. *Tu* is a grammar word with several functions: it forms possessives (*A tu B* corresponds to "A's B" or "the B of A"), and it is also an all-purpose object pronoun, translatable equally as him, her, it, them. In Ode 76 we find four-word stichs in the first two verses matched in the third verse by the stich *ouy nin tu tày ngan*, "I'm afraid of people's gossip", where *nin tu*, "people's", may have sounded in practice like little more than a single syllable, *nin t'*. Several frequent grammar words consist of a consonant followed by the vowel -u, which is the "neutral" vowel, like the -a of English "rota, camera", and was clearly often heavily reduced. (In other cases, though, *tu* did count metrically as a beat: evidently it was not always reduced.)

In other cases again, metrical irregularities may have been introduced through editorial changes to the original texts. I am not talking here about copying errors, but alterations made for what seemed to editors good reasons, perhaps at a time when the spoken language had changed so much that the speech-music of the Odes had evaporated and the poems were conceived as purely written works.

One example occurs in Ode 59, where every stich has four words except for a stich which runs *wans hwrang dìc bac muc* "distancing herself from elder brother(s) and younger brother(s), father and mother". (Old Chinese—and indeed modern Chinese—has no single word for "brother" or for "sister"; different words are used, depending on whether the relative is older or younger.) No word here is a little grammar word that might have been discounted for scansion. What surely must have happened is that one of the four kinship terms, probably *dìc* "younger brother", was not there originally, but the pair of words *hwrang dìc* "brothers" was such a cliché that an editor used it in full despite the damage it does to the metre. I have even seen an edition of this poem where the sequence of generations is reversed: *wans bac muc hwrang dìc*, "... father and mother, elder and younger brothers". An editor doubtless felt that it was only proper for seniors to precede juniors. This destroys the rhyme between *muc* "mother" and *wuc* "right-hand" in an earlier stich; but in the modern language these words no longer rhyme. I have adjusted the text I print to reflect the wording as I believe it was originally.

A subtler example occurs in Ode 260, which is a praise-song about a king's chief minister, named *Droungs Shàn-pac*. This name occurs eleven times in the received text, and although in general the poem contains normal four-word stichs, each stich containing the name, other than the first of them and one other, has five words. (One of them has six words, but the last word in that stich is the unstressed *tu*, so the stich has five beats.) What seems to have happened is this. At the time, *pac* was an honorific suffix: an Old Chinese name *A B-pac* was rather like an English name "Sir B A" (with A and B the other way round, because in Chinese family surname comes before individual name). The poet will have given *Shàn* his full name complete with honorific at first mention, but later, except where *Shàn* is reintroduced after a digression, he dropped the honorific, as an English historian might write "King Henry entered the court ... Henry summoned his counsellor ...". Then at a later period, after this use of *pac* ceased to be current, it was reinterpreted as part of the man's proper name: *Droungs Shàn-pac* looked as though it fitted the usual modern naming pattern of single-syllable surname followed

22

by two-syllable individual name. And if so, *pac* could not be dropped (no-one would call Mao Zedong "Mao Ze"). So the missing *pac*'s were inserted, despite this doing violence to the metre. I have taken them out again.

Apart from cases where apparent deviations from the predominant four-beat rhythm can be explained away, there is also a residue of cases where, from our point of view, the poet appears to have made a mistake. For instance, Ode 262 has 48 stichs, all but one comprising four syllables; but in the middle of the poem is one five-syllable stich, *Ma wat "Lac syawc tzuc"*, "Don't say 'I am just a boy' ". No word here seems likely to have been so reduced as not to constitute a beat. But with such early verse we cannot know how rigidly the poets felt bound by "rules" of scansion, and hence whether what look to us like "mistakes" would have been regarded as such at the time.

As a side issue, one of the great nineteenth-century experts on the far more complex metres of Greek and Latin verse, Ulrich von Wilamowitz-Moellendorff, held that these descended from an abstract primordial four-syllable metre, which is never observed "at the surface" because word inflexion and quantity and stress differences among syllables led to the many metrical subtleties of the Greek epic hexameter and other classical European metres. Old Chinese had no inflexion, the European phonological concept of syllable quantity had no obvious relevance to it, and its telegraphic grammar made wholly unstressed syllables infrequent; and we find that the predominant metre of the Odes matches Wilamowitz's "primordial" metre. Wilamowitz did not mention Chinese verse, and I surmise that he knew nothing about it. Whether the match is more than coincidental I cannot guess.

Free translation

Translators often discuss arguments for and against "free" versus literal translation. But the stripped-down quality of Old Chinese language structure gives the translator of this language no choice: translation must be free.

Consider Ode 31, which describes a scene in a state which is preparing for war with a neighbour; the capital of the state is called *Dzòu*. The second line runs: *thàc kwùk geng Dzòu, ngàyc dòk nùm gràng*—word for word, "earth state wall *Dzòu*, I/we alone south walk". The second stich is unproblematic: "we alone march south". The first stich evidently describes what is being done by other people, who are not marching to war; but what are they doing? We cannot write "earth state wall *Dzòu*" and call it a literal rather than free "translation".

According to the commentary tradition, the words for "earth" and "wall", though both commonly function as nouns, are used here as verbs—my translation is "They are fortifying the state with earthworks and walling *Dzòu* town". The two stichs describe preparations for defence and attack, respectively. This translation supplies a great deal which is not explicit in the original—it is a very "free" rendering; but any less free and it could scarcely be meaningful English.

In this case there is little difference of opinion among commentators about the correct interpretation, despite the austerity of the language. But in many other cases quite different renderings of a passge are each defensible, and defended by various authorities.

That often happens because verbs lack subjects. In European languages it is compulsory for sentences to have subjects, and even if the subject is only a pronoun, the ranges of different pronouns—first, second, or third person, singular or plural, "he", "she", or "it"—require a decision on who or what the subject is in any given case. Old Chinese does not require subjects, and commonly a sentence lacks one. Heavy use of subjects (or of pronouns generally) is described by Martin Kern as "a feature typical of liturgical speech ... a conscious stylistic choice that adds rhythm, intensity, and a rhetorical emphasis on personality". Most Odes are not liturgical, and they often omit subject and other pronouns.

Sometimes it is easy to infer the subject from the context, but often it is not. Indeed, there are cases where a Chinese reader might think the question pointless: the poem is what it is, it makes some things explicit and leaves others vague. (It is often said that in this respect Chinese poetry resembles Chinese landscape painting. In a European painting, every inch is covered with paint; but a Chinese painter will place a mountain here, a tree there, a stream over there, and leave the blanks for the viewer to fill in from imagination.) There are other cases, though, where the poet surely had a particular subject in mind, but we cannot be certain what it was.

Take a stich in Ode 19, by a woman whose man has gone away and who longs for his return: the stich runs *màk kàmp wùk wàng* (repeated with slight variations in later verses). Translated word for word, this says "not-have/there-isn't dare something leisure"—but that isn't a translation, it is just a jumble of English words. Earlier translators, so far as I have seen, have all taken the subject of "dare" to be the man. He probably holds an official position, and the woman could be asking whether he doesn't dare take a little leave from the task which is keeping him away. (Nothing in the language tells us whether the words are a statement or a question.) I have preferred to take the phrase as an assertion about the woman herself, so I translate as "I cannot rest for a moment".

My reasoning is that this Ode presents the woman as awestruck by the majesty of her absent man. Realistically, in a situation like that the woman would probably not see the man as "daring" to take time off: to her he seems all-powerful, even if in reality he is subject to superiors' orders. But it is psychologically realistic that the woman might feel she cannot allow herself to relax.

Or again, Ode 33 is another woman's appeal for support to a nobleman who has done her wrong (presumably, got her pregnant, though this is not spelled out) and then abandoned her. Its last line runs: *pu kes pu gou, gày longs pu tzàng*—"not malign not seek, because-of-what not good". I take the first stich to have first-person reference, and the second stich to refer to "you", so I translate: "I'm not a nasty girl, not a gold-digger: so why can't you act decently?" In the context of the poem as a whole, this interpretation feels rather compelling to me; if I hesitated, it would be about whether the second stich should also be understood in the first person, "why am I no good (in your eyes)?"

Yet all traditional commentators have taken this line quite differently, as having a third-person subject throughout: the poetess is not addressing a man who has left her, but describing him to the reader, and in positive terms. As Legge translates it: "He hates none; he covets nothing;—What does he which is not good?" No less an authority than Confucius quoted this line as an illustration of ideal conduct. Obviously I do not claim to know Confucius's mother tongue better than he knew it himself. But the point is that there is nothing, *in the language*, which anyone could point to as showing that Confucius's interpretation is correct and mine wrong—or *vice versa*. No English translation could leave such an issue vague, but it can be resolved only by considering the poem as a whole in terms of the balance of human probabilities. In that domain I do feel entitled to back my judgement against that of the great sage.

These examples are not special cases. Choices between radically different interpretations of wording arise over and over again, with respect not just to subjects of verbs but to all kinds of translation issues. William Empson has argued that ambiguity is of the essence of all poetry. Even if that is true, though, ambiguity is certainly more salient in Chinese poetry than in any European language. Not just the lack of subjects, but the fewness of grammatical devices of any sort, mean that there is far more room than we are used to for the reader to interpret a line one way or another way. The logical explicitness of European languages forces a translator to choose one reading and impose it, but alternative readings will often be fully defensible.

So the translator must necessarily put quite a lot into the translation which is not there in the original. One can be cautious, and search for English wording that adds as little as possible to what is explicit in the Chinese. I prefer to be bolder, and make my versions as humanly plausible and comprehensible as possible. Sometimes I add words that a Chinese reader of the period would not have needed, because he was familiar with the culture, but the absence of which would leave the poem mysterious to a 21st-century Westerner. And the ambiguities in the original mean that sometimes one just has to guess—any translator would have to guess.

When my interpretation of a passage conflicts with other translators' versions, as an academic I was often tempted to spell out the linguistic or other considerations that have led me to prefer my rendering. Many readers would find that kind of discussion tedious, so I have tried to resist the temptation—but yes, I am aware of alternatives to my interpretations, and I do have reasons for my translation choices.

An overriding consideration for me, which in itself eliminates some previous interpretations of particular passages, is that anything written by an Odes poet must have made sense at the time. A poem (Ode 36, for instance) may puzzle us because we don't know the circumstances behind it, but it will not assert absurdities. I gave up looking in Arthur Waley's popular Odes translation for suggestions about the meaning of difficult passages when I saw that Waley rendered a stich *Traw tzì wa si* in Ode 51 as "There is dawnlight mounting in the west". Day breaking in the west is nonsense; faced with seeming nonsense, I look for a nonstandard graph use, or a plausible scribal distortion. If all else fails I signal a gap with an ellipsis mark and explain that the original is irretrievable: anything rather than turn apparent Chinese nonsense into real English nonsense. (In fact the Ode 51 stich is unproblematic if one realizes that *tzì* can mean "rainbow", but perhaps the reference books available to Waley in the 1930s did not tell him that. Word for word the line runs "morning rainbow at west", the natural place for it.)

In some cases I have preferred to avoid literal translation even when the English language would allow it. Another contrast between Chinese and European languages is that Chinese has limited resources for expressing what logicians call "universal quantification". Where in English we say "all Xs" or "every X", in Chinese we tend to find phrases like "the hundred Xs", "the ten thousand Xs"—giving a specific round number which is commonly larger than the true total number of Xs. Instead of "Everyone did X", in Chinese we find *màk pu X*, "there was no-one who did not do X". Rather than "the whole world", the usual Odes phrase is *Slits Pang*, "the Four Quarters". A line in Ode 33 complains about the behaviour of noblemen as a class: the poetess calls them *pràk nec kwun-tzuc*, literally "hundred you princely-men", or as we would say "you hundred princely-men". She does not mean there were precisely one hundred of them, it is just a conventional way of referring to a class: "you noblemen", or "all you noblemen".

Normally there is no difficulty about imitating these Chinese turns of phrase in English, if a translator wants to do that. But in many contexts the result sounds quaint. My aim is to offer readers a window onto a world which is very different, physically and socially, from the world of any 21st-century Westerner, and I want the window to be as transparent as possible: which means translating into natural-sounding modern English. If I were creating a window onto Tudor England, I would not use wrinkly, imperfect glass just because that was the kind of glass found in Tudor windows.

Clothes, journeys, and bronzes

Many Odes passages require knowledge of some concrete feature of *Tiw* society to make them understandable. My plan in this book is to deal with such points as they arise, by means of brief explanations accompanying the poems. But some issues recur so frequently that it will be efficient to deal with them once for all here.

Finding English words for the clothes mentioned is difficult, because traditional Chinese dress was different from ours. The main elements, for either sex, were the *dang*, which wrapped round the body and in particular covered the legs in the manner of a skirt, and the *uy*, which covered the upper body in the manner of a jacket. Both sexes held their clothes together with a sash or belt (*gums*, or *tàts*). I do not know whether trousers existed at this early period, but more recently trousers were associated specifically with manual workers (men or women). If we wanted to use consistent translations for these terms, the obvious word for *dang* would be "skirt", but it gives a strange impression in English if a woman comments admiringly on her male lover's skirt. To avoid these difficulties, I tend to use vague words like "robe".

A mystifying element of *Tiw*-dynasty dress is the ear-stoppers worn by gentlemen (*thoung nuc*, literally "fill-ear"). These were evidently decorative, often being made of semi-precious stone, but we don't know what they were for. Already in the Han dynasty (206 B.C. to A.D. 220) we find commentators expressing puzzlement about ear-stoppers. Were naked earholes thought indecent?

Another decorative element of dress was *bès*. Chinese robes did not have pockets; people hung their kit on cords from their sash or belt, using toggles to stop the cords slipping through. The toggles, *bès*, were often carved from jade and might be little works of art in their own right. My translations call them "netsuke", the Japanese term used by Western collectors.

Some things that we think of as typical of China were not yet central to Chinese life. Rice was known, but it was a luxury food. The ordinary staple food was millet of several varieties, though wheat had been introduced to eastern areas by the beginning of the Odes period. Not that the Chinese were fussy about their diet—living in unfriendly terrain, with early technology, they needed to eat whatever was edible. Many Odes make it clear that famine was a permanent threat. To learn about some of the food crops mentioned, I visited websites which advise modern Man on wilderness survival.

A feature of Chinese etiquette is that when a guest departed, the host was expected to accompany him (*sòngs*, to escort) for the first part of his journey. Goodbyes were said where the host turned back, which for an important guest might be a day's journey away. It was for the host to provide a farewell feast (*dzans*) and perhaps parting gifts, at that place.

A specially important journey was the one a woman made to get married. As in the West, brides went to live in their husbands' homes rather than *vice versa*, and among the gentry these will typically have been some distance away. But whereas a Western bridegroom travels to where the bride lives, and her family lays on the ceremony and a reception for guests before the husband takes her away with him, in *Tiw* China when a marriage had been agreed (using the services of a go-between) the man fetched his bride away, or sent for her, to marry her at his home. The ceremony was entirely a matter for the groom's family.

Consequently women are often said to "go on their journey" as a reference to marriage. The word *kwuy* is often glossed as "return, go home", but more precisely it meant "go where one belongs", and a woman on her marriage journey is said to *kwuy*—she is going where she now belongs, although she never lived there before. Ode 28 shows us a father bidding a tearful farewell after accompanying his daughter on the first stage of her marriage journey, perhaps never to see her again.

The Odes contain many words for food and drink vessels, and these have far more cultural resonance than words like "dish" or "jar" have for us. In some contexts these words may refer to objects made of pottery or other workaday materials and serving purely functional purposes —so far as I know, a *pèn* only ever meant a covered fruit basket, though the fruit in a *pèn* might be an offering to the spirits. But other words often referred to ritual objects cast in bronze in a range of highly distinctive shapes, each of which has its own name. A *dòs*, for instance, is a food bowl that with its lid forms a slightly flattened sphere, standing on a flared circular foot. In the bronze cases it is not clear that the objects were ever used for non-ritual purposes. Indeed, the science-fiction shape of the *tzyawk* goblet, with an egg-shaped body standing on three long triangular legs, with two mushroom-shaped pillars rising from the rim on either side of a large flat spout opposite a protruding horn, and with a handle on one side, is not easy to explain in terms of function (though the legs may have enabled the wine to be warmed—it was probably used as a decanter). We know that a *tzyawk* might be awarded by a ruler as the equivalent of a European patent of nobility—the word *tzyawk* is in fact ambiguous between the concrete sense "goblet" and the abstract sense "nobility"; and in Ode 220 we see a *tzyawk* conferred as a prize in an archery competition, as in the West a sportsman might receive a silver cup. (The archery may have had a religious overtone absent from Western sport.)

As Christian Deydier says in an excellent illustrated book on these ritual vessels, they "were regarded by the Chinese as tangible symbols of their possessors' heaven-bestowed right to wield political power, as well as to worship and supplicate heaven, the spirits, and the ... ancestors ..., thereby ensuring peace, prosperity and heavenly protection from natural disasters". (Deydier's and other books refer to the vessel types by their modern pronunciations, so my Glossary includes these.) The durable nature of bronze means that for us today these beautiful objects are probably the most inspiring products of *Un* and *Tiw* China. As well as complex decoration many carry long inscriptions, which comprise much of our earliest evidence for written Chinese (the only earlier examples are the "oracle bones" I shall mention with Ode 50). And the quality of their workmanship is astonishing. William Willets, in *Chinese Art*, quotes Herrlee Creel commenting in the 1930s "We think of the work of Benvenuto Cellini as superlatively fine, but those who have examined his castings say that they are full of [imperfections repaired after casting] ... a very few of the best living craftsmen in Europe and America, aided by all the resources of modern science and technology, may be able to equal the casting of the [*Un*-dynasty] bronze workers, they can do no better".

The structure of the language

We have seen that an English translation must be specific about many issues left vague in the Chinese original. But this not mean that one can make the original say whatever one wants. The language does have rules of grammar, which a translator must respect. In examples discussed earlier, it was reasonable for me to differ from other translators because alternative renderings are equally compatible with the Chinese wording. In another case, though, there might be some English turn of phrase loosely related to the Chinese wording which, in itself, would seem a plausible, artistically fitting thing for the poet to say, but adopting it as a translation would ignore the normal rules of Chinese grammar. In such cases I have chosen the more defensible rendering, even if that feels less satisfying poetically.

Many of the main Old Chinese grammatical rules resemble those of English, for instance adjectives come before nouns rather than after, as in French: "white house" rather than *maison blanche*. But, naturally, understanding this language does involve a few special linguistic wrinkles, apart from the optionality of subjects. If the object is a pronoun it often precedes the verb—here Old Chinese is like French (*je le vois* versus "I see him"). Adjectives as predicates require no word comparable to "to be": for "John is wise" Old Chinese would normally say the equivalent of "John wise". If a descriptive predicate is tangible and physical, the word for it is commonly doubled. For instance, *tzàng* and *phàts* are two of the many words meaning "luxuriant": in Ode 140, the idea "its leaves are thick" is expressed in the first verse as *gu lap tzàng-tzàng*, and in the second verse as *gu lap phàts-phàts*. (The Glossary lists words as single syllables even if in the poems they only occur doubled.) When a descriptive word is a two-syllable compound, each syllable is doubled separately: *oy-lay* "submissive" becomes *oy-oy-lay-lay*.

There is no singular/plural distinction. The word for "leaf" can equally mean "leaves", and indeed a word for "I, me" (there are several alternative first-person and second-person pronouns) can equally mean "we, us".

But these are very minor hurdles to the task of grasping how Old Chinese words combine to express thoughts. They do not compare with the difficulty of mastering verb endings even in a modern European language, let alone Latin or Greek.

The one respect in which European languages are easier for us is that, normally, many of their words are recognizably similar to their English equivalents. European languages share a common origin, and they have borrowed vocabulary from one another heavily. Chinese is an entirely separate language; its speakers had no contacts with speakers of the Indo-European family of languages to which English belongs. So, naturally, every word, whether a rare word or a frequent word, is totally unrelated to its English equivalent. Someone who approaches this literature unaided has a great deal of dictionary work to do.

But, for readers of these translations, that work is already done. All words used in the Odes are listed in my Glossary.

Strictly, I should add, it may be an overstatement to say that Old Chinese speakers never had any cultural contacts with Indo-European speakers. We know nowadays that one group of Indo-Europeans, the Tocharians (now long extinct), lived in what is now Xinjiang, north of Tibet, at least as early as the Odes period. (A very readable book on the Tocharians is by Elizabeth Wayland Barber, *The Mummies of Ürümchi*.) There are tantalizing suggestions that some words may have been exchanged between the respective languages. For instance, "honey" was *mit* in both Old Chinese and the "Tocharian B" language, and this is claimed not to be a coincidence: Chinese is said to have borrowed the Tocharian word. (If so, the Chinese for "honey" would ultimately stem from the same root as English "mead", a drink made from honey.) But cases like this, though fascinating, are so marginal that for practical purposes the general point stands.

Titles and opening images

A title is an essential element of an English poem. The Odes have traditional Chinese titles, but they are less essential: it is unlikely that they were chosen by the poets, and not all Chinese editions of the Odes print the titles. Commonly the titles are derived rather mechanically from the opening words of the poems. (Occasionally the traditional title has no discernable link with the poem content. The title of Ode 194 translates as "Uncontrolled Rain", but rain is not mentioned in the poem.)

Where translating a Chinese title yields a reasonable title in English, I use that as the English title. Often, though, this does not work, and I have invented a suitable title. I have also made my English titles unique across the whole anthology (sometimes Odes in different subsections share the same Chinese title).

Even when a Chinese title translates into a title-like English phrase, this will often seem strangely disconnected from the overall poem topic. This is because the Odes commonly begin with what I shall call an "opening image" (the Chinese term is 'xing', "arousal"), and as the Chinese titles are derived from the first words of their Ode, they usually refer to that image. Opening images are allusions to some aspect of nature, such as a particular plant, bird, or animal, which is described in a line or two and then, often, never mentioned again. (Sometimes, later verses have their own opening images.)

In some cases one can see that an opening image establishes a mood appropriate to the topic of the poem. Ode 35 begins with a line about rainy, depressing weather, and then turns into a lament by a loyal wife of long standing who is neglected by her husband in favour of a new second wife. One of the mysteries about the Odes, though, for us who come to them today, is the many cases where we can detect no link between an opening image and the body of its poem. And this is not just because we are 21st-century Westerners. The longstanding traditions of Chinese scholarly commentary sometimes claim to explain the relevance of an opaque opening image, but in such an implausible fashion that we are forced to conclude that, in reality, the commentators knew no more about it than we do. (Look at my discussion of Ode 60, for instance.) And in other cases even early commentators admitted defeat, saying of Ode 115, for instance, that the tree names in the first lines of successive verses do nothing more than establish rhymes for their verses.

The subtitle of this book includes the word "demystified", but the opening images are an aspect of the Odes where mystery remains and is never likely to be dispelled. I choose to see that as part of the fascination of these poems. Readers must decide for themselves whether they are willing to share that view.

Prudishness as a barrier to understanding

Sometimes aspects of an Ode's meaning can be concealed from us by prudishness. There is no reason to expect *Tiw* Chinese to share the same hang-ups about sex which in the West probably stem largely from the teachings of St Paul, and these poets can seem surprisingly down-to-earth.

Take the opening line of Ode 1, which as a whole describes a young man's desire to find a girlfriend. The line runs *Kròn, kròn, tsa-kou, dzùc Gày tu tou*, which I translate as "*Kròn, kròn*, calls the fish-hawk on an islet in the River". The nature of Chinese script means that animal sounds can only be represented by writing a Chinese word that sounds similar, as we represent the sound of a duck by writing an English word for an incompetent doctor, "quack". The word *kròn* (which happens to mean "barrier") sounds reasonable to me as an imitation of a bird call—though the particular species called *tsa-kou* is said to be the osprey, which I believe makes no *kròn*-like sound, and for that reason I translate the term as "fish-hawk", which is a synonym for osprey but sounds conveniently vague.

Reviewing my 2006 translation of a small selection of the Odes, the distinguished Sinologist Edward Shaughnessy took me to task here, arguing that I had missed the point of the opening image. Shaughnessy pointed out, first, that fish motifs are often associated in the Odes with sex, so the fact that the bird "is a fish eater immediately alerts the reader that this poem has to do with a man looking for romance". Furthermore, as Shaughnessy sees it, onomatopoeic words like *kròn* must have been chosen not just for sound but also for meaning; and although the meaning "barrier" is irrelevant, he pointed out that there was a similar-sounding word, *kòns*, "which primarily means 'to pass through' but has an extended sense of sexual penetration", and these two words are often exchanged. The first words of Ode 1 make explicit what the young man wants to do with his hypothetical girlfriend, as he tosses and turns on his lonely bed.

I was initially sceptical. This idea smacked of film directors who sex up Jane Austen novels to increase box-office takings, and the chain of linguistic links seemed tenuous. But that was before I studied Ode 218, where a sexual interpretation of *kròn* seems inescapable. And other Odes scholarship which I have since read confirms that Shaughnessy is correct about Ode 1. Some readers may find it startling, even offensive, to be told that the opening words of this ancient and greatly-revered monument of world literature might be most faithfully rendered into English as "Fuck, fuck!" Offensive or not, it appears to be true.

Modern Chinese editions of the Odes commonly do treat *kròn* in Ode 1 as onomatopoeic and nothing more. But I don't mean to suggest that prudishness leading to misunderstandings lies all on the Chinese side. Traditional Chinese commentary could be quite un-prudish. Consider Ode 226, where a woman bewails the fact that her man was due home the previous day after five days away, but has not shown up. People have wondered why a relatively short absence should provoke such a response. But Mao Heng (one of two men, both surnamed Mao, who compiled what is now the received edition of the Odes) believed he knew why. According to Mao, a wife made love with her husband once every five days and she would look forward to it, so if she went unsatisfied for longer she would get upset. Legge responded to this with a fit of the Victorian vapours, refusing even to state Mao's "filthy and absurd view".

I certainly find Mao's theory hard to accept. I wonder whether Chinese couples three thousand years ago truly took their pleasure by numbers like that (and how Mao could have known it even if they did). But this is a matter of plausibility, not prudishness.

Probably most languages have words which, alongside their "official" meanings, are also used in sexual senses that every adult speaker knows but which often fail to find their way into dictionaries. As I read the Odes, other words in this category are *kòc* and *rouc*, both of which have the dictionary meaning "fish-trap", and *rang*, "dam". Various passages make sense if these words are interpreted as sexual allusions, whereas translators who have taken the words in their dictionary meanings have produced peculiar or nonsensical renderings of the passages, and they resort to describing the wording with comments like "so general and vague that it allows of the most varying interpretations" (quoting Legge on Ode 199). The Odes poets lived millennia ago, but they were rational human beings like you and me; if they wrote something, it must have made definite sense of one kind or another.

I endeavour to offer whatever interpretation of particular passages seems to me most plausible on balance—if this involves a sexual allusion, my English wording reflects that, but I avoid dragging sex in gratuitously where I find such an interpretation far-fetched. (In the Ode 1 case I copped out, leaving *kròn* as simple onomatopoeia for fear of giving readers who bypass this Introduction and go straight to the poems too abrupt a jolt.)

Text emendations

I need to say a little, mainly for the benefit of those who can read it, about the Chinese text I have translated.

In the Odes period, Chinese script was less fully developed than it later became. Often words would have no graphs of their own, and were written using the graph for some other word that sounded the same or similar. If these words were never given distinctive graphs of their own, then a single graph has stood subsequently for any of a set of unrelated but similar-sounding words. (If one identifies words with their written forms, as Chinese tend to do, then one would say that a single word has a range of unrelated meanings. As a Western linguist I think of the identity of a word as residing in its etymological history, so I would say that separate words share the same graph, and I give them separate Glossary entries.) Commonly, though, the words in question were later given their own graphs. In that case, for us who live after the standardization of the written language, the form which appears for one of these words in the received Odes text is "wrong", and represents the intended word by the graph for a different word.

Even though many of these substitutions of one graph for another are nowadays quite uncontroversial among the scholarly community, it has been usual for published editions of the Odes to show the received text with its non-standard graph uses. This is unlike what is usually done in editions of early Western literature. Suppose, say, that in the original manuscript of some pre-modern English literary work we read of someone cooking "a stake of beef". Clearly, "stake" here stands for the word that is nowadays spelled "steak". A modern edition will normally print the word as "steak"—if it is a scholarly edition for readers interested in the history of the language, perhaps there might be a footnote about the original spelling, but an edition for general readers will change "stake" to "steak" silently. If English-language editors took the approach commonly taken in editions of ancient Chinese texts, on the other hand, they would print "stake of beef"—in a scholarly edition adding a footnote explaining that "stake" meant what is now spelled "steak", but in a general edition leaving "stake" unexplained, or at most marking it with a symbol meaning "this form does not stand here for the obvious word".

For readers of this book, I believe the Western editorial approach will be more helpful, so I have replaced graphs that occur in the received Odes text with the graphs that became usual for the words in question.

Sometimes, in the long centuries before printing, copyists made mistakes, and some of those mistaken writings became accepted in place of the correct originals. One example is in the fourth verse of Ode 261, where the received text reads 不顯其光, *pu hènt gu kwàng*, literally "his light was not splendid". In context this makes no sense: it is contradictory. But alongside the word *pu*, written 不, which remains the usual word for "not" in modern Chinese (and hence is an extremely common word), Old Chinese also had a word *phru* (now long-obsolete), meaning "great, very" (though it was not the most usual word for those concepts) which happened to be written quite similarly: 丕. "His light was very splendid" fits the context well, so evidently some scribe (who was perhaps unfamiliar with the word *phru*) misread 丕 as 不. The same apparent misreading appears at several other points. So in these cases my Chinese text has 丕, *phru*, rather than 不.

Other cases are more debatable. Ode 203 is about differences between the comfortable life of those who inhabit the *Tiw* dynastic capital in the West—the "sons of *Tiw*"—with the impoverished life of the "sons of the East". At one point the received text says that the sons of 舟人 *tou nin*, literally "boat men", dress in bearskins, with a word for "boat" which in modern Chinese is a perfect homophone of the modern pronunciation of *Tiw*, and sounded similar in Old Chinese. Here one cannot say that "boatmen" is meaningless or contradictory, but it hardly fits the context well: there is nothing else about boats or water in Ode 203. Some commentators have held that the poet was referring literally to boatmen, but other scholars believe that the "boat" graph, 舟, was on this occasion borrowed to write *Tiw*: the phrase is intended as another reference to the sons of *Tiw*. It is not that the graph for "boat" had to be borrowed because the dynasty-name *Tiw* had no graph of its own: *Tiw* already had a distinctive graph, 周, which is used elsewhere in the same poem. But the suggestion is that, for some reason, in this particular line (and in one other Ode) the scribe represented *Tiw* by the "boat" graph rather than by its proper graph. I find this convincing, so I have replaced 舟 with 周 in the Chinese text.

Some debates about alternatives to the received text appear oddly disconnected from the practical realities described. Odes 169 and 236 describe troops on or returning from military service, and call the vehicles conveying them *dàn ka*, "sandalwood carriages". One influential commentator took the *dàn* graph as having been substituted for the word *djànt*, which merely refers to the box made of interwoven laths on a vehicle which accommodates the passengers or goods. Later editors have seen this as a gratuitous speculation, saying that "carriage made of sandalwood" makes good sense. They apparently do not realize that sandalwood is a precious aromatic substance used mainly to yield essential oil for cosmetics or religious rites. It is not the kind of stuff one would use to knock up a carriage, least of all a troop carrier. *Dàn* must be wrong, so I expect that *djànt* is right.

Or consider Ode 178, where a rural yokel appears overwhelmed by witnessing the arrival of a large army on its way to deal with restive tribesmen. Its second verse ends with four words which I spell *Wuc tsang chòng gràng* and translate as "There was a mighty sound of waggons rolling". But while the graph which I read as *chòng* "waggon" can mean that, it was originally invented to write the near-homophone *tsòng* "onion"; and in the received text, the graph for *gràng* "travel, road" has an extra graphic element which turns it into the perfect homophone *gràng* "netsuke gem". Accordingly, earlier Chinese and Western expositors of the Odes have taken the phrase as describing the tinkling of onion-coloured netsuke. This seems absurd: netsuke are not noise-makers, and if a couple of them did chink together the sound would be too trivial for the poet to notice, surrounded by beating drums, jingling harness, and officers barking orders. (And what particular colour are onions anyway?) I cannot guarantee that my translation is faithful to the poet's idea, but at least it could be right, requiring only the hypothesis of a minor copyist's error of a kind which frequently occurs.

I do not claim to have eliminated every graphic unclarity. Yu Xingwu observed in the 1930s that there are a number of cases where the two very common words *tu* and *tuc* are confused (their graphs were much more similar in the early script than in modern Chinese script). In some places I have changed one of these words to the other, but there are probably further cases where a change would be desirable. And recent scholarship in China has proposed various other candidates for text emendation, some of which I would surely wish to adopt if I were aware of them; but these proposals are scattered in various scholarly publications, and so far as I know there is no source which conveniently summarizes them.

To keep things simple I do not regularly include notes on modifications of the received text. Any reader keen to check what appears in that text can easily get hold of an edition of the Odes which uses it. (On the rare occasions when I amend the received text on my own initiative rather than in response to a suggestion in the published literature, I usually draw attention briefly to that.)

Because the traditional Chinese poem titles are derived from the opening words of each Ode, in a few cases these textual emendations would logically imply changing the title. I have not done that: I retain the traditional titles, because that is what Chinese readers know the poems by. Numbering the Odes from 1 to 305 is a Western innovation; Chinese editions do not include numbers—and if they did the numbering would be different, because at several points they list Odes whose title is known but which are otherwise lost. I have ignored the lost Odes.

I have been discussing the "received text" of the Odes as if there were only one early version, to which scholars have proposed occasional amendments long after the poems were originally composed. For most of Chinese history, that was broadly the situation. Recent archaeological discoveries, though, show that there was masses of textual variation in very early times, though this was eventually eliminated through circulation of an edition that was treated as authoritative. Martin Kern has examined these early textual variations. Happily (for the present-day translator), he finds that overwhelmingly they are either alternative ways of writing the same word, or substitutions of a synonym or near-synonym for a word in the received text. There are very few cases where a textual variant might require even a minor difference in the English translation.

The calendar

Many Odes refer to times of year, so I need to say a little about the Chinese calendar (which is still maintained, though for everyday purposes the Chinese now use our Western calendar).

Nature offers two obvious ways to group days into meaningful, predictable sequences: the cycle of the seasons, say from one shortest day (winter solstice) to the next, and the phases of the moon. The problem faced by any calendar design is that a lunation (new moon to new moon period) is about 29½ days long, and no whole multiple of that figure comes close to fitting into the 365¼ days of the seasonal cycle. Our own calendar bases itself on the seasonal cycle and ignores the moon. The word "month" derives from "moon", and a month is very roughly as long as a lunation, but in fact all months but February are longer; in consequence, new moons can occur at any point in a Western month. By ignoring the moon, our calendar need only insert a leap day every four years to keep pace with the cycle of seasons.

The Chinese calendar takes the opposite tack. Its months are new-moon-to-new-moon periods—the same word *ngwat* means both "moon" and "month". Chinese months or moons are numbered rather than named; my translations call them "moons" to make it clear that, say, "the third moon" is not identifiable with any particular Western month. Twelve lunations fall many days short of 365¼ days, so every few years a "leap moon" is inserted to catch up with the seasonal cycle.

Obviously, then, a Chinese date such as "day *N* of the *M*-th moon" equates to no particular date in our calendar. The two calendars slide against one another by several weeks from year to year, though never getting more than a few weeks out of synch.

Still, for poetry it is only months rather than individual dates that have much significance, and one could give a rough correspondence between Chinese moons and Western months, if one knew which new moon began the year. For most of Chinese history, this has been the second new moon after the winter solstice, so the Chinese New Year is celebrated some time in late January or February. But this has been the China-wide rule only since 104 B.C., long after the Odes period. Before that, different new-year rules were used at different periods, or even in different Chinese states at the same time.

All one is safe to say is that the new year always fell in winter, which is handy for historians because it makes sense to translate Chinese year names into specific dates B.C.: a Chinese year and a year of our calendar will always overlap heavily, though the Chinese year can never run precisely from 1st January to 31st December. But the year might begin with the first new moon after the winter solstice, or the new moon preceding the solstice. Each poet took for granted the calendar in use where he lived, and they don't tell us which new-year rule it used. (A rather inexplicit passage by Henri Maspero claims to explain confusing references to moons in Ode 154 by saying that the same moons are being identified by different calendars, though I am not sure that idea works.)

Probably the most widely-used rule at the Odes period was to begin the year with the first new moon after the solstice. That implies that, in the absence of contrary evidence, the best bet is to take "*N*th moon" as very roughly matching the Western month with the same number. But this can easily be more than a month out in a given case. When Ode 204 says "By the fourth moon we are in summer; in the sixth moon its heat is abating", the poet's calendar must surely begin with a later moon.

Individual days have names from a set of sixty names which, like the seven days of the Western week, cycle endlessly, independently of the division of time into months and years. Thus when Ode 193 describes an eclipse of the sun as occurring on a *sin-mròuc* day, the 28th day of the cycle, astronomers have been able to identify this as an eclipse which occurred on 29 August 775 B.C. The elements of these two-syllable names have astrological significance, and the same cycle of sixty is also used for years (A.D. 2011 was a *sin-mròuc* year).

The sounds of Old Chinese

Since Chinese has never been written alphabetically, one might wonder how we can tell what it sounded like thousands of years ago. In fact there are several sources of information. For one thing, while the script is not alphabetic, it does contain large clues to how words were said at the time when the script was developed. (It would take us too far from our theme to discuss Chinese script in detail here, but readers interested in pursuing the topic might like to look at relevant chapters in my book *Writing Systems*; and for those interested in the aesthetics of the script, Chiang Yee's *Chinese Calligraphy* is an excellent introduction.) Another kind of data is the forms Chinese words took when they were borrowed by other languages. Because of the immense, longstanding cultural dominance of China in the East Asian area, languages like Korean, Japanese, and Vietnamese, though belonging originally to separate language-families, are full of vocabulary borrowed from Chinese at early dates (rather as much of English vocabulary is derived from Latin and Greek). Often the words in the receiving languages preserve aspects of pronunciation which were lost in Chinese long ago. And borrowings happened into Chinese too. When Buddhism reached China from India, many Sanskrit terms arrived with it; looking at how the Chinese used their own script to write those terms gives us information about how the graphs were said at the time. When I began to study the language, it puzzled me that the name "Buddha" was 'Fo' in Chinese. Why 'Fo'?—the words seemed to have nothing in common. But we believe that modern Chinese 'fó' derives, via a long series of sound changes, from an earlier *but*, which may well have been the closest a Chinese mouth could get to the sounds of Sanskrit *buddha*.

There are further kinds of evidence too. I shall not give more detail here, but readers wanting to pursue the issue could consult, for instance, William Baxter's 1992 *Handbook of Old Chinese Phonology*.

The fact that Chinese at the Odes period was pronounced differently from modern Mandarin (or from any other present-day Chinese dialect) is of course rather obvious simply because lines which are clearly intended to rhyme often, now, don't. Chinese scholars realized more than a thousand years ago that sounds must have changed; and in the Qing dynasty (the last imperial dynasty, A.D. 1644–1911) the topic was studied more systematically. The pioneer of this study in the West was the Swede Bernhard Karlgren, whose 1957 book *Grammata Serica Recensa* became for many years the standard authority on Old Chinese pronunciation.

In the past quarter-century there has been an explosion of research in this area. Various scholars have built on the foundation laid by Karlgren, and (to quote from the announcement of an academic conference on Old Chinese held in Germany in 2018), "reconstruction systems [recently] proposed independently by different scholars ... resemble each other much more than earlier reconstructions". By now it seems fair to say that we have a reasonably clear idea of the original pronunciation of most words in the Odes. There naturally remain differences of opinion about details, and nobody would suggest that if we could go back in a time machine we could pass for native speakers of the language—that would be too much to expect for any language without living speakers. But my guess is that we probably could make ourselves understood, doubtless with some difficulty (whereas there is no chance at all that an Old Chinese speaker could understand Mandarin).

So it makes sense to print the Odes in our reconstructed version of their original pronunciation. And that is the only way that anyone can fully appreciate them as poetry, a form of literature in which not just the ideas but the physical sounds of words matter.

I said that scholars continue to differ over details. To proceed, we must pick out one particular reconstruction of Old Chinese for our transcriptions. The obvious choice is the version published by Axel Schuessler in books which appeared in 2007 and 2009. Schuessler's reconstruction follows Baxter's *Handbook* closely but improves on it in a number of respects, and it seems destined to replace Karlgren's system as the standard account of Old Chinese. One reason for saying that is that Schuessler's books (unlike Baxter's) are arranged as dictionaries, in which one can straightforwardly look up any particular word and see its Old Chinese pronunciation.

Schuessler's system is attractive also because of the modesty of his claims. He calls it "Minimal Old Chinese", meaning that it includes those features which most scholars agree on, without succumbing to the temptation to postulate speculative refinements.

Furthermore, if I had treated Baxter rather than Schuessler as the authority to follow, it would have been logical to keep up with developments in Baxter's thinking since his *Handbook*. That book was a very sensible, uncontroversial treatment, but more recently Baxter has changed his mind. He has teamed up with the Frenchman Laurent Sagart to publish, in 2014, a quite different reconstruction which is full of features that can only be described as at best highly speculative. (I note that my own reaction to Baxter and Sagart's new theory is shared by various expert reviewers.)

I am sure that, if we want to hear the Odes as they sounded when they were new, our most reasonable approach is to transcribe them according to Schuessler's system. Having said that there are differences of scholarly opinion, I shall write from now on as if Schuessler's version of the language were the unchallengeable truth. That is not so, but it would be unprofitable to draw attention to uncertainties wherever they arise in the text of individual Odes. This is intended to be a readable book of poetry, not a densely scientific work of philology.

Having settled on Schuessler's version of Old Chinese, in a book addressed to the general reader it is necessary to modify his spelling conventions slightly. Schuessler uses several phonetic symbols, which are the best way to indicate sounds unambiguously to professional linguists, but are offputting to readers who have not studied phonetics. In this book it is important that Old Chinese should not just be pronounceable but look pronounceable, spelled with ordinary letters arranged in reasonably ordinary combinations. So I have replaced Schuessler's phonetic symbols with suitable letters of the Roman alphabet. Naturally, Old Chinese cannot look precisely like English, because it has some different sounds, and even when sounds are the same they occur in different combinations. In English the "ng" sound occurs only after vowels, but in Old Chinese it often begins a syllable: "fish" is *nga*. (*Ng* is always the single sound of "singer", not the "ngg" of "finger".) Some aspects of Old Chinese pronunciation will look quite surprising to Chinese-speakers today—over a gap of three millennia, that is only to be expected.

Old Chinese had six simple vowels, which I spell *a e i o ou u*. The first four have their usual Continental values, and *ou* is as in French, the vowel of English *boot*. The letter *u* represents the vowel written "er" by English people (who do not sound the letter *r* after a vowel) or "uh" by Americans (who do). There are diphthongs, *ay aw oy* as in English *bite, bout, Boyd*; *ouy* as in

English *gooey*; *iw* is "ee-oo" run together as one syllable, and *uy* is "er-ee" (for Americans, "uh-ee") again as one syllable.

Turning to consonants: while English and other European languages commonly have a two-way contrast between "voiceless" and "voiced" stop consonants—p/b, t/d, k/g—Old Chinese, like Ancient Greek, had a three-way contrast between "aspirated", "unaspirated", and "voiced": *ph/p/b, th/t/d, kh/k/g*. The aspirated stops, *ph th kh*, are like English p t k, which are normally pronounced with aspiration, whereas unaspirated *p t k* are like those letters as pronounced in French. Note that *ph, th* are not the sounds of English *phone, thin*. (Sounds like those are not thought to have occurred in Old Chinese, and these absences may not be a matter of chance. Few ancient languages have the F sound—Swiss linguists have shown that it arose as a consequence of anatomical changes caused by modern dietary habits; and it has been argued, though controversially, that there is a genetic component in the propensity of various populations to use "th" sounds.) Of course, if anyone cares to make reading aloud easier by pronouncing Old Chinese *ph, th* as in English, why not? It will not affect the rhymes, and it is what we usually do in reading Ancient Greek.

I use *ts* and *tz* to represent aspirated and unaspirated t + s combinations, rather than writing the former cumbersomely and ambiguously as *tsh*.

The sounds I spell *sh ch j dj* were originally sequences of *s ts tz dz* respectively followed by *r*, and they may still have been sequences of separate sounds at the Odes period. At some stage the sequences merged into the single sounds which they are in the modern language, like the English sounds spelled "sh ch j" except that they are "retroflex"—made with the tip of the tongue curled back towards the roof of the mouth. I have assumed that the sequences had already merged by the Odes period, an assumption which simplifies my Old Chinese spellings.

Like Welsh, Old Chinese had voiceless counterparts to the voiced sounds *l r m n ng*; I spell the voiceless consonants *lh rh mh nh ngh*—*lh* is the sound spelled *ll* in Welsh place names like *Llanelli*. As the first letter of a word, on the other hand, the letter *h* represents the sound which is written ch in Scots "loch" or as J in Spanish *Juan*—I will call it the "loch" sound. (*Hl* and *hr* are different from *lh* and *rh*—the former spellings each represent a sequence of two sounds, the first in each case being the "loch" sound.) Marginally, there is also a "voiced h", which I spell as *gh*.

The letter *s* always has the sound of S rather than Z: *dans* "cooked food" is like English *dance*, not *Dan's*, and *dàws* "robber" is like *douse*, not *dowse*.

The sequences *kw-, gw-, ngw-* at the beginning of a syllable each represent a single consonant, *k, g,* or *ng* said with the lips rounded as for *w*, and the first and third of these are the same sound that I write *-wk, -wng* at the end of a syllable (*-wg* does not occur). Similarly, *hw-* is the "loch" sound said with rounded lips.

Schuessler uses a hyphen to separate prefixes from roots. These hyphens usually have no relevance for pronunciation, in which case my spellings ignore them. However, when a *k-* prefix is attached to a root beginning with *h*, representing the "loch" sound, I write this sequence as *k'h*, to distinguish it from *kh* as the aspirated stop.

The most awkward aspect of the Old Chinese spelling system relates to the glottal stop: the sound which occurs instead of T in a Cockney utterance of, say, *meat* as *mea'*. All the experts agree that the glottal stop was frequent in Old Chinese, and functioned as a separate consonant, not a variant of another consonant as in the Cockney case. Alongside *khak* "coarse cloth" and *khat* "martial-looking" there was *khaʔ* "eliminate", where *ʔ* is the phonetic symbol for glottal stop.

For the general reader a spelling system which used the sign ʔ would be unacceptable, and even a page littered with apostrophes would be unattractive, looking as though many letters had been left out. Yet the Roman alphabet offers no letter for the glottal stop.

Where a glottal stop occurs before a vowel, there is no contrast in Schuessler's Old Chinese between presence and absence of glottal stop: if a syllable has no other initial consonant, he always writes it with the glottal stop symbol. So in those cases there is no need for my spelling to include anything at all. English words whose spelling begins with a vowel are often said with an initial glottal stop in practice, and we can leave it to be understood that in Old Chinese that was always so. Where the glottal stop follows a nasal consonant *m n* or *ng* at the end of a syllable, I spell the combinations as *mp nt nk* (which amount to much the same, phonetically).

There remain many cases of glottal stop following a vowel, where there is a contrast between presence and absence of the stop. We saw that *khaʔ* is "eliminate"; on the other hand *kha* is "ruins". My solution here may look strange, but I believe it is preferable to alternatives: I write these glottal stops as *-c*, for instance I spell "eliminate" as *khac*. The resulting spellings look reasonably natural as sequences of letters; the obvious interpretation of a final *-c* is as a K sound, and while Old Chinese *-c* is not a K sound (that is always spelled *k*) it is at least another kind of stop—the syllable is cut off abruptly rather than fading gradually, potentially an important feature in the context of poetry. And there are hints in the Odes that speakers of Old Chinese heard the two sounds as similar. In Ode 209 *sluc* "sacrifice" appears in a rhyming position in a verse where all the other rhyme words end in *–uk*.

Unfortunately, we have not quite finished with glottal stops. Although Schuessler's reconstruction involves no contrasts between presence and absence of this sound before vowels, he does have such a contrast before the sounds *r*, *w*, and *y*: for instance "excellent" is *rang*, while "ornament, gem" is *rang* preceded by glottal stop. My problem here is that I find it hard to believe that any language would distinguish between presence and absence of glottal stop just before "semivowels" but not before full vowels—that is not, I would have said, how human languages work. I understand the reasoning which led Schuessler to reconstruct Old Chinese that way, but I believe there must be another explanation. However, there must have been some difference between these pairs of syllables: I mark the contrast in a neutral fashion by writing *rr*, *ww*, *yy* double where Schuessler has a preceding glottal stop. Thus I spell "ornament" as *rrang*.

I have deviated in one minor way from my policy of spelling everything with the 26 letters of our alphabet. There is one phonetic contrast running through Old Chinese which we know to have existed, but whose nature is unknown: all Old Chinese syllables are classified as Type A or Type B, depending on how they later developed, but we do not know what the original difference between the two types was. There are plenty of theories, for instance several scholars suggest it was a difference between long and short vowels. But one of these men suggests that Type A syllables had long vowels and Type B short, while another has it the other way round. I myself think it unlikely that the distinction related to vowel length, because syllables of the two types rhyme with one another freely—I would expect a vowel-length contrast to interfere with rhyming. It seems more likely that the difference related to the consonants beginning a syllable, and there are theories along those lines too. But, since we do not know what the distinction was (and the theory which strikes me as most plausible—consonants in Type A syllables were "pharyngealized"—is too technical to go into here), it is best to mark the distinction unobtrusively and noncommittally. Schuessler marks Type A syllables (the less frequent type) with a circumflex accent; I prefer grave, as less obtrusive. Whatever the difference between Type A and Type B syllables was, it did not affect rhyming or scansion, so anyone who reads the Odes aloud can safely ignore the accents.

Finally, in one respect even Schuessler's spellings involve an unnecessary speculation; to avoid this I have adopted his own suggestion of rewriting his -s as -ts and his -h as -s. That point apart, I do not give details on the rules by which I convert Schuessler's phonetic symbols to my reader-friendly spellings: to anyone who compares our books, these will be obvious.

For a minority of words, Schuessler is undecided between alternative reconstructions. In such cases I pick one to use here, more or less at random. Occasionally I have been persuaded by some scholar's discussion of the etymology of a particular word to spell that word differently from Schuessler's reconstruction. Schuessler's 2009 dictionary seems to confuse the alternative readings of the very common graph 其, and I have rearranged these to agree with Karlgren's dictionary. And in one case I have preferred Baxter's to Schuessler's reconstruction of a word for a frankly non-scholarly reason. An ancient musical instrument resembling the zither plays an important role in the romantic poem which is the very first of the Odes, and I found myself unwilling to spell its Old Chinese name as *shit*.

While Schuessler's version of Old Chinese pronunciation is about as close to the reality as we are ever likely to get, there may well have been a few further sounds which the evidence we have does not allow us to reconstruct. Schuessler suggests this by calling his reconstruction "Minimal Old Chinese"; and there are several factors in the reconstruction which point in this direction. One is the number of homophones—words listed in my Glossary with the same pronunciation but different meanings. As an extreme case, the syllable *gou* can have any of seven seemingly unrelated senses, each written differently in Chinese script—some of them are: "urgent; long and curved; to seek; a chisel". True, any language has some homophones. In English, "right" can mean "correct, proper; opposite of left; an entitlement", and the same spoken syllable can be spelled "rite", "write", "wright", with further meanings. It is not self-evident that the incidence of homophony is greater in Schuessler's Old Chinese than in English, but impressionistically it does seem suspiciously high. Then there is the fact that homophones are occasionally allowed to rhyme. In Western poetry, rhymes must sound alike from the last stressed vowel onwards, but we expect them to sound *different* before that point—if a poet were to rhyme *feet* with *feat*, say, I think we would see that as verging on the childish. Yet in Ode 180 we find three different words all reconstructed as *wuc* (and meaning "have", "friend", and "right"), all used as rhymes for one another. And in the opening stich of Ode 194, *Gòuc-gòuc Gòuc Thin*, we find two words both reconstructed as *gòuc* and meaning respectively "vast" and "bright" used contrastively: "Bright Sky in its vastness".

We cannot know whether *Tiw* Chinese had the same feelings about speech-music as we in the 21st-century West. Perhaps "over-rhyming" sounded perfectly acceptable to them. But there is an alternative possibility: that some words which Schuessler reconstructs as homophones in reality differed in ways invisible to us. That might easily be so. For instance, Schuessler's Old Chinese has many words ending in voiceless stops: *-p, -t, -k, -wk*; but none at all ending in their voiced counterparts—no *-b, -d, -g, -wg*. Suppose that in reality there were such words, but some time after the Odes period word-final voiced stops all dropped; then when the poems were written the numerous *gou* words would actually have been said *goub, goud*, and so forth, and there would have been far fewer homophones, but Schuessler, and we, would have no way of discovering that. (I am not saying that this particular development did happen, only that it is the *kind* of thing which easily could have happened.) The three *wuc* words of Ode 180 might have had some unreconstructable difference in their initial consonants.

Perhaps it sounds implausible that a language could change in ways which mean that huge numbers of different words come to sound exactly the same. But it shouldn't sound implausible, because we know with certainty that, more recently, Chinese behaved in exactly that way. Modern Chinese not only has no words ending in voiced stops—it has no final stops at all, the –p –t –k of Old Chinese have all dropped out, leaving masses of words that sounded different at the Odes period now sounding exactly the same. And many other sound-changes on the road from Old Chinese to the modern language have merged what used to be distinct pronunciations. Whether or not the incidence of homophones in Schuessler's Old Chinese reconstruction is unusually high, the incidence in modern Chinese is truly colossal, and the language has had to take drastic steps to avoid communication breaking down through ambiguity. It has replaced what was an almost entirely monosyllabic vocabulary with two-syllable compound words. In Old Chinese the words *bùng* and *wuc* both meant something like "friend", and more than one Ode uses them together as a phrase, *bùng wuc*. In modern Chinese that is the only way they can be used—the phrase *bùng wuc* has turned into a single word 'péngyǒu' for "friend", and neither 'péng' nor 'yǒu' can be used on its own—ten different Old Chinese words are each said 'péng' in the modern language, and thirteen are each said 'yǒu', so as independent words they would be too ambiguous. One of the most characteristic features of the history of Chinese has been the replacement of a monosyllabic vocabulary with a vocabulary that is predominantly disyllabic. It is as if, in modern English, we regularly said things like "It's timehour to gowalk homehouse", and "time" or "hour" as separate words had become meaningless.

This is another reason why I show names in the Old Chinese forms which were actually used by the bearers of the names. Chinese names in any form tend to be confusing to Westerners because of unfamiliarity; but, alphabetized in their modern pronunciations, they are far more confusing because the modern language has so few different-sounding syllables. The same few syllables, Li, Fu, Yi, and so on, recur again and again. We have seen that three rivers mentioned in the Odes, *Wuts*, *Wets*, and *Wruc*, all come out in modern pronunciation as 'Wei'. For Chinese readers the problem is solved by their script, which assigns distinct graphs to separate roots whether or not they sound alike. For Western readers to whom Chinese script is impenetrable, spelling names in their Old Chinese form helps to keep the *dramatis personae* straight.

Rhymes

Almost all the Odes rhyme, and for stichs to "rhyme" means the same as in a European language: the sounds of the stichs from their last stressed vowel onwards are the same. As we saw when considering metre, most words receive some stress, so that commonly only the last words of stichs are relevant for rhyming. But there are cases where an unstressed last word causes rhyming to begin with the preceding word. In Ode 1 we find *tsùc tu* "gather them" rhyming with *wuc tu* "befriend her", where *tu* is the all-purpose object pronoun. And, like English folk-songs, the Odes had syllables which were inserted for the sake of rhythm rather than meaning: *ì*, or *luc*. Again these cause rhyming to begin with the preceding word, so in Ode 3 we find the last four stichs rhyming in *tsa luc* "rocks, oh", *dà luc* "ill, oh", *pha luc* "sick, oh", *hwa luc* "sad, oh".

Rhyming often seems a little looser than would be usual in Western poetry. We must be cautious here: the reconstruction of Old Chinese pronunciation is not likely to be perfect, so if a pair of lines which "ought" to rhyme appear to do so poorly, this could be because there is a mistake in the reconstruction of one of the rhyming words. It would be remarkable if there were not some cases like that. I do not believe, though, that there are numerous cases. Even when rhymes look imperfect, there is often system in the imperfections.

In some cases the appearance of imperfect rhyming is a consequence of my Old Chinese spelling system. Syllables ending in –*i* often rhyme with syllables in –*uy*, and –*iw* syllables with

-*ou* syllables. But *uy* spells a diphthong "uh-ee" while *i* spells the "ee" sound, so there is no reason not to see these as matching phonetically; and likewise for "ee-oo" (*iw*) and "oo" (*ou*).

In other cases there are real discrepancies. The *s* sound and the glottal stop (which I spell *c*) seem to count less than other consonants: it is very common for syllables in –*s* or –*c* to rhyme with syllables having the same vowel with no following –*s* or –*c*, or with one another. It is not that these sounds count for nothing at all: more often than not, –*s* syllables rhyme with –*s* syllables and –*c* syllables with –*c* syllables—but the alternative happens often enough that it must have been heard as an acceptable deviation from perfect rhyming. Neither consonant still occurs at the end of modern Chinese syllables; they have both dropped out of the language, though in doing so they created some of the tone distinctions which make modern Chinese phonetically so different from Western languages. It may be that when some of the Odes were composed, –*s* and –*c* were already weaker than other consonant sounds.

Some other pairs of sounds which we know to have been different were on occasion not so different that they could not be rhymed. We looked at the occasional rhyming of glottal stop with –*k* on p. 37, but there are other examples; for instance it is not uncommon for *ou* to rhyme with *u*, or *e* with *i*. Phonetically this makes sense: these pairs of vowels are closer to one another than either member of the pairs is to most other vowels.

Consider verse 2 of Ode 257, which contains eight stichs, with the rhyme-scheme A B A B A B A B. The A words are *gwruy*, *luy*, *rì*, *ùy*, and it is only my spelling system that makes *rì* look like an imperfect rhyme for –*uy*. But the B words are *phen*, *mint*, *dzins*, *bin*. Not one of these words ends with precisely the same sounds as any other. Taking *bin* as the basic rhyme, *phen* differs by having the vowel *e* rather than *i*; *mint*, by having a glottal stop after the *n*; and *dzins* by the addition of *s*. Yet all of these were evidently acceptable rhymes.

The other aspect of Odes rhyming which strikes us as imperfect or tentative is the variability of rhyme schemes within single Odes. The verse just discussed has a very regular scheme in which alternative stichs rhyme, even if the rhyming is not always exact. But verse 1 of the same Ode has a slight variation: A B A B A B B B. Verse 3 has one stich which rhymes with none of the others: A B C B A B A B; and verse 4 moves the "odd" rhyme to a later stich: A B A B C B A B. The rhyme scheme of verse 6 is quite different: A B A B C C D D. Later verses have six rather than eight stichs, and by the last verse rhyming seems to have gone right off the rails: A B C D E C.

If rhyming poetry was novel when the Odes were written, then this variability is perhaps to be expected: poets were feeling their way. We may be looking at the very birth of a technique which later became central to poetry in many parts of the world.

A first step

I should like to end this Introduction with some personal remarks on why I found this book worth the labour of producing.

These poems are one accessible introduction to a civilization which is one of the most complex and most successful that has ever evolved on our planet, and one which, until the last 150 years or less of its three-thousand-year history, was completely untouched by the European-based civilization familiar to Western readers.

Yet the enormous vastness and richness of China, in time, numbers, and cultural complexity, has been hidden from the average Westerner by a remarkably low level of interest in the country. For most Westerners, China falls into a similar category to Siberia: everyone knows it is there, they know it is big, but few care to go into details. This astonishing narrow-mindedness was brought home to me when I studied Chinese language and culture as an undergraduate in one of the West's most distinguished academic centres of Sinology. My graduating class in 1965 numbered three students. Three!—when, elsewhere in the same university, hundreds were studying the far smaller-scale, Johnny-come-lately cultures of France and Germany. (Today students of Chinese are more numerous, but they focus mainly on the modern Mandarin language, which has been a standard written language for only the past hundred years, and these have hardly been the most inspiring or instructive hundred years of China's history.)

In the globalized societies of the 21st century, it is not easy to learn about sophisticated ways of life that are thoroughly separate from ours. We hear a lot today about multiculturalism and diversity. In my experience, those who mouth these slogans loudest tend to be wholly innocent of any real knowledge of cultures other than their own.

This cannot be healthy. When I graduated, I took away from my studies a deep respect for Chinese civilization, and also, through comparison and contrast, a much clearer understanding and valuation than I had before of my own cultural inheritance as an Englishman. As the decades have passed, it has become increasingly clear to me that these lessons—both of them—were the right ones to draw. And they have been joined by consternation at how the distinctive approaches to social organization characteristic of my own nation are being eroded or unthinkingly discarded.

Human cultures are not trivial veneers. They are, or can be, deeply different from one another. They are not casually interchangeable; they vary greatly in the extent to which they satisfy individuals' aspirations, and in the aims which they prioritize at the expense of others. Anyone who has influence over the general nature of his or her society, which in a democracy means all of us, needs to understand this. The only way I know to grasp it viscerally as well as just theoretically is to soak oneself in knowledge of a thoroughly separate civilization. Education used to encourage this, via study of the Greeks and Romans. China is arguably a better case, because more separate.

Clearly, reading an anthology of ancient poetry could be no more than a tiny first step; but it might be that. The Odes show us a rich, subtle civilization at a period when Britain had none at all. For the next three thousand years, China went on deepening and broadening its degree of sophistication and complexity. Many readers will read these poems for their inherent charm and pass on, and that in itself is good. One or two, though, might perhaps be moved to learn more about traditional China. If so, then they are in for an intellectual feast. And my work in compiling this book will have been richly rewarded.

Appendix: Unprintable Graphs

The Odes contain a handful of words which are so thoroughly obsolete that their graphs are not included in printing fonts. These are represented in the poems and the Glossary by the symbol ○; I spell out the obsolete graphs here using Unicode "ideographic description characters", with which for instance 字 can be shown as ⿱宀子.

dòuk₂	⿲艹⿱□氵 毒
grùk₂	⿰革羽
khes	⿰匕支
khòy	⿰亻過
mou₄	⿰髟敄
ryawks	⿰广樂
tzi₄	⿱齊皿

List of Works Consulted

Allen, J.R., "A literary history of the *Shi Jing*". In Allen, ed., *The Book of Songs: The Ancient Chinese Classic of Poetry*, Grove Press, New York, 2000, pp. 336–83.
Barber, Elizabeth W., *The Mummies of Ürümchi*, paperback edn. Pan, London, 2000.
Baxter, W.H., *A Handbook of Old Chinese Phonology*. Mouton de Gruyter, Berlin, 1992.
Baxter, W.H. and L. Sagart, *Old Chinese: a New Reconstruction*. Oxford University Press, 2014.
Blasi, D.E. et al., "Human sound systems are shaped by post-Neolithic changes in bite configuration". *Science*, vol. 363, issue 6432, 2019.
Boltz, W.G., *The Origin and Early Development of the Chinese Writing System*. American Oriental Society, New Haven, Conn., 1994.
Brosnahan, L.F., *The Sounds of Language*. Heffer, Cambridge, 1961.
Chen Kuangyu, "The Book of Odes: a case study of the 2600 years Chinese hermeneutic tradition". In Tu Ching-i, ed., *Interpretation and Intellectual Change*, Transaction Publishers, New Brunswick, N.J., 2005, pp. 47–62.
Chiang Yee, *Chinese Calligraphy*, 3rd edn. Harvard University Press, Cambridge, Mass., 1972.
Article on "Chinese Calendar". At <www.newworldencyclopedia.org/entry/Chinese_calendar>, accessed 9 Dec 2019.
Confucius, 論語 (*The Analects*). Edition published by 廣智書局 (Kwong Chi Book Company), Hong Kong, 1966.
Cook, Constance A., "Ancestor worship during the Eastern Zhou", 2011. In Lagerwey and Kalinowski, pp. 237–79.
Davidson, J., *Courtesans and Fishcakes*. St Martin's Press, New York, 1997.
Dawson, R., ed., *The Legacy of China*. Clarendon Press, Oxford, 1964.
Deydier, C., *Understanding Ancient Chinese Bronzes*. Privately published at <www.deydier.com/livres/iaba/Livre EN.pdf>, accessed 28 Oct 2019.
Eifring, H., "Emotions and the conceptual history of *qíng* 情". In Eifring, ed., *Love and Emotions in Traditional Chinese Literature*, Brill, Leiden, 2004, pp. 1–36.
Empson, W., *Seven Types of Ambiguity*, 3rd edn. Penguin, Harmondsworth, Mddx, 1961.
Grigson, G., *The Englishman's Flora*. Reprinted by Helicon Publishing, Oxford, 1996.
Harbsmeier, C., "Irrefutable conjectures" (review article on Baxter and Sagart). *Monumenta Serica*, vol. 64, 2016, pp. 445–504.
Herrmann, A., *An Historical Atlas of China*, new edn. Edinburgh University Press, 1966.
Ho Dah-an, "Such errors could have been avoided" (review article on Baxter and Sagart). *Journal of Chinese Linguistics*, vol. 44, 2016, pp. 175–230.
Karlgren, B., *Glosses on the Book of Odes*. Bulletin of the Museum of Far Eastern Antiquities, Stockholm, no. 14, 1942, pp. 71–247, no. 16, 1944, pp. 25–169, and no. 18, 1946, pp. 1–198.
Karlgren, B., *Glosses on the Book of Documents*. Bulletin of the Museum of Far Eastern Antiquities, Stockholm, no. 20, 1948, pp. 39–315, and no. 21, 1949, pp. 63–206.
Karlgren, B., *The Book of Odes: Chinese Text, Transcription and Translation*. Museum of Far Eastern Antiquities, Stockholm, 1950.
Karlgren, B., *Grammata Serica Recensa*. Bulletin of the Museum of Far Eastern Antiquities, Stockholm, vol. 29, 1957, pp. 1–332.

Karlgren, B., *Sound and Symbol in Chinese*, revised edn. Hong Kong University Press, 1962.
Keightley, D., "The Bamboo Annals and Shang-Chou chronology". *Harvard Journal of Asiatic Studies*, vol. 38, 1978, pp. 423–38.
Kern, M., " 'Shi Jing' songs as performance texts: a case study of 'Chu ci' (Thorny Caltrop)". *Early China*, vol. 25, 2000, pp. 49–111.
Kern, M., "The Odes in excavated manuscripts". In Kern, ed., *Text and Ritual in Early China*, University of Washington Press, 2005, pp. 149–93.
Kern, M., "Excavated manuscripts and their Socratic pleasures: newly discovered challenges in reading the 'Airs of the States' ". *Etudes Asiatiques/Asiatische Studien*, vol. 61, 2007, pp. 775–93.
Kern, M., "Bronze inscriptions, the *Shijing* and the *Shangshu*", 2011. In Lagerwey and Kalinowski, pp. 143–200.
Le Roy Ladurie, E., *Montaillou*, paperback edn. Penguin, Harmondsworth, Mddx, 1980.
Lagerwey, J. and M. Kalinowski, eds, *Early Chinese Religion, part one: Shang through Han* (2 vols). Brill, Leiden, 2011.
Lee, Lily A.H. and A.D. Stefanowska, eds, *Biographical Dictionary of Chinese Women: Antiquity through Sui*. University of Hong Kong Libraries Publications, no. 21, 2007.
Legge, J., *The Chinese Classics*, vol. III: *The Shoo King*, 1865. Reprinted by SMC Publishing, Taipei, 2000.
Legge, J., *The Chinese Classics*, vol. IV: *The She King*, 1871. Reprinted by 文星書店 (Wen Xing Shudian), Taipei, 55th year of the Republic (i.e. 1966).
Legge, J., *The Chinese Classics*, vol. V: *The Ch'un Ts'ew with the Tso Chuen*, 1872. Reprinted by FB&c, London, n.d.
Liu, J.J.Y., *The Art of Chinese Poetry*. Routledge and Kegan Paul, London, 1962.
Loewe, M., ed., *Early Chinese Texts*. Institute of East Asian Studies, Berkeley, Calif., 1993.
Loewe, M. and E.L. Shaughnessy, eds, *The Cambridge History of Ancient China: From the Origin of Civilization to 221 B.C.* Cambridge University Press, 1999.
毛詩正義 (*Mao Shi Zheng Yi*). Online at <ctext.org/library.pl?if=gb&res=77714>, accessed 9 Dec. 2019.
Maspero, J., *La Chine antique*, new edn. Imprimerie Nationale, Paris, 1955.
Needham, J., *Science and Civilisation in China*, vol. 3. Cambridge University Press, 1959.
Nivison, D., "An interpretation of the 'Shao gao' ". *Early China*, vol. 20, 1995, pp. 177–93.
Nivison, D., "The key to the chronology of the Three Dynasties: the 'Modern Text' Bamboo Annals". *Sino-Platonic Papers*, no. 93, 1999, <www.sino-platonic.org/complete/spp093_bamboo_annals.pdf>, accessed 9 Dec 2019.
Norman, J., *Chinese*. Cambridge University Press, 1988.
Pulleyblank, E.G., "The locative particles yu 于, yu 於, hu 乎". *Journal of the American Oriental Society*, vol. 106, 1986, pp. 1–12.
Pulleyblank, E.G., *Outline of Classical Chinese Grammar*. University of British Columbia Press, Vancouver, 1995.
Pullum, G.K, *The Great Eskimo Vocabulary Hoax*. University of Chicago Press, 1991.
Reischauer, E.O. and J.K. Fairbank, *East Asia: the Great Tradition*. Houghton Mifflin, Boston, Mass., 1960.
Riegel, J., "Eros, introversion, and the beginnings of *Shijing* commentary". *Harvard Journal of Asiatic Studies*, vol. 57, 1997, pp. 143–77.
Sagart, L., *The Roots of Old Chinese*. John Benjamins, Amsterdam, 1999.
Sampson, G.R., *Love Songs of Early China*. Shaun Tyas, Donington, Lincs., 2006.
Sampson, G.R., *Writing Systems*, 2nd edn. Equinox, Sheffield, 2015.

de Saussure, L., *Les Origines de l'astronomie chinoise*. *T'oung Pao* vol. 10, 1909, pp. 121–82 & 255–305; vol. 11, 1910, pp. 221–92, 457–88, & 583–648; vol. 12, 1911, pp. 347–74; vol. 14, 1913, pp. 388–426; vol. 15, 1914, pp. 645–96; vol. 20, 1921, pp. 86–116; and vol. 21, 1922, pp. 251–318.

Schuessler, A., *ABC Etymological Dictionary of Old Chinese*. University of Hawai'i Press, Honolulu, 2007.

Schuessler, A., *Minimal Old Chinese and Later Han Chinese: a companion to* Grammata Serica Recensa. University of Hawai'i Press, Honolulu, 2009.

Schuessler, A., "New Old Chinese" (review of Baxter and Sagart). *Diachronica*, vol. 32, 2015, pp. 571–98.

Shaughnessy, E., review of Sampson, *Love Songs of Early China*. *Modern Philology*, vol. 106, 2008, pp. 197–200.

Shaughnessy, E., "Writing and rewriting the *Poetry*". Paper presented to the International Symposium on Excavated Manuscripts and the Interpretation of the *Book of Odes*, Chicago, 2009.

舒新城 (Shu Xincheng) et al., eds-in-chief, 辭海. 中華書局 (Zhonghua Shuju), Kunming, 27th year of the Republic (i.e. 1938).

Starostin, G., review of Baxter and Sagart. *Journal of Language Relationship*, vol. 13, 2015, pp. 383–389.

Stenton, F., *The First Century of English Feudalism, 1066-1166*, 2nd edn. Clarendon Press, Oxford, 1961.

Thurgood, G. and R.J. LaPolla, eds., *The Sino-Tibetan Languages*. Routledge, London, 2003.

Waley, A., *The Book of Songs*, 2nd edn. Allen and Unwin, London, 1952.

Wheatley, P., *The Pivot of the Four Quarters*. Edinburgh University Press, 1971.

v. Wilamowitz-Moellendorff, U., "Choriambischer Dimeter". *Sitzungsberichte der Königlich Preussischen Akademie der Wissenschaften*, vol. 34, 1902, pp. 864–96.

Willetts, W., *Chinese Art* (2 vols). Penguin, Harmondsworth, Mddx, 1958.

Wong, L.K.P., "Image-making in classical Chinese poetry and in Western poetry". In M. Gálik, ed., *Proceedings of the 2nd International Sociological Symposium*, Bratislava, 1993, pp. 177–89; reprinted in Wong, *Thus Burst Hippocrene: Studies in the Olympian Imagination*, Cambridge Scholars Publishing, Newcastle-upon-Tyne, 2018, pp. 230–57.

許慎 (Xu Shen), 説文解字. Reprint of Song dynasty edn by 徐鉉 (Xu Xuan), 中華書局 (Zhonghua Shuju), Kowloon, 1972.

張允中 (Zhang Yunzhong), 白話註解詩經. 商務印書館 (Commercial Press), Taipei, 60th year of the Republic (i.e. 1971).

PREDYNASTIC PERIOD

"Yellow Emperor" r. 2287–2188

"White Emperor", father of Millet Lord, r. 2100–2038

2000 BC

Ngyáw r. 2026–1969
Hwins r. 1968–35
Wac founds Ghàc dynasty, r. 1934–07

GHÀC

Lhàng founds Un dynasty, r. 1554–43

1500 BC

UN

Mac Teng r. 1250–1189

Drouc r. 1069–40, last Un king; Mun ruler of Tiw state 1101–1050, succeeded by Mac
Battle of Herdsman's Heath, 1040; Mac becomes king of China, d. 1038
1000 BC   Deng r. 1037–06; Khàng r. 1005–978

W. *TIW*

Rats r. 859–28 (*de jure*, exiled 841)
Swan r. 827–784
Iw r. 783–; conquered by father-in-law allied with barbarians, 771
Capital moves east; Breng r. 770–18

E. *TIW*

599: latest historical event referred to in the *Odes*

500 BC

A Timeline of Early Chinese History and Myth

VOICES FROM EARLY CHINA

The Airs of the States

State of *Tiw* and Southwards

Tiw here refers to the area around modern Xi'an which was the Western *Tiw* "royal domain", and "Southwards", it is presumed, to minor states further south.

1

The Fish-Hawk 關雎

Kròn, kròn, calls the fish-hawk on an islet in the River.
A girl who's alluring and lithe is the fit match for a princely man.

Kròn, kròn, tsa-kou, dzùc Gày tu tou.　　關關雎鳩　在河之洲
Ìwc-lìwc diwk nrac kwun-tzuc hòuc gou.　　窈窕淑女　君子好仇

Unevenly grow the floating-hearts, to left and right we pick them.
A girl who's alluring and lithe, waking and sleeping I search for her.

Chum-chay grànk tsùs, tzàyc wuc riw tu.　　參差荇菜　左右流之
Ìwc-lìwc diwk nrac, ngàs mits gou tu.　　窈窕淑女　寤寐求之

I search for her but don't find her; waking and sleeping I brood about her.
Ah, longing! Ah, longing! Restlessly I toss and turn.

Gou tu pu tùk, ngàs mits sus buk.　　求之不得　寤寐思服
You tzù! You tzù! Trent-tront pant juk.　　悠哉悠哉　輾轉反側

Unevenly grow the floating-hearts, to left and right we gather them.
A girl who's alluring and lithe, with lute and zither I'll befriend her.

Chum-chay grànk tsùs, tzàyc wuc tsùc tu.　　參差荇菜　左右采之
Ìwc-lìwc diwk nrac, gum sprit wuc tu.　　窈窕淑女　琴瑟友之

Unevenly grow the floating-hearts, to left and right we reap them.
A girl who's alluring and lithe, with bells and drums I'll delight her.

Chum-chay grànk tsùs, tzàyc wuc màws tu.　　參差荇菜　左右芼之
Ìwc-lìwc diwk nrac, tong kàc ngràwks tu.　　窈窕淑女　鍾鼓樂之

Floating-hearts, scientifically *Nymphoides*, are river plants like miniature water lilies; their shoots are edible. On the fish-hawk and the sound *kròn*, see pp. 29–30.

2

The Spreading Lablab Vine 葛覃

How the lablab vine spreads! It covers all the middle of the valley.
Its leaves are dense.
There are orioles on the wing—they are settling in the copse.
They sing harmoniously.

Kàt tu lùm ì! Lhay wa troung klòk.	葛之覃兮　施于中谷
Wi lap tsì-tsì.	維葉萋萋
Gwàng tìwc wa puy, dzup wa kwàns mòk.	黃鳥于飛　集于灌木
Gu mreng krì-krì.	其鳴喈喈

How the lablab vine spreads! It covers all the middle of the valley.
It's thick with leaves.
We cut them and boil them, to make fine cloth and coarse cloth
—people never tire of wearing it.

Kàt tu lùm ì! Lhay wa troung klòk.	葛之覃兮　施于中谷
Wi lap màk-màk.	維葉莫莫
Dec ngats, dec gwàk, way thruy, way khak.	是刈是濩　為絺為綌
Buk tu ma lak.	服之無斁

I shall talk to the mistress about going home for a visit.
Let's see: I must wash my undies, and launder my dresses.
Which ones shall I launder, which ones not? When I go home, it will put Mum and Dad's minds at rest.

Ngan kòuk shi gec, ngan kòuk ngan kwuy.	言告師氏　言告言歸
Bàk wwà ngàyc si, bàk gwànt ngàyc uy.	薄污我私　薄澣我衣
Gàt gwànt, gàt puc? Kwuy nèng bac muc.	曷澣曷否　歸寧父母

A girl in service away from home plans a visit back to her parents.

Kàt is a family of bean-bearing vine plants, notably including the lablab bean or hyacinth bean (*Lablab purpureus*), which is both useful and a showily ornamental plant, with pink flowers and purple pods on vines up to thirty feet long. *Kàt* vines can be plaited into cords, the beans and other parts are edible, and fibres from the leaves were woven into cloth. I do not know why "people never tire of wearing it", but then I don't know what the alternatives then available felt like on the body. There is no single English name covering the range of vines called *kàt*, so for simplicity I translate this word as "lablab" wherever it occurs in the Odes; but cloth was probably made from the fibres of *Pachyrhizus tuberosus* (yam bean, or potato bean).

Gwàng tìwc, "yellow bird", was a name for the black-naped oriole, *Oriolus sinensis*, regarded by the Chinese as having an outstandingly lovely song.

3

The Mouse-Ears 卷耳

Picking the mouse-ears, I'm not even filling my slanted-basket.
Alas, my beloved, they have sent him on the *Tiw* road.

Tsùc-tsùc kont-nuc, pu leng kwheng-kwhang. 采采卷耳　不盈頃筐
Tzay ngàyc gròuy nin, tets payc Tiw gràng. 嗟我懷人　寘彼周行

I'd go up that crag, but my horse is worn out.
I'll just pour some wine into the bronze jar,
to stop my endless yearning.

Truk payc dzòuy-ngòuy, ngàyc mràc gòuyc-dòuy. 陟彼崔嵬　我馬虺隤
Ngàyc kà tyawk payc kum ròuy, 我姑酌彼金罍
wi luc pu wrank gròuy. 維以不永懷

I'd go up that high ridge, but my horse has the black-and-yellow sickness.
I'll just pour some wine into the water-buffalo drinking horn,
to stop my endless grieving.

Truk payc kàw kàng, ngàyc mràc gwìn-gwàng. 陟彼高岡　我馬玄黃
Ngàyc kà tyawk payc syuyc kwràng, 我姑酌彼兕觥
wi luc pu wrank lhang. 維以不永傷

I'd go up those rocks, oh, but my horse is sick, oh,
my driver is disabled, oh—how miserable I am, oh!

Truk payc tsa luc, ngàyc mràc dà luc. 陟彼砠矣　我馬瘏矣
Ngàyc bòk phà luc. Wun gày hwa luc! 我僕痡矣　云何吁矣

Kont-nuc, "rolled ears", is the Chinese name for the edible plant mouse-ear chickweed, *Cerastium vulgatum*. A *kwheng-kwhang*, "slanted-basket", was used for harvesting. The *Tiw* road was the road to the dynastic capital, so a young man sent that way had been taken to serve, probably as a soldier. The poet hopes that if she could get to the top of the hill she might see him returning.

The word *tziwc* referred to any alcoholic drink. The poet may have meant wine, though not wine made from grapes (which were not known in China at the time), or this *tziwc* may have been spirits distilled from some type of grain. We have no general term in English, so when *tziwc* occurs in the Odes I translate it as "wine" for simplicity, but one should bear in mind that this is over-specific.

We don't know what *gwìn-gwàng*, "black and yellow", referred to, but in the context it seems likely to be some illness of horses.

4

Sagging Branches 樛木

In the south are trees with sagging branches, weighed down by ropes of vine and creeper.
May our lord be happy—may he relax in the enjoyment of good fortune and respect.

Nùm wuc kiw mòk, kàt rouyc rouy tu.　　　　　　　南有樛木　葛藟纍之
Ngràwks kec kwun-tzuc, puk ric snouy tu.　　　　樂只君子　福履綏之

In the south are trees with sagging branches, smothered in vines and creepers.
May our lord be happy—may good fortune and respect make him a great man.

Nùm wuc kiw mòk, kàt rouyc mhàng tu.　　　　　南有樛木　葛藟荒之
Ngràwks kec kwun-tzuc, puk ric tzang tu.　　　　樂只君子　福履將之

In the south are trees with sagging branches, wound round by vines and creepers.
May our lord be happy—may good fortune and respect make him the complete ruler.

Nùm wuc kiw mòk, kàt rouyc wweng tu.　　　　　南有樛木　葛藟縈之
Ngràwks kec kwun-tzuc, puk ric deng tu.　　　　樂只君子　福履成之

The sagging branches might seem wholly unrelated to the lines about a *kwun-tzuc* (in this case an actual nobleman), until one appreciates that creepers hanging from the branches of a tree were a standard metaphor for subjects' dependence on the support of their ruler.

5

Locusts 螽斯

Locusts are numberless, oh;
it will be fitting that you have similarly numerous descendants.

Toung se wac shun-shun ì.　　　　　　　　　　　螽斯羽　詵詵兮
Ngay nec tzuc sòun tun-tun ì.　　　　　　　　　宜爾子孫　振振兮

Locusts are countless, oh;
it will be fitting that your lineage too continues endlessly into the future.

Toung se wac mhùng-mhùng ì.　　螽斯羽　薨薨兮
Ngay nec tzuc sòun mlung-mlung ì.　　宜爾子孫　繩繩兮

Locusts occur in swarms, oh;
it will be fitting that your descendants are similarly multitudinous.

Toung se wac jup-jup ì.　　螽斯羽　揖揖兮
Ngay nec tzuc sòun drup-drup ì.　　宜爾子孫　蟄蟄兮

An uninspiring little poem which expresses the same simple wish in three slightly different ways. (The poet literally says that locusts' wings are numerous.)

6

The Delicate Peach-Tree　桃夭

How delicate is the peach-tree: its flowers blaze bright.
This young lady is off to her new home; she will put in order her chamber and her household.

Làw tu aw-aw: tyawk-tyawk gu wà.　　桃之夭夭　灼灼其華
Tu tzuc wa kwuy; ngay gu lhit krà.　　之子于歸　宜其室家

How delicate is the peach-tree: its fruit are very well-set.
This young lady is off to her new home; she will put in order her household and her chamber.

Làw tu aw-aw: wuc bun gu mlit.　　桃之夭夭　有蕡其實
Tu tzuc wa kwuy; ngay gu krà lhit.　　之子于歸　宜其家室

How delicate is the peach-tree: its leaves grow in profusion.
This young lady is off to her new home; she will put in order her household staff.

Làw tu aw-aw: gu lap dzin-dzin.　　桃之夭夭　其葉蓁蓁
Tu tzuc wa kwuy; ngay gu krà nin.　　之子于歸　宜其家人

A poem of optimism about a new bride's future. A peach-tree is delicately lovely, but it knows its business.

7

The Rabbit Net 兔罝

They hammer the pegs of the rabbit net in—*tèng, tèng* they beat them down.
Handsome are the warriors: protective bulwarks to their prince.

Siwk-siwk lhàs-tza—tròk tu tèng tèng.　　　肅肅兔罝　椓之丁丁
Kaw-kaw mac pa, klòng gò gàns geng.　　　嬌嬌武夫　公侯干城

They hammer the pegs of the rabbit net in—they set it out where many roads meet.
Handsome are the warriors: good comrades to their prince.

Siwk-siwk lhàs-tza—lhay wa troung grou.　　肅肅兔罝　施于中逵
Kaw-kaw mac pa, klòng gò hòuc gou.　　　　嬌嬌武夫　公侯好仇

They hammer the pegs of the rabbit net in—they set it out in the middle of the copse.
Handsome are the warriors: their prince's guts and heart.

Siwk-siwk lhàs-tza—lhay wa troung rum.　　肅肅兔罝　施于中林
Kaw-kaw mac pa, klòng gò pouk sum.　　　　嬌嬌武夫　公侯腹心

This Ode may have been intended as an illustration of social mobility under the *Tiw*. According to the records, *Mun* "raised from their rabbit nets" two named men and made them ministers in his government.

8

Gathering Plantains 芣苢

Here we go gathering plantains, yea, we're gathering them.
Here we go gathering plantains, yea, we've got them.

Tsùc tsùc bu-luc, bàk-ngan tsùc tu.　　　　采采芣苢　薄言采之
Tsùc tsùc bu-luc, bàk-ngan wuc tu.　　　　采采芣苢　薄言有之

Here we go gathering plantains, yea, we're picking them.
Here we go gathering plantains, yea, we're plucking them.

Tsùc tsùc bu-luc, bàk-ngan tòt tu.　　　　采采芣苢　薄言掇之
Tsùc tsùc bu-luc, bàk-ngan ròt tu.　　　　采采芣苢　薄言捋之

Here we go gathering plantains, yea, we're carrying them in our skirts.
Here we go gathering plantains, yea, we're tucking our skirts up to carry them.

Tsùc tsùc bu-luc, bàk-ngan krìt tu. 采采芣苢 薄言袺之
Tsùc tsùc bu-luc, bàk-ngan gìt tu. 采采芣苢 薄言襭之

Was it a nursery rhyme, or perhaps a work song?

Plantains are a genus of low-lying weeds, which have many and various uses in folk medicine.

9

The Wide River Han 漢廣

Here in the south there are tall trees—too tall to rest under.
Here by the river Han are girls of leisure—not for the likes of us to pursue.
How wide the Han is—too wide to wade across.
How long the Yangtze is—too long to take a raft down.

Nùm wuc gaw mòk, pu khàyc hou su. 南有喬木 不可休思
Hàns wuc you nrac, pu khàyc gou su. 漢有游女 不可求思
Hàns tu kwànk luc, pu khàyc wrangs su. 漢之廣矣 不可泳思
Kròng tu yangs luc, pu khàyc pang su. 江之永矣 不可方思

The dense brushwood has grown high; we cut the thorn-trees.
These girls go off on their wedding journeys, and we feed their horses.
How wide the Han is—too wide to wade across.
How long the Yangtze is—too long to take a raft down.

Gyaw-gyaw tsàk sin, ngan ngats gu chac. 翹翹錯薪 言刈其楚
Tu tzuc wa kwuy, ngan màt gu mràc. 之子于歸 言秣其馬
Hàns tu kwànk luc, pu khàyc wrangs su. 漢之廣矣 不可泳思
Kròng tu yangs luc, pu khàyc pang su. 江之永矣 不可方思

The dense brushwood has grown high; we cut the *rò* wood.
These girls go off on their wedding trips, and we feed their colts.
How wide the Han is—too wide to wade across.
How long the Yangtze is—too long to take a raft down.

Gyaw-gyaw tsàk sin, ngan ngats gu rò. 翹翹錯薪 言刈其蔞
Tu tzuc wa kwuy, ngan màt gu ko. 之子于歸 言秣其駒
Hàns tu kwànk luc, pu khàyc wrangs su. 漢之廣矣 不可泳思
Kròng tu yangs luc, pu khàyc pang su. 江之永矣 不可方思

VOICES FROM EARLY CHINA

A song of young men who recognize that the local gentry girls are out of their league. Trees can be so tall that they offer no shade or shelter; rivers so broad or long that those with no proper boat at their command cannot hope to navigate them. These girls will marry, but the poet's only roles will be to cut firewood for their parents' houses (we don't know what *rò* wood was), and to look after the girls' horses as they prepare to leave.

The Yangtze and Han rivers are both well to the south of the original *Tiw* area, on the far side of the Qinling range. This is one of several cases that leave us wondering about the basis for dividing the Airs of the States into subsections.

10

On the Embankment of the *Nac* 汝墳

I walk along the embankment of the *Nac*, cutting back encroaching growth.
I haven't yet seen my prince: I hunger as one hungers for breakfast at daybreak.

Tzoun payc Nac bun, bat gu lìw mùy.　　遵彼汝墳　伐其條枚
Muts kèns kwun-tzuc; nìwk na trous kri.　　未見君子　惄如調飢

I walk along the embankment of the *Nac*, cutting back dead branches.
Now I have seen my prince: he wasn't distant, he didn't reject me!

Tzoun payc Nac bun, bat gu lìw lits.　　遵彼汝墳　伐其條肄
Kuts kèns kwun-tzuc; pu ngàyc grà khits!　　既見君子　不我遐棄

The tail of the bream is red. The royal household blazes in glory like a fire.
But although it is glorious as a fire, Mum and Dad will be very close.

Bang nga threng muyc. Wang lhit na mhayc.　　魴魚赬尾　王室如燬
Swi-tzùk na mhayc, bac muc khònk nec.　　雖則如燬　父母孔邇

I take this as the poem of a girl with hopes of marrying a member of the ruling family but unsure of her situation: when the grandeur of the palace feels frightening, she comforts herself with the thought that her parents are always on her side.

The river *Nac* (now Ru) is a minor river in south-east Henan—again a long way from the *Tiw* royal domain.

11

A Unicorn's Hooves 麟之趾

A unicorn's hooves!
Tally-ho, you mighty duke's sons: it's a unicorn!

Rin tu tuc! 麟之趾
Tun-tun klòng tzuc, hwa-tzay rin ì! 振振公子　吁嗟麟兮

A unicorn's forehead!
Tally-ho, you mighty men of the duke's family: it's a unicorn!

Rin tu tèng! 麟之定
Tun-tun klòng sengs, hwa-tzay rin ì! 振振公姓　吁嗟麟兮

A unicorn's horn!
Tally-ho, you mighty men of the duke's clan: it's a unicorn!

Rin tu kròk! 麟之角
Tun-tun klòng dzòk, hwa-tzay rin ì! 振振公族　吁嗟麟兮

The word *rin* or *gu-rin* (in modern Chinese 'lin' or 'qilin') has in recent times referred to a mythical beast, and is conventionally translated as "unicorn". But at this early period a *rin* was a real, though rare, deer-like animal. (Famously, the last entry in a historical work called *Spring and Autumn Annals* records the capture of a *rin* in 480 B.C., implying that by then it was very rare indeed.) It was re-imagined as a mythical animal after becoming extinct in reality.

Gu-rin is among a number of two-syllable terms for exotic fauna and flora, which perhaps entered Chinese from neighbouring languages whose vocabularies were polysyllabic. In Chinese the assumption that words are monosyllables is so entrenched that these terms were reinterpreted as pairs of words: according to the scholars, *gu* and *rin* meant respectively "male unicorn" and "female unicorn". This is a rationalization, not likely to have any etymological basis.

State of *Daws* and Southwards

When *Mun* shifted his capital from Qishan to *Phoung*, he divided *Tiw* into two, bestowing the western half, around modern Baoji, Shaanxi, on one of his leading supporters (who may have been his son by a concubine) and calling it *Daws*; the eastern half, which retained the name *Tiw*, would go to his heir *Mac*. The ruler of *Daws*, known to history as the Duke of *Daws*, played an important role in establishing the new dynasty, and he may have been effectively co-regent with the Duke of *Tiw* after *Mac*'s death.

By the time when the Airs of the States were written, *Daws* was merely a place within the Western *Tiw* royal domain. This is one of several ways in which the division of the Airs of the States into subsections seems to have been done anachronistically.

12

Magpie and Dove   鵲巢

> It's the magpie that builds the nest, but the pearl-necked dove that inhabits it.
> This young lady is going to her new home, and there are a hundred carriages to meet her.

Wi tsak wuc jàw: wi kou kas tu.   　　維鵲有巢　維鳩居之
Tu tzuc wa kwuy, pràk rangs ngràs tu.　之子于歸　百兩御之

> It's the magpie that builds the nest, but the pearl-necked dove that occupies it.
> This young lady is going to her new home, and there are a hundred carriages to escort her.

Wi tsak wuc jàw: wi kou pang tu.   　　維鵲有巢　維鳩方之
Tu tzuc wa kwuy, pràk rangs tzang tu.　之子于歸　百兩將之

> It's the magpie that builds the nest, but the pearl-necked dove that fills it.
> This young lady is going to her new home, and there are a hundred carriages to complete her entourage.

Wi tsak wuc jàw: wi kou leng tu.   　　維鵲有巢　維鳩盈之
Tu tzuc wa kwuy, pràk rangs deng tu.　之子于歸　百兩成之

The magpie is a common bird in China. *Kou* often occurs as a suffix to a specific bird-name (as in the first line of Ode 1), but as an independent word it is thought to refer to the pearl-necked dove, *Streptopelia* or *Spilopelia chinensis*. This is more colourful and rather smaller than a magpie, and the Chinese believed (mistakenly, I understand) that it commonly invaded and occupied a magpie's nest rather than taking the trouble to build its own. Thus the poem is effectively an unflattering image of a marriage among the nobility, involving much pomp; but the essence of the occasion is that the bride is taking the benefits of a grand position to which she is not entitled through any merit of her own. The bride will "fill" her new nest with maidservants and so forth. To make the metaphor even less flattering, the Chinese also believed that doves were unusually stupid birds, which was all right because, as a Song-dynasty commentator remarked, "The duties of a wife are few and confined; there is no harm in her being stupid." (His words, not mine.)

13

Gathering Mugwort 采蘩

She goes out to gather mugwort, by the ponds and on the islets.
She goes so that it can be used in the prince's sacrifices.

Wa luc tsùc ban, wa tawc, wa tuc.   于以采蘩　于沼于沚
Wa luc longs tu, klòng gò tu shuc.   于以用之　公侯之事

She goes out to gather mugwort, by the stream in the ravine.
She goes so that it can be used in the prince's temple.

Wa luc tsùc ban, wa kràns tu troung.   于以采蘩　于澗之中
Wa luc longs tu, klòng gò tu koung.   于以用之　公侯之宮

How full her head-dress is!—morning and evening she is at the palace.
How large her head-dress is!—and then she returns home.

Bays tu dòng-dòng! Souk yas dzùc klòng.   被之童童　夙夜在公
Bays tu gri-gri! Bàk-ngan swen kwuy.   被之祁祁　薄言還歸

Mugwort was used in sacrificial rites; it was burned like incense, and caused participants to see visions.

14

Insects in the Grass 草蟲

Insects in the grass shrill *yyaw-yyaw*; grasshoppers jump about.
When I haven't yet seen my man, my sad heart is agitated;
but when I've seen him, when I've met him, then my heart settles down.

Yyaw-yyaw tsòuc droung; lhyàwk-lhyàwk bouc-toung.   喓喓草蟲　趯趯阜螽
Muts kèns kwun-tzuc, ou sum throung-throung;   未見君子　憂心忡忡
yak kuts kèns tu, yak kuts kòs tu, ngàyc sum tzùk gròung.   亦既見之　亦既覯之
    我心則降

I climb the Southern Mountains to gather the turtle-foot fern that grows there.
When I've not yet seen my man, my sad heart is grieved;
but when I've seen him, when I've met him, then my heart is glad.

Truk payc Nùm shàn, ngan tsùc gu kot.   陟彼南山　言采其蕨
Muts kèns kwun-tzuc, ou sum trot-trot;   未見君子　憂心惙惙
yak kuts kèns tu, yak kuts kòs tu, ngàyc sum tzùk lot.   亦既見之　亦既覯之
                   我心則悅

I climb the Southern Mountains to gather the royal fern that grows there.
When I've not yet seen my man, my sad heart is afflicted;
but when I've seen him, when I've met him, then my heart is at peace.

Truk payc Nùm shàn, ngan tsùc gu muy.   陟彼南山　言采其薇
Muts kèns kwun-tzuc, ou sum lhang pruy;   未見君子　我心傷悲
yak kuts kèns tu, yak kuts kòs tu, ngàyc sum tzùk luy.   亦既見之　亦既覯之
                   我心則夷

A wife waits for her husband's return. We shall see that the trope "before I have seen my *kwun-tzuc*, I am sad, but when I have seen him I am happy" recurs frequently in the Odes. It perhaps sounds unduly abject—could an adult woman not manage on her own for a while without collapsing into misery? But this was a world without telephones, postal service, or modern medicine—and where a wife was entirely dependent on her husband for the means of subsistence. Perhaps her heart really would be in her mouth in case some accident or disease carried him off. It may also be that women wrote poems expecting their husbands to read them, and it was in their interest to exaggerate their emotional dependence.

(In most cases of this trope, including this one, I take *kwun-tzuc* to mean "my prince, my lord" in the sense "my husband", though where similar wording occurred in Ode 10 it seemed more likely that the *kwun-tzuc* was an actual ruling-family member.)

The "Southern Mountains", often mentioned in the Odes, are the range today called Qinling, south of the Wei valley. It has peaks rising to 5000 feet, and even higher at its western end; obviously this lady was walking only in the foothills. *Kot* and *muy* are two edible ferns; *muy* is "royal fern", *Osmunda regalis*—I do not know precisely what *kot* is, but in Chinese it is commonly called "turtle's foot".

15

Gathering Water Clover   采蘋

We go and gather water clover by the bank of the stream in the southern gully.
We go and gather ditch-grass from the puddles by the road.

Wa luc tsùc bin, nùm kràns tu pin.   于以采蘋　南澗之濱
Wa luc tsùc tzàwc, wa payc gràng ràwc.   于以采藻　于彼行潦

We go and collect them into baskets square and round.
Then we go and boil them in pots and cauldrons.

Wa luc deng tu, wi kwhang gup kac.   于以盛之　維筐及筥
Wa luc sang tu, wi gayc gup bac.   于以湘之　維錡及釜

We go and set them out as sacrificial offerings below the window of the ancestral temple.
Who will be the Corpse? We have a ritually-pure young girl.

Wa luc dìns tu, tzòung lhit louc gràc.   于以奠之　宗室牖下
Douy gu lhi tu? Wuc jì kwits nrac.   誰其尸之　有齋季女

Bin and *tzàwc* are both aquatic plants: *tzàwc* is probably "ditch-grass", *Ruppia maritima* (not a marine species despite its Latin name), *bin* is water clover (*Marsilea* spp.), which has parts called sporocarps that can be eaten, though if not correctly prepared they are poisonous. (It is thought that water clover, in Australia called "nardoo", was what killed the explorers Burke and Wills.)

What we don't know is why cooked water-weeds were a suitable offering to the ancestors. Usually, ritual sacrifices involve the best that people have to offer, whereas one authority comments that ditch-grass is "eaten only in times of famine". We may have here a glimpse of a desperate community on the edge of starvation.

On the other hand, the mention of a corpse is less dramatic than it sounds—it doesn't imply human sacrifice. An offering of food to an ancestral spirit would hardly be successful if it was left uneaten, so a teenage descendant represented the ancestor and ate the offering, or a sample of it. That person was called the "Corpse".

16

The Birchleaf Pear　甘棠

Pleasantly shady is that birchleaf pear tree.
Don't trim it, don't cut it down: this is where the lord of *Daws* bivouacked.

Pets-puts kàm dàng.   蔽芾甘棠
Mut tzent, mut bat: Daws pràk shac bàt.   勿翦勿伐　召伯所茇

Pleasantly shady is that birchleaf pear tree.
Don't trim it, don't destroy it: this is where the lord of *Daws* stopped to rest.

Pets-puts kàm dàng.   蔽芾甘棠
Mut tzent, mut pràts: Daws pràk shac khats.   勿翦勿敗　召伯所憩

Pleasantly shady is that birchleaf pear tree.
Don't trim it, don't bend its branches: this is where the lord of *Daws* halted for the night.

Pets-puts kàm dàng. 蔽芾甘棠
Mut tzent, mut prèts: Daws pràk shac lhots. 勿翦勿拜　召伯所說

The later inhabitants of *Daws* are protecting a living memorial to the founder of their society. The birchleaf pear, *Pyrus betulifolia*, is grown as an ornamental tree rather than for fruit. Its habit is high and broad enough to make the bivouacking tale entirely plausible.

17

Dew on the Road　行露

The road is wet with dew:
morning or evening, when is it not?
I'll say there's too much dew on the road.

Ep-up gràng ràks: 厭浥行露
khuyc pu, souk yas? 豈不夙夜
Wuts gràng tày ràks. 謂行多露

Who says a sparrow has no beak? How else does it make a hole in our roof?
Who says you have no family behind you? How else could you be pressing a
　　lawsuit on us?
But though you press your lawsuit, your family won't win.

Douy wuts tzyawk ma kròk? Gày luc thon ngàyc òk? 誰謂雀無角　何以穿我屋
Douy wuts nac ma krà? Gày luc sòk ngàyc ngok? 誰謂汝無家　何以速我獄
Swi sòk ngàyc ngok, lhit krà pu tzok. 雖速我獄　室家不足

Who says a rat has no teeth? How else does it make a hole in our wall?
Who says you have no family behind you? How else could you press your case
　　against us?
But though you press your case, still I shan't go to you.

Douy wuts nhac ma ngrà? Gày luc thon ngàyc long? 誰謂鼠無牙　何以穿我墉
Douy wuts nac ma krà? Gày luc sòk ngàyc slong? 誰謂汝無家　何以速我訟
Swi sòk ngàyc slong, yak pu nac dzong. 雖速我訟　亦不汝從

A girl's father has promised her in marriage to a man from an influential family; now the time has come to marry him, she is determined not to, despite his trying to use the law to make her fulfil the bargain. (Karlgren remarked that "Conflicts like this [were] not uncommon" in the China of his day.) The dew is quoted as an always-available excuse for being unable to make the wedding journey—hardly a plausible excuse, but the girl is clutching at straws. Sparrows, like rats, were despised creatures.

18

Braids of White Silk 羔羊

On his lamb furs, five braids of white silk.
He has withdrawn from the court to dine. How gracious he is!

Kàw yang tu bay, sàs su ngàc lày.　　　　　　　　羔羊之皮　素絲五紽
Thòuts mluk dzis klòng; oy-lay, oy-lay!　　　　退食自公　委蛇委蛇

On his lambskins, five plaits of white silk.
How gracious he is! He has retired from the court to eat.

Kàw yang tu krùk, sàs su ngàc hwuk.　　　　　羔羊之革　素絲五緎
Oy-lay, oy-lay! Dzis klòng thòuts mluk.　　　　委蛇委蛇　自公退食

Over the seams in his lamb furs, five tresses of white silk.
How gracious he is! He has withdrawn from the court to dine.

Kàw yang tu bongs, sàs su ngàc tzònk.　　　　羔羊之縫　素絲五總
Oy-lay, oy-lay! Thòuts mluk dzis klòng.　　　　委蛇委蛇　退食自公

Someone's head has been turned by the behaviour and dress of a distinguished arrival at court. The lambswool is likely to have been naturally dark in colour, so if white silk braids were sewn over the seams to hide them, they would stand out well.

19

The Sound of Thunder 殷其靁

Unt sounds the thunder from beyond the Southern Mountains.
Why have you left me so completely? I can't rest for a moment.
Oh, my awesome prince: come home, come home!

Unt kus ròuy dzùc Nùm shàn tu lang.　　　　殷其靁　在南山之陽
Gày ses wuy se? Màk kàmp wùk wàng.　　　　何斯違斯　莫敢或遑
Tuns-tuns kwun-tzuc: kwuy tzù, kwuy tzù!　　振振君子　歸哉歸哉

Unt sounds the thunder from the side of the Southern Mountains.
Why have you left me so completely? I can't relax at all.
Oh, my awesome prince: come home, come home!

Unt kus ròuy dzùc Nùm shàn tu juk.　　　　　殷其靁　在南山之側
Gày ses wuy se? Màk kàmp wàng suk.　　　　何斯違斯　莫敢遑息
Tuns-tuns kwun-tzuc: kwuy tzù, kwuy tzù!　　振振君子　歸哉歸哉

Unt sounds the thunder from below the Southern Mountains.
Why have you left me so completely? I can't be still for a moment.
Oh, my awesome prince: come home, come home!

Unt kus ròuy dzùc Nùm shàn tu gràc.　　殷其靁　在南山之下
Gày ses wuy se? Màk wùk wàng k'hlac.　　何斯違斯　莫或遑處
Tuns-tuns kwun-tzuc: kwuy tzù, kwuy tzù!　　振振君子　歸哉歸哉

The word "awesome" has been devalued in recent English, but here it is meant in its etymological sense, awe-inspiring: *tuns-tuns*, literally something or someone that shakes the world—like those thunderclaps from the distant mountains, which the poetess optimistically hears as getting closer.

20

The Plum Tree is Shedding　摽有梅

The plum tree is shedding: it has seven fruit left.
Various gentlemen are courting me: may good fortune arrive!

Byawc wuc mùc; gu mlit tsit ì.　　摽有梅　其實七兮
Gou ngàyc lhaks shuc; lùc gu kit ì!　　求我庶士　迨其吉兮

The plum tree is shedding: it has three fruit left.
Various gentlemen are courting me: may the time arrive!

Byawc wuc mùc; gu mlit sùm ì.　　摽有梅　其實三兮
Gou ngàyc lhaks shuc; lùc gu kum ì!　　求我庶士　迨其今兮

The plum tree is shedding: I gather the fruit in my slanted-basket.
Various gentlemen are courting me: may a proposal arrive!

Byawc wuc mùc; kwheng-kwhang huts tu.　　摽有梅　頃筐墍之
Gou ngàyc lhaks shuc; lùc gu wuts tu!　　求我庶士　迨其謂之

21

Little Stars　小星

Those little stars are twinkling, the Three and the Five in the east.
Early and late, we scurry off on our night-expeditions at the palace.
Truly, our fate is not the same as hers.

Hwìts payc syawc sèng, Sùm Ngàc dzùc tòng. 嘒彼小星　三五在東
Siwk-siwk syaw teng, souk yas dzùc klòng. 肅肅宵征　夙夜在公
Dit mreng pu dòng. 寔命不同

Those little stars are twinkling—only Orion's Belt and the Pleiades are left.
We scurry away on our night-expeditions, carrying quilt and nightdress.
Truly, our fate is not like hers.

Hwìts payc syawc sèng, wi Shum lac Mròuc. 嘒彼小星　維參與昴
Siwk-siwk syaw teng, bòuc khum lac driw. 肅肅宵征　抱衾與裯
Dit mreng pu you. 寔命不猶

A concubine's life was inferior to that of a ruler's principal wife, who lived in the fine rooms of the palace by day as well as night. The concubines visit the master when he summons them and then hasten back to the women's quarters through the cold night air in the small hours.

The Chinese divide the night sky into constellations differently from Westerners; Chinese constellations tend to be smaller, for instance Orion's Belt is seen as a complete unit rather than part of a larger array. The Chinese zodiac is divided into 28 rather than twelve houses. The "Three Stars", or "Heart", comprises Antares and two lesser stars in our constellation of Scorpio. I cannot identify the "Five".

22

Sidestreams of the Yangtze　江有汜

The Yangtze has its sidestreams.
My lady has come to her new home, but she won't use us
—she won't use us, but let's hope that later she changes her mind.

Kròng wuc sluc. 江有汜
Tu tzuc kwuy, pu ngàyc luc 之子歸　不我以
—pu ngàyc luc, gu ghòc layc mhùs. 不我以　其後也悔

The Yangtze has its islets.
My lady has come to her new home, but she won't mix with us
—she won't mix with us, but let's hope that later she settles down.

Kròng wuc tac. 江有渚
Tu tzuc kwuy, pu ngàyc lac 之子歸　不我與
—pu ngàyc lac, gu ghòc layc k'hlac. 不我與　其後也處

The Yangtze has its leats.
My lady has come to her new home, but she won't go near us
—she won't go near us, but let's hope that her hissing noises will change to singing.

Kròng wuc dray.
Tu tzuc kwuy, pu ngàyc kòy
—pu ngàyc kòy, gu sìws layc kày.

江有沱
之子歸　不我過
不我過　其嘯也歌

A principal wife would prefer to be the only woman in her husband's life, and is sulkily refusing to accept that she must share him with her "younger sisters" (p. 16), for instance she is not organizing their work as the mistress of a household should.

The opening images stand for the relationship between principal and subsidiary wives. A *sluc*, "sidestream", is a stream which departs from the main course of the river and later rejoins it. A *dray*, "leat", is an artificial sidestream, such as might power a water-mill.

The word *sìws* in the last line may be onomatopoeic. It is defined as making a sound with pursed lips; I interpret this as the kind of tsk, tsk noises which someone might make to express disapproval of the company she finds herself in while at least pretending that they cannot hear.

23

A Dead Deer in the Fields　野有死麕

There is a dead fallow-deer in the fields; wrap it in white cogon grass.
There is a girl full of springtime yearnings; lucky man, seduce her!

Lac wuc sic koun; bràk mròu pròu tu.
Wuc nrac gròuy thoun; kit shuc, louc tu.

野有死麕　白茅包之
有女懷春　吉士誘之

There is undergrowth in the forest; there is a dead sika deer in the fields.
Tie it into a bundle with white cogon grass. There is a girl like jade!

Rum wuc pòk-sòk; lac wuc sic ròk.
Bràk mròu dòun lhok. Wuc nrac na ngok.

林有樸樕　野有死鹿
白茅純束　有女如玉

Nice and slowly, now!
Don't flutter my neckerchief!
Don't let the dog bark!

Lha nu lhòts-lhòts ì!
Ma kùmp ngàyc tsots ì!
Ma shuc mròng layc bats.

舒而脫脫兮
無感我帨兮
無使尨也吠

A hunter is talking to himself: he has brought down two deer, and he likens the task of enticing an attractive girl to the task of dealing with the next deer—both are all too easily frightened away.

Cogon grass, *Imperata*, is a long reedy type of grass with silky white plumes, still used as a packing material today.

24

How Rich the Cherry Blossom　何彼襛矣

How rich it is, the blossom of the cherry trees.
How could we fail to offer a respectful welcome to the carriage of the royal *Kyu* clan?

Gày payc nong luc, glang-lìts tu wà.　　　何彼襛矣　唐棣之華
Gàt pu siwk ong, wang Kyu tu ka?　　　　曷不肅雝　王姬之車

How rich they are, the peach and plum trees in flower.
Oh, the granddaughter of king *Breng*, and the son of the marquis of *Dzì*!

Gày payc nong luc, wà na làw ruc.　　　　何彼襛矣　華如桃李
Breng wang tu sòun, Dzì gò tu tzuc!　　　　平王之孫　齊侯之子

What does one use for fishing? The line is made of nothing more than silk.
Oh, the son of the marquis of *Dzì*, and the granddaughter of king *Breng*!

Ku tyàwks wi gày? Wi su i moun.　　　　其釣維何　維絲伊緡
Dzì gò tu tzuc, Breng wang tu sòun!　　　　齊侯之子　平王之孫

A girl from the royal family has arrived in *Dzì* to marry the son of its ruler; she is lovely as fruit trees in flower. (*Glang-lìts* is a kind of cherry, thought to be the great white cherry, *Prunus taihaku*, which has particularly showy blossom.) *Breng* was the first Eastern *Tiw* king. As it takes a slender silken line to catch a solid fish, so it takes a delicate young girl to create a valuable alliance with royalty.

25

Tally-ho!　騶虞

By the sprouting rushes! One volley, five sows!
Tally-ho, you grooms and gamekeepers!

Payc jot tac krà! It pat ngàc prà!　　　　彼茁者葭　壹發五豝
Hwa-tzay ghà, jo ngwa!　　　　　　　吁嗟乎騶虞

By the sprouting fleabane! One volley, five piglets!
Tally-ho, you grooms and gamekeepers!

Payc jot tac bòng! It pat ngàc tzòng!　　　彼茁者蓬　壹發五豵
Hwa-tzay ghà, jo ngwa!　　　　　　　吁嗟乎騶虞

VOICES FROM EARLY CHINA

State of *Bùks*

After the battle of Herdsman's Heath, the victorious king *Mac* divided what had been the royal domain of the *Un* dynasty into three states: *Bùks* in the north, *Long* in the south, and *Wets* in the east. But again it is unclear why each of these is allotted a separate section of the "Airs of the States", because the first two were annexed by *Wets* well before the Airs are likely to have been written. *Bùks* became merely the name of a small place south of present-day Anyang in the far north-east of Henan.

26

Drifting With the Current   柏舟

That cypress-wood boat floats about, just drifting with the current.
I lie wide awake, unable to sleep, as one does with a secret sorrow.
It isn't that I have no wine to keep me jolly and amuse myself.

Bum payc pràk tou, yak bum gu riw.   汎彼柏舟　亦汎其流
Krènk-krènk pu mits, na wuc unt ou.   耿耿不寐　如有隱憂
Muy ngàyc ma tziwc, luc ngàw, luc you.   微我無酒　以敖以遊

My heart is not a mirror: you can't look into it.
Yes, I have brothers, but I can't rely on them
—look, if I try complaining to them about my situation, all I get from them is anger.

Ngàyc sum puyc gràms: pu khàyc luc nas.   我心匪鑒　不可以茹
Yak wuc hwrang dìc, pu khàyc luc kas: 亦有兄弟　不可以據
Bàk-ngan wank sngàks, bong payc tu nàc.   薄言往愬　逢彼之怒

My heart is not a stone: you can't throw it away.
My heart is not a mat: you can't roll it up.
I have been punctilious about maintaining my dignity—no-one could fault me there.

Ngàyc sum puyc dak: pu khàyc tron layc.   我心匪石　不可轉也
Ngàyc sum puyc slak: pu khàyc kont layc.   我心匪席　不可卷也
Ouy-ngay lùts-lùts; pu khàyc sònt layc.   威儀棣棣　不可選也

My grieving heart puts me constantly on edge, and I am disliked by my inferiors.
Plenty of distressing things have happened to me; not a few episodes have left me feeling insulted.
I brood about these things in silence; I lie awake, beating my breast in frustration.

Ou sum tsyawc-tsyawc, ouns wa gwun syawc.
Kòs mrunt kuts tày, douc moc pu hyawc.
Dzenk ngan sus tu, ngàs bek wuc phyàw.

憂心悄悄　慍于群小
覯閔既多　受侮不少
靜言思之　寤辟有摽

Sun, Moon, why do you periodically let yourselves be eclipsed?
My grieving heart feels like an unwashed dress sticking to me.
I brood about all this in silence, since I can't just spread my wings and fly off out of it.

Nit ka, Ngwat ta, gà lìt nu muy?
Sum tu ou luc, na puyc gwànt uy.
Dzenk ngan sus tu, pu nùc puns puy.

日居月諸　胡迭而微
心之憂矣　如匪澣衣
靜言思之　不能奮飛

Ode 26 and the next four Odes were traditionally held to be about a specific episode in the history of *Wets*. Duke *Jang* succeeded to the rulership of *Wets* in 756 and married a woman from the *Kyang* clan of *Dzì* state—she is known to history as *Jang Kyang*, from her husband's name and her clan name. Because *Jang Kyang* had no child, the duke adopted as heir a son, *Gon*, that he had with another lady of the harem, *Tùs Kway*, and *Jang Kyang* brought *Gon* up as if he were her own. But a third harem girl also had a son, *Tou-hwa*, who turned into a dashing but unscrupulous young man, and became a favourite with the duke. When the duke died in 734, *Gon* succeeded him, but in 718 *Tou-hwa* assassinated *Gon* and tried (unsuccessfully) to take his place. One consequence was that *Tùs Kway* had to leave *Wets* for her original state of *Dzin*. Each of these Odes is claimed to relate to this story; Ode 26 was supposed to be a complaint by *Jang Kyang* about being neglected by her husband.

However, there is little in this group of poems to support a link with that story. I needed to introduce *Jang Kyang* somewhere, because Ode 57 will be about her, but I am sceptical in this case. Behind the line about "disliked by my inferiors" one glimpses the type of lady who stands on her dignity and "can't keep servants"; and I suppose if she were a ruler's consort, that might explain the reference to sun and moon in verse 5—perhaps the writer was saying that she could never be mistreated if proper order were maintained in the heavens, whereas if even sun and moon allow themselves to be eclipsed, then a mere human must be vulnerable even if a duchess. It doesn't help with the opaque opening image of drifting boats, though; and while different commentators have agreed in linking this group of poems to historical figures, they have disagreed about who the figures were; for instance the Mao commentary claimed they were about the wife of the man who became ruler after *Tou-hwa* was defeated. So I have ignored the various theories and translated these Odes in their own terms, without introducing historical allusions.

27

The Green Jacket　綠衣

Ah, that green jacket—green jacket with yellow lining!
The grief in my heart: what will ever cure it?

Rok ì uy ì—rok uy, gwàng ruc! 綠兮衣兮　綠衣黃裏
Sum tu ou luc, gàt wi gu luc? 心之憂矣　曷維其已

Ah, that green jacket—green jacket and yellow skirt!
The grief in my heart: when will it ever fade?

Rok ì uy ì—rok uy, gwàng dang! 綠兮衣兮　綠衣黃裳
Sum tu ou luc, gàt wi gu mang? 心之憂矣　曷維其亡

Ah, that green silk, which you sewed with your own hands!
I contemplate the men of old, so as to be a decent man.

Rok ì su ì, nac shac dru ì! 綠兮絲兮　汝所治兮
Ngàyc sus kàc nin, pec ma wu ì. 我思古人　俾無訧兮

Ah, fine cloth, coarse cloth: in the wind both are chilly.
I contemplate the men of old, so that I can truly take command of my heart.

Thruy ì, khak ì: tsì kus luc pum. 絺兮綌兮　淒其以風
Ngàyc sus kàc nin, dit wàk ngàyc sum. 我思古人　實獲我心

He has lost the girl; much is unsaid, but the end of verse 3 perhaps implies that he blames himself for that. *Tiw*-dynasty Chinese tried to achieve a proper attitude by thinking about the ancestors, in something of the same spirit in which we might contemplate the life of Jesus. Dressing in thin fabrics, metaphorically, was fine in the summer days when the girl was with him, but now the season has changed he needs more robust psychological clothing.

28

Swallows　燕燕

Swallows wheel through the air—their wings seem to flicker.
This young lady is travelling to her new home, and I have accompanied her deep into the wilds.
I gaze after her till she vanishes from view, and my silent tears fall like rain.

Èns-èns wa puy—chay-dray gu wac. 燕燕于飛　差池其羽
Tu tzuc wa kwuy, want sòngs wa lac. 之子于歸　遠送于野
Tam mang put gup; khrup thìc na wac. 瞻望弗及　泣涕如雨

Swallows are on the wing, stretching out their necks.
This young lady is travelling to her new home, and I have escorted her a long stretch of the way.
I gaze after her till she vanishes from view, and I stand there, weeping.

Èns-èns wa puy—gìt tu, gàng tu. 燕燕于飛　頡之頏之
Tu tzuc wa kwuy, want wa tzang tu. 之子于歸　遠于將之
Tam mang put gup; drac rup luc khrup. 瞻望弗及　佇立以泣

Swallows are flying, calling as they now swoop down, now soar high.
This young lady is travelling to her new home, and I have brought her far to the south.
I gaze after her till she vanishes from view; my heart is truly sad.

Èns-èns wa puy—gràs dyank gu um. 燕燕于飛　下上其音
Tu tzuc wa kwuy, want sòngs wa nùm. 之子于歸　遠送于南
Tam mang put gup; dit ràw ngàyc sum. 瞻望弗及　寔勞我心

May you be strong, Second-Daughter! She has a sincere, deep heart;
she is a thoroughly gentle and kind girl, with a lithe, well-cared-for body.
I think about the rulers of old, to draw strength for my life as a lonely man.

Droungs-gec num kec! Gu sum sùk wwìn; 仲氏任只　其心塞淵
toung òun tsac wìts, diwk dins gu lhin. 終溫且惠　淑慎其身
Sùn kwun tu su, luc hok kwràc nin. 先君之思　以勗寡人

Swallows migrate, just as daughters go far from home to be married.

29

Oh Sun, oh Moon!　日月

Oh Sun, oh Moon! You shine down on the earth below.
Such a man: it has come to where he doesn't give me my old place any more.
How can things be resolved? Why does he ignore me?

Nit ka, Ngwat ta, tyaw rum gràc thàc. 日居月諸　照臨下土
Nùc na tu nin ì: dats pu kàc k'hlac. 迺如之人兮　逝不古處
Gà nùc wuc dèngs? Nèng pu ngàyc kàs? 胡能有定　寧不我顧

Oh Sun, oh Moon! You gaze down on the earth below.
Such a man: it has come to where the love between us is gone.
How can things be resolved? Why doesn't he do right by me?

Nit ka, Ngwat ta, gràc thàc dec mòus. 日居月諸　下土是冒
Nùc na tu nin ì: dats pu sang hòus. 迺如之人兮　逝不相好
Gà nùc wuc dèngs? Nèng pu ngàyc pòus? 胡能有定　寧不我報

Oh Sun, oh Moon! You rise out of the east.
Such a man: there is nothing good about his reputation.
How can things be resolved, so that I can forget about him?

Nit ka, Ngwat ta, k'hlout dzis tòng pang. 　　日居月諸　出自東方
Nùc na tu nin ì: tùk um ma rang. 　　迺如之人兮　德音無良
Gà nùc wuc dèngs, pec layc khàyc mang? 　　胡能有定　俾也可忘

Oh Sun, oh Moon! Out of the east you rise.
Father, mother, it seems you haven't finished looking after me.
How can things be resolved? It isn't right, the way he treats me.

Nit ka, Ngwat ta, tòng pang dzis k'hlout. 　　日居月諸　東方自出
Bac ì, muc ì, rhouk ngàyc pu tzout. 　　父兮母兮　畜我不卒
Gà nùc wuc dèngs? Pòus ngàyc pu mlout. 　　胡能有定　報我不述

30

Ceaseless Wind　終風

Ceaseless wind and cloudbursts. When you look at me, you smile,
but your joking goes too far, your laughter is arrogant. In my heart I'm sad.

Toung pum tsac bàwks. Kàs ngàyc tzùk saws, 　　終風且暴　顧我則笑
nghawk ràngs saws ngàw. Troung sum dec dàwks. 　　謔浪笑敖　中心是悼

Ceaseless wind and duststorms. Sweetly, you agree to come to me,
but there's no coming and going. Longingly I brood about you.

Toung pum tsac mrù. Wìts nan khènk rù, 　　終風且霾　惠然肯來
màk wank, màk rù. You-you ngàyc sus. 　　莫往莫來　悠悠我思

Ceaseless wind and overcast skies, no sun: it's thoroughly overcast.
When I go to bed I can't sleep; when I yearn for you, I feel chagrin.

Toung pum tsac ìts; pu nit, wuc ìts. 　　終風且曀　不日有曀
Ngàs ngan pu mits; ngons ngan tzùk thrits. 　　寤言不寐　願言則嚔

Oh, the gloom of the clouds; the rumbling of the thunder!
When I go to bed I can't sleep; when I yearn for you, I feel love.

Ìts-ìts gu um; hwuyc-hwuyc gu ròuy! 　　曀曀其陰　虺虺其靁
Ngàs ngan pu mits; ngons ngan tzùk gròuy. 　　寤言不寐　願言則懷

31

The Drumbeat 擊鼓

He: Hark, the boom of the beating drum. Men are jumping to and brandishing weapons.
They are fortifying the state with earthworks and walling *Dzòu* town. We alone march south!

Kèk kàc gu thàng, lonk lhyàwk longs prang.   擊鼓其鏜　踊躍用兵
Thàc kwùk, geng Dzòu; ngàyc dòk nùm gràng.   土國城漕　我獨南行

Our leader is *Sòun Tzuc-droungs*. We march to bring peace to the states of *Drin* and *Sòungs*.

Dzong Sòun Tzuc-droungs; breng Drin lac Sòungs.   從孫子仲　平陳與宋

... But *Sòun* will not be returning with us; we are dejected, deeply grieved.

... Pu ngàyc luc kwuy; ou sum wuc throung.   不我以歸　憂心有忡

And now we stop, and again we halt; and now we've lost our horses.
We go searching for them, down in the forests.

Wan kac, wan k'hlac; wan sàngs gu mràc.   爰居爰處　爰喪其馬
Wa luc gou tu, wa rum tu gràc.   于以求之　于林之下

She: Whether you are dead or alive, we are far apart. With you, I was perfectly happy;
I held your hand. I was going to grow old together with you.

Sic sheng khèt-khòt. Lac tzuc deng lot;   死生契闊　與子成悅
tup tzuc tu nhouc. Lac tzuc krìc ròuc.   執子之手　與子偕老

Alas, separation! You will not be supporting me.
Alas, distance! You will not be going on with me.

Hwa-tzay, kwhàt ì! Pu ngàyc gwàt ì.   吁嗟闊兮　不我活兮
Hwa-tzay, hwìn ì! Pu ngàyc lhin ì.   吁嗟洵兮　不我申兮

Sòungs and *Drin* were immediately south of *Wets*; the *Wets* city of *Dzòu* was close to the *Sòungs* border, so presumably vulnerable. (In modern terms *Dzòu* was at Huaxian, east of Xinxiang in northern Henan.) This Ode may relate to a known campaign of 718.

32

The Gentle Breeze 凱風

This gentle breeze from the south reaches into the heart of the jujube bush.
Its inner shoots are delicate and lovely. Our lady mother is burdened with toil.

Khùyc pum dzis nùm, thoy payc kuk sum.   凱風自南　吹彼棘心
Kuk sum aw-aw. Muc gec go ràw.   棘心夭夭　母氏劬勞

This gentle breeze from the south sets the outer branches of the jujube aquiver.
Our lady mother is both wise and good. Yet there's not one decent man among us.

Khùyc pum dzis nùm, thoy payc kuk sin.   凱風自南　吹彼棘薪
Muc gec lhengs dant. Ngàyc ma reng nin.   母氏聖善　我無令人

Below *Syouns* town there's a cool spring.
Here are seven sons; yet our lady mother is laden with bitter toil.

Wan wuc gàn dzwan, dzùc Syouns tu gràc.   爰有寒泉　在浚之下
Wuc tzuc tsit nin, muc gec ràw khàc.   有子七人　母氏勞苦

The oriole is a beautiful bird, and we love listening to its song.
Here are seven sons; but not one of us is a comfort to our mother's heart.

Gènt-gwrànt gwàng tìwc, tzùs hòus gu um.   睍睆黃鳥　載好其音
Wuc tzuc tsit nin, màk outs muc sum.   有子七人　莫慰母心

The opening image here, of the breeze in the jujube bush, comes close to taking over the Ode and leaving little space to develop its real theme, which seems to be the guilt of a set of brothers who enjoy the pleasant things of life at their leisure while taking their mother for granted, not lifting a finger to lighten her burdens. (The jujube, *Ziziphus jujuba*, is an ornamental tree with date-like fruit that are used to treat sore throats.) *Gec* is an honorific suffix to a lady's name; I try to capture its force here with the phrase "lady mother".

Syouns was a town of *Wets* state, in western Shandong. The spring there was famous, and it seems to be included as another example associated with the good life, in contrast with the hard life of the mother.

33

Cock Pheasants 雄雉

Cock pheasants are flying—their wingbeats are leisurely.
Oh, my dear, it's you who got me into this mess.

Wung dric wa puy—lats-lats gu wac. 雄雉于飛　洩洩其羽
Ngàyc tu gròuy luc, dzis lu i jac. 我之懷矣　自詒伊阻

Cock pheasants are flying—listen to the rise and fall of their wings.
Truly, sir, you have filled my heart with trouble.

Wung dric wa puy—gràs dyank gu um. 雄雉于飛　下上其音
Trant luc kwun-tzuc, dit ràw ngàyc sum. 展矣君子　寔勞我心

I contemplate the days and the months, and I ponder long-broodingly.
You said "It's a long way"; when will you say "Now I can come to you"?

Tam payc nit ngwat; you-you ngàyc su. 瞻彼日月　悠悠我思
Lòuc tu wun "want"; gàt wun "nùc rù"? 道之云遠　曷云能來

You gentry folk—none of you know how to behave.
I'm not a nasty girl, not a gold-digger: so why can't you act decently?

Pràk nec kwun-tzuc, pu tre tùk gràng. 百爾君子　不知德行
Pu kes, pu gou: gày longs pu tzàng? 不忮不求　何用不臧

The opening image here perhaps suggests the leisurely style of noblemen who lead their lives on a plane above the troubles of lesser people, even when they have caused those troubles.

34

The Gourds have their Bitter Leaves 匏有苦葉

The gourds have their bitter leaves, the ford has deep wading.
Where it's deep it is wetting people's clothes; where it's shallow they are lifting up their skirts.

Bròu wuc khàc lap, tzìs wuc nhum dap. 匏有苦葉　濟有深涉
Nhum tzùk rats, tsent tzùk khats. 深則厲　淺則揭

Heavy flows are filling up the ford. The hen pheasant is calling, *wuc-wic*.
The depth is not yet up to the carriage axles; the hen-pheasant is calling for her mate.

Wuc mec tzìs leng; wuc-wic dric mreng. 有瀰濟盈　有鷕雉鳴
Tzìs leng pu no krouc. Dric mreng gou gu mouc. 濟盈不濡軌　雉鳴求其牡

Ong, ong calls the wild goose; the warm sun is just rising.
If the man is to come back to his wife, it should be before the ice melts.

Ong-ong mreng ngràns. Hos nit lhuc tàns. 雝雝鳴鴈　煦日始旦
Shuc na kwuy tsùy, lùc prung muts phàns. 士如歸妻　迨冰未泮

The ferryman is beckoning, people are crossing—but not me.
People are crossing, but not me. I wait for my beloved.

Taw-taw tou tzuc; nin dap, ngàng puc.　　招招舟子　人涉卬否
Nin dap, ngàng puc; ngàng sno ngàyc wuc.　人涉卬否　卬須我友

The gourds being in leaf, the ice melted, and the pheasant calling all show that the season is advanced past the point where her man should have come for her; but the water is not too deep yet, it is still possible.

The wild goose to the Chinese symbolizes solitude.

35

Grey Skies and Rain　谷風

Slup, slup gusts the east wind, with grey skies and rain;
I strive to make my heart agreeable, it isn't right to harbour anger.
Lifting a turnip or a radish, one can't know what their body will be like.
My reputation is unsullied; I am with you until death.

Slup, slup klòk pum, luc um, luc wac.　　習習谷風　以陰以雨
Mrunt-mrant dòng sum, pu ngay wuc nàc.　黽勉同心　不宜有怒
Tsùc phong, tsùc phuyc, ma luc gràc rhìc.　采葑采菲　無以下體
Tùk um màk wuy, gup nec dòng sic.　　　德音莫違　及爾同死

But I go my road haltingly, and in my heart there is rebellion.
Not far, just a little way, you trailed to the door with me.
Who says dandelion is bitter? It's as sweet as shepherd's-purse.
You are enjoying your new bride, as close as a pair of brothers.

Gràng lòuc dri-dri, troung sum wuc wuy.　行道遲遲　中心有違
Pu want i nec, bàk sòngs ngàyc guy.　　不遠伊邇　薄送我畿
Douy wuts là khàc? Gu kàm na dzìc.　　誰謂荼苦　其甘如薺
Èns nec sin mhùn, na hwrang, na dìc.　　宴爾新昏　如兄如弟

The Wei river is turbulent when the *Kèng* joins it, but then it slows down and
　　becomes clear.
You are enjoying your new bride, and you can't be bothered with me.
Don't you touch me down there, then! Don't you grope my quim!
If my body is unsatisfactory, I'll devote my time to our children.

Kèng luc Wuts dròk; duk-duk gu tuc.　　涇以渭濁　湜湜其沚
Èns nec sin mhùn, pu ngàyc slit luc.　　宴爾新昏　不我屑以
Mu dats ngàyc rang! Mu pat ngàyc kòc!　毋逝我梁　毋發我笱
Ngàyc koung pu lot, wàng swit ngàyc ghòc.　我躬不閱　遑恤我後

When we reached deep water, we got through on a raft or a boat;
when we came to where it was shallow, we waded, or we swam.
What did we have, what did we lack? I strove to supply our needs.
If any of our people had a bereavement, I would crawl on my knees to help them.

Dzous gu nhum luc, pang tu, tou tu;	就其深矣　方之舟之
dzous gu tsent luc, wrangs tu, you tu.	就其淺矣　泳之游之
Gày wuc, gày mang? Mrunt-mrant gou tu.	何有何亡　黽勉求之
Bam min wuc sàng, bà-ba kous tu.	凡民有喪　匍匐救之

You didn't look after me or cherish me—far from it, you treated me as an enemy;
now you've cast aspersions on my virtue, a merchant couldn't even sell me as a concubine.
In the old days, growing up, I was poor and scared; I joined you and we were destitute.
Now I've lived and grown up, and you liken me to poison.

Pu ngàyc nùc houk, pant luc ngàyc way dou.	不我能慉　反以我為讎
Kuts jac ngàyc tùk, kàc longs pu dous.	既阻我德　賈用不售
Sak louk khonk kouk, gup nec tìn phouk.	昔育恐鞠　及爾顛覆
Kuts sheng, kuts louk, pic lac wa dòuk.	既生既育　比予于毒

I keep a fine larder to get us through the winter;
but you're enjoying your new bride, and I'm just your guarantee against hunger.
You are fierce and violent, and your only gift to me has been toil.
You don't remember the old days, when it was me you came to for rest.

Ngàyc wuc kic rhouks, yak luc ngas tòung.	我有旨蓄　亦以御冬
Èns nec sin mhùn, luc ngàyc ngas goung.	宴爾新昏　以我御窮
Wuc kwàng, wuc gwùts, kuts lu ngàyc lits.	有洸有潰　既詒我肄
Pu nìms sak tac, i la rù huts.	不念昔者　伊余來墍

Marriage is for life, and one cannot know how a wife or husband will turn out any more than one knows what the body of a root vegetable will be like before pulling it out of the ground.

The lines I translate as "Not far, just a little way ..." seem to refer to the polite Chinese custom of going part of the way on the road with someone who departs: this husband accompanied the writer for the bare minimum distance. But I doubt that a wife of long standing has literally been turned out of her home to wander the roads. Perhaps she was demoted to less desirable quarters within the family compound, and the husband was dismissive about the new arrangements; or possibly the "door" is purely metaphorical.

Dandelion and shepherd's-purse look rather similar (before they flower, at least). Shepherd's-purse is thoroughly edible, and rather pretty with its heart-shaped seed cases; in East Asia it is cultivated for food today. Dandelion leaves certainly can be eaten, but it is less sought after as a food plant, and less attractive.

The lines about rivers flowing together plainly mean that the man is in a frenzy of sexual excitement which will not last. (The title *klòk pum* literally means "valley wind", but in the Wei valley, a valley wind was an east wind; and the east was the direction of the ocean, so this was the wind which brought gloomy skies and rain. The *Kèng*, modern Jing, is a tributary which meets the Wei near Xi'an.) In the passage about rafts and wading, the poetess is perhaps reminding the husband how, when the two of them were young and poor, they managed as a team to deal with whatever life threw at them.

36

It's No Use 式微

It's no use, it's no use; why not come home?
It isn't His Highness's fault. What are you doing in the middle of the road?

Lhuk muy, lhuk muy; gà pu kwuy?   式微式微　胡不歸
Muy kwun tu kàs. Gà way ghà troung ràks?   微君之故　胡為乎中路

It's no use, it's no use; why not come home?
It isn't down to His Highness. What are you doing out in the mud?

Lhuk muy, lhuk muy; gà pu kwuy?   式微式微　胡不歸
Muy kwun tu koung. Gà way ghà nì troung?   微君之躬　胡為乎泥中

37

The Lablab Beans 旄丘

The lablab beans on *Màw* Hill, how rampantly their vines spread!
Younger brother, elder brother, how many days will he be?

Màw kwhu tu kàt ì, gày lànt tu tzìt ì.   旄丘之葛兮　何誕之節兮
Nhouk ì, pràk ì, gày tày nit layc?   叔兮伯兮　何多日也

What's keeping him? He must have someone with him.
How much longer will he be? He must be up to something.

Gày kus k'hlac layc? Pit wuc lac layc.   何其處也　必有與也
Gày kus kwuc layc? Pit wuc luc layc.   何其久也　必有以也

The foxfur coats are shaggy. It isn't that no carriages are travelling east,
younger brother, elder brother, only there's no-one for me to travel with.

Gwà gwu mròng-nong. Puyc ka pu tòng,   狐裘蒙茸　匪車不東
nhouk ì, pràk ì, mayc shac lac dòng.   叔兮伯兮　靡所與同

76

Oh, how tiny, how cute, the owl chicks!
Younger brother, elder brother, in full dress, as if your ears were stopped!

Sòyc ì, muyc ì, riw-ray tu tzuc! 　　瑣兮娓兮　流離之子
Nhouk ì, pràk ì, yous na thoung nuc.　叔兮伯兮　褎如充耳

As often, the opening image has limited relevance to the main theme. If *Màw* is the proper name of a hill (it could be a description), we do not know where it was.

Pràk and *nhouk* mean respectively eldest son and third son: in this case probably the girl's brothers, or her uncles, rather than her own sons. She is suspicious about the prolonged absence of her husband, or the man she is expecting to marry, and wants to go after him—but a girl cannot go travelling on her own, and it sounds as though her relatives are not disposed to help.

Why does the poetess suddenly break off to comment on the fur coats, and the owl chicks? Can this be intended to suggest a charming butterfly mind, or does that read 21st-century judgements into a world where they are alien? *Muyc* seems to be a baby-talk version of *mouyc*, "beautiful", so the connotations of "cute" may be appropriate.

38

The Scorpion Dance 　簡兮

Oh, so nonchalant! They are just going to dance the scorpion dance
—the sun is just at its zenith. He takes the leading place in the front rank.

Krènt ì, krènt ì: pang tzang màns mac.　　簡兮簡兮　方將萬舞
Nit tu pang troung; dzùc dzèn dyangs k'hlac.　日之方中　在前上處

The great man is tall, dancing the scorpion dance in the royal courtyard.
He has strength like a tiger; he grasps reins as if they were mere strings.

Dak nin ngwac-ngwac, klòng lèng màns mac.　碩人俁俁　公庭萬舞
Wuc ruk na hlàc: tup prus na tzàc.　　　　　有力如虎　執轡如組

In his left hand he holds a flute, in his right he brandishes pheasant feathers.
He gleams red as if freshly-painted. The prince announces a noble title for him.

Tzàyc nhouc tup yawk, wuc nhouc prank lyàwk.　左手執籥　右手秉翟
Hràk na rròk tac; klòng ngan slàk tzyawk.　　　赫如渥赭　公言錫爵

On the hill there are hazels, in the wet ground there are cockleburs.
Pray, who am I thinking about? The handsome man of the West.
That handsome man, he is a man from the West!

Shàn wuc jin, slup wuc rìn.　　　　　　　　山有榛　隰有苓
Wun douy tu su? Sì pang mouyc nin.　　　云誰之思　西方美人
Payc mouyc nin ì, sì pang tu nin ì.　　　　彼美人兮　西方之人兮

Arthur Waley assembled the sparse evidence we have for the nature of the scorpion dance, in an appendix to his Odes translation. He believed it was a dance of love, though others think it was a ritual war dance involving battleaxes and shields.

The word *tzyawk* in verse 3 refers both to a title of nobility, and to one of the ritual bronze vessels discussed on p. 27. Just as the Queen makes men knights by tapping them on the shoulder with a sword, so it seems that a *Tiw* prince made someone noble by presenting him with a bronze wine-vessel. Various translators render this line as "ordered him to be given a jar of wine", "ordered him to be given a wine-vessel", and "ordered a title of nobility to be bestowed on him", but these are probably not alternatives: all are simultaneously correct.

The word *slup* in the last verse occurs in many of the Odes; it is hard to translate, because Chinese rivers were often different from the managed watercourses we know in the 21st century, with clear streams flowing swiftly between neatly-defined banks. A river in *Tiw* China would often be a broad expanse within which the moving stream itself might be lost among a congeries of boggy ground, standing pools, backwaters, and islets of different degrees of firmness. All this low, wet ground was *slup*, in contrast to the slopes or hills.

In the *Tiw* period, the west of China was the rich and powerful area of the country.

39

Spring Water 泉水

The water bubbling up in this very spring will flow into the river *Gu*.
I have a love in the state of *Wets*: not a day but I think about him.
The *Kyu*'s are lovely people, I must involve them in the planning.

Pits payc dzwan lhouyc, yak riw wa Gu.	毖彼泉水　亦流于淇
Wuc gròuy wa Wets; mayc nit pu su.	有懷于衛　靡日不思
Ront payc ta Kyu; rìw lac tu mu.	孌彼諸姬　聊與之謀

If we make the first overnight stop on the river *Tzìc*, we can hold the farewell
　　party at *Nèc*.
A girl must make her journey, going far away from parents and brothers.
I must get advice from my aunts, and from my girl-cousins, too.

K'hlout souk wa Tzìc, ums dzans wa Nèc.	出宿于濟　飲餞于禰
Nrac tzuc wuc gràng, wans bac muc hwrang dìc.	女子有行　遠父母兄弟
Muns ngàyc ta kà, swits gup pràk tzic.	問我諸姑　遂及伯姊

Or if we stop overnight at *Kàn*, we can have the farewell party at *Ngan*.
Then comes the axle-grease! Then comes servicing the linchpins! There, the
　　returning carriages will leave us.
If we are in too much of a rush to reach *Wets*, there is sure to be a breakdown.

K'hlout souk wa Kàn, ums dzans wa Ngan.	出宿于干　飲餞于言
Tzùs ki, tzùs gràt; swen ka ngan mràts.	載脂載舝　還車言邁
Don jin wa Wets, pu grà wuc gàts.	遄臻于衛　不瑕有害

78

I am thinking about Fat Spring, I am for ever sighing for that place.
I am thinking about *Sno* and *Dzòu* towns; my heart longs [...]

Ngàyc su Buy Dzwan; tzu tu wrank nhàn.   我思肥泉 茲之永歎
Su Sno lac Dzòu. Ngàyc sum you-you ...   思須與漕 我心悠悠

The writer looks forward to marrying into the large and powerful state of *Wets*. As we saw on p. 26, the *dzans* was a party on the road to bid the bride farewell. The main part of the journey began once the escort had turned back, so that was the time for fettling the vehicles to face the rigours of the road. The North China plain has changed too much to reconstruct the geography of the journey.

The received text of this Ode ends with eight words which are identical to the last line of Ode 59. In that poem the wording fits its context, but here it feels out of place and "tacked on". I believe the line was inserted here mistakenly, in place of wording now irretrievably lost, by someone reconstructing this Ode from memory; so I omit the line.

40

The North Gate 北門

I go out of the North Gate, filled with woe.
I am out of money and resources. Nobody understands the situation I'm in.
I've had it!
It's Sky that has got me into this, so what can I say?

K'hlout dzis pùk mùn, ou sum un-un.   出自北門 憂心殷殷
Toung groc tsac brun. Màk tre ngàyc krùn.   終窶且貧 莫知我艱
Luc an tzù!   已焉哉
Thìn dit way tu, wuts tu gày tzù?   天寔為之 謂之何哉

The king's business lands on me—my admin duties are for ever being piled higher,
and when I get home, my family all join in criticizing me.
I've had it!
It's Sky that has got me into this, so what can I say?

Wang shuc lhek ngàyc—tengs shuc it be ek ngàyc.   王事適我 政事一埤益我
Ngàyc nup dzis ngwàts, lhit nin kryàw pèns trèk ngàyc.   我入自外 室人交徧讁我
Luc an tzù!   已焉哉
Thìn dit way tu, wuts tu gày tzù?   天寔為之 謂之何哉

The king's business is heaped onto me—tasks are always being shuffled off in my direction,
and when I get home, my family all join in scorning me.
I've had it!
It's Sky that has got me into this, so what can I say?

Wang shuc tòun ngàyc—tengs shuc it be wi ngàyc. 王事敦我　政事一埤遺我
Ngàyc nup dzis ngwàts, lhit nin kryàw pèns dzòuy ngàyc. 我入自外　室人交徧摧我
Luc an tzù! 已焉哉
Thìn dit way tu, wuts tu gày tzù? 天實為之　謂之何哉

A low-grade official feels overworked and unappreciated.

41

The North Wind　北風

The north wind is so chill, and it's snowing so thickly.
If you are sweet and love me, I'll hold your hand and go with you.
—He's so shy, he's so slow, but it's urgent now!

Pùk pum gu rang, was sot gu phàng. 北風其涼　雨雪其雱
Wìts nu hòus ngàyc, wè nhouc dòng gràng. 惠而好我　攜手同行
Gu ha, gu sla, kuts kuk kec tza! 其虛其徐　既亟只且

The north wind is so cold, and the snow is so heavy.
If you are sweet and love me, I'll hold your hand and you can take me home.
—He's so shy, he's so slow, but it's urgent now!

Pùk pum gu krì, was sot gu phuy. 北風其喈　雨雪其霏
Wìts nu hòus ngàyc, wè nhouc dòng kwuy. 惠而好我　攜手同歸
Gu ha, gu sla, kuts kuk kec tza! 其虛其徐　既亟只且

The only red to see is foxes, the only black to see is crows.
If you are sweet and love me, I'll hold your hand and get in your carriage.
—He's so shy, he's so slow, but it's urgent now!

Màk khlak puyc gwà, màk mhùk puyc à. 莫赤匪狐　莫黑匪烏
Wìts nu hòus ngàyc, wè nhouc dòng ka. 惠而好我　攜手同車
Gu ha, gu sla, kuts kuk kec tza! 其虛其徐　既亟只且

42

The Red Flute　靜女

That demure girl, how sweet she is; she was going to wait for me by the corner of the town wall.
I love her, but I don't see her. Scratching my head I pace back and forth.

Dzenk nrac gu tho; shuc ngàyc a geng ngo. 靜女其姝　俟我於城隅
Ùts nu pu kèns. Sou lhouc dre-dro. 愛而不見　搔首踟躕

That demure girl, how beautiful she is; she gave me a red flute.
Red flute, you are really bright, and I delight in your loveliness.

Dzenk nrac gu ront; lu ngàyc lòung kònt. 靜女其孌　貽我彤管
Lòung kònt wuc wuyc, lot lak nac mouyc. 彤管有煒　悅懌女美

You've come to me like a tendril from the field, and you are really lovely and unusual;
but it isn't because you are lovely—it's because a lovely girl gave you to me.

Dzis muk kwuy dì, swin mouyc tsac luks; 自牧歸荑　恂美且異
puyc nac tu ways mouyc—mouyc nin tu lu. 匪汝之為美　美人之貽

43

The New Tower　新臺

The New Tower is decorated brightly, and the waters of the River are in full flow.
She had looked for someone handsome: this mat-roll of a man is nothing special.

Sin Dù wuc tsèc, Gày lhouyc mec-mec. 新臺有泚　河水瀰瀰
Èns-ont tu gou: ga-dra pu sent. 嬿婉之求　籧篨不鮮

The New Tower is freshly cleaned, and the waters of the River are flowing smoothly.
She had looked for someone handsome: this mat-roll of a man is no good.

Sin Dù wuc sìc, Gày lhouyc mùyc-mùyc. 新臺有洒　河水浼浼
Èns-ont tu gou: ga-dra pu thùnt. 嬿婉之求　籧篨不殄

She set up her fish-net, but what it trapped was a toad.
She had looked for someone handsome: she got this paddock!

Nga mank tu nhet, gòng tzùk ray tu. 魚網之設　鴻則離之
Èns-ont tu gou: tùk tsec tsìwk-lhay. 嬿婉之求　得此戚施

The New Tower looks promising as the home of a good match, but the man who lives there is a disappointment. A *ga-dra* is a rough bamboo mat; it would often be kept rolled up, in which case it is seen as resembling a stiff, clumsy man.

The word *gòng* in the last verse normally means "wild goose", but the early twentieth-century scholar Wen Yiduo argued that in this case it was a synonym for *tsìwk-lhay*, "toad". I haven't seen his argument, but it makes better sense of the poem; so I use "paddock" as an English synonym for "toad".

44

Two Young Men Board Boats 二子乘舟

Two young men board boats, and float far away.
Longingly I think about you—there is grief in my heart.

Nits tzuc mlung tou, bum-bum kus kwrank. 　　二子乘舟　汎汎其憬
Ngons ngan sus tzuc—troung sum yangs-yangs. 　願言思子　中心養養

Two young men board boats, and float down river.
Longingly I think about you—disaster is close now.

Nits tzuc mlung tou, bum-bum kus dats. 　　二子乘舟　汎汎其逝
Ngons ngan sus tzuc—pu grà wuc gàts. 　　　願言思子　不瑕有害

This brief poem alludes in a guarded fashion to an episode which occurred in 703 (and is considerably more interesting than the poem itself). The brothers *Shok* and *Douc* were sons of duke *Swan*, ruler of *Wets*; their mother *Swan Kyang* came from the ruling family of the next-door state, *Dzì*. (*Swan Kyang*, in modern pronunciation Xuan Jiang, is the name by which the lady is known to history, but it simply means that she was born a member of the *Kyang* clan and became wife of *Swan*; a lady's personal name was a private matter, I don't suppose the poet would have known it.) The duke had brought *Swan Kyang* to *Wets* as a bride for his heir *Kup*, son by an incestuous relationship with one of his father's concubines, but when the duke saw how beautiful *Swan Kyang* was he took her to be his own concubine instead. In due course *Swan Kyang* drove the duke's principal wife to suicide, and plotted with the duke and with *Shok* to do away with *Kup*, leaving the way free for *Shok* to become heir. The duke sent *Kup* on a mission to *Dzì*, and arranged for hit-men to kill him after he disembarked from the voyage down the Yellow River. *Shok*'s brother *Douc* got wind of the plan and urged *Kup* to save himself by going to some other state, but *Kup* was unwilling to violate the obligation of *hràws*, filial piety: "If I ignore my father's command, how can I call myself a son? If there were some state where there were no such things as fathers, I could go there." Finding *Kup* obdurate, *Douc* changed tack: he got *Kup* too drunk to travel, then went on ahead to *Dzì*, carrying the banner intended to identify *Kup*. The hit-men killed him. But *Kup* went to *Dzì* in his turn. He told the hit-men: "It is me that you seek. What crime was this? Please kill me." So they did.

When *Shok* succeeded his father in 700, he had no children, so *Swan Kang* took another of her stepsons as lover, to produce children to continue her influence into later generations. According to her biographer, the end result of all this was that *Wets* state "went to ruin and for five generations there was no peace".

We have seen that, often, interpretations in terms of politics have been imposed on Odes despite the poems containing no real evidence for such interpretations. This Ode, on the other hand, would make little sense unless the poet was alluding to a specific episode, so I take the traditional interpretation to be right.

VOICES FROM EARLY CHINA

State of *Long*

As we saw on p. 66, when the Airs of the States were written *Long* was a place within *Wets* state. It was at modern Jixian, Henan.

45

This was Going to be the Right One 柏舟

Boats of cypress wood are drifting in the middle of the River.
A youth's two hair-tufts hanging down: this was going to be the right one for me.
Till death, he swore, he would have no other.
Oh mother, oh Sky: what an untrustworthy man!

Bum payc pràk tou, dzùc payc troung Gày.   汎彼柏舟　在彼中河
Dùmp payc rank mou: dit wi ngàyc ngay.   髧彼兩○　寔維我儀
Tu sic lhic mayc lhày.   之死矢靡它
Muc layc, Thìn kec: pu rangs nin kec!   母也天只　不諒人只

Boats of cypress wood are drifting at the side of the River.
A youth's two hair-tufts hanging down: this was going to be my special one.
Till death, he swore, he would never wrong me.
Oh mother, oh Sky: what an untrustworthy man!

Bum payc pràk tou, dzùc payc Gày juk.   汎彼柏舟　在彼河側
Dùmp payc rank mou: dit wi ngàyc dùk.   髧彼兩○　寔維我特
Tu sic lhic mayc nhùk.   之死矢靡慝
Muc layc, Thìn kec: pu rangs nin kec!   母也天只　不諒人只

Two tufts of a child's hair were bound up and not cut until he became an adult.

46

The Creeper-Encrusted Wall 牆有茨

The wall is encrusted with creepers; they can't be brushed away.
What is said within the lattice can't be repeated
—what could be repeated would be ugly enough.

Dzang wuc dzi; pu khàyc sòus layc.
Troung kòs tu ngan pu khàyc lòus layc
—shac khàyc lòus layc, ngan tu k'hyou layc.

牆有茨　不可埽也
中冓之言　不可道也
所可道也　言之醜也

The wall is encrusted with creepers; it can't be cleared.
What is said within the lattice can't be spelled out
—what could be spelled out would be a tedious story.

Dzang wuc dzi; pu khàyc snang layc.
Troung kòs tu ngan pu khàyc syang layc
—shac khàyc syang layc, ngan tu drang layc.

牆有茨　不可襄也
中冓之言　不可詳也
所可詳也　言之長也

The wall is encrusted with creepers; they can't be bundled away.
What is said within the lattice can't be reported
—what could be reported would be disgraceful enough.

Dzang wuc dzi; pu khàyc lhok layc.
Troung kòs tu ngan pu khàyc lòk layc
—shac khàyc lòk layc, ngan tu nok layc.

牆有茨　不可束也
中冓之言　不可讀也
所可讀也　言之辱也

Life in a harem—"within the lattice". Just as it is physically impractical to lay the wall bare, so it would be socially unacceptable to lay bare the women's backbiting and intrigues.

47

Utterly Submissive　君子偕老

The prince's consort: the hairpin in her headdress bears six gems.
She is utterly submissive;
she is majestic as the hills and the River;
the figured dress is right for her.
For this lady not to be good, pray, how could that be?

Kwun-tzuc krìc ròuc, phuks kì rouk kràiy.
Oy-oy-lay-lay;
na shàn, na Gày;
syank buk dec ngay.
Tzuc tu pu diwk, wun na tu gày?

君子偕老　副笄六珈
委委佗佗
如山如河
象服是宜
子之不淑　云如之何

Bright, shining bright, is her pheasant feather.
Her black hair is like the clouds; she scorns false hair.
Her earstoppers of jade! Her hairpin of ivory!
The whiteness of her forehead!
How can she be so celestial? How can she be such a goddess?

Tsèc ì, tsèc ì, kus tu lyàwk layc.
Tint pat na wun; pu slit slek layc.
Ngok tu thìns layc! Syank tu thès layc!
Lang tza tu sèk layc!
Gà-nan nu thìn layc? Gà-nan nu tès layc?

玼兮玼兮　其之翟也
鬒髮如雲　不屑髢也
玉之瑱也　象之揥也
揚且之晳也
胡然而天也　胡然而帝也

White, gleaming white, is her ritual robe.
It covers the crushed linen of her plain undergarment.
The lady's clear forehead! The colour of her forehead!
Truly, a person like this is the belle of the nation.

Tsàyc ì, tsàyc ì, kus tu trans layc.
Mòng payc jous thruy, dec snet ban layc.
Tzuc tu tseng lang! Lang tza tu ngràn layc!
Trant na tu nin ì pròng tu wens layc.

瑳兮瑳兮　其之展也
蒙彼縐絺　是紲袢也
子之清揚　揚且之顏也
展如之人兮　邦之媛也

A satire on *Swan Kyang*, whom we met in Ode 44.

Krìc ròuc, "grow old together", was a conventional way of referring to marriage. In the first line here the phrase is used as a noun—the one with whom one grows old, i.e. one's partner.

48

Among the Mulberry Trees　桑中

Pulling up dodder to the south of *Mùts*,
pray who am I thinking about? It's the lovely eldest daughter of the *Kyang* family!
She made a date with me among the mulberry trees,
she met me at the upper temple,
she walked out with me along the river *Gu*.

Wan tsùc glang luc, Mùts tu hangs luc.
Wun douy tu su? Mouyc mràngs Kyang luc!
Gu ngàyc ghà sàng troung;
yaw ngàyc ghà dyangs koung;
sòngs ngàyc ghà Gu tu dyangs luc.

爰采唐矣　沬之鄉矣
云誰之思　美孟姜矣
期我乎桑中
要我乎上宮
送我乎淇之上矣

Harvesting wheat to the north of *Mùts*,
pray who am I thinking about? It's the lovely eldest daughter of the *Luk* family!
She made a date with me among the mulberry trees,
she met me at the upper temple,
she walked out with me along the river *Gu*.

Wan tsùc mrùk luc, Mùts tu pùk luc.
Wun douy tu su? Mouyc mràngs Luk luc!
Gu ngàyc ghà sàng troung;
yaw ngàyc ghà dyangs koung;
sòngs ngàyc ghà Gu tu dyangs luc.

爰采麥矣　沬之北矣
云誰之思　美孟弋矣
期我乎桑中
要我乎上宮
送我乎淇之上矣

Pulling up turnips to the east of *Mùts*,
pray who am I thinking about? It's the lovely eldest daughter of the *Long* family!
She made a date with me among the mulberry trees,
she met me at the upper temple,
she walked out with me along the river *Gu*.

Wan tsùc phong luc, Mùts tu tòng luc. 爰采葑矣　沬之東矣
Wun douy tu su? Mouyc mràngs Long luc! 云誰之思　美孟庸矣
Gu ngàyc ghà sàng troung; 期我乎桑中
yaw ngàyc ghà dyangs koung; 要我乎上宮
sòngs ngàyc ghà Gu tu dyangs luc. 送我乎淇之上矣

Dodder is a parasitic weed that has to be removed early in the growing season, before it can destroy the food value of crops. Wheat is harvested in summer. Turnips are lifted when the cold weather has arrived.

Mùts was a town in the area of modern Qixian, south-east of Kaifeng in eastern Henan. The river *Gu* is mentioned in several Odes: there is a problem about identifying it. The river which bears the name today is a minor tributary of another river named after *Wets*, the state through whose former territory it runs. (On Western maps *Gu* and *Wets* are of course spelled in their modern forms, as Qi and Wei.) The *Gu* which these poets knew seems to have been a more important river. We know that there have been large changes to the geography of the North China plain, and that certainly applies to the *Gu*: a dictionary dating from A.D. 100 said that it had once been a tributary of the Yellow River but at that period followed a different course.

49

Quails are Fiercely Uxorious 鶉之奔奔

Quails are fiercely uxorious, and magpies defend their mates boldly.
This most worthless of human beings, I must treat as my elder brother.

Doun tu pùn-pùn; tsak tu kang-kang. 鶉之賁賁　鵲之彊彊
Nin tu ma rang, ngàyc luc way hwrang. 人之無良　我以為兄

Magpies defend their mates boldly, and quails are fiercely uxorious.
This most worthless of human beings, I must treat as a noble.

Tsac tu kang-kang; doun tu pùn-pùn. 鵲之彊彊　鶉之奔奔
Nin tu ma rang, ngàyc luc way kwun. 人之無良　我以為君

Verse 2 of this little poem is held to refer to *Swan Kyang* (see Ode 44) and verse 1 to her stepson and lover.

There is controversy about the meanings of *pùn-pùn* and *kang-kang*. On one tradition both simply meant "faithful to their mates", which these birds were believed to be; however the evidence is weak, and Karlgren held that both meant "fierce". But the latter interpretation

VOICES FROM EARLY CHINA

creates no link with the following lines, whereas "faithful" makes the opening images easily understandable as irony. Since I cannot resolve the issue, my translation combines both interpretations.

50

Building a Palace 定之方中

When the Forehead had just culminated, he set about building the *Chac* palace.
He oriented its foundations by the sun, and proceeded to build the great house at *Chac*.
He planted there hazels and chestnuts, igiri trees, tung trees, catalpas, and lacquer trees,
so later he could play the lute and zither.

Tèng tu pang troung, tzàk wa Chac koung.　　　定之方中　作于楚宮
Gwic tu luc nit, tzàk wa Chac lhit.　　　　　　　揆之以日　作于楚室
Doc tu jin rit, ay dòng tzuc tsit.　　　　　　　　樹之榛栗　椅桐梓漆
Wan bat gum sprit.　　　　　　　　　　　　　爰伐琴瑟

He walked up the hill of ruins to inspect *Chac*.
He surveyed *Chac* and *Dàng*, the high mountains and the hills.
Then he went down to look over the mulberry plantations.
The turtle-shell oracle was favourable—in all respects it was truly positive.

Lhung payc kha luc, luc mang Chac luc.　　　　升彼虛矣　以望楚矣
Mang Chac lac Dàng, krank shàn lac krang.　　望楚與堂　景山與京
Kròungs kwàn wa sàng.　　　　　　　　　　　降觀于桑
Pòk wun kus kit, toung an yount tzàng.　　　　卜云其吉　終焉允臧

After a divine rain had fallen, he told his groom:
"Once the weather clears, yoke up my horses in the early morning; I'll spend the night among the mulberry plantations and the fields."
Was he not a down-to-earth man? His mind was steadfastly sincere and deep.
He had three thousand large stallions and mares.

Rèng wac kuts rìn, mreng payc kòn nin:　　　　靈雨既零　命彼倌人
dzeng ngan souk kràys, lhots wa sàng lìn.　　　星言夙駕　說于桑田
Puyc druk layc nin? Prank sum sùk wwìn.　　　匪直也人　秉心塞淵
Rù bint sùm tsìn.　　　　　　　　　　　　　　騋牝三千

This is about a ruler *Mhayc* who set the state of *Wets* back on its feet after it had been almost wiped out in 659 by an invasion of *Lèk* tribesmen from the north. That involved creating a new capital for the state at a place called *Chac*, near the present-day Chengwu, western Shandong.

The Forehead is a Chinese constellation comprising part of our Pegasus, including the bright star Markab. The commentators explain that we have to understand the first line as referring to the position of the stars at nightfall, and in the *Tiw* dynasty it was at the beginning of winter that the Forehead culminated (reached its highest position in the sky) at nightfall, which was taken as a signal that agricultural work was over for the year and people should turn to building work.

The list of trees sounds as though *Mhayc* were creating an ornamental park, and certainly several of these species are ornamental. But also, all have (or had) economic value. Hazel and chestnut are food sources, and so were the berries of the igiri tree. The oil of the tung tree, *Vernicia fordii*, was burned in lamps, and also provided a tough varnish. The use of lacquer is well known, and the lacquer tree also had medicinal uses. Both tung-tree wood and wood of the Chinese catalpa were needed for the manufacture of *gum* lutes, as in the last line of the verse.

The *kha* of verse 2 perhaps implies something like a Middle Eastern *tell*—the site of an earlier city at *Chac* which had been wrecked by the barbarian invasion. (*Dàng* was a settlement close to *Chac*.) In verse 3 the language becomes very obscure. Spending time among the mulberries and the fields is said to indicate *Mhayc*'s willingness to get involved with his subjects at the grassroots level rather than ruling them distantly from a luxurious palace; but various commentators and translators have very diverse ideas about the stich I translate as "Was he not a down-to-earth man?", and I cannot claim my rendering is more than guesswork. We do not know why the rain was "divine" (if that is the right shade of meaning for *rèng* here), nor do we understand the relevance of the three thousand horses. (One translator sees these not as horses owned by *Mhayc*, but as a measure of the number of enthusiastic subjects who come to join him at *Chac*. That is quite imaginative.)

Turtle or tortoise shells were standard tools for foretelling the future in early China. A question was written on a shell (ox shoulderblades were also used), a notch was made and a heated metal point applied to it, and the resulting pattern of cracks gave the answer to the question. Our knowledge of the beginning of written Chinese is entirely dependent on this practice. When a question was put to the oracle, it was written on the shell or bone, and the response as interpreted from the cracks was written alongside it. The earliest surviving examples of Chinese writing, dating from about 1200 B.C. onwards, are all instances of this divination technique.

51

Rainbows 蝃蝀

There is a rainbow in the east—no-one dares point at it.
A girl must go on a wedding journey, taking her far from parents and brothers.

Tèts-tòng dzùc tòng—màk tu kàmp kic.   蝃蝀在東　莫之敢指
Nrac tzuc wuc gràng, wans bac muc hwrang dìc.   女子有行　遠父母兄弟

In the morning there is a rainbow in the west: it will rain all morning.
A girl must go on a wedding journey, taking her far from brothers and parents.

Traw tzì wa sì; djoung traw gu wac.   朝隮于西　崇朝其雨
Nrac tzuc wuc gràng, wans hwrang dìc bac muc.   女子有行　遠兄弟父母

But what a piece of work this girl is: she is so enthusiastic about marital relations that she is being entirely sneaky. She does not acknowledge Sky's ordinance.

Nùc na tu nin layc: gròuy mhùn in layc,
dàts ma sins layc, pu tre mreng layc.

迺如之人也　懷昏姻也
大無信也　不知命也

The commentary tradition gives this poem a sexual interpretation which is not obvious from the surface of the words. But a surface translation would give a pointless-sounding rendering, so I take the traditional interpretation to be right.

This depends on the significance of rainbows to the Chinese. In the Christian world, the Noah story gives rainbows positive associations, but in China they were evil omens. Someone who pointed at a rainbow could expect injury to his hand. And in particular, being produced through a combination of sunshine and rain, rainbows were seen as an irregular mixing of Yang and Yin principles (light and dark, male and female), and hence they symbolized irregular sexual liaisons. This girl is mad about men, and the proper solution to that is for her elders to arrange a marriage, which among the gentry class is likely to be with a man living distantly. But the girl is jumping the gun by enjoying herself with a local young man, and she is reckless about Sky signalling that its will is being flouted.

52

Look at the Rat 相鼠

Look at the rat, it has skin; but the man has no dignity.
If a man has no dignity, why doesn't he just die?

Sangs nhac, wuc bay. Nin nu ma ngay.
Nin nu ma ngay, pu sic gày way?

相鼠有皮　人而無儀
人而無儀　不死何為

Look at the rat, it has teeth; but the man has no manners.
If a man has no manners, why is he hanging around instead of dying?

Sangs nhac, wuc k'hyuc. Nin nu ma tuc.
Nin nu ma tuc, pu sic gày shuc?

相鼠有齒　人而無止
人而無止　不死何俟

Look at the rat, it has limbs; but the man doesn't know how to behave.
If a man doesn't know how to behave, why doesn't he hurry up and die?

Sangs nhac, wuc thìc. Nin nu ma rìc.
Nin nu ma rìc, gà pu don sic?

相鼠有體　人而無禮
人而無禮　胡不遄死

Even a rat has everything a rat should have, whereas the man lacks what a man should have. (But the only parallel between the rat's qualities and those lacking in the man is that they rhyme.)

53

The Ox-Tail Pennon 干旄

Aloft on its pole is the ox-tail pennon, in the outskirts of *Syouns*.
It is braided with white silk; there are fine horses—four of them.
This open-hearted gentleman: what can I give him?

Kat-kat kàn màw, dzùc Syouns tu kràw. 孑孑竿旄　在浚之郊
Sàs su bis tu; rang mràc slits tu. 素絲紕之　良馬四之
Payc tho tac tzuc, gày luc pits tu? 彼姝者子　何以畀之

Aloft on its pole is the falcon flag, within the outer wall of *Syouns*.
It is corded with white silk; there are fine horses—five of them.
This open-hearted gentleman: what can I present to him?

Kat-kat kàn la, dzùc Syouns tu tà. 孑孑竿旟　在浚之都
Sàs su tzàc tu; rang mràc ngàc tu. 素絲組之　良馬五之
Payc tho tac tzuc, gày luc lac tu? 彼姝者子　何以予之

Aloft on its pole is the feather-pennon, within the inner wall of *Syouns*.
It is bound with white silk; there are fine horses—six of them.
This open-hearted gentleman: what honour can I announce for him?

Kat-kat kàn tzeng, dzùc Syouns tu geng. 孑孑竿旌　在浚之城
Sàs su touk tu; rang mràc rouk tu. 素絲祝之　良馬六之
Payc tho tac tzuc, gày luc kòuk tu? 彼姝者子　何以告之

The arrival of a great man in China was heralded by displays of animal trophies. According to James Legge, a *màw* was a pole "adorned with feathers. It was carved with the figure of some animal, or had such a figure set upon it; and the pennon hung down, consisting of ox-tails, dressed and strung together". A *tzeng* was similar "but instead of the ox-tails, the pennon was composed of feathers of different colours, skilfully disposed in spreading plumes". Legge explains the growing number of fine horses by suggesting that they are the horses of *Syouns* dignitaries gathering to welcome the distinguished visitor. (For *Syouns*, see Ode 32.)

54

Canter, Horses 載馳

Canter, horses, hurry, horses, taking me home to comfort the lord of *Wets*.
The horses have come at the trot a long, long way, and I am reaching *Dzòu* town
... but your courtier cuts me off by coming across country, and so my heart is full
　of grief.

Tzùs dray, tzùs kho, kwuy ngrans Wets gò. 　　載馳載驅　歸唁衛侯
Kho mràc you-you, ngan tits a Dzòu 　　　　驅馬悠悠　言至于漕
... dàts-pa bàt-dàp, ngàyc sum tzùk ou. 　　　大夫跋涉　我心則憂

Now you have disapproved of me, I cannot turn and go back.
I see you as in the wrong, and my thoughts will not shift from that.
Now you have disapproved of me, I cannot turn and cross the *Tzìc* again.
I see you as in the wrong, and my thoughts will not cease.

Kuts pu ngàyc kràr, pu nùc swen pant. 　　既不我嘉　不能旋反
Gic nec pu tzàng, ngàyc su pu want. 　　　視爾不臧　我思不遠
Kuts pu ngàyc kràr, pu nùc swen Tzìc. 　　既不我嘉　不能旋濟
Gic nec pu tzàng, ngàyc su pu pits. 　　　視爾不臧　我思不閟

Walking up that slope, I gather snake's-head lilies.
Womenfolk are kind and loving, so we all need to go on visits;
but your people of *Nghac* object to that: the whole lot of them are childish and silly.

Truk payc ày kwhu, ngan tsùc gu mràng. 　　陟彼阿丘　言采其蝱
Nrac tzuc dant gròuy, yak kàk wuc gràng. 　女子善懷　亦各有行
Nghac nin wu tu; toungs dris tsac gwang. 　　許人尤之　眾穉且狂

I walk in these fields; the wheat is growing thick.
I would throw myself on some great state—but who can I trust? Who can I flee to?
Courtiers and nobles, it is not I who am blameworthy.
The hundred things you are thinking are not going to stand in my way.

Ngàyc gràng kus lac; bùm-bùm gu mrùk. 　　我行其野　芃芃其麥
Khòngs wa dàts pròng—douy in? douy guk? 　控于大邦　誰因誰極
Dàts-pa, kwun-tzuc, ma ngàyc wuc wu. 　　大夫君子　無我有尤
Pràk nec shac su, pu na ngàyc shac tu. 　　百爾所思　不如我所之

After her husband's death, *Swan Kyang* of *Wets* (see Odes 44, 47) had children with one of her stepsons, and this Ode was written by their daughter. She married duke *Mouk* of the small state of *Nghac*, while after the barbarian invasion of *Wets* mentioned with Ode 50 and the death of her brother who then ruled *Wets*, her other brother *Mhayc* ruled what was left of his people, initially from the town of *Dzòu* where they had taken refuge. The poetess was unhappy in her marriage and used her brother's difficulties as an excuse for escape, but her husband sent a courtier to fetch her back; history tells us that in her despair she fatally wounded herself, writing this poem before dying. In the poem she seems to waver between pretending that she was making an innocent visit to support her brother, and admitting that she had fled an intolerable marriage.

Snake's-head lilies (*Fritillaria*) were believed in China to make a medicine good for dissipating sadness. For a woman to go on a journey, as in verse 3, usually refers to marriage; here, though, it makes better sense to interpret it as referring to family visits after marriage.

VOICES FROM EARLY CHINA

State of *Wets*

For the first several centuries of the existence of *Wets* as a *Tiw* vassal state, it was based on the old *Un*-dynasty capital whose name translates as "Song of the Morning", and which was located at Qixian, north-east Henan. After the *Lèk* invasion in 659 (Ode 50), the capital was moved for greater safety—first to *Dzòu*, and two years later to modern Caozhou in south-west Shandong.

55

The Inlet in the River　淇奧

Look at that inlet in the river *Gu*: how profusely the lentils and *dòuk* creepers
　　grow there.
We have an elegant Prince!
His looks are like a gem that has been cut and filed, chiselled and polished.
He looks so fresh and refined, so imposing and conspicuous.
We have an elegant Prince; once seen, he can never be forgotten.

Tam payc Gu ouk: rok dòuk àyc-àyc.　　　　瞻彼淇奧　菉○猗猗
Wuc phuyc kwun-tzuc!　　　　　　　　　　有斐君子
Na tsìt, na tsày, na tròk, na mày.　　　　　　如切如磋　如琢如磨
Sprit ì, grènt ì; hràk ì, hwant ì.　　　　　　瑟兮僩兮　赫兮咺兮
Wuc phuyc kwun-tzuc! Toung pu khàyc hwan ì.　有匪君子　終不可諼兮

Look at that inlet in the river *Gu*: how green its lentils and *dòuk* creepers are.
We have an elegant Prince!
His ear-stoppers are of *siws* and *wreng* gems; his skullcap is like a star.
He looks so fresh and refined, so imposing and conspicuous.
We have an elegant Prince; once seen, he can never be forgotten.

Tam payc Gu ouk: rok dòuk tsèng-tsèng.　　　瞻彼淇奧　菉○青青
Wuc phuyc kwun-tzuc!　　　　　　　　　　有斐君子
Thoung-nuc siws wreng, gòts brans na sèng.　充耳琇瑩　會弁如星
Sprit ì, grènt ì; hràk ì, hwant ì.　　　　　　瑟兮僩兮　赫兮咺兮
Wuc phuyc kwun-tzuc! Toung pu khàyc hwan ì.　有斐君子　終不可諼兮

Look at that inlet in the river *Gu*: its lentils and *dòuk* creepers are thick as a mat.
We have an elegant Prince!
His looks are like gold, like tin—like a *kwè* or *pek* jade emblem.
He's open-hearted and easy-going, leaning on the double sidebars of his chariot.
He's witty and amusing, but he's never cruel.

Tam payc Gu ouk: rok dòuk na jèk.
Wuc phuyc kwun-tzuc!
Na kum, na slèk; na kwè, na pek.
Kwhàn ì, thàwk ì, ayc drong kràwk ì.
Dant hays nghawk ì, pu way ngawk ì.

瞻彼淇奧　菉〇如簀
有斐君子
如金如錫　如圭如璧
寬兮綽兮　倚重較兮
善戲謔兮　不為虐兮

The subject here is believed to be a man who became ruler of *Wets* state by killing his elder brother on the death of their father, the previous ruler, and proceeded to enjoy a long and successful reign from 811 to 757 under the name Duke *Mac*. (Not to be confused with king *Mac*—*Mac*, "brave, warlike", was a common name.) After king *Iw* was killed in 771 (p. 9), Duke *Mac* of *Wets* was instrumental in restoring that king's son *Breng* to the throne.

We do not know what *dòuk* creepers were, and the translation "lentils" for *rok* is far from certain (a river-bank is not the likeliest place for lentils to grow); likewise we cannot now identify the specific gems called *siws* or *wreng*. *Kwè* and *pek* are jade emblems of authority, discussed elsewhere.

56

We Attained Ecstasy　考槃

We attained ecstasy by the hidden stream. Oh, the generosity of the great man!
I go to bed alone and prattle when I wake. Never, he swears, will he forget me.

Khòuc bàn dzùc kràns. Dak nin tu kwhàn!
Dòk mits, ngàs ngan. Wrank lhic put hwan.

考槃在澗　碩人之寬
獨寐寤言　永矢弗諼

We attained ecstasy on the slope. Oh, the beauty of the great man!
I go to bed alone and sing when I wake. Never, he swears, will he let me go.

Khòuc bàn dzùc ày. Dak nin tu khòy!
Dòk mits, ngàs kày. Wrank lhic put kòy.

考槃在阿　碩人之〇
獨寐寤歌　永矢弗過

We attained ecstasy on the hilltop. Oh, the eminence of the great man!
I go to bed alone, and when I wake I long to see him again. Never, he swears, will he tell others of our love.

Khòuc bàn dzùc rouk. Dak nin tu lìwk!
Dòk mits, ngàs siwk. Wrank lhic put kòuk.

考槃在陸　碩人之迪
獨寐寤宿　永矢弗告

Or is it she who is giving her word to him? As usual, the grammatical subjects are left vague.

57

A Stately Lady 碩人

How tall this stately lady is; she wears an embroidered dress with a simple hempen tunic over it.
Daughter of the marquis of *Dzì*, now to be wife of the marquis of *Wets*,
sister of the heir of *Dzì*, and sister-in-law to the marquis of *Gèng*,
the lord of *Lùm* is her brother-in-law.

Dak nin gu guy; uys kump kwhènk uy. 碩人其頎　衣錦褧衣
Dzì gò tu tzuc, Wets gò tu tsùy, 齊侯之子　衛侯之妻
tòng koung tu mùts, Gèng gò tu luy, 東宮之妹　邢侯之姨
Lùm klòng wi si. 譚公維私

Her fingers are like soft young shoots; her skin like lard.
Her neck is like a beetle larva, and her teeth like rows of melon seeds.
With her cicada's forehead and silkworm-moth eyebrows,
her artful smiles show such pink lips, and how the whites of her lovely eyes set off the black irises!

Nhouc na nou dì, pra na ngung ki. 手如柔荑　膚如凝脂
Renk na dziw-dzì, k'hyuc na gwàs sì. 領如蝤蠐　齒如瓠棲
Dzin lhouc, ngayc mouy. 螓首蛾眉
Khròus saws tsìns ì! Mouyc mouk phrìns ì! 巧笑倩兮　美目盼兮

This stately lady is tall; she halts for the night in a rural suburb.
Her team of four stallions is robust, each of their bits adorned with vermilion bit-plaques.
Now she is off to court in her carriage with its pheasant-feather screen.
The courtiers withdraw at an early hour, not wishing to tire this noble visitor.

Dak nin ngàw-ngàw. Lhots wa nòung kràw. 碩人敖敖　說于農郊
Slits mouc wuc khaw, to phun paw paw. 四牡有驕　朱幩鑣鑣
Lyàwk put luc draw. 翟茀以朝
Dàts-pa souk thòuts, ma shuc kwun ràw. 大夫夙退　無使君勞

The waters of the Yellow River are mighty, rippling as they flow northwards.
Men are dropping nets—*hwàt! hwàt!*—and the sturgeon are thrashing their tails—*pàt! pàt!*
The rushes and silvergrass are tall.
My lady's attendants wear high hairdos, and her gentlemen-in-waiting are every inch warriors.

Gày lhouyc yang-yang, pùk riw kwàt-kwàt. 河水洋洋　北流活活
Lhay kwà hwàt-hwàt; tran wruc pàt-pàt. 施罛濊濊　鱣鮪發發
Krà lhàmp kat-kat. 葭菼揭揭
Lhaks Kyang ngat-ngat; lhaks shuc wuc khat. 庶姜孽孽　庶士有朅

The poem is believed to describe the arrival of *Jang Kyang* in the state of *Wets* in 756 to marry its ruler (see Ode 26). *Tòng koung*, "the eastern palace", was the building in a ruler's compound where his heir lived, so in the third line it refers to the heir. *Gèng* and *Lùm* were two small states, respectively at modern Xingtai, south-west Hebei, and to the east of Jinan, Shandong.

The similes used to reveal *Jang Kyang*'s beauty are remarkable. *Gwàs sì* is literally "melon nest": the rows of seeds seen when a melon is cut open. A cicada has a notably broad, square forehead.

The frequent phrase *slits mouc*, occurring here in verse 3, literally means "four male animals". In this case I take the animals to be horses, but oxen were also used as draught animals, and in some later cases oxen will be the more plausible rendering.

In the last line, *Kyang* is the lady's clan name, so these *Kyangs* are her "younger sisters"—ladies-in-waiting for *Jang Kyang* and secondary wives for her husband. It is very likely one of these girls who was destined to supplant *Jang Kyang* in the marquis's affections.

58

A Jolly Man of the People 氓

You were a jolly man of the people, bringing funds to buy silk;
but you weren't here to buy silk: once you arrived it was me you were after.
We went paddling in the *Gu* river together, we went all the way to *Dòuns* hill.
It wasn't I who delayed things; you had no satisfactory go-between.
I begged you not to be angry, and we fixed the date for autumn.

Mrùng tu thu-thu, bòuc pàs mòus su.	氓之蚩蚩　抱布貿絲
Puyc rù mòus su: rù kuts ngàyc mu.	匪來貿絲　來即我謀
Sòngs tzuc dap Gu, tits wa Dòuns kwhu.	送子涉淇　至于頓丘
Puyc ngàyc khryan gu: tzuc ma rang mù.	匪我愆期　子無良媒
Tsang tzuc ma nàc, tsiw luc way gu.	將子無怒　秋以為期

I would climb that ruined wall to watch for you returning to the town gate.
If I didn't see you coming to the gate, my tears fell, drop after drop;
once I'd seen you come to the gate, then I was laughing, then I was chattering.
I cast your omens by turtleshell and by yarrow, and they contained nothing worrying.
You arrived with your carriage; I moved house with my valuables.

Mlung payc kwayc wan, luc mang bouk kròn.	乘彼垝垣　以望復關
Pu kèns bouk kròn, khrup thìc ran-ran.	不見復關　泣涕漣漣
Kuts kèns bouk kròn, tzùs saws, tzùs ngan.	既見復關　載笑載言
Nec pòk, nec dats, rhìc ma gouc ngan.	爾卜爾筮　體無咎言
Luc nec ka rù; luc ngàyc mhùc tsan.	以爾車來　以我賄遷

While the mulberries remain unwithered, the leaves are so glossy.
Ah, pigeons! Don't eat the mulberry fruit.
Ah, women! Don't take your pleasure with men.
If a man takes his pleasure, that can always be excused.
If a woman takes her pleasure, that's inexcusable.

Sàng tu muts ràk, gu lap àwk nak.   桑之未落　其葉沃若
Hwa-tzay, kou ì: ma mluk sàng dump!   吁嗟鳩兮　無食桑葚
Hwa-tzay, nrac ì: ma lac shuc tùm!   吁嗟女兮　無與士耽
Shuc tu tùm ì, you khàyc lhot layc.   士之耽兮　猶可說也
Nrac tu tùm ì, pu khàyc lhot layc.   女之耽兮　不可說也

When the mulberry leaves wither, they go yellow and fall.
Since the time I came to you, for three years I've tasted poverty.
The *Gu* river is in spate, it soaks the bottom of my carriage curtains.
Myself, I wasn't disloyal, but your behaviour was two-faced.
You: you were utterly deceitful, your character quite unreliable.

Sàng tu ràk luc, kus gwàng nu wrunt.   桑之落矣　其黃而隕
Dzis ngàyc dzà nec, sùm swats mluk brun.   自我徂爾　三歲食貧
Gu lhouyc lhang-lhang, tzam ka wri dang.   淇水湯湯　漸車帷裳
Nrac layc pu shank; shuc nits gu gràngs.   女也不爽　士貳其行
Shuc layc mank guk, nits sùm gu tùk.   士也罔極　二三其德

For three years I've been your wife; I didn't treat the housework as a burden.
I got up early and went to bed in the dark, with no mornings relaxing with friends.
I kept my promises, but you came to violence.
My brothers don't understand, their laughter is scornful.
Though I talk demurely, I brood, feeling sorry for myself.

Sùm swats way buc, mayc lhit ràw luc.   三歲為婦　靡室勞矣
Souk hung, yas mits; mayc wuc draw luc.   夙興夜寐　靡有朝矣
Ngan kuts swits luc, tits wa bàwks luc.   言既遂矣　至于暴矣
Hwrang dìc pu tre, dìt gu saws luc.   兄弟不知　咥其笑矣
Dzenk ngan sus tu; koung dzis dàwks luc.   靜言思之　躬自悼矣

The two of us were to grow old together, but age led you to resent me.
Even the *Gu* river has a further bank—even a swamp has a far side!
While my hair was bound up in girl's tufts, I talked and laughed happily,
I swore earnest oaths of sincerity. I had no thought that things could go wrong like this.
Going wrong, this I had no thought of. But ah, all that is over now.

Gup nec krìc ròuc; ròuc shuc ngàyc ons.   及爾偕老　老使我怨
Gu tzùk wuc ngàns; slup tzùk wuc phàns.   淇則有岸　隰則有泮
Tzònk kròk tu kròns, ngan saws rràns-rràns.   總角之宴　言笑晏晏
Sins dats tàns-tàns; pu su kus pant.   信誓旦旦　不思其反
Pant, dec pu su; yak luc an tzù.   反是不思　亦已焉哉

Some cultural references here need explanation. *Pàs*, in the first line, is literally "cloth", but at this period cloth was used as a currency. The delicate matter of arranging a marriage depended crucially, then and much more recently in Chinese history, on the services of a go-between neutral between the two families. The passage in verse 4 about her carriage curtains getting wet in a crossing of the *Gu* suggests that the woman has given up on the marriage and left the man.

We saw in Ode 50 how tortoise shells were used to tell the future. Another technique used sections of yarrow stalk, either having a joint in the middle (Yin) or unjointed and straight (Yang). Various rituals produced a sequence of six of these pieces, and whichever of the 64 possible "hexagrams" emerged was looked up in a book, the Yi Jing or *Book of Changes*. This offers an oracular statement for each hexagram which one can describe as mystical or nonsensical, depending on one's level of tolerance for that kind of thing. (The *Book of Changes* that we have is later than the *Odes* period, but evidently some forerunner of it must already have existed.) The eight trigrams which paired off to give 64 hexagrams can be seen today surrounding the Yin–Yang symbol on the flag of South Korea.

From our point of view, these techniques are superstitious—meaning that we know, now, that they do not work. In the *Tiw* dynasty, they were reasonable attempts to make sense of a mysterious and difficult world.

59

Bamboo Rods　竹竿

Slender are the bamboo rods they use for fishing in the *Gu*.
How can I not think about you? But there's no reaching you so far off.

Lyawk-lyawk trouk kàn luc tyàwks wa Gu.　籊籊竹竿　以釣于淇
Khuyc pu nec su? Want màk trits tu.　豈不爾思　遠莫致之

On the left are the springs, on the right are the waters of *Gu*.
A daughter must journey, going far away from her family.

Dzwan ngwan dzùc tzàyc, Gu lhouyc dzùc wuc.　泉源在左　淇水在右
Nrac tzuc wuc gràng, wans hwrang bac muc.　女子有行　遠兄父母

On the right are the waters of *Gu*, on the left are the springs.
The gleam of your intelligent smile! The richness of your jade netsuke!

Gu lhouyc dzùc wuc, dzwan ngwan dzùc tzàyc.　淇水在右　泉源在左
Khròus saws tu tsàyc! Bès ngok tu nàyc!　巧笑之瑳　佩玉之儺

The river *Gu* flows on, with oars of juniper they are rowing boats of pine.
I harness words to wander abroad, as a way to release my grief.

Gu lhouyc you-you; kòt tzap slong tou.　淇水滺滺　檜楫松舟
Kràys ngan k'hlout you, luc sac ngàyc ou.　駕言出遊　以寫我憂

A married woman remembers the place where she grew up on the banks of the *Gu*, and the lover she left behind there.

In Europe, junipers are shrubby plants that could not be used for oars, but the Chinese juniper, *Juniperus chinensis*, is a tree.

Earlier translators have taken the last line of this Ode to mean "Harnessing [my carriage] I shall go out for an excursion, so as to dissipate my grief". This might seem bathetic as a response to lost love, but *Tiw* Chinese were more down-to-earth than romantic Europeans. However there is also a linguistic problem. The word *ngan* is ambiguous between "I, me" and "speech, words"; and the conventional interpretation of *kràys ngan* as "harnessing, I ..." reads oddly. If the subject "I" needs to be mentioned here, it is hard to see why it is placed so as to split *kràys* from the other two verbs. I find it more natural to take *ngan* as "words", object of *kràys* and subject of the other verbs. But my version could in turn be criticized on the ground that "harnessing words" is too metaphorical. In European poetry it would raise no eyebrows, but the Odes commonly use language more literally than that.

Questions like this reduce to balances of obscure probabilities, with little chance of definitive resolution.

60

The Rough-Potato Plant 芄蘭

Oh, the branches of the rough-potato plant! My boy is wearing a marlinspike at his belt.
Even though he is wearing a marlinspike, can he fail to know me?
Oh, the ceremonial dagger! The jade emblem! Oh, the trembling of his sash-ends!

Wàn-ràn tu ke! Dòng tzuc bès hwe.	芄蘭之支　童子佩觿
Swi-tzùk bès hwe, nùc pu ngàyc tre?	雖則佩觿　能不我知
Long ì, syouts ì, doy tàts gwits ì!	容兮遂兮　垂帶悸兮

Oh, the leaves of the rough-potato plant! My boy is wearing an archer's thimble at his belt.
Even though he is wearing an archer's thimble, can he fail to be friends with me?
Oh, the ceremonial dagger! The jade emblem! Oh, the trembling of his sash-ends!

Wàn-ràn tu lap! Dòng tzuc bès lhep.	芄蘭之葉　童子佩韘
Swi-tzùk bès lhep, nùc pu ngàyc kràp?	雖則佩韘　能不我甲
Long ì, syouts ì, doy tàts gwits ì!	容兮遂兮　垂帶悸兮

A boy has become a man, wearing the accoutrements of adult manhood. (A *hwe* was a spike of bone or horn used to undo knots. A *lhep* protected an archer's finger from bowstring burns.) The young man's girl is afraid that he has become too important to bother with her.

Some of the "opening images" in the *Odes* have traditionally been given explanations that seem scarcely plausible. This case is extreme. The rough-potato plant, *Metaplexis japonica*, is a creeper with showy leaves and flowers; the stalks are edible, and contain a white milky juice. It is claimed that the poet is contrasting the lad's present appearance of manhood with his having only recently been a milk-drinking infant. Really? I suspect one would need to be a *Tiw*-dynasty Chinese to understand this image.

61

The Wide Yellow River 河廣

Who calls the Yellow River wide? A single reed could float across it.
Who calls *Sòungs* distant? If I stood on tiptoe I could see it.

Douy wuts Gày kwànk? It wuyc gàng tu.   誰謂河廣　一葦杭之
Douy wuts Sòungs want? Khec lac mang tu.   誰謂宋遠　跂予望之

Who calls the Yellow River wide? It has no room for even a canoe.
Who calls *Sòungs* distant? It wouldn't take me a morning.

Douy wuts Gày kwànk? Tzùng pu long tàw.   誰謂河廣　曾不容舠
Douy wuts Sòungs want? Tzùng pu djoung traw.   誰謂宋遠　曾不崇朝

This Ode is believed to be by another daughter of *Swan Kyang* of *Wets*. This daughter married the duke of *Sòungs*, on the other side of the Yellow River, and they had a son; but later she was divorced and sent back to *Wets*. In due course the son succeeded as ruler of *Sòungs*, and his mother longed to cross the river to be with him—but as a divorcee, she couldn't. Hence the Ode is saying that *Sòungs* is not far, but barred to her: she is not allowed to board any boat, though the crossing would take no time.

62

My Warlike Lord 伯兮

How warlike my lord looked! He is the hero of the nation.
My lord grasped his lance; he rode in the king's vanguard.

Pràk ì, khat ì, pròng tu gat ì.   伯兮朅兮　邦之桀兮
Pràk layc tup do, ways wang dzèn kho.   伯也執殳　為王前驅

Since my lord rode east, my hair has been like fleabane flying in the wind.
I have lotions and shampoos, of course—but who cares to put effort into appearance?

Dzis pràk tu tòng, lhouc na puy bòng.   自伯之東　首如飛蓬
Khuyc ma kàws mòk, douy lhek way long.   豈無膏沐　誰適為容

How it rains, how it rains! Let the sun shine out brightly.
Longingly I think of my lord; there is sweetness in my heart, but my head aches.

Gu wac, gu wac: kòuc-kòuc k'hlout nit.　　其雨其雨　杲杲出日
Ngons ngan sus pràk; kàm sum, lhouc dzit.　　願言思伯　甘心首疾

Where can I get the herb of forgetfulness? I would plant it at the back of the house.
Longingly I think of my lord; it makes my heart distressed.

An tùk hwan tsòuc? Ngan doc tu pùks.　　焉得諼草　言樹之背
Ngons ngan sus pràk; shuc ngàyc sum mùs.　　願言思伯　使我心痗

Her husband is away on a long campaign, which has been identified with a specific episode in 706.

We do not know for sure what plant *bòng* was; one suggestion is hairy fleabane, *Conyza bonariensis*. The traditional commentaries say that *bòng* was a plant with hairy seeds which dispersed on the wind, hence the analogy with messy hair—but the force of the simile may have stemmed from the fact that Chinese happened to have another word *bòng* which meant "disorderly". The herb of forgetfulness was said to be a plant that one could cook, flowers and leaves together, to make a potion that led to forgetting one's sorrows. Probably this species was mythical, though some have identified it with one of the shade-loving hostas. The rear of the house is where the women's quarters are, so the herb would be handy for use.

63

A Fox　有狐

A fox is quietly creeping across the weir on the river *Gu*.
Oh, how sad: this young person has no skirt.

Wuc gwà snouy-snouy, dzùc pàyc Gu rang.　　有狐夂夂　在彼淇梁
Sum tu ou luc, tu tzuc ma dang.　　心之憂矣　之子無裳

A fox is quietly creeping through the ford on the river *Gu*.
Oh, how sad: this young person has no girdle.

Wuc gwà snouy-snouy, dzùc pàyc Gu rats.　　有狐夂夂　在彼淇厲
Sum tu ou luc, tu tzuc ma tàts.　　心之憂矣　之子無帶

A fox is quietly creeping along the side of the river *Gu*.
Oh, how sad: this young person is naked.

Wuc gwà snouy-snouy, dzùc pàyc Gu juk.　　有狐夂夂　在彼淇側
Sum tu ou luc, tu tzuc ma buk.　　心之憂矣　之子無服

All it seems safe to say about this mysterious little Ode is that the old fox is having his wicked way with the young person.

64

The Quince 木瓜

She threw me a quince; I paid her with a netsuke gem.
It wasn't payment: it was to represent my love for ever.

Dò ngàyc luc mòk gwàs; pòus tu luc gweng ka.　　投我以木瓜　報之以瓊琚
Puyc pòus layc: wrank luc way hòus layc.　　匪報也　永以為好也

She threw me a peach; I paid her with a gem of jasper.
It wasn't payment: it was to represent my love for ever.

Dò ngàyc luc mòk làw; pòus tu luc gweng yaw.　　投我以木桃　報之以瓊瑤
Puyc pòus layc: wrank luc way hòus layc.　　匪報也　永以為好也

She threw me a plum; I paid her with a gem of obsidian.
It wasn't payment: it was to represent my love for ever.

Dò ngàyc luc mòk ruc; pòus tu luc gweng kwuc.　　投我以木李　報之以瓊玖
Puyc pòus layc: wrank luc way hòus layc.　　匪報也　永以為好也

The Royal Domain

This refers to the Eastern *Tiw* royal domain, around modern Luoyang.

65

The Hanging Millet Ears 黍離

The foxtail-millet ears hang down—oh, the sprouts of broomcorn-millet!
I walk slowly: in my heart's core I am shaken.
Those who know me say I'm sad;
those who don't know me ask what I'm searching for.
Oh, you distant blue Sky: what kind of man is he?

Payc nhac ray-ray—payc tzuk tu maw!　　彼黍離離　彼稷之苗
Gràng mràts mayc-mayc; troung sum yaw-yaw.　　行邁靡靡　中心搖搖
Tre ngàyc tac, wuts ngàyc sum ou;　　知我者　謂我心憂
pu tre ngàyc tac, wuts ngàyc gày gou.　　不知我者　謂我何求
You-you tsàng Thìn, tsec gày nin tzù?　　悠悠蒼天　此何人哉

The foxtail-millet ears hang down—oh, the broomcorn-millet come into ear!
I walk slowly: in my heart's core I feel dizzy.
Those who know me say I'm sad;
those who don't know me ask what I'm searching for.
Oh, you distant blue Sky: what kind of man is he?

Payc nhac ray-ray—payc tzuk tu swits!　　彼黍離離　彼稷之穗
Gràng mràts mayc-mayc; troung sum na tzouts.　　行邁靡靡　中心如醉
Tre ngàyc tac, wuts ngàyc sum ou;　　知我者　謂我心憂
pu tre ngàyc tac, wuts ngàyc gày gou.　　不知我者　謂我何求
You-you tsàng Thìn, tsec gày nin tzù?　　悠悠蒼天　此何人哉

The foxtail-millet ears hang down—oh, the ripe grains of broomcorn-millet!
I walk slowly: in my heart's core it's as if I'm choking.
Those who know me say I'm sad;
those who don't know me ask what I'm searching for.
Oh, you distant blue Sky: what kind of man is he?

Payc nhac ray-ray—payc tzuk tu mlit!　　彼黍離離　彼稷之實
Gràng mràts mayc-mayc; troung sum na ìt.　　行邁靡靡　中心如噎
Tre ngàyc tac, wuts ngàyc sum ou;　　知我者　謂我心憂
pu tre ngàyc tac, wuts ngàyc gày gou.　　不知我者　謂我何求
You-you tsàng Thìn, tsec gày nin tzù?　　悠悠蒼天　此何人哉

Foxtail and broomcorn are two millet varieties, which ripen at different times.

66

My Man Has Been Called Up 君子于役

My man has been called up: I don't know when his release will be
—oh, when will it come?
The fowls go to roost in their nest-holes;
it's the evening of the day, and the sheep and cattle come down from the pasture.
But my man has been called up—how can I fail to worry about him?

Kwun-tzuc wa wek; pu tre gu gu   君子于役 　不知其期
—*gàt tits tzù?*   曷至哉
Kè sì wa du;   雞棲于塒
nit tu syak luc, yang ngwu gràs rù.   日之夕矣 　羊牛下來
Kwun-tzuc wa wek—na tu gày mut sus?   君子于役 　如之何勿思

My man has been called up: not just for days, not just for months
—when will he rejoin me?
The fowls go to roost on their perches;
it's the evening of the day, and the sheep and cattle gather from the hillside.
But my man has been called up—oh, don't let him be going hungry or thirsty!

Kwun-tzuc wa wek, pu nit, pu ngwat   君子于役 　不日不月
—*gàt gu wuc gwàt?*   曷其有佸
Kè sì wa gat;   雞棲于桀
nit tu syak luc, yang ngwu gràs kwàt.   日之夕矣 　羊牛下括
Kwun-tzuc wa wek—kòc ma kri khàt!   君子于役 　苟無飢渴

Her man—her *kwun-tzuc*, her lord—has been taken for state service, in the army or the like.
    A farmstead was surrounded by simple earthen walls in which it was easy to scoop out holes, *du*, for hens to roost in.

67

My Lord is Elated 君子陽陽

My lord is elated.
In his left hand he holds his reed-organ, with his right he beckons me to his room.
Oh, the joy in him!

Kwun-tzuc lang-lang.
Tzàyc tup gwàng, wuc taw ngàyc you bang.
Gu ngràwks kec tza!

君子陽陽
左執簧　右招我由房
其樂只且

My lord is pleased with himself.
In his left hand he holds his feather-stick, with his right he beckons me to the pleasure-land.
Oh, the joy in him!

Kwun-tzuc law-law.
Tzàyc tup dòu, wuc taw ngàyc you ngàw.
Gu ngràwks kec tza!

君子陶陶
左執翿　右招我由敖
其樂只且

68

Rising Water　揚之水

Rising water won't float apart sticks that are tied together.
That lady there is not here with me as I guard the *Lhin* border.
Oh love, oh love! What month will I get home?

Lang tu lhouyc pu riw lhok sin.
Payc kus tu tzuc, pu lac ngàyc hyos Lhin.
Gròuy tzay, gròuy tzay! Gàt ngwat lac wèn kwuy tzay?

揚之水　不流束薪
彼其之子　不與我戍申
懷哉懷哉　曷月予還歸哉

Rising water won't float apart brushwood that is tied together.
That lady there is not here with me as I guard the *Pac* border.
Oh love, oh love! What month will I get home?

Lang tu lhouyc pu riw lhok chac.
Payc kus tu tzuc, pu lac ngàyc hyos Pac.
Gròuy tzay, gròuy tzay! Gàt ngwat lac wèn kwuy tzay?

揚之水　不流束楚
彼其之子　不與我戍甫
懷哉懷哉　曷月予還歸哉

Rising water won't float apart reeds that are tied together.
That lady there is not here with me as I guard the *Nghac* border.
Oh love, oh love! What month will I get home?

Lang tu lhouyc pu riw lhok bà.
Payc kus tu tzuc, pu lac ngàyc hyos Nghac.
Gròuy tzay, gròuy tzay! Gàt ngwat lac wèn kwuy tzay?

揚之水　不流束蒲
彼其之子　不與我戍許
懷哉懷哉　曷月予還歸哉

Although the rising tide of war is keeping the couple apart, it cannot break the marriage bond.

69

Parched Motherwort 中谷有蓷

In the middle of the valley there is motherwort; its dry stems are scorched.
There is a girl who has been sent away; her sighs are sad.
Her sighs are sad, experiencing human misery.

Troung klòk wuc thòuy; hànt gu kàn luc.	中谷有蓷　暵其乾矣
Wuc nrac bric ray; khùts gu nhàn luc.	有女仳離　嘅其嘆矣
Khùts gu nhàn luc, ngos nin tu krùn nàns luc.	嘅其嘆矣　遇人之艱難矣

In the middle of the valley there is motherwort; its withered stems are scorched.
There is a girl who has been sent away; her wailing is long-drawn-out.
Her wailing is long-drawn-out, encountering human wickedness.

Troung klòk wuc thòuy; hànt gu siw luc.	中谷有蓷　暵其脩矣
Wuc nrac bric ray; lìw gu sìws luc.	有女仳離　條其歗矣
Lìw gu sìws luc, ngos nin tu pu diwk luc.	條其歗矣　遇人之不淑矣

In the middle of the valley there is motherwort; its parched stems are scorched.
There is a girl who has been sent away; her sobs are convulsive.
Her sobs are convulsive, but where will "alas" get her?

Troung klòk wuc thòuy; hànt gu khup luc.	中谷有蓷　暵其㬂矣
Wuc nrac bric ray; trot gu khrup luc.	有女仳離　啜其泣矣
Trot gu khrup luc, gày "tzay" gup luc?	啜其泣矣　何嗟及矣

Motherwort, *Leonurus cardiaca,* is a weed of the mint family. If it is parched even in the middle of the valley, where water should normally flow, this must be a bad season with a poor harvest expected. This has led some to suggest that the girl is a servant turned out because her master cannot keep her on; but it seems more likely that this rather heartless poem is about a girl rejected by a husband or lover, rather than by an employer.

It might seem excessive to translate *pu diwk*, literally "not good", as "wicked". But even in modern Chinese the concept "bad" is standardly expressed in this roundabout way. Stalin or Hitler in Mandarin would be 'hen bu hao ren', "very not good men".

70

The Slow-Moving Rabbit 兔爰

There is a rabbit moving slowly, while a pheasant is caught fast in a *ràiy*-net.
When I was a young man, if only I hadn't done what I did!
Now I'm older, I have to cope with all these difficulties.
If only I could fall asleep and stay that way!

Wuc lhàs wan-wan; dric ray wa ràiy.　　有兔爰爰　雉離于羅
Ngàyc sheng tu cha, dangs ma way!　　我生之初　尚無為
Ngàyc sheng tu ghòc, bong tsec pràk ray.　　我生之後　逢此百罹
Dangs mits ma ngòy!　　尚寐無吪

There is a rabbit moving slowly, while a pheasant is caught fast in a *phou*-net.
When I was a young man, if only I hadn't acted!
Now I'm older, I have to cope with all these sorrows.
If only I could fall asleep and never wake up!

Wuc lhàs wan-wan; dric ray wa phou.　　有兔爰爰　雉離于罦
Ngàyc sheng tu cha, dangs ma dzòuc!　　我生之初　尚無造
Ngàyc sheng tu ghòc, bong tsec pràk ou.　　我生之後　逢此百憂
Dangs mits ma kròuk!　　尚寐無覺

There is a rabbit moving slowly, while a pheasant is caught fast in a *thong*-net.
When I was a young man, if only I hadn't meddled!
Now I'm older, I have to cope with all these horrors.
If only I could fall asleep and be deaf to the world!

Wuc lhàs wan-wan; dric ray wa thong.　　有兔爰爰　雉離于罿
Ngàyc sheng tu cha, dangs ma long!　　我生之初　尚無庸
Ngàyc sheng tu ghòc, bong tsec pràk hong.　　我生之後　逢此百凶
Dangs mits ma tsòng!　　尚寐無聰

Too late, he wishes he had been a cautious rabbit rather than an impetuous pheasant. (*Ràiy*, *phou*, and *thong* were three kinds of net for trapping birds.)

71

Creepers　葛藟

Creepers run along the ground on the bank of the River.
Separated for ever from my kin, I call a stranger "father".
I call a stranger "father", and no-one pays me heed.

Ment-ment kàt rouyc, dzùc Gày tu nghàc.　　緜緜葛藟　在河之滸
Toung wans hwrang dìc, wuts lhày nin bac.　　終遠兄弟　謂他人父
Wuts lhày nin bac, yak màk ngàyc kàs.　　謂他人父　亦莫我顧

Creepers run along the ground beside the River.
Separated for ever from my kin, I call a stranger "mother".
I call a stranger "mother", and no-one is my friend.

Ment-ment kàt rouyc, dzùc Gày tu shuc.　　緜緜葛藟　在河之涘
Toung wans hwrang dìc, wuts lhày nin muc.　　終遠兄弟　謂他人母
Wuts lhày nin muc, yak màk ngàyc wuc.　　謂他人母　亦莫我友

Creepers run along the ground on the lip of the River bank.
Separated for ever from my kin, I call a stranger "elder brother".
I call a stranger "elder brother", and no-one asks after me.

Ment-ment kàt rouyc, dzùc Gày tu mdoun.　　縣縣葛藟　在河之漘
Toung wans hwrang dìc, wuts lhày nin kòun.　終遠兄弟　謂他人昆
Wuts lhày nin kòun, yak màk ngàyc muns.　　謂他人昆　亦莫我問

72

Gathering Beans　采葛

I'll go and gather lablab beans there;
a whole day without seeing him is like three months.

Payc tsùc kàt ì;　　　　　　　　　彼采葛兮
it nit pu kèns, na sùm ngwat ì.　　一日不見　如三月兮

I'll go and gather lad's-love there;
a whole day without seeing him is like three autumns.

Payc tsùc sìw ì;　　　　　　　　　彼采蕭兮
it nit pu kèns, na sùm tsiw ì.　　一日不見　如三秋兮

I'll go and gather mugwort there;
a whole day without seeing him is like three years.

Payc tsùc ngàts ì;　　　　　　　　彼采艾兮
it nit pu kèns, na sùm swats ì.　　一日不見　如三歲兮

The plants mentioned are discussed in notes to other Odes.

73

The Big Carriage　大車

My big carriage rumbles, my patterned robe is like young silvergrass.
How can I not long for you—but I'm afraid you won't dare.

Dàts ka gàmp-gàmp, chots uy na lhàmp.　　大車檻檻　毳衣如菼
Khuyc pu nec sus—ouys tzuc pu kàmp.　　　豈不爾思　畏子不敢

My big carriage roars, my patterned robe is like red millet.
How can I not long for you—but I'm afraid you won't run away with me.

Dàts ka thòun-thòun, chots uy na mùn.　　　　　　大車啍啍　毳衣如璊
Khuyc pu nec sus—ouys tzuc pu pùn.　　　　　　豈不爾思　畏子不奔

While we live you shall have your own room; when we die we shall share one grave.
Will you say I'm not to be trusted? By the bright sun, I am!

Kòk tzùk luks lhit; sic tzùk dòng wìt.　　　　　　穀則異室　死則同穴
Wuts lac pu sins? Wuc na kyàwc nit!　　　　　　謂予不信　有如皦日

Lhàmp is said to refer to young Chinese silvergrass (*Miscanthus*). This is a plant often grown ornamentally—its leaves catch the light to create an impression of cool green shot through with silver. Red millet, likewise, is a showy variety. The roaring and rumbling was road noise rather than a motor, but the idea of big cars and smart clothes as routes to a girl's heart is familiar.

74

Hemp on the Hill　丘中有麻

On that hill, hemp grows; Mr *Tzay* is still there.
Mr *Tzay* is still there; please, let him come and bring me a present.

Kwhu troung wuc mràly; payc rou tzuc Tzay.　　　丘中有麻　彼留子嗟
Payc rou tzuc Tzay; tsang kus rù lhays.　　　　　彼留子嗟　將其來施

On that hill, wheat grows; Mr *Kwùk* is still there.
Mr *Kwùk* is still there; please, let him come and feast me.

Kwhu troung wuc mrùk; payc rou tzuc Kwùk.　　　丘中有麥　彼留子國
Payc rou tzuc Kwùk; tsang kus rù sluks.　　　　　彼留子國　將其來食

On that hill there are plum trees; that young gentleman is still there.
That young gentleman is still there; let him give me an obsidian netsuke.

Kwhu troung wuc ruc; payc rou tu tzuc.　　　　　丘中有李　彼留之子
Payc rou tu tzuc; lu ngàyc bès kwuc.　　　　　　彼留之子　貽我佩玖

Was the author a courtesan? She seems not even to remember the name of lover number three.

State of *Drengs*

Drengs was one of the most powerful *Tiw* vassal states; originally based on Huazhou, central Shaanxi, its ruler was killed in the conflict which ended the Western *Tiw* dynasty in 771, and it was re-established from a new base at Xinzheng ("New *Drengs*") in central Henan.

75

The Black Robe 緇衣

How well that black robe suits you! When it wears out, I'll make you a new one.
When I move in with you, I shall be prompt about serving your dinner.

Ju uy tu ngay ì, bets lac wus kùc way ì.　　　緇衣之宜兮　敝予又改為兮
Lhek tzuc tu kòns ì, swen lac dous tzuc tu tsàns ì.　適子之館兮　還予授子之粲兮

How lovely that black robe is! When it wears out, I'll run you up another.
When I move in with you, I shall be prompt about serving your dinner.

Ju uy tu hòuc ì, bets lac wus kùc dzòuc ì.　　　緇衣之好兮　敝予又改造兮
Lhek tzuc tu kòns ì, swen lac dous tzuc tu tsàns ì.　適子之館兮　還予授子之粲兮

How full that black robe is! When it wears out, I'll make you a replacement.
When I move in with you, I shall be prompt about serving your dinner.

Ju uy tu slak ì, bets lac wus kùc tzàk ì.　　　緇衣之蓆兮　敝予又改作兮
Lhek tzuc tu kòns ì, swen lac dous tzuc tu tsàns ì.　適子之館兮　還予授子之粲兮

76

Please, Second-Son 將仲子

Please, Second-Son,
don't trespass into our compound—don't break the matrimony-vines we planted.
Of course I don't care about them, but I'm afraid of my parents.
Second-Son is someone to love,
but the words of my parents: they are something to fear.

Tsang, Droungs-tzuc ì,
ma lo ngàyc ruc—ma tet ngàyc doc khuc!
Khuyc kàmp ùts tu; ouys ngàyc bac muc.
Droungs khàyc gròuy layc;
bac muc tu ngan, yak khàyc ouys layc.

將仲子兮
無踰我里　無折我樹杞
豈敢愛之　畏我父母
仲可懷也
父母之言　亦可畏也

Please, Second-Son,
don't trespass over our wall—don't break the mulberries we planted.
Of course I don't care about them, but I'm afraid of my brothers.
Second-Son is someone to love,
but the words of my brothers: they are something to fear.

Tsang, Droungs-tzuc ì,
ma lo ngàyc dzang—ma tet ngàyc doc sàng!
Khuyc kàmp ùts tu; ouys ngàyc ta hwrang.
Droungs khàyc gròuy layc;
ta hwrang tu ngan, yak khàyc ouys layc.

將仲子兮
無踰我墻　無折我樹桑
豈敢愛之　畏我諸兄
仲可懷也
諸兄之言　亦可畏也

Please, Second-Son,
don't trespass into our garden—don't break the sandalwoods we planted.
Of course I don't care about them, but I'm afraid of people's gossip.
Second-Son is someone to love,
but people's gossip: that is something to fear.

Tsang, Droungs-tzuc ì,
ma lo ngàyc wan—ma tet ngàyc doc dàn!
Khuyc kàmp ùts tu; ouys nin tu tày ngan.
Droungs khàyc gròuy layc;
nin tu tày ngan, yak khàyc ouys layc.

將仲子兮
無踰我園　無折我樹檀
豈敢愛之　畏人之多言
仲可懷也
人之多言　亦可畏也

Matrimony-vine or boxthorn (*Lycium chinense*) is a shrub which can be grown as a hedge. It is the plant which gives us goji berries, and has medicinal and other uses.

Many cultures use birth order as a basis for personal names; such names were frequent in *Tiw* China.

77

Nobody Left　叔于田

Third-Son has taken the field—nobody is left living in our lane.
How do you mean, nobody living in the lane?
Nobody to compare with Third-Son, truly handsome and kind.

Nhouk wa lìn; gròngs ma kas nin.
Khuyc ma kas nin?
Pu na Nhouk layc, swin mouyc tsac nin.

叔于田　巷無居人
豈無居人
不如叔也　恂美且仁

Third-Son has gone hunting—nobody is left drinking wine in our lane.
How do you mean, nobody drinking wine?
Nobody to compare with Third-Son, truly handsome and fine.

Nhouk wa hyouc; gròngs ma um tziwc.   叔于狩　巷無飲酒
Khuyc ma um tziwc?   豈無飲酒
Pu na Nhouk layc, swin mouyc tsac hòuc.   不如叔也　恂美且好

Third-Son is away in the wilds—there are no horsemen left in our lane.
How do you mean, no horsemen?
None to compare with Third-Son, truly handsome and brave.

Nhouk lhek lac; gròngs ma buk mràc.   叔適野　巷無服馬
Khuyc ma buk mràc?   豈無服馬
Pu na Nhouk layc, swin mouyc tsac mac.   不如叔也　恂美且武

78

Driving his Team　大叔于田

Third-Son has taken the field, driving a team of four horses.
The reins are as light in his grasp as ribbons; the two outer horses step as if dancing.
Third-Son is in the marshes; fires blaze up everywhere.
Stripped to the waist, he wrestles a tiger to the ground, and presents it to the duke in person.
I'm begging you, Third-Son, don't ever do that again—beware of it mauling you!

Nhouk wa lìn, mlung mlungs mràc.   叔于田　乘乘馬
Tup prus na tzàc; rank tsùm na mac.   執轡如組　兩驂如舞
Nhouk dzùc sòc; mhùyc rat gos klac.   叔在藪　火烈具舉
Dànt-slèk bàwks lhàc, nghans wa klòng shac.   襢裼暴虎　獻于公所
Tsang Nhouk ma nrouc—krùs gu lhang nac!   將叔無狃　戒其傷汝

Third-Son has taken the field, driving a team of four bays.
The inner horses rear their heads; as in a skein of wild geese, the outer horses trot slightly behind.
Third-Son is in the marshes; fires flare up everywhere.
Third-Son is a fine archer, as well as a skilled driver.
Now he sounds the musical stone and pulls his horses up; now he releases the bowstring and follows the course of the arrow.

Nhouk wa lìn, mlung mlungs gwàng.   叔于田　乘乘黃
Rank buk dyank snang, rank tsùm ngràns gràng.   兩服上襄　兩驂雁行
Nhouk dzùc sòc; mhùyc rat gos lang.   叔在藪　火烈具揚
Nhouk dant mlak kus, wus rang ngas kus.   叔善射忌　又良御忌
Uk khèngs khòngs kus; uk tzongs sòngs kus.   抑磬控忌　抑縱送忌

Third-Son has taken the field, driving a team of four piebalds.
The inner horses' heads are level with one another; the outer horses flank them like arms.
Third-Son is in the marshes; the fires are full and wide everywhere.
Third-Son's horses are slower now, and he shoots only an occasional arrow.
Now he sets aside his quiver. And now he puts his bow away in its case.

Nhouk wa lìn, mlung mlungs pòuc.   叔于田　乘乘鴇
Rank buk dzì lhouc, rank tsùm na nhouc.   兩服齊首　兩驂如手
Nhouk dzùc sòc; mhùyc rat gos bouc.   叔在藪　火烈具阜
Nhouk mràc mràns kus; Nhouk pat nghànt kus.   叔馬慢忌　叔發罕忌
Uk lhak prung kus, uk trhangs kwung kus.   抑釋掤忌　抑鬯弓忌

Traditionally Odes 77 and 78 were believed to be about the same man, brother of the man who ruled *Drengs* from 742. But although the Third-Son of Ode 78 is evidently close enough to his ruler to present him with a tiger, the Third-Son of Ode 77 sounds to me more like a "boy next door" type. They may have been one and the same, but we need not assume this.

The word *sòc*, which I have translated as "marshes", specifically means a marshy area abundant in game birds. Fires were lit to do the job done by beaters in a shoot on dry land: to flush birds into the air.

In a team of four horses, the inner horses were yoked to the shaft of the carriage, while the outer horses were attached to the carriage itself by long straps. Thus the four were arranged in a configuration a little like the V shape of a skein of geese (though geese will normally have a single lead bird), and if we think of the carriage as a body one can see the inner horses as head and the outer horses as hands or arms reaching forward.

In battle, signals for various tactics were given by musical instruments, including boomerang-shaped sounding stones, and the same method was used in hunting.

79

Men of *Tseng*   清人

The men of *Tseng* are at *Bràng*. Their teams of four mailed horses thunder over the ground.
The pair of lances in each chariot have double ornaments. They promenade back and forth on the bank of the River.

Tseng nin dzùc Bràng. Slits krèts pàng-pàng.   清人在彭　駟介旁旁
Nits mou drong rrang. Gày dyangs ghà ngòu-syang.   二矛重英　河上乎翱翔

The men of *Tseng* are at *Syaw*. Their teams of four mailed horses are cantering.
The pair of lances in each chariot are decorated with pheasant-feather pennons.
They drive about at their leisure on the bank of the River.

Tseng nin dzùc Syaw. Slits krèts paw-paw.
Nits mou drong-gaw. Gày dyangs ghà syaw-yaw.

清人在消　駟介儦儦
二矛重鷮　河上乎逍遙

The men of *Tseng* are at *Driwk*. Their teams of four mailed horses are at the gallop. Wheeling to his left hand while drawing his weapon with his right hand, the commander is making himself admired.

Tseng nin dzùc Driwk. Slits krèts lòus-lòus.
Tzàyc swen wuc rhiw, troung-kwun tzàk hòus.

清人在軸　駟介陶陶
左旋右抽　中軍作好

The key to this Ode is the historical context in which it was written, which was the tribal invasion of *Wets* mentioned with Ode 50. Although his own state was not the one invaded, the ruler of *Drengs* felt vulnerable, and raised troops from the city of *Tseng* (a site on the east of Zhengzhou) to defend his frontier. (*Bràng*, *Syaw*, and *Driwk* were places on the Yellow River—the first, and probably the other two, were to the east of modern Xinxiang.) But this army never did anything beyond parading and looking martial, until eventually the men melted away back to their homes, and the commander fled in disgrace. It possibly added to the piquancy of the satire that the name *Tseng* means "pure"; the Ode title, *Tseng Nin*, literally means "pure people"—too pure to get their hands dirty with fighting, perhaps? To be fair, it is not clear that the tribesmen ever tried to enter *Drengs*.

80

Glistening Lamb Fur　羔裘

His lambskin jacket glistens as if dewy; truly he is a straight, princely man.
This gentleman will be steadfast until death.

Kàw gwu na no; swin druk tsac gò.
Payc kus tu tzuc, lhac mreng pu lo.

羔裘如濡　洵直且侯
彼其之子　舍命不渝

His lambskin jacket has leopard-fur cuffs; he is very valiant and tough.
This gentleman sets the standard of uprightness for our state.

Kàw gwu pràwks lhuk; khònk mac wuc ruk.
Payc kus tu tzuc, pròng tu su druk.

羔裘豹飾　孔武有力
彼其之子　邦之司直

His lambskin jacket is so bright! Its three gems form a trinity of beauty.
This gentleman is the ornament of the state.

Kàw gwu rràns ì, sùm rrang tsàns ì!
Payc kus tu tzuc, pròng tu ngans ì.

羔裘晏兮　三英粲兮
彼其之子　邦之彥兮

VOICES FROM EARLY CHINA

Legge tells us that lambskin jackets were court dress, and the leopard-fur cuffs distinguished courtiers from ruler.

81

Heading for the High Road 遵大路

You were heading for the high road, but I wouldn't let go of your sleeve.
Don't hate me—our old feelings shouldn't be dismissed.

Tzoun dàts ràks ì, shùmp tup tzuc tu kha ì.　　遵大路兮　掺執子之袪兮
Ma ngàyc àks ì—pu dzap kàs layc.　　　　　　無我惡兮　不寁故也

You were heading for the high road, but I wouldn't let go of your hand.
Don't be hostile—love shouldn't be shrugged off.

Tzoun dàts ràks ì, shùmp tup tzuc tu nhouc ì.　　遵大路兮　掺執子之手兮
Ma ngàyc dou ì—pu dzap hòus layc.　　　　　　無我魗兮　不寁好也

82

The Girl Says "The Cock is Crowing" 女曰雞鳴

The girl says "The cock is crowing". The man says "It's not light yet."
She: "Sir, get up and look at the night!" *He:* "The Morning Star is still bright."
She: "Please, stir yourself, please get going, go and shoot wild duck and geese."

Nrac wat "Kè mreng". Shuc wat "Mùts tàns."　　女曰雞鳴　士曰昧旦
"Tzuc hung gic yas." "Mrang Sèng wuc ràns."　　子興視夜　明星有爛
"Tsang ngòu, tsang syang, luk bo lac ngràns."　　將翱將翔　弋鳧與鴈

She: "When you've hit one, I'll prepare it for you.
When it's ready, I'll pour you wine. I shall be your companion into old age.
There will be lute and zither when we are served; everything will be pure and
　　lovely."

"Luk ngan kràny tu, lac tzuc ngay tu.　　弋言加之　與子宜之
Ngay ngan ums tziwc, lac tzuc krìc ròuc.　　宜言飲酒　與子偕老
Gum sprit dzùc ngràs, màk pu dzenk hòuc."　　琴瑟在御　莫不靜好

He: "If I know you are coming to me, I'll present you with an assortment of
　　netsuke.
If I know you'll be obedient, I'll sort out an assortment of netsuke.
If I know that you love me, I shall repay you with an assortment of netsuke."

"Tre tzuc tu rù tu, dzùp bès luc dzùngs tu. 知子之來之　雜佩以贈之
Tre tzuc tu mlouns tu, dzùp bès luc muns tu. 知子之順之　雜佩以問之
Tre tzuc tu hòus tu, dzùp bès luc pòus tu." 知子之好之　雜佩以報之

To *luk* was to shoot arrows with strings attached, so they could easily be retrieved. Why such emphasis on an "assortment" of netsuke? Well, one possible reason is that Chinese has no plural; *bès*, "netsuke", alone could be just one—with *dzùp* the man assures her there will be several, without committing himself to a figure.

83

A Girl in my Carriage　有女同車

I have a girl in my carriage whose face is like a hibiscus flower.
We shall promenade here and there, with precious jade netsuke at her girdle.
This lovely Eldest-Daughter *Kyang*: truly she is both lovely and refined.

Wuc nrac dòng ka, ngràn na hwins wà. 有女同車　顏如舜華
Tzang ngòu, tzang syang, bès ngok gweng ka. 將翱將翔　佩玉瓊琚
Payc mouyc Mràngs Kyang, swin mouyc tsac tà. 彼美孟姜　洵美且都

I have a girl walking with me whose face is like a hibiscus blossom.
We shall promenade to and fro, with her jade netsuke chinking together.
This lovely Eldest-Daughter *Kyang*: her fame will be immortal.

Wuc nrac dòng gràng, ngràn na hwins rrang. 有女同行　顏如舜英
Tzang ngòu, tzang syang, bès ngok tsang-tsang. 將翱將翔　佩玉瑲瑲
Payc mouyc Mràngs Kyang, tùk um pu mang. 彼美孟姜　德音不忘

84

Rose-Mallows　山有扶蘇

There are rose-mallow bushes on the hill, and lotus blossoms in the wetland.
I don't see Master *Tà*, only some daft oaf.

Shàn wuc ba-sngà, slup wuc gày wà. 山有扶蘇　隰有荷華
Pu kèns tzuc Tà, nùc kèns gwang tza. 不見子都　迺見狂狙

There are tall pines on the hill, and floating-dragons in the wetland.
I don't see Master *Thoung*, only a sly boy.

Shàn wuc gaw slong, slup wuc you rong.
Pu kèns tzuc Thoung, nùc kèns kràwc dòng.

山有喬松　隰有游龍
不見子充　迺見狡童

A girl is out for a walk, hoping to be picked up by one of the eligible young men she knows, but she only encounters youths who don't interest her.

The rose mallow or "China rose", *Hibiscus rosa-sinensis*, is a shrub with red blooms. *You rong*, "floating-dragons", are probably the plant amphibious bistort, *Persicaria amphibia*.

85

Dead Leaves　蘀兮

Oh, dead leaves, dead leaves: how the wind rustles you.
Oh, junior uncle, senior uncle: you give the note and I'll sing in tune.

Lhàk ì, lhàk ì, pum gu thoys nac.
Nhouk ì, pràk ì, k'hlangs lac wàys nac.

蘀兮蘀兮　風其吹汝
叔兮伯兮　倡予和汝

Oh, dead leaves, dead leaves: how the wind blows you down.
Oh, junior uncle, senior uncle: you give the note and I'll harmonize with you.

Lhàk ì, lhàk ì, pum gu phyaw nac.
Nhouk ì, pràk ì, k'hlangs lac yaw nac.

蘀兮蘀兮　風其飄汝
叔兮伯兮　倡予要汝

A girl reluctantly agrees to a marriage arranged by her elders. A *nhouk* is a third son, and *pràk* is one word for the eldest brother; both words are commonly used by the next generation to refer to their uncles. The dead leaves reflect the mood of a girl whose hopes for a bright future have withered, and singing in tune with the uncles means accepting their uncongenial plans for her.

The graph I spell in the first line as *thoys*, which means a musical concert, can represent either that derived form, or the root *thoy*, "to blow". Here I believe the poet intends us to hold both meanings in mind, with the creative ambiguity that Empson saw as characteristic of poetry: the wind is literally blowing the dead leaves about, but metaphorically the uncles are inducing the girl to behave "in tune" with them.

86

The Sly Boy　狡童

That sly boy has stopped talking to me.
This is your fault; it's preventing me swallowing my food.

Payc kràwc dòng ì, pu lac ngàyc ngan ì.
Wi tzuc tu kàs; shuc ngàyc pu nùc tsàn ì.

彼狡童兮　不與我言兮
維子之故　使我不能餐兮

That sly boy has stopped eating next to me.
This is your fault; it's preventing me sleeping.

Payc kràwc dòng ì, pu lac ngàyc mluk ì.
Wi tzuc tu kàs; shuc ngàyc pu nùc suk ì.

彼狡童兮　不與我食兮
維子之故　使我不能息兮

The girl is evidently losing her young man, but who is "you"—another woman? Does the poetess see the boy as deliberately playing one girl off against the other?

87

Tucking Up My Skirt 褰裳

If you think of me fondly, I'd tuck up my skirt and wade across the river *Jin*.
But if you don't think about me, do you imagine there's no-one else out there?
You really are the silliest of silly boys!

Tzuc wìts su ngàyc, khran dang dap Jin.
Tzuc pu ngàyc su, khuyc ma lhày nin?
Gwang dòng tu gwang layc tza!

子惠思我　褰裳涉溱
子不我思　豈無他人
狂童之狂也且

If you think of me fondly, I'd tuck up my skirt and wade across the river *Wruc*.
But if you don't think about me, do you imagine there are no other men out there?
You really are the silliest of silly boys!

Tzuc wìts su ngàyc, khran dang dap Wruc.
Tzuc pu ngàyc su, khuyc ma lhày shuc?
Gwang dòng tu gwang layc tza!

子惠思我　褰裳涉洧
子不我思　豈無他士
狂童之狂也且

The *Jin* and *Wruc* (modern Zhen and Wei) are streams which rise in the hills south-west of Zhengzhou, flow south-eastwards, and meet, eventually flowing into the Jialu.

88

If Only 丰

How handsome you were!
You waited for me in the lane;
if only I had walked with you.

Tzuc tu phong ì! 子之丰兮
Shuc ngàyc ghà gròngs ì; 俟我乎巷兮
mhùs lac pu sòngs ì. 悔予不送兮

How splendid you were!
You waited for me in the hall;
if only I had gone to you.

Tzuc tu k'hlang ì! 子之昌兮
Shuc ngàyc ghà dàng ì; 俟我乎堂兮
mhùs lac pu tzang ì. 悔予不將兮

I shall wear a brocaded silk top with an unlined hemp jacket; my skirt will be brocaded silk with an unlined hemp overskirt.
Junior uncle, senior uncle: yoke me to him so we go away together!

Uys kump kwhènk uy; dang kump kwhènk dang. 衣錦褧衣 裳錦褧裳
Nhouk ì, pràk ì: kràys lac lac gràng! 叔兮伯兮 駕予與行

My skirt will be brocaded silk with an unlined hemp overskirt; I shall wear a brocaded silk top with an unlined hemp jacket.
Junior uncle, senior uncle: yoke me to him so we go to his home!

Dang kump kwhènk dang; uys kump kwhènk uy. 裳錦褧裳 衣錦褧衣
Nhouk ì, pràk ì: kràys lac lac kwuy! 叔兮伯兮 駕予與歸

She hopes, perhaps fantasizes, that it may not be too late for the men of her family to arrange the marriage.

89

By the Sacrifice-Ground   東門之墠

By the sacrifice-ground at the East Gate, madder grows on the bank.
Your home is quite near, but you yourself are so distant.

Tòng mùn tu dant, na-ra dzùc brànt. 東門之墠 茹藘在阪
Gu lhit tzùk nec; kus nin dums want. 其室則邇 其人甚遠

The chestnuts at the East Gate grow among low-fenced houses.
How can I not brood over you? But you don't come to me.

Tòng mùn tu rit wuc tsent krà lhit. 東門之栗 有淺家室
Khuyc pu nec sus?—Tzuc pu ngàyc tzit. 豈不爾思 子不我即

A *dant* was an area of hard level ground used for offering sacrifices. The madder and the chestnuts are easy for anyone to gather; likewise the girl is ready and waiting, if the man would only come.

90

Wind and Rain 風雨

The wind and rain are chilly; the cocks are all crowing together.
But since I've been with my man, tell me, how can I fail to feel easy?

Pum wac tsì-tsì, kè mreng krì-krì.　　　　風雨淒淒　雞鳴喈喈
Kuts kèns kwun-tzuc, wun gà pu luy?　　　既見君子　云胡不夷

The wind and rain are bitter; the cocks are crowing, *krìw, krìw*.
But since I've been with my man, tell me, how can I fail to be refreshed?

Pum wac sìw-sìw, kè mreng krìw-krìw.　　　風雨蕭蕭　雞鳴膠膠
Kuts kèns kwun-tzuc, wun gà pu rhiw?　　　既見君子　云胡不瘳

With the wind and rain it scarcely looks like day; the cocks are crowing non-stop.
But since I've been with my man, tell me, how can I fail to rejoice?

Pum wac na mhùc, kè mreng pu luc.　　　　風雨如晦　雞鳴不已
Kuts kèns kwun-tzuc, wun gà pu huc?　　　既見君子　云胡不喜

It's a morning of filthy weather, but all that matters is that her man has spent the night with her.

91

The Green Collar 子衿

Green, green is your collar; longing, longing is my heart.
True, I'm making no move towards you—but why do you send no more messages to me?

Tsèng-tsèng tzuc kum; you-you ngàyc sum.　　　青青子衿　悠悠我心
Tzongs ngàyc pu wank—tzuc nèng pu slus um?　　縱我不往　子寧不嗣音

Green, green are your netsuke; longing, longing are my thoughts.
True, I'm making no move towards you—but why do you not come to me?

Tsèng-tsèng tzuc bès; you-you ngàyc su.　　　青青子佩　悠悠我思
Tzongs ngàyc pu wank—tzuc nèng pu rù?　　　縱我不往　子寧不來

Pacing back and forth, oh, on the town lookout tower, oh,
one day not seeing you is like three months, oh.

Lhàw ì, thàt ì, dzùc geng khot ì.
It nit pu kèns na sùm ngwat ì.

挑兮達兮　在城闕兮
一日不見　如三月兮

We are told that a green or blue collar (*tsèng*, like Welsh *glas*, covered both colours) was a student's uniform.

92

Just Me and You　揚之水

Even eddying water can't float away brushwood that's tied into a bundle.
In the end we brothers are few: just me and you.
Don't believe the things others are saying—truly, they're deceiving you.

Lang tu lhouyc, pu riw lhok chac.
Toung sent hwrang dìc: wi lac lac nac.
Ma sins nin tu ngan—nin dit gwank nac.

揚之水　不流束楚
終鮮兄弟　維予與汝
無信人之言　人實迋汝

Even eddying water can't float away sticks that are tied into a bundle.
In the end we brothers are few: just the two of us.
Don't believe the things others are saying—truly, they're not to be trusted.

Lang tu lhouyc, pu riw lhok sin.
Toung sent hwrang dìc: wi lac nits nin.
Ma sins nin tu ngan—nin dit pu sins.

揚之水　不流束薪
終鮮兄弟　維予二人
無信人之言　人實不信

93

As I Go Out by the East Gate　出其東門

As I go out by the East Gate, there are girls as thickly-packed as clouds.
Although they're like clouds, my mind is on none of them.
Plain silk dress and black-mottled grey headcloth: she will make me happy!

K'hlout kus tòng mùn, wuc nrac na wun.
Swi-tzùk na wun, puyc ngàyc su dzùn.
Kàwc uy, gu krun: rìw ngràwks ngàyc wun!

出其東門　有女如雲
雖則如雲　匪我思存
縞衣綦巾　聊樂我員

As I go out by the barbican, there are girls as crowded as dandelions.
Although they're like dandelions, my mind turns to none of them.
Plain silk dress and crimson sash: I can be joyful with her!

K'hlout kus in-tà, wuc nrac na là. 出其闉闍　有女如荼
Swi-tzùk na là, puyc ngàyc su dzà. 雖則如荼　匪我思且
Kàwc uy, na-ra: rìw khàyc lac ngwa! 縞衣茹藘　聊可與娛

Madder gives a crimson dye; according to the commentators, it was understood that the crimson garment was a sash. The clothes described are those of a poor girl.

94

Dew on the Creepers　野有蔓草

The fields are covered with creepers; the falling dew is heavy.
Here is a certain lovely person—her clear forehead is beautiful.
In carefree mood we happen to meet, and she falls in with my desire.

Lac wuc mans tsòuc; rìn ràks dòn ì. 野有蔓草　零露漙兮
Wuc mouyc it nin—tseng lang ont ì. 有美一人　清揚婉兮
Grès-gròs sang ngos, lhek ngàyc ngons ì. 邂逅相遇　適我願兮

The fields are covered with creepers; the falling dew is thick.
Here is a certain lovely person—beautiful is your clear forehead.
In carefree mood we happen to meet. You and I are good together.

Lac wuc mans tsòuc; rìn ràks nang-nang. 野有蔓草　零露瀼瀼
Wuc mouyc it nin—ont na tseng lang. 有美一人　婉如清揚
Grès-gròs sang ngos. Lac tzuc krì tzàng. 邂逅相遇　與子偕臧

95

Two Rivers　溱洧

In the rivers *Jin* and *Wruc*, just now the water is high.
Men and girls just now are holding orchids.
A girl says "Shall we take a look?" The man says "I already have!"
"Shall we go and look again?"
Beyond the *Wruc*, the view is wide and pleasant.
Men and girls, this is how they tease each other,
and one gives the other a peony.

Jin lac Wruc, pang hwàns-hwàns ì.　　溱與洧　方渙渙兮
Shuc lac nrac pang prank krèn ì.　　士與女　方秉蘭兮
Nrac wat "Kwàn ghà?" Shuc wat "Kuts tzac!"　　女曰觀乎　士曰既且
"Tsac wank kwàn ghà?"　　且往觀乎
Wruc tu ngwàts, swin hwa tsac ngràwks.　　洧之外　恂訏且樂
Wi shuc lac nrac, i gu sang nghawk,　　維士與女　伊其相謔
dzùngs tu luc dyawk-yawk.　　贈之以勺藥

In the rivers *Jin* and *Wruc*, the water is deep and clear.
Men and girls are there in great crowds.
A girl says "Shall we take a look?" The man says "I already have!"
"Shall we go and look again?"
Beyond the *Wruc*, the view is wide and pleasant.
Men and girls, this is how they tease each other,
and one gives the other a peony.

Jin lac Wruc, rouc gu tseng luc.　　溱與洧　瀏其清矣
Shuc lac nrac un gu leng luc.　　士與女　殷其盈矣
Nrac wat "Kwàn ghà?" Shuc wat "Kuts tzac!"　　女曰觀乎　士曰既且
"Tsac wank kwàn ghà?"　　且往觀乎
Wruc tu ngwàts, swin hwa tsac ngràwks.　　洧之外　恂訏且樂
Wi shuc lac nrac, i gu tzang nghawk,　　維士與女　伊其將謔
dzùngs tu luc dyawk-yawk.　　贈之以勺藥

In *Drengs* there was a spring festival, held at the meeting of rivers running high with snow melted in the mountains, and intended to banish ill omens and promote fertility. (For *Jin* and *Wruc*, see Ode 87.) According to Maspero, the theme of the festival meant that normal social constraints between young men and girls were suspended; the flowers were gifts from the men to the girls whose favours they had enjoyed.

State of *Dzì*

Dzì was a large state which had been granted as a fief to one of *Mac*'s henchmen who helped him conquer *Un*. It was based on modern Linzi, on the north of the Shandong hills; at the beginning of the *Tiw* dynasty it was the only Chinese state with a sea-coast.

96

Cock-Crow 雞鳴

She: The cock has crowed, the court will be filling up!
He: It wasn't the cock crowing, it was just the buzzing of bluebottles.

"*Kè kuts mreng luc: draw kuts leng luc!*"　　　雞既鳴矣　朝既盈矣
"*Puyc kè tzùk mreng; tsàng lung tu hyeng.*"　　匪雞則鳴　蒼蠅之聲

She: It's daybreak in the east, the court will be swept and garnished!
He: It isn't daybreak in the east, it's just the light of the moon rising.

"*Tòng pang mrang luc: draw kuts k'hlang luc!*"　　東方明矣　朝既昌矣
"*Puyc tòng pang tzùk mrang; ngwat k'hlout tu kwàng.*"　匪東方則明　月出之光

She: Crowds of insects are on the wing! *He*: It's sweet dreaming alongside you.
She: The assembly will reconvene soon; we don't want them being malicious
　　　about the pair of us.

"*Droung puy mhùng-mhùng!*" "*Kàm lac tzuc dòng mung.*"　蟲飛薨薨　甘與子同夢
"*Gòts tsac kwuy luc! Ma lhaks lac tzuc tzùng.*"　　　會且歸矣　無庶予子憎

97

Athletic 還

How athletic you are, oh!
We met not far from Mount *Nràw*, oh!
Side by side we galloped after a pair of boar, oh!
Bowing, you told me I was smart, oh!

Tzuc tu swen ì!
Tzòu ngàyc ghà Nràw tu krèn ì!
Bènk kho dzong rank kèn ì!
Up ngàyc wuts ngàyc hwen ì!

子之還兮
遭我乎峱之間兮
並驅從兩肩兮
揖我謂我儇兮

How handsome you are, oh!
We met on the road to mount *Nràw*, oh!
Side by side we rode after a pair of bucks, oh!
Bowing, you told me I was lovable, oh!

Tzuc tu mous ì!
Tzòu ngàyc ghà Nràw tu lòuc ì!
Bènk kho dzong rank mouc ì!
Up ngàyc wuts ngàyc hòuc ì!

子之茂兮
遭我乎峱之道兮
並驅從兩牡兮
揖我謂我好兮

How splendid you are, oh!
We met to the south of mount *Nràw*, oh!
Side by side we rode after a pair of wolves, oh!
Bowing, you told me I was good, oh!

Tzuc tu k'hlang ì!
Tzòu ngàyc ghà Nràw tu lang ì!
Bènk kho dzong rank ràng ì!
Up ngàyc wuts ngàyc tzàng ì!

子之昌兮
遭我乎峱之陽兮
並驅從兩狼兮
揖我謂我臧兮

This piece is thought to be intended satirically. The ruler of *Dzì* was said to be foolishly passionate about hunting and to have encouraged his court to share this passion. By pretending to report one of their conversations, the poem portrays this enthusiasm as empty-headed.

Mount *Nràw* is in the south of Linzi district.

98

Within the Gate-Screen   著

He waited for me within the gate-screen, ah-nu;
his ear-stoppers were white, ah-nu;
on them he wore floral jewels, ah-nu.

Shuc ngàyc a traks, ghà-nu;
thoung-nuc luc sàs, ghà-nu;
dangs tu luc gweng wà, ghà-nu.

俟我於著乎而
充耳以素乎而
尚之以瓊華乎而

He waited for me in the courtyard, ah-nu;
his ear-stoppers were green, ah-nu;
on them he wore *wreng* gems, ah-nu.

Shuc ngàyc a lèng, ghà-nu;　　　　俟我於庭乎而
thoung-nuc luc tsèng, ghà-nu;　　　充耳以青乎而
dangs tu luc gweng wreng, ghà-nu.　尚之以瓊瑩乎而

He waited for me in the hall, ah-nu;
his ear-stoppers were yellow, ah-nu;
on them he wore blossom jewels, ah-nu.

Shuc ngàyc a dàng, ghà-nu;　　　　俟我於堂乎而
thoung-nuc luc gwàng, ghà-nu;　　充耳以黃乎而
dangs tu luc gweng rrang, ghà-nu.　尚之以瓊英乎而

The gateway between a family compound and the street would have a small screening wall built directly inside it, for privacy and to avoid giving evil spirits easy access. The *traks* was the area between the gate and the screening wall.

The repeated *ghà-nu*, which I have Anglicized as "ah-nu", must have expressed some emotion, but was it admiration, or a wistful thought of what might have been?

99

The Sun in the East　東方之日

The sun in the east: that willing young lady
is in my room—she's in my room!
Stepping towards me, she approaches.

Tòng pang tu nit ì: payc tho tac tzuc　　東方之日兮　彼姝者子
dzùc ngàyc lhit ì, dzùc ngàyc lhit ì!　　在我室兮　在我室兮
Ric ngàyc tzit ì.　　　　　　　　　　　　履我即兮

The moon in the east: that willing young lady
is at my door—she's at my door.
Stepping past me, she leaves.

Tòng pang tu ngwat ì: payc tho tac tzuc　東方之月兮　彼姝者子
dzùc ngàyc thàt ì, dzùc ngàyc thàt ì.　　在我闥兮　在我闥兮
Ric ngàyc pat ì.　　　　　　　　　　　　履我發兮

Why does she visit in the daytime? Because she is married?

100

Before Dawn 東方未明

The east is not bright yet. She throws off her clothes,
ripping them off, chucking them down—the call has come from the duke.

Tòng pang muts mrang: tìn tàwc uy-dang,   東方未明　顛倒衣裳
tìn tu, tàwc tu—dzis klòng draws tu.   顛之倒之　自公召之

It is not yet first light in the east. She throws off her clothes,
chucking them down, ripping them off—the command has come from the duke.

Tòng pang muts huy: tìn tàwc uy-dang,   東方未晞　顛倒裳衣
tàwc tu, tìn tu—dzis klòng rin tu.   倒之顛之　自公令之

He breaks through the defences of her lady-garden—the lust-maddened fellow is frantic.
He cannot last all night; but he doesn't come too soon, indeed he takes his time.

Tet rouc ban pàs—gwang pac kwaks-kwaks.   折霤樊圃　狂夫瞿瞿
Pu nùc dun yas; pu souk tzùc màks.   不能辰夜　不夙則莫

The duke's concubines do not keep him waiting.
My translation might sound like the kind of "sexing up Jane Austen" that I criticized in the Introduction; but the poem must have made some kind of sense originally, and if it did not mean something broadly similar to my version, then what could it have meant? Others' translations sound nonsensical to me. Karlgren sees the person summoned as an official called to a meeting: "he turns his clothes upside down; he turns them upside down", and having done that he breaks through the willow fence of his garden in preference to leaving by the gate. It is true that nothing in the Chinese is explicit about the sex of the person described, but I wonder whether *Tiw*-dynasty rulers went in for the 21st-century habit of breakfast meetings, whichever way up the participants wore their clothes. It is reasonable to take *rouc* "willow" in the received text to represent the graphically-related homophone *rouc* "fish-trap", a concept used in a sexual sense elsewhere: that is the kind of graph-substitution which is frequent in these poems, written long before script standardization.

101

Mount Tai 南山

Mount Tai is high and craggy; the dog-fox walks slyly.
The road to *Ràc* is smooth, and the young lady of *Dzì* followed it to her new home.
She's gone, so why are you still yearning for her?

Nùm shàn dzòuy-dzòuy; wung gwà snouy-snouy. 南山崔崔　雄狐夊夊
Ràc lòuc wuc lànk, Dzì tzuc you kwuy. 魯道有蕩　齊子由歸
Kuts wat kwuy tuc, gàt wus gròuy tu? 既曰歸止　曷又懷之

Five pairs of bean-fibre sandals, and a couple of cap-tassels.
The road to *Ràc* is smooth, and the young lady of *Dzì* took it.
She's taken it, so why are you still mooning after her?

Kàt kros ngàc rank, kòn nouy shòng tuc. 葛屨五兩　冠緌雙止
Ràc lòuc wuc lànk, Dzì tzuc long tu. 魯道有蕩　齊子庸之
Kuts wat long tu, gàt wus dzong tu? 既曰庸之　曷又從之

How is hemp sown? You plough your acre longways and crossways.
How does one take a wife? You must make an announcement to her parents.
He made the announcement, so why are you still sending your addresses?

Nyot mràj na tu gày? Gwràng tzong gu mùc. 藝麻如之何　衡從其畝
Tsos tsùy na tu gày? Pit kòuk bac muc. 娶妻如之何　必告父母
Kuts wat kòuk tu, gàt wus kouk tu? 既曰告之　曷又鞠之

How is firewood split? Without an axe it can't be done.
How does one take a wife? Without a go-between it isn't possible.
But he had one, so why are you still so distraught?

Sèk sin na tu gày? Puyc pac pu khùk. 析薪如之何　匪斧不克
Tsos tsùy na tu gày? Puyc mù pu tùk. 娶妻如之何　匪媒不得
Kuts wat tùk tu, gàt wus guk tuc? 既曰得之　曷又極止

A young man of *Dzì* is hankering after a girl who has left to marry a man from *Ràc*. (Mount Tai, the great mountain of eastern China, lies between these states; the sly fox may represent the outsider who has won the girl.) The man from *Ràc* has married her fair and square, presenting her father with the bridegroom's traditional gifts of sandals and cap-tassels—which symbolize marriage, since they come in pairs.

102

Too Large a Field　甫田

Don't try to till too large a field, or you'll just end up with weeds growing tall.
Don't keep brooding on that far-away person, or you'll put your heart through sorrow.

Ma lìns pac lìn, wi youc kaw-kaw. 無田甫田　維莠驕驕
Ma sus want nin, ràw sum tàw-tàw. 無思遠人　勞心忉忉

Don't try to till too large a field, or you'll just end up with weeds shoulder-high.
Don't keep brooding on that far-away person, or you'll put your heart through grief.

Ma lìns pac lìn, wi youc gat-gat.　　無田甫田　維莠揭揭
Ma sus want nin, ràw sum tàt-tàt.　　無思遠人　勞心怛怛

Yes, he was bonny, he was handsome, with his hair tied up in youthful horns.
But in just a little while when you see him again, suddenly he'll be wearing the cap of manhood.

Ont ì, ront ì, tzònk kròk kròns ì;　　婉兮孌兮　總角丱兮
muts kuyc kèns ì, thòut nu brans ì.　　未幾見兮　突而弁兮

As said with Ode 45, children wore their hair tied up in two horns or bunches; when a boy became adult, his hair was cut and he donned a *brans* cap (and a girl put her hair up with pins). The girl is yearning for a boy she knew before he went away, but marriages are arranged by elders: when she sees the young man again, chances are he will have been committed elsewhere. Like an over-ambitous farmer, she is being unrealistic.

103

The Hounds' Bells　盧令

The hounds' bells are jingling; their master is good-looking and kind.
The hounds have double rings; their master is good-looking and attractive.
The hounds have double collars; their master is good-looking and tough.

Rà rin-rin; gu nin mouyc tsac nin.　　盧令令　其人美且仁
Rà drong wèn; gu nin mouyc tsac gwren.　　盧重環　其人美且鬈
Rà drong mà; gu nin mouyc tsac tsà.　　盧重鋂　其人美且偲

Like Ode 97, this brief poem is held to have been a satire on the excessive, empty-headed addiction of the *Dzì* court to hunting (not a very sharp satire, surely?)

The commentators' explanations about the dogs' collars and "rings" are not comprehensible to me.

104

Broken Fish-Traps 敝笱

There are broken fish-traps by the dam—the fish are bream and widower-fish.
The young lady of *Dzì* is going home, surrounded by clouds of attendants.

Bets kòc dzùc rang, gu nga bang kwrùn. 敝笱在梁　其魚魴鰥
Dzì tzuc kwuy tuc, gu dzongs na wun. 齊子歸止　其從如雲

There are broken fish-traps by the dam—the fish are bream and tench.
The young lady of *Dzì* is going home, with an entourage as numerous as raindrops.

Bets kòc dzùc rang, gu nga bang slac. 敝笱在梁　其魚魴鱮
Dzì tzuc kwuy tuc, gu dzongs na wac. 齊子歸止　其從如雨

There are broken fish-traps by the dam—the fish are swimming about freely.
The young lady of *Dzì* is going home, with a whole river of attendants.

Bets kòc dzùc rang, gu nga tsouyc-tsouyc. 敝笱在梁　其魚唯唯
Dzì tzuc kwuy tuc, gu dzongs na lhouyc. 齊子歸止　其從如水

There are two ways of understanding this Ode. It could simply be about a bride travelling (*kwuy*, see p. 26) to her new home. In that case the fish, which in China were a symbol of sex and fertility, express the hope that the woman will have many children. But traditionally the poem was taken to be about a particular young woman, *Mun Kyang*, and to carry a less innocent interpretation. *Mun Kyang* was a daughter of the *Dzì* ruling house, who had an incestuous relationship with her brother. In 708 she married the ruler of *Ràc*, but when her brother became lord of *Dzì* she took her husband to visit him; in *Dzì* the husband was assassinated, allowing incest to resume. Thus the Ode is seen as describing that visit—*kwuy* as returning to her original home. The broken baskets fail to stop the fish swimming around freely, i.e. sex has broken through conventional restraints. (We don't know what fish a *kwrùn* was, but in Chinese the word for "widower" was used for it.)

Ode 101 was also traditionally seen as relating to this episode, in which case it would be about the brother in *Dzì* missing his lover-sister; but in that case I see less reason to reject the more straightforward reading.

105

Bowling Along 載驅

Bowling along, clip-clop, her carriage has bamboo mats and red leather screens.
The *Ràc* road is smooth, and the young lady of *Dzì* sets off in the evening.

Tzùs kho phàk-phàk, lìmp put to kwhàk. 载驱薄薄 簟茀朱鞹
Ràc lòuc wuc lànk; Dzì tzuc pat syak. 鲁道有荡 齐子发夕

Handsome are the four black horses, with their many rein-ends dangling.
The *Ràc* road is smooth, and the young lady of *Dzì* is feeling good.

Slits rè tzìc-tzìc, doy prus nèc-nèc. 四骊济济 垂辔濔濔
Ràc lòuc wuc lànk; Dzì tzuc khùyc dìc. 鲁道有荡 齐子岂弟

The river *Muns* is in spate; *pàng, pàng* sound the feet of the footmen.
The *Ràc* road is smooth, and the young lady of *Dzì* comes and goes as she pleases.

Muns lhouyc lhang-lhang; gràng nin pàng-pàng. 汶水汤汤 行人彭彭
Ràc lòuc wuc lànk; Dzì tzuc ngòu-syang. 鲁道有荡 齐子翱翔

The river *Muns* is brim-full of water; the footmen are running alongside.
The *Ràc* road is smooth, and the young lady of *Dzì* enjoys her excursion.

Muns lhouyc lhòu-lhòu; gràng nin paw-paw. 汶水滔滔 行人儦儦
Ràc lòuc wuc lànk; Dzì tzuc you ngàw. 鲁道有荡 齐子游敖

If the "young lady of *Dzì*" in Ode 104 was *Mun Kyang*, this Ode must be about the same woman. With her husband out of the way, she is nonchalant about trips to take her pleasure with her brother.

The river *Muns* (modern Wen) rises at Laiwu in the Shandong mountains and flows south-westwards. It formed the border between *Ràc* and *Dzì* states.

106

Ay-tzay! 猗嗟

Ay-tzay! How splendid! He is tall and long-legged.
Oh, such a forehead: beautiful eyes and forehead!
Nimble is his footwork; when he shoots, he's skilled.

Ay-tzay, k'hlang ì! Guy nu drang ì. 猗嗟昌兮 颀而长兮
Uk nak lang ì: mouyc mouk lang ì. 抑若扬兮 美目扬兮
Khròus cho-tsang ì; mlaks tzùk tzàng ì. 巧趋跄兮 射则臧兮

Ay-tzay! How illustrious! His beautiful eyes are clear;
his manners are consummate. All day he shoots at the target,
and never misses the bullseye. He's a true nephew of mine!

Ay-tzay, meng ì! Mouyc mouk tseng ì; 猗嗟名兮 美目清兮
ngay kuts deng ì. Toung nit mlak gò, 仪既成兮 终日射侯
pu k'hlout teng ì. Trant ngàyc sheng ì! 不出正兮 展我甥兮

Ay-tzay! How handsome! His clear forehead is gentle.
Dancing, he keeps time; shooting, he pierces the centre of the target.
His flight of four arrows each find their way to it: he could put down a rebellion!

Ay-tzay, ront ì! Tseng lang ont ì. 　猗嗟孌兮　清揚婉兮
Mac tzùk sònt ì; mlaks tzùk kòns ì. 　舞則選兮　射則貫兮
Slits lhic pant ì: luc ngac ròns ì! 　四矢反兮　以禦亂兮

Archery contests were rituals that involved dancing as well as shooting; the archers may have been required to co-ordinate their shots with steps of a dance, making for a greater challenge than shooting from a fixed position.

VOICES FROM EARLY CHINA

State of Ngwuy

Ngwuy was a small state based on Xiaxian in southern Shanxi, annexed by *Tzins* in 660.

107

Delicate Hands 葛屨

All twisty [*is the lablab-vine footwear we use for walking in icy terrain*].
Delicate are the girl's hands: with them she can sew a robe.
She attaches its waistband, she attaches its collar, and a handsome man wears it.

Kiwc-kiwc kàt kros, khàyc luc ric sheng.   糾糾葛屨　可以履霜
Shàm-shàm nrac nhouc, khàyc luc bong dang.   摻摻女手　可以縫裳
Yyaw tu, kuk tu, hòuc nin buk tu.   要之襋之　好人服之

The handsome man is suave, and polite in the way he steps aside to let others pass.
At his girdle he wears an ivory comb-pin.
It is just his priggishness: that's what makes him a butt of sarcasm.

Hòuc nin dè-dè, ont nan tzàyc beks.   好人提提　宛然左避
Bès kus syank thès.   佩其象揥
Wi dec pent sum, dec luc way tsek.   維是褊心　是以為刺

The first eight words are identical to a passage in Ode 203; I suspect they belong there, and occur here only because some scribe has made an error. If this Ode did originally begin *kiwc-kiwc*, and this misled the scribe into continuing with words remembered from another Ode which began that way, then millennia later there is no chance of recovering the correct version. Perhaps *kiwc-kiwc* described some feature of the sewing, or maybe the girl's hair was plaited.

The gentleman is well-dressed, good to look at, and polished in his manners; but to little avail, if he is a prig.

108

In the *Bun* Marshes 汾沮洳

In the marshes of the river *Bun* we were gathering sorrel.
That young man with the baskets:
he was beautiful beyond measure ... beautiful beyond measure
—very different from the Prince's charioteers.

Payc Bun tzas-nas, ngan tsùc gu màks.　　彼汾沮洳　言采其莫
Payc ku tu tzuc:　　彼箕之子
mouyc ma dàks, mouyc ma dàks　　美無度　美無度
do luks ghà klòng ràks.　　殊異乎公輅

By the side of the river *Bun* we were picking mulberries.
That young man with the baskets:
he was beautiful as a flower ... beautiful as a flower
—very different from the Prince's bodyguards.

Payc Bun it pang, ngan tsùc gu sàng.　　彼汾一方　言采其桑
Payc ku tu tzuc:　　彼箕之子
mouyc na rrang, mouyc na rrang　　美如英　美如英
do luks ghà klòng gàng.　　殊異乎公行

By the bend in the river *Bun* we were gathering water-plantains.
That young man with the baskets:
he was beautiful as jade ... beautiful as jade
—very different from the Prince's clansmen.

Payc Bun it khok, ngan tsùc gu slok.　　彼汾一曲　言采其藚
Payc ku tu tzuc:　　彼箕之子
mouyc na ngok, mouyc na ngok　　美如玉　美如玉
do luks ghà klòng dzòk.　　殊異乎公族

The young man is described in surprisingly feminine terms. *Tzuc* can occasionally refer to a young lady, but if that were so here, why would she be compared to the hard men of the Prince's retinue? I follow other translators in taking the subject as male. On the other hand the "baskets" are my idea. The word I spell *ku* could alternatively be a synonym for *payc*, "that", and others have taken it that way here. But this gives a rather flat poem; and there must have been someone in charge of handing out baskets and perhaps keeping track of how many basketfuls each worker gathered.

The *Bun* is a tributary of the Yellow River, which flows southwards through Shanxi province. The translation "sorrel" for *màks* is not certain, but it is plausible: that plant has many culinary uses, for instance in soup, for salads, and as a flavouring agent. *Slok*, "water-plantain", is probably *Alisma orientale*, the roots of which have various uses in Chinese medicine, for instance in cases of urine retention and dropsy.

109

Peach Trees in my Garden 園有桃

In my garden I have peach trees; their fruit is my food.
Oh, the grief in my heart! I sing, sometimes I play music,
and people who don't know me say I'm a haughty official
—indeed, they're justified. You ask "What is all this?"
Oh, the grief in my heart: who knows it,
who knows it? In truth, no-one has any idea.

Wan wuc làw; gu mlit tu gràw.	園有桃　其實之殽
Sum tu ou luc! Ngàyc kày tsac yaw.	心之憂矣　我歌且謠
Pu tre ngàyc tac, wuts ngàyc shuc layc kaw	不我知者　謂我士也驕
—payc nin dec tzù. Tzuc wat "gày kus?"	彼人是哉　子曰何其
Sum tu ou luc! Ku douy tre tu,	心之憂矣　其誰知之
ku douy tre tu? Kàts yak mut su.	其誰知之　蓋亦勿思

In my garden I have jujube trees; their fruit is my nourishment.
Oh, the grief in my heart! I take time off for country walks,
and people who don't know me say I'm being unprofessional
—indeed, they're justified. You ask "What is all this?"
Oh, the grief in my heart: who knows it,
who knows it? In truth, no-one has any idea.

Wan wuc kuk; gu mlit tu mluk.	園有棘　其實之食
Sum tu ou luc! Rìw luc gràng kwùk.	心之憂矣　聊以行國
Pu tre ngàyc tac, wuts ngàyc shuc layc mank guk	不我知者　謂我士也罔極
—payc nin dec tzù. Tzuc wat "gày kus?"	彼人是哉　子曰何其
Sum tu ou luc! Ku douy tre tu,	心之憂矣　其誰知之
ku douy tre tu? Kàts yak mut su.	其誰知之　蓋亦勿思

Some private grief is leading the poet to mishandle or neglect his official duties. He tells himself that if others understood what turmoil he is going through, they would make allowances. To an English reader, peaches are luxuries which grow only in hothouses, but the commentators suggest that the poet is putting forward a fruit diet as evidence of the austere life he is leading, despite appearing arrogant to outsiders.

In the second line, *kày* and *yaw* both mean "sing", but we are told that the former is singing with an instrumental accompaniment, the latter without.

110

On the Wooded Hill 陟岵

He walks up that wooded hill, and gazes towards where his father is.
And his father is saying "Alas, my son
is on manoeuvres. From morning to night he's getting no rest.
Oh, do let him look after himself, and let him come back home again without hold-ups."

Truk payc gàc ì, tam mang bac ì.   陟彼岵兮　瞻望父兮
Bac wat "Tzay, lac tzuc   父曰嗟予子
gràng wek. Souk yas ma luc.   行役　夙夜無已
Dangs dins tan tzù; you rù ma tuc."   尚慎旃哉　猶來無止

He walks up that bare hill, and gazes towards where his mother is.
And his mother is saying "Alas, my youngest child
is on manoeuvres. Neither in the dawn nor at night am I getting a wink of sleep.
Oh, do let him look after himself, and let him not go missing but come home again."

Truk payc khuc ì, tam mang muc ì.   陟彼屺兮　瞻望母兮
Muc wat "Tzay, lac kwits   母曰嗟予季
gràng wek. Souk yas ma mits.   行役　夙夜無寐
Dangs dins tan tzù; you rù ma khits."   尚慎旃哉　猶來無棄

He walks up that ridge, and gazes towards where his brother is.
And his brother is saying "Alas, my younger brother
is on manoeuvres. From morning to night he has to fall in with his comrades.
Oh, do let him look after himself, and let him come back home and not get killed."

Truk payc kàng ì, tam payc hwrang ì.   陟彼岡兮　瞻望兄兮
Hwrang wat "Tzay, lac dìc   兄曰嗟予弟
gràng wek. Souk yas pit krìc.   行役　夙夜必偕
Dangs dins tan tzù; you rù ma sic."   尚慎旃哉　猶來無死

This poem has an unusual metre, in which the line-division suggested by the rhymes conflicts with the breaks of sense. I have set the lines out as implied by the rhymes.

111

Within the Ten-Acre 十畝之間

Within the ten-acre, the mulberry-leaf pickers are moving lazily.
The two of us are safe to turn aside together.

Gip mùc tu krèn ì, sàng tac grèn-grèn ì.   十畝之間兮　桑者閑閑兮
gràng lac tzuc wèn ì.   行與子還兮

Beyond the ten-acre, the mulberry-leaf pickers are slow and spread out.
The two of us are safe to slip off together.

Gip mùc tu ngwàts ì, sàng tac lats-lats ì.   十畝之外兮　桑者泄泄兮
Gràng lac tzuc dats ì.   行與子逝兮

Silkworms live on mulberry leaves, which must be gathered in the heat of summer (other crops wait till summer is turning into autumn). The gatherers are relaxed; no one will notice two people slipping away.

The Chinese measure land by the *mùc*, sometimes called a "Chinese acre". In fact it is smaller: ten *mùc* is about one and a half English acres, but the translation might sound excessively pedantic if it took account of this.

112

Felling Trees 伐檀

Khùmp, khùmp sounds his axe on the tree-trunks, and he piles them on the bank of the River.
Clear are the rolling River waters.
You do not sow, neither do you reap;
so how is it that the harvest of three hundred farms comes to you?
You never go hunting or trapping vermin;
so how is it that I see badger corpses hanging in your yards?
Now that princely man, he earns his dinners.

Khùmp-khùmp bat dàn ì, tets tu Gày tu kàn ì.   坎坎伐檀兮　寘之河之干兮
Gày lhouyc tseng tsac ran ay.   河水清且漣猗
Pu kràs, pu shuk: 不稼不穡
gà tsoc wày sùm pràk dran ì?   胡取禾三百廛兮
Pu hyouc, pu rap: 不狩不獵
gà tam nec lèng wuc gwèn hwàn ì?   胡瞻爾庭有縣貆兮
Payc kwun-tzuc ì, pu sàs tsàn ì.   彼君子兮　不素餐兮

Khùmp, khùmp sounds his axe as he carves wheel-spokes, which he piles by the side of the River.
Clear are the straight-flowing River waters.
You do not sow, neither do you reap;
so how is it that thirty million ears of grain come to you?
You never go hunting or trapping vermin;
so how is it that I see sides of venison hanging in your yards?
Now that princely man, he earns his food.

Khùmp-khùmp bat puk ì, tets tu Gày tu juk ì.	坎坎伐輻兮　寘之河之側兮
Gày lhouyc tseng tsac druk ay.	河水清且直猗
Pu kràs, pu shuk:	不稼不穡
gà tsoc wày sùm pràk uk ì?	胡取禾三百億兮
Pu hyouc, pu rap:	不狩不獵
gà tam nec lèng wuc gwèn dùk ì?	胡瞻爾庭有縣特兮
Payc kwun-tzuc ì, pu sàs mluk ì.	彼君子兮　不素食兮

Khùmp, khùmp sounds his axe as he makes wheels, and he piles them on the lip of the Yellow River bank.
Clear are the rippling River waters.
You do not sow, neither do you reap;
so how is it that you get three hundred granaries filled?
You never go hunting or trapping vermin;
so how is it that I see quail hanging in your yards?
Now that princely man, he earns his meals.

Khùmp-khùmp bat roun ì, tets tu Gày tu mdoun ì.	坎坎伐輪兮　寘之河之漘兮
Gày lhouyc tseng tsac roun ay.	河水清且淪猗
Pu kràs, pu shuk:	不稼不穡
gà tsoc wày sùm pràk khoun ì?	胡取禾三百囷兮
Pu hyouc, pu rap:	不狩不獵
gà tam nec lèng wuc gwèn doun ì?	胡瞻爾庭有縣鶉兮
Payc kwun-tzuc ì, pu sàs sòun ì.	彼君子兮　不素飧兮

The labour of an honest working man is contrasted with the self-indulgence of a lazy official who lives off the toil of many workers. In the last line of each verse, the *kwun-tzuc* is not, literally, a prince's son but refers to the labourer as a "princely man", one of nature's gentlemen. It is very uncertain what the *dùk* hanging in the courtyard in verse 2 are; the commentary tradition claims that the word can mean "a three-year-old animal", so presumably meat carcasses rather than vermin like the badgers, and if hunted then not cattle or sheep—I have taken them to be sides of venison. And there is a large question about the word *dàn* in the first stich. *Dàn* means "sandalwood", but as said on p. 32, this is not the kind of stuff used for everyday carpentry. I can only think that *dàn* was a copyist's error for some other tree.

113

Sir Rat 碩鼠

Sir rat, sir rat, don't eat our millet!
Three years we've been serving you, and you've never granted us any consideration.
It has come to the point that we're going to leave you, and move away to the happy land.
Happy land, oh, happy land: there will be a place for us there.

Dak nhac, dak nhac, ma mluk ngàyc nhac! 　　碩鼠碩鼠　無食我黍
Sùm swats kòns nac, màk ngàyc khènk kàs. 　三歲貫汝　莫我肯顧
Dats tzang khas nac, lhek payc ngràwks thàc. 　逝將去汝　適彼樂土
Ngràwks thàc, ngràwks thàc: wan tùk ngàyc shac! 　樂土樂土　爰得我所

Sir rat, sir rat, don't eat our wheat!
Three years we've been serving you, and you've never been willing to treat us decently.
It has come to the point that we're going to leave you, and move away to the happy country.
Happy country, oh, happy country: there we shall be right at last.

Dak nhac, dak nhac, ma mluk ngàyc mrùk! 　　碩鼠碩鼠　無食我麥
Sùm swats kòns nac, màk ngàyc khènk tùk. 　三歲貫汝　莫我肯德
Dats tzang khas nac, lhek payc ngràwks kwùk. 　逝將去汝　適彼樂國
Ngràwks kwùk, ngràwks kwùk: wan tùk ngàyc druk! 　樂國樂國　爰得我直

Sir rat, sir rat, don't eat our sprouting grain!
Three years we've been serving you, and you've never been willing to reward our toil.
It has come to the point that we're going to leave you, and move away to the happy demesne.
Happy demesne, oh, happy demesne: who goes there and sings sad songs for long?

Dak nhac, dak nhac, ma mluk ngàyc maw! 　　碩鼠碩鼠　無食我苗
Sùm swats kòns nac, màk ngàyc khènk ràws. 　三歲貫汝　莫我肯勞
Dats tzang khas nac, lhek payc ngràwks kràw. 　逝將去汝　適彼樂郊
Ngràwks kràw, ngràwks kràw: douy tu wrangs ghàw? 　樂郊樂郊　誰之永號

The "rat" is a rapacious official who uses his position to squeeze people for money rather than further their welfare. There is some evidence that *dak nhac* was a particular species of rodent, though, if so, it is not known what species that was; since *dak* is a positive word, I take it as a polite form of address to a powerful man.

VOICES FROM EARLY CHINA

State of *Glang*

"*Glang*" was an antiquarian name for the state normally called *Tzins*, which covered much of the territory east of the Yellow River, in modern terms southern Shanxi, and was probably the most powerful of all *Tiw* vassal states (until the eventual rise of *Dzin*, which was destined to found the Chinese Empire in the third century). The name *Glang* alluded to a legendary ruler who was believed to have used that title when he ruled the area a thousand years earlier.

114

The Cricket　蟋蟀

There is a cricket in the hall: it is the evening of the year.
If we don't enjoy ourselves now, the days and months will have passed, never to return.
But we mustn't relax too much—just think of our position.
In our love of pleasure we mustn't go to excess. A good official is circumspect.

Shit-shout dzùc dàng: swats lout gu màks.　蟋蟀在堂　歲聿其莫
Kum ngàyc pu ngràwks, nit ngwat gu dras.　今我不樂　日月其除
Ma luc thàts khàng—tuk su gu kas.　無已太康　職思其居
Hòus ngràwks ma mhàng. Rang shuc kwaks-kwaks.　好樂無荒　良士瞿瞿

There is a cricket in the hall: the year is on its way out.
If we don't enjoy ourselves now, the days and months will disappear.
But we mustn't relax too much—just think of how we look to others.
In our love of pleasure we mustn't go to excess. A good official is guarded in his behaviour.

Shit-shout dzùc dàng: swats lout gu dats.　蟋蟀在堂　歲聿其逝
Kum ngàyc pu ngràwks, nit ngwat gu mràts.　今我不樂　日月其邁
Ma luc thàts khàng—tuk su gu ngwàts.　無已太康　職思其外
Hòus ngràwks ma mhàng. Rang shuc gots-gots.　好樂無荒　良士蹶蹶

There is a cricket in the hall: the troop transports are at rest.
If we don't enjoy ourselves now, the days and months will be lost for ever.
But we mustn't relax too much—just think of our responsibilities.
In our love of pleasure we mustn't go to excess. A good official is sedate.

Shit-shout dzùc dàng: wek ka gu hou.　蟋蟀在堂　役車其休
Kum ngàyc pu ngràwks, nit ngwat gu lhòu.　今我不樂　日月其慆
Ma luc thàts khàng—tuk su gu ou.　無已太康　職思其憂
Hòus ngràwks ma mhàng. Rang shuc hou-hou.　好樂無荒　良士休休

The cold weather has arrived, driving crickets indoors, and the season of military activities is over for the year. In any culture, this is a time for fun and relaxation. But, as a Chinese would have recognized at any time for the past three thousand years, a gentleman has a social duty not to relax too much.

115

Thorn-Elms 山有樞

There are thorn-elms on the high ground, and David elms in the wetland.
You have a full wardrobe, yet you don't show off your clothes.
You have carriage-horses, yet you don't go for drives.
You will wither away and die, leaving others to enjoy these things.

Shàn wuc ò, slup wuc lo.   山有樞　隰有榆
Tzuc wuc uy dang, put lats, put ro.   子有衣裳　弗曳弗婁
Tzuc wuc ka mràc, put dray, put kho.   子有車馬　弗馳弗驅
Out gu sic luc, lhày nin dec lo.   宛其死矣　他人是愉

There are *khòuc* trees on the high ground, and *nrouc* trees in the wetland.
You have courtyards and rooms, yet you don't keep them swept and sprinkled against dust.
You have bells and drums, yet you don't play them.
You will wither away and die, leaving these things in others' hands.

Shàn wuc khòuc, slup wuc nrouc.   山有栲　隰有杻
Tzuc wuc lèngs nòuts, put shìc, put sòus.   子有廷內　弗洒弗埽
Tzuc wuc tong kàc, put kàc, put khòuc.   子有鐘鼓　弗鼓弗考
Out gu sic luc, lhày nin dec pòuc.   宛其死矣　他人是保

There are lacquer trees on the high ground, and chestnut trees in the wetland.
You have wine and food, so why don't you have the zither played daily?
And that way you could have some fun and pleasure, that way your days would last far into the night.
You will wither away and die, and other people will take over your house.

Shàn wuc tsit, slup wuc rit.   山有漆　隰有栗
Tzuc wuc tziwc mluk, gày pu nit kàc sprit?   子有酒食　何不日鼓瑟
Tsac luc huc ngràwks, tsac luc wrank nit.   且以喜樂　且以永日
Out gu sic luc, lhày nin nup lhit.   宛其死矣　他人入室

Khòuc may be *Ailanthus fordii* (for which I know no English name), and *nrouc* is some variety of cherry or similar species.
    A noble family's meals would be accompanied by music.

116

The Wild River 揚之水

Washed by the wild river waters, the white rocks gleam in the sun.
In my white dress with its collar embroidered in red, I shall come to you at *Àwk*.
Once I have met my lord, how can I fail to be joyful?

Lhang tu lhouyc, bràk dak tzàwk-tzàwk.   揚之水　白石鑿鑿
Sàs uy to pàwk, dzong tzuc wa Àwk.   素衣朱襮　從子于沃
Kuts kèns kwun-tzuc, wun gày pu ngràwks?   既見君子　云何不樂

Washed by the wild river waters, the white rocks are clean and bright.
In my white dress with red embroidery, I shall come to you at *Gòuk*.
Once I have met my lord, how could I still feel sad?

Lhang tu lhouyc, bràk dak kòuc-kòuc.   揚之水　白石皓皓
Sàs uy to siwks, dzong tzuc wa Gòuk.   素衣朱繡　從子于鵠
Kuts kèns kwun-tzuc, wun gày ku ou?   既見君子　云何其憂

The white rocks are worn into fretted shapes by the wild river waters.
I have received your instructions—I wouldn't think of telling anyone about them.

Lhang tu lhouyc, bràk dak rins-rins.   揚之水　白石磷磷
Ngàyc mun wuc mreng; pu kàmp luc kòuk nin.   我聞有命　不敢以告人

Like some other translators, I read this as the poem of a girl agreeing a secret assignation with her lover—"my lord" in the sense "my man". However, the traditional commentaries give it a political interpretation which is better motivated than in the case of some Odes. *Àwk* and *Gòuk* are believed to be alternative names for a then-significant city in the east of what is now Wenxi county, south-west Shanxi, and the claim is that the poem relates to a known occasion when the ruler of that city conspired to rebel against his feudal overlord, the ruler of *Tzins*. The red-embroidered white garment sounds similar to a robe which only a state ruler was entitled to wear; the conspirators could be promising to bring one to their leader and thus raise him to this status. I prefer the more straightforward reading, but this may be my mistake.

117

The Peppers 椒聊

The fruit of the pepper plants have swollen up beyond all bounds, any one of them would fill a quart pot.
That gentleman there is a very great man—he is without peer.
Oh, the pepper plants, how they have spread!

Tziw-rìw tu mlit, ban yant leng lhung.
Payc kus tu tzuc, dak dàts ma bùng.
Tziw-rìw tza, want lìw tza!

椒聊之實　蕃衍盈升
彼其之子　碩大無朋
椒聊且　遠條且

The fruit of the pepper plants have swollen up beyond all bounds, any one of them would fill your two cupped hands.
That gentleman there is a very great man, and solidly established.
Oh, the pepper plants, how they have spread!

Tziw-rìw tu mlit, ban yant leng kouk.
Payc kus tu tzuc, dak dàts tsac tòuk.
Tziw-rìw tza, want lìw tza!

椒聊之實　蕃衍盈匊
彼其之子　碩大且篤
椒聊且　遠條且

118

Tied Together　綢繆

The bundle of sticks are tied together; the Three Stars are in the sky.
What a night tonight will be, meeting these lovely women!
Such girls, such girls: what women are as lovely as these!

Driw-miws lhok sin; Sùm Sèng dzùc thìn.
Kum syak gày syak, kèns tsec rang nin!
Tzuc ì, tzuc ì: na tsec rang nin gày!

綢繆束薪　三星在天
今夕何夕　見此良人
子兮子兮　如此良人何

The bundle of hay is tied together; the Three Stars are at the corner.
What a night tonight will be, embracing this carefree joy!
Such girls, such girls: what joy is as carefree as this!

Driw-miws lhok cho; Sùm Sèng dzùc ngo.
Kum syak gày syak, kèns tsec grès-gròs!
Tzuc ì, tzuc ì: na tsec grès-gròs gày!

綢繆束芻　三星在隅
今夕何夕　見此邂逅
子兮子兮　如此邂逅何

The bundle of brushwood is tied together; the Three Stars are at the door.
What a night tonight will be, getting together with this beauty-threesome!
Such girls, such girls: what three are as beautiful as this!

Driw-miws lhok chac; Sùm Sèng dzùc gàc.
Kum syak gày syak, kèns tsec tsàns tac!
Tzuc ì, tzuc ì: na tsec tsàns tac gày!

綢繆束楚　三星在戶
今夕何夕　見此粲者
子兮子兮　如此粲者何

The poet has married a principal wife and two "younger sisters", who are now tied to him in marriage as a bundle of sticks is tied with cord. He compares them with the constellation of Three Stars, on which see Ode 21.

119

Solitary 杕杜

There's a lone pear-tree: how thick its leaves are!
Solitary and forlorn I go my road.
Why do I have no-one else with me?—but they wouldn't be like sons of my own father.
Ah me, you travellers: why don't you share my company?
People who have no brothers yourselves, why don't you support me?

Wuc dèts tu dac: gu lap shac-shac! 有杕之杜 其葉湑湑
Dòk gràng kwac-kwac. 獨行踽踽
Khuyc ma lhày nin?—pu na ngàyc dòng bac. 豈無他人 不如我同父
Tzay, gràng tu nin, gà pu bis an? 嗟行之人 胡不比焉
Nin ma hwrang dìc, gà pu tsis an? 人無兄弟 胡不佽焉

There's a lone pear-tree: how profuse its leaves are!
I go my solitary road, scared and helpless.
Why do I have no-one else with me?—but they wouldn't be like members of my own clan.
Ah me, you travellers: why don't you share my company?
People who have no brothers yourselves, why don't you support me?

Wuc dèts tu dac: gu lap tzèng-tzèng! 有杕之杜 其葉菁菁
Dòk gràng gweng-gweng. 獨行睘睘
Khuyc ma lhày nin?—pu na ngàyc dòng sengs. 豈無他人 不如我同姓
Tzay, gràng tu nin, gà pu bis an? 嗟行之人 胡不比焉
Nin ma hwrang dìc, gà pu tsis an? 人無兄弟 胡不佽焉

120

Lambskin Coat with Leopard Sleeves 羔裘

In his lambskin coat with leopard sleeves, this man of mine is so big-headed.
Why don't I go out with someone else? Because it's only you I have history with.

Kàw gwu, pràwks kha; dzis ngàyc nin kas-kas. 羔裘豹袪 自我人居居
Khuyc ma lhày nin? Wi tzuc tu kàs. 豈無他人 維子之故

In his lambskin coat with leopard sleeves, this man of mine is so extravagant.
Why don't I go out with someone else? Because it's only you I love.

Kàw gwu, pràwks syous; dzis ngàyc nin kous-kous. 羔裘豹褎 自我人究究
Khuyc ma lhày nin? Wi tzuc tu hòus. 豈無他人 維子之好

121

The Bustards' Wings 鴇羽

The bustards' wings sound, *siwk-siwk*, as they settle in a dense stand of cork-oaks.
There's no skimping the king's service; but it means I can't sow the broomcorn millet and the foxtail millet.
How will my parents manage?
Oh, you far-away Blue Sky, when will all this be resolved?

Siwk-siwk pòuc wac, dzup wa pròu hwac.	肅肅鴇羽　集于苞栩
Wang shuc mayc kàc; pu nùc ngets tzuk nhac.	王事靡盬　不能蓺稷黍
Bac muc gày gàc?	父母何怙
You-you Tsàng Thìn, gàt kus wuc shac?	悠悠蒼天　曷其有所

The bustards' pinions sound, *siwk-siwk*, as they settle in a dense stand of thorn trees.
There's no skimping the king's service; but it means I can't sow the foxtail millet and the broomcorn millet.
What are my parents going to eat?
Oh, you far-away Blue Sky, when will there be an end to all this?

Siwk-siwk pòuc yuk, dzup wa pròu kuk.	肅肅鴇翼　集于苞棘
Wang shuc mayc kàc; pu nùc ngets nhac tzuk.	王事靡盬　不能蓺黍稷
Bac muc gày mluk?	父母何食
You-you Tsàng Thìn, gàt kus wuc guk?	悠悠蒼天　曷其有極

The skeins of bustards sound, *siwk-siwk*, as they settle in a dense stand of mulberries.
There's no skimping the king's service; but it means I can't sow the rice or sorghum.
What will my parents live on?
Oh, you far-away Blue Sky, when will things get back to normal?

Siwk-siwk pòuc gàng, dzup wa pròu sàng.	肅肅鴇行　集于苞桑
Wang shuc mayc kàc; pu nùc ngets lòuc rang.	王事靡盬　不能蓺稻粱
Bac muc gày dyang?	父母何嘗
You-you Tsàng Thìn, gàt kus wuc dyang?	悠悠蒼天　曷其有常

Believed to date from the late eighth century, when there was a decades-long armed power struggle in *Tzins*.
 The bustard is a kind of goose. Some varieties, including the one found in China, have mainly black and white plumage, hence the same word *pòuc* is also used for a piebald horse. The tree name I translate for simplicity as "cork-oak" may have been jolcham oak, *Quercus serrata*, or Chinese cork-oak, *Q. variabilis*.

122

How Could I Say I Had Nothing to Wear 無衣

How could I say I had nothing to wear? I had seven robes,
but not as good as the one you've given me: it's comfortable and smart.

Khuyc wat ma uy? Tsit ì,
pu na tzuc tu uy: àn tsac kit ì.

豈曰無衣　七兮
不如子之衣　安且吉兮

How could I say I had nothing to wear? I had six robes,
but not as good as the one you've given me: it's comfortable and warm.

Khuyc wat ma uy? Rouk ì,
pu na tzuc tu uy: àn tsac ouk ì.

豈曰無衣　六兮
不如子之衣　安且燠兮

I follow Karlgren in guessing that this poem is effectively a thank-you note for the gift of a robe —but "you have given me" is my phrase, the Chinese just says "your robe". And I had to guess what the poet meant by calling the garment *kit*, literally "lucky": apart from comfort and warmth the obvious remaining criterion for clothes is to look smart.

123

The Pear Tree by the Road 有杕之杜

There is a lone pear tree growing to the left of the road.
That prince of a boy: we've got to where he's keen to come and see me.
In my heart I love him—what am I going to give him to eat and drink?

Wuc dèts tu dàc, sheng wa lòuc tzàyc.
Payc kwun-tzuc ì, dats khènk lhek ngàyc.
Troung sum hòus tu—gàt ums sluks tu?

有杕之杜　生于道左
彼君子兮　逝肯適我
中心好之　曷飲食之

There is a lone pear tree growing at a bend in the road.
That prince of a boy: we've got to where he's keen to come and take me out.
In my heart I love him—what am I going to give him to eat and drink?

Wuc dèts tu dàc, sheng wa lòuc tiw.
Payc kwun-tzuc ì, dats khènk rù you.
Troung sum hòus tu—gàt ums sluks tu?

有杕之杜　生于道周
彼君子兮　逝肯來遊
中心好之　曷飲食之

Chinese pears are a sweet delicacy, so the tree could be a metaphor for a girl without a boyfriend.

124

Overgrown Bushes 葛生

The thorn bushes are overgrown with lablab vines, and snake-gourd plants have covered the rough ground.
You aren't here any more, my lovely; who can I be with, living alone as I do?

Kàt sheng mòng chac; ramp mans wa lac.   葛生蒙楚　薟蔓于野
Lac mouyc mang tsec: douy lac, dòk k'hlac?   予美亡此　誰與獨處

The jujube trees are overgrown with lablab vines, and snake-gourd plants have invaded the graveyard.
You aren't here any more, my lovely; who can I be with, in my times of solitary leisure?

Kàt sheng mòng kuk; ramp mans wa wuk.   葛生蒙棘　薟蔓于域
Lac mouyc mang tsec: douy lac, dòk suk?   予美亡此　誰與獨息

The horn-inlaid pillow is splendid, and the brocaded quilt is bright.
But you aren't here any more, my lovely; who can I be with, waking as I do to lonely dawns?

Kròk kimp tsàns ì, kump khum ràns ì.   角枕粲兮　錦衾爛兮
Lac mouyc mang tsec: douy lac, dòk tans?   予美亡此　誰與獨旦

Summer days, winter nights;
a hundred years will have passed, before I join him in his resting-place.
Winter nights, summer days;
a hundred years will have passed, before I join him in his mansion.

Gràs tu nit; tòung tu yas.   夏之日　冬之夜
Pràk swats tu ghòc, kwuy wa gu kas.   百歲之後　歸於其居
Tòung tu yas; gràs tu nit.   冬之夜　夏之日
Pràk swats tu ghòc, kwuy wa gu lhit.   百歲之後　歸於其室

A widow contemplates her lot. To an English ear, "summer days and winter nights" sounds like a contrast between pleasant and unpleasant times, but the heat of a Chinese summer is itself oppressive (the "good" times are spring and autumn). Some commentators claim that a hundred years stood conventionally for a lifetime, so verse 4 is a flat statement that the poet will be with her husband when she dies. To my mind, rather, the poet is saying that the wretched time she must endure, before joining her husband in the grave, will *feel* like a hundred years.

  Chinese slept on wooden pillows. The woman's bedchamber is fine, however every morning when she wakes in it she faces anew the misery of loneliness. The vines and snake-gourd plants are perhaps an image of physical desolation and neglect, reflecting the desolation in the poetess's heart.

125

Gathering Cocklebur 采苓

We gather cocklebur, we gather cocklebur, on top of Mount *Lhouc-lang*.
People's false stories—you really mustn't believe them.
Ignore them, ignore them! You really mustn't approve them.
People's false stories—what good will they do you?

Tsàc rìn, tsàc rìn, Lhouc-lang tu tìn.　　　采苓采苓　首陽之巔
Nin tu ngways ngan—kòc yak ma sins.　　　人之偽言　苟亦無信
Lhac tan, lhac tan! Kòc yak ma nan.　　　舍旃舍旃　苟亦無然
Nin tu ngways ngan, gà tàk an?　　　人之偽言　胡得焉

We gather sowthistles, we gather sowthistles, below Mount *Lhouc-lang*.
People's false stories—you really mustn't get involved with them.
Ignore them, ignore them! You really mustn't approve them.
People's false stories—what good will they do you?

Tsàc khàc, tsàc khàc, Lhouc-lang tu gràc.　　　采苦采苦　首陽之下
Nin tu ngways ngan—kòc yak ma lac.　　　人之偽言　苟亦無與
Lhac tan, lhac tan! Kòc yak ma nan.　　　舍旃舍旃　苟亦無然
Nin tu ngways ngan, gà tàk an?　　　人之偽言　胡得焉

We pull up turnips, we pull up turnips, to the east of Mount *Lhouc-lang*.
People's false stories—you really mustn't go along with them.
Ignore them, ignore them! You really mustn't approve them.
People's false stories—what good will they do you?

Tsàc phong, tsàc phong, Lhouc-lang tu tòng.　　　采葑采葑　首陽之東
Nin tu ngways ngan—kòc yak ma dzong.　　　人之偽言　苟亦無從
Lhac tan, lhac tan! Kòc yak ma nan.　　　舍旃舍旃　苟亦無然
Nin tu ngways ngan, gà tàk an?　　　人之偽言　胡得焉

A condemnation of the slanders and backbiting endemic in small closed communities.

There are several mountains in China called *Lhouc-lang* (modern Shouyang). This is thought to be the one on the border of Yongji county, south-west Shanxi. There are uncertainties about the plants being gathered, but likely equations are: *rìn* cocklebur (*Xanthium strumarium*), a plant used in Chinese medicine, but which contains toxins and has been responsible for many deaths; *khàc* sowthistle (*Sonchus oleraceus* or similar), an edible vegetable; *phong* turnip.

VOICES FROM EARLY CHINA

State of *Dzin*

Dzin was the state, seen as semi-barbarian by the Home States, which was destined to conquer all China in the third century. Its earliest known base was in south-east Gansu, but its seat moved progressively eastwards into the Chinese heartland.

126

Rumbling Carriages 車鄰

Carriages are rumbling, there are horses with silver blazes.
I haven't seen my lord yet; I give orders to the attendant eunuch.

Wuc ka rin-rin, wuc mràc bràk tìn.   有車鄰鄰　有馬白顛
Muts kèns kwun-tzuc; slus nin tu rin.   未見君子　寺人之令

On the slopes there are lacquer-trees, by the river there are chestnuts.
When I've seen my lord, we shall sit together playing the zither.
If we don't enjoy ourselves today, in the future old age awaits.

Brànt wuc tsit, slup wuc rit.   阪有漆　隰有栗
Kuts kèns kwun-tzuc, bènk dzòyc kàc sprit.   既見君子　並坐鼓瑟
Kum tac pu ngràwks, dats tac gu dìt.   今者不樂　逝者其耋

On the slopes there are mulberry trees, by the river there are poplars.
When I've seen my lord, we shall sit together playing the reed-organ.
If we don't enjoy ourselves today, in the future we shall be gone.

Brànt wuc sàng, slup wuc lang.   阪有桑　隰有楊
Kuts kèns kwun-tzuc, bènk dzòyc kàc gwàng.   既見君子　並坐鼓簧
Kum tac pu ngràwks, dats tac gu mang.   今者不樂　逝者其亡

On one interpretation, while she cools her heels in the great man's waiting room the poetess is trying to convince herself that he will be as interested in seeing her again as she is in seeing him.

127

Hunting Deer 駟驖

The teams of four black horses are robust. Six reins in hand,
the duke's favourites follow him to the hunting field.

Slits lèt khònk bouc. Rouk prus dzùc nhouc, 駟驖孔阜　六轡在手
klòng tu mouys tzuc dzong klòng wa hyouc. 公之媚子　從公于狩

The gamekeepers lead them to that herd of does and buck—they're well-grown
    deer.
The duke shouts "Left wheel!"—when he releases an arrow, it finds its mark.

Phonk dit dun mouc; dun mouc khònk dak. 奉寎麌牡　麌牡孔碩
Klòng wat "Tzàyc tuc!"—lhac bàt tzùk wàk. 公曰左止　舍拔則獲

They are hunting in the North Park. The four-horse teams are well trained,
the carriages are light, and there are bells at the horses' bits. They let slip the
    hounds.

You wa Pùk Wan. Slits mràc kuts gràn, 遊于北園　四馬既閑
you ka, ròn paw. Tzù ram hat-haw. 輶車鑾鑣　哉獫歇驕

Ram, and *hat-haw*, were types of dog. "Six reins in hand" will be explained with the next Ode.

128

The Short War-Chariot 小戎

His short war-chariot has five ornamental straps to its carriage-pole;
it has slip-rings, side-shields, covered traces and silver-washed attachments,
a tigerskin rug, and protruding wheel-hubs. Harnessed up are our dappled grey
    and *tos* horses.
I am thinking about my man. He must look so suave, like jade,
among those shacks. The thought of him flutters every corner of my heart.

Syawc noung dzant hyou, ngàc mòk rang trou. 小戎俴收　五楘梁輈
You wèn hap kho, um lins àwk slok, 游環脅驅　陰靷鋈續
mun in, thrangs kòk. Kràys ngàyc gu tos. 文茵暢轂　駕我騏馵
Ngan nìms kwun-tzuc; òun kus na ngok 言念君子　溫其如玉
dzùc kus prànt òk. Ròns ngàyc sum khok. 在其板屋　亂我心曲

The four stallions are robust—six reins in hand.
The dappled and black-maned greys, those are the inside horses, and the black-muzzled bay and the black horse are the outers.
He has a full set of dragon shields, and there are silver-washed buckles to the fixed reins.
I am thinking about my man. He must look so suave, among those rural dorps.
How long will he be? Oh, how I miss him!

Slits mouc khònk bouc, rouk prus dzùc nhouc. 　四牡孔阜　六轡在手
Gu rou dec troung, kròy rè dec tsùm. 　騏駵是中　騧驪是驂
Rong mlount tu gùp, àwk luc kwèt nùp. 　龍盾之合　鋈以觼軜
Ngan nìms kwun-tzuc; òun kus dzùc up. 　言念君子　溫其在邑
Pang gày way gu? Gà-nan ngàyc nìms tu! 　方何為期　胡然我念之

The four mailed horses make a fine team. His three-sided lance has a silver-washed butt-cap;
the cover of his shield is richly ornamented, and he has a tigerskin bowcase and an engraved breastplate.
A pair of bows are crossed within the case, tied to bamboo stretchers.
I think about my man when I lie down to sleep and when I rise.
May that good man be as serene as his reputation is unsullied.

Dzant slits khònk gwun. Gwu mou àwk dòuyc, 　俴駟孔羣　厹矛鋈錞
mòng bat wuc wunt, hlàc thrangs ròs ung. 　蒙伐有苑　虎韔鏤膺
Kryàw thrangs nits kwung, trouk prit kòunt lùng. 　交韔二弓　竹柲緄縢
Ngan nìms kwun-tzuc, tzùs tsump, tzùs hung. 　言念君子　載寢載興
Em-em rang nin, drit-drit tùk um. 　厭厭良人　秩秩德音

A woman comforts herself in her husband's absence by musing about how he must be dazzling the yokels with his splendid equipage in whatever rural backwater he is posted to. Her vocabulary stretches our knowledge of *Tiw*-dynasty vehicle technology to and beyond its limit. We know, or think we know, that when a carriage was drawn by four horses, rather than being harnessed two behind two they were arranged in a single fan of four, and one rein of each of the two outer horses was attached directly to the carriage, so the driver had six rather than eight reins in hand. The "slip-rings" may have played a part in leading the two fixed reins to their place. But we are left with much guesswork. Even the descriptions of the horses are uncertain. The commentary tradition tells us that single words were used for horses with different colours or patterns of coat, and these definitions have been repeated from edition to edition down the centuries, but there is no independent way to check them. It is easy to believe that *rè* meant "black horse", and not implausible that *gu* could have meant "dappled grey horse". But the Odes include two different Chinese graphs both pronounced *rou* which the commentators distinguish as "yellow horse with black mane" and "white horse with black mane"; these must be two ways of writing the same word, which perhaps meant a horse with a black mane contrasting with a pale coat. Then, when it comes to *tos*, I really do not believe that any language would use a single word to mean "horse with a white left hind leg"—so I leave it untranslated.

Mun as a description of the rug is literally "striped", but since it is mentioned as a luxury it is a good guess that it is a tiger skin. The lance is presumably triangular in cross-section.

129

Reeds 蒹葭

The reeds are green; the white dew is turning to frost.
He I call "the one and only" is somewhere about the river.
I go after him upstream; the track is difficult and long.
I go after him downstream; he eludes me in the middle of the river.

Kèm-krà tsàng-tsàng; bràk ràks way shang.　　蒹葭蒼蒼　白露為霜
Shac wuts "i nin" dzùc lhouyc it pang.　　　　所謂伊人　在水一方
Sngàks wùy dzong tu; lòuc jac tsac drang.　　　遡洄從之　道阻且長
Sngàks you dzong tu; ont dzùc lhouyc troung ang.　遡遊從之　宛在水中央

The reeds are dense; the sun hasn't yet dried the white dew.
He I call "the one and only" is on the margin of the river.
I go after him upstream; the track is difficult and steep.
I go after him downstream; he eludes me among the islets in the stream.

Kèm-krà tsì-tsì; bràk ràks muts huy.　　　　蒹葭淒淒　白露未晞
Shac wuts "i nin" dzùc lhouyc tu mouy.　　　所謂伊人　在水之湄
Sngàks wùy dzong tu; lòuc jac tsac tzì.　　　遡洄從之　道阻且躋
Sngàks you dzong tu; ont dzùc lhouyc troung dri.　遡遊從之　宛在水中坻

The reeds are colourful; the white dew hasn't yet dispersed.
He I call "the one and only" is on the bank of the river.
I go after him upstream; the track is difficult and overgrown.
I go after him downstream; he eludes me among the eyots in the river.

Kèm-krà tsùc-tsùc; bràk ràks muts luc.　　　蒹葭采采　白露未已
Shac wuts "i nin" dzùc lhouyc tu shuc.　　　所謂伊人　在水之涘
Sngàks wùy dzong tu; lòuc jac tsac gwu.　　　遡洄從之　道阻且芫
Sngàks you dzong tu; ont dzùc lhouyc troung tuc.　遡遊從之　宛在水中沚

A girl hopes to encounter a man whose name she is perhaps too shy to utter. Struggling along the rough tracks where he is working, she fails to catch him up—because he is avoiding her, or because he is unaware of her presence?

No commentary I have seen makes plausible sense of the last word of the penultimate line, which in the received text reads *wuc*, "right-hand". I have ventured very tentatively to amend it to the near-homophone *gwu* "wilderness".

130

The *Toung-nùm* Mountains 終南

What is there in the *Toung-nùm* Mountains? There are rowans and plum trees.
Our prince has arrived, in a brocaded jacket trimmed with fox fur,
looking as though he's dyed his face vermilion—he's every inch a prince!

Toung-nùm gày wuc? Wuc lìw, wuc mù.   終南何有　有條有梅
Kwun-tzuc tits tuc, kump uy, gwà gwu,   君子至止　錦衣狐裘
ngràn na rròk tàn—kus kwun layc tzù!   顏如渥丹　其君也哉

What is there in the *Toung-nùm* Mountains? There are boxthorns and pear trees.
Our prince has arrived, in a jacket with emblems of nobility over an embroidered
   gown,
and netsuke jades chinking at his belt. May he live long and never be forgotten!

Toung-nùm gày wuc? Wuc khuc, wuc dàng.   終南何有　有杞有棠
Kwun-tzuc tits tuc, put uy, siwks dang,   君子至止　黻衣繡裳
bès ngok tsang-tsang. Douc khòuc pu mang!   佩玉瑲瑲　壽考不忘

The *Toung-nùm* (modern Zhongnan) Mountains are outliers of the Qinling range, not far southeast of the *Tiw* capital *Gàwc* and of modern Xi'an. As a wild area close to the heart of civilization, they became a favoured place for Daoist hermits to reside—the sage Laozi lived there. The "emblems of nobility" were a particular pattern of border, a little like the Greek-key pattern, reserved for clothes of men of rank (the last of the rows of motifs discussed with Ode 222 below).

  "Dyed his face vermilion" is undoubtedly meant admiringly. It can be difficult to appreciate other cultures' ideas of beauty.

131

Orioles on the Jujube Trees 黃鳥

Hither and thither fly the orioles, before settling on the jujube trees.
Who was to accompany duke *Mouk*?—*Amp Suk* of the *Tzuc-ka* clan.
Now this *Amp Suk* was a man in a hundred,
yet when he arrived and looked down at his grave, he was shaking with fear.
Blue Sky destroys our best men.
Oh, if only we could ransom *Amp Suk*, his price would be a hundred ordinary men.

Kryàw-kryàw gwàng tìwc, tuc wa kuk.   交交黃鳥　止于棘
Douy dzong Mouk klòng?—Tzuc-ka Amp Suk.   誰從穆公　子車奄息
Wi tsec Amp Suk, pràk pa tu dùk.   維此奄息　百夫之特
Rum gu wìt, toys-toys gu rit.   臨其穴　惴惴其慄
Payc tsàng tac Thìn tzam ngàyc rang nin.   彼蒼者天　殲我良人
Na khàyc mlok ì, nin pràk gu lhin.   如可贖兮　人百其身

Hither and thither fly the orioles, before settling on the mulberry trees.
Who was to accompany duke *Mouk*?—*Droungs Gàngs* of the *Tzuc-ka* clan.
Now this *Droungs Gàngs* was a match for a hundred men,
yet when he arrived and looked down at his grave, he was shaking with fear.
Blue Sky destroys our best men.
Oh, if only we could ransom *Droungs Gàngs*, his price would be a hundred ordinary men.

Kryàw-kryàw gwàng tìwc, tuc wa sàng.　　交交黃鳥　止于桑
Douy dzong Mouk klòng?—Tzuc-ka Droungs Gàngs.　　誰從穆公　子車仲行
Wi tsec Droungs Gàngs, pràk pa tu bang.　　維此仲行　百夫之防
Rum gu wìt, toys-toys gu rit.　　臨其穴　惴惴其慄
Payc tsàng tac Thìn tzam ngàyc rang nin.　　彼蒼者天　殲我良人
Na khàyc mlok ì, nin pràk gu lhin.　　如可贖兮　人百其身

Hither and thither fly the orioles, before settling on the thorn trees.
Who was to accompany duke *Mouk*?—Tiger *Kim* of the *Tzuc-ka* clan.
Now this Tiger *Kim* could hold his own against a hundred men.
Yet when he came and looked down at his grave, he was shaking with fear.
Blue Sky destroys our best men.
Oh, if only we could ransom Tiger *Kim*, his price would be a hundred ordinary men.

Kryàw-kryàw gwàng tìwc, tuc wa chac.　　交交黃鳥　止于楚
Douy dzong Mouk klòng?—Tzuc-ka Kim Hlàc.　　誰從穆公　子車鍼虎
Wi tsec Kim Hlàc, pràk pa tu ngac.　　維此鍼虎　百夫之禦
Rum gu wìt, toys-toys gu rit.　　臨其穴　惴惴其慄
Payc tsàng tac Thìn tzam ngàyc rang nin.　　彼蒼者天　殲我良人
Na khàyc mlok ì, nin pràk gu lhin.　　如可贖兮　人百其身

When duke *Mouk* of *Dzin* died in 621 he asked for these cousins to be sent to keep him company in the afterlife, buried alive. In total 170 men and women were sacrificed at that funeral; most will have been wives and servants, but these three were distinguished men, who could ill be spared. (Others saw this practice as evidence of the semi-barbarian nature of *Dzin* state. Eventually, in 384, it was banned by the then *Dzin* ruler.)

132

The Falcon 晨風

A falcon is flying swiftly above this dense northern forest.
I haven't seen my man, and my heart is struck deep with grief.
Where are we—where are we? Truly, sir, you neglect me too much.

Wit payc mdun-pum; out payc pùk rum.   鴥彼晨風　鬱彼北林
Muts kèns kwun-tzuc, ou sum khum-khum.   未見君子　憂心欽欽
Na gày, na gày? Mang ngàyc dit tày.   如何如何　忘我實多

On the slopes, oaks are flourishing, and in the wetland there are yellow catalpas.
I haven't seen my man, and there's no music in my heart.
Where are we—where are we? Truly, sir, you neglect me too much.

Shàn wuc pròu ryàwk, slup wuc rouk-pràwk.   山有苞櫟　隰有六駮
Muts kèns kwun-tzuc, ou sum mayc ngràwk.   未見君子　憂心靡樂
Na gày, na gày? Mang ngàyc dit tày.   如何如何　忘我實多

On the slopes, cherry trees are flourishing, and birchleaf pears are planted in the wetland.
I haven't seen my man, and I feel hung over with depression.
Where are we—where are we? Truly, sir, you neglect me too much.

Shàn wuc pròu lìts, slup wuc doc syouts.   山有苞棣　隰有樹檖
Muts kèns kwun-tzuc, ou sum na tzouts.   未見君子　憂心如醉
Na gày, na gày? Mang ngàyc dit tày.   如何如何　忘我實多

The repeated phrase *na gày* means "how is X?"—X is not specified here but is evidently the state of the lady's marriage, hence "Where are we?" The mention of "northern forest" perhaps implies that the marriage has removed her far from her own people.

Mdun-pum in the opening line, literally "morning breeze", is a poetic name for the falcon, which can fly free while the lady is stuck where she is. *Rouk-pràwk*, literally "six colours", is some kind of tree—possibly the yellow catalpa, *Catalpa ovata*, but this identification, and that of *syouts* as birchleaf pear, are uncertain.

133

I'll Share With You　無衣

How can you say you have nothing to wear? I'll share my quilted coats with you.
The king is raising troops: we'll fettle our halberds and lances,
and anyone who attacks you will have to face me too.

Khuyc wat ma uy? Lac tzuc dòng bòu.   豈曰無衣　與子同袍
Wang wa hung shi. Siw ngàyc kwày mou,   王于興師　修我戈矛
lac tzuc dòng gou.   與子同仇

How can you say you have nothing to wear? I'll share my underclothes with you.
The king is raising troops: we'll fettle our lances and swords,
and we'll stand shoulder to shoulder.

Khuyc wat ma uy? Lac tzuc dòng làk.
Wang wa hung shi. Siw ngàyc mou krak,
lac tzuc krìc tzàk.

豈曰無衣　與子同澤
王于興師　修我矛戟
與子偕作

How can you say you have nothing to wear? I'll share my robes with you.
The king is raising troops: we'll fettle our body-armour and weaponry,
and we'll march together.

Khuyc wat ma uy? Lac tzuc dòng dang.
Wang wa hung shi. Siw ngàyc kràp prang,
lac tzuc krìc gràng.

豈曰無衣　與子同裳
王于興師　修我甲兵
與子偕行

A surprising little poem. Who ever offered "I've nothing to wear" as an excuse for dodging military service?

134

Escorting my Cousin 渭陽

I escorted my cousin on his way; I took him as far as *Wuts-lang*.
What did I give as his parting gift? A team of bays for his state carriage.

Ngàyc sòngs gouc gec; wat tits Wuts-lang.
Gày luc dzùngs tu? Ràks ka mlungs gwàng.

我送舅氏　曰至渭陽
何以贈之　路車乘黃

I escorted my cousin on his way—he'll have remembered me when we were far apart.
What did I give as his parting gift? Jewels and jade netsuke.

Ngàyc sòngs gouc gec; you-you ngàyc sus.
Gày luc dzùngs tu? Gweng kòuy, ngok bès.

我送舅氏　悠悠我思
何以贈之　瓊瑰玉佩

Said to have been written by *Khàng*, son of *Mouk* whose funeral we read about in Ode 131. *Khàng*'s mother had a nephew *Drong-nuc* ("Double Ears") who was the rightful heir to the neighbouring dukedom of *Tzins*, but was forced into exile at *Dzin* through skulduggery at the *Tzins* court. With *Mouk*'s support *Drong-nuc* eventually mounted a successful expedition to recover his dukedom, and *Khàng* escorted him on this return to *Tzins* in 636.

The name *Wuts-lang* should mean "north bank of the Wei". The whole journey was north of that river, but doubtless at some stage it passed close to a crossing-point with that name.

135

What I Was Used To 權輿

Woe is me! In the great house, things were on a spacious scale.
But now, whenever I eat there's never any food to spare.
Alas and alack, this isn't what I was used to.

À ngàyc ghà! Ghàc òk ga-ga. 　　　　　於我乎　夏屋渠渠
Kum layc mùc mluk ma la. 　　　　　今也每食無餘
Wa tzay ghà, pu dung gon-la. 　　　　于嗟乎　不承權輿

Woe is me! At every meal there used to be four *krouc* pots on the mat.
But now, I never get to eat my fill.
Alas and alack, this isn't what I was used to.

À ngàyc ghà! Mùc mluk slits krouc. 　　　於我乎　每食四簋
Kum layc mùc mluk pu pròuc. 　　　　　今也每食不飽
Wa tzay ghà, pu dung gon-la. 　　　　于嗟乎　不承權輿

Said to have been written by some favoured retainer of duke *Mouk*, who found himself edged out of favour under *Mouk*'s successor *Khàng*. A *krouc* was the vessel in which millet or other grain was served at a meal, from which the diners would help themselves; four *kroucs*, with other dishes in proportion, would be a lavish meal.

State of Drin

Drin was a south-eastern state, with its capital in what is now Huaiyang, eastern Henan.

136

Ont Hill 宛丘

You are so reckless, there on *Ont* Hill.
I'm fond of you, it's true, but I don't admire you.

Tzuc tu lànk ì, Ont kwhu tu dyangs ì. 子之惕兮　宛丘之上兮
Swin wuc dzeng ì, nu ma mang ì. 洵有情兮　而無望兮

Thump goes the beating of the drum below *Ont* Hill.
In season and out, your egret's feathers are waving.

Khùmp kus kèk kàc, Ont kwhu tu gràc. 坎其擊鼓　宛丘之下
Ma tòung, ma gràs, druks gu ràks wac. 無冬無夏　植其鷺羽

Thump goes the beating of the pot on the road to *Ont* Hill.
In season and out, your egret's-plume stick is waving.

Khùmp kus kèk pouc, Ont kwhu tu lòuc. 坎其擊缶　宛丘之道
Ma tòung, ma gràs, druks gu ràks dòu. 無冬無夏　植其鷺翿

Ont Hill was a rich man's partying place near the *Drin* capital. The egret's plumes were waving in a dance.

137

The Elms of the East Gate 東門之枌

Below the elms of the East Gate and below the cork-oaks of *Ont* Hill,
you, Second-Son's daughter, led us in the *bày-sày*.

Tòng mùn tu bun, Ont kwhu tu hwac, 東門之枌　宛丘之栩
tzuc Droungs tu tzuc bày-sày gu gràc. 子仲之子　婆娑其下

On an auspicious morning we came forward to choose one to lead us: you, miss
    Ngwan of the south quarter.
We left off spinning hemp and we danced the *bày-sày* in the market square.

Kòk tàns wa chày: nùm pang tu Ngwan.   穀旦于差　南方之原
Pu tzèk gu mrày, duc layc bày-sày.   不績其麻　市也婆娑

On that auspicious morning we came forward, and you led off the dance.
To look at you were like a mallow blossom. You gave us a handful of pepper
    plants.

Kòk tàns wa dats, wat-luc tzòng mràts.   穀旦于逝　越以鬷邁
Gic nec na gyaw. Lu ngàyc rròk tziw.   視爾如荍　貽我握椒

The *bày-sày* was a ritual dance performed by girls—it will have been danced to invoke some favour from Sky or the spirits. (Pepper plants with their distinctive fragrance were used to persuade the spirits to descend.) Like other rituals, the dance needed to be done on a date identified by the astrologers as auspicious (*kit*, or here *kòk*). The *Ngwan* family are known to have been leading citizens of *Drin* state, indeed there is a record of this lady's father, Second-Son *Ngwan*.

The elms of the first line were not the elms we used to know in Britain, but probably lacebark elm, *Ulmus parvifolia*; for the *hwac* oaks see Ode 121.

138

Beneath My Rustic Lintel　衡門

Beneath my rustic lintel I can feel at ease.
The bubbling of the spring will assuage my hunger pangs.

Gràng mùn tu gràc khàyc luc sì dri.   衡門之下　可以棲遲
Pits tu yang-yang khàyc luc ryawks kri.   泌之洋洋　可以○飢

If one eats a fish, why does it have to be a Yellow River bream?
If one takes a wife, why must she be a *Kyang* of *Dzì*?

Khuyc gu mluk nga, pit Gày tu bang?   豈其食魚　必河之魴
Khuyc gu tsos tsùy pit Dzì tu Kyang?   豈其娶妻　必齊之姜

If one eats a fish, why does it have to be a Yellow River carp?
If one takes a wife, why must she be a *Tzuc* of *Sòungs*?

Khuyc gu mluk nga, pit Gày tu ruc?   豈其食魚　必河之鯉
Khuyc gu tsos tsùy pit Sòungs tu Tzuc?   豈其娶妻　必宋之子

Bream and carp from the Yellow River were prized by gourmets; the *Kyangs* and *Tzucs* of *Dzì* and *Sòungs* states respectively were distinguished families. The poet is resisting pressure to make a "good marriage".

The opening word, *gràng*, means a horizontal crossbeam; a "crossbeam-door" implied a doorway formed from a treetrunk as lintel—hence the doorway of a simple rustic home.

139

The Pond by the East Gate 　東門之池

The pond by the East Gate is used for soaking hemp.
That lovely Third-Daughter *Kyu*, I could sing to her face to face.

Tòng mùn tu dray, khàyc luc òs mràiy.　　　　　東門之池　可以漚麻
Payc mouyc Nhouk Kyu, khàyc lac ngàs kày.　　彼美叔姬　可與晤歌

The pond by the East Gate is used for soaking ramie.
That lovely Third-Daughter *Kyu*, I could speak to her face to face.

Tòng mùn tu dray, khàyc luc òs drac.　　　　　東門之池　可以漚紵
Payc mouyc Nhouk Kyu, khàyc lac ngàs ngac.　　彼美叔姬　可與晤語

The pond by the East Gate is used for soaking red-grass.
That lovely Third-Daughter *Kyu*, I could chat with her face to face.

Tòng mùn tu dray, khàyc luc òs kràn.　　　　　東門之池　可以漚菅
Payc mouyc Nhouk Kyu, khàyc lac ngàs ngan.　　彼美叔姬　可與晤言

If the girls come to the pool to work, a lad might get his chance to make the acquaintance of one he has noticed. Ramie is a nettle-like plant comparable to flax: its fibres are woven into grasscloth. Red-grass (in Australia called kangaroo grass) is a colourful, tough grass species used to make mats and ropes.

140

The Poplars by the East Gate 　東門之楊

The poplars by the East Gate, their leaves are thick.
Sundown was the time we agreed; now the Evening Star is gleaming.

Tòng mùn tu lang, gu lap tzàng-tzàng.　　東門之楊　其葉牂牂
Mhùn luc way gu; Mrang Sèng wàng-wàng.　昏以為期　明星煌煌

The poplars by the East Gate, their leaves are dense.
Sundown was the time we agreed; now the Evening Star is brilliant.

Tòng mùn tu lang, gu lap phàts-phàts.   東門之楊　其葉肺肺
Mhùn luc way gu; Mrang Sèng tats-tats.   昏以為期　明星哲哲

The lady has not shown up.

141

By the Graveyard Gate 墓門

There are jujube trees by the graveyard gate; they are lopped with axes.
My man is wicked, and everyone hereabouts knows it.
They know it, but that doesn't stop him. Who has been this way for a long time now?

Màks mùn wuc kuk; pac luc se tu.   墓門有棘　斧以斯之
Pa layc pu rang, kwùk nin tre tu.   夫也不良　國人知之
Tre nu pu luc. Douy sak nan luc?   知而不已　誰昔然矣

There are plum trees by the graveyard gate, and owls gather and settle on them.
My man is wicked, and this song is his rebuke.
I rebuke him, but he ignores me. When he gets his comeuppance, then he'll pay me heed.

Màks mùn wuc mù, wuc waw dzouts tuc.   墓門有梅　有鴞萃止
Pa layc pu rang, kày luc souts tu.   夫也不良　歌以訊之
Souts lac pu kàs. Tìn tàwc su lac.   訊予不顧　顛倒思予

"Who has been this way …?" seems to be a rhetorical question implying that *he* has been like this.

Several different bird names in the Odes are debatably translated as "owl". *Waw* in verse 2 here occurs in Ode 155 as part of a two-syllable word *thi-waw*, which sounds so close to "tu-whoo" that the identification seems inescapable; so it is natural to take *thi* and *waw*, when they occur separately here and in Ode 264, as short names for the same bird. Yet Ode 299 has a *waw* eating mulberries—owls are carnivorous. If these birds were owls, we should note that in China they were birds of ill omen.

142

Magpies' Nests 防有鵲巢

There are magpies' nests on the embankment, and sweet *dyàw* plants on the hillock.
Who is leading my lover astray? Oh, my heart is full of misery.

Bang wuc tsak jàw, gong wuc kic dyàw.　　防有鵲巢　邛有旨苕
Douy trou lac mouyc? Sum an tàw-tàw.　　誰侜予美　心焉忉忉

The middle of the temple path is paved with tiles; there are sweet pheasant-plants on the hillock.
Who is leading my lover astray? Oh, my heart is full of grief.

Troung glang wuc bèk; gong wuc kic ngèk.　　中唐有甓　邛有旨鷊
Douy trou lac mouyc? Sum an lhèk-lhèk.　　誰侜予美　心焉惕惕

Dyàw is thought to be some variety of pea, but since "sweet pea" means something else in English, I have left it untranslated. In the case of *ngèk*, no-one now knows what plant it was; but the same word is used for a species of pheasant, so I have called it "pheasant-plant".

143

The Moon Comes Out　月出

The moon comes out in her brightness—oh, how fine that fair one is: serene, elegant. But oh, my troubled heart is anxious.

Ngwat k'hlout kyàwc ì—kràwc nin ryàwc ì:　　月出皎兮　佼人僚兮
lha, ìwc-kiwc ì. Ràw sum tsyawc ì.　　舒窈糾兮　勞心悄兮

The moon comes out in her radiance—oh, how queenly that fair one is: serene, tranquil. But oh, my troubled heart is concerned.

Ngwat k'hlout kòuc ì—kràwc nin rouc ì:　　月出皓兮　佼人懰兮
lha, ouc-douc ì. Ràw sum sòuc ì.　　舒懮受兮　勞心慅兮

The moon comes out in her brilliance—oh, how that fair one shines: she is serene, delicately lovely. But oh, my troubled heart is filled with grief.

Ngwat k'hlout tyaw ì—kràwc nin ryaws ì:　　月出照兮　佼人燎兮
lha, aw-dawc ì. Ràw sum tsàwc ì.　　舒夭紹兮　勞心慘兮

I read the "fair one" as the moon itself, so that the poem contrasts the serene heavenly body with the disturbed poet. But *kràwc nin* is literally "beautiful person", and personifying an inanimate object in that way is unusual in Old Chinese. Others have understood the "fair one" to be some human being, and the moon to be merely an opening image.

144

Stump Wood 株林

What will I be doing at Stump Wood? Going to see *Ghàc Nùm*.
It's not that I specially want to go to Stump Wood: I'm just going to see *Ghàc Nùm*.

Gà way ghà Tro Rum? Dzong Ghàc Nùm.   胡為乎株林　從夏南
Puyc lhek Tro Rum: dzong Ghàc Nùm.   匪適株林　從夏南

I'll yoke my team of four horses, and I'll stop overnight somewhere in the Stump area.
I'll drive my team of four colts, and tomorrow I'll be breakfasting at Stump.

Kràys ngàyc mlungs mràc; lhots wa Tro lac.   駕我乘馬　說于株野
Mlung ngàyc mlungs ko; traw mluk wa Tro.   乘我乘駒　朝食于株

This little poem is cryptic, but whoever wrote it might not have dared be more explicit. It is worded as if spoken by *Rèng*, ruler of *Drin*, and refers to happenings in the year 599 (making it one of the latest, perhaps the very last Ode to be composed). The full story is in a later historical work called Zuo Zhuan, literally "Left-Hand Commentary".

Tro Rum, "Stump Wood" (at present-day Zhecheng, eastern Henan) was the seat of the *Ghàc* family, and *Ghàc Nùm* was the son of a high officer of *Drin* state; by 599 the father was dead. But the point of the poem is that it wasn't really *Ghàc Nùm* that *Rèng* was going to see. It was his mother, the merry widow *Ghàc Kyu*, who was sleeping not just with *Rèng* but also with two of his ministers. On one occasion these three men were fooling about at court, each wearing an item of *Ghàc Kyu*'s underclothes. A leading courtier, *Slat Lac*, ventured to reprove *Rèng* for setting such a poor example, and was fobbed off with a promise of amendment; but the other two suggested killing *Slat Lac*, and *Rèng* "did not forbid". That was the end of *Slat Lac*.

145

On the Edge of the Marsh 澤陂

On the edge of that marsh there are reeds and lotus plants;
there is a certain lovely person: how painful it is!
Waking and sleeping I don't know what to do. My tears and snivel flow freely.

Payc drak tu pay, wuc bà lac gày;   彼澤之陂　有蒲與荷
wuc mouyc it nin, lhang na tu gày!   有美一人　傷如之何
Ngàs mits ma way. Thìc sits phàng lày.   寤寐無為　涕泗滂沱

On the edge of that marsh there are reeds and water-lilies;
there is a certain lovely person, regal and handsome.
Waking and sleeping I don't know what to do. In my inmost heart I grieve.

Payc drak tu pay, wuc bà lac rèn;   彼澤之陂 　有蒲與蓮
wuc mouyc it nin, dak dàts tsac gwren.   有美一人 　碩大且卷
Ngàs mits ma way. Troung sum wwen-wwen.   寤寐無為 　中心悁悁

On the edge of that marsh there are reeds and lotus blossoms;
there is a certain lovely person, regal and majestic.
Waking and sleeping I don't know what to do. Lying on my pillow I toss and turn.

Payc drak tu pay, wuc bà gùmp-lùmp;   彼澤之陂 　有蒲菡萏
wuc mouyc it nin, dak dàts tsac ngamp.   有美一人 　碩大且儼
Ngàs mits ma way. Trent-tront buk kimp.   寤寐無為 　輾轉伏枕

State of Kòt

Kòt was a small state in Henan, annexed by Drengs in the eighth century.

146

Lambskin and Fox Fur 羔裘

In your lambskin coat you saunter at leisure; you attend court in fox fur.
How could I fail to be thinking about you? My troubled heart is full of grief.

Kàw gwu syaw-yaw; gwà gwu luc draw.   羔裘逍遙 狐裘以朝
Khuyc pu nec su? Ràw sum tàw-tàw.   豈不爾思 勞心忉忉

In your lambskin coat you mooch around; you appear in Hall in fox fur.
How could I fail to be thinking about you? My heart is sad and hurt.

Kàw gwu ngòu-syang; gwà gwu dzùc dàng.   羔裘翱翔 狐裘在堂
Khuyc pu nec su? Ngàyc sum ou lhang.   豈不爾思 我心憂傷

Your lambskin coat glistens like grease, it gleams bright when the sun is out.
How could I fail to be thinking about you? In my inmost heart I worry about you.

Kàw gwu na kàws, nit k'hlout wuc lyawks.   羔裘如膏 日出有曜
Khuyc pu nec su? Troung sum dec dàwks.   豈不爾思 中心是悼

One theory about this is that specific fur garments were properly worn only on prescribed formal occasions; the poet worries because the man addressed is careless about these rules, and might suffer for it.

147

His White Cap 素冠

Oh, I wish I could see his white cap. He'll be losing weight in his distress.
My troubled heart is full of grief.

Lhaks kèns sàs kòn ì. Kuk nin ròn-ròn ì.   庶見素冠兮 棘人欒欒兮
Ràw sum dòn-dòn ì.   勞心慱慱兮

Oh, I wish I could see your white jacket. My heart is sad and pained.
Would that I could go home with you.

Lhaks kèns sàs uy ì. Ngàyc sum lhang pruy ì.　　庶見素衣兮　我心傷悲兮
Rìw lac tzuc dòng kwuy ì.　　聊與子同歸兮

Oh, I wish I could see your white knee-covers. I am all blocked and knotted up inside.
Would that I could be one with you.

Lhaks kèns sàs pit ì. Ngàyc sum ount kit ì.　　庶見素韠兮　我心蘊結兮
Rìw lac tzuc na it ì.　　聊與子如一兮

White is the colour of mourning; evidently she is missing a man who has had to part from her because of a bereavement.

148

Starfruit Trees　隰有萇楚

There are starfruit trees by the river: their branches are luxuriant,
glossy with youth. I'm delighted that you have no boyfriend.

Slup wuc drang-chac, àyc-nàyc gu ke,　　隰有萇楚　猗儺其枝
aw tu àwk-àwk. Ngràwks tzuc tu ma tre.　　夭之沃沃　樂子之無知

There are starfruit trees by the river: their blossoms are luxuriant,
glossy with youth. I'm delighted that you're not the lady of a house.

Slup wuc drang-chac, àyc-nàyc gu wà,　　隰有萇楚　猗儺其華
aw tu àwk-àwk. Ngràwks tzuc tu ma krà.　　夭之沃沃　樂子之無家

There are starfruit trees by the river: their fruit are luxuriant,
glossy with youth. I'm delighted that you have no married-woman's chamber.

Slup wuc drang-chac, àyc-nàyc gu mlit,　　隰有萇楚　猗儺其實
aw tu àwk-àwk. Ngràwks tzuc tu ma lhit.　　夭之沃沃　樂子之無室

The poet hopes to supply the deficiencies himself.
　　Starfruit tree (carambola) is one idea about the identity of *drang-chac*.

149

It Isn't the Wind　匪風

It isn't that the wind is getting up—ah no;
it isn't that the carriage is moving off—ah no.
Looking back at the road to *Tiw*: that's what's making this grief in my heart.

Puyc pum pat ì,　　　　　　　　匪風發兮
puyc ka khat ì;　　　　　　　　匪車揭兮
kàs tam Tiw lòuc, troung sum tàt ì.　顧瞻周道　中心怛兮

It isn't that the wind is growing wild—ah no;
it isn't that the carriage is rattling and jolting—ah no.
Looking back at the road to *Tiw*, that's what's making this sadness in my heart.

Puyc pum pyaw ì,　　　　　　　　匪風飄兮
puyc ka phyaw ì;　　　　　　　　匪車嘌兮
kàs tam Tiw lòuc, troung sum tyàwk ì.　顧瞻周道　中心弔兮

Who could cook me a fish? For him I'd wash the great boiling-pan out with my own hands.
Who's headed home to the West? Him I'd serve by promoting his good name.

Douy nùc phràng nga? Kùts tu bac slum.　誰能烹魚　溉之釜鬵
Douy tzang sì kwuy? Gròuy tu hòuc um.　誰將西歸　懷之好音

Someone, perhaps on royal service, has had to leave behind the comfortable life of the *Tiw* capital, and yearns for what he has lost. Fish is a luxury food, so the poet expresses himself as willing to do a servant's work in exchange for it; and in a sort of parallel, he would abase himself on behalf of someone destined for life at court, doubtless with the hope that the favour would be returned when a vacancy arises.

State of *Dzòu*

Dzòu was a small state centred on modern Dingtao, south-west Shandong (not to be confused with *Dzòu* city in Ode 31—the names are written differently in Chinese).

150

The Mayfly 蜉蝣

Like the mayfly's wings, your dress is splendid.
My heart is so sad; come home with me.

Bou-you tu wac, uy-dang chac-chac.	蜉蝣之羽　衣裳楚楚
Sum tu ou luc; a ngàyc kwuy k'hlac.	心之憂矣　於我歸處

Like the wings of the mayfly, your clothes are brightly coloured.
My heart is so sad; come and sleep with me.

Bou-you tu yuk, tsùc-tsùc uy-buk.	蜉蝣之翼　采采衣服
Sum tu ou luc; a ngàyc kwuy suk.	心之憂矣　於我歸息

Like the mayfly bursting forth from its burrow, your hempen robe is as the snow.
My heart is so sad; come and spend the night with me.

Bou-you khòut lot, mràу uy na sot.	蜉蝣掘閱　麻衣如雪
Sum tu ou luc; a ngàyc kwuy lhots.	心之憂矣　於我歸說

After it emerges in adult form, the mayfly mates and dies within a single day. This young man is hoping for a similarly short-term relationship.

151

Halberds and Clubs 候人

The men of the escort bear halberds and clubs.
This youth is a "red knee-cover" with three hundred men under him.

Payc gòs nin ì gàyc kwày lac tòts.	彼候人兮　何戈與祋
Payc kus tu tzuc, sùm pràk khlak put.	彼其之子　三百赤市

The cormorant by the weir isn't getting its wings wet;
this youth isn't taking his responsibilities seriously.

Wi dì dzùc rang, pu no gu yuk.   維鵜在梁　不濡其翼
Payc kus tu tzuc, pu k'hlungs gu buk.   彼其之子　不稱其服

The cormorant by the weir isn't getting its beak wet;
this youth isn't going to continue in favour.

Wi dì dzùc rang, pu no gu tòks.   維鵜在梁　不濡其咮
Payc kus tu tzuc, pu swits gu kòs.   彼其之子　不遂其媾

Veils of morning mist are concealing the Southern Mountains
—oh, but she's fair, she's lovely, that young miss he hungers for.

Òts ì, outs ì, Nùm shàn tràw tzì.   薈兮蔚兮　南山朝隮
Ont ì, ront ì, kwits nrac se kri.   婉兮孌兮　季女斯飢

A young officer is neglecting his duties because he is mooning over a girl. Cormorants are used for catching fish, so one that fails to dive into a pond is similarly work-shy.

Red knee-covers were an element of military dress identifying senior officers. A *kwày* seems to have been the standard weapon carried by a *Tiw*-dynasty soldier. Ancient pictures show a knifeblade projecting forward from a short handle, with a crescent-shaped axe-blade attached to the side, points outward. The word is commonly given in English as "dagger-axe"; but the weapon was somewhat similar to what in mediaeval Europe was called a halberd.

152

The Cuckoo　鳲鳩

The cuckoo's in the mulberry tree; it has seven chicks.
Our prince is an excellent man, consistent in his decorum.
He's consistent in his decorum, with his emotions tightly controlled.

Lhi-kou dzùc sàng, gu tzuc tsit ì.   鳲鳩在桑　其子七兮
Diwk nin kwun-tzuc, gu ngay it ì.   淑人君子　其儀一兮
Gu ngay it ì, sum na kìt ì.   其儀一兮　心如結兮

The cuckoo's in the mulberry tree; its chicks are in the plum tree.
Our prince is an excellent man; he wears a silken girdle.
He wears a silken girdle, and his cap is mottled grey.

Lhi-kou dzùc sàng, gu tzuc dzùc mù.   鳲鳩在桑　其子在梅
Diwk nin kwun-tzuc, gu tàts i su.   淑人君子　其帶伊絲
Gu tàts i su, gu brans i gu.   其帶伊絲　其弁伊騏

The cuckoo's in the mulberry tree; its chicks are in the thorn bush.
Our prince is an excellent man; his decorum is faultless.
His decorum is faultless, and he sets a standard for the states of the whole world.

Lhi-kou dzùc sàng, gu tzuc dzùc kuk.　　鳲鳩在桑　其子在棘
Diwk nin kwun-tzuc, gu ngay pu lhùk.　　淑人君子　其儀不忒
Gu ngay pu lhùk, tengs dec Slits kwùk.　其儀不忒　正是四國

The cuckoo's in the mulberry tree; its chicks are in the hazel.
Our prince is an excellent man; he sets a standard for the people of our land.
He sets a standard for the people of our land—how can he not live ten thousand years?

Lhi-kou dzùc sàng, gu tzuc dzùc jin.　　鳲鳩在桑　其子在榛
Diwk nin kwun-tzuc, tengs dec kwùk nin.　淑人君子　正是國人
Tengs dec kwùk nin, gà pu màns nìn?　　正是國人　胡不萬年

153

Cold Spring Water   泉

Chill is the water streaming down from this spring, and overflowing the thickly-growing darnel.
Ah me, I sigh as I lie awake, thinking about the *Tiw* capital.

Rat payc gràs ngwan, tzums payc pròu ràng.　洌彼下泉　浸彼苞稂
Khùts ngàyc ngàs nhàn, nìms payc Tiw krang.　愾我寤嘆　念彼周京

Chill is the water streaming down from this spring, and overflowing the thickly-growing lad's-love.
Ah me, I sigh as I lie awake, thinking about *Tiw* city.

Rat payc gràs ngwan, tzums payc pròu sìw.　洌彼下泉　浸彼苞蕭
Khùts ngàyc ngàs nhàn, nìms payc krang Tiw.　愾我寤嘆　念彼京周

Chill is the water streaming down from this spring, and overflowing the thickly-growing yarrow.
Ah me, I sigh as I lie awake, thinking about the metropolis.

Rat payc gràs ngwan, tzums payc pròu hi.　洌彼下泉　浸彼苞蓍
Khùts ngàyc ngàs nhàn, nìms payc krang shi.　愾無寤歎　念彼京師

The millet is sprouting richly, fattened up by the dreary rain.
It's the season when rulers of all states are visiting the court, and the lord of *Swin* is rewarding them.

Bùm-bùm nhac maw, um wac kàws tu.
Slits kwùk wuc wang, Swin pràk ràws tu.

芃芃黍苗　陰雨膏之
四國有王　郇伯勞之

An official posted to some dismal rural backwater yearns for the life of the capital. (Darnel, *Lolium temulentum*, is a poisonous weed of cereal crops.) To twist the knife, the poet knows that, as he writes, the vassal rulers are required to visit the court to demonstrate loyalty, and are being recompensed for their trouble.

Swin was a small state at modern Puzhou on the east bank of the Yellow River, just above its junction with the Wei. Its ruling family descended from *Mun*, and evidently the current ruler had a role supervising the other state rulers on the king's behalf.

State of *Prun*

Listing *Prun* among the *Tiw* "states" is another unexplained anachronism. As we saw on p. 7, *Prun* was a name with historical resonance, having been the home of the *Tiw* people before their migration to the Wei valley. But in the *Tiw* dynasty *Prun* was just a remote town within the western royal domain.

154

The Seventh Moon 七月

In the seventh moon, Fire descends; in the ninth moon we hand out clothes.
During the first moon we'll get gales; during the second moon it'll be bitterly cold.
Without clothes and blankets, how would folk get through the year?
During the third moon they fettle the ploughs; during the fourth they set to and turn the ground with them.
We women and children together carry food out to the hands in the southerly fields.
The field-inspector arrives and is highly satisfied.

Tsit ngwat riw mhùyc; kouc ngwat dous uy.	七月流火　九月授衣
It tu nit pit-pat, nits tu nit rit-rat.	一之日觱發　二之日栗烈
Ma uy ma gàt, gày luc tzout swats.	無衣無褐　何以卒歲
Sùm tu nit wa sluc; slits tu nit klac tuc.	三之日于耜　四之日舉趾
Dòng ngàyc buc tzuc wap payc nùm mùc.	同我婦子　饁彼南畝
Lìn tzyouns tits huc.	田畯至喜

In the seventh moon, Fire descends; in the ninth moon we hand out clothes.
In springtime days we get sunshine; the orioles begin singing.
With our deep baskets, we girls stroll along hidden paths, searching for tender young mulberry leaves.
The springtime days draw out longer, and crowds gather hoary mugwort.
A girl's heart is vulnerable; perhaps one of the young noblemen will take me home with him.

Tsit ngwat riw mhùyc; kouc ngwat dous uy.	七月流火　九月授衣
Thoun nit tzùs lang, wuc mreng tsàng-kràng.	春日載陽　有鳴倉庚
Nrac tup its kwhang, tzoun payc muy gràng, wan gac nou sàng.	女執懿筐　遵彼微行　爰求柔桑
Thoun nit dri-dri, tsùc ban gri-gri.	春日遲遲　采蘩祁祁
Nrac sum lhang pruy, lùc gup klòng tzuc dòng kwuy.	女心傷悲　殆及公子同歸

In the seventh moon, Fire descends; the eighth is the season of rushes and reeds.
In the silkworm moon they strip leaves from the mulberry trees; taking axes and saws,
they lop off branches which have grown too long or too high. The pruned trees are flourishing.
In the seventh moon the butcher bird shrieks.
The eighth moon is the time for spinning; we make black cloth and yellow.
Our red dye is particularly vivid. We make robes for the young nobles.

Tsit ngwat riw mhùyc; prèt ngwat gwàn wuyc.	七月流火　八月萑葦
Dzùm ngwat lhìw sàng, tsoc payc pac tsang,	蠶月條桑　取彼斧斨
luc bat want lang; ayc payc nrac sàng.	以伐遠揚　猗彼女桑
Tsit ngwat mreng tsa.	七月鳴鵙
Prèt ngwat tzùs tzèk, tzùs gwìn tzùs gwàng.	八月載績　載玄載黃
Ngàyc to khònk lang. Way klòng tzuc dang.	我朱孔陽　為公子裳

In the fourth moon the milkworts flower and set seed. In the fifth moon the cicadas begin shrilling.
The eighth moon is harvest-time; in the tenth moon the dead leaves fall.
During the first moon people go after badgers
and catch foxes and wildcats, to make furs for the young noblemen to wear.
During the second moon comes the hunt meet, which helps the men maintain their prowess in warfare.
They keep the young piglets for us, and present the older ones to the prince.

Slits ngwat siws yyaw; ngàc ngwat mreng dìw.	四月秀葽　五月鳴蜩
Prèt ngwat kus gwàk; gip ngwat wrunt lhàk.	八月其穫　十月隕蘀
Its tu nit wa gàk,	一之日于貉
tsòc payc gwà ru, way klòng tzuc gwu.	取彼狐狸　為公子裘
Nits tu nit gu dòng, tzùs tzònt mac kòng.	二之日其同　載纘武功
Ngan si gu tzòng; nghans kèn wa klòng.	言私其豵　獻豜于公

In the fifth moon, grasshoppers are buzzing with their hind legs. In the sixth moon, katydids are buzzing with their wings.
In the seventh moon we sleep in field shelters; in the eighth, below our house-eaves; in the ninth we go back indoors.
In the tenth moon, crickets take up residence under our beds.
With holes stopped up, we smoke out the rats. We block up the north-facing windows and plaster the doors.
We hear "Now, you womenfolk and children of ours: the year's on the turn, come and stop inside."

Ngàc ngwat se toung dònk kàc; rouk ngwat shày-kè tuns wac.	五月斯螽動股　六月莎雞振羽
Tsit ngwat dzùc dac; prèt ngwat dzùc wac; kouc ngwat dzùc gàc.	七月在野　八月在宇　九月在戶
Gip ngwat shit-shout nup ngàyc djang gràc.	十月蟋蟀　入我牀下
Kwhung tìt hwun nhac; sàk hangs gruns gàc.	穹窒熏鼠　塞向墐戶

"Tzay ngàyc buc tzuc", wat "Way kùc swats; nup tsec lhit k'hlac." 嗟我婦子　日為改歲　入此室處

In the sixth moon we eat bush-cherries and wild grapes;
in the seventh we cook mallow and beans.
In the eighth moon we pick jujubes. In the tenth we reap rice,
and make that spring wine which leads to a more vigorous old age.
In the seventh moon we eat melons; in the eighth we cut bottle-gourds.
In the ninth moon we stack straw, and gather dandelion leaves, firewood, and sumach bark to supply to our farmhands.

Rouk ngwat mluk out gup ouk; 六月食鬱及薁
tsit ngwat phràng gwi gup nhouk. 七月烹葵及菽
Prèt ngwat pròk tzòuc. Gip ngwat gwàk lòuc, 八月剝棗　十月穫稻
way tsec thoun tziwc, luc krèts muyc douc. 為此春酒　以介眉壽
Tsit ngwat mluk kwrà; prèt ngwat tònt gà. 七月食瓜　八月斷壺
Kouc ngwat nhouk tsa; tsàc là sin thra, sluks ngàyc nòung pa. 九月叔苴　采荼薪樗　食我農夫

In the ninth moon we pound the soil of the vegetable plot to turn it into a threshing floor. In the tenth moon we harvest grain:
foxtail and broomcorn millet, slow-ripening and fast-ripening cereals—grain, together with hemp, beans, and wheat.
And the word is: "Now then, you farmhands of ours:
now you've got our grain in, you need to go up and get to work on the palace.
By day you'll gather cogon grass, and in the evenings you'll twist it into rope.
As a priority, climb up on the roof and repair any leaks. Then you can start sowing the grain crops."

Kouc ngwat trouk drang pàs, gip ngwat nùp wày kràs: 九月築場圃　十月納禾稼
nhac tzuk drong rouk—wày mràу nhouk mràk. 黍稷重穋　禾麻菽麥
"Tzay ngàyc nòung pa: 嗟我農夫
ngàyc kràs kuts dòng, dyank nup tup koung kòng. 我稼既同　上入執宮功
Trous nec wa mròu, syaw nec sàk lòu. 晝爾于茅　宵爾索綯
Kuk gu mlung òk, gu lhuc pàys pràk kòk." 亟其乘屋　其始播百穀

During the second moon we chisel ice out of the ponds, with a *droung droung* sound;
in the third moon we store it in the ice-house.
During the fourth moon, early in the morning, a sacrificial dish of lamb and garlic is offered.
In the ninth moon, plants wither and we get hoar-frost; in the tenth, we sweep the threshing-floor clean.
A pair of jars of wine are contributed for a feast, and we hear "Lambs have been slaughtered, come up to the meeting hall!"
Raising the water-buffalo horn of wine, the toast is "Ten thousand years of life without end!"

Nits tu nit dzàwk prung, droung-droung; 二之日鑿冰沖沖
sùm tu nit nùp wa rung ums. 三之日納于凌陰
Slits tu nit gu tzòuc, nghans kàw tzats kouc. 四之日其蚤 獻羔祭韭
Kouc ngwat siwk shang; gip ngwat lìwk drang. 九月肅霜 十月滌場
Bùng tziwc se hang, wat "Shàt kàw yang, tzì payc klòng dàng!" 朋酒斯饗 曰殺羔羊 躋彼公堂
K'hlung payc syuyc kwràng, "Màns douc ma kang!" 稱彼兕觥 萬壽無疆

"Fire descends" means that the reddish Fire Star, Antares, passed its highest point in the sky by nightfall. The movements of Antares were taken to signal the proper dates for various agricultural activities.

The poem deals with many items of everyday rural life three millennia ago using words which are sometimes thoroughly obsolete, and some of the traditional explanations are easier to accept than others. So for instance the tools which are used to prune mulberry trees (verse 3, stich 4) are called *pac* and *tsang*, and there is little doubt that *pac* means "axe"—it remains the word for "axe" in the modern language. But *tsang* is an obsolete word. The Chinese tradition claims that *tsang*, too, was a kind of axe, and that the difference between *pac* and *tsang* was the shape of the holes where the handle fitted through the head. That sounds like a desperate invention by someone who had no idea what a *tsang* was; and in my experience axes are not the most useful tools for pruning trees. I notice that what is now the usual word for "saw" (in modern Chinese, 'ju') never occurs in the *Odes*—that proves nothing, but it does at least create a possibility that *tsang* meant "saw".

In verse 2, hoary mugwort, or "Dusty Miller" plants, *Artemisia stelleriana*, have leaves which are used to flavour dumplings. In verse 3, "silkworm moon" refers to the time when silkworms emerge from their cocoons, which they do in spring, to coincide with mulberry trees coming into leaf—their only food. *Dzùm*, "silkworm", sounds very like *sùm*, "three", so it may be that "silkworm moon" was an informal synonym for "third moon".

In verse 5 katydids, here probably the species *Mecopoda nipponensis*, are a group of insects known in Britain as "bush crickets", but since true crickets are mentioned later I have preferred the simple American name. This line displays careful observation of Nature. All these insects stridulate, but grasshoppers do this by rubbing hind legs against their wings, while crickets and katydids rub their wings together.

Sleeping in field shelters was done to guard valuable crops against predators, human or otherwise. Sleeping outside, under the house eaves, will have been done to catch some moving air on nights of sweltering heat. Windows will have been empty holes and outside doorways protected in summer by flimsy hangings; plaster turned these into better defences against winter cold.

Out and *ouk*, which the poet looked forward to eating in the sixth moon, were wild fruit: *out* were Oriental bush cherries (*Prunus japonica*), which are sour but good for cooking, while *ouk* was the dark red, grape-like fruit of *Vitis bryoniifolia*, which has no English name that I can discover; for the translation I call it "wild grape". For jujubes, see Ode 32. The bottle-gourd is also called "calabash", *Lagenaria siceraria*; it is eaten as a vegetable, or it can be hollowed out, dried, and used as a bottle. On *là*, translated here and in the next Ode as "dandelion", see Ode 237. *Thra*—Tree of Heaven, or Chinese sumach, *Ailanthus altissima*—is poisonous, but its bark and other parts of it have many medicinal uses—some important, for instance dealing with tapeworms, but ranging as far as curing baldness.

Many British readers will be familiar with the written form of the closing words, which I translate as "Ten thousand years of life without end!"—a wish we might see as contradictory, but the Chinese blurred the difference between eternity and a very long time. In the late twentieth century a huge number of cheap and colourful bowls were imported from China which had four Chinese graphs in circular cartouches spaced round their circumference, and they were these words *màns douc ma kang*.

These vignettes of rural life are delightful. But the overall impression created by this Ode seems oddly fumbling and amateurish. One might expect the months to be discussed in sequence, but sometimes a verse dodges back and forth (though see p. 33). There is some attempt to make individual verses cover coherent ranges of subject-matter, for instance verse 6 is largely about food and drink, but why does verse 2 repeat the point about issuing winter clothes when the rest of it is about the warm days of spring? And why is the point about Antares said three times? (A possible explanation, admittedly, would be textual corruption; if the *Odes* had to be reconstructed from memory, this one with its many repetitions of numbered moons would have been exceptionally difficult to get right.) Most activities mentioned are fairly major elements of a farming year, but surely sweeping the threshing floor could not take long? Perhaps the reason for including that was simply that the word for "threshing-floor" offered a convenient rhyme for "hoar frost"; but the rhyming and metre of the Ode are clumsy too. Verses 6 and 8 vary the four-beat rhythm by beginning with a pair of longer stichs—but why just those verses? Each verse has eleven stichs: sometimes we have a succession of stichs grouped by rhyming into pairs, interrupted by one stich that rhymes with nothing; other verses handle the odd number by including a sequence of three stichs all rhyming with one another.

155

Tu-whoo! 鴟鴞

Tu-whoo, tu-whoo! You have taken my chicks,
don't destroy my nest!
I cared for them, I devoted myself to them: you should have pity for my brood.

Thi-waw, thi-waw! Kuts tsoc ngàyc tzuc,　　　鴟鴞鴟鴞　既取我子
ma mhayc ngàyc lhit.　　　無毀我室
Ùn se, gun se; louk tzuc tu mrunt se.　　　恩斯勤斯　育子之閔斯

While the weather was still fair I tugged those mulberry roots free,
twining them to make window and door;
now, you base folk, do any of you dare scorn me?

Làc thìn tu muts um wac, thret payc sàng dàc,　　　迨天之未陰雨　撤彼桑土
driw-miws louc gàc.　　　綢繆牖戶
Kum nac gràc min, wùk kàmp moc lac?　　　今汝下民　或敢侮予

It was my claws that pulled up dandelions;
the straw bedding I gathered has left me with a poorly beak.
Are you telling me I haven't earned the right to my own nest?

Lac nhouc kit ka, lac shac ròt là;   予手拮据　予所捋荼
lac shac rhouks tzà, lac khòc tzout dà.   予所蓄租　予口卒瘏
Wat lac muts wuc lhit krà?   曰予未有室家

My feathers are worn, my tail is frayed.
My high perch is perilous, shaken by wind and rain.
All that's left for me is to make alarm calls.

Lac wac dzaw-dzaw, lac muyc syaw-syaw.   予羽譙譙　予尾消消
Lac lhit gyaw-gyaw, pum wac shac phyaw yaw.   予室翹翹　風雨所飄搖
Lac wi um hyàw-hyàw.   予維音嘵嘵

In the guise of an owl, a wife complains about her husband throwing her out while keeping their children.

Thi-waw seems so close to "tu-whoo", the standard English rendering of the call of the female tawny owl ("tu-whit" is the male's call), that the identification is hard to doubt. Why the bird metaphor, which might seem frivolous in the context of the woman's tragic situation? Could she be reminding the man of a carefree, fluffy nickname from courting days?

156

The Eastern Mountains 東山

We marched away to the eastern mountains—we went far away, with no home leave.
Now we're returning from the east, how dark and drizzly the weather is.
When we were out east, talking about home, our hearts yearned for the west
—we'd say "Let's run up some civvy clothes, and stop serving in the ranks with gags in our mouths".
This mulberry grove is crawling with caterpillars,
and now it's full of us soldiers, each lonely man sleeping under a cart for shelter.

Ngàyc dzà tòng shàn—lhòu-lhòu, pu kwuy.   我徂東山　慆慆不歸
Ngàyc rù dzis tòng, rìn wac gu mòng.   我來自東　零雨其濛
Ngàyc tòng wat kwuy, ngàyc sum sì pruy: 我東曰歸　我心西悲
"Kets payc dang uy, mut shuc gàng mùy".   制彼裳衣　勿士行枚
Went-went tac dok tung dzùc sàng lac.   蜎蜎者蠋　烝在桑野
Dòn payc dòk souk, yak dzùc ka gràc.   敦彼獨宿　亦在車下

We marched away to the eastern mountains—we went far away, with no home leave.
Now we're returning from the east, how dark and drizzly the weather is.
At home, cucumber-vines laden with fruit will be brushing against the eaves; there will be woodlice in the room, and spiders by the door.
The threshing-floor will be trampled by deer. Fireflies will be shining in the dusk
—they might look frightening, but really they are lovable.

Ngàyc dzà tòng shàn—lhòu-lhòu, pu kwuy.　　我徂東山　慆慆不歸
Ngàyc rù dzis tòng, rìn wac gu mòng.　　　　我來自東　零雨其濛
Kòyc-ròyc tu mlit yak lhays wa wac;　　　　　果臝之實　亦施于宇
i-ouy dzùc lhit, syòu-shyàw dzùc gàc.　　　　伊威在室　蠨蛸在戶
Thènt-thònt ròk drang. Wup lyawks syaw-gràng　町畽鹿場　熠燿宵行
—yak khàyc ouys luc, i khàyc gròuy luc.　　　亦可畏也　伊可懷也

We marched away to the eastern mountains—we went far away, with no home leave.
Now we're returning from the east, how dark and drizzly the weather is.
A heron is calling from an anthill. A wife is sighing in her chamber;
she's sprinkling and sweeping the floor, and stopping up the cracks. We march; and finally we arrive.
Masses of bitter melons are growing over the firewood pile of chestnut logs.
Since we last saw this scene, three years have passed.

Ngàyc dzà tòng shàn—lhòu-lhòu, pu kwuy.　　我徂東山　慆慆不歸
Ngàyc rù dzis tòng, rìn wac gu mòng.　　　　我來自東　零雨其濛
Kwàns mreng wa dìt. Buc nhàn wa lhit;　　　鸛鳴于垤　婦歎于室
shìc sòus, kwhung tit. Ngàyc teng; lout tits.　灑掃穹窒　我征聿至
Wuc dòn kwrà khàc, tung dzùc rit sin.　　　　有敦瓜苦　烝在栗薪
Dzis ngàyc pu kèns, wa kum sùm nìn.　　　　自我不見　于今三年

We marched away to the eastern mountains—we went far away, with no home leave.
Now we're returning from the east, how dark and drizzly the weather is.
An oriole is on the wing: its plumage is brilliant.
Here's a young bride about to leave for her new home, behind roan and skewbald horses.
Her mother's tying her apron in place; nine, ten rules she must follow now.
This new marriage is a very happy occasion. But how will things stand with our old marriages?

Ngàyc dzà tòng shàn—lhòu-lhòu, pu kwuy.　　我徂東山　慆慆不歸
Ngàyc rù dzis tòng, rìn wac gu mòng.　　　　我來自東　零雨其濛
Tsàng-kràng wa puy: wup lyawks gu wac.　　　倉庚于飛　熠燿其羽
Tu tzuc wa kwuy, wàng pràwk gu mràc.　　　　之子于歸　皇駁其馬
Tsin kìt gu ray; kouc gip gu ngay.　　　　　親結其縭　九十其儀
Kus sin khònk kràv—kus gwuc na tu gày?　　　其新孔嘉　其舊如之何

A troop of soldiers has longed to get home to their families; when they finally see their village after years away, they wonder how things will be between them and their wives.

Some authorities claim that serving soldiers were physically gagged to discourage chatter in the ranks. I cannot believe that. More likely, the gags were metaphorical: soldiers felt gagged because they could not talk back to officers, discuss orders, or perhaps even be heard to grumble.

The "cucumbers" of verse 2 are not the cucumbers we know, but members of the same family—probably one or other species of the genus *Trichosanthes*, some of which are eaten and others used in Chinese medicine. Fireflies seemed frightening because they were reminiscent of the will-o'-the-whisp phenomenon, which (according to Karlgren) the Chinese took to be "an emanation from the blood of killed men". But in reality fireflies are harmless, homely creatures. "Bitter melon" (verse 3) nowadays refers to *Momordica charantia*, but this only arrived in China in the fourteenth century A.D., so some other gourd-like plant must have been meant.

157

Broken Axes   破斧

Our axes were broken and our saws cracked.
The Duke of *Tiw* led his troops east; he brought order to the states of the world.
He had pity for our people, and enabled us to flourish mightily.

Kuts phàys ngàyc pac, wus kwhet ngàyc tsang.   既破我斧　又缺我斨
Tiw klòng tòng teng; Slits kwùk dec wàng.   周公東征　四國是皇
Ùy ngàyc nin se, yak khònk tu tzang.   哀我人斯　亦孔之將

Our axes were broken and our chisels cracked.
The Duke of *Tiw* led his troops east; he reformed the states of the world.
He had pity for our people, and bestowed great good fortune on us.

Kuts phàys ngàyc pac, wus kwhet ngàyc gay.   既破我斧　又缺我錡
Tiw klòng tòng teng; Slits kwùk dec ngòy.   周公東征　四國是吪
Ùy ngàyc nin se, yak khònk tu krày.   哀我人斯　亦孔之嘉

Our axes were broken and our chisels cracked.
The Duke of *Tiw* led his troops east; he united the states of the world.
He had pity for our people, and made us greatly blessed.

Kuts phàys ngàyc pac, wus kwhet ngàyc gou.   既破我斧　又缺我銶
Tiw klòng tòng teng; Slits kwùk dec dziw.   周公東征　四國是遒
Ùy ngàyc nin se, yak khònk tu hou.   哀我人斯　亦孔之休

For the Duke of *Tiw*, see p. 8. I have seen no good explanation of why broken tools should be an apt image for miserable conditions in the closing years of *Un* rule.

158

Shaping an Axe-Handle 伐柯

How do you shape an axe-handle? Without using another axe, you can't.
How do you get a wife? Without using a go-between, it's impossible.

Bat kày na gày? Puyc pac pu khùk.   伐柯如何　匪斧不克
Tsos tsùy na gày? Puyc mù pu tùk.   娶妻如何　匪媒不得

So, shaping an axe-handle, shaping an axe-handle, you don't have to look far for the pattern to follow.
This young lady is with me, and the *pèn* baskets and *dòs* bowls are filled with food for the wedding sacrifice.

Bat kày, bat kày, gu tzùk pu want.   伐柯伐柯　其則不遠
Ngàyc kòs tu tzuc, pèn dòs wuc dzans.   我覯之子　籩豆有踐

The idea seems to be: there is a right and wrong way to do anything, but doing it the right way is straightforward enough; and to prove it, here I am about to get married, with everything ready for the appropriate ritual.

159

The Netted Fish 九罭

The fish in the nine nets are salmon and bream.
You, when we met, wore a royal dragon coat and an embroidered robe.

Kouc wuc tu nga, dzòunt bang.   九罭之魚　鱒魴
Ngàyc kòs tu tzuc, kòunt uy siwks dang.   我覯之子　袞衣繡裳

The wild goose flies along the island.
When the duke goes home, there will be no place for us there; I can stay with you one more night.

Gòng puy tzoun tac.   鴻飛遵渚
Klòng kwuy ma shac; a nac sins k'hlac.   公歸無所　於汝信處

The wild goose flies along the scarp.
When the duke goes home, he won't come back here; I can sleep with you once more.

Gòng puy tzoun rouk.   鴻飛遵陸
Klòng kwuy pu bouk; a nac sins souk.   公歸不復　於汝信宿

So, you of the dragon coat,
don't go back with our duke,
don't make my heart grieve!

Dec luc wuc kòunt uy ì,　　是以有袞衣兮
ma luc ngàyc klòng kwuy ì,　無以我公歸兮
ma shuc ngàyc sum pruy ì!　無使我心悲兮

The poetess has become involved with a nobleman who arrived in the duke's retinue, but the duke and he are now due to depart.

Dzòunt is a Pacific salmon species, *Oncorhynchus masou*—Americans call it cherry salmon.

160

The Wolf　狼跋

The wolf treads on his dewlap and trips on his tail.
The prince's grandson is mighty fine, in his red slippers with silk bobbles.

Ràng bàt gu gà, tzùs trits gu muyc.　　狼跋其胡　載疐其尾
Klòng sòun dak pra, khlak sak kric-kric.　公孫碩膚　赤舄几几

The wolf trips on his tail and treads on his dewlap.
The prince's grandson is mighty fine—his reputation is unblemished.

Ràng trits gu muyc, tzùs bàt gu gà.　　狼疐其尾　載跋其胡
Klòng sòun dak pra, tùk um pu grà.　　公孫碩膚　德音不瑕

Karlgren sees this as a comparison between a young nobleman (whose red slippers show that he is ruler of a state) and a "fiercely springing wolf". To me, treading and tripping on his own body makes the wolf sound clownish rather than fierce.

Lesser Clarions

161

The Deer Bark 鹿鳴

Iw, iw, bark the deer, as they browse on lad's-love in the wild.
I have a distinguished guest; we strum the zither and blow the reed-organ.
We blow the reed-organ so its tongues vibrate; baskets of delicacies are served, and we partake.
This man who likes me, he's going to show me the ways of *Tiw*.

Iw-iw ròk mreng, mluk lac tu breng.	呦呦鹿鳴　食野之苹
Ngàyc wuc kràyc pin. Kàc sprit thoy sheng.	我有嘉賓　鼓瑟吹笙
Thoy sheng kàc gwàng, dung kwhang dec tzang.	吹笙鼓簧　承筐是將
Nin tu hòus ngàyc, gis ngàyc Tiw gràng.	人之好我　示我周行

Iw, iw, bark the deer, as they browse on wormwood in the wild.
I have a distinguished guest; his reputation is highly illustrious
—but he doesn't look down on us ordinary people. Yet noblemen treat him as a model and imitate him.
I have fine wine, and my distinguished guest is enjoying himself at our banquet.

Iw-iw ròk mreng, mluk lac tu hàw.	呦呦鹿鳴　食野之蒿
Ngàyc wuc kràyc pin, tùk um khònk kyaw.	我有嘉賓　德音孔昭
Gic min pu lhyàw, kwun-tzuc dec tzùk dec gràws.	視民不恌　君子是則是傚
Ngàyc wuc kic tziwc, kràyc pin lhuk ès luc ngàw.	我有旨酒　嘉賓式燕以敖

Iw, iw, bark the deer, as they browse on reeds in the wild.
I have a distinguished guest; we play the zither and the lute.
We play the zither and the lute; together we celebrate and soak ourselves in pleasure.
I have fine wine; my banquet is delighting my distinguished guest's heart.

Iw-iw ròk mreng, mluk lac tu gum.	呦呦鹿鳴　食野之芩
Ngàyc wuc kràyc pin. Kàc sprit kàc gum.	我有嘉賓　鼓瑟鼓琴
Kàc sprit kàc gum, wày ngràwks tsac tùm.	鼓瑟鼓琴　和樂且湛
Ngàyc wuc kic tziwc, luc èns ngràwks kràyc pin tu sum.	我有旨酒　以燕樂嘉賓之心

A provincial revels in playing host to a swell from the capital. The great man is actually treating him as a valued companion, and condescending to enjoy the host's best wines and food; and the host hopes to pick up tips on how they behave at the royal court.

Lad's-love, or southernwood, is a shrubby plant, *Artemisia abrotanum*. In Ode 245 it is burned to mask the stink of burning fat at a ritual sacrifice.

162

The Four Stallions 四牡

The four stallions are cantering steadily, but the *Tiw* road is long and winding.
Of course I long to go home,
but there's no skimping the king's service: my heart is full of grief.

Slits mouc phuy-phuy, Tiw lòuc oy-lay.	四牡騑騑　周道倭遲
Khuyc pu gròuy kwuy?	豈不懷歸
Wang shuc mayc kàc, ngàyc sum lhang pruy.	王事靡盬　我心傷悲

The four stallions are cantering steadily, but these black-maned greys are exhausted now.
Of course I long to go home,
but there's no skimping the king's service: I have no time free to relax.

Slits mouc phuy-phuy, thàn-thàn ràk mràc.	四牡騑騑　嘽嘽駱馬
Khuyc pu gròuy kwuy?	豈不懷歸
Wang shuc mayc kàc, pu wàng khìc-k'hlac.	王事靡盬　不遑啟處

Wood-pigeons are flying back and forth—some are on the wing, others on the ground.
They settle in a dense stand of cork-oaks.
There's no skimping the king's service, so I have no time free to look after my father.

Phen-phen tac touy, tzùs puy, tzùs gràc.	翩翩者鵻　載飛載下
Dzup wa pròu hwac.	集于苞栩
Wang shuc mayc kàc, pu wàng tzang bac.	王事靡盬　不遑將父

Wood-pigeons are flying back and forth—some are on the wing, others standing still.
They settle in a dense stand of boxthorn.
There's no skimping the king's service, so I have no time free to look after my mother.

Phen-phen tac touy, tzùs puy, tzùs tuc.	翩翩者鵻　載飛載止
Dzup wa pròu khuc.	集于苞杞
Wang shuc mayc kàc, pu wàng tzang muc.	王事靡盬　不遑將母

These four greys in harness are really flying along now.
Of course I long to go home.
I'll make a song about all this, and raise my mother's need for care when I report for duty.

Kràys payc slits ràk, tzùs djos chum-chum.
Khuyc pu gròuy kwuy?
Dec longs tzàk kày, tzang muc rù nhimp.

駕彼四駱　載驟駸駸
豈不懷歸
是用作歌　將母來諗

This Ode seems derivative. Not only the theme of royal service interfering with the poet's duty of care to his parents, but chunks of wording—the refrain "there is no skimping the king's service", and the birds "settling in a dense stand of cork-oaks", are word for word identical to passages in Ode 121 (though the former phrase recurs elsewhere too and must have been a standard slogan), and we shall see that "of course I/we long to go home", and "I/we have no time free to relax", are identical to passages in Ode 168.

163

Brilliant Flowers 皇皇者華

Brilliant are the flowers growing in the boggy area by the spring.
The field is full of troops, each man worrying that he won't make the grade.

Wàng-wàng tac wà wa payc ngwan slup.
Shun-shun teng pa, mùc gròuy mayc gup.

皇皇者華　于彼原隰
駪駪征夫　每懷靡及

My horses are colts; their six reins are as glossy as if wet.
Now I canter, now I trot, answering questions and discussing tactics with everyone.

Ngàyc mràc wi ko, rouk prus na no.
Tzùs dray, tzùs kho, tiw wan tzi tzo.

我馬維駒　六轡如濡
載馳載驅　周爰咨諏

My horses are dappled greys; their six reins are smooth as silk.
Now I canter, now I trot, talking with everyone about the plan of action.

Ngàyc mràc wi gu, rouk prus na su.
Tzùs dray, tzùs kho, tiw wan tzi mu.

我馬維騏　六轡如絲
載馳載驅　周爰咨謀

My horses are greys with black manes; their six reins gleam as if moist.
Now I canter, now I trot, sorting out decisions with everyone.

Ngàyc mràc wi ràk, rouk prus àwk nak.
Tzùs dray, tzùs kho, tiw wan tzi dàk.

我馬維駱　六轡沃若
載馳載驅　周爰咨度

My horses are piebalds; their six reins have been well matched.
Now I canter, now I trot, consulting and planning with everyone.

Ngàyc mràc wi in, rouk prus kuts kwin. 　　我馬維駰　六轡既均
Tzùs dray, tzùs kho, tiw wan tzi swin. 　　載馳載驅　周爰咨詢

I interpret the *teng pa* in this brief vignette as soldiers preparing for a battle, and the poet as a general going round ostensibly to check that everyone is on the same page with respect to the plan of attack, though just as importantly, no doubt, to hearten his men through personal contact with their leader—"a little touch of Harry in the night".

The dictionaries claim that *dray* and *kho* in the repeating stich both mean "gallop". But they are used contrastively here, and in more than one Ode they are applied to carriage horses, making "gallop" implausible. I wonder whether the experts on Old Chinese philology were also experts on the gaits of horses; here and elsewhere I take *kho* as "trot" and *dray* as "canter".

164

Cherry Trees　常棣

Suddenly the cherry trees show a dense flush of bright blossom.
Among all our contemporaries, there are none to match our brothers.

Dyang-lìts tu wà, ngàk phru wuyc-wuyc. 　　常棣之華　鄂不韡韡
Bam kum tu nin, màk na hwrang dìc. 　　凡今之人　莫如兄弟

When the tragedies of death and mourning arise, brothers really care;
gathering from highlands and lowlands, brothers seek one another out.

Sic sàng tu ouy, hwrang dìc khònk gròuy. 　　死喪之威　兄弟孔懷
Ngwan slup bòu luc, hwrang dìc gou luc. 　　邍隰裒矣　兄弟求矣

There are wagtails by the spring. Brothers rush to help when trouble strikes.
You may have good friends, and they may feel distressed, but all they'll do is sigh
　　endlessly.

Tzek-reng dzùc ngwan. Hwrang dìc kup nàns. 　　脊令在原　兄弟急難
Swi wuc rang bùng, hwank layc wrank nhàn. 　　每有良朋　況也永歎

Within four walls, brothers may wrangle; outside the house, they defend each
　　other against insult.
You may have good friends, perhaps many of them, but they don't help.

Hwrang dìc nghèk wa dzang: ngwàts ngac gu moc. 　　兄弟鬩于牆　外禦其侮
Swi wuc rang bùng, tung layc ma noung. 　　每有良朋　烝也無戎

Once death or disorder have been dealt with, peace and calm take over;
and although one has brothers, now they seem less important than one's friends!

Sàng ròns kuts breng, kuts àn tsac nèng. 　　喪亂既平　既安且寧
Swi wuc hwrang dìc, pu na wuc sheng. 　　雖有兄弟　不如友生

Set out your *pèn* baskets and *dòs* bowls, and drink your fill of wine.
When brothers are gathered together, all is peace, joy, and gentleness.

Pins nec pèn dòs, um tziwc tu os: 　　儐爾籩豆　飲酒之飫
hwrang dìc kuts gos, wày ngràwks tsac nos. 　　兄弟既具　和樂且孺

When wives and children are loving and united, it's like playing zither and lute.
When brothers have been getting on with one another, they have peace and joy
　　and are soaked in pleasure.

Tsùy tzuc hòus gùp, na kàc sprit gum. 　　妻子好合　如鼓瑟琴
Hwrang dìc kuts hup, wày ngràwks tsac tùm. 　　兄弟既翕　和樂且湛

Run your household well; give joy to your wives and children.
Study these things, plan for them—truly, isn't this the way?

Ngay nec lhit krà, ngràwks nec tsùy nà. 　　宜爾室家　樂爾妻帑
Dec kous, dec dà—tànt kus nan ghà? 　　是究是圖　亶其然乎

165

Trees are Felled　伐木

Trees are being felled, *tèng, tèng*; a bird calls, *rrèng, rrèng*.
It flies out from a dark gorge to settle in a tall tree.
That *rrèng* sound is the call it uses to make contact with its fellows.
Look at this bird: just as it responds to the call of its fellow,
　　how much more will humans not seek out their friends?
Provided the Spirits hear, then for sure everything will be harmony and peace.

Bat mòk tèng-tèng; tìwc mreng rrèng-rrèng. 　　伐木丁丁　鳥鳴嚶嚶
K'hlout dzis iw klòk, tsan wa gaw mòk. 　　出自幽谷　遷于喬木
Rrèng gu mreng luc, gou gu wuc hyeng. 　　嚶其鳴矣　求其友聲
Sangs payc tìwc luc, you gou wuc hyeng, 　　相彼鳥矣　猶求友聲
lhint i nin luc pu gou wuc sheng? 　　矧伊人矣　不求友生
Mlin tu lhèng tu, toung wày tsac breng. 　　神之聽之　終和且平

Trees are being felled, *hàc, hàc*. The strained wine is really delicious.
Now I have a fat lamb, I can invite my father's brothers.
Even if it happens that they can't come, that's better than ignoring them.

Oh, the food! And the floors sprinkled and swept! The delicacies I'm offering are set out in eight *krouc* bowls.
Now I have a fat bullock, I can invite my mother's brothers.
Even if it happens that they can't come, that's better than letting myself look mean.

Bat mòk hàc-hàc; she tziwc wuc slac. 伐木許許 釃酒有藇
Kuts wuc buy drac, luc sòk ta bac. 既有肥羜 以速諸父
Nèng lhek pu rù, muy ngàyc put kàs. 寧適不來 微我弗顧
À, tsàns shìc sòus, drin gouts prèt krouc. 於粲洒掃 陳饋八簋
Kuts wuc buy mouc, luc sòk ta gouc. 既有肥牡 以速諸舅
Nèng lhek pu rù, muy ngàyc wuc gouc. 寧適不來 微我有咎

Trees are being felled on the slope. There are lashings of strained wine,
the *pèn* baskets and *dòs* bowls are full of good food, and the uncles haven't stayed away.
It's when people have strayed from the path of right living that they have to make do with eating dry biltong.
As long as the wine lasts, they strain it for us, and when that runs out, they give us must.
Khùmp, khùmp, they beat drums for us, and with move after move they dance for us.
Now we're at leisure, we drink up this bounty.

Bat mòk wa brànt, she tziwc wuc yant. 伐木于阪 釃酒有衍
Pèn dòs wuc dzans; hwrang dìc ma want. 籩豆有踐 兄弟無遠
Min tu lhit tùk, kàn gò luc khryan. 民之失德 乾餱以愆
Wuc tziwc, shac ngàyc; ma tziwc, gàc ngàyc. 有酒湑我 無酒酤我
Khùmp-khùmp kàc ngàyc, tsoun-tsoun mac ngàyc. 坎坎鼓我 蹲蹲舞我
Lùc ngàyc gràs luc, um tsec shac luc. 迨我暇矣 飲此湑矣

A gentleman revels in entertaining his relatives (and in being the kind of right-living man who is in a position to offer hospitality).

Alcoholic drinks needed to be strained before they were good to drink. *Gàc*, in the fourth line of verse 3, was "must"—wine that has only just begun to ferment.

166

Sky Protects You　天保

Sky protects you and keeps you secure, and it does so very reliably.
It causes you to be generously provided for—what variety of good fortune is not heaped upon you?
It causes great increase in your resources, so that in no respect do you go short.

Thìn pòuc dèngs nec, yak khònk tu kàks. 　　天保定爾　亦孔之固
Pec nec tàn gòc—gày puk pu dra? 　　　　俾爾單厚　何福不儲
Pec nec tày ek, luc màk pu lhaks. 　　　　俾爾多益　以莫不庶

Sky protects you and keeps you secure; it enables you to reap your harvests.
In no respect is anything amiss: from Sky you receive a hundred blessings.
It showers wide-ranging good fortune upon you—days are all too short to enjoy it to the full.

Thìn pòuc dèngs nec; pec nec tzint kòk. 　天保定爾　俾爾戩穀
Khèngs ma pu ngay; douc Thìn pràk ròk. 　罄無不宜　受天百祿
Kròungs nec grà puk—wi nit pu tzok. 　　降爾遐福　維日不足

Sky protects you and keeps you secure, so that you have nothing which doesn't rise in prosperity
like a hill, like a mountain, like a ridge, like a lofty height,
like a river just at the top of its flood: so that nothing fails to increase.

Thìn pòuc dèngs nec, luc màk pu hung 　　天保定爾　以莫不興
na shàn, na bouc, na kàng, na rung, 　　　如山如阜　如岡如陵
na k'hloun tu pang tits: luc màk pu tzùng. 　如川之方至　以莫不增

Auspicious and ritually pure are the foodstuffs you offer to your forefathers
—the sacrifices of the four seasons to the princes and past kings.
The princes say "We foresee for you ten thousand years of endless life".

Kit kwèn way k'hyuc, dec longs hràws hang 　吉蠲為饎　是用孝享
—yawk, slu, tung, dyang, wa klòng sùn wang. 　禴祠烝嘗　于公先王
Kwun wat "Pòk nec màns douc ma kang". 　　君曰卜爾　萬壽無疆

The sympathy of the Spirits grants you many kinds of good fortune.
The straightforward honesty of the people yields your daily food and drink.
All the multitude of the Hundred Names emulate your "virtue" throughout the land.

Mlin tu tyàwk luc lu nec tày puk. 　　　　神之弔矣　詒爾多福
Min tu tut luc, nit longs um mluk. 　　　　民之質矣　日用飲食
Gwun rì Pràk Sengs pèns way nec tùk. 　　群黎百姓　徧為爾德

Like the brightness of the moon, like the rising of the sun,
like the durability of the Southern Mountains, which are never damaged, never fall,
like the evergreen quality of pine and cypress: for you, nothing by any chance can be less than eternal.

Na ngwat tu hwant, na nit tu lhung, 　　　如月之恒　如日之升
Na Nùm Shàn tu douc, pu kryan, pu pùng, 　如南山之壽　不騫不崩
na slong pràk tu mous: ma pu nec wùk dung. 　如松柏之茂　無不爾或承

A praise-song to the king. For centuries, Chinese kings and emperors were never really convinced that they needed to die; some put great efforts into searching for an elixir of eternal life.

The phrase "Hundred Names" in verse 5 needs explanation. Chinese names work differently from European names. Rather than selecting individual Christian names from a limited stock while having an endless variety of inherited family surnames, as in Europe, in China any words can be used for an individual's name (commonly two words are used, but they are not expected to fit together as a meaningful phrase), while there is a small fixed range of surnames. Hence "the Hundred Names" was a way of referring to the gentry collectively (the same phrase is used today for the Chinese population in general).

167

Gathering Fiddleheads 采薇

Gathering fiddleheads, gathering fiddleheads: the fiddleheads were just sprouting.
Do you call this coming home, is that what you call it? It's late in the year already,
and I have no house, no home to return to—thanks to the *Hamp-sòn*;
I have no chance to relax—thanks to the *Hamp-sòn*.

Tsùc muy, tsùc muy: muy yak tzàk tuc.   采薇采薇　薇亦作止
Wat kwuy, wat kwuy? Swats yak màks tuc,   曰歸曰歸　歲亦莫止
mayc lhit, mayc krà—Hamp-sòn tu kàs;   靡室靡家　玁狁之故
pu wàng khìc-kac—Hamp-sòn tu kàs.   不遑啟居　玁狁之故

Gathering fiddleheads, gathering fiddleheads: the fiddleheads were tender.
Do you call this coming home, is that what you call it? My heart is full of grief
—grief chills my heart. I'm hungry and thirsty.
There's no end in sight to my army duty, and I've never been given leave to go home and check on my family's fate.

Tsùc muy, tsùc muy: muy yak nou tuc.   采薇采薇　薇亦柔止
Wat kwuy, wat kwuy? Sum yak ou tuc.   曰歸曰歸　心亦憂止
Ou sum rat-rat; tzùs kri, tzùs khàt.   憂心冽冽　載飢載渴
Ngàyc noung muts dèngs, mayc shuc kwuy phengs.   我戍未定　靡使歸聘

Gathering fiddleheads, gathering fiddleheads: the fiddleheads are tough by now.
Do you call this coming home, is that what you call it? The year has reached midwinter.
There's no skimping the king's service, so I have no time to take a rest.
My grieving heart is truly sore. We marched away, without returning.

Tsùc muy, tsùc muy: muy yak kàng tuc.
Wat kwuy, wat kwuy? Swats yak lang tuc.
Wang shuc mayc kàc, pu wàng khìc-k'hlac.
Ou sum khònk kwus; ngàyc gràng, pu rù.

采薇采薇　薇亦剛止
曰歸曰歸　歲亦陽止
王事靡盬　不遑啟處
憂心孔疚　我行不來

What's that blossom? Just ordinary flowers.
What's that on the road? The prince's carriage.
Once our war-chariot was harnessed to a team of four strong stallions,
who dared to be inactive? In one month we fought and won three battles.

Payc nèc wi gày? Wi dyang tu wà.
Payc ràks se gày? Kwun-tzuc tu ka.
Noung ka kuts kràys, slits mouc ngap-ngap,
khuyc kàmp dèngs kac? It ngwat sùm dzap.

彼爾維何　維常之華
彼路斯何　君子之車
戎車既駕　四牡業業
豈敢定居　一月三捷

Our four-horse team is in harness—four sturdy stallions
which carry the prince, while we ordinary men follow on foot.
The team of horses is well trained; there are ivory-tipped bows and sharkskin
　　quivers.
Who dares not stand to arms each day, when the *Hamp-sòn* are so aggressive?

Kràys payc slits mouc—slits mouc gwruy-gwruy,
kwun-tzuc shac uy, syawc nin shac buy.
Slits mouc yuk-yuk, syank mec nga buk.
Khuyc pu nit noung, Hamp-sòn khònk kuk.

駕彼四牡　四牡騤騤
君子所依　小人所腓
四牡翼翼　象弭魚服
豈不日戒　玁狁孔棘

When we marched off, the poplars and willows were in glorious leaf.
Now we're on our way back, sleety snow is pelting down.
We plod slowly along the road, thirsty and hungry.
My heart is wracked with misery—no-one knows my woe!

Sak ngàyc wank luc, lang rouc uy-uy.
Kum ngàyc rù su, wac sot phuy-phuy.
Gràng lòuc dri-dri, tzùs khàt, tzùs kri.
Ngàyc sum lhang pruy—màk tre ngàyc ùy!

昔我往矣　楊柳依依
今我來思　雨雪霏霏
行道遲遲　載渴載飢
我心傷悲　莫知我哀

The *Hamp-sòn* were a nomadic tribe in the territory beyond China's northern border, who periodically made destructive incursions and had to be thrown back. On some accounts, *Hamp-sòn* was an alternative name for the Xiongnu, who were a major factor in Chinese history in the following period, and are thought in turn to be identifiable with the people which irrupted into Europe in the fourth century A.D. as the "Huns". The poet here seems to be on campaign against the *Hamp-sòn* while they have destroyed his home.

Like a number of fern varieties, royal fern, *muy*, produces sprouts which begin curled up like the head of a violin; young "fiddlehead greens" are edible.

It seems paradoxical that *lang*, i.e. Yang, "bright, sunny", as opposed to Yin, "shady", stands for the winter solstice in verse 3. The logic perhaps was that when the sun is furthest south, in winter, Yang is at its maximum.

The question and answer about blossom in verse 4 is certainly odd. Others have taken *dyang*

189

not as "ordinary" but in its other sense of "cherry tree", however this is no clearer: who could fail to recognize a cherry in bloom, and how could it be flowering in midwinter? In any case, what is the relevance of flowers here?

168

Bringing Out Our Carriages 出車

We bring out our carriages and draw them up here in the pasture.
Orders have come from the royal residence, bidding us to turn out.
We summon our men and tell them to load up.
The king's service is full of hardships—but it is urgent.

Ngàyc k'hlout ngàyc ka, wa payc muk luc.	我出我車 于彼牧矣
Dzis Thìn Tzuc shac, wuts ngàyc rù luc.	自天子所 謂我來矣
Draws payc bòk pa, wuts tu dzùs luc.	召彼僕夫 謂之載矣
Wang shuc tày nàns, wi kus kuk luc.	王事多難 維其亟矣

We bring out our carriages and draw them up here by the city wall.
We set up our tortoise-and-snake flag and our ox-tail pennons.
Our falcon banner and our tortoise-and-snake flag, how they flutter in the breeze!
My sad heart is full of anxiety, and my men are miserable and weary.

Ngàyc k'hlout ngàyc ka, wa payc kràw luc.	我出我車 于彼郊矣
Nhet tsec drawc luc, kans payc màw luc.	設此旐矣 建彼旄矣
Payc la drawc se, gà pu bàts-bàts!	彼旟旐斯 胡不旆旆
Ou sum tsyawc-tsyawc; bòk pa hwank dzouts.	憂心悄悄 僕夫況瘁

The king has commanded Second-Son *Nùm* to go and fortify *Pang*.
We bring out our carriages with a mighty rumble, our dragon and tortoise-and-snake flags gleaming in the sun.
Sky's Son has commanded us to fortify the *Shok* region.
Second-Son *Nùm* is magnificent: the invading *Hamp-sòn* are pushed out.

Wang mreng Nùm Droungs wank geng wa Pang.	王命南仲 往城于方
K'hlout ka pàng-pàng, guy drawc rrang-rrang.	出車彭彭 旂旐央央
Thìn Tzuc mreng ngàyc geng payc Shok pang.	天子命我 城彼朔方
Hràk-hràk Nùm Droungs; Hamp-sòn wa snang.	赫赫南仲 獫狁于襄

When we went away all that time ago, the millet had just come into flower.
Now, as we come back from battle, unkempt and unshaven, snow is falling and settling in the mud.
The king's service is full of hardships—we have no time free to relax.
Of course we long to go home, but we fear those bamboo slips bearing orders.

Sak ngàyc wank luc, nhac tzuk pang wà. 昔我往矣　黍稷方華
Kùm ngàyc rù sù, was sot tzùs là. 今我來思　雨雪載塗
Wang shuc tày nàns, pu wàng khìc-kac. 王事多難　不遑啟居
Khuyc pu gròuy kwuy?—ouys tsec krènt lha. 豈不懷歸　畏此簡書

[...]
Second-Son *Nùm* is magnificent, as he presses the attack against the Western Noung.
[...]
Hràk-hràk Nùm Droungs, bàk bat Sì Noung. 赫赫南仲　薄伐西戎

The days of spring are drawing out, and plants and trees are donning their fresh foliage.
Orioles are singing in harmony, and the mugwort gatherers are out in force.
We've seized prisoners for interrogation—we've captured a crowd of them. And now we can go home.
Second-Son *Nùm* is magnificent, and the *Hamp-sòn* won't be giving any more trouble.

Thoun nit dri-dri, hwuys mòk tsì-tsì. 春日遲遲　卉木萋萋
Tsàng-kràng krì-krì, tsùc ban gri-gri. 倉庚喈喈　采蘩祁祁
Tup sins wàk k'hyou; bàk-ngan swen kwuy. 執訊獲醜　薄言還歸
Hràk-hràk Nùm Droungs; Hamp-sòn wa luy. 赫赫南仲　獫狁于夷

Another (or perhaps the same) campaign against invasion from the north. We do not know exactly where *Pang* or *Shok* were, but we know that they were in this northern region of China—*Pang* will be mentioned again in Ode 177. The *Noung* of verse 5 were another non-Chinese people, whose territory lay west of the *Hamp-sòn*.

The flags and pennons described were typical for early China. Leaders commonly used animal tails to decorate their weaponry. Falcon flags, and doubtless also flags showing tortoise and snake (the pattern called *drawc*), were symbols of high rank.

The word *sù*, "bearded", in line 2 of verse 4 is written with a graph that is much more commonly pronounced *su* and functions in that pronunciation as a fairly empty grammar word. Most commentators have taken the graph that way here, and they may well be right to do so; the "bearded" reading of the graph applies only once elsewhere (and is questioned even there). But taking the word as "bearded" adds so much vividness to the image of soldiers on the road back from a campaign that I allowed myself to adopt that interpretation.

The *Odes* were written long before the invention of paper. The everyday surface used for writing was strips of bamboo, like those on which the army here receives its orders.

The received text of verse 5 begins with three lines that are almost identical to the opening lines of Ode 14, and they are out of place here; they have probably been copied into this Ode by mistake, in the same way as I suggested in earlier cases.

169

Glossy Pears 杕杜

See that lone pear-tree: how glossy its fruit are!
There's no skimping the king's service, but our days drag on one after another.
The calendar has come round to the tenth moon; my womanly heart is full of worry
—but by now the troops must have been released.

Wuc dèts tu dàc: wuc gwrànt gu mlit! 　　有杕之杜　有睆其實
Wang shuc mayc kàc, kès slus ngàyc nit. 　王事靡盬　繼嗣我日
Nit ngwat làng tuc; nrac sum lhang tuc; 　日月陽止　女心傷止
teng pa wàng tuc. 　　　　　　　　　征夫遑止

See that lone pear-tree: how abundant its foliage is!
There's no skimping the king's service, but my heart is sad and care-laden.
Trees and shrubs are looking lovely, only my womanly heart is sad
—but the troops will be on their way home.

Wuc dèts tu dàc: gu lap tsì-tsì! 　　　　有杕之杜　其葉萋萋
Wang shuc mayc kàc, ngàyc sum lhang pruy. 王事靡盬　我心傷悲
Hwuys mòk tsì tuc, nrac sum pruy tuc; 　卉木萋止　女心悲止
teng pa kwuy tuc. 　　　　　　　　征夫歸止

I walk up the northern hill, to gather the goji berries that grow there.
There's no skimping the king's service, but our parents are in a poor way.
Those ox-carts are slow, and the teams of beasts pulling them will be worn out;
but the troops can't be far off now.

Truk payc pùk shàn, ngan tsùc gu khuc. 　陟彼北山　言采其杞
Wang shuc mayc kàc, ou ngàyc bac muc. 　王事靡盬　憂我父母
Djànt ka thant-thant, slits mouc kwànt-kwànt; 棧車嘽嘽　四牡痯痯
teng pa pu want. 　　　　　　　　征夫不遠

Perhaps they haven't started yet?—they haven't arrived. In my misery I'm really on the ropes.
We've passed the date that was announced, yet they aren't here—creating a great deal of anxiety.
But the turtle-shell and yarrow oracles agree: both say the troops are near.
They must be close now.

Puyc tzùs, puyc rù; ou sum khònk kwus. 　匪載匪來　憂心孔疚
Gu dats, pu tits, nu tày way swit. 　　　期逝不至　而多為恤
Pòk dats krìc tuc, gòts ngan gunt tuc: 　卜筮偕止　會言近止
teng pa nec tuc. 　　　　　　　　征夫邇止

A woman yearns for the return of her man from military service, and tries to convince herself that she has not long left to wait. Apart from the fact that she misses him, the enforced absence of the young men at harvest time will have made things very difficult for the women and old people left at home.

170

Fish in the Traps 魚麗

There are fish in the fish-traps: *dyang*-fish and gobies.
Our noble host has wine, delicious and plenty of it.

Nga rès wa rouc: dyang shày.   魚麗于罶　鱨鯊
Kwun-tzuc wuc tziwc, kic tsac tày.   君子有酒　旨且多

There are fish in the fish-traps: bream and blennies.
Our noble host has wine, plenty of it and delicious.

Nga rès wa rouc: bang rìc.   魚麗于罶　魴鱧
Kwun-tzuc wuc tziwc, tày tsac kic.   君子有酒　多且旨

There are fish in the fish-traps: *ant*-fish and carp.
Our noble host has wine, delicious—truly delicious.

Nga rès wa rouc: ant ruc.   魚麗于罶　鰋鯉
Kwun-tzuc wuc tziwc, kic tsac wuc.   君子有酒　旨且有

How abundant it all is—how abundant, and how good it tastes!
How good it all tastes—how good it tastes, and how plentiful!
How much he has—how much, and how well-chosen!

Mout gu tày luc, wi gu kràv luc.   物其多矣　維其嘉矣
Mout gu kic luc, wi gu krìc luc.   物其旨矣　維其偕矣
Mout gu wuc luc, wi gu du luc.   物其有矣　維其時矣

A simple poem; but for most of human history, most people were hungry most of the time—so the situation portrayed here was worth "writing home about".

Some fish mentioned can be identified with more certainty than others. *Dyang* and *ant* seem to be different kinds of catfish: *dyang* may be a bagrid, perhaps *Pseudobagrus auranticus*, and *ant* may be a silurid, perhaps the Amur catfish, *Silurus asotus*. *Shày* may have been yellowfin goby, *Acanthogobius flavimanus*.

171

Barbel in the South Country 南有嘉魚

There are barbel in the south country: with baskets they're caught in great numbers.
Our noble host has wine; and his fine guests, they feast and enjoy themselves.

Nùm wuc kràynga: tung nan tràwks-tràwks.   南有嘉魚　烝然罩罩
Kwun-tzuc wuc tziwc; kràypin lhuk èns luc ngràwks.   君子有酒　嘉賓式燕以樂

There are barbel in the south country: with wicker traps they're caught in great numbers.
Our noble host has wine; and his fine guests, they feast and make merry.

Nùm wuc kràynga: tung nan shàns-shàns.   南有嘉魚　烝然汕汕
Kwun-tzuc wuc tziwc; kràypin lhuk èns luc khàns.   君子有酒　嘉賓式燕以衎

The trees in the south country have branches laden with fruit, and sweet melon vines climbing over them.
Our noble host has wine; and his fine guests, they feast and hearten him.

Nùm wuc kiw mòk, kàm gwàs rouy tu.   南有樛木　甘瓠纍之
Kwun-tzuc wuc tziwc; kràypin lhuk èns snouy tu.   君子有酒　嘉賓式燕綏之

There are wood-pigeons flying about; they're arriving in great numbers.
Our noble host has wine; and his fine guests, they feast and support him.

Phen-phen tac touy, tung nan rù su.   翩翩者鵻　烝然來思
Kwun-tzuc wuc tziwc; kràypin lhuk èns wus su.   君子有酒　嘉賓式燕佑思

Another celebration of a hospitable local ruler. *Kràynga* literally means "fine fish", but Legge tells us that this was a name for the barbel, and that barbel abound in the waters between Han and Yangtze rivers (which is what "south country" refers to).

A *tràwks* was a basket that was inverted and clapped down on a fish, which could then be extracted through a hole in the middle of the basket.

172

Sedge in the Southern Hills 南山有臺

Sedge grows in the hills of the south, and goosefoot in the hills of the north.
May you be happy, prince, the foundation of the nation!
May you be happy, prince, and live for ten thousand years, eternally!

Nùm shàn wuc dù; pùk shàn wuc rù. 　　南山有薹　北山有萊
Ngràwks kec kwun-tzuc, pròng krà tu ku!　　樂只君子　邦家之基
Ngràwks kec kwun-tzuc, màns douc ma gu!　　樂只君子　萬壽無期

Mulberries grow in the hills of the south, and poplars in the hills of the north.
May you be happy, prince, the light of the nation!
May you be happy, prince, and live for ten thousand years without end!

Nùm shàn wuc sàng; pùk shàn wuc lang.　　南山有桑　北山有楊
Ngràwks kec kwun-tzuc, pròng krà tu kwàng!　　樂只君子　邦家之光
Ngràwks kec kwun-tzuc, màns douc ma kang!　　樂只君子　萬壽無疆

Boxthorn grows in the hills of the south, and plum trees in the hills of the north.
May you be happy, prince, father and mother of the people!
May you be happy, prince; may your fame never cease to spread!

Nùm shàn wuc khuc; pùk shàn wuc ruc.　　南山有杞　北山有李
Ngràwks kec kwun-tzuc, min tu bac muc!　　樂只君子　民之父母
Ngràwks kec kwun-tzuc, tùk um pu luc!　　樂只君子　德音不已

Khòuc trees grow in the hills of the south, and *nrouc* trees in the hills of the north.
May you be happy, prince; how should your old age not be vigorous?
May you be happy, prince, and may your fame ever flourish!

Nùm shàn wuc khòuc; pùk shàn wuc nrouc.　　南山有栲　北山有杻
Ngràwks kec kwun-tzuc, gà pu muyc douc?　　樂只君子　胡不亹壽
Ngràwks kec kwun-tzuc, tùk um dec mous!　　樂只君子　德音是茂

Raisin-trees grow in the hills of the south, and catalpas in the hills of the north.
May you be happy, prince; how should you not live to a grey-haired old age?
May you be happy, prince, and may you protect and govern well your descendants!

Nùm shàn wuc koc; pùk shàn wuc yoc.　　南山有枸　北山有楰
Ngràwks kec kwun-tzuc, gà pu gwàng kòc?　　樂只君子　胡不黃耇
Ngràwks kec kwun-tzuc, pòuc ngats nec ghòc!　　樂只君子　保乂爾後

A routine expression of loyalty to the ruler. This will be the ruler of a *pròng*, a state, rather than the king of China. But the expression *pròng krà*, equating the state with a family, is reminiscent of the modern Chinese word for "nation", 'guojia' (from Old Chinese *kwùk krà*); only "nation" in English carries this family overtone, "state" would be too bloodless in this context.

As in the case of the fish of Ode 170, here we cannot always identify the plants and trees with certainty. (And in this Ode the opening images seem to have no function beyond establishing rhyme words for the successive verses.) *Rù*, goosefoot or *Chenopodium*, is a genus of weedy plants (quinoa is one goosefoot species, though quinoa does not occur in China). For boxthorn see Ode 76, and for *khòuc* and *nrouc* trees see Ode 115. *Koc*, the oriental raisin tree (*Hovenia dulcis*), is a tree bearing a raisin-like fruit, and *yoc* is some kind of catalpa, perhaps Manchurian catalpa (*Catalpa bungei*).

The closing wish, about governing descendants well, sounds to a Westerner like a reference merely to the ruler's children. But after the ruler dies, he becomes an ancestor, and ancestors continued to rule their descendants from generation to generation.

173

Lad's-Love 蓼蕭

The lad's-love grows tall; everything is soaked in dew.
I've met my lord now, and my heart is unburdened.
We talk and laugh happily, so that we have real joy and tranquillity.

Riwk payc sìw se; rìn ràks shac ì.　　　蓼彼蕭斯　零露湑兮
Kuts kèns kwun-tzuc, ngàyc sum sac ì.　　既見君子　我心寫兮
Èns saws ngac ì, dec luc wuc las k'hlac ì.　燕笑語兮　是以有譽處兮

The lad's-love grows tall; everything is weighed down with dew.
I've met my lord now; he fills life with good feeling and brightness.
May his strength never fail—long life to him, and may his fame never perish!

Riwk payc sìw se; rìn ràks nang-nang.　　蓼彼蕭斯　零露瀼瀼
Kuts kèns kwun-tzuc, way rhonk, way kwàng.　既見君子　為龍為光
Gu tùk pu shank, douc khòuc pu mang!　　其德不爽　壽考不忘

The lad's-love grows tall; everything is wet with dew.
I've met my lord now, and I'm totally relaxed and happy.
He is an example to his brothers; Sky, give him strength, long life, and happiness!

Riwk payc sìw se; rìn ràks nìc-nìc.　　　蓼彼蕭斯　零露泥泥
Kuts kèns kwun-tzuc, khònk èns khùyc dìc.　既見君子　孔燕豈弟
Ngay hwrang, ngay dìc. Reng tùk, douc, khùyc!　宜兄宜弟　令德壽豈

The lad's-love grows tall; dew lies thick everywhere.
I've met my lord now. The harmonious jingle of his harness bells
　was answered by the tinkle of his metal-ornamented reins. He is the one in whom
　　countless blessings are united.

Riwk payc sìw se; rìn ràks nòng-nòng.　　蓼彼蕭斯　零露濃濃
Kuts kèns kwun-tzuc, lìw rùk droung-droung　既見君子　鞗勒沖沖
wàys ròn ong-ong. Màns puk you dòng!　　和鸞雝雝　萬福攸同

An anxious wife welcomes her husband home. For lad's-love see Ode 161.

174

Soaked in Dew 湛露

Everything is soaked in dew—until sun-up it won't dry.
Quietly we drink the night away, and no-one withdraws before he's drunk.

Drùmp-drùmp ràks se—puyc lang pu huy.　　湛湛露斯　匪陽不晞
Em-em yas um, pu tzouts ma kwuy.　　厭厭夜飲　不醉無歸

The thick vegetation is all soaked in dew.
Quietly we drink the night away, rounding off the feast in our clan hall.

Drùmp-drùmp ràks se, dzùc payc phoung tsòuc.　　湛湛露斯　在彼豐草
Em-em yas um, dzùc tzòung tzùs khòuc.　　厭厭夜飲　在宗載考

The goji-berry and jujube trees are soaked in dew.
The assembled nobles are both illustrious and loyal—great-hearted, every one of them.

Drùmp-drùmp ràks se, dzùc payc khuc kuk.　　湛湛露斯　在彼杞棘
Hènt yount kwun-tzuc—màk pu reng tùk.　　顯允君子　莫不令德

The tung trees and igiri trees are weighed down with fruit.
The nobles are at ease and merry—admirably behaved, every one of them.

Kus dòng, kus ay, gu mlit ray-ray.　　其桐其椅　其實離離
Khùyc dìc kwun-tzuc—màk pu reng ngay.　　豈弟君子　莫不令儀

The ruler is feasting his nobles.

175

The Red Bow 彤弓

The red bow is unstrung—he has accepted it and stored it away.
I have a distinguished guest, and I bestowed it on him with all my heart.
The bells and drums are set up, and all morning long I feast him.

Lòung kwung thaw ì—douc ngan dzàng tu.　　彤弓弨兮　受言藏之
Ngàyc wuc kràyc pin, troung sum hwangs tu.　　我有嘉賓　中心貺之
Tong kàc kuts nhet, it traw hang tu.　　鐘鼓既設　一朝饗之

The red bow is unstrung—he has accepted it and attached a frame to it.
I have a distinguished guest, and I rejoice in him with all my heart.
The bells and drums are set up, and all morning long I honour and serve him.

Lòung kwung thaw ì—douc ngan tzùs tu.　　彤弓弨兮　受言載之
Ngàyc wuc kràyc pin, troung sum huc tu.　　我有嘉賓　中心喜之
Tong kàc kuts nhet, it traw wus tu.　　鐘鼓既設　一朝右之

The red bow is unstrung—he has taken it and put it in its case.
I have a distinguished guest, and I love him with all my heart.
The bells and drums are set up, and all morning long I drink his health.

Lòung kwung thaw ì—douc ngan kòu tu.　　彤弓弨兮　受言櫜之
Ngàyc wuc kràyc pin, troung sum hòus tu.　　我有嘉賓　中心好之
Tong kàc kuts nhet, it traw dou tu.　　鐘鼓既設　一朝醻之

A red bow was a ceremonial gift, presented by the king to a nobleman as a symbol of royal favour. Among the verbs applied to the bow in successive verses, *tzùs* in verse 2 is a vague, ambiguous word; one idea is that it refers here to attaching the bow to a bamboo frame which prevents it from warping.

176

Flourishing Mugwort　菁菁者莪

Mugwort plants are flourishing in the middle of the slope.
Now I've seen my man, I rejoice and treat him with ceremony.

Tzèng-tzèng tac ngày, dzùc payc troung ày.　　菁菁者莪　在彼中阿
Kuts kèns kwun-tzuc, ngràwks tsac wuc ngay.　　既見君子　樂且有儀

Mugwort plants are flourishing in the middle of the islet.
Now I've seen my man, my heart is filled with joy.

Tzèng-tzèng tac ngày, dzùc payc troung tuc.　　菁菁者莪　在彼中沚
Kuts kèns kwun-tzuc, ngàyc sum tzùk huc.　　既見君子　我心則喜

Mugwort plants are flourishing on the middle of the hillock.
Now I've seen my man, he presents me with a hundred strings of cowries.

Tzèng-tzèng tac ngày, dzùc payc troung rung.　　菁菁者莪　在彼中陵
Kuts kèns kwun-tzuc, slèk ngàyc pràk bùng.　　既見君子　錫我百朋

Poplar-wood boats are floating about, some low in the water, others riding high.
Now I've seen my man, my heart is at ease.

Bum-bum lang tou, tzùs drum, tzùs bou. 汎汎楊舟　載沉載浮
Kuts kèns kwun-tzuc, ngàyc sum tzùk hou. 既見君子　我心則休

A routine expression of a wife's relief when her husband returns home safely. Cowrie shells were valuable items, indeed the graphic element 貝 which occurs in many Chinese words for valuable objects, or concepts related to value, began as a picture of a cowrie. Strings of a standard number of cowrie shells were an early form of currency—and when the Chinese made metal coins, until recently they were made with holes in the middle so they could be held on strings.

177

The Sixth Moon　六月

In the sixth moon the world goes to sleep to escape the summer heat—yet we were fettling the war chariots!
Our teams of stallions were sturdy; we loaded up the uniform suits of armour.
The *Hamp-sòn* were thoroughly ablaze, so that we were hard pressed.
The king arrived to send off an expedition, to rescue his Royal Domain.

Rouk ngwat sì-sì; noung ka kuts rhuk. 六月棲棲　戎車既飭
Slits mouc gwruy-gwruy, dzùs dec dyang buk. 四牡騤騤　載是常服
Hamp-sòn khònk thuks, ngàyc dec longs krùs. 玁狁孔熾　我是用急
Wang wa k'hlout teng, luc kwhang wang kwùk. 王于出征　以匡王國

We formed teams of four black horses, matched by ability, and we trained them as laid down in regulations.
Only in this sixth moon was our armour completed
—our armour was completed in the Thirty Li factory.
The king arrived to send off an expedition, to help Sky's Son.

Bis mout slits rè, gràn tu wi tzùk. 比物四驪　閑之維則
Wi tsec rouk ngwat, kuts deng ngàyc buk 維此六月　既成我服
—ngàyc buk kuts deng, wa sùm gip ruc. 我服既成　于三十里
Wang wa k'hlout teng, luc tzàys Thìn Tzuc. 王于出征　以佐天子

Our four-stallion teams were long- and wide-bodied; their size was imposing.
We pressed our attack on the *Hamp-sòn*—and we achieved marvellous feats of prowess.
We perform military service in a highly disciplined, well-trained fashion
—we perform military service to safeguard the Royal Domain.

Slits mouc siw kwànk, gu dàts wuc ngong. 四牡脩廣　其大有顒
Bàk bat Hamp-sòn, luc tzòs pra kòng. 薄伐玁狁　以奏膚功
Wuc ngam, wuc yuk, kong mac tu buk 有嚴有翼　共武之服
—kong mac tu buk, luc dèngs wang kwùk. 共武之服　以定王國

The *Hamp-sòn* have no strategic sense. They just poured through *Tzaw* and *Gwàk*,
and overran *Gàwc* and *Pang*, even getting as far as the north side of the *Kèng*
    valley.
But we of the bird-embroidered banners, our white pennons shining in the sun,
used our ten largest war-chariots to open up a path for our army.

Hamp-sòn puyc dàk, tenk kac Tzaw Gwàk,	獫狁匪度　整居焦穫
tsum Gàwc gup Pang, tits wa Kèng lang.	侵鎬及方　至于涇陽
Tuk mun tìwc tang, bràk bàts rrang-rrang,	織文鳥章　白旆央央
ngon noung gip mlungs, luc sùns khìc gràng.	元戎十乘　以先啟行

The war-chariots advanced steadily, without jolting, impressing with their size.
The four-stallion teams advanced unswerving—unswerving, and well-disciplined.
Whoosh, we fell on the *Hamp-sòn*, and pushed them right back to the Great Plain.
Our general *Kit-pac*, great in peacetime and in war, showed himself a model for
    the myriad States.

Noung ka kuts àn, na trits, na nghan.	戎車既安　如輊如軒
Slits mouc kuts git—kuts git tsac gràn.	四牡既佶　既佶且閑
Phàk bat Hamp-sòn, tits wa Thàts Ngwan.	薄伐獫狁　至于大原
Mun mac Kit-pac, màns pròng way nghans.	文武吉甫　萬邦為憲

Kit-pac feasted and rejoiced, having been blessed with great good fortune.
We had got home from *Gàwc* after an enormously long march.
Kit wined and dined those close to him, on roast turtle and minced carp.
Now, who do you suppose was there? Yes, yours filially and fraternally, Second-
    Son *Trang*!

Kit-pac èns huc, kuts tày douc thruc.	吉甫燕喜　既多受祉
Rù kwuy dzis Gàwc, ngàyc gràng wrank kwuc.	來歸自鎬　我行永久
Ums ngas ta wuc, bròu pet kòts ruc.	飲御諸友　炰鱉膾鯉
Gò douy dzùc luc? Trang Droungs hràws wuc.	侯誰在矣　張仲孝友

A warrior reminisces about a campaign to deal with a *Hamp-sòn* incursion into the *Tiw* royal domain—believed to have occurred in 827. In terms of the larger China of today, the *Hamp-sòn* homeland was in and around Shanxi province; the "Great Plain" (in modern Chinese, Taiyuan) was on their border—it is now the name of the largest city of Shanxi. The campaign was led by *Wint Kit-pac*, who is known to history independently—we shall meet him again as author of two later Odes. This Ode was evidently written by one Second-Son *Trang*, who introduces himself rather archly in the closing lines.

The tribesmen are described in verse 4 as getting as far south as *Kèng lang*, that is, the "sunny" (i.e. northern) side of the valley of the river *Kèng* (see Ode 35). In its modern pronunciation, Jingyang, this is the name of a town twenty miles north of Xi'an. Other places mentioned cannot all be identified (at least, identifications in the commentary tradition seem contradictory); *Gàwc* although sharing its name with the dynastic capital must refer here to some other place.

The closing words of verse 2 sound as though "Sky's Son" refers to someone other than the *Tiw* king, yet these would normally be different ways of speaking about the same man. And more problematically, nobody knows what the line in that verse about "thirty li" (a distance of some ten miles) is saying. Traditional commentators held that it referred to the distance troops march in a day, which might be so but fails to make sense in context. My suggestion that it was the proper name of a battledress factory is probably wrong, but feels at least as plausible as others' offerings. Then, the word *buk* has several different meanings, and Karlgren held that since the instances in verses 1 and 2 clearly refer to garments (military uniforms, probably incorporating armour, thus worn during battle itself rather than on the march), the word must be given the same interpretation in verse 3, where he translates the repeated line as "we provided the war clothes". But that would be a bathetic boast; surely *buk* there must be taken in its other sense of "serve, service"? The *na trits, na nghan* line in verse 5 is another mystery, where again my translation is offered very tentatively.

178

Harvesting White Millet 采芑

Well, we were harvesting white millet
in the new stretch of land—in those acres that were first ploughed this year.
Then Third-Son *Pang* arrived to pitch camp.
He's got three thousand chariots, every one of them helping to protect us.
Third-Son *Pang*'s a real leader.
He had his four dappled grey horses harnessed to his chariot—they step immaculately.
His great chariot is bright red.
It has a bamboo-mat cover, fishscale hangings, and his horses have hooked breastplates and metal-ornamented reins.

Bàk-ngan tsùc khuc,	薄言采芑
wa payc sin lìn, wa tsec ju mùc.	于彼新田　于此菑畝
Pang Nhouk ruts tuc.	方叔涖止
Gu ka sùm tsìn, shi gàns tu lhuks.	其車三千　師扞之試
Pang Nhouk shout tuc.	方叔率止
Mlungs gu slits gu, slits gu yuk-yuk.	乘其四騏　四騏翼翼
Ràks ka wuc huk.	路車有奭
Lìmp put nga buk, kò ung lìw rùk.	簟笰魚服　鉤膺鞗勒

Yes, we were harvesting white millet in the new stretch of land
—in that central section.
Then Third-Son *Pang* arrived to pitch camp.
He's got three thousand chariots. His dragon flags and tortoise-and-snake flags shine in the sun.
Third-Son *Pang*'s a real leader.
There were cords round his wheel-hubs, his carriage-yokes were ornamented, and his eight harness bells were jingling.

He was in his officer's uniform
—his red knee-covers looked splendid. There was a mighty sound of waggons rolling.

Bàk-ngan tsùc khuc,
wa payc sin lìn, wa tsec troung hang.
Pang Nhouk ruts tuc.
Gu ka sùm tsìn, guy drawc rrang-rrang.
Pang Nhouk shout tuc.
Yyawk ge tsàk gràng, prèt ròn tsang-tsang.
Buk gu mreng buk,
to put se wàng. Wuc tsang chòng gràng.

薄言采芑
于彼新田　于此中鄉
方叔涖止
其車三千　旂旐央央
方叔率止
約軝錯衡　八鸞瑲瑲
服其命服
朱芾斯皇　有瑲蔥珩

See how fast that hawk flies—it's flown right up to the sky!
But now it stoops, and pounces.
Third-Son *Pang* arrived to pitch camp. He's got three thousand chariots,
every one of them helping to protect us.
Third-Son *Pang*'s a real leader.
His bell-men were beating their drums; they fell the troops in, and Third-Son *Pang* addressed them.
He's a great man, Third-Son *Pang*—one you can trust.
They were beating the bass drums, bom bom, marshalling the troops, and the side-drums were sounding, bim bim.

Wit payc puy snount—gu puy rìts thìn!
Yak dzup wan tuc.
Pang Nhouk ruts tuc. Gu ka sùm tsìn,
shi gàns tu lhuk.
Pang Nhouk shout tuc.
Teng nin bat kàc, drin shi kouk rac.
Hènt yount Pang Nhouk.
Bat kàc wwìn-wwìn, tuns rac dìn-dìn.

鴥彼飛隼　其飛戾天
亦集爰止
方叔涖止　其車三千
師干之試
方叔率止
鉦人伐鼓　陳師鞠旅
顯允方叔
伐鼓淵淵　振旅闐闐

You can wriggle, you *Kreng* tribe of southern barbarians—now our great nation is going to deal with you!
Third-Son *Pang*, our top man, knows how to make his plans watertight.
Third-Son *Pang*'s a real leader. He is going to take prisoners to interrogate—he'll capture loads of you.
He has masses of war-chariots
—masses of them, and good solid ones too! They sound like thunderclaps, like rolls of thunder.
He's a great man, Third-Son *Pang*—one you can trust.
He's already taken on the *Hamp-sòn* and smashed them. Come on, you *Kreng* people of the south: come and be terrified!

Thount nec Mròn Kreng—dàts pròng wi dou!
Pang Nhouk ngon ròuc, khùk jangs gu you.
Pang Nhouk shout tuc. Tup sins wàk k'hyou.

蠢爾蠻荊　大邦為讎
方叔元老　克壯其猶
方叔率止　執訊獲醜

Noung ka thàn-thàn
—thàn-thàn, thòun-thòun, na lèng, na ròuy.
Hènt yount Pang Nhouk.
Teng bat Hamp-sòn. Mròn Kreng rù ouy.

戎車嘽嘽
嘽嘽焞焞　如霆如雷
顯允方叔
征伐玁狁　蠻荊來威

The poet writes as a rural yokel overwhelmed by the sudden irruption into his world of an army expedition led by a famous general, on his way to deal with unrest among a southern tribe. Probably because of the mention of the *Hamp-sòn*, it is supposed that Third-Son *Pang*, who is celebrated here, took part in the northern expedition which was the subject of Ode 177, and has now been promoted into overall command for this campaign against the *Kreng* tribe of the Hubei area in the following year, 826.

Nga buk in verse 1 might be something like chain mail, which could look like fish scales; however *buk* can mean an archer's quiver, and the consensus has been that *nga buk* is a quiver covered with fishskin, perhaps shark's skin. (But would a quiver be large enough to strike this onlooker's notice?) There are various ideas about the "hooked breastplates" (which were clearly important in *Tiw* China—they crop up in other Odes).

The hawk seems to be a variation on the usual opening image, in this case delayed to verse 3. The idea seems to be that Third-Son *Pang*'s troops will swoop out of nowhere unerringly on the *Kreng*, like a hawk dropping out of the sky onto its prey.

The word *thount* which opens verse 4 means "to move" (and hence refers here to whatever barbarian activity has triggered this campaign), but it more particularly means to wriggle like an insect—hence a suitable verb to describe activity by "barbarians".

Legge points out that the figure of three thousand war-chariots must have been a gross exaggeration: there was no way that *Tiw* China could have put this many in the field. But that makes the phrase all the more realistic as uttered by a garrulous peasant who has never seen anything in his life before to match Third-Son *Pang*'s army.

179

Well-Built Carriages　車攻

Our carriages are well-built, and our horses well-matched.
Our four-horse teams are well-nourished; we harness them up and head east.

Ngàyc ka kuts kòung, ngàyc mràc kuts dòng.　我車既攻　我馬既同
Slits mouc ròng-ròng; kràys ngan dzà tòng.　四牡龐龐　駕言徂東

Our hunting chariots are fine, and our four-horse teams very robust.
In the east are the royal hunting-grounds; we harness our horses and go off to hunt.

Lìn ka kuts hòuc, slits mouc khònk bouc.　田車既好　四牡孔阜
Tòng wuc pàc tsòuc; kràys ngan gràng hyouc.　東有甫草　駕言行狩

Here are the gentlemen at the meet. Amid a hubbub they're checking off the footmen;
they set up the tortoise-and-snake flag and the oxtail pennon, so all is ready to hunt at *Ngàw*.

Tu tzuc wa maw. Sònt dà hàw-hàw;   之子于苗　選徒囂囂
kans drawc nhet màw. Bàk hyous wa Ngàw.   建旐設旄　薄獸于敖

We harness up our four-horse team—mighty stallions they are!
Amid red knee-covers and gilt slippers, the hunt meet is a splendid affair.

Kràys payc slits mouc—slits mouc yak-yak!   駕彼四牡　四牡奕奕
Khlak put kum sak, gòts dòng wuc lak.   赤市金舄　會同有繹

Thimbles and armlets have been donned in turn; bowstrings have been tightened and arrows fletched.
The bowmen have been grouped into matched teams; they'll help us build up a stack of game.

Kwèt gip kuts tsis, kwung lhic kuts dìw.   決拾既次　弓矢既調
Mlaks-pa kuts dòng, djas ngàyc klac dzes.   射夫既同　助我舉柴

Our four bays are in harness—the outer horses run straight and true,
not missing their step at the canter; and when the bowmen loose their arrows, they find their targets.

Slits gwàng kuts kràys—rank tsùm pu ayc,   四黃既駕　兩驂不猗
pu lhit gu dray; lhac lhic na phàys.   不失其馳　舍矢如破

The horses are neighing, *sìw sìw*, and the pennons flutter in long streamers.
Unless footmen and charioteers are diligent, the great royal kitchen will be short of meat.

Sìw-sìw mràc mreng; you-you bàts tzeng.   蕭蕭馬鳴　悠悠旆旌
Dà ngas pu kreng, dàts bròu pu leng.   徒御不驚　大庖不盈

The gentlemen are on foot now—all ears are pricked, no-one speaks.
Truly, these are princely men; and the day is a real success!

Tu tzuc wa teng—wuc mun, ma lhèng.   之子于征　有聞無聲
Yount luc kwun-tzuc; trant luc dàts deng!   允矣君子　展也大成

When *Mac* founded the *Tiw* dynasty, he planned to give it a new capital at *Ràk* (modern Luoyang). *Mac* soon died and *Ràk* did not become the capital until after the downfall of king *Iw* (p. 9), but during much of the Western *Tiw* there were regular royal visits to the eastern royal domain, with meetings of vassal rulers and grand hunting parties. This poem is thought to describe such an occasion under king *Swan*, who revived the *Ràk* visits after a lapse. *Ngàw* (verse 3) was a hill and district on the west side of modern Zhengzhou, sixty miles east of Luoyang.

Thimbles and armlets were archery accoutrements: the ivory thimble protected the thumb from being grazed by the bowstring, and the leather armlet had a similar function.

180

Auspicious Days 吉日

The auspicious day was a *mous* day: we sacrificed to the Spirits of the Soil and prayed.
Our hunting chariots were fine, and our four-horse teams very robust.
We went up the large hill to go after the deer herd.

Kit nit wi mous. Kuts mràs, kuts tòuc. 吉日維戊　既禡既禱
Lìn ka kuts hòuc, slits mouc khònk bouc. 田車既好　四牡孔阜
Lhung payc dàts bouc, dzong kus gwun k'hyou. 升彼大阜　從其群醜

The auspicious day was a *kràng-ngàc* day. We selected our horses.
Where herds gathered, does and stags were there in numbers.
We pursued them by the *Tsit* and *Tzas* rivers, the hunting-ground of Sky's Son.

Kit nit kràng-ngàc. Kuts chày ngàyc mràc. 吉日庚午　既差我馬
Hyous tu shac dòng, ou ròk ngwac-ngwac. 獸之所同　麀鹿麌麌
Tsit Tzas tu dzong—Thìn Tzuc tu shac. 漆沮之從　天子之所

Look at the middle of the plain—how broad and full of game it is!
Now the deer run, now they pause—some in groups, some in pairs.
We all head the herd off from escaping to left or right, to make things easy for Sky's Son.

Tam payc troung ngwan—gu gri khònk wuc! 瞻彼中邍　其祁孔有
Paw-paw, shuc-shuc, wùk gwun, wùk wuc. 儦儦俟俟　或群或友
Sit shout tzàyc wuc, luc èns Thìn Tzuc. 悉率左右　以燕天子

We've drawn our bows, arrows steadied between our fingers.
Now we shoot at a piglet; now we down a large water-buffalo,
so we can serve them up to our guests, while we pour them goblets of young wine.

Kuts trang ngàyc kwung, kuts gèp ngàyc lhic. 既張我弓　既挾我矢
Pat payc syawc prà; its tsec dàts syuyc, 發彼小豝　殪此大兕
luc ngas pin khràk, tsac luc tyawk rìc. 以御賓客　且以酌醴

The opening word, *kit*, is commonly translated "lucky", but it means more than just a day which happened to go well: *kit* is "auspicious" in the sense that astrology or other soothsaying techniques predicted good fortune. *Mous* days were the fifth, fifteenth, 25th, etc. of each sixty-day cycle; *kràng-ngàc* days were the seventh of each cycle. (I do not understand why the

205

activities of verse 1 happened on a different day from those of the following verses—perhaps the omens were consulted separately for sacrificing and for hunting?) *Mràs* was a sacrifice offered by expeditions where they camped, to ask pardon for disturbing the land by marching over it. (Some versions have a different word at this point, meaning that the sacrifice was offered to the ancestors of the huntsmen's horses.) The *Tsit* and *Tzas* were minor rivers of Shaanxi province, which flow together at modern Yaoxian, 48 miles north of Xi'an.

181

Wild Geese 鴻雁

Wild geese are flying—hear the *siwk*, *siwk* of their wingbeats.
We young men are on campaign, toiling wearily through the wilds.
If you pity us, spare a sigh too for the widowed mothers and solitary fathers we left behind.

Gòng ngràns wa puy; siwk-siwk gu wac.	鴻雁于飛　肅肅其羽
Tu tzuc wa teng, go ràw wa lac.	之子于征　劬勞于野
Wan gup grin nin, ùy tsec kwrùn kwràc.	爰及矜人　哀此鰥寡

Wild geese are flying—they are settling in the marshes.
We young men are on wall-building duty: we've completed a full eight thousand feet.
But while we do exhausting work, our minds are busy with thoughts of our peaceful homes.

Gòng ngràns wa puy; dzup wa troung drak.	鴻雁于飛　集于中澤
Tu tzuc wa wan: pràk tàc krì tzàk.	之子于垣　百堵皆作
Swi-tzùk go ràw, gu kous àn dràk.	雖則劬勞　其究安宅

Wild geese are flying, making their *ngàw-ngàw* distress call.
Intelligent people recognize that we are hard-working men;
stupid folk just call us cocky, overbearing soldiery.

Gòng ngràns wa puy, ùy mreng ngàw-ngàw.	鴻雁于飛　哀鳴嗷嗷
Wi tsec trat nin wuts ngàyc go ràw;	維此哲人　謂我劬勞
wi payc ngo nin wuts ngàyc swan kaw.	維彼愚人　謂我宣驕

According to the commentators, *gòng* and *ngràns* are large and small varieties of wild goose, but I suspect this was another case like *gu-rin* for "unicorn" (see Ode 11), and that *gòng-ngràns* may have begun as a single word for "goose".

182

Torches in the Courtyard 庭燎

What of the night?—It's not yet midnight.
The torches in the courtyard are burning bright.
The prince is on his way: his harness bells are tinkling.

Yas na gày ku?—Yas muts ang.   夜如何其 夜未央
Lèng ryaws tu kwàng.   庭燎之光
Kwun-tzuc tits tuc; ròn hyeng tsang-tsang.   君子至止 鸞聲鏘鏘

What of the night?—It's not over yet.
The torches in the courtyard are brilliant.
The prince is getting here: his harness bells are jingling.

Yas na gày ku?—Yas muts ngats.   夜如何其 夜未刈
Lèng ryaws tats-tats.   庭燎晣晣
Kwun-tzuc tits tuc; ròn hyeng hwàts-hwàts.   君子至止 鸞聲噦噦

What of the night?—It's almost morning.
The torches in the courtyard are still aflame.
The prince has arrived: I can see his dragon banners.

Yas na gày ku?—Yas hangs mdun.   夜如何其 夜鄉晨
Lèng ryaws wuc hwuy.   庭燎有輝
Kwun-tzuc tits tuc; ngan kwàn gu guy.   君子至止 言觀其旂

This Ode contains an interesting issue of poetics. The first two verses establish a rhyme scheme involving three rhyme words, in *-ang* and in *-ats* respectively. But there is no way that *mdun* "morning" in verse 3 could be heard as rhyming with *guy* "dragon banner". However, the graph in the central rhyming position of verse 3, which I have spelled *hwuy* to rhyme with *guy*, actually stands for either of two words each meaning roughly "flame, brightness"—the other is *wuns*, which could count as a rhyme for *mdun* (since an extra *-s* is commonly not seen as spoiling a rhyme). Chinese script gives a reader no basis for choosing between these two words, so can the graph be said to stand for both at once and hence, in a sense, all three words rhyme?

The progression between "on his way", "getting here", and "has arrived" is introduced into my translation to make sense of the poem. The original has the same phrase *tits tuc* in each verse.

VOICES FROM EARLY CHINA

183

The River in Spate 沔水

The river is in spate, flowing to pay court to the sea.
That hawk is rapid on the wing; now it hovers, now it stoops.
Ah, brothers, and all friends of the state:
nobody wants to think about the present disorders, yet who hasn't got parents?

Ment payc riw lhouyc, draw tzòung wa mhùc.　　沔彼流誰　朝宗于海
Wit payc puy snount; tzùs puy, tzùs tuc.　　　　鴥彼飛隼　載飛載止
Tzay, ngàyc hwrang dìc, pròng nin ta wuc:　　　嗟我兄弟　邦人諸友
màk khènk nìms ròns, douy ma bac muc?　　　莫肯念亂　誰無父母

The river is in spate, it's in full flow.
That hawk is rapid on the wing; now it hovers, now it soars.
When I think about the dissidents, I can't sit still—I stand up and pace about.
The grief in my heart can't be dissipated or ignored.

Ment payc riw lhouyc, gu riw lhang-lhang.　　沔彼流水　其流湯湯
Wit payc puy snount; tzùs puy, tzùs lang.　　　鴥彼飛隼　載飛載揚
Nìms payc pu tzek, tzùs khuc, tzùs gràng.　　　念彼不蹟　載起載行
Sum tu ou luc pu khàyc mec mang.　　　　　　心之憂矣　不可彌忘

That hawk is rapid on the wing; it's flying along the middle hill.
People's lying gossip: why does no-one stamp it out?
My friends, be careful. How fast troublemaking talk is growing!

Wit payc puy snount, shout payc troung rung.　鴥彼飛隼　率彼中陵
Min tu ngòy ngan, nèng màk tu drung?　　　　民之訛言　寧莫之懲
Ngàyc wuc, krengs luc. Djàms ngan gu hung!　　我友敬矣　讒言其興

Now the snows have melted, the seaward-flowing river is like a vassal demonstrating loyalty by travelling to the royal court with a baggage-train loaded with tribute.
　　The poet and his audience can look after themselves if unrest grows, but their parents are elderly and defenceless.

184

A Crane is Calling 鶴鳴

A crane is calling in the Nine Marshes—the sound carries over the countryside.
A fish dives to the bottom of the pond ... or perhaps it swims in the shallows by the islet.

I delight in this garden!
Sandalwood trees grow here, with a litter of dead leaves below them.
Stones from other hills can serve as whetstones!

Gàwk mreng wa Kouc Drak, hyeng muns wa lac. 鶴鳴于九澤　聲聞于野
Nga dzem dzùc wwìn, wùk dzùc wa tac. 魚潛在淵　或在于渚
Ngràwks payc tu wan. 樂彼之園
Wan wuc doc dàn, gu gràc wi lhàk. 爰有樹檀　其下維蘀
Lhày shàn tu dak, khàyc luc way tsàk. 他山之石　可以為錯

A crane is calling in the Nine Marshes—the sound carries up to the sky.
A fish swims in the shallows by the islet ... or perhaps it dives to the bottom of the pond.
I delight in this garden!
Sandalwood trees grow here, with paper-mulberry bushes below them.
Stones from other hills can serve to work jade!

Gàwk mreng wa Kouc Drak, hyeng muns wa thìn. 鶴鳴于九澤　聲聞于天
Nga dzùc wa tac, wùk dzem dzùc wwìn. 魚在于渚　或潛在淵
Ngràwks payc tu wan. 樂彼之園
Wan wuc doc dàn, gu gràc wi kòk. 爰有樹檀　其下維穀
Lhày shàn tu dak, khàyc luc kòung ngok. 他山之石　可以攻玉

A poem celebrating the joys of retirement, when a Chinese gentleman traditionally moved away from towns and areas of intensive agriculture to some hilly district (we don't know where the Nine Marshes were), where cultural pursuits and the beauties of Nature could be enjoyed undisturbed. The poet compares himself to a piece of rock: even stones can have economic value, but if you are looking for one to do a job of work, look elsewhere! In the poet's lazy garden no-one is under pressure. A fish can swim in the shallows or in the deep, just as the whim takes it. The dead leaves perhaps reinforce this picture: this is not the kind of garden that is kept obsessively tidy.

185

War Minister　祈父

War Minister, you are the king's claws and teeth:
why have you plunged us into anxiety, and given us no chance to stop and rest?

Guy-pac, wi wang tu jòuc ngrà: 祈父　維王之爪牙
gà tron lac wa swit, mayc shac tuc kac? 胡轉予于恤　靡所止居

War Minister, you are the king's defence officer:
why have you plunged us into anxiety, and given us no chance of respite?

Guy-pac, wi wang tu jòuc shuc: 祈父　維王之爪士
gà tron lac wa swit, mayc shac tic tuc? 胡轉予于恤　靡所底止

War Minister, this really isn't clever.
Why have you plunged us into anxiety? There are mothers having to preside over
    the sacrificial dishes themselves.

Guy-pac, tànt pu tsòng.   圻父　亶不聰
Gà tron lac wa swit? Wuc muc tu lhi ong.   胡轉予于恤　有母之尸饔

This Ode is believed to relate to an episode in 787, the year after king *Swan*'s forces had suffered a heavy defeat by northern tribes. Since *Swan* was running out of ordinary troops, he ordered the royal guard to take part in the campaign to reverse the defeat, and the poem is said to express the guards' resentment of a task which was no part of their normal duty of defending the king's person: the complaint is nominally against the minister of war, but really against the king. "No chance to rest" suggests that the troops are being sent north immediately after some previous demanding assignment.

    Sacrificial rites were normally carried out by men, and there seems to have been a rule that parents old enough to need care would not have all their sons called up for military service. Part of the complaint may have been that this rule was being ignored.

186

The White Colt　白駒

The pure white colt can feed on the new growth in my vegetable yard.
Hobble it, or tether it, so this morning visit can continue a long time,
and the one I call "The Man" can take his ease here.

Kyàwc-kyàwc bràk ko, mluk ngàyc drang maw.   皎皎白駒　食我場苗
Trup tu, wi tu, luc wrank kum draw,   縶之維之　以永今朝
shac wuts I Nin a an syaw-yaw.   所謂伊人　於焉逍遙

The pure white colt can feed on the bean shoots in my vegetable yard.
Hobble it, or tether it, so this evening can continue a long time,
with the one I call "The Man" as my distinguished guest.

Kyàwc-kyàwc bràk ko, mluk ngàyc drang hwàk.   皎皎白駒　食我場藿
Trup tu, wi tu, luc wrank kum syak,   縶之維之　以永今夕
shac wuts I Nin a an kràv khràk.   所謂伊人　於焉嘉客

The pure white colt has arrived, brightly caparisoned.
To me you are a nobleman, a lord: relax and enjoy yourself as long as you like!
Don't let yourself be pushed around: insist on taking some time out.

Kyàwc-kyàwc bràk ko, pays nan rù su.   皎皎白駒　賁然來思
Nec klòng, nec gò; lit las ma gu!   爾公爾侯　逸豫無期
Dins nec ou-you; mrant nec lòunt su.   慎爾優游　勉爾遁思

The pure white colt is down in the ravine,
with a bundle of fresh hay.—This man is as fine as jade!
Don't distance yourself from me mentally, making your words as rare as gold.

Kyàwc-kyàwc bràk ko, dzùc payc kwhung klòk,   皎皎白駒   在彼穹谷
sheng cho it lhok. Kus nin na ngok!   生芻一束   其人如玉
Mu kum nec um, nu wuc grà sum.   毋金爾音   而有遐心

The poet has an impressive guest and is anxious for him not to rush off too soon.

In the received text the last line runs "rare as gold or jade"; but including the word *ngok*, "jade", spoils the metre, and I take this word to be a mistaken repetition from the line before.

187

Don't Peck at My Grain   黃鳥

Oh you orioles, you yellow orioles:
don't settle on the paper-mulberries; don't go pecking at my grain.
The people of this state aren't willing to treat me decently.
I'm going to turn and head home, back to my own state and my own clan.

Gwàng tìwc, gwàng tìwc: 黃鳥黃鳥
ma dzup wa kòk, ma tròk ngàyc sok.   無集于穀   無啄我粟
Tsec pròng tu nin, pu ngàyc khènk kòk.   此邦之人   不我肯穀
Ngan swen, ngan kwuy, bouk ngàyc pròng dzòk.   言旋言歸   復我邦族

Oh you orioles, you yellow orioles:
don't settle on the mulberry trees; don't go pecking at my sorghum.
The people of this state are impossible to deal with.
I'm going to turn and head home, back to my brothers.

Gwàng tìwc, gwàng tìwc: 黃鳥黃鳥
ma dzup wa sàng, ma tròk ngàyc rang.   無集于桑   無啄我梁
Tsec pròng tu nin, pu khàyc lac mrang.   此邦之人   不可與盟
Ngan swen, ngan kwuy, bouk ngàyc ta hwrang.   言旋言歸   復我諸兄

Oh you orioles, you yellow orioles:
don't settle on the cork-oaks; don't go pecking at my millet.
The people of this state are impossible to live with.
I'm going to turn and head home, back to my father and uncles.

Gwàng tìwc, gwàng tìwc: 黃鳥黃鳥
ma dzup wa hwac, ma tròk ngàyc nhac.   無集于栩   無啄我黍
Tsec pròng tu nin, pu khàyc lac k'hlac.   此邦之人   不可與處
Ngan swen, ngan kwuy, bouk ngàyc ta bac.   言旋言歸   復我諸父

This and the next Ode are about women who have married unhappily, far from home.

188

Walking in the Countryside 我行其野

I'm walking in the countryside—it's shady below the Trees of Heaven.
Marriage brought me to live with you,
but you don't cherish me. I shall go back to my own state and family.

Ngàyc gràng kus lac—pets-puts gu thra.　　我行其野　蔽芾其樗
Mhùn in tu kàs ngan dzous nec kac.　　昏姻之故　言就爾居
Nec pu ngàyc houk. Bouk ngàyc pròng krà.　　爾不我畜　復我邦家

I'm walking in the countryside, gathering dock leaves.
Marriage brought me to stay with you,
but you don't cherish me. I shall go back home.

Ngàyc gràng kus lac; ngan tsùc gu hriwk.　　我行其野　言采其蓫
Mhùn in tu kàs ngan dzous nec souk.　　昏姻之故　言就爾宿
Nec pu ngàyc houk. Ngan kwuy su bouk.　　爾不我畜　言歸思復

I'm walking in the countryside, gathering pokeweed.
You spare no thought for your old marriage, you're only concerned to find a new wife.
But truly, she won't give you a better life: she'll just be different.

Ngàyc gràng kus lac; ngan tsùc gu puk.　　我行其野　言采其葍
Pu su gwuc in: gou nec sin dùk.　　不思舊姻　求爾新特
Deng pu luc puks; yak ke luc luks.　　誠不以富　亦祇以異

For "Tree of Heaven" see Ode 154. *Hriwk*, Japanese dock (*Rumex japonicus*), and *puk*, pokeweed (*Phytolacca decandra*), are plants used medicinally: the former for skin diseases, the latter for rheumatism, arthritis, and various other conditions.

189

Bright Waters 斯干

The waters of this beck are clear and bright; the Southern Mountains are dark,
massed together like stands of bamboo, lovely as pine trees.
Brothers should love one another
—they shouldn't plot against each other.

Dret-dret se kàn; iw-iw Nùm shàn　　澈澈斯干　幽幽南山
na trouk pròu luc, na slong mous luc.　　如竹苞矣　如松茂矣
Hwrang gup dìc luc, lhuk sang hòus luc.　　兄及弟矣　式相好矣
Ma sang you luc.　　無相猶矣

Our prince is like his female and male ancestors returned to life. He's building an 8000-foot residence.
Its doors face west and south.
There he'll stay, there he'll live; he will laugh there, he will talk there.

Sluc slok pis tzàc. Trouk lhit pràk tàc.   似續妣祖　築室百堵
Sì nùm gu gàc.   西南其戶
Wan kac, wan k'hlac; wan saws, wan ngac.   爰居爰處　爰笑爰語

The frames are tied into place one above another, and earth is pounded into them, with a *thàk! thàk!* sound.
Wind and rain will be shut out from here, birds and rats kept at bay.
It will be our prince's haven.

Yyawk tu kàk-kàk, tròk tu thàk-thàk.   約之閣閣　椓之橐橐
Pum wac you dra, tiwc nhac you khac.   風雨攸除　鳥鼠攸去
Kwun-tzuc you wac.   君子攸芋

Reverent as one who stands on tiptoe, rapid as an arrow,
winged like a bird,
soaring like a pheasant: this is our prince when he arises.

Na khec se yuk, na lhic se kuk,   如跂斯翼　如矢斯棘
na tiwc se grùk,   如鳥斯○
na hwuy se puy, kwun-tzuc you tzì.   如翬斯飛　君子攸躋

The courtyard is level, and the pillars perfectly vertical.
The main hall is spacious, and the private rooms ample.
Here, our prince will know peace.

Duk-duk gu lèng, wuc kròuk gu leng.   殖殖其庭　有覺其楹
Khròts-khròts gu teng, hwàts-hwàts gu mènk.   噲噲其正　噦噦其冥
Kwun-tzuc you nèng.   君子攸寧

Rushes on the floor, with bamboo mats laid over them. He'll sleep peacefully here.
Now he'll sleep, now wake, and say "Interpret my dream!"
What are the tokens of an auspicious dream?
They are: bears—black, and brown-and-white; and snakes, little and large.

Gràc gwàn, dyangs lìmp: nùc àn se tsump.   下莞上簟　迺安斯寢
Nùc tsump, nùc hung, nùc "Tem ngàyc mung!"   迺寢迺興　迺占我夢
Kit mung wi gày?   吉夢維何
Wi wum, wi pay, wi hwuyc, wi mlay.   維熊維羆　維虺維蛇

The Big Man interprets the dream:
The bears of various colours foretell boy children.
The snakes of different sizes foretell girls.

Thàts Nin tem tu:
wi wum, wi pay, nùm tzuc tu syang;
wi hwuyc, wi mlay, nrac tzuc tu syang.

太人占之
維熊維羆　男子之祥
維虺維蛇　女子之祥

When a boy child is born, he's laid to sleep in a bed;
he's dressed in a loincloth, and given precious jades to play with.
He cries lustily, *hwàng hwàng!*
He's destined to wear brilliant red knee-covers, as a ruler of noble houses, or even king.

Nùc sheng nùm tzuc: tzùs tsump tu djang,
tzùs uys tu dang; tzùs ròngs tu tang.
Gu khrup hwàng-hwàng.
To put se wàng; lhit krà kwun wang.

迺生男子　載寢之床
載衣之裳　載弄之璋
其泣喤喤
朱芾斯皇　室家君王

But when a girl child is born, she's laid to sleep on the floor;
she's thoroughly swaddled in clothes, and given tiles to play with.
She mustn't be naughty, but it isn't for her to decide what's right.
Her business will just be to learn to take care of food and drink, and not to give her parents anxiety.

Nùc sheng nrac tzuc: tzùs tsump tu drays,
tzùs uys tu lhèks, tzùs ròngs tu ngròyc.
Ma puy, ma ngay.
Wi tziwc mluk dec ngays, ma bac muc lu ray.

迺生女子　載寢之地
載衣之裼　載弄之瓦
無非無儀
唯酒食是議　無父母詒罹

A ruler is building himself a palace. (If we knew which ruler this was, we might understand the lines in verse 1 about brothers plotting against each other.) A grand residence in China was a set of buildings in a compound surrounded by a high wall (at this time made of pounded earth), so the outward evidence of grandeur was the length of the wall.

Thàts Nin, the "Big Man", was evidently a title for the chief soothsayer or shaman.

To avoid wasting resources on weakly family members, a newborn baby was shut away for three days; only if it was robust enough to survive this was it fed and accepted into the family. During that period of isolation, a boy baby was laid on a bed but a girl on the floor. The point about clothes, I believe, is that in the sweltering heat of a Chinese summer a boy could be comfortable in minimal clothing, but a girl had to be fully covered up.

There is a longstanding debate about the penultimate line, *ma puy, ma ngay*, which resonates so strongly with present-day issues about women's roles that it is worth explaining here. Following one interpretative tradition, I punctuate the line as two phrases: on the one hand a girl should not *puy*, do wrong, but on the other she should not, or could not, *ngay*. The basic sense of *ngay* is "decorum, dignified behaviour", and it would be odd to suggest that this is forbidden to girls; but by extension it can mean to judge what is decorous, so (on this intepretation) the poet is saying that girls must obey the rules but have no say in deciding what the rules are.

However, another ancient tradition groups *ma puy ma* as a single phrase: the girl child has "nothing which does not lack" dignity, hence everything about her is simple rather than grand —no jade toys or red knee-covers for a girl. Karlgren condemns the reading I have adopted as "very scholastic", and prefers this alternative as "simple and plausible". I find nothing simple in a triple negative.

190

No Sheep 無羊

Who says you have no sheep? There are three hundred in your flock.
Who says you have no cattle? You have ninety *noun* oxen.
Here come your sheep—all one sees is a mass of horns.
Here come your cattle, flapping their ears.

Douy wuts nec ma yang? Sùm pràk wi gwun.	誰謂爾無羊　三百維群
Douy wuts nec ma ngwu? Kouc gip kus noun.	誰謂爾無牛　九十其犉
Nec yang rù su, gu kròk jup-jup.	爾羊來思　其角濈濈
Nec ngwu rù su, gu nuc chup-chup.	爾牛來思　其耳濕濕

Some are grazing down the slope, some drinking from the pond,
some are asleep, others on their feet moving about.
Here come your herdsmen,
with their straw raincoats and bamboo hats, some with their lunch-bags on their backs.
There are thirty beasts per colour category, so you have all you need for sacrifices.

Wùk kròungs wa ày, wùk um wa dray;	或降于阿　或飲于池
wùk tsump, wùk ngòy.	或寢或訛
Nec muk rù su,	爾牧來思
gàyc sòy, gàyc rup, wùk buc gu gò.	何蓑何笠　或負其餱
Sùm gip wi mout: nec sheng tzùk gos.	三十維物　爾牲則具

Here come your herdsmen,
with firewood and kindling, with cock and hen birds.
Here come your sheep,
vigorous and robust—none are injured, and there's no murrein in the flock.
With arm-waving they're all got up into the sheepfold.

Nec muk rù su,	爾牧來思
luc sin, luc tung, luc tse, luc wung.	以薪以蒸　以雌以雄
Nec yang rù su,	爾羊來思
grin-grin, gung-gung, pu kryan, pu pùng.	矜矜兢兢　不騫不崩
Mhay tu luc kwùng, pit rù kuts lhung.	麾之以肱　畢來既升

And then the herdsmen dream:
they dream that locusts turn into fish, they dream that tortoise-and-snake flags turn into falcon flags.

The Big Man interprets the dreams:
locusts turning into fish, that means there will be bumper harvests;
tortoise turning into falcon flags, that means the household will have abundant offspring.

Muk nin nùc mung: 牧人迺夢
toung wi nga luc, drawc wi la luc.   螽維魚矣 旐維旟矣
Thàts Nin tem tu: 太人占之
toung wi nga luc, dit wi phoung nìn;   螽維魚矣 寔維豐年
drawc wi la luc, lhit krà jin-jin.   旐維旟矣 室家溱溱

The commentary tradition offers explanations for the rhetorical questions in the opening lines, and for the dreams in the last verse; but these explanations are too implausible to inflict on the reader. Then again, should we expect to follow the ideas of a 3000-year-old shaman about dreams?

When a set of animals were ritually sacrificed, they had to be all the same colour. If the herd has thirty beasts per colour category, it won't be difficult to assemble suitable sacrifices.

191

The Southern Mountain Crests 節南山

In crests rise those Southern mountains, high and rocky.
Majestic Sire *Wint*, the people are all looking to you.
Their hearts are as if aflame with grief; not one cheery word passes their lips.
The states are utterly run down; why do you not carry out an inspection?

Dzìt payc Nùm shàn, wi dak ngràm-ngràm.   節彼南山 維石巖巖
Hràk-hràk shi Wint, min gos nec tam.   赫赫師尹 民具爾瞻
Ou sum na làm, pu kàmp hays làm.   憂心如惔 不敢戲談
Kwùk kuts tzout jàmp. Gày longs pu kràm?   國既卒斬 何用不監

In crests rise those Southern mountains, smothered in luxuriant greenery.
Majestic Sire *Wint*, what does this irregularity mean?
Sky is sending down repeated epidemics in our time; deaths and discord are many and widespread.
In the people's talk there's never a loyal word, yet no-one is rebuking them for their moans.

Dzìt payc Nùm shàn, wuc mlit gu àyc.   節彼南山 有實其猗
Hràk-hràk shi Wint, pu breng wuts gày?   赫赫師尹 不平謂何
Thìn pang dzùns dzày, smàngs ròns gwùng tày.   天方薦瘥 喪亂弘多
Min ngan ma krày, tsùmp màk drung tzay!   民言無嘉 憯莫懲嗟

Great Master of the line of *Wint*, you should be the rock on which *Tiw* rests.
It should be you holding the states on an even keel; you should be binding together the Four Quarters.
You should be supporting Sky's Son, and making sure the people don't go astray.
Pitiless Bright Sky shouldn't be left to lay our population low.

Wint gec dàts shi, wi Tiw tu tì.   尹氏大師　維周之氐
Prank kwùk tu kwin, Slits Pang dec wi.   秉國之均　四方是維
Thìn Tzuc dec bi, pec min pu mì.   天子是毗　俾民不迷
Pu tyàwk Gòuc Thìn, pu ngay khòngs ngàyc shi.   不弔昊天　不宜空我師

You don't show yourself, you don't act in person, and the people have lost trust in you.
You don't look into problems, but you don't delegate, either—don't cheat the gentlefolk!
Stick to procedure, practise forbearance; don't let yourself get entangled with low-lifes,
or we'll end up with all the top posts filled by your wife's worthless kin.

Put koung put tsin, lhaks min put sins;   弗躬弗親　庶民弗信
put muns put shuc, mut mank kwun-tzuc.   弗問弗仕　勿罔君子
Lhuk luy lhuk luc, ma syawc nin lùc.   式夷式已　無小人殆
Sòyc-sòyc in rràks, tzùk ma mac shuc.   瑣瑣姻亞　則無膴仕

Bright Sky is not fair, it's sending down this full measure of discord;
Bright Sky is not kind, it's sending down these great assaults.
If their betters behave with moderation, that gives the common people easy minds.
If the gentlefolk stick to routine, hatred and resentments fade away.

Gòuc Thìn pu khlong, kròungs tsec kouk hong;   昊天不傭　降此鞠訩
Gòuc Thìn pu wìts, kròungs tsec dàts rìt.   昊天不惠　降此大戾
Kwun-tzuc na krìts, pec min sum kwhìt.   君子如屆　俾民心闋
Kwun-tzuc na luy, àks nàc dec wuy.   君子如夷　惡怒是違

Bright Sky is pitiless, and discords are not being resolved;
indeed they're growing month by month, putting the people under stress.
If you drown your grief in drink, who'll take on the task of restoring harmony in the states?
If you won't yourself govern, then you'll just load more misery and toil onto the Hundred Names.

Pu tyàwk Gòuc Thìn, ròns mayc wuc dèngs;   不弔昊天　亂靡有定
lhuk ngwat se sheng, pec min pu nèng.   式月斯生　俾民不寧
Ou sum na rheng, douy prank kwùk deng?   憂心如酲　誰秉國成
Pu dzis way tengs, dzouts ràw pràk sengs.   不自為政　瘁勞百姓

I yoke these four oxen—they stretch their necks for the yoke.
I consider the Four Quarters: but they're all in deep trouble, and there's nowhere for me to drive.

Kràys payc slits mouc, slits mouc grònk renk.　　駕彼四牡　四牡項領
Ngàyc tam Slits Pang, tziwk-tziwk mayc shac rhenk.　　我瞻四方　蹙蹙靡所騁

For the moment you're able to impose your heartlessness, we see your lances;
but once order and welfare are restored, then it'll be payback time.

Pang mòus nec àk, sangs nec mou luc;　　方懋爾惡　相爾矛矣
kuts luy kuts lak, na sang dou luc.　　既夷既懌　如相酬矣

Bright Sky is not just, and our king is under stress.
But you don't correct your attitude, on the contrary you resent those who correct you.

Gòuc Thìn pu breng, ngàyc wang pu nèng.　　昊天不平　我王不寧
Pu drung gu sum, phouk ons gu tengs.　　不懲其心　覆怨其正

The father of a family has written this poem, as a review of discord at the royal court.
You need to change your attitude, so as properly to care for the many states.

Krà bac tzàk slongs, luc kous wang hong.　　家父作誦　以究王訩
Lhuk ngòy nec sum, luc rhouk màns pròng.　　式訛爾心　以畜萬邦

The head of government, who wields actual power under a quasi-sacred king or "Sky's Son", because of some personal grief is ignoring his duties and even showing active hostility towards the population whose welfare is in his charge. (The latter, at least, seems to be the implication of the phrase about lances.) On the "Hundred Names", see Ode 166. *Wint*, in modern pronunciation Yin, still occurs as a surname today, and we know that the *Wint* clan provided *Tiw* kings with many high officers.

Chinese script has no device like capitalization to mark words as proper names. According to tradition the two opening words of the last verse are to be read as a name (in modern pronunciation it would be Jia Fu). However the literal meaning of *krà bac*, "father of a family", makes good sense in the context—and I wonder how prudent it would have been for the writer of a piece like this to identify himself openly.

192

The First Moon　正月

It's the first moon, and the frost is heavy; I'm sick at heart,
and people's false words are making me more so.
They remind me how isolated I am, and my heart-sickness is immense.
Alas for my worries; grief is making me ill.

Teng ngwat ban shang. Ngàyc sum ou lhang,   正月繁霜　我心憂傷
min tu ngòy ngan yak khònk tu tzang.   民之訛言　亦孔之將
Nìms ngàyc dòk ì, ou sum krang-krang.   念我獨兮　憂心京京
ùy ngàyc syawc sum. Nhac ou luc yang.   哀我小心　瘋憂以痒

Father, mother, why did you make me suffer by bringing me into the world?
This misery wasn't there before my time, and it won't be there after I'm gone.
Sometimes flattering words come from people's mouths, sometimes hurtful words;
my heart-sickness increases, and I'm made to feel like a pariah.

Bac muc sheng ngàyc: gà pec ngàyc loc?   父母生我　胡俾我瘉
Pu dzis ngàyc sùn; pu dzis ngàyc ghòc.   不自我先　不自我後
Hòus ngan dzis khòc, youc ngan dzis khòc;   好言自口　莠言自口
ou sum loc-loc, dec luc wuc moc.   憂心愈愈　是以有侮

In my sickness of heart I'm alone and helpless, pondering on how I lack status.
Those who aren't complicit with the authorities are all reduced to serfdom.
Woe to us—how can we pursue a good life?
I watch a crow stooping to settle—whose roof will it land on?

Ou sum gweng-gweng, nìms ngàyc ma ròk;   憂心惸惸　念我無祿
min tu ma kà peng kus gin bòk.   民之無辜　并其臣僕
ùy ngàyc nin se: wa gày dzongs ròk?   哀我人斯　于何從祿
Tam à wan tuc: wa douy tu òk?   瞻烏爰止　于誰之屋

Consider what's in that forest: just brash and kindling.
Now, when the people are in peril, they see that Sky is blind to their needs.
Can the situation ever be resolved? There's no-one who isn't beaten by it.
The Almighty is there on high: which of us does he hate so much?

Tam payc troung rum: gò sin gò tung.   瞻彼中林　侯薪侯蒸
Min kum pang lùc, gic Thìn mòng-mòng.   民今方殆　視天夢夢
Kuts khùk wuc dèngs? Mayc nin put lhungs.   既克有定　靡人弗勝
Wuc wàng Dyangs Tès, i douy wun tzùng?   有皇上帝　伊誰云憎

"They" say, yes indeed, the hills are low—but in reality there are steep ridges and cliffs!
Why does no-one refute people's false words?
Men of experience are called in and bidden to interpret dreams.
They all just say "We may be wise men, but who can tell the sex of a crow?"

Wuts shàn kàts pe, way kàng way rung.   謂山蓋卑　為岡為陵
Min tu ngòy ngan nèng màk tu drung?   民之訛言　寧莫之懲
Draws payc kàs ròuc, sins tu tem mung.   召彼故老　訊之占夢
Gos wat "Lac lhengs, douy tre à tu tse wung?"   具曰予聖　誰知烏之雌雄

"They" say, yes indeed, the sky is high—yet in reality who dares go without stooping?
They say, yes indeed, the ground is solid—yet who dares not to tread gingerly?
They clamour that their assertions are principled and have backbone
—alas for the men of today: why are they such creeps?

Wuts thìn kàts kàw, pu kàmp pu gok. 　謂天蓋高　不敢不局
Wuts drays kàts gòc, pu kàmp pu tzek. 　謂地蓋厚　不敢不蹐
Wi ghàw se ngan, wuc roun wuc tzek 　維號斯言　有倫有脊
—ùy kum tu nin, gà way hwuyc lek? 　哀今之人　胡為虺蜴

Look at that steeply-sloping field: its crop is growing well and straight.
Sky can shake me, but it can't crush me.
"They" try to emulate me but they can't match me.
They grapple with me like wrestlers, but they can't impose their strength on me.

Tam payc brànt lìn: wuc out gu dùk. 　瞻彼阪田　有菀其特
Thìn tu ngòut ngàyc, na pu ngàyc khùk. 　天之抓我　如不我克
Payc gou ngàyc tzùk, na pu ngàyc tùk. 　彼求我則　如不我得
Tup ngàyc gou-gou, yak pu ngàyc ruk. 　執我仇仇　亦不我力

My heart is sick; it feels as though someone has knotted a cord tight round it.
These present-day authorities, why are they so cruel?
Yet now the torch has been raised, how can anyone put it out?
Majestic was the *Tiw* royal lineage, but now *Bòu Sluc* has brought it to collapse.

Sum tu ou luc, na wùk kìt tu. 　心之憂矣　如或結之
Kum tzu tu tengs, gà nan rats luc? 　今茲之正　胡然厲矣
Ryaws tu pang lang, nèng wùk met tu? 　燎之方揚　寧或滅之
Hràk-hràk Tzòung Tiw, Bòu Sluc mhet tu. 　赫赫宗周　褒姒威之

This constant anxiety is relentless, and on top of that gloomy downpours are making us miserable.
—Once your waggon is loaded, you throw away the side-guards,
and then when the waggon sheds its load you beg your superiors: "Help us".

Toung kus wrank gròuy, wus gount um wac. 　終其永懷　又窘陰雨
Gu ka kuts tzùs, nùc khits nec bac. 　其車既載　乃棄爾輔
Tzùs lho nec tzùs, tsang pràk "Djas lac". 　載輸爾載　將伯助予

Don't throw the side-guards away, or the load will fall down onto the wheels!
Keep an eye on your driver, and don't let the waggon overturn
—that way, in the end you'll get past the most precipitous spot. But you haven't thought about that.

Ma khits nec bac, wrunt wa nec puk. 　無棄爾輔　員于爾輻
Ros kàs nec bòk, pu lho nec tzùs. 　屢顧爾僕　不輸爾載
Toung lo dzot nghramp. Dzùng dec pu uks. 　終踰絕險　曾是不意

220

A fish lives in a pond, but it can't relax:
although it can lie on the bottom, it will still be clearly visible.
My heart-sickness is grievous as I think of the cruelties being practised in the nation.

Nga dzùc wa tawc, yak puyc khùk ngràwks. 　魚在于沼　亦匪克樂
Dzem swi buk luc, yak khònk tu tyawk. 　潛雖伏矣　亦孔之灼
Ou sum tsàwc-tsàwc, nìms kwùk tu way ngawk. 　憂心慘慘　念國之為虐

"They" have fine wines and delicious food.
They invite their neighbours to frequent parties, and they have numerous relatives.
I consider how isolated I am, and my heart-sickness is miserable.

Payc wuc kic tziwc, wus wuc kràygràw. 　彼有旨酒　又有嘉殽
Grùp bis gu rin, mhùn in khònk wun. 　洽比其鄰　昏姻孔云
Nìms ngàyc dòk ì, ou sum un-un. 　念我獨兮　憂心慇慇

"They" are worthless men, but they have residences; they are rubbish men, but they have nice salaries.
If the people nowadays lack any quality of life, that's down to Sky's destructive assaults.
The rich are all right, but alas for those who are powerless and isolated.

Tsec-tsec payc wuc òk, sòk-sòk pang wuc kòk. 　佌佌彼有屋　蔌蔌方有穀
Min kum tu ma ròk, Thìn awc dec tròk. 　民今之無祿　天夭是椓
Kày luc puks nin; ùy tsec gweng dòk. 　哿矣富人　哀此惸獨

The poet sees his time as uniquely wretched, with good government abandoned in favour of a régime under which the rich become richer but the poor are left to fester, and those who ought to speak out instead parrot the complacent falsehoods of the authorities' party line. The poet himself has higher standards, but as a lone voice he feels helpless to achieve change. And yet he has flashes of hope: "now the torch has been raised, how can anyone put it out?"

The "before my time/after I'm gone" passage is puzzling: people who see society as ruined are not usually confident that better times will come (if they were, they might feel less despairing). It seems fair to detect a certain ambiguity about whether the poet's misery is because the nation is suffering, or because he personally is going without the material rewards available to those—the anonymous "they"—who are willing to go along with an oppressive régime.

Later verses contain metaphors which require considerable glossing. The crow is a bird of ill omen, so the poet is asking in verse 3 who will be next to find his life destroyed by the régime— it may be anyone. The forest is society, which ought to contain able men of integrity, just as a forest should contain tall, well-grown trees usable for roof-beams or shipbuilding, but the current society has only worthless yes-men. The régime is requiring people to go along with lie after lie, like Orwell's "war is peace, ignorance is strength", and people are obediently saying "yes, the ground is level and walking easy" although they well know that the reverse is the truth. The poet shares with his society a belief that dreams are a source of information relevant for good government, so when the authorities ask soothsayers for help with this, if they were honest they would say things that the régime does not want to hear: instead they cop out by claiming that interpretation is impossible. (For some bird species cock and hen are easily distinguished by their plumage, but in crows there is no visible difference.)

In verse 7 the poet grows defiant. One might imagine that a slope would affect the direction that plants grow in, but in fact they stand straight up just as they do on level ground; likewise he maintains his integrity in adverse circumstances. The tight cord of verse 8 sounds rather like the sensation which precedes a heart attack. Perhaps "heart-sickness" is more than purely metaphorical.

For *Tiw*-dynasty Chinese, adverse weather and adverse social conditions were all alike imposed by Sky on mankind, so the downpours of verse 9 reinforce the inference that Sky has it in for the people. The poet seems anxious to repeat the point that it is Sky who is the ultimate source of society's misery, perhaps to avoid any dangerous suggestion that a human ruler is to blame.

The loaded waggon metaphor is essentially saying "For society to function well you ought to be using the ability and honesty of people like me—but I'm being marginalized". A waggon had side-guards to form a box holding the load in place, and perhaps they were heavy so that it was tempting to make haulage easier by leaving them off—but they were there for a reason. The fish represents someone who hopes to escape oppression by keeping a low profile, but nobody can keep himself safe that way, just as a heron can spot a fish even on the bottom of a pond. The point about the yes-men's numerous relatives is not the biological fact that they have many kinsmen, but that they are able to help their in-laws into nice jobs, entertain them lavishly, and so forth. The worthless men's residences are probably good accommodation that comes with an official position.

193

Eclipse 十月之交

The eclipse in the seventh moon happened on the first day of the moon, a *sin-mròuc* day.
The sun was eaten: a very ominous event.
The moon had been invisible, and now the sun was invisible.
The common people of today bewail it heartily.

Tsit ngwat tu kryàw, shok nit sin-mròuc.	七月之交　朔日辛卯
Nit wuc mluk tu: yak khònk tu k'hyou.	日有食之　亦孔之醜
Payc ngwat nu muy, tsec nit nu muy.	彼月而微　此日而微
Kum tsec gràc min, yak khònk tu ùy.	今此下民　亦孔之哀

Sun and moon were announcing calamities, failing to follow their normal orbits.
The states of the world are without good government, failing to make proper use of their able men.
For the moon to become invisible happens regularly,
but for the sun to be eclipsed ... we ask where the evil will hit us?

Nit ngwat kòuk hong, pu longs gu gràng.　　日月告凶　不用其行
Slits kwùk ma tengs, pu longs gu rang.　　四國無政　不用其良
Payc ngwat nu mluk, tzùk wi gu dyang;　　彼月而食　則維其常
tsec nit nu mluk ... wa gày pu tzàng?　　此日而食　于何不臧

Flash, flash sizzled lightning bolts along with thunderclaps; there was no calm, no good order.
A hundred new streams gushed forth; mountain peaks tottered and collapsed.
High bluffs turned into valleys, and deep valleys into hills.
Alas for the people of today: why has no-one put things right?

Wap-wap tuns lìns; pu nèng, pu reng.　　爗爗震電　不寧不令
Pràk k'hlòun put lùng; shàn tronk sòuts pùng.　　百川沸騰　山冢崒崩
Kàw ngàns way klòk, nhum klòk way rung.　　高岸為谷　深谷為陵
Ùy kum tu nin: gà tsùmp màk drung?　　哀今之人　胡憯莫懲

Wàng-pac is prime minister, *Phan* is minister of labour;
Krà Pràk is chief steward, and *Droungs Yount* is master of the royal kitchens.
Master *Jou* is keeper of the private records; *Gots* is master of the royal horse;
Kwac is commander of the clans; and lady Blaze, the lovely royal consort, is at the king's side.

Wàng-pac khrang-shuc, Phan wi su-dà;　　皇父卿士　番維司徒
Krà Pràk tronk tzùc; Droungs Yount dans-pa;　　家伯冢宰　仲允膳夫
Jou-tzuc nòuts-shuc; Gots wi tsòc-mràc;　　棸子內史　蹶維趣馬
Kwac wi shi-gec. Yams tsùy Nhans pang k'hlac.　　楀維師氏　豔妻煽方處

However, this *Wàng-pac*: how can I find words to express his wrongfulness?
Why doesn't he come and help me plan my work?
He's pulling down our walls and roofs, and our fields are thoroughly weed-infested.
He says "I am not mistreating you, this is what the law requires".

Uk tsec Wàng-pac, khuyc wat pu du?　　抑此皇父　豈曰不時
Gà ways ngàyc tzàk, pu tzit ngàyc mu?　　胡為我作　不即我謀
Thret ngàyc dzang òk, lìn tzout wwà rù;　　徹我牆屋　田卒汙萊
wat "Lac pu dzang, rìc tzùk nan luc".　　曰予不戕　禮則然矣

Wàng-pac is a very clever man. He has founded a capital at *Yangs*,
and selected three administrators for it. But these men are utterly rapacious.
They won't spare even a single greybeard in carrying out their work of guarding the king.
They seek out people who own carriages and horses to settle *Yangs*.

Wàng-pac khònk lhengs. Tzàk tà wa Yangs.　　皇父孔聖　作都于向
Drak sùm wuc-shuc; tànt gò tày dzàng.　　擇三有事　亶侯多藏
Pu ngrins wi it ròuc, pec hyouc ngàyc wang.　　不憖遺一老　俾守我王
Drak wuc ka mràc, luc kas dzà Yangs.　　擇有車馬　以居徂向

I slave away at my job, not daring to complain that I'm overworked;
I've done nothing wrong, yet I hear a hubbub of slanderous gossip against me.
It isn't Sky that has sent down calamities on the people;
there's malicious gossip behind one's back—it's human beings alone who are creating strife.

Mrunt-mrant dzong shuc, pu kàmp kòuk ràw. 黽勉從事 不敢告勞
Ma dzòuyc ma kà, djàms khòc ngàw-ngàw. 無罪無辜 讒口囂囂
Gràc min tu ngat, puyc kròungs dzis Thìn: 下民之孽 匪降自天
tzòunt lùp pùks tzùng—tuk grangs you nin. 噂沓背憎 職競由人

My suffering is something I can't help brooding on, and the distress caused is great.
On all sides there is affluence; I alone dwell in misery.
Every one of the population is at ease with life—I alone dare not relax.
Sky's edicts are impenetrable.
I dare not imitate my acquaintances and take things easy myself.

You-you ngàyc ruc, yak khònk tu mùs. 悠悠我里 亦孔之痗
Slits Pang wuc slans; ngàyc dòk kas ou. 四方有羨 我獨居憂
Min màk pu lit, ngàyc dòk pu kàmp hou. 民莫不逸 我獨不敢休
Thìn mreng pu thret. 天命不徹
Ngàyc pu kàmp gràws, ngàyc wuc dzis lit. 我不敢傚 我友自逸

This Ode begins with a clear statement about an eclipse of the sun, which was followed by seismic disturbances (no doubt greatly exaggerated). Obviously, no-one understood the mechanism of eclipses; we don't need to take seriously the idea that the earthquakes were linked to the eclipse, any more than we think of an eclipse as occurring because sun or moon has deviated from its normal orbit. We saw on p. 34 that this eclipse occurred in August 775, which was just four years before the downfall of king *Iw* and the Western *Tiw* dynasty. (The traditional Chinese title has the eclipse happening in the "tenth moon", but there is good reason to think that "ten" was a scribal error for "seven".) The poem suggests that the dynasty has now fallen, and the poet is harking back to the recent eclipse to explain that. Clearly the poet is complaining about bad government; but what exactly has happened?

The new king, *Breng*, ruled from a new capital in the area of modern Luoyang. Through the mists of time and language, we dimly see that the king's first minister, having decided on this move, is giving the new town a population through forcible resettlement, rendering people's previous places of residence uninhabitable. (*Yangs* was a location corresponding to present-day Jiyuan city, which is separate from Luoyang but close to it.) If that is right, others might not have agreed that this was misgovernment. It could be that by the standards of the time this was a proper thing to do, and it was the duty of a subject to co-operate with good grace. Hence *Wàng-pac*'s remark "This is what the law requires". (*Rìc* would normally be translated as "ritual, propriety" rather than "law", but there may have been little concept of law as a system separate from ritual obligations associated with religious concepts—there is controversy about whether China already had formal written laws in the Western *Tiw*.)

There was certainly little concept (as there was not in mediaeval Europe) of a distinction between the government of the state, and the organization of the king's personal household. The names in verse 4 are presumably listed as responsible along with *Wàng-pac* for the way society is being mismanaged; this might be reasonable when directed against a minister whose title I have rendered as "minister of labour" (literally, "controller of the common people"), but we might see it as misdirected as against the man responsible for the food on the royal table. According to Karlgren, the "commander of the clans" was in charge of the royal guard.

Later verses become harder to follow, because we don't know what the poet's job was, or why tongues were wagging about him. Was he perhaps an administrator who couldn't grasp, as pen-pushers sometimes cannot, that work to which he had devoted his career had been rendered largely irrelevant by wider social changes? Can we reconcile the poet's statements that he is unique in being unable to rest and relax, and that everyone around him is affluent, with "Alas for the people of today" and the statement that the common people are beset by calamities? Perhaps the poet's "everyone" doesn't extend to the common people, and his "alas" means not that those around him are miserable but that they are corrupt, using power to live well rather than provide for the general welfare.

194

Destruction 雨無正

Bright Sky, in its vastness, has withdrawn its favour.
It's sending down destruction and famine; it has attacked and ruined the states of the whole world.
Bright Sky is terrible; it doesn't act by reason or calculation.
It spares people who have done wrong, though they may even have admitted their own guilt,
while the innocent are all indiscriminately made to suffer.

Gòuc-gòuc Gòuc Thìn, pu tzyouns gu tùk.   浩浩昊天 不俊其德
Kròungs sàngs kri gruns; jàmp bat Slits kwùk.   降喪飢饉 斬伐四國
Gòuc Thìn dzit-ouy, put ras, put dà.   昊天疾威 弗慮弗圖
Lhac payc wuc dzòuyc, kuts buk gu kà,   舍彼有罪 既伏其辜
nak tsec ma dzòuyc, roun-sa luc phà.   若此無罪 淪胥以痛

The dynastic capital has been sacked, and we have nowhere to settle.
The chief officers of the court have scattered. Nobody knows what we're going through.
The three ministers and the court officials are none of them willing to attend regularly.
The rulers of fiefs, and the nobles, are none of them willing to be on hand day in, day out.
People all talk about "taking the good as their model", then they go off and do wrong.

Tiw tzòung kuts met, mayc shac tuc rìts.   周宗既滅 靡所止戾
Teng dàts-pa ray kac. Màk tre ngàyc lat.   正大夫離居 莫知我勩
Sùm shuc, dàts-pa, màk khènk souk yas.   三事大夫 莫肯夙夜
Pròng kwun, ta gò, màk khènk traw syak.   邦君諸侯 莫肯朝夕
Lhaks wat "lhuk tzàng", phouk k'hlout way àk.   庶曰式臧 覆出為惡

Bright Sky, what's happening? What rulers say can't be trusted.
They are behaving like voyagers who lack a destination.
All you lordships are focusing on keeping your own skins safe.
Why don't you respect one another? You don't even respect Sky.

Na gày, Gòuc Thìn? Pek ngan pu sins.   如何昊天　辟言不信
Na payc gràng mràts tzùk mayc shac jin.   如彼行邁　則靡所臻
Bam pràk kwun-tzuc kàk krengs nec lhin.   凡百君子　各敬爾身
Gà pu sang ouys? Pu ouys wa Thìn.   胡不相畏　不畏于天

The fact is that weapons haven't yet been laid aside, nor have we seen the end of famine;
so even an aide like me is plunging deeper into distress with every day that passes.
None of you lordships are willing to heed reproofs.
When speech is loyal, respond to it! When you hear troublemaking, ignore it.

Noung deng pu thòuts, kri deng pu swits,   戎誠不退　飢誠不遂
tzùng ngàyc snet ngas tsùmp-tsùmp nit dzouts.   曾我替御　憯憯日瘁
Bam pràk kwun-tzuc màk khènk longs souts.   凡百君子　莫肯用訊
Lhèngs ngan tzùk tùp; jums ngan tzùk thòuts.   聽言則答　譖言則退

Ah me, not to be able to speak—not to be able to exercise one's tongue,
how wearing it is. It's good to be able to speak:
well-chosen words are like a free-flowing river—they leave one at ease with oneself.

Ùy-tzù, pu nùc ngan, puyc mlat dec k'hlouts,   哀哉不能言　匪舌是出
wi koung dec dzouts! Kày luc nùc ngan: 維躬是瘁　哿矣能言
khròus ngan na riw, pec koung k'hlac hou.   巧言如流　俾躬處休

You say that taking an official post entails great trouble and risk.
But then, if you decline the appointment, you offend against Sky's Son
—though if you accept it, you'll incur hostility towards you and towards your associates.

Wi wat wa shuc khònk kuk tsac lùc.   維曰于仕　孔棘且殆
Wun pu khàyc shuc, tùk dzòuyc wa Thìn Tzuc;   云不可使　得罪于天子
yak wun khàyc shuc, ons gup bùng wuc.   亦云可使　怨及朋友

When I ask you to move to the royal capital,
you say "But I have no household set up".
I'm so overcome with worry that I'm weeping blood. I don't ask for anything unless it is crucial.
When in the past you went to live somewhere new, who did you ever have to set up house for you?

Wuts nec tsan wa wang tà,   謂爾遷于王都
wat "Lac muts wuc lhit krà".   曰予未有室家

Nhac sus khrup hwìt. Ma ngan pu dzit.　　瘋思泣血　無言不疾
Sak nec k'hlout kac, douy dzongs tzàk nec lhit?　　昔爾出居　誰從作爾室

This again is set around the time of the collapse of the Western *Tiw*. The poet is a royal aide who is attempting to re-create the machinery of government, but this requires a number of the ruling class to come and reside at the new capital and accept various ministerial roles. While something like a civil war is going on, they are making feeble excuses to avoid leaving their own strongholds.

I take verse 5 to say that expressing his frustrations in poetry gives the writer relief from the stress of a post which requires him to guard his tongue (others have taken it differently). The words I render as "exercise one's tongue" literally mean "stick one's tongue out": evidently *Tiw* Chinese believed that speaking involved protruding the tongue from the mouth.

195

Sky is Fearsome　小旻

Sky in its severity is fearsome, dominating the whole earth below.
Our policies and plans are misguided—when will this situation end?
When policies are good, they aren't carried out; on the other hand when they're
    bad, they are implemented.
Contemplating our policies and plans, I really despair.

Mrun Thìn dzit-ouy, pha wa gràc thàc.　　旻天疾威　敷于下土
Mu you wùy-wit—gày nit se dzac?　　謀猶回遹　何日斯沮
Mu tzàng, pu dzong; pu tzàng, phouk longs.　　謀臧不從　不臧覆用
Ngàyc gic mu you, yak khònk tu gong.　　我視謀猶　亦孔之邛

There is an atmosphere of plotting and back-biting—I really can't stand it.
Where we have good policies, everyone disobeys them,
    whereas they all follow the bad ones.
Contemplating our policies and plans, I ask myself what we're coming to.

Hup-hup, tzec-tzec—yak khònk tu ùy.　　翕翕訿訿　亦孔之哀
Mu tu gu tzàng, tzùk gos dec wuy;　　謀之其臧　則具是違
mu tu pu tzàng, tzùk gos dec uy.　　謀之不臧　則具是依
Ngàyc gic mu you, i wa gà tic?　　我視謀猶　伊于胡底

Our tortoises have had enough—they won't pronounce on our plans.
We have so very many policy-makers that we're getting nowhere.
The court is full of advice being offered, but who's willing to take responsibility
    for the outcomes?
It's like travellers who spend so much time discussing their route that they never
    progress along the road.

VOICES FROM EARLY CHINA

Ngàyc kwru kuts ems—pu ngàyc kòuk you. 我龜既厭　不我告猶
Mu pa khònk tày, dec longs pu dzous. 謀夫孔多　是用不就
Pat ngan leng lèng; douy kàmp tup gu gouc? 發言盈庭　誰敢執其咎
Na payc gràng mràts mu, dec longs pu tùk wa lòuc. 如彼行邁謀　是用不得于道

The way plans are being made—oh dear!
They don't treat our ancestors as having set the standards; they don't treat established leading policies as norms.
The ideas they listen to and debate are just shallow words.
It's like someone building a house, who asks advice from anyone he bumps into on the street, and so never buckles down to getting the job done.

Ùy-tzù, way you. 哀哉為猶
Puyc sùn min dec dreng; puyc dàts you dec kèng. 匪先民是程　匪大猶是經
Wi nec ngan dec lhèngs, wi nec ngan dec jèng. 維邇言是聽　維邇言是爭
Na payc trouk lhit wa lòuc mu, dec longs pu gwùts wa deng. 如彼築室于道謀　是用不潰于成

The nation may be unsettled, but it does contain wise people and high-flyers.
The population may not be large, but it contains clever people and wise counsellors,
solid citizens, and people who are orderly in their conduct.
Let them not all be indiscriminately ruined, like the water flowing from that spring and smashing on the rocks.

Kwùk swi mayc tuc, wùk lhengs, wùk puc. 國雖靡止　或聖或不
Min swi mayc mù, wùk trat, wùk mu, 民雖靡膴　或哲或謀
wùk siwk, wùk ngats. 或肅或乂
Na payc dzwan riw: ma roun-sa luc bràts. 如彼泉流　無淪胥以敗

I wouldn't dare attack a tiger with my hands, or try to ford the Yellow River.
People are conscious of one issue, but they're oblivious to other dangers.
We need to be wary, to be cautious,
as if we were standing at the edge of an abyss, or treading on thin ice.

Pu kàmp bàwks hlàc; pu kàmp brung Gày. 不敢暴虎　不敢馮河
Nin tre gu it, màk tre gu lhày. 人知其一　莫知其他
Tans-tans, kung-kung, 戰戰兢兢
na rum nhum wwìn, na ric bàk prung. 如臨深淵　如履薄冰

The tortoises of verse 3 refer to the tortoise-shell oracle explained with Ode 50: when advisers suggested alternative plans, it would have been normal to use a tortoise to check which alternative was best, but now the tortoises have been so over-used that they have effectively gone on strike.

In verse 5, others have taken *puc* at the end of the first line in its usual meaning, "not", so that the stich says that some people are wise, some aren't. But this is the first of three stichs each of the form "some are X, some are Y", and in the other cases both X and Y seem to be positive words. Surely either positive should contrast with negative in each case, or else all six of the terms should be positive? The *puc* graph has another meaning, "to soar", so I have translated it as "high-flyers". This may be wrong—the metaphor might well be alien to *Tiw* China—but I find it less forced than other interpretations.

Very odd things happen to the metre in verses 3 and 4. The first stich containing more than four syllables is the question *douy kàmp tup gu gouc?*, where *gu* is the kind of "little" unstressed word that might well not have counted for metrical purposes. But it would be hard to argue the same for a number of the following over-long stichs, one of which has as many as seven syllables. Did a stich which was extra-long for good reason suspend a poet's sense of the right length for later stichs?

196

The Turtle-Dove 小宛

That little turtle-dove is flying right up to the sky.
My heart is afflicted with sadness, through thinking about my forefathers.
Even by daybreak I can't get to sleep—remembering my parents makes me so emotional.

Ont payc mreng kou, gàn puy rìts thìn.	宛彼鳴鳩　翰飛戾天
Ngàyc sum ou lhang, nìms sak sùn nin.	我心憂傷　念昔先人
Mrang pat pu mits—wuc gròuy nits nin.	明發不寐　有懷二人

People who are wise and intelligent remain gentle and self-controlled when drinking wine,
but the ignorant thickoes just get drunk, and grow daily more assertive.
Always be careful to maintain your dignity, people—Sky doesn't give second chances.

Nin tu dzì lhengs um tziwc òun khùk;	人之齊聖　飲酒溫克
payc mhùn pu tre, it tzouts nit puks.	彼昏不知　壹醉日富
Kàk krengs nec ngay: Thìn mreng pu wus.	各敬爾儀　天命不又

There are beans growing in the middle of the plain, and the people harvest them.
When the cotton bollworm produces offspring, the potter wasp adopts them.
Teach your children how to behave, and they will be similarly virtuous.

Troung ngwan wuc nhouk, lhaks min tsùc tu.	中邍有菽　庶民采之
Mèng-rèng wuc tzuc, kòyc-ròyc buc tu.	螟蛉有子　蜾蠃負之
Kràws mhùs nec tzuc, lhuk kòk sluc tu.	教誨爾子　式穀似之

Look at that pied wagtail—it never stops flying and singing.
If, by pushing ahead a bit each day, we make progress every month,
if we get up with the lark and wait till dark to go to bed, then we shan't disgrace those who brought us into the world.

Dès payc tzek-rèng—tzùs puy tzùs mreng.	題彼脊令　載飛載鳴
Ngàyc nit se mràts, nu ngwat se teng,	我日斯邁　而月斯征
souk hung yas mits: ma lhèmp nec shac sheng.	夙興夜寐　無忝爾所生

The grosbeaks fly to and fro, pecking stray grains up from one threshing floor after another.
Woe is me, feverish and alone in the world, liable to be treated as a criminal by the authorities.
I go out with a handful of grain to tell my fortune—where can I look for happiness?

Kryàw-kryàw sàng-gàc, shout drang tròk sok.   交交桑扈　率場啄粟
Ùy ngàyc thruns kwràc, ngay ngàns ngay ngok.   哀我瘨寡　宜岸宜獄
Rròk sok k'hlout pòk—dzis gày nùc kòk?   握粟出卜　自何能穀

Be gentle and respectful towards others, like birds settling in a tree.
Be anxious and careful, as if you were looking down from the top of a cliff.
Be timid and cautious, as if you were stepping on thin ice.

Òun-òun krong nin, na dzup wa mòk.   溫溫恭人　如集于木
Toys-toys, syawc sum, na rum wa klòk.   惴惴小心　如臨于谷
Tans-tans, kung-kung, na ric bàk prung.   戰戰兢兢　如履薄冰

The poet is plunged into misery by the fact of his parents having died, and he preaches to others about the importance of living in ways that would not shame their own parents. It is easy to infer that he feels he has failed in this himself—though that is not explicit (indeed, it is not said explicitly that the parents are dead). We cannot tell whether the poet's feelings of guilt have some realistic basis or are purely neurotic symptoms: it may be that authorities in *Tiw* China had little respect for social isolates lacking the support of a family around them, but surely that alone would not have led to the risk of prison?

A Westerner would hardly counsel people deliberately to cultivate anxiety. But even today East Asians are often brought up to put a level of effort into detecting and avoiding possibilities of minor social friction that goes far beyond anything seen as desirable in the West.

Several verses begin with opaque "arousals". The wagtail of verse 4 may be a metaphor for someone who is constantly busy, as the poet feels a man worthy of his parents ought to be; but I don't see the point of the turtle-dove in verse 1 or the beans in verse 3. (Nor do I know how one used grain for fortune-telling.) However, I can explain the insects of verse 3. The potter wasp carries bollworm caterpillars off to its own nest, and at this period the Chinese supposed that it transformed them into the new generation of wasps which emerged subsequently. Thus the process was an image of how careful rearing causes a child to acquire desirable character traits which might be very different from what would develop without parental guidance. (This was a misunderstanding of natural history. The wasp lays its eggs in the caterpillars, which serve as food for the new wasps.)

197

The Ravens 小弁

See those ravens flying, flocking home to their roosts.
Among the people none are unlucky, except me alone in my trouble.

How have I offended Sky? What am I guilty of?
My heart is filled with grief; what's to be done?

Phan payc las se, kwuy puy de-de.   翻彼鶌斯　歸飛提提
Min màk pu kòk, ngàyc dòk wa ray.   民莫不穀　我獨于罹
Gày kà wa Thìn, ngàyc dzòuyc i gày?   何辜于天　我罪伊何
Sum tu ou luc, wun na tu gày?   心之憂矣　云如之何

The *Tiw* road is smooth, but it's all overgrown with grass.
I'm sick at heart, the situation makes me feel as though my guts were griping.
When I snatch a few moments' sleep, I can't leave off sighing; misery is ageing me.
My heart is filled with grief; I ache as though my head were fevered.

Dìwk-dìwk Tiw lòuc, kouk way mous tsòuc.   踧踧周道　鞠為茂草
Ngàyc sum ou lhang, nìwk an na tròuc.   我心憂傷　怒焉如祷
Kràc mits wrank nhàn, wi ou longs ròuc.   假寐永嘆　維憂用老
Sum tu ou luc, thruns na dzit lhouc.   心之憂矣　疢如疾首

Mulberry and catalpa trees, these we are bound to respect.
One has nobody to look up to, if one has no father; nobody to depend on, if one has no mother.
Yet I have no attachments, either on Yang or Yin side.
What unlucky time can it have been, when Sky gave me birth?

Wi sàng lac tzuc, pit krong krengs tuc.   維桑與梓　必恭敬止
Mayc tam puyc bac; mayc uy puyc muc.   靡瞻匪父　靡依匪母
Pu tok wa màw, pu ray wa ruc.   不屬于毛　不離于裏
Thìn tu sheng ngàyc, ngàyc dun àn dzùc?   天之生我　我辰安在

Those willows are in luxuriant leaf, and the cicadas are shrilling.
The water is deep, and sedge and rushes abound in it.
I feel like that boat drifting along: who can tell where it's heading?
My heart is filled with grief; I can't relax enough to snatch even brief sleep.

Out payc rouc se, mreng dìw hwìts-hwìts.   菀彼柳斯　鳴蜩嘒嘒
Wuc tsòuyc tac wwìn, gwàn wuyc phìts-phìts.   有漼者淵　萑葦淠淠
Pheks payc tou riw: pu tre shac krìts.   譬彼舟流　不知所屆
Sum tu ou luc, pu wàng kràc mits.   心之憂矣　不遑假寐

When deer run, they are sure-footed;
the dawn call of the cock pheasant still summons its mate.
I feel like that decayed tree, which blight has left without branches.
My heart is grief-stricken; why does no-one understand this?

Ròk se tu pùn, wi tzok gre-gre.   鹿斯之奔　維足伎伎
Dric tu traw kòs, dangs gou gu tse.   雉之朝雊　尚求其雌
Pheks payc gròuys mòk, dzit longs ma ke.   譬彼壞木　疾用無枝
Sum tu ou luc, nèng màk tu tre?   心之憂矣　寧莫之知

See that hare which has been started from cover: something might still head it off from the hunter's net.
In the road there's a dead man: someone could still bury the body.
But that heart of my lord's, he keeps it hard.
My heart is filled with grief, and my tears have been flowing.

Sangs payc dò lhàs, dangs wùk sùns tu.　　相彼投兔　尚或先之
Gràng wuc sic nin, dangs wùk gruns tu.　　行有死人　尚或墐之
Kwun-tzuc prank sum, wi kus nunt tu.　　君子秉心　維其忍之
Sum tu ou luc, thìc kuts wrunt tu.　　心之憂矣　涕既隕之

My lord believes the slanders against me, as reflexively as if he were responding to a toast.
My lord is ungenerous; he doesn't take time to look into the facts.
When a tree is felled, people pull it in the direction it needs to fall; when chopping firewood, they split it along the grain.
But my lord ignores the people who are really guilty, and lays the burden on me.

Kwun-tzuc sins djàms, na wùk dou tu.　　君子信讒　如或酬之
Kwun-tzuc pu wìts, pu lha kous tu.　　君子不惠　不舒究之
Bat mòk kayc luc, sèk sin drayc luc.　　伐木掎矣　析薪杝矣
Lhac payc wuc dzòuyc, lac tu lhàys luc.　　舍彼有罪　予之佗矣

Nothing is higher than a mountain, nothing deeper than a spring.
My lord shouldn't casually let his tongue run away with him: ears are listening at walls.
[...]

Màk kàw puyc shàn; màk syouns puyc dzwan.　　莫高匪山　莫浚匪泉
Kwun-tzuc ma leks you ngan, nuc dok wa wan.　　君子無易由言　耳屬于垣
[...]

In the received text of this Ode, the last two lines (sixteen words) of the last verse are identical to the fifth and sixth lines in verse 3 of Ode 35. The lines fit well in Ode 35, where a wife is complaining to a cruel husband, but in Ode 197 we are not, I think, being addressed by a woman. This seems to be another case where lines have been inserted mistakenly in place of wording which is now lost, so I have omitted them.

This Ode contains a lot of metaphor, some obscure. The line about the overgrown road to *Tiw* is mysterious, unless perhaps it means that the poet's difficulties with his local ruler are putting the kybosh on his ambition of moving to the fleshpots of the dynastic capital. In verse 3, mulberry and catalpa symbolize a family homestead: they introduce the poet's lament about lack of family to support him in adversity. The third line literally says that the poet is unattached either to "fur" or to "lining", in other words to either side of a coat. Outside and inside are one of the many contrasts bound up in the concepts Yang and Yin: male v. female, sunny v. shady, etc. The poet is saying that he lacks family support, through either father or mother, or perhaps through either blood or marriage.

Verses 4 and 5 simply say that everything in the world around is proceeding naturally and happily, while the poet has lost his way in life. Even when disasters loom for others (verse 6), they still have chances to escape, but the poet sees no way forward for himself. The line in

VOICES FROM EARLY CHINA

verse 7 about felling trees and chopping firewood tells us that there is a right and a wrong way to do anything, and the ruler is going about things wrongly.

The first line of verse 8 is probably intended to contrast this ruler's approach with that of a true *kwun-tzuc*, "princely man". The rest of the verse would perhaps have enlarged on this theme.

198

Artful Words 巧言

Oh, you distant Bright Sky—you whom we call "father and mother":
we haven't offended, we are guilty of nothing, yet rebellion has spread this widely!
Oh, Bright Sky, you are fearsome—but truly, we have done nothing wrong.
Bright Sky, you are mighty—but truly, we are innocent.

You-you Gòuc Thìn—wat "bac muc" tza:　　悠悠昊天　曰父母且
ma dzòuyc, ma kà, ròns na tsec mac.　　無罪無辜　亂如此幠
Gòuc Thìn luc ouy—lac tin ma dzòuyc.　　昊天已威　予眞無罪
Gòuc Thìn thàts mac—lac tin ma kà.　　昊天泰幠　予眞無辜

When unrest first arose, initially the bad ideas were refuted.
But when it continued to grow, our prince came to believe the troublemaking talk.
If the prince were to show anger, probably he'd soon root out mutinous behaviour.
If he were to reward those loyal to him, probably rebellion would quickly fade away.

Ròns tu cha sheng, tzèms lhuc kuts krùmp.　　亂之初生　僭始既涵
Ròns tu wus sheng, kwun-tzuc sins djàms.　　亂之又生　君子信讒
Kwun-tzuc na nàc, ròns lhaks don dzac.　　君子如怒　亂庶遄沮
Kwun-tzuc na thruc, ròns lhaks don luc.　　君子如祉　亂庶遄已

Our prince often makes bargains, and that just leads to rebellion spreading.
Our prince believes what he's told by scoundrels, and that leads to unrest growing violent.
Scoundrels use honeyed words which entice people into rebellion.
They don't give respect where it's due—they are the king's bane.

Kwun-tzuc ros mrang, ròns dec longs trank.　　君子屢盟　亂是用長
Kwun-tzuc sins dàws, ròns dec longs bàwks.　　君子信盜　亂是用暴
Dàws ngan khònk kàm, ròns dec longs lam.　　盜言孔甘　亂是用餤
Puyc gu tuc krong—wi wang tu gong.　　匪其止恭　維王之邛

233

Grand is the temple which our prince erected.
Well-chosen are the leading policies which our wise men thought out.
Others have their various intentions, but I can work out what's in their minds.
A crafty hare may jump about, but even a stupid dog can catch it.

Yak-yak tsump mraws, kwun-tzuc tzàk tu. 奕奕寢廟　君子作之
Drit-drit dàts you, lhengs nin màk tu. 秩秩大猷　聖人莫之
Lhày nin wuc sum, lac tsòunt dàk tu. 他人有心　予忖度之
Lhyàwk-lhyàwk djàm lhàs, ngo kwhìnt wàk tu. 躍躍毚兔　愚犬獲之

Soft and pliable are the trees which our prince has planted.
From the talk current among people who get around, we can assess what's in their minds.
Their grandiose, loyal-sounding remarks are only lip-service.
Their artfully-chosen words are blather, going to show how brazen they are.

Nump-namp nou mòk, kwun-tzuc doc tu. 荏染柔木　君子樹之
Wank rù gràng ngan, sum an shoc tu. 往來行言　心焉數之
Lay-lay dak ngan, k'hlout dzis khòc luc; 詍詍碩言　出自口矣
Khròus ngan na gwàng, ngràn tu gòc luc. 巧言如簧　顏之厚矣

What kind of men are these! They are poised on the brink of the River
—they have no real strength or courage of their own, they are just stirrers.
You are swelled-up nonentities: how brave are you really?
You make grand plans and many of them, but how many troops are at your disposal?

Payc gày nin se! Kac Gày tu mouy. 彼何人斯　居河之湄
Ma gon, ma lonk, tuk way ròns krì. 無拳無勇　職為亂階
Kuts muy tsac donk; nec lonk i gày? 既微且尰　爾勇伊何
Way you tzang tày; nec kac dà kuyc gày? 為猶將多　爾居徒幾何

The disaster which Chinese government aimed to avoid at all costs was *ròns*, often translated "disorder"; it meant chiefly disorder arising from disobedience to established authority, so "rebellion" or "mutiny" might be clearer English terms. The poet feels that his ruler could easily have nipped the current rebellion in the bud, but instead responded in ways that just helped it to grow. The *mrang* at the beginning of verse 3 are literally "treaties" or "covenants": I suppose that when disaffected subjects made demands, rather than refusing and using a strong hand to choke off rebellion, the ruler tried to offer compromises which led to further demands. And he is naively credulous. The "hare and dog" passage in verse 4 says that it is not difficult to see through someone who tries to conceal mutinous ideas, so why can't he do this?

I do not know why "soft and pliable" should be desirable attributes of trees, but the line in verse 5 is evidently intended that way. The people giving lip-service to loyalty are literally "thick-faced", meaning that they have no shame in concealing their real intentions. But if the ruler took the rebels on, they would be easy to deal with; they are "poised on the brink of the River", it would not take much for them to fall in and be swept away.

199

What Kind of Man? 何人斯

What kind of man is he? He must have some serious hang-up.
Why does he explore as far as my waist, and then not go all the way?
Who is content just to keep company, when it's time for action?

Payc gày nin se? Gu sum khònk krùn.	彼何人斯　其心孔艱
Gà dats ngàyc rang, pu nup ngàyc mùn?	胡逝我梁　不入我門
I douy wun dzong, wi bàwks tu wun?	伊誰云從　維暴之云

When two people have got together, why would anyone make such a fiasco of it?
Why does he explore as far as my waist, and then not do what would leave me satisfied?
I didn't think it was going to be like this. Is there something making him incapable with me?

Nits nin dzong gràng, douy way tsec gòyc?	二人從行　誰為此禍
Gà dats ngàyc rang, pu nup ngrans ngàyc?	胡逝我梁　不入唁我
Lhuc tac pu na kum. Wun pu ngàyc khàyc?	始者不如今　云不我可

What kind of man is he? Why does he even approach my lady-garden?
I listen to his talk, but I never see his body.
Yet he's not someone who can't face his fellow men—and he's not frightened of Sky.

Payc gày nin se? Gà dats ngàyc drin?	彼何人斯　胡逝我陳
Ngàyc mun gu lhèng, pu kèns gu lhin.	我聞其聲　不見其身
Pu kouys wa nin—pu ouys wa Thìn.	不愧于人　不畏于天

What kind of man is he? He stirs an emotional whirlwind in me.
Why doesn't he take me, any which way he likes?
Why does he explore as far as my waist, and then just leave me frustrated?

Payc gày nin se? Kus way pyaw pum.	彼何人斯　其為飄風
Gà pu dzis pùk? Gà pu dzis nùm?	胡不自北　胡不自南
Gà dats ngàyc rang, ke kròuc ngàyc sum?	胡逝我梁　祇攪我心

Sometimes you visit in a leisurely fashion, yet you say you haven't got time to stay the night.
Sometimes you say you're in a hurry, yet you find the time to fettle your carriage.
Every time you visit, how anguished you leave me!

Nec tu àn gràng, yak pu wàng lhas.	爾之安行　亦不遑舍
Nec tu kuk gràng, wàng ki nec ka.	爾之亟行　遑脂爾車
It tac tu rù, wun gày gu hwa.	壹者之來　云何其盱

If you came round and took me, I could relax.
But you come round and don't take me, and I just can't understand why not.
Each time I see you, you make me ill.

Nec swen nu nup, ngàyc sum leks luc.   爾還而入　我心易也
Swen nu pu nup, puc nàn tre luc.   還而不入　否難知也
It tac tu rù, pec ngàyc ge luc.   壹者之來　俾我疧也

There is First-Daughter playing her ocarina, and Second-Daughter playing her flute.
Until you have had me you won't properly know me.
I shall get out the Three Things to cast a spell on you.

Pràk gec thoy hwan; Droungs gec thoy dre.   伯氏吹壎　仲氏吹篪
Gup nec na kòns, rangs pu ngàyc tre.   及爾如貫　諒不我知
K'hlouts tsec Sùm Mout, luc jas nec se.   出此三物　以詛爾斯

If you were some devil or water-demon, you would have no chance with me.
But you have an ordinary human face and eyes—I see you as a man, who need have no restraint with me.
So I have written this sexy song, to spill out all my frustration.

Way kwuyc, way wuk, tzùk pu khàyc tùk.   為鬼為蜮　則不可得
Wuc thènt mens mouk—gic nin mank guk.   有靦面目　視人罔極
Tzàk tsec hòus kày, luc guk pant-juk.   作此好歌　以極反側

This Ode is probably the one where my reading departs most radically from those of previous commentators and translators; but if it didn't mean this, what did it mean? Previous translators haven't made much sense of it.

Accepting my reading does not solve all the translation problems. I am not sure of the role of the ocarina and flute players; are they women the poetess sees as competition that she can only eliminate by getting the man into bed at last? No commentator seems to know what the Three Things were, but they must have been objects regarded as effective for casting a love spell.

200

The Eunuch's Song   巷伯

Rich and ornate, indeed, is this shell brocade;
as for these troublemakers, they really are too much, far too much.

Tsì ì, phuyc ì, deng dec pàts kump.   萋兮斐兮　誠是貝錦
Payc jums nin tac, yak luc thàts dums.   彼譖人者　亦已大甚

Gaping wide, indeed, is the mouth of the Southern Winnowing-Basket;
as for these troublemakers, who cares to listen to them?

236

Khlac ì, khlayc ì, deng dec Nùm Ku. 哆兮移兮 誠是南箕
Payc jums nin tac, douy lhek lac mu? 彼譖人者 誰適與謀

Tittle-tattlers, smooth-tongued men, you plan how best to bad-mouth people;
you choose your words carefully, saying things you don't yourselves believe.

Tsup-tsup, ben-ben, mu lok jums nin; 晢晢諞諞 謀欲譖人
dins nec ngan layc, wuts nec pu sins. 慎爾言也 謂爾不信

Quick to suit your opinions to your audience, you plan how best to word your slanders.
How would people fail to accept them from you?—but afterwards they'll have had enough of you.

Dzap-dzap, phan-phan, mu lok jums ngan. 捷捷翻翻 謀欲譖言
Khuyc pu nec douc? Kuts kus nac tsan. 豈不爾受 既其汝遷

High-placed men are so refined, while working men are rough and simple.
But oh, blue Sky, blue Sky, look at those high-placed men
—and then pity the working men!

Kaw nin hòuc-hòuc, ràw nin tsòuc-tsòuc. 驕人好好 勞人草草
Tsàng Thìn, tsàng Thìn, gic payc kaw nin 蒼天蒼天 視彼驕人
—*grin tsec ràw nin!* 矜此勞人

The troublemakers: who cares to listen to them?
Take the troublemakers and throw them to the wolves and tigers.
And if the wolves and tigers won't eat them, throw them to the Lord of the North;
if the Lord of the North won't have them, throw them to the Lord of Outer Space!

Payc jums nin tac, douy lhek lac mu? 彼譖人者 誰適與謀
Tsoc payc jums nin, dò pits djù hlàc. 取彼譖人 投畀豺虎
Djù hlàc pu mluk, dò pits Wuc Pùk; 豺虎不食 投畀有北
Wuc Pùk pu douc, dò pits Wuc Gòuc. 有北不受 投畀有昊

The Poplar Park road goes round by *Mùc* Hill.
The eunuch Master *Mràngs* has made this song
—may your various lordships find it worth listening to!

Lang Wan tu lòuc, ayc wa Mùc Kwhu. 楊園之道 倚于畝丘
Slus nin Mràngs-tzuc, tzak way tsec lhu. 寺人孟子 作為此詩
Bam pràk kwun-tzuk, krengs nu lhèngs tu! 凡百君子 敬而聽之

The opening image of this Ode is not obviously relevant: shell brocade is patterned like the close-set veins of a cowrie shell. Perhaps it is intended to suggest the feminine preoccupations of a poet who, as we learn from the last verse, was a eunuch. In verse 2, the Southern Winnowing-Basket is a Chinese zodiac sign (part of our Sagittarius), and its shape with a mouth gaping wide is doubtless intended to reflect the ever-open mouths of *jums nin*—malicious gossips who run others down behind their backs, what the French call *mauvaises langues*.

The Lords of the North and of Space were not standard bogeyman figures in later Chinese mythology, but that is evidently what they are here. (*Gòuc* is the "Bright" of "Bright Sky", written with "sun" above "sky": in this context, outer space seems as good a rendering as any.)

201

The East Wind 谷風

Slup, slup gusts the east wind, there's nothing but gales and rain.
When we faced worries or fears only I was there to support you,
but when calm and joyful times came you changed and turned from me.

Slup, slup, klòk pum, wi pum gup wac.	習習谷風　維風及雨
Tzang khonk tzang gwaks, wi lac lac nac,	將恐將懼　維予與汝
tzang àn tzang ngràwks, nac tront khits lac.	將安將樂　汝轉棄予

Slup, slup gusts the east wind, there's nothing but gales and whirlwinds.
When we faced worries or fears you held me close to your heart,
but when calm and joyful times came you turned away and rejected me.

Slup, slup, klòk pum, wi pum gup dòuy.	習習谷風　維風及頹
Tzang khonk tzang gwaks, tets lac wa gròuy,	將恐將懼　寘予于懷
tzang àn tzang ngràwks, khits lac na wi.	將安將樂　棄予如遺

Slup, slup gusts the east wind, there's nothing but rocky hillsides.
The grass is all dead, the trees are all blighted.
You forget the great kindness you had from me, but you brood on the little faults
    you find in me.

Slup, slup, klòk pum, wi shàn dzòuy-ngòuy.	習習谷風　維山崔嵬
Ma tsòuc pu sic, ma mòk pu oy.	無草不死　無木不萎
Mang ngàyc dàts tùk, sus ngàyc syawc ons.	忘我大德　思我小怨

202

Tall Mugwort 蓼莪

Tall-growing are the *ngày* plants—those aren't *ngày*, they're only *hàw* plants.
Woe, woe, my father and mother! How they toiled to give me life.

Riwk-riwk tac ngày—puyc ngày, i hàw;	蓼蓼者莪　匪莪伊蒿
ùy-ùy bac muc, sheng ngàyc go ràw.	哀哀父母　生我劬勞

Tall-growing are the *ngày* plants—those aren't *ngày*, they're only *outs* plants.
Woe, woe, my father and mother! What effort and weariness my life cost them.

Riwk-riwk tac ngày, puyc ngày i outs; 蓼蓼者莪　匪莪伊蔚
ùy-ùy bac muc, sheng ngàyc ràw dzouts. 哀哀父母　生我勞瘁

If the jug is empty, shame on the storage jar.
Rather than an orphan's life, better to have died long ago.
With no father, who is there to rely on? With no mother, who is there to turn to?
When I go out, I taste anxiety in my mouth; when I come home, there's no-one to come home to.

Bèng tu khèngs luc, wi ròuy tu rhuc; 缾之罄矣　維罍之恥
sent min tu sheng, pu na sic tu kwuc luc. 鮮民之生　不如死之久矣
Ma bac gày gàc, ma muc gày duc? 無父何怙　無母何恃
K'hlout tzùk gràm swit, nup tzùk mayc tits. 出則銜恤　入則靡至

My father gave me life; my mother nourished me,
cuddled me and cherished me, reared me and brought me up,
looked after me and constantly attended to my needs, held me close, indoors and out.
If only I could repay their goodness. But there's no limit to the cruelty of Bright Sky.

Bac ì sheng ngàyc, muc ì kouk ngàyc, 父兮生我　母兮鞠我
phoc ngàyc, rhouk ngàyc, trank ngàyc, louk ngàyc, 拊我畜我　長我育我
kàs ngàyc, bouk ngàyc, k'hlout nup pouk ngàyc. 顧我復我　出入腹我
Lok pòus tu tùk. Gòuc Thìn mank guk. 欲報之德　昊天罔極

The southern mountains rise in ridge beyond ridge, winds whistling around.
Among the people, every one is happy: why am I alone made so wretched?

Nùm shàn rat-rat, pyaw pum pat-pat. 南山列列　飄風發發
Min màk pu kòk, ngàyc dòk gày gàts? 民莫不穀　我獨何害

The southern mountains rise in row after row of peaks, with gusty winds eddying about.
Among the people, every one is happy: why am I alone denied a full life?

Nùm shàn rout-rout, pyaw pum put-put. 南山律律　飄風弗弗
Min màk pu kòk, ngàyc dòk pu tzout. 民莫不穀　我獨不卒

The opening image suggests that while things may seem outwardly to be going well, in reality it is a different story. *Ngày*, *hàw*, and *outs* are three similar-looking plants of the Artemisia family; the young stems of *ngày* (perhaps mugwort) are good to eat, but the other two were seen as worthless. (*Hàw* may be wormwood, *A. absinthium*, and *outs* is identified with *A. japonica*.)

Before piped water, a household would store water in a large Ali-Baba-type jar, and fill jugs from it as needed. The poet likens his (or her?) need for family support to the jug's need of a source for filling. The rugged mountains and rushing winds reflect the poet's low spirits.

Pu tzout, "not finish", was an idiom for not being granted a normal lifespan leading to a natural death. The English reader might want to reply "We all have our troubles, do buck up a bit." But "filial piety", *hràws*, has traditionally been so central a virtue for the Chinese that this lament for an orphan's state may have seemed only right and proper. Legge tells us that the line about Bright Sky "is in the mouth of every Chinese, when speaking of what is due to parents".

203

East and West　大東

There are *krouc* bowls loaded with cooked rice, and long, curved thornwood spoons.
The *Tiw* road is level as a whetstone, and straight as an arrow.
It's the route on which gentlemen travel, while the little people look on.
Longingly I gaze over towards it, tears falling from my eyes.

Wuc mòng krouc sòun, wuc gou kuk pic.　　有饛簋飧　有捄棘匕
Tiw lòuc na dri, kus druk na lhic.　　周道如砥　其直如矢
Kwun-tzuc shac ric; syawc nin shac gic.　　君子所履　小人所視
Konts ngan kàs tu, shànt an k'hlout thìc.　　睠言顧之　潸焉出涕

Throughout the lesser and the greater Eastern states, how empty are the shuttles and cylinders of the looms.
All twisty is the lablab-vine footwear we use for walking in icy terrain.
Sons of princely houses come and go, travelling the *Tiw* road.
Seeing all that coming and going depresses me.

Syawc tòng dàts tòng, drac drouk gu khòng.　　小東大東　杼柚其空
Kiwc-kiwc kàt kros, khàyc luc ric shang.　　糾糾葛屨　可以履霜
Lyàw-lyàw klòng tzuc, gràng payc Tiw gràng.　　佻佻公子　行彼周行
Kuts wank kuts rù, shuc ngàyc sum kwus.　　既往既來　使我心疚

There's icy water pouring from the rock face; it mustn't wet the timber I cut for firewood.
At a distance I lie awake sighing—woe, I'm a worn-out man.
When that felled wood is chopped up, I wish it could be got home on wheels.
Woe, I'm a worn-out man, and I'd be glad to take my ease as gentlemen do.

Wuc rat kwruc dzwan, ma tzums gwàk sin.　　有冽氿泉　無浸穫薪
Khèts-khèts ngàs nhàn, ùy ngàyc tàys nin.　　契契寤歎　哀我憚人
Sin dec gwàk sin, dangs khàyc tzùs layc.　　薪是穫薪　尚可載也
Ùy ngàyc tàys nin, yak khàyc suk layc.　　哀我憚人　亦可息也

The sons of the East just have to labour, unappreciated,
while the sons of the West wear fine clothes.

The sons of *Tiw* dress in black or brown-and-white bear furs,
and their young relatives fill all the official posts.

Tòng nin tu tzuc, tuk ràw pu rùs;	東人之子　職勞不勑
Sì nin tu tzuc, tsàns-tsàns uy-buk;	西人之子　粲粲衣服
Tiw nin tu tzuc, wum pay dec gwu;	周人之子　熊羆是裘
si nin tu tzuc, pràk ryàwc dec lhuks.	私人之子　百僚是試

They know what to do with their wine, I agree—but they have no use for congee.
Their jade netsuke are flawless—but they don't make worthwhile use of their high positions.
There in the sky is the Milky Way; it looks down on us, and it's a brilliant thing.
The Weaving Girl is there, on a slant. After 24 hours she's risen seven stages.

Wùk luc gu tziwc, pu luc gu tzang.	或以其酒　不以其漿
Gwènt-gwènt bès syouts, pu luc gu trank.	鞙鞙佩璲　不以其長
Wi thìn wuc Hàns, kràm yak wuc kwàng.	維天有漢　監亦有光
Khes payc Tuk Nrac, toung nit tsit snang.	○彼織女　終日七襄

But despite the seven stages, she's produced no woven pattern.
The Draught Ox shines brightly—but you can't harness it to a carriage.
In the east is the Morning Star, in the west the Evening Star,
and then there's the hornlike Heavenly Fork: they have no duties beyond arraying themselves in their ranks.

Swi-tzùk tsit snang, pu deng pòus tang.	雖則七襄　不成報章
Gwrànt payc Khìn Ngwu; pu luc buc-sang.	睆彼牽牛　不以服箱
Tòng wuc Khìc Mrang, sì wuc Drang Kràngs,	東有啟明　西有長庚
wuc gou Thìn Pit. Tzùs lhay tu gàng.	有捄天畢　載施之行

In the south is the Winnowing Basket, but you can't winnow with it.
In the north is the Ladle, but it doesn't ladle out any wine or congee.
The Winnowing Basket in the south—its only duty is to stick out its Tongue,
while the Ladle in the north raises its handle westwards.

Wi nùm wuc Ku; pu khàyc luc pàyc-lang;	維南有箕　不可以簸揚
wi pùk wuc Toc; pu up tziwc tzang.	維北有斗　不挹酒漿
Wi nùm wuc Ku; tzùs hup gu mlat.	維南有箕　載翕其舌
Wi pùk wuc Toc; sì prangs tu kat.	維北有斗　西柄之揭

At this period, wealth and power in China were concentrated in the West, around the dynastic capital; the East, where this poet lived, was a poor hinterland. He looks with longing on the road to the West and the well-to-do gentlemen travelling on it. They have fine clothes and sturdy shoes, while in the East there is not even much cloth being produced. Congee is a kind of porridge made from rice, and in the East it is an important element of nutrition, but for westerners it is beneath consideration.

In the Himalayas, shoes of twisted grass rope over leather socks have been used for walking in ice and snow in our own time. Verse 2 seems to describe something like that, perhaps suggesting the primitive conditions in the East.

The poet resents the westerners not just for their affluence but because, as he sees it, they are useless: they hold lucrative official posts and achieve nothing in them. Hence the extended comparison with the stars in the night sky, which are beautiful but do nothing for mankind.

We have seen that the Chinese partitioned the night sky into constellations differently from us. The Milky Way is of course common to all cultures: the Chinese call it the "heavenly Han river", mirroring the Han river on earth, after which the Chinese race is named. Some other references, though, are mysterious. The Weaving Girl is a constellation including the bright star Vega; the "seven stages" must relate in some way to the rotation of the stars across the firmament, but I do not know enough about traditional Chinese astronomy to say how. The Draught Ox is part of our Capricorn. Nowadays we know that the Morning and Evening Stars are the same thing, the planet Venus, but evidently at this time the Chinese took *Khìc Mrang*, "the inaugurator of brightness", and *Drang Kràng*, "the long continuation", to be separate phenomena—as did we. The Heavenly Fork is a set of stars in the Hyades, which together form a Y shape. The Winnowing Basket is part of our Sagittarius; the Ladle is our Plough.

Two stars in the Winnowing Basket were called the Heel and two others the Tongue. Most commentators translate *hup* as "draw in" rather than "stick out" the Tongue, but while one can imagine an array of stars being seen as having a protruding tongue, I cannot think that any arrangement would be seen as a retracted tongue.

In the last verse, the first line seems to have one syllable too many for the metre; *khàyc luc*, "be able to", was a frequent set phrase (and still is: in Mandarin it is pronounced 'kěyǐ'), and probably *luc* could be so de-emphasized in this phrase that it did not count as a beat. In the received text, the following line is even worse, with two extra syllables. But when successive passages are parallel, it is a common copyist's error to repeat wording from the first passage into the second; I suspect that happened here, and have mended the metre accordingly.

204

000000000Th000e0000 Fourth Moon　　四月

By the fourth moon we are in summer; in the sixth moon its heat is abating.
Are the ancestors inhuman? Why are they so unfeeling towards me?

Slits ngwat wi gràs; rouk ngwat dzà lhac.　　四月維夏　六月徂暑
Sùn tzàc puyc nin? Gà nèng nunt lac?　　先祖匪人　胡寧忍予

Autumn days are chilly, and every kind of plant is withered.
Disorder and scattering of families are creating distress. Where can I find sanctuary?

Tsiw nit tsì-tsì, pràk hwuys gos buy.　　秋日淒淒　百卉具腓
Ròns ray màk luc. Gè ku lhek kwuy?　　亂離瘼矣　奚其適歸

In winter, days are bitterly cold, and winds are strong and gusty.
The entire population is prospering; why am I alone made to suffer?

Tòung nit rat-rat, pyaw pum pat-pat.
Min màk pu kòk; ngàyc dòk gày gàts?

冬日冽冽　飄風發發
民莫不穀　我獨何害

In the hills there is fine vegetation—there are chestnut trees, and plum trees.
People are mutilating them severely. Yet no-one knows how the trees are guilty.

Shàn wuc kràḥ hwuys, gò rit, gò mù.
Pat way dzàn dzùk—màk tre gu wu.

山有嘉卉　侯栗侯梅
廢為殘賊　莫知其尤

Look at the water in the spring: now it is clear, now turbid.
I meet disasters every day; how, pray, can I change my luck?

Sangs payc dzwan lhouyc: tzùs tseng, tzùs dròk.
Ngàyc nit kòs gòyc; gàt wun nùc kòk?

相彼泉水　載清載濁
我曰構禍　曷云能穀

The Yangtze and the Han are mighty rivers, chief arteries of the southern states.
I'm knocking myself out to serve the public—why is nobody on my side?

Lhòu-lhòu Kròng Hàns, nùm kwùk tu kuc.
Dzint dzouts luc shuc: nèng màk ngàyc wuc?

滔滔江漢　南國之紀
盡瘁以仕　寧莫我友

I'm no eagle, no kite, that could soar up to the sky.
I'm no switchtail or mikado-fish, that could escape by diving into the deep.

Puyc dòn, puyc yon, gàn puy rìts thìn.
Puyc tran, puyc wruc, dzem làw wa wwìn.

匪鶉匪鳶　翰飛戾天
匪鱣匪鮪　潛逃于淵

In the hills there are royal ferns and turtle's-foot ferns; in the wetlands, matrimony-vines and tawkins.
I, a nobleman, have composed this song, to make the world aware of my woe.

Shàn wuc kot muy, slup wuc khuc li.
Kwun-tzuc tzàk kày, wi luc kòuk ùy.

山有蕨薇　隰有杞桋
君子作歌　維以告哀

A routine exercise in self-pity by a member of the gentry, who feels he is not receiving adequate recognition for his efforts on behalf of his people, either from the people themselves or from his ancestral spirits. It is not clear how the "disorder" of verse 2 is consistent with the statement that the population is prospering—and if there is a relationship between these lines and the autumn and winter images, it is not apparent. My rendering of the stich about "sanctuary" may be wrong; the Chinese text has a variant which would make this stich a statement rather than a question, though this would scarcely be clearer. The damaged trees in verse 4 are even more mysterious.

Verse 5 with its image of clear and turbid water may be saying that most people have ups and downs in life, but the poet feels his life is all downs.

In verse 7, *yon* is the black kite, *Milvus melanotis*. Switchtail and mikado-fish are two species of sturgeon, respectively *Scaphirhynchus platorhyncus* and *Acipenser mikadoi*. Tawkins (*Orontium aquaticum*), a kind of arum, are little more than a guess at the plant the poet calls *li*.

VOICES FROM EARLY CHINA

205

The North Hill 北山

We go up the north hill, gathering the goji berries that grow there.
Early and late, the many officials are all at work.
There's no skimping the king's service; but I grieve for my parents.

Truk payc pùk shàn, ngan tsùc gu khuc.　　　涉彼北山　言采其杞
Krì-krì shuc tzuc, traw syak dzong shuc.　　皆皆士子　朝夕從事
Wang shuc mayc kàc; ou ngàyc bac muc.　　王事靡盬　憂我父母

Under Sky's vast expanse, there's no land which is not the king's.
Of those who visit the court from every land, none but is the king's servant.
But the high officials are not all equally diligent: I'm really the only one doing his job properly.

Phàc Thìn tu gràc, màk puy wang thàc.　　溥天之下　莫非王土
Shout thàc tu pin, màk puy wang gin.　　率土之賓　莫非王臣
Dàts pa pu kwin; ngàyc dzong shuc dòk gìn.　大夫不均　我從事獨賢

My team of four stallions thunders over the ground, and on every hand I deal with tasks for the king.
It's fine that I'm not yet old—it's splendid that I'm just at my peak,
and my spine and sinews are tough as ever. I'm setting all parts of the world to rights.

Slits mouc pàng-pàng, wang shuc bàng-bàng.　　四牡彭彭　王事旁旁
Kràt ngàyc muts ròuc, sen ngàyc pang tzang.　　嘉我未老　鮮我方將
Rac-ruk pang kàng; kèng-weng Slits Pang.　　脊力方剛　經營四方

Some officials spend their time feasting and quietly relaxing, but some of us wear ourselves out in state service.
Some stretch themselves out on their couches, but some are for ever on the road.

Wùk èns-èns kas suk; wùk dzint dzouts shuc kwùk.　或燕燕居息　或盡瘁事國
Wùk suk ant dzùc djang; wùk pu luc wa gràng.　　或息偃在床　或不已于行

Some never know the sound of a summons to duty, but some make themselves wretched with hard work.
Some lie for hours gazing at the ceiling, but some are at their wits' end in the king's service.

Wùk pu tre kìws ghàw; wùk tsùmp-tsùmp go ràw.　或不知叫號　或慘慘劬勞
Wùk sì dri ant ngank; wùk wang shuc ank-thank.　或棲遲偃仰　或王事鞅掌

Some soak themselves in pleasure and wine, but some torment themselves with the fear of incurring criticism.
Some just complain wherever they are, but for some there's no task they fail to tackle.

Wùk tùm ngràwks um tziwc; wùk tsùmp-tsùmp ouys gouc. 或湛樂飲酒　或慘慘畏咎
Wùk k'hlout nup pums ngays; wùk mayc shuc pu way. 或出入諷議　或靡事不為

To self-pity is added brazen boasting. Where does he find time to gather goji berries?
Worry that public responsibilities are preventing one from looking after aged parents properly (end of verse 1) is a recurrent Odes trope.

206

Don't Try to Shift the Big Waggon　無將大車

Don't try to shift the big waggon: you'll only get yourself dusty.
Don't brood on your many sorrows: you'll only make yourself ill.

Ma tzang dàts ka: ke dzis drun ì. 無將大車　祇自塵兮
Ma sus pràk ou: ke dzis tì ì. 無思百憂　祇自疧兮

Don't try to shift the big waggon: you'll be black with dust.
Don't brood on your many sorrows: you'll never escape into the light.

Ma tzang dàts ka: wi drun mènk-mènk. 無將大車　維塵冥冥
Ma sus pràk ou: pu k'hlout wa kwènk. 無思百憂　不出于熲

Don't try to shift the big waggon: you'll be covered in dust.
Don't brood on your many sorrows: you'll only weigh yourself down.

Ma tzang dàts ka: wi drun onk ì. 無將大車　維塵雝兮
Ma sus pràk ou: ke dzis dronk ì. 無思百憂　祇自重兮

207

On Campaign　小明

Bright is Sky above, shining down on the earth below.
We have come west on campaign, and reached a remote waste.
Since early in the second moon we've experienced biting cold and then sweltering heat.

Oh, the misery in my heart—the poison of it is very bitter.
Thinking of my family, tears flow like rain.
How could I not yearn to go home? But I fear getting enmeshed in the net of
    guilt.

Mrang-mrang dyangs Thìn, tyaw rum gràc thàc.   明明上天　照臨下土
Ngàyc teng dzà sì, tits wa gwu lac.   我征徂西　至于艽野
Nits ngwat cha kit, tzùs ray gàn lhac.   二月初吉　載離寒暑
Sum tu ou luc; gu dòuk thàts khàc.   心之憂矣　其毒大苦
Nìms payc gongs nin: thìc rìn na wac.   念彼共人　涕零如雨
Khuyc pu gròuy kwuy? Ouys tsec dzòuyc kàc.   豈不懷歸　畏此罪罟

Back when we set off, the old year was just drawing to its close.
When, pray, shall we return? This year will itself have grown old.
Contemplating my loneliness, and the burden of my many duties,
oh, the misery in my heart—I'm exhausted, and never get any respite.
Thinking of my family, I look back at them fondly.
How could I not yearn to go home? But I fear official reprimands and anger.

Sak ngàyc wank luc, nit ngwat pang dras.   昔我往矣　日月方除
Gàt wun gu wèn? Swats lout wun màks.   曷云其還　歲聿云莫
Nìms ngàyc dòk ì, ngàyc shuc khònk lhaks,   念我獨兮　我事孔庶
sum tu ou luc, tàys ngàyc pu gràs.   心之憂矣　憚我不暇
Nìms payc gongs nin, kons-kons gròuy kàs.   念彼共人　睠睠懷顧
Khuyc pu gròuy kwuy? Ouys tsec khens nàc.   豈不懷歸　畏此譴怒

Back when we set off, the weather was still clement.
When, pray, shall we return? My responsibilities are ever more demanding.
The year will have grown old, and they'll be gathering lad's-love and harvesting
    beans.
Oh, the misery in my heart—but I've brought this grief on myself.
Thinking of my family, I can't sleep: I get up and spend the night out of bed.
How could I not yearn to go home? But I fear the come-back if I did.

Sak ngàyc wank luc, nit ngwat pang ouk.   昔我往矣　日月方奧
Gàt wun gu wèn? Tengs shuc loc tziwk.   曷云其還　政事愈蹙
Swats lout wun màks, tsùc sìw, gwàk nhouk.   歲聿云莫　采蕭穫菽
Sum tu ou luc; dzis lu i tsìwk.   心之憂矣　自詒伊戚
Nìms payc gongs nin, hung ngan k'hlout souk.   念彼共人　興言出宿
Khuyc pu gròuy kwuy? Ouys tsec pant phuk.   豈不懷歸　畏此反覆

Ah, your lordships, don't perpetually take it easy.
Take your official roles seriously and thoughtfully; associate with people who are
    honest and straight.
The Spirits will hear you—they'll treat you with favour.

Tzay nec kwun-tzuc, ma gùng àn k'hlac.   嗟爾君子　無恆安處
Dzenk krong nec wruts; tengs druk dec lac.   靖恭爾位　正直是與
Mlin tu lhèng tu, lhuk kòk luc nac.   神之聽之　式穀以汝

Ah, your lordships, don't let yourselves perpetually relax.
Take your official roles seriously and thoughtfully; love those who are honest and straight.
The Spirits will hear you, and they'll make your happy situation happier still.

Tzay nec kwun-tzuc, ma gùng àn suk. 嗟爾君子 無恆安息
Dzenk krong nec wruts; hòus dec tengs druk. 靖恭爾位 好是正直
Mlin tu lhèng tu, kréts nec krank puk. 神之聽之 介爾景福

The poet is leading a military campaign, and missing home. But by identifying the people he misses as his family, my translation flies in the face both of the Chinese commentary tradition, and of previous Western translations. They, without exception so far as I know, represent the poet as missing the company of his polished fellow courtiers, by contrast with the rough soldiery under his command. The received text repeatedly describes the poet as missing *payc gongs nin*. *Payc* is just "that, those, the", and *nin* is "person" or "people". *Gongs* in the standard script means "together", and the graph can alternatively stand for *konk* "join hands", but neither seems to fit this context—to think of one's wife as the person one holds hands with might work for a cheesy 21st-century rom-com, but scarcely for *Tiw* China. So it is assumed that the *gongs* graph was being used as a substitute for some graph written similarly (as did often happen): either *krong* "polite, respectful", or *kong* "serve, provide". "Serving people" could mean office-holders at court, and "courteous people" might be a way of referring to polished courtiers. Neither is a standard locution, but the poem is taken that way for lack of an obvious alternative. However I find that reading too implausible to go along with. To call one's family one's "together people" is not a usual idiom either, but at least it would explain the tearfulness. Or perhaps the poet really did think of his wife as the one he held hands with.

Kit in the third line normally means "lucky", but it is believed here to refer either to the first day or the first ten-day period of a month.

There is another textual difficulty about the last word of verse 1: to a Western mind, "the net of guilt" is a plausible metaphor (all the more so because criminals in ancient China were sometimes confined in nets), but others take the word *kàc* "net" to have been substituted for an original *kà*, which is a close synonym of the preceding word *dzòuyc*, "guilt, crime". Again I have preferred to take the received text as correct. Either way, it is plain that the poet could decide to lead his troops home, but having been given responsibility for the campaign he will be in trouble if he abandons it. Yet he knows he has brought his trouble on himself—he did not have to accept command.

We are familiar in the West with soldiers who see the politicians who have sent them to war as irresponsible.

208

They Sound the Bells 鼓鍾

They sound the bells, *tsang tsang*; the river *Wì* is in spate.
My heart is full of grief and pain.
I think about my lord, that good man; truly he is never out of my mind.

Kàc tong tsang-tsang; Wì lhouyc lhang-lhang.
Ou sum tsac lhang.
Diwk nin kwun-tzuc, gròuy yount pu wang.

鼓鍾鏘鏘　淮水湯湯
憂心且傷
淑人君子　懷允不忘

They sound the bells in harmony; the waters of the *Wì* are cold.
My heart is full of grief and sorrow.
My lord, that good man: his character never goes astray.

Kàc tong krì-krì; Wì lhouyc grì-grì.
Ou sum tsac pruy.
Diwk nin kwun-tzuc, gu tùk pu wùy.

鼓鍾喈喈　淮水湝湝
憂心且悲
淑人君子　其德不回

They sound the bells and beat the big drum; in the river *Wì* there are three islets.
My heart is full of grief and anxiety.
My lord, that good man: his character is unmatched.

Kàc tong bat kòu; Wì wuc sùm tou.
Ou sum tsac t'hliw.
Diwk nin kwun-tzuc, gu tùk pu you.

鼓鍾伐鼛　淮有三洲
憂心且妯
淑人君子　其德不猶

They sound the bells most solemnly; they play zither and lute.
The reed-organ and the musical stones blend their notes.
With this accompaniment dancers perform the *ngràc* and the *nùm*, handling their
    flutes faultlessly.

Kàc tong khum-khum; kàc sprit, kàc gum.
Sheng khèngs dòng um.
Luc ngràc, luc nùm, luc yawk pu tzèms.

鼓鍾欽欽　鼓瑟鼓琴
笙磬同音
以雅以南　以籥不僭

We saw in Ode 38 that there was a type of ritual dance where the dancers held a flute in one hand and a plume in the other; *ngràc* and *nùm* are two such dances. But that does not tell us what the point of this poem might be. The *Wì* (modern Huai) is a river of the south-east, but what had it to do with the music and dancing? Is there any reason to mention the islets in that river, beyond the fact that *tou* "islet" provides a rhyme to *kòu* "big drum"?

209

The Vigorous Puncture-Vine　楚茨

Ode 209 gives us the fullest picture we have of the rite in which a clan head offered a sacrifice to an ancestral spirit. Although the Chinese text comprises just a series of spoken words with few "stage directions", it seems that the words divide into speeches by various participants in the ritual, occasionally interrupted by scene-setting narration. The translation here is my own, but in ascribing successive lines and verses to particular speakers I follow the analysis by Martin Kern. Kern identifies the following participants: the Descendant (the living head of the clan); the Corpse (the living proxy for the ancestor being honoured, see Ode 15); what Kern calls the "Invocator", who leads participants through the ritual—I shall call him the "Priest"; and the male clan members speaking in chorus.

The Priest addresses the Corpse on behalf of the Descendant:
"The puncture-vine has spread vigorously, and we're pulling out its thorns.
What have we done since time immemorial?—we have grown millet.
Our foxtail millet has cropped abundantly, and our broomcorn millet is coming along nicely.
Our grain store is full already, and we have countless outdoor stacks.
We shall make wine from it, and eat it; it will give us feasts, and sacrifice-offerings.
It will let us quaff at our ease; it will enlarge our shadows, and increase our welfare."

Chac-chac tac dzi; ngan rhiw gu kuk.	楚楚者茨	言抽其棘
Dzis sak gày way? Ngàyc tzup nhac tzuk.	自昔何為	我蓺黍稷
Ngàyc nhac la-la; ngàyc tzuk yuk-yuk.	我黍與與	我稷翼翼
Ngàyc tsàng kuts leng, ngàyc yoc wi uk.	我倉既盈	我庾維億
Luc way tziwc mluk, luc hang, luc sluc.	以為酒食	以饗以祀
Luc nhòyc, luc wus, luc krèts krank puk.	以妥以侑	以介景福

The Priest addresses the Descendant:
"Stately are the movements and pure the colours of the cattle and sheep which you offer at the seasonal sacrifices.
Some are cutting up meat while others are boiling it; some are setting it out, and others bringing it forward.
I, the priestly celebrant, make the offering by the temple gate. The rite of sacrifice is very bright.
You have caused your ancestor to return, and this guardian Spirit is enjoying his feast.
His pious Descendant will be blessed
—he will be rewarded with increased good fortune, ten thousand years of life unending."

Tzìc-tzìc tsang-tsang, kèt nec ngwu yang, luc wank tung dyang.	濟濟蹌蹌 烝嘗	潔爾牛羊 以往
Wùk pròk, wùk phràng, wùk sits, wùk tzang.	或剝或烹	或肆或將
Touk tzats wa pràng. Sluc shuc khònk mrang.	祝祭于祊	祀事孔明
Sùn tzàc dec wank. Mlin pòuc dec hang,	先祖是往	神保是饗
hràws sòun wuc khrangs	孝孫有慶	
—pòus luc krèts puk, màns douc ma kang.	報以介福	萬壽無疆

The Priest continues speaking to the Descendant:
"The barbecues are attended assiduously, and the sacrificial tables are set out impressively. Some people are roasting, others broiling.
The noblewomen have fallen respectfully silent, as they serve food into numerous *dòs* bowls.

There are guests, there are visitors. People are toasting one another in all
 directions.
The rituals and ceremonies are just as they should be, the laughter and chatter is
 entirely fitting to the occasion.
The guardian Spirit is here.
His response to your rite will be ever-growing good fortune: ten thousand years
 of life will be your reward."

Tup tsòns tsak-tsak; way jac khònk dak. Wùk ban, wùk tak.	執爨踏踏	為俎孔碩　或燔或炙
Kwun buc mràk-mràk, way dòs khònk lhaks.	君婦嘆嘆	為豆孔庶
Way pin, way khràk. Nghans dou kryàw tsàk.	為賓為客	獻酬交錯
Rìc ngay tzout dàk, saws ngac tzout wàk.	禮儀卒度	笑語卒獲
Mlin pòuc dec kràk.	神保是格	
Pòus luc krèts puk, màns douc you dzàk.	報以介福	萬壽攸酢

The Descendant says: "We are in great awe, seeing the rituals executed without
 mistakes."
Then the Priest makes the announcement, he comes forward and addresses the
 pious Descendant:
"This pious sacrifice is fragrant. The Spirit relishes the drink and food,
and promises good luck coming your way a hundredfold, in the proper quantity
 and following the proper norms.
You have provided the grain for sacrifice, in particular you have provided millet;
 you have brought baskets of vegetables and arranged them.
The utmost you could wish for will be bestowed on you, ten thousand-fold, a
 hundred thousand-fold, for ever."

Ngàyc khònk nant luc, lhuk rìc màk khryan.	我孔戁矣	式禮莫愆
Kòng touk trits kòuk, dzà rùks hràws sòun:	工祝致告	徂賚孝孫
"Bìt phun hràws sluc; Mlin gis um mluk,	苾芬孝祀	神嗜飲食
pòk nec pràk puk, na kuyc na lhuk.	卜爾百福	如幾如式
Kuts tzi, kuts tzuk, kuts kwhang, kuts rhuk;	既○既稷	既匡既敕
wrank slèk nec guk, du màns, du uk."	永錫爾極	時萬時億

Descendant: "The rituals and ceremonies are now complete. The drums and bells
 have sounded for attention."
The pious Descendant goes to his place of honour, and the Priest makes the
 announcement:
"The Spirits are all thoroughly drunk. The august Corpse may now rise!"
The Corpse is escorted away with drums and bells, whereupon the guardian
 Spirit returns whence he came.
The attendants and the noblewomen clear things away promptly,
and (the Spirit having been served) the menfolk are ready for their own feasting.

"Rìc ngay kuts bruks; tong kàc kuts krùs."	禮儀既備	鍾鼓既戒
Hràws sòun dzà wruts. Kòng touk trits kòuk:	孝孫徂位	工祝致告
"Mlin gos tzouts tuc. Wàng Lhi tzùs khuc."	神具醉止	皇尸載起

Kàc tong sòngs Lhi, Mlin pòuc lout kwuy.   鼓鍾送尸　神保聿歸
Ta tzùc kwun buc, pats thret pu dri;   諸宰君婦　廢徹不遲
ta bac hwrang dìc, bruks ngan èns si.   諸父兄弟　備言燕私

The musicians all come in and hasten to their places, so that participants may relax as they enjoy the good things which are coming.
Priest to Descendant: "Your food has been served out. No-one is dissatisfied, all are happy."
Clan members: "We are sozzled and stuffed with food. Young men and old, we bow our heads to the ground.
The Spirit relished the drink and food, so he will grant the prince a long, long life."
Priest to Descendant: "Things have gone off very conformably and *comme il faut*, and now all is complete.
May sons and grandsons follow you in unbroken succession."

Ngràwk gos nup tzòs, luc snouy ghòc ròk.   樂具入奏　以綏後祿
"Nec gràw kuts tzang. Màk ons, gos khrangs."   爾殽既將　莫怨具慶
"Kuts tzouts, kuts pròuc. Syawc dàts khìc lhouc.   既醉既飽　小大稽首
Mlin gis um mluk, shuc kwun douc khòuc."   神嗜飲食　使君壽考
"Khònk wìts, khònk du; wi kus dzint tu.   孔惠孔時　維其盡之
Tzuc tzuc, sòun sòun, mut thìs lint tu."   子子孫孫　勿替引之

Puncture-vine (*Tribulus terrestris*) is a ground-hugging plant with tough thorns which are well able to puncture bike tyres, let alone bare feet. It has uses, as a medicine and an aphrodisiac, but here it seems to function to contrast the pain of growing millet with the pleasures that follow the harvest. (Why this is a suitable way to introduce a solemn ritual is as mysterious as opening images commonly are.) Millet wine was an important element of early East Asian rituals.

I take "enlarge our shadows" to mean "make us fat"—which in the 21st century West is nothing to look forward to, but attitudes were different in a society never far from hunger.

To read the description of this ceremony sympathetically, we must forget our modern associations with concepts like "spirit", "pious". For most of us today, ghosts are a joke; but for *Tiw* Chinese the idea that they were watched over by the spirits of their dead ancestors, and needed to treat them well, was very serious. Arguably, later Chinese thinkers were well ahead of their Western counterparts in discarding such ideas, but they were a perfectly reasonable early attempt to make sense of the happy or disastrous events occurring in the Chinese world.

Again, "pious" has slightly mocking overtones in the 21st century, but I am using it here in something more like its etymological Latin sense. When Virgil called the hero of the *Aeneid* "pious Aeneas", he did not mean that that warrior went about with a prayerful expression on his face mouthing well-meaning platitudes; he meant something like "public-spirited"—Aeneas cared about the welfare of his people and strove to do the things needed to promote that welfare. Old Chinese *hràws* was like that, with an emphasis on serving one's ancestors, which for a ruler was seen as very much to society's as well as his own benefit.

210

The Extensive Southern Uplands 信南山

The southern uplands are extensive; it was *Wac* who prepared them for cultivation,
clearing the plateaus and draining the wetlands. Now his Descendant cultivates them.
We are defining boundaries and marking out fields, orienting them to the cardinal points.

Lhin payc nùm shàn; wi Wac lìns tu,	伸彼南山　維禹甸之
win-win ngwan slup. Tzùng sòun lìns tu.	畇畇邊隰　曾孫田之
Ngàyc kang, ngàyc ruc, nùm tòng gu mùc.	我疆我理　南東其畝

Sky on High masses together the clouds, sending down heavy snow.
Then follows drizzling rain: amply it moistens the land
—it soaks the land in good measure, giving life to our various grain crops.

Dyangs Thìn dòng wun, was sot phun-phun.	上天同雲　雨雪紛紛
Uk tu luc mrèk-mròk: kuts ou, kuts rròk	益之以霢霂　既優既渥
—kuts trem, kuts tzok; sheng ngàyc pràk kòk.	既霑既足　生我百穀

The field boundaries and the dykes subdividing them are well arranged, and the millet is richly developed.
The Descendant harvests it, to turn it into food and wine.
He offers these to our Corpse and our guests, with wishes for long life, ten thousand years.

Kang lek yuk-yuk, nhac tzuk ouk-ouk.	疆場翼翼　黍稷彧彧
Tzùng sòun tu shuk, luc way tziwc sluks.	曾孫之穡　以為酒食
Pits ngàyc Lhi pin, douc khòuc, màns nìn.	畀我尸賓　壽考萬年

In the middle of the fields are huts, while gourds grow along the edges.
These we cut up and pickle, offering them to the divine Ancestors.
May the Descendant have long life, and receive Sky's blessing.

Troung lìn wuc ra; kang lek wuc gwàs.	中田有廬　疆場有瓜
Dec pròk, dec ja, nghans tu wàng tzàc.	是剝是菹　獻之皇祖
Tzùng sòun douc khòuc, douc Thìn tu gàc.	曾孫壽考　受天之祜

As sacrifice the Descendant offers clear wine, and follows that with a red stallion,
presenting these to the Ancestors.
He takes the bell-knife and opens up the horse's hide,
to get the blood and fat.

Tzats luc tseng tziwc, dzong luc seng mouc,
hang wa tzàc khòuc.
Tup gu ròn tàw, luc khìc gu màw,
tsoc gu hwìt ryàw.

祭以清酒　從以騂牡
享于祖考
執其鸞刀　以啟其毛
取其血膋

He offers these things, he presents them—they smell good, they are fragrant.
The business of sacrifice is carried off splendidly. The ancestors are divine indeed,
rewarding the Descendant with great felicity—ten thousand years of endless life.

Dec tung, dec hang, bìt-bìt, phun-phun.
Sluc shuc khònk mrang. Sùn tzàc dec wàng,
pòus luc krèts puk, màns douc ma kang.

是烝是享　苾苾芬芬
祀事孔明　先祖是皇
報以介福　萬壽無疆

Wac's "Descendant" refers to the current ruler. Obviously he did not personally grow and harvest the crops, but he probably did do symbolic things like ploughing the first furrow.

British field boundaries run in all sorts of directions, determined largely by the lie of the land. But that kind of geographic anarchy is alien to the Chinese, for whom field boundaries (or city walls) not running north–south and east–west would be uncivilized.

The sacrificial *seng mouc* of verse 5 may have been a stallion, or a bull.

211

Broad Fields　甫田

These broad fields are first-rate: they crop a thousand measures of grain for each ten measures sown.
We use the old grain to feed our farm-hands.
We've been getting harvests in since olden times; and now we've moved on to the southerly acres.
Some are weeding, some are hoeing earth up round the growing plants; our foxtail- and broomcorn-millet are both doing splendidly.
We are being enriched, we are being made prosperous, so we can bestow bonuses on our fine officials.

Tràwk payc pac lìn: swats tsoc gip tsìn.
Ngàyc tsoc gu drin, sluks ngàyc nòung nin.
Dzis kàc wuc nìn; kum lhek nùm mùc.
Wùk wun, wùk tzuc; nhac tzuk nguc-nguc.
You krèts, you thruc, tung ngàyc màw shuc.

倬彼甫田　歲取十千
我取其陳　食我農人
自古有年　今適南畝
或耘或耔　黍稷薿薿
攸介攸止　烝我髦士

With our bright grain and our sacrificial lambs
we make our offering to the Spirit of the Soil, to the Four Quarters.
The excellence of our fields is our farm-hands' joy.
We play lutes and zithers, and beat drums, to make welcome the Spirit of Agriculture,

to pray for sweet rain to enlarge our millet harvest,
and thus to further the welfare of our men and women.

Luc ngàyc tzi mrang, lac ngàyc nghay yang, 以我○明　與我犧羊
luc Dac, luc Pang. 以社以方
Ngàyc lìn kuts tzàng, nòung pa tu khrangs. 我田既臧　農夫之慶
Gum sprit, kèk kàc, luc ngràs Lìn Tzàc, 琴瑟擊鼓　以御田祖
luc guy kàm wac, luc krèts ngàyc tzuk nhac, 以祈甘雨　以介我稷黍
luc kòk ngàyc shuc nrac. 以穀我士女

The Descendant has come:
via the women and children he arranges for food to be taken out to the men in the southern acres.
The field inspector arrives, and he's delighted with what he sees.
He thrusts aside his assistants and tastes personally to check whether the grain is sweet.
The grain has been well tended throughout these acres—it's both good quality and abundant.
There's nothing here to irritate the Descendant: the farm-hands have shown themselves well capable of hard work.

Tzùng Sòun rù tuc: 曾孫來止
luc gu buc tzuc, wap payc nùm mùc. 以其婦子　饁彼南畝
Lìn tzyouns tits huc. 田畯至喜
Nang gu tzàyc-wuc, dyang kus kic puc. 攘其左右　嘗其旨否
Wày leks drang mùc—toung dant tsac wuc. 禾易長畝　終善且有
Tzùng Sòun pu nàc: nòung pa khùk mùc. 曾孫不怒　農夫克敏

The Descendant's grain stands thick as thatch, sturdy as poles.
His open-air grain stacks are like islands rising from the sea, like hills.
He's going to need to find a thousand granaries to store it all—to find ten thousand carts to transport it.
The foxtail- and broomcorn-millet, the rice, and the sorghum are the farm-hands' joy.
May the Descendant be rewarded with ever-increasing good fortune, and ten thousand years of life without end!

Tzùng Sòun tu kràs, na dzi, na rang. 曾孫之稼　如茨如梁
Tzùng Sòun tu yoc, na dri, na krang. 曾孫之庾　如坻如京
Nùc gou tsìn ses tsàng, nùc gou màns se sang. 迺求千斯倉　迺求萬斯箱
Tzuk nhac lòuc rang, nòung pa tu khrangs. 黍稷稻粱　農夫之慶
Pòus luc krèts puk, màns douc ma kang. 報以介福　萬壽無疆

The ruler has arrived in the poet's neck of the woods, where the harvest is more than satisfactory. The point about "old grain", I take it, is that last year's crop was so good that there still remains enough for the workers' rations, without trenching into the new harvest. (Why the ruler needs to arrange for the workers to get lunch is mysterious: if he had not visited, would they have been expected to work through the day without a break?)

212

Seed-Time and Harvest 大田

May our wide fields yield a good crop of grain!
We have readied our seed-grain and our tools; once all is prepared, we set to work.
With sharp ploughshares we begin on the southern acres;
we sow the various kinds of grain, and they grow straight and well.
The Descendant approves.

Dàts lìn tày kràs!	大田多稼
Kuts tonk, kuts grùs; kuts bruks, nùc shuc.	既種既械　既備迺事
Luc ngàyc lemp sluc, thiwk tzùs nùm mùc.	以我覃耜　俶載南畝
Pàys kot pràk kòk; kuts lèng tsac dak.	播厥百穀　既庭且碩
Tzùng sòun dec nak.	曾孫是若

The crop develops as it should, and the kernels are tender;
then they harden and begin to swell. The plants are free of darnel and other weeds,
and we have suppressed the caterpillars and eelworm.
Nothing is damaging the young crops in our fields; strong is the magic of the Father of Agriculture.
We throw handfuls of weeds onto the blazing bonfire.

Kuts pang, kuts dzòuc;	既方既皁
kuts kìn, kuts hòuc—pu ràng, pu youc.	既堅既好　不稂不莠
Khac gu mèng-lùk, gup gu mou dzùk.	去其螟螣　及其蟊賊
Ma gàts ngàyc lìn dris; Lìn Tzàc wuc mlin.	無害我田穉　田祖有神
Prank pits wam mhùyc.	秉畀炎火

Clouds gather and thicken, bringing on heavy rain.
First it rains on the common fields, and then it reaches our individual plots.
Over there is some grain not cut because it was late ripening, here are some sheaves that were never gathered up;
here are some forgotten handfuls, there are some discarded ears.
These will be the widows' share.

Wuc amp tsì-tsì, hung wac gri-gri.	有渰萋萋　興雨祁祁
Was ngàyc kòng lìn, swits gup ngàyc si.	雨我公田　遂及我私
Payc wuc pu gwàk dris; tsec wuc pu rams dzìs.	彼有不穫穉　此有不斂穧
Payc wuc wi prank; tsec wuc drets swits.	彼有遺秉　此有滯穗
I kwràc buc tu ris.	伊寡婦之利

The Descendant arrives.
He has his womenfolk and children bring food to the men working the south acres.

VOICES FROM EARLY CHINA

The field inspector comes and he's happy with what he sees, so the Descendant organizes the *in* and *sluc* sacrifices.
Using these red cattle and black cattle, and this millet of two sorts,
he makes offerings, he sacrifices, and thus ensures us ever greater welfare.

Tzùng sòun rù tuc.	曾孫來止
Luc gu buc tzuc, wap payc nùm mùc.	以其婦子　饁彼南畝
Lìn Tzyouns tits huc; rù pang in sluc.	田畯至喜　來方禋祀
Luc kus seng mhùk, lac kus nhac tzuk,	以其騂黑　與其黍稷
luc hang, luc sluc, luc krèts krank puk.	以享以祀　以介景福

The Father of Agriculture is a reference to a god Shen Nong, inventor of agriculture and medicine. The farmhands will not have relied solely on spirit influence to combat crop pests such as eelworms, which destroy cereal crops by attacking their roots; even today in the West, eelworm is sometimes tackled by digging chopped marigolds into the soil. (We don't know exactly what pest is meant by *mèng-lùk*, but some sources suggest a type of caterpillar—or possibly *mèng* and *lùk* are different pests.)

213

See the River *Ràk*　瞻彼洛矣

See the *Ràk*, that deep and powerful river!
The Prince has arrived; it's as if good fortune and blessings are piled high upon him.
His knee-covers are dyed bright red, because he's raising his six regiments.

Tam payc Ràk luc, wi lhouyc ang-ang.	瞻彼洛矣　維水泱泱
Kwun-tzuc tits tuc, puk ròk na dzi.	君子至止　福祿如茨
Mùts kùp wuc huk, luc tzàk rouk shi.	韎韐有奭　以作六師

See the *Ràk*, that deep and powerful river!
The Prince has arrived; his scabbard decoration sparkles brightly.
May the Prince live ten thousand years, and may his family and house be preserved!

Tam payc Ràk luc, wi lhouyc ang-ang.	瞻彼洛矣　維水泱泱
Kwun-tzuc tits tuc, pènk-pònk wuc pit.	君子至止　鞞琫有珌
Kwun-tzuc màns nìn, pòuc gu krà lhit.	君子萬年　保其家室

See the *Ràk*, that deep and powerful river!
The Prince has arrived; good fortune and blessings are united in him.
May the Prince live ten thousand years, and may his family and state be preserved!

Tam payc Ràk luc, wi lhouyc ang-ang. 瞻彼洛矣　維水泱泱
Kwun-tzuc tits tuc, puk ròk kuts dòng. 君子至止　福祿既同
Kwun-tzuc màns nìn, pòuc gu krà pròng. 君子萬年　保其家邦

The *Ràk* (modern Luo) is the Yellow River tributary adjacent to the Eastern *Tiw* capital at Luoyang—Luoyang is named after this river. *Kwun-tzuc*, "princely man", refers here to the king; rulers of different ranks were allowed to maintain different numbers of military units ("regiments" in my translation), and the king alone kept six. The scabbard is a good example of how traditional Odes commentators sometimes tied themselves in knots through guesswork and over-interpretation. They were sure that the stich had something to do with the decoration on the king's scabbard; they took *pènk* to mean "scabbard", and then they said that *pònk* was the decoration at the top of the scabbard and *pit* that at the bottom: the prince's scabbard was "decorated at the top and at the bottom too". But separate words for top and bottom trim is implausible, and *pènk-pònk* surely has to be one of the alliterative phrases which are common in the Odes; I am willing to accept that as a whole it refers to the decoration on a scabbard, but then *pit* must have some adjectival meaning—since it is written with a jade element I guess it meant something like "sparkling, glittering".

214

Glorious Flowers　裳裳者華

The flowers are glorious, with lovely foliage!
I've met the young lord now, and a load is lifted from my heart.
A load is lifted from my heart, leaving me happy and calm.

Dang-dang tac wà, gu lap shac ì!　裳裳者華　其葉湑兮
Ngàyc kòs tu tzuc, ngàyc sum sac ì.　我覯之子　我心寫兮
Ngàyc sum sac ì, dec luc wuc las k'hlac ì.　我心寫兮　是以有譽處兮

The flowers are glorious—how rich their yellow is!
I've met the young lord now—how refined he is!
He's so refined, which makes me thoroughly joyful!

Dang-dang tac wà, wuns gu gwàng ì!　裳裳者華　芸其黃矣
Ngàyc kòs tu tzuc, wi kus wuc tang ì.　我覯之子　維其有章矣
Wi kus wuc tang ì, dec luc wuc khrangs ì.　維其有章矣　是以有慶矣

The flowers are glorious—some yellow, some white!
I've met the young lord now, driving his four black-maned greys;
driving his four black-maned greys, with his six reins so glossy they look wet.

Dang-dang tac wà, wùk gwàng wùk bràk.　裳裳者華　或黃或白
Ngàyc kòs tu tzuc, mlung gu slits ràk.　我覯之子　乘其四駱
Mlung gu slits ràk, rouk prus àwk nak.　乘其四駱　六轡沃若

He veers them left, and again left: the young lord is skilful.
He veers them right, and again right: the young lord has what it takes.
He has what it takes—everything about him shows it.

Tzàyc tu, tzàyc tu, kwun-tzuc ngay tuc. 左之左之 君子宜止
Wuc tu, wuc tu, kwun-tzuc wuc tuc. 右之右之 君子有止
Wi kus wuc tu, dec luc sluc tuc. 維其有之 是以似止

The load lifted from the poet's heart suggests that she is a girl whose father has promised her to the young lord in marriage. If we care to give our imagination free rein, we might even guess that the flowers are the young man's first gift to her.

215

The Grosbeaks 桑扈

Grosbeaks are flying in all directions; how colourful their wings are!
The nobles are enjoying one another's company, blessed by Sky as they are.

Kryàw-kryàw sàng-gàc; wuc rrèng gu wac! 交交桑扈 有鶯其羽
Kwun-tzuc ngràwks shac, douc Thìn tu gàc. 君子樂胥 受天之祜

Grosbeaks are flying in all directions; how colourful their collars are!
The nobles are enjoying one another's company; they are the bulwarks of their states.

Kryàw-kryàw sàng-gàc; wuc rrèng gu renk! 交交桑扈 有鶯其領
Kwun-tzuc ngràwks shac, màns pròng tu bèng. 君子樂胥 萬邦之屏

They protect the states, and they support them—the nobles are models for their people.
They aren't rapacious, but they're fearless; if fortune favours them, that's no more than they deserve.

Tu bèng, tu gàn, pràk pek way nghans. 之屏之翰 百辟為憲
Pu jup, pu nant; douc puk pu này. 不戢不難 受福不那

How long and curved is the water-buffalo drinking horn! The fine wine in it is soft on the tongue.
The nobles are mingling without standing on ceremony. May ten thousand blessings come and meet in them!

Syuyc kwràng gu giw! Kic tziwc su nou. 兕觥其觩 旨酒思柔
Payc kryàw puyc ngàws. Màns puk rù gou! 彼交匪傲 萬福來遒

216

Mandarin Ducks 鴛鴦

Mandarin ducks are on the wing; we catch them in hand-nets and fixed nets.
May our prince live ten thousand years, with happiness and prosperity his due!

On-ang wa puy; pit tu, ràv tu. 鴛鴦于飛　畢之羅之
Kwun-tzuc màns nìn, puk ròk ngay tu. 君子萬年　福祿宜之

There are mandarin ducks on the weir, with their left wings folded up.
May our prince live ten thousand years—he's entitled to happiness in full measure!

On-ang dzùc rang, jup gu tzàyc yuk. 鴛鴦在梁　戢其左翼
Kwun-tzuc màns nìn, ngay gu grà puk. 君子萬年　宜其遐福

Teams of horses are in the stables, and we feed them cut grass and grain.
May our prince live ten thousand years, made secure in happiness and prosperity!

Mlungs mràc dzùc kous; dzòuy tu, màt tu. 乘馬在廄　摧之秣之
Kwun-tzuc màns nìn, puk ròk ngats tu. 君子萬年　福祿艾之

Teams of horses are in the stables, and we feed them grain and cut grass.
May our prince live ten thousand years, with happiness and prosperity granting him inner peace!

Mlungs mràc dzùc kous; màt tu, dzòuy tu. 乘馬在廄　秣之摧之
Kwun-tzuc màns nìn, puk ròk snouy tu. 君子萬年　福祿綏之

Mandarin ducks are known for fidelity to their mates, and the line about "left wings folded up" refers to an idea that they roost in pairs, left side to left side, with their right wings free to ward off intruders. Hand-nets were like old-fashioned butterfly nets on long handles, while fixed nets would have been set up in places such as a dip in a ridge where ducks would fly close to the ground.

217

Split Bands 頍弁

There are caps with split bands: who are these men?
Your wine is delicious, your dishes of food ambrosial:
how could they be for strangers? No, they're for brothers and no-one else.

Mistletoe and dodder spread among the pines and cypresses.
When we have yet to see our prince, our hearts are full of great sadness,
but when we do see him, there will surely be pleasure and gladness.

Wuc kwhec tac brans: dit wi i gày? 有頍者弁 寔維伊何
Nec tziwc kuts kic, nec gràw kuts kràe. 爾酒既旨 爾殽既嘉
Khuyc i luks nin? Hwrang dìc, puyc lhày. 豈伊異人 兄弟匪他
Tìws lac nrac-ràey lhay wa slong pràk. 蔦與女蘿 施于松柏
Muts kèns kwun-tzuc, ou sum yak-yak; 未見君子 憂心弈弈
kuts kèns kwun-tzuc, lhaks-kuy lot lak. 既見君子 庶幾悅懌

There are caps with split bands: what occasion is this?
Your wine is delicious, your dishes of food just what they should be:
how could they be for strangers? No, it's your brothers who are here.
Mistletoe and dodder spread over the pine trees.
When we have yet to see our prince, our hearts are full of grief,
but when we do see him, things will surely be good.

Wuc kwhec tac brans: dit wi gày gu? 有頍者弁 寔維何期
Nec tziwc kuts kic, nec gràw kuts du. 爾酒既旨 爾殽既時
Khuyc i luks nin? Hwrang dìc gos rù. 豈伊異人 兄弟具來
Tìws lac nrac-ràey lhay wa slong dyangs. 蔦與女蘿 施于松上
Muts kèns kwun-tzuc, ou sum prangs-prangs; 未見君子 憂心怲怲
kuts kèns kwun-tzuc, lhaks-kuy wuc tzàng. 既見君子 庶幾有臧

There are caps with split bands, on men's heads.
Your wine is delicious, your dishes of food ample:
how could they be for strangers? No, they're for brothers, nephews, and uncles.
Life is like a fall of snow: before it comes sleet.
We're given no date for our death or burial, but we're together only briefly.
This will be a night of music and wine; our prince is holding a feast!

Wuc kwhec tac brans, dit wi dzùc lhouc. 有頍者弁 寔維在首
Nec tziwc kuts kic, nec gràw kuts bouc. 爾酒既旨 爾殽既阜
Khuyc i luks nin? Hwrang dìc sheng gouc. 豈伊異人 兄弟甥舅
Na payc was sot: sùn dzup wi sèns. 如彼雨雪 先集維霰
Sic sàng ma nit, ma kuy sang kèns. 死喪無日 無幾相見
Ngràwk tziwc kum syak, kwun-tzuc wi èns! 樂酒今夕 君子維宴

Kwhec tac brans are caps with bands attached that are split down the middle, so that they can be used to gather up hair outside the cap and tie it up neatly. The poet has noticed that a lot of men from outside have arrived at court. (One might think it unnecessary to mention that the caps are on heads, but it establishes a rhyme for verse 3.)

Mistletoe and dodder are parasitic plants, and hence a metaphor for the way in which junior members of a ruler's family depend on the head of the family. In English the overtones of the word "parasite" are negative, but here the relationship of dependence is seen as healthy (compare Ode 4). Sleet turning into snow is a metaphor for old age and infirmity leading to death—a snowfall makes a good symbol for death, because white is the colour of mourning.

VOICES FROM EARLY CHINA

218

The Linchpin 車舝

Thrusting the carriage linchpin home in its socket puts me in mind of the lovely young girl I'm off to see.
It's not that she hungers or thirsts for my body, but my social standing attracts her to me.
Though I have no boon companions to join us, we shall feast and make merry.

Krèn kròn ka tu gràt ì, sus ront kwits nrac dats ì.   間關車之舝兮　思孌季女逝兮
Puyc kri puyc khàt, tùk um rù kwàt.   匪飢匪渴　德音來括
Swi ma hòuc wuc, lhuk èns tsac huc.   雖無好友　式燕且喜

The forest in the plain is broad, and pheasants settle in it.
This ripe girl, thanks to my status, really is coming to let me teach her.
With feasting and fun, I shall never weary of loving you.

Uy payc breng rum, wuc dzup wi gaw.   依彼平林　有集維鷮
Trant payc dak nrac, reng tùk rù kràws.   展彼碩女　令德來教
Lhuk èns tsac las, hòus nec ma lak.   式燕且譽　好爾無射

Though I have no fine wines, we shall have something or other to drink.
Though I have no gourmet foods, we shall have something or other to eat.
Although you're a girl of no social status, we shall have singing and dancing.

Swi ma kic tziwc, lhuk um lhaks-kuy.   雖無旨酒　式飲庶幾
Swi ma kràw gràw, lhuk mluk lhaks-kuy.   雖無嘉殽　式食庶幾
Swi ma tùk lac nac, lhuk kày tsac mac.   雖無德與汝　式歌且舞

I climbed that high ridge to split oak logs for firewood.
I was splitting oak logs for firewood; the oaks were in full leaf.
Lonely, I came across you—and my heart shed its burdens.

Truk payc kàw kàng, sèk gu dzàk sin.   陟彼高岡　析其柞薪
Sèk gu dzàk sin, gu lap shac ì.   析其柞薪　其葉湑兮
Sent ngàyc kòs nec, ngàyc sum sac ì.   鮮我覯爾　我心寫兮

I gaze up at the lofty mountains as I bowl along the high road.
My four stallions trot tirelessly, and the six reins are like lute-strings in my hand.
I'm off to meet my bride, and so bring peace to my heart.

Kàw shàn ngank tuc, krank gràng gràng tuc.   高山仰止　景行行止
Slits mouc phuy-phuy, rouk prus na gum.   四牡騑騑　六轡如琴
Kòs nec sin mhùn, luc outs ngàyc sum.   覯爾新昏　以慰我心

Nothing in the Chinese of the second line of verse 1 says who is spoken about, and other translators have taken the one who is not hungry to be the poet himself, and the *tùk um*,

261

" 'virtuous' reputation" or high social standing, to belong to the girl. But, uncontroversially, the hunger and thirst here stand for sexual attraction, and the first line has made clear that the poet has an appetite. So I take him to be saying that the girl is marrying him not because of sexual chemistry but for the position he can give her. Then the first line of verse 2 has been translated by others in ways that make little sense to me. Some have taken *rù kràws* to mean that the girl is coming to teach the poet, which does not seem consistent with usual social assumptions. I read the phrase as, literally, "come to instruction", in other words come to be taught by the poet; I take the Ode as written by a gentleman (if, evidently, a gentleman of modest means) who is marrying a peasant girl for her looks and youth, and because he is lonely, and who expects to have to teach her the proper behaviour for a lady.

For 21st-century sensibilities, of course, all this might seem appallingly condescending. But I believe a nineteenth-century Englishman would find it entirely understandable; and it makes sense of the lines, while doing no more violence to the original language than others have done in producing less comprehensible readings. (All the same, I do wonder whether the girl will find this marriage as satisfying as the poet assumes.)

219

Bluebottles　青蠅

Bluebottles buzz around, and settle on the fence.
Oh, my happy prince, don't believe the malicious gossip you hear.

Weng-weng tsèng lung, tuc wa ban.　　　營營青蠅　止于樊
Khùyc dìc kwun-tzuc, ma sins djàms ngan.　豈弟君子　無信讒言

Bluebottles buzz around, and settle on the jujube tree.
The troublemakers know no restraint; they're setting the states of the whole world by the ears.

Weng-weng tsèng lung, tuc wa kuk.　　　營營青蠅　止于棘
Djàms nin mank guk, kryàw ròns Slits kwùk.　讒人罔極　交亂四國

Bluebottles buzz around, and settle on the hazel.
The troublemakers know no restraint; they're turning us two against one another.

Weng-weng tsèng lung, tuc wa jin.　　　營營青蠅　止于榛
Djàms nin mank guk, kòs ngàyc nits nin.　讒人罔極　構我二人

A courtier tries to shore up his vulnerable position. The bluebottles are clearly a metaphor for the gossips; anyone may be their next victim.

220

When the Guests First Take their Places 賓之初筵

When the guests first take their places, to left and right all is decorous.
The table is laden with *pèn* baskets and *dòs* bowls; there are savoury dishes and piles of stone fruit galore.
The wine is well blended and delicious, and there's plenty of it to drink.
The bells and drums have been set up; relaxing, the guests raise their cups and return one another's toasts.
The great target has been set in place, the bows with their arrows are strung,
the archers have been grouped into heats. Show your prowess at shooting,
aim at that bullseye, and try to win yourself the *tzyawk* goblet!

Pin tu cha lan, tzàyc wuc drit-drit.	賓之初筵　左右秩秩
Pèn dòs wuc chac; gràw grùk wi rac.	籩豆有楚　殽核維旅
Tziwc kuts wày kic, um tziwc khònk krìc.	酒既和旨　飲酒孔偕
Tong kàc kuts nhet; klac dou lit-lit.	鐘鼓既設　舉醻逸逸
Dàts gò kuts khàngs, kwung lhic se trang.	大侯既抗　弓矢斯張
Mlaks pa kuts dòng: nghans nec pat kòng,	射夫既同　獻爾發功
pat payc wuc tyàwk, luc guy nec tzyawk!	發彼有的　以祈爾爵

There's flute music, and dancing to reed-organ and drums—the music is played in perfect harmony.
We offer our acclaim to the illustrious Ancestors, so as to fulfil the hundred rituals.
The hundred rituals are fully elaborated—they are grand, they are intricate.
They bring you the blessings of fellowship and plenty. You descendants can rejoice:
rejoice and be happy, each of you displaying your skill.
Then the guests offer their hand to their opponents, and the servants come forward to assist
by pouring the winding-down goblets to celebrate those of you who shot well.

Yawk mac sheng kàc—ngràwk kuts wày tzòs.	籥舞笙鼓　樂既和奏
Tung khàns rat tzàc, luc grùp pràk rìc.	烝衎烈祖　以洽百禮
Pràk rìc kuts tits—wuc num, wuc rum.	百禮既至　有壬有林
Slèk nec dòun kràc. Tzuc sòun gu tùm:	錫爾純嘏　子孫其湛
gu tùm wat ngràwks, kàk tzòs nec nùc.	其湛曰樂　各奏爾能
Pin tzùs nhouc gou; lhit nin nup wus,	賓載手仇　室人入又
tyawk payc khàng tzyawk, luc tzòs nec du.	酌彼康爵　以奏爾時

When the guests first take their places, their attitude is warmly respectful.
They are still sober, and they behave with complete dignity.
But when they get tipsy, their dignity totters.

They get up from their places and move around; they take to capering wildly to the music.
Those who are still sober are careful to preserve their dignity,
but those who get drunk cease to care about dignity.
Once tipsy, they no longer know what good behaviour is.

Pin tu cha lan, òun-òun gu krong. 　賓之初筵　溫溫其恭
Kus muts tzouts tuc; ouy-ngay pràent-pràent. 　其未醉止　威儀昄昄
Wat kuts tzouts tuc, ouy-ngay phan-phan. 　曰既醉止　威儀幡幡
Lhac gu dzòys tsan; ros mac san-san. 　舍其坐遷　屢舞僊僊
Gu muts tzouts tuc, ouy-ngay uk-uk 　其未醉止　威儀抑抑
wat kuts tzouts tuc, ouy-ngay bit-bit. 　曰既醉止　威儀怭怭
Dec wat kuts tzouts pu tre gu drit. 　是曰既醉　不知其秩

Guests who are drunk start shouting and making a racket.
They play havoc with the food dishes laid out on my table, and persist in dancing around with faces like devil-masks.
The ones who are drunk don't even realize they're misbehaving.
They let their caps slip awry, and keep dancing foolishly.
If someone leaves the room once he gets tipsy, he shares the benefit of the good party mood.
But if someone is drunk and doesn't leave, I call that wrecking the atmosphere.
Drinking wine is a fine thing, but only provided one behaves properly.

Pin kuts tzouts tuc, tzùs ghàw, tzùs nràw. 　賓既醉止　載號載呶
Ròns ngàyc pèn dòs, ros mac khu-khu. 　亂我籩豆　屢舞僛僛
Dec wat kuts tzouts pu tre gu wu. 　是曰既醉　不知其郵
Juk brans tu ngày, ros mac sày-sày. 　側弁之俄　屢舞傞傞
Kuts tzouts nu k'hlout, bènk douc kus puk. 　既醉而出　並受其福
Tzouts nu pu k'hlout, dec wuts bat tùk. 　醉而不出　是謂伐德
Um tziwc khònk kràk, wi gu reng ngay. 　飲酒孔嘉　維其令儀

Among all those who drink, some get tipsy and others don't.
So I've appointed an inspector, with an assistant to take notes.
When the drunkards misbehave, the sober ones for their part feel embarrassed.
So don't go along with them, don't talk to them! Don't encourage them to lose self-control even further.
If words shouldn't be spoken, don't speak them. If topics shouldn't be raised, don't discuss them.
If you give a hearing to drunkards' talk, you just make them reveal themselves to be immature animals.
Three *tzyawk* goblets are enough to make a man forget himself; so how can anyone dare drink even more?

Bam tsec um tziwc, wùk tzouts, wùk puc. 　凡此飲酒　或醉或否
Kuts rup tu kràm, wùk tzàys tu shuc. 　既立之監　或佐之史
Payc tzouts pu tzàng, pu tzouts pant rhuc. 　彼醉不臧　不醉反恥
Lhuk mut dzong wuts, ma pec thàts lùc. 　式勿從謂　無俾大怠
Puyc ngan, mut ngan; puyc you, mut ngas. 　匪言勿言　匪由勿語

You tzouts tu ngan, pec k'hlout dòng kàc.
Sùm tzyawk pu tuks; lhint kàmp tày wus?

由醉之言　俾出童羖
三爵不識　矧敢多又

221

The Fish in the Water-Weed 魚藻

The fish lives in the water-weed; how large its head is!
The King lives at *Gàwc*, merrily drinking wine.

Nga dzùc dzùc tzàwc; wuc bun gu lhouc!
Wang dzùc dzùc Gàwc; khùyc ngràwks um tziwc.

魚在在藻　有頒其首
王在在鎬　豈樂飲酒

The fish lives in the water-weed; how long its tail is!
The King lives at *Gàwc*, drinking wine merrily.

Nga dzùc dzùc tzàwc; wuc shin gu muyc!
Wang dzùc dzùc Gàwc; um tziwc ngràwks khùyc.

魚在在藻　有莘其尾
王在在鎬　飲酒樂豈

The fish lives in the water-weed, close up against the reeds.
The King lives at *Gàwc*, in his stately home.

Nga dzùc dzùc tzàwc, uy wa kus bà.
Wang dzùc dzùc Gàwc; wuc này gu kac!

魚在在藻　依于其蒲
王在在鎬　有那其居

This was surely more of a nursery rhyme than a poem for an adult audience.

222

Picking Beans 采菽

They're picking beans, picking beans, into baskets square and round.
The noblemen are coming to court; what is there to give them?
There's nothing to give them—except state chariots and teams of horses.
And what else is there to give them? Black robes embroidered with every emblem from dragons down to axes.

Tsùc nhouk, tsùc nhouk, kwhang tu, kac tu.
Kwun-tzuc rù draw: gày slèk lac tu?
Swi ma lac tu, ràks ka, mlungs mràc.
Wus gày lac tu? Gwìn kòunt gup pac.

采菽采菽　筐之筥之
君子來朝　何錫予之
雖無予之　輅車乘馬
又何予之　玄袞及斧

The spring gushes up in a jet; we gather the watercress that grows there.
The noblemen are coming to court—I can see their dragon banners,
masses of dragon banners fluttering in the breeze. Their harness bells are shrilling.
I see the outside horses; and now I see the entire teams. This is where the nobles will arrive.

Pit-put gràmp dzwan; ngan tsùc gu gun. 觱沸檻泉 言采其芹
Kwun-tzuc rù draw; ngan kwàn gu guy, 君子來朝 言觀其旂
gu guy phìts-phìts. Ròn hyeng hwìts-hwìts. 其旂淠淠 鸞聲嘒嘒
Tzùs tsùm, tzùs slits—kwun-tzuc shac krìts. 載驂載駟 君子所屆

Red knee-covers on their legs, with puttees criss-crossed below them.
They avoid all discourtesy, all casualness, coming to be rewarded by Sky's Son.
Three cheers for the noblemen, holding Sky's Son's commission!
Three cheers for the noblemen—may their happiness and prosperity long continue!

Khlak put dzùc kàc, ya pruk dzùc gràc. 赤市在股 邪幅在下
Puyc kràwc, puyc mla, Thìn Tzuc shac lac. 匪絞匪紓 天子所予
Ngràwks kec kwun-tzuc; Thìn Tzuc mreng tu. 樂只君子 天子命之
Ngràwks kec kwun-tzuc; puk ròk lhin tu. 樂只君子 福祿申之

The branches of the oak trees are brimming with foliage.
Three cheers for the noblemen, protectors of Sky's Son's realm!
Three cheers for the noblemen, round whom ten thousand felicities gather!
May the supporters following in their train be ever diligent in serving them.

Wi dzàk tu ke, gu lap bòng-bòng. 維柞之枝 其葉蓬蓬
Ngràwks kec kwun-tzuc, tuns Thìn Tzuc tu pròng. 樂只君子 殿天子之邦
Ngràwks kec kwun-tzuc, màns puk you dòng. 樂只君子 萬福攸同
Bren-bren tzàyc-wuc, yak dec shout dzong. 采采左右 亦是率從

There's a poplar-wood boat drifting about, but it has a painter mooring it to the bank.
Three cheers for the noblemen, supervised by Sky's Son!
Three cheers for the noblemen—may happiness and prosperity magnify them!
How open-handed, how easy-going they are as they arrive!

Bum-bum lang tou, put re wi tu. 汎汎楊舟 紼纚維之
Ngràwks kec kwun-tzuc, Thìn Tzuc gwic tu. 樂只君子 天子揆之
Ngràwks kec kwun-tzuc, puk ròk bi tu. 樂只君子 福祿膍之
Ou tzù, you tzù, yak dec rìts luc. 優哉游哉 亦是戾矣

The king prepares to receive his noble vassals on one of the periodic visits they were expected to make to court. Under European feudalism, vassals supplied service and goods to their overlords, but the overlord's duty in the other direction was to protect those under him: feudalism was essentially a way of fulfilling society's need for defence. In China defence was important, but also the flow of material goods was a two-way affair: there was more emphasis on superiors giving prestigious things to their vassals.

"There's nothing to give them" must have been mock modesty, if the speaker was the king: state carriages and teams of horses sound like very good gifts. And the robes were more valuable than is perhaps apparent. They were not just smart suits of clothes, but indicators of the wearers' high rank. According to the early commentators, noblemen were entitled to wear robes embroidered with rows of some or all of twelve different emblems. From top to bottom, the twelve rows contained: suns; moons; stars; mountains; dragons; pheasants; temple cups; water-weeds; flames; grains of rice; axes; and an angular geometrical design reminiscent of the Greek key pattern. The king alone had all twelve rows. Dukes omitted sun, moon, and stars. The next two ranks began with pheasants, and the lowest two ranks of nobility began with temple cups. Hence "dragons down to axes" implies that the visiting nobles were dukes. (*Kòunt* is standardly glossed as "dragon robe" but doubtless included the mountains too, and the geometrical row was perhaps taken for granted.)

223

The Inlaid Bow 角弓

The materials of the horn-inlaid bow are neatly fitted together; but, if it warps, it
    sends its shots awry.
Relatives by blood or marriage ought not to be distanced from one another.

Seng-seng kròk kwung; phen gu pant luc.　　　　　解解角弓　偏其反矣
Hwrang dìc mhùn in ma sa wans luc.　　　　　　　兄弟昏姻　無胥遠矣

If you keep them at a distance, people will be distant towards you;
if you set them a good example, people will imitate it.

Nec tu wans luc, min se nan luc;　　　　　　　　爾之遠矣　民斯然矣
nec tu kràws luc, min se gràws luc.　　　　　　爾之教矣　民斯傚矣

Good brothers are gentle and forbearing;
but bad brothers create misery for one another.

Tsec reng hwrang dìc thàwk-thàwk wuc loks;　　此令兄弟　綽綽有裕
pu reng hwrang dìc kryàw sang way loc.　　　　不令兄弟　交相為瘉

Inferior people maintain one-sided grudges against one another;
they accept the benefits of high rank without moderating their own behaviour
    accordingly, and in the end they destroy themselves.

Min tu ma rang sang ons it pang.　　　　　　　民之無良　相怨一方
Douc tzyawk, pu nangs; tits wa luc se mang.　　受爵不讓　至于已斯亡

Old horses take themselves to be colts again, and don't think of the consequences.
If they're served food, they think it fine to stuff themselves; if they're offered drink they take a lot.

Ròuc mràc pant way ko, pu kàs gu ghòc. 老馬反為駒　不顧其後
Na sluks, ngay os; na tyawk, khònk tsoc. 如食宜饇　如酌孔取

Don't try teaching a monkey to climb trees; if you plaster a wall, the plaster will stick naturally.
When noble men have meritorious policies, the common people will gladly go along with them.

Mu kràws nòu lhung mòk; na là, là bos. 毋教猱升木　如塗塗附
Kwun-tzuc wuc mhuy you, syawc min lac tok. 君子有徽猷　小人與屬

There may be heavy snow, but when it encounters warm sunshine the snow melts.
On the other hand, none of these wretches are willing to resign their places—no, they cling to them, useless but arrogant.

Was sot paw-paw, kèns nèns wat syaw. 雨雪瀌瀌　見晛曰消
Màk khènk gràs dòuy, lhuc kac rò kaw. 莫肯下隧　式居婁驕

There may be deep snow, but when it encounters warm sunshine the snow flows away in streams.
These men are like the *Mròn* and *Màw* barbarians—and hence my sadness.

Was sot bou-bou, kèns nèns wat riw. 雨雪浮浮　見晛曰流
Na Mròn, na Màw, ngàyc dec longs ou. 如蠻如髦　我是用憂

An Ode directed against men who use high office as an opportunity to feather their own nests without any attempt to do a good job. Perhaps surprisingly, the poet links this selfish attitude to a lack of family feeling. A family should ideally fit together tightly like the marquetry of a bow with inlaid decoration, but if the elements forming the bow do not fit together properly then the bow will not shoot straight. The "you" addressed seems to be the king, who is admonished to set a good example to those under him through the way he treats his own relatives.

The "old horses" verse seems not so much to be about the need to be public-spirited, as about how those with ageing bodies must accept that they can no longer indulge in the physical excesses which may be allowable in young men. But in the poet's mind these things were perhaps all related to one another. Likewise the following verse, about monkeys and plastering, seems to be teaching a quite different lesson—"don't teach your grandmother to suck eggs"; but we should perhaps see it as a foreshadowing of what became a leading political principle in imperial China, that the ideal behaviour for an emperor is 'wu wei', "inactivity", so that again this is advice about how to be a good ruler. The world, it was believed, has a natural balance, so, while it is well run, the ruler should not need to interfere. If he does need to step in, that is because the world has been thrown off balance by something or someone, perhaps by the ruler himself.

Then verses 7 and 8 return to the theme of the selfish officials, who insist on clinging to their lucrative positions though it would be better for them to retire voluntarily when it is clear that they are serving no useful purpose, as snow melts of its own accord when spring weather arrives.

Mròn and *Màw* were tribes of the south and west, respectively, seen by the Chinese as particularly wild and devoid of civility. (*Màw* meant "shaggy".)

224

Willows in Leaf 菀柳

The willows are in glorious leaf—wouldn't I love to take a rest among them!
The Almighty is too unpredictable—best that I avoid interfering.
But suppose I did let things drift: eventually I'd find myself in dire straits.

Wuc out tac rouc—pu dangs suk an!	有菀者柳　不尚息焉
Dyangs Tès dums lòus; ma dzis nruk an.	上帝甚蹈　無自暱焉
Pec lac dzenk tu: ghòc lac guk an.	俾予靖之　後予極焉

The willows are in glorious leaf—wouldn't I love to relax among them!
The Almighty is too unpredictable—best avoid putting myself in the firing line.
But suppose I did let things drift: eventually I'd find myself out of favour.

Wuc out tac rouc—pu dangs khats an!	有菀者柳　不尚愒焉
Dyangs Tès dums lòus; ma dzis jèts an.	上帝甚蹈　無自瘵焉
Pec lac dzenk tu: ghòc lac mràts an.	俾予靖之　後予邁焉

There is a bird flying high, it soars all the way up to the sky.
These men's hearts: what is the highest they might rise to?
How can I let things drift? I would end up wretched and pitiable.

Wuc tìwc kàw puy, yak bas wa thìn.	有鳥高飛　亦傅于天
Payc nin tu sum: wa gày ku jin?	彼人之心　于何其臻
Gàt lac dzenk tu? Kac luc hong grin.	曷予靖之　居以凶矜

A high official faces a standard dilemma: his duty is to speak out to address some current abuse by "these men", but he would be safer settling for a quiet life, in the short term at least.

Tès, or *Dyangs Tès*, commonly refers to God, but here it refers to the king. My phrase "the Almighty" aims to capture this vagueness.

225

Gentlemen from the Capital　都人士

These gentlemen from the capital wear rich tawny fox furs.
Their faces are impassive; when they speak, their words are elegant.
As they travel to and from *Tiw*, the multitudes gaze at them admiringly.

Payc tà nin shuc gwà gwu gwàng-gwàng.　　　彼都人士　狐裘黃黃
Gu long pu kùc; k'hlout ngan wuc tang.　　　其容不改　出言有章
Gràng kwuy wa Tiw, màns min shac mang.　　行歸于周　萬民所望

These gentlemen from the capital wear reed rain-hats or black skullcaps.
As for their noble ladies, their hair is long and thick.
If I can't see them, I'm sad at missing the sight.

Payc tà nin shuc, dù rup ju tsòt.　　　彼都人士　臺笠緇撮
Payc kwun-tzuc nrac, driw druk na pat.　　彼君子女　綢直如髮
Ngàyc pu kèns ì, ngàyc sum pu lot.　　　我不見兮　我心不悅

These gentlemen from the capital wear ear-stoppers fashioned from large *siws*
　stones.
Their noble ladies are known for being upright and blessed by fortune.
If I can't see them, my heart is knotted with frustration.

Payc tà nin shuc, thoung-nuc siws mlit.　　彼都人士　充耳琇實
Payc kwun-tzuc nrac, wuts tu wint kit.　　　彼君子女　謂之尹吉
Ngàyc pu kèns ì, ngàyc sum out kìt.　　　我不見兮　我心苑結

These gentlemen from the capital wear their sashes with ends trailing down.
As for their noble ladies, their hair curls like a scorpion's tail.
If I can't see them, I chase after them on foot.

Payc tà nin shuc, doy tàts nu rats.　　　彼都人士　垂帶而厲
Payc kwun-tzuc nrac, gon pat na rhàts.　　彼君子女　卷髮如蠆
Ngàyc pu kèns ì, ngan dzong tu mràts.　　我不見兮　言從之邁

It isn't that the gentlemen arrange their sashes specially: they're made extra-
　long.
It isn't that the ladies roll their hair: it has a natural wave.
If I can't see them, how very pained I feel!

Puyc i doy tu: tàts tzùk wuc la.　　　匪伊垂之　帶則有餘
Puyc i kont tu: pat tzùk wuc la.　　　匪伊卷之　髮則有旟
Ngàyc pu kèns ì, wun gày hwa luc!　　我不見兮　云何吁矣

A country-dweller is impressed by fashionable metropolitan types, rather as film stars are mobbed by fans in our own time.

It is hard to grasp the fine points of sharp dressing after a hundred years, let alone three millennia. When it comes to the sash-ends I am lost, but I am sure it made sense at the time.

226

Gathering Lentils 采綠

All morning I've been gathering lentils, but I haven't found enough to fill my cupped hands once.
My hair is a mess; heigh-ho, I'll go home and wash it.

Toung traw tsùc rok, pu leng it kouk. 終朝采菉　不盈一匊
Lac pat khok-gok; bàk-ngan kwuy mòk. 予髮曲局　薄言歸沐

All morning I've been gathering indigo, but I haven't managed to fill my apron once.
He should have come back after five days; this is the sixth day, and I still haven't seen him.

Toung traw tsùc rok, pu leng it tham. 終朝采藍　不盈一襜
Ngàc nit way gu, rouk nit pu tam. 五日為期　六日不瞻

This man of mine went hunting, and I put his bow in its case for him.
This man of mine went fishing, and I twisted his line for him.

Tu tzuc wa hyouc, ngan thrangs gu kwung. 之子于狩　言韔其弓
Tu tzuc wa tyàwks, ngan roun tu mlung. 之子于釣　言綸之繩

What is he fishing for? Bream and tench.
Bream and tench—but heigh-ho, whether I'll ever see them ...

Kus tyàwks wi gày? Wi bang gup slac. 其釣維何　維魴及鱮
Wi bang gup slac; bàk-ngan kwàn tac ... 維魴及鱮　薄言觀者

227

Sprouting Millet 黍苗

Bushy are the millet sprouts—the rain of overcast days is swelling them out.
This has been a long expedition to the south—but the lord of *Daws* is rewarding us accordingly.

271

Bùm-bùm nhac maw; um wac kàws tu. 芃芃黍苗　陰雨膏之
You-you nùm gràng; Daws pràk ràws tu. 悠悠南行　召伯勞之

We loaded up our handcarts, and harnessed oxen to our carriages.
Now we've accomplished our mission, so we're free to go back.

Ngàyc num ngàyc rant, ngàyc ka ngàyc ngwu. 我任我輦　我車我牛
Ngàyc gràng kuts dzup, kàts wun kwuy tzù. 我行既集　蓋云歸哉

We appointed runners to our chariot-teams, and organized our troops into platoons.
Now we've accomplished our mission, so we're free to go home.

Ngàyc dà ngàyc ngas, ngàyc shi ngàyc rac. 我徒我御　我師我旅
Ngàyc gràng kuts dzup, kàts wun kwuy k'hlac. 我行既集　蓋云歸處

The work at *Slaks* has gone smoothly, planned by the lord of *Daws*.
Our expeditionary force is splendid, its capabilities perfected by the lord of *Daws*.

Siwk-siwk Slaks kòng, Daws pràk weng tu. 肅肅謝功　召伯營之
Rat-rat teng shi, Daws pràk deng tu. 烈烈征師　召伯成之

We've cleared and levelled the high ground and the low ground, we've cleaned out the springs and watercourses.
The lord of *Daws* has been thoroughly successful, so the king's heart can rest easy.

Ngwan slup kuts breng, dzwan riw kuts tseng. 遝隰既平　泉流既清
Daws pràk wuc deng, wang sum tzùk nèng. 召伯有成　王心則寧

King *Swan* commissioned the lord of *Daws* to form a new state, *Lhin*, as a bulwark against the tribes of the southwest: its capital was established at *Slaks*, in the area of modern Xinyang in the far south of Henan. (Ode 259 will deal with the same event at greater length.)

228

Mulberries in the Wetland　隰桑

The mulberries in the wetland are lovely, their leaves are rich.
Once I've seen my man, how joyful that will be!

Slup sàng wuc àyc, gu lap wuc nàyc. 隰桑有猗　其葉有難
Kuts kèns kwun-tzuc, ku ngràwks na gày! 既見君子　其樂如何

The mulberries in the wetland are lovely, their leaves are glossy.
Once I've seen my man, how can I fail to be joyful?

Slup sàng wuc àyc, gu lap wuc àwk.　　隰桑有猗　其葉有沃
Kuts kèns kwun-tzuc, wun gày pu ngràwks?　既見君子　云何不樂

The mulberries in the wetland are lovely, their leaves are dark.
Once I've seen my man, his fine reputation will bind us together.

Slup sàng wuc àyc, gu lap wuc iw.　　　隰桑有猗　其葉有幽
Kuts kèns kwun-tzuc, tùk um khònk krìw.　既見君子　德音孔膠

In my heart I love him—why would I not say it?
In my inmost heart I treasure him; when could I ever forget him?

Sum ghà ùts luc—gà pu wuts luc?　　　心乎愛矣　胡不謂矣
Troung sum dzàng tu: gày nit mang tu?　中心藏之　何日忘之

229

White Flowers　白華

Red-grass with its white flowers is tied into bundles using white stalks.
He's going away, leaving me alone.

Bràk wà kràn ì, bràk mròu lhok ì.　　白華菅兮　白茅束兮
Tu tzuc tu wans, pec ngàyc dòk ì.　　之子之遠　俾我獨兮

The white clouds shine brilliantly; there's dew on the red-grass and the lawn.
Sky's present course is disastrous, and he's made no plans to address that.

Rrang-rrang bràk wun; ràks payc kràn mròu.　英英白雲　露彼菅茅
Thìn bàs krùn nàn, tu tzuc pu you.　　　　天步艱難　之子不猶

The *Biw-dray* brook is flowing northwards, flooding the paddy-field.
I croon a song with wounded heart, thinking about the great man.

Biw-dray pùk riw, tzums payc lòuc lìn.　滮池北流　浸彼稻田
Sìws kày lhang gròuy, nìms payc dak nin.　嘯歌傷懷　念彼碩人

We gathered mulberry branches for firewood; now I burn them in our stove.
Oh, that great man: he troubles my heart.

Dzaw payc sàng sin, ngàng hòng wa dum.　樵彼桑薪　卬烘于煁
Wi payc dak nin, dit ràw ngàyc sum.　　維彼碩人　寔勞我心

In the palace they're playing bells—the sound carries out here.
I'm thinking about you miserably, but you don't care about me a bit.

Kàc tong wa koung—lhèng muns wa ngwàts.
Nìms tzuc tsàwc-tsàwc; gic ngàyc mràts-mràts.

鼓鍾于宮　聲聞于外
念子懆懆　視我邁邁

There's a stork on the weir, and cranes in the woodland.
Oh, that great man: he troubles my heart.

Wuc tsiw dzùc rang, wuc gàwk dzùc rum.
Wi payc dak nin, dit ràw ngàyc sum.

有鶩在梁　有鶴在林
維彼碩人　寔勞我心

Mandarin ducks are on the weir, folding up their left wings.
There's no decency in him—he's completely unreliable.

On-ang dzùc rang, jup gu tzàyc yuk.
Tu tzuc ma rang—nits sùm gu tùk.

鴛鴦在梁　戢其左翼
之子無良　二三其德

These rocks are too flat and thin: even standing on them I'm not tall enough.
He's going away, leaving me to suffer.

Wuc pènt se dak, ric tu pe ì.
Tu tzuc tu wans, pec ngàyc ge ì.

有扁斯石　履之卑兮
之子之遠　俾我疧兮

The poem is about someone who is referred to several times as *tu tzuc*, "this young man" or "this gentleman"—I just write "he". In verse 3 he is called *dak nin*, which might mean literally "tall man", but I find it more plausible to take it as "great man" in the social rather than physical sense. Circumstance ("Sky's course", i.e. fate) is parting him from the girl, and he is doing nothing to avoid the parting. (For red-grass see Ode 139; for the mandarin ducks "folding up their left wings", see Ode 216. *Biw-dray* is an ancient name for a minor watercourse in the north-west of modern Xi'an.) The girl is trying to climb onto rocks for a last glimpse of the departing man, but she can't get high enough.

230

Delicate Orioles　綿蠻

Delicate are the orioles; they settle on the slope of the hill.
The road is so long—how tired we are!
Give us drink, feed us—train us, teach us!
Tell the baggage-train drivers to pick us up so we can ride!

Ment-mròn gwàng tìwc, tuc wa kwhu ày.
Lòuc tu wun want; ngàyc ràw na gày.
Ums tu, sluks tu—kràws tu, mhùs tu!
Mreng payc ghòc ka, wuts tu tzùs tu.

綿蠻黃鳥　止于丘阿
道之云遠　我勞如何
飲之食之　教之誨之
命彼後車　謂之載之

Delicate are the orioles; they settle at the corner of the hill.
It's not that we don't want to march, of course, but we're afraid of not keeping
　up.

Give us drink, feed us—train us, teach us!
Tell the baggage-train drivers to pick us up so we can ride!

Ment-mròn gwàng tìwc, tuc wa kwhu ngo. 綿蠻黃鳥　止于丘隅
Khuyc kàmp dàns gràng?—ouys pu nùc cho. 豈敢憚行　畏不能趨
Ums tu, sluks tu—kràws tu, mhùs tu! 飲之食之　教之誨之
Mreng payc ghòc ka, wuts tu tzùs tu. 命彼後車　謂之載之

Delicate are the orioles; they settle on the side of the hill.
It's not that we don't want to march, of course, but we're afraid of not lasting the distance.
Give us drink, feed us—train us, teach us!
Tell the baggage-train drivers to pick us up so we can ride!

Ment-mròn gwàng tìwc, tuc wa kwhu juk. 綿蠻黃鳥　止于丘側
Khuyc kàmp dàns gràng?—ouys pu nùc guk. 豈敢憚行　畏不能極
Ums tu, sluks tu—kràws tu, mhùs tu! 飲之食之　教之誨之
Mreng payc ghòc ka, wuts tu tzùs tu. 命彼後車　謂之載之

Doubtless the infantry would be glad of some training sessions because anything is less tiring than marching.

We saw in the Introduction that personal pronouns are less tightly defined in Old Chinese than in European languages. *Tu* commonly refers to a third person (male or female, singular or plural) but can on occasion stand for "me" or "you"; here, in the repeated refrain *wuts tu tzùs tu* it varies between third person (the drivers) and first person within a single stich.

231

Melon Leaves　瓠葉

The melon leaves are stirring in the breeze; we'll pick them and boil them.
Our lord has wine; he pours a cup and tastes it.

Phan-phan gwàs lap; tsùc tu, phràng tu. 幡幡瓠葉　采之烹之
Kwun-tzuc wuc tziwc; tyawk ngan dyang tu. 君子有酒　酌言嘗之

We have this one hare; we'll bake it, or roast it.
Our lord has wine; he pours it into cups and hands them round.

Wuc lhàs se lhouc; bròu tu, ban tu. 有兔斯首　炮之燔之
Kwun-tzuc wuc tziwc; tyawk ngan nghans tu. 君子有酒　酌言獻之

We have this one hare; we'll roast it, or broil it.
Our lord has wine; he fills the cups and we toast him.

Wuc lhàs se lhouc; ban tu, tak tu. 有兔斯首　燔之炙之
Kwun-tzuc wuc tziwc; tyawk ngan dzàk tu. 君子有酒　酌言酢之

We have this one hare; we'll roast it, or bake it.
Our lord has wine; he fills the cups and toasts us back.

Wuc lhàs se lhouc; ban tu, bròu tu. 　　有兔斯首　燔之炮之
Kwun-tzuc wuc tziwc; tyawk ngan dou tu. 　君子有酒　酌言醻之

This is so jingly and repetitive that perhaps it functioned as a nursery rhyme or a drinking song, with the meaning relatively unimportant. The commentaries explain it as expressing how gentlemen preserve good manners even when near starvation: boiled melon leaves and one hare between several people is a meagre dinner, but proper wine-drinking etiquette is observed nevertheless. (As in England not many centuries ago, one did not just quaff away at one's own pace, but "took wine with" individual fellow diners.)

232

Lofty Crags 漸漸之石

Rugged and lofty are the crags—how high they are!
But those mountains and streams are far from here; how hard our service is!
We soldiers are on the march eastwards, with never a morning's freedom.

Djàm-djàm tu dak—wi gu kàw luc! 　　漸漸之石　維其高矣
Shàn k'hloun you want—wi gu ràw luc. 　山川悠遠　維其勞矣
Mac nin tòng teng, pu wàng traw luc. 　　武人東征　不遑朝矣

Rugged and lofty are the crags—how sharp their pinnacles are!
But those mountains and streams are far from here. When would one ever tire of them?
We soldiers are on the march eastwards, and there is never leave to fall out.

Djàm-djàm tu dak—wi gu dzout luc! 　　漸漸之石　維其崒矣
Shàn k'hloun you want—gàt kus mòut luc? 　山川悠遠　曷其沒矣
Mac nin tòng teng, pu wàng k'hlout luc. 　武人東征　不遑出矣

There, a herd of pigs with white trotters is splashing through the ripples!
Now, the Moon is in the Heavenly Fork, so we are in for soaking rain.
We soldiers are on the march eastwards, with never a chance to do anything else.

Wuc lhec bràk tèk tung dap pày luc! 　　有豕白蹢　烝涉波矣
Ngwat ray wa Pit, pec phàng lày luc. 　　月離于畢　俾滂沱矣
Mac nin tòng teng, pu wàng lhày luc. 　　武人東征　不遑他矣

A man on military service in the uninspiring landscape of eastern China thinks longingly of the mountains and streams of his western homeland. For the Heavenly Fork see Ode 203.

233

The Bloom of the Trumpet Vine　苕之華

How rich is the orange of the trumpet vine blossoms;
how painful the grief in my heart.

Dyàw tu wà, wuns gu gwàng luc.　　　　苕之華　芸其黃矣
Sum tu ou luc, wi gu lhang luc.　　　　心之憂矣　維其傷矣

The leaves of the trumpet vine are luxuriant;
if I'd known how it would be for me, better never to have been born.

Dyàw tu wà, gu lap tzèng-tzèng.　　　　苕之華　其葉菁菁
Tre ngàyc na tsec, pu na ma sheng.　　　知我如此　不如無生

The ewes have swollen heads; in a fish trap I see the Three Stars.
People may find a bit to eat, but rarely can they eat their fill.

Tzàng yang bunt lhouc; Sùm Sèng dzùc rouc.　　牂羊墳首　三星在罶
Nin khàyc-luc mluk, sent khàyc-luc pròuc.　　　人可以食　鮮可以飽

A brief elegy for a starving society. The sheep appear to have oversized heads by comparison with their emaciated bodies; and one would not notice stars reflected in a fish trap, if there were live fish thrashing about in it.

234

What Grass is not Withered?　何草不黃

What grass is not withered? When do we get a day without marching?
Who isn't under orders to bring about peace in the Four Quarters?

Gày tsòuc pu gwàng? Gày nit pu gràng?　　何草不黃　何日不行
Gày nin pu tzang kèng-weng Slits Pang?　　　何人不將　經營四方

What grass is not frost-blackened? Which man isn't in poor shape?
Woe, we're on military service—we alone have to live as non-people.

Gày tsòuc pu gwìn? Gày nin pu grin?　　何草不玄　何人不矜
Ùy ngàyc teng pa, dòk way puyc min.　　哀我征夫　獨為匪民

We aren't water-buffaloes or tigers, yet we must trek through this desolate
　　wilderness.
Woe, we're on military service; morning and evening we get no respite.

Puyc syuyc, puyc hlàc, shout payc kwhàngs lac.
Ùy ngàyc teng pa, traw syak pu gràs.

匪兕匪虎　率彼曠野
哀我征夫　朝夕不暇

There is a thick-furred fox, slipping through the dark undergrowth.
There are carriages, moving along the *Tiw* road.

Wuc bùm tac gwà, shout payc you tsòuc;
wuc djànt tu ka, gràng payc Tiw lòuc.

有芃者狐　率彼幽草
有棧之車　行彼周道

A lament for the hardships of military service, with the conscripts heading off to put down unrest at some godforsaken place deep in the "Four Quarters". The poet's discomfort is sharpened through glimpses of freer creatures. The fox has thick fur to keep him warm, and the carriages on the highroad are heading to the capital, where the poet would love to be.

VOICES FROM EARLY CHINA

Greater Clarions

235

Mun Dwells on High 文王

Mun dwells on high—oh, he shines in the sky!
Although as a state *Tiw* was old, its mandate to rule China is new.
Since the house of *Tiw* had become pre-eminent, was God's mandate not right?
Mun ascends to Sky and descends to mankind: he's on God's left and right hands.

Mun wang dzùc dyangs—à tyaw wa thìn!	文王在上　於昭于天
Tiw swi gwuc pròng, gu mreng wi sin.	周雖舊邦　其命維新
Wuc Tiw phru hènt: Tès mreng pu du?	有周丕顯　帝命不時
Mun wang truk kròungs; dzùc Tès tzàyc wuc.	文王陟降　在帝左右

Mun was a vigorous man, and his fine reputation is immortal.
Oh, *Mun* lavished gifts on *Tiw*, namely his descendants.
Mun's descendants will be the roots and boughs of the nation for a hundred generations,
and the officers serving *Tiw* will themselves be eminent for generations.

Muyc-muyc Mun wang, reng muns pu luc.	亹亹文王　令聞不已
Drin slèk tzay Tiw: gò Mun wang sòun tzuc.	陳錫哉周　侯文王孫子
Mun wang sòun tzuc, pùnt ke pràk lhats,	文王孫子　本支百世
bam Tiw tu shuc phru hènt yak lhats.	凡周之士　丕顯奕世

They have been eminent for generations, due to their well-thought-out policies.
Many august officers have been produced in this king's state of *Tiw*.
Tiw has been able to produce them, and they have been its supports.
Thanks to these many impressive officers, *Mun* can rest securely.

Lhats tu phru hènt, kot you yuk-yuk.	世之丕顯　厥猶翼翼
Su wàng tày shuc sheng tsec wang kwùk.	思皇多士　生此王國
Wang kwùk khùk sheng, wi Tiw tu treng.	王國克生　維周之楨
Tzìc-tzìc tày shuc, Mun wang luc nèng.	濟濟多士　文王以寧

Mun was august—ah, he was constantly bright and reverent.
Mighty, indeed, was Sky's mandate. The descendants of the house of *Un*
—and those descendants, did they not number a hundred thousand?
—but their destiny was decided by God on High, who made them subject to *Tiw*.

Mouk-mouk Mun wang—à tsup hu krengs tuc.	穆穆文王　於緝熙敬止
Kràc tzay Thìn mreng. Wuc Lhang sòun tzuc	假哉天命　有商孫子

—Lhang tu sòun tzuc, gu rès pu uk? 商之孫子　其麗不億
—Dyangs Tès kuts mreng, gò wa Tiw buk. 上帝既命　侯于周服

Yes, they were made subject to *Tiw*: Sky's mandate doesn't last for ever.
Un's officers were admirable and energetic, yet even so they have to pour ritual libations in our capital,
and when they perform the libation rites, they wear our uniform of *hwac* caps and robes embroidered with axe-heads.
You who are favoured with high positions under our king, don't you be thinking about your own ancestors.

Gò buk wa Tiw: Thìn mreng mayc dyang. 侯服于周　天命靡常
Un shuc pra mùc; kòns tzang wa krang. 殷士膚敏　祼將于京
Kot tzàk kòns tzang, dyang buk pac hwac. 厥作祼將　常服黼冔
Wang tu dzins gin, ma nìms nec tzàc. 王之藎臣　無念爾祖

Don't think about your own ancestors, which would lead to your adopting their attitudes.
You need always to be making yourself worthy of Sky's new mandate, and you can look for abundant prosperity that way.
Before the *Un* forces were destroyed, that dynasty had been the earthly counterpart to God on High.
You should reflect on the fate of *Un*. Sky's lofty mandate is not an easy thing.

Ma nìms nec tzàc, lout siw kot tùk. 無念爾祖　聿修厥德
Wrank ngan phùts mreng, dzis gou tày puk. 永言配命　自求多福
Un tu muts sàngs shi, khùk phùts Dyangs Tès. 殷之未喪師　克配上帝
Ngay kràms wa Un. Syouns mreng pu leks. 宜鑒于殷　峻命不易

Sky's mandate is not easy: don't let it come to an end with yourselves.
Make your upright reputations visible and burnish them. It was from Sky that power came to the house of *Ngwa* and later to *Un*,
but Sky's initiatives have no sound, no smell.
You should model yourself on *Mun*, and then all the many states will trust you.

Mreng tu pu leks: ma àt nec lhin. 命之不易　無遏爾躬
Swan tyaw ngays muns. Wuc Ngwa Un dzis Thìn. 宣昭義問　有虞殷自天
Dyangs Tès tu tzùs ma hyeng, ma k'hyous. 上天之載　無聲無臭
Ngay gèng Mun wang, màns pròng tzàk phou. 儀形文王　萬邦作孚

After *Tiw* conquered *Un*, it must have needed to continue in post many administrators who had been serving the old régime. I read this Ode as an exercise in political re-education, aimed at extinguishing obsolete loyalties to *Un* which might sap the legitimacy of *Tiw* rule. If the Ode were addressed to people of the conquered generation, it would have to be very early, perhaps implausibly so; but old loyalties could have survived into later generations, particularly among families which traced their own ancestry to the *Un* ruling house.

The "house of *Ngwa*" (verse 7) was a shadowy dynasty which may or may not have existed, separate from *Ghàc*, before the *Un* dynasty. (In the *Tiw* dynasty *Ngwa* was a small state in the area of Pinglu and Xiaxian, southern Shanxi.) "No sound, no smell" is a way of saying that Sky moves in a mysterious way: one cannot decide on correct actions by scrutinizing Sky directly, so one should do so by modelling oneself on *Mun*, who as a spirit mediates ("ascends and descends") between Sky and Man.

236

Illuminating the World 大明

Illuminating the world below, and majestic on high,
Sky can't be taken for granted: it is not easy to be a king.
Sky had given the *Un* heir a distinguished position, yet didn't allow him to come into possession of the world.

Mrang-mrang dzùc gràc, hràk-hràk dzùc dyangs,	明明在下　赫赫在上
Thìn nàns dum se: pu leks wi wang.	天難忱斯　不易維王
Thìn wruts Un tèk, shuc pu gèp Slits Pang.	天位殷適　使不挾四方

Second-daughter *Num* of *Tuts* was a member of the *Un* royal family.
She came and was married in *Tiw*, at the capital,
and with her husband *Kwits* she settled down to cultivate the ways of "virtue".
The lady *Num* became pregnant, and gave birth to *Mun*.

Tuts droungs gec Num dzis payc Un-Lhang.	摯仲氏任　自彼殷商
Rù kràs wa Tiw, wat bin wa krang.	來嫁于周　曰嬪于京
Nùc gup Wang Kwits wi tùk tu gràng.	迺及王季　維德之行
Thàts Num wuc lhin, sheng tsec Mun wang.	太任有身　生此文王

Now *Mun* was a circumspect and a reverent man.
He served God on High in brightness, thus aspiring to great good fortune.
He never deviated from the path of righteousness, and in consequence he would be given mastery of the world's states.

Wi tsec Mun wang syawc sum, yuk-yuk.	維此文王　小心翼翼
Tyaw shuc Dyangs Tès, lout gròuy tày puk.	昭事上帝　聿懷多福
Kot tùk pu wùy, luc douc Pang kwùk.	厥德不回　以受方國

Sky inspected the earth below, and the mandate alighted on *Mun*.
And when *Mun* began his career, Sky made a mate for him,
south of *Grùp* city, beside the Wei river.
Mun was a fine man, and in a large state there was a young lady ...

Thìn kràm dzùc gràc, wuc mreng kuts dzup.	天監在下　有命既集
Mun wang cha tzùs, Thìn tzàk tu gùp	文王初載　天作之合
dzùc Grùp tu lang, dzùc Wuts tu shuc.	在洽之陽　在渭之涘
Mun wang kràysc tuc, dàts pròng wuc tzuc ...	文王嘉止　大邦有子

... in a large state there was a young lady who looked like Sky's younger sister.
Mun fixed an auspicious date, and travelled in person to meet her at the Wei.
He constructed a pontoon of boats—his brightness was indeed illustrious.

... dàts pròng wuc tzuc, khèns Thìn tu mùts.	大邦有子　倪天之妹
Mun dèngs kot syang, tsin ngrangs wa Wuts.	文定厥祥　親迎于渭
Dzòuc tou way rang—phru hènt gu kwàng.	造舟為梁　丕顯其光

A mandate came down from Sky, and it was conferred on *Mun*
in *Tiw*—in the capital. The new queen's clan was *Shin*.
She, its eldest daughter, was a strong girl, and she gave birth sturdily to king
  Mac.
Sky told *Mac*: "I shall protect and aid you, and confer on you my Mandate". So
  Mac marched on great *Un*.

Wuc mreng dzis Thìn, mreng tsec Mun wang	有命自天　命此文王
wa Tiw, wa krang. Tzònt nrac wi Shin.	于周于京　纘女維莘
Trank tzuc wi gàngs, tòuk sheng Mac wang.	長子維行　篤生武王
"Pòuc wus mreng nec": sèp bat dàts Lhang.	保右命爾　燮伐大商

The troops of *Un* were massed together like a forest.
At Herdsman's Heath *Mac* made a solemn proclamation: "We are now rising up!
God on High is looking down at you: do not hold back."

Un-Lhang tu rac, gu gòts na rum.	殷商之旅　其會如林
Lhic wa Muk Lac: "Wi lac gò hung!	矢于牧野　維予侯興
Dyangs Tès kràm nac: ma nits nec sum."	上帝臨汝　無貳爾心

Herdsman's Heath was broad. The battle wagons were brightly coloured,
and the four-horse teams pounded the earth. The troops were commanded by
  sire *Dangs*
and he was an eagle, a hawk. King *Mac* shone,
falling furiously on great *Un*. The morning of the encounter was clear and bright.

Muk Lac yang-yang. Djànt ka wàng-wàng,	牧野洋洋　棧車煌煌
slits ngwan pàng-pàng. Wi shi Dangs-pac,	駟騵彭彭　維師尚父
du wi ung lang. Rangs payc Mac wang,	時維鷹揚　亮彼武王
sits bat dàts Un. Gòts traw tseng mrang.	肆伐大商　會朝清明

In this Ode about the conquest of *Un*, that dynasty is referred to variously as *Un*, *Lhang*, or *Un-Lhang*. As explained on p. 7, my translations always call the dynasty *Un*.

Tuts, the home of *Mun*'s mother, is believed to have been a small district within the *Un* royal domain. *Grùp* may have been a town or a river, and is placed by the reference books in the angle between the Wei and Yellow rivers, in eastern Shaanxi. That would put it within the *Tiw*-dynasty state of *Nots* (though *Nots* was not a very large state).

In verse 8, the dictionaries define *ngwan* as "a red horse with a white belly"; but (as mentioned earlier) I am sceptical about these words for very specific colour combinations in horse's coats, so I have left the word untranslated.

237

Sinuous 緜

Long and sinuous are the melon vines.
The origin of our people lay in the country of the *Dàc*, *Tzas*, and *Tsit* rivers.
The duke of olden time, sire *Tànt*, made shelters for them out of clay and in caves,
since they had no houses yet.

Ment-ment kwrà lìt. 緜緜瓜瓞
Min tu cha sheng dzis Dàc, Tzas, Tsit. 民之初生　自杜沮漆
Kàc klòng Tànt-pac lòu phouks, lòu wìt, 古公亶父　陶覆陶穴
muts wuc krà lhit. 未有家室

At break of day the old duke, sire *Tànt*, galloped his horse
along the bank of the western river, till he reached the land below Mount *Ge*.
There he met a girl of the *Kyang* clan; and so he tarried, and took up residence.

Kàc klòng Tànt-pac rù traw tzòc mràc, 古公亶父　來朝走馬
shout sì lhouyc nghàc, tits wa Ge gràc. 率西水滸　至于岐下
Wan gup Kyang nrac, lout rù sa wac. 爰及姜女　聿來胥宇

The plain of *Tiw* was broad and lush—its violet-cress and *là* plants tasted like sweet rice cakes.
So there *Tànt* set to and made plans. He made notches in our tortoise shells,
and they said "Stay, stop! Build houses here."

Tiw ngwan mù-mù; kunt là na lu. 周原膴膴　堇荼如飴
Wan lhuc, wan mu, wan khèts ngàyc kwru, 爰始爰謀　爰契我龜
"Wat tuc, wat druc; trouk lhit wa tzu." 曰止曰時　築室于茲

Tànt quietened down and settled. He scouted to left and to right,
he made boundaries and marked out fields, surveying by the yard and the acre.
West to east, everywhere he put work in hand.

Nùc outs, nùc tuc, nùc tzàyc, nùc wuc. 迺慰迺止　迺左迺右
Nùc kang, nùc ruc, nùc swan, nùc mùc. 迺疆迺理　迺宣迺畝
Dzis sì dzà tòng, tiw wan tup shuc. 自西徂東　周爰執事

And then he summoned his Master of Works and his Master of Labour,
to arrange for a residence to be erected.
Their plumblines were straight; they lashed boards together into shuttering,
and with reverence they constructed a temple.

Nùc draws su-khòng, nùc draws su-dà, 迺召司空　迺召司徒
pec rup lhit krà. 俾立室家

Gu mlung tzùk druk, shouk prànt luc dzùs.   其繩則直　縮版以栽
Tzàk mraws yuk-yuk.   作廟翼翼

They collected soil into long rows, checking measurements continually,
They pounded it into walls, higher and higher, scraping them repeatedly into solidity.
Eight thousand feet of walls rose together, ignoring the timing of the drums.

Kou tu nung-nung, dàk tu mhùng-mhùng.   捄之陾陾　度之薨薨
Trouk tu tùng-tùng, syawk ros brung-brung.   築之登登　削屢馮馮
Pràk tàc krì hung; kòu kàc put lhung.   百堵皆興　鼛鼓弗勝

Then they constructed the outer citadel gate, very high,
and the inner gate to the palace, very grand,
and they built the Altar of the Earth, from which troops would march to war.

Nùc rup kòu mùn, kòu mùn wuc khàngs.   迺立皋門　皋門有伉
Nùc rup ungs mùn, ungs mùn tzang-tzang.   迺立應門　應門將將
Nùc rup tronk thàc, noung k'hyou you gràng.   迺立冢土　戎醜攸行

The troops' fighting spirit was indomitable, and their renown was never dimmed.
Rides were cut through the oak forests and roads opened up.
The *Kòun Luy* tribesmen fled—how they panted in their haste!

Sits pu dùnt kot ouns, yak pu wrunt kot muns.   肆不殄厥慍　亦不隕厥聞
Dzàk wuk bàts luc, gràng lòuc lòts luc.   柞棫拔矣　行道兌矣
Kòun Luy lhòts luc—wi gu thots luc!   混夷駾矣　維其喙矣

Ngwa and *Nots* states agreed peace treaties, giving pledges of good faith, and *Mun* set their animal-offerings on the sacrificial altar.
And so: we had allies in distant parts; we had buffers supporting us on either side;
we had friends who would rush to our aid if need be; we had defences against insult.

Ngwa Nots tuts kot deng; Mun wang gots kot sheng.   虞芮質厥成　文王蹶厥牲
Lac wat wuc sha bos; lac wat wuc sùns ghòs;   予曰有疏附　予曰有先後
lac wat wuc pùn tzòc; lac wat wuc ngac moc.   予曰有奔走　予曰有禦侮

In this poem about the origin of the *Tiw* nation, *Tànt* (also known as *Thàts wang*) was the grandfather of *Mun*. The *Dàc*, *Tzas*, and *Tsit* rivers rise in the hills north of the Wei valley—the latter two were discussed with Ode 180, the *Dàc* flows through modern Fufeng, some sixty miles west of Xi'an.

The "western river" was the Wei. Mount *Ge* is modern Qishan, fifteen miles or so west of Fufeng; the "plain of *Tiw*" was to its south, and was the *Tiw* people's base before *Mun* led them east (p. 8). Of the plants that grew there, I believe *kunt* may have been modern Chinese 'zhuge cai', "February orchid" or "Chinese violet cress" (*Orychophragmus violaceus*), which is eaten as salad leaves or cooked like spinach. The case of *là* is more complicated. The word normally stands for a range of plants in the sowthistle and dandelion family (my translations use "dandelion", as the member of the family most familiar to English-speakers). Though edible, these are bitter rather than sweet, indeed *là* can be used to mean "bitter". However, some editions of the Odes show a variant form of the Chinese graph at this point, standing for *dra* "tea" (this word, in modern pronunciation 'cha', is the source of the English word "tea" and the slangy "char"). The words *dra* and *là* may themselves be related within Chinese, and I wonder whether, before the tea plant was available, the Chinese made a hot drink by infusing leaves of some dandelion-like plant.

For the tortoise-shell oracle see Ode 50.

Buildings were constructed of pounded earth, and wooden shuttering was used to hold it in place while it was pounded into solidity. The "scraping" was probably to smooth bumps of loose soil into place. There are different theories about the drums: one idea is that they were used to establish a working rhythm, but these workers were so eager that they worked faster, another idea is that the drums announced knocking-off time but the workers carried on anyway.

The last verse skips forward two generations to the time of *Mun*. *Ngwa* and *Nots* were states discussed with Odes 235 and 236 respectively; those states alone could not have been said to protect *Tiw* "on all sides", but perhaps other allies went unmentioned. The "pledges of good faith" may have been hostages.

238

Stands of Oaks 棫樸

Dense are the stands of oaks—we chop them into firewood for storing in the woodshed.
Stately is our sovereign king, and on all sides people hasten to join him.

Bùm-bùm wuk pòk—sin tu, yous tu.   芃芃棫樸　薪之槱之
Tzìc-tzìc pek wang, tzàyc wuc tsos tu.   濟濟辟王　左右趣之

Stately is our sovereign king, and on all sides people display *tang* emblems.
They raise their *tang* emblems high, as is fitting for officers of such eminence.

Tzìc-tzìc pek wang, tzàyc wuc phonk tang;   濟濟辟王　左右奉璋
phonk tang ngày-ngày, màw shuc you ngay.   奉璋峨峨　髦士攸宜

On the *Kèng* boats are crowded, and their oarsmen are many.
The *Tiw* king is on the march, and his six regiments are rallying to him.

Phìts payc Kèng tou, tung dà tzap tu.   淠彼涇舟　烝徒楫之
Tiw wang wa mràts, rouk shi gup tu.   周王于邁　六師及之

The Milky Way is brilliant, making a *tang* emblem in the sky.
Long live the *Tiw* king—is he not truly a man!

Tràwk payc Wun Hàns, way tang wa thìn.   倬彼雲漢　為章于天
Tiw wang douc-khòuc—grà pu tzàk nin!   周王壽考　遐不作人

His exterior is as if carved—his appearance is like gold or jade.
Energetic is our king: he keeps the world in line.

Tòuy tròk gu tang—kum ngok gu sangs.　　追琢其章　金玉其相
Mrant-mrant ngàyc wang; kàng kuc Slits Pang.　　勉勉我王　綱紀四方

A *tang* was a ritual symbol of authority, like the larger *kwè* emblem mentioned in other Odes; both were tall, flat rectangles of jade with a pointed or rounded top, which the bearer would hold with both hands against his chest—or, during an audience with the king, before his mouth to avoid his breath polluting the royal presence.

For the river *Kèng* see Ode 35.

239

The Wooded Slopes of *Gànt*　旱麓

See the wooded slopes of mount *Gànt*, full of hazels and *gàc* trees.
Joyous is our prince—in calling down blessings he is joyous.

Tam payc Gànt ròk, jin gàc tzìc-tzìc.　　瞻彼旱麓　榛楛濟濟
Khùyc dìc kwun-tzuc, kàn ròk khùyc dìc.　　豈弟君子　干祿豈弟

Bright is the jade libation-ladle, full of yellow liquid.
Joyous is our prince, on whom blessings and good fortune are bestowed.

Sprit payc ngok dzànt, gwàng riw dzùc troung.　　瑟彼玉瓚　黃流在中
Khùyc dìc kwun-tzuc, puk ròk you kròungs.　　豈弟君子　福祿攸降

A hawk flies right up to the sky; a fish leaps in the deep pool.
Joyous is our prince—is he not truly a man?

Yon puy rìts thìn, nga lhyàwk wa wwìn.　　鳶飛戾天　魚躍于淵
Khùyc dìc kwun-tzuc, grà pu tzàk nin.　　豈弟君子　遐不作人

The clear wine has been delivered; the red stallion has been prepared for sacrifice.
He will be a burnt-offering, and so will further increase our good fortune.

Tseng tziwc kuts tzùs, seng mouc kuts bruks,　　清酒既載　騂牡既備
luc hang luc sluc, luc krèts krank puk.　　以享以祀　以介景福

See those oak logs, which the people will use for the sacrificial bonfire.
Joyous is our prince, sustained by the Spirits.

Sprit payc dzàk wuk, min shac ryaws luc.　　瑟彼柞棫　民所燎矣
Khùyc dìc kwun-tzuc, Mlin shac ràws luc.　　豈弟君子　神所勞矣

Luxuriant are the lablab vines and lianas, spreading like netting over the boughs.
Joyous is our prince; when supplicating for blessings he never botches the rites.

Màk-màk kàt rouyc, lhay wa lyòu mùy. 莫莫葛藟　施于條枚
Khùyc dìc kwun-tzuc, gou puk pu wùy. 豈弟君子　求福不回

The poet revels in the demeanour of his prince as the latter prepares to intercede with Sky for the prosperity of his society by making a burnt offering of a male animal, perhaps a horse, together with a libation of wine. Mount *Gànt* is about forty miles south of present-day Hanzhong city, Shaanxi.

The *gwàng riw*, "yellow liquid", might simply be white wine (modern Chinese calls that "yellow wine"), but the commentators suggest that it was wine infused with turmeric or a similar spice.

Whatever relevance the opening image of the wooded hillsides had is now lost (and no-one today knows what tree a *gàc* was). But the creepers of the final verse are the standard metaphor for the dependence of society's members on its leader's prowess.

240

The Pure Lady *Num*　思齊

Pure was the lady *Num*, mother of *Mun*;
lovable was *Kyang* of *Tiw*, lady of the capital's royal residence.
The lady *Sluc* continued their excellent reputation; and now we find a hundred princes have sprung from these.

Su jì Thàts Num, Mun wang tu muc; 思齊泰任　文王之母
su mouys Tiw Kyang, krang lhit tu buc. 思媚周姜　京室之婦
Thàts Sluc slus mhuy um, tzùk pràk se nùm. 泰姒嗣徽音　則百斯男

Mun being obedient to the Spirits of his past clan heads, not one of them was dissatisfied with him, not one of the Spirits was unhappy with him.
He was a model for his queen and for his brothers too, so he could manage his family and his state.

Wìts wa tzòung klòng, Mlin mank du ons, Mlin mank 惠于宗公　神罔時怨　神罔
du thòng. 時恫
Gèng wa kwràc tsùy, tits wa hwrang dìc, luc ngas wa 形于寡妻　至于兄弟　以御
krà pròng. 于家邦

Keeping the peace at court and reverent in the temple,
he was illustrious in monitoring his people's welfare, protecting them tirelessly.

Ong-ong dzùc koung, siwk-siwk dzùc mraws, 雝雝在宮　肅肅在廟
phru hènt yak rum, ma lak yak pòuc. 丕顯亦臨　無射亦保

His great energy was unquenchable, and there was no flaw in his brilliance and
    greatness.
He made use even of information he hadn't been told directly, and took on board
    even criticisms not formally addressed to him.

Sits noung dzit pu dùnt, rat kràc pu grà.   肆戎疾不殄　烈假不瑕
Pu muns yak lhuk, pu kràns yak nup.   不聞亦式　不諫亦入

As an adult *Mun* was highly "virtuous"; as a boy he was thoroughly trained in his
    role.
The men of old were indefatigable; praise to this fine nobleman!

Sits deng nin wuc tùk; syawc tzuc wuc dzòuc.   肆成人有德　小子有造
Kàc tu nin ma lak; las màw se shuc!   古之人無斁　譽髦斯士

Num and *Kyang* were respectively *Mun*'s mother and his grandmother; *Sluc* was his wife—their marriage was described in Ode 236. (Some or all of the ladies' names will have been clan names rather than individual names. *Thàts* is an honorific prefix—etymologically it means "great", I translate it here as "lady".)

My wording "sprung from these" at the end of verse 1 suggests vaguely that the hundred princes descend from one or more of these ladies; the Chinese is itself vague but could more naturally be read as saying they are all sons of *Sluc*. That might sound absurd, but Legge explains that while *Sluc* had only ten sons, "her freedom from jealousy so encouraged the fruitfulness of the harem, that all the sons born in it are ascribed to her".

By prefacing verses about the excellence of *Mun* with a verse praising his grandmother, mother, and wife, the poem suggests that his virtues stemmed from their influence. The traditional commentators noticed this implication, and found it objectionable.

241

Almighty was God   皇矣

Almighty was God on High; he looked down in majesty,
scrutinizing the world and seeking tranquillity for the people.
Two dynasties' government had failed.
So he investigated and assessed the world's states.
God on High settled matters. Hating the existing states' extravagant ways,
he turned to gaze with favour towards the west, and granted land for a new
    settlement.

Wàng luc Dyangs Tès, rum gràc wuc hràk;   皇矣上帝　臨下有赫
kràm kwàn Slits Pang, gou min tu mràk.   監觀四方　求民之莫
Wi tsec nits kwùk, gu tengs pu wàk.   維此二國　其政不獲
Wi payc Slits kwùk wan kous, wan dàk.   維彼四國　爰究爰度
Dyangs Tès tic tu. Dzùng gu lhuk kwhàk,   上帝耆之　憎其式廓
nùc kons sì kàs, tsec wi lac dràk.   迺眷西顧　此維與宅

The men of *Tiw* cleared the land, its standing dead trees, its fallen trees;
they made it tidy and levelled it, with its bushy clumps and its saplings.
They opened it up and cleared it, with its tamarisks and its walking-stick trees.
They cleared them away and cut them down, its wild-mulberry trees and its mountain-mulberry trees.
God transferred bright virtue to *Tiw*, and its customs and institutions became marked by greatness.
Sky established a partner for itself on Earth, and the mandate granted to *Tiw* became securely fixed.

Jàk tu, penk tu, gu jus, gu ìts;　　　柞之屏之　其菑其殪
siw tu, breng tu, gu kwàns, gu rets.　　修之平之　其灌其栵
Khìc tu, bek tu, gu rheng, gu kas;　　啟之闢之　其檉其椐
nang tu, lhèk tu, gu emp, gu taks.　　攘之剔之　其檿其柘
Tès tsan mrang tùk, kròns luy tzùs ràks.　帝遷明德　串夷載路
Thìn rup kot phùts, douc mreng kuts kàks.　天立厥配　受命既固

God inspected the mountains;
the oaks were thinned out, the pine and cypress groves were opened up.
God made a state, and he made a king to be his counterpart, springing from the line of *Thàts Pràk* and *Kwits*.
Now, this *Kwits*,
in his trusting nature he was a friendly man. He was a good friend to his elder brother *Thàts Pràk*,
and worked to promote his welfare; consequently glory was conferred on him.
He received blessings which he was never to forfeit, and he took full possession of the world.

Tès senk gu shàn;　　　　　　　　帝省其山
dzàk wuk se bàts, slong pràk se lhòt.　柞棫斯拔　松柏斯兌
Tès tzàk pròng, tzàk tòuts, dzis Thàts Pràk Wang Kwits.　帝作邦作對　自大伯王季
Wi tsec Wang Kwits,　　　　　　　維此王季
in sum tzùk wuc; tzùk wuc gu hwrang,　因心則友　則友其兄
tzùk tòuk gu khrangs. Tzùs slèk tu kwàng.　則篤其慶　載錫之光
Douc ròk ma smàngs, amp wuc Slits Pang.　受祿無喪　奄有四方

Now we come to his son, *Mun*.
God probed his heart: he had an established reputation,
by nature he was capable of enlightened behaviour
—he was capable of enlightened and decent behaviour; he was able to preside and to rule,
to be king over a great state. He was worthy to be followed and obeyed.
When the people co-operated with *Mun* his character was such that no-one was left with regrets.
And once *Mun* was granted divine favour, it would continue to his descendants.

Wi tsec Mun Wang,　　　　　　　　維此文王
Tès dàk gu sum. Mràk gu tùk um,　　帝度其心　嘆其德音

gu tùk khùk mrang
—*khùk mrang, khùk routs, khùk trank, khùk kwun,*
wang tsec dàts pròng. Khùk mlouns, khùk dzong.
Dzong wa Mun Wang, gu tùk mayc mhùs.
Kuts douc Tès thruc, lhay wa sòun tzuc.

其德克明
克明克類　克長克君
王此大邦　克順克從
從于文王　其德靡悔
既受帝祉　施于孫子

God spoke to *Mun*:
"Don't be so easy-going, don't be so self-indulgent."
So after he had climbed to a high lookout post,
he saw that the men of *Mrit* were disloyal: they were daring to rebel against his great fiefdom.
They had invaded *Wens* and were marching on *Konk*. In his majesty, *Mun* was angered by this.
So he marshalled his troops, and in order to put down the rebels he marched to *Kac*,
so as to confirm *Tiw* as divinely chosen, and to respond to the whole world's wishes.

Tès wuts Mun Wang:
"*Ma nan bàns-wans, ma nan hum slans.*"
Lànt sùn tùng wa ngàns:
Mrit nin pu krong, kàmp gac dàts pròng.
Tsum Wens dzà Konk. Wang hràk se nàc.
Wan tenk gu rac, luc àns dzà Kac,
luc tòuk Tiw gàc, luc tòuts wa thìn gràc.

帝謂文王
無然畔援　無然歆羨
誕先登于岸
密人不恭　敢距大邦
侵阮徂共　王赫斯怒
爰整其旅　以按徂莒
以篤于周祜　以對于天下

Mun was firmly established in his capital.
The enemy invaded across the *Wens* border and climbed our high ridge,
but they were unable to form up on our heights—on our heights, our slopes;
and they couldn't reach our springs to water their troops—our springs, or our pools.
Mun resided on the bright plateau to the south of mount *Ge*,
on the course of the river *Wei*: for the myriad states a model,
and for the common people their sovereign.

Uy gu dzùc krang.
Tsum dzis Wens kang, truk ngàyc kàw kàng;
ma drit ngàyc rung—ngàyc rung, ngàyc ày;
ma ums ngàyc dzwan—ngàyc dzwan, ngàyc dray.
Dràk kus sen ngwan kas Ge tu lang,
dzùc Wuts tu tzang—màns pròng tu pang,
gràc min tu wang.

依其在京
侵自阮疆　陟我高岡
無矢我陵　我陵我阿
無飲我泉　我泉我池
宅其鮮原　居岐之陽
在渭之將　萬邦之方
下民之王

God spoke to *Mun*: "I cherish your bright virtue.
You do not make a show of your great renown;
you have not let your pre-eminent greatness change you.
Instinctively, without study or thought, you obey God's laws."
And again God spoke to *Mun*:

"Make plans with your allied states: unite with your brothers.
With your grappling-hooks and ladders, your siege-engines and battering-rams,
attack the walls of *Djoung*."

Tès wuts Mun Wang: "*Lac gròuy mrang tùk.*	帝謂文王　予懷明德
Pu dàts hyeng luc shuk,	不大聲以色
pu trank ghàc luc krùk.	不長夏以懌
Pu lhuk pu tre mlouns Tès tu tzùk."	不識不知　順帝之則
Tès wuts Mun Wang:	帝謂文王
"*Swin nec gwu pang, dòng nec dìc hwrang.*	詢爾仇方　同爾弟兄
Luc nec kò wan lac nec rum thong,	以爾鉤援　與爾臨衝
luc bat Djoung long."	以伐崇墉

Slowly but steadily the siege-engines and battering-rams moved forward. The walls of *Djoung* were lofty and thick.
One after another captives were taken for interrogation, before their severed heads were solemnly
offered as a sacrifice to God—an open-air sacrifice. They were brought forward and added to the offerings.
Throughout the world there were already none who lacked respect for *Mun*.
His siege-engines and battering-rams were massive. The walls of *Djoung* were solid;
but he attacked them, he smashed them, he broke them down and utterly annihilated them.
And after that, throughout the world none dared say him nay.

Rum thong gràn-gràn; Djoung long ngant-ngant.	臨衝閑閑　崇墉巘巘
Tup sins ran-ran, you kwrùk àn-àn	執訊連連　攸馘安安
dec routs, dec mràs, dec trits, dec bos.	是類是禡　是致是附
Slits Pang luc ma moc.	四方以無侮
Rum thong put-put. Djoung long ngut-ngut;	臨衝茀茀　崇墉仡仡
dec bat, dec sits, dec dzot, dec mhùt.	是伐是肆　是絕是忽
Slits Pang luc ma but.	四方以無拂

The poet describes the beginnings of the *Tiw* state in the twelfth century. *Tiw* is presented as a tribe which moved into China proper from the west, and proceeded both to conquer the effete polities then in power and to adopt civilized Chinese ways. The idea that a conquering nation is fulfilling the wishes of God—and perhaps, in a distant second place, the wishes of the populations affected—is familiar enough from European history.

Kas, which I have translated as "walking-stick tree", was called the "tree of longevity" because it provided walking sticks as used by the elderly. I do not know what modern species name it corresponds to.

Most place-names mentioned in the later verses are long obsolete, but with one exception their locations have been identified in the area to the west of modern Xi'an. *Mrit* was around modern Lingtai, across the provincial boundary in Gansu a hundred miles northwest of Xi'an. *Wens* and *Konk* were around Jingchuan, twenty miles further northwest. I cannot locate *Kac*. Mount *Ge* is the modern Qishan, see p. 8. *Djoung* state (which *Mun* conquered during the expedition on which he would die, see p. 7) is standardly held to have been in the area of modern Huxian, twenty miles south-west of Xi'an. (Edward Shaughnessy has suggested that *Djoung* was much further east, near Luoyang, but I don't understand how he squares that with the content of the Odes.)

According to the Chinese commentary tradition, *rum* and *thong* were two separate elements of military equipment. Etymologically, the words link to the ideas "approach" and "knock" respectively. It is easy to surmise that a "knocker" was a battering-ram. I imagine an "approacher" as the kind of vehicle with a roof which was used in European sieges to protect attackers from the arrows of the defenders.

242

The Magic Tower 靈臺

He planned the Magic Tower and put the work in hand—he planned it and marked out the foundations.
The people set to work on it, and in less than a day it was finished.
He planned it and put the work in hand with no special urgency, but the people arrived and went to work with a will.

Kèng lhuc Rèng Dù—kèng tu, weng tu.	經始靈臺　經之營之
Lhaks min kòung tu, pu nit deng tu.	庶民攻之　不日成之
Kèng lhuc mut kuk, lhaks min tzu rù.	經始勿亟　庶民孜來

The king was in the Magic Park, where does were sleeping.
The does had glossy coats; the plumage of the white birds gleamed.
The king was at the Magic Pool—oh, it was full of leaping fish.

Wang dzùc Rèng Wuks, ou ròk you buk.	王在靈囿　麀鹿攸伏
Ou ròk dryawk-dryawk; bràk tìwc hràwk-hràwk.	麀鹿濯濯　白鳥翯翯
Wang dzùc Rèng Tawc—à, nuns nga lhyàwk.	王在靈沼　於牣魚躍

Suspended from the uprights and sawtooth crossbeams of their stands were the great drums and bells.
Oh, how the drums and bells were massed together! Oh, how joyous the Hall of the Circular Moat!

Kha ngap wi tsong, bun kàc wi long.	虡業維樅　賁鼓維鏞
À, roun kàc tong; à, ngràwks Pek Ong!	於論鼓鐘　於樂辟廱

Oh, how the drums and bells were massed together! Oh, how joyous the Hall of the Circular Moat!
The alligator-skin drums sounded, *bòng, bòng,* as blind musicians performed their work.

À, roun kàc tong; à, ngràwks Pek Ong!	於論鼓鐘　於樂辟廱
Dày kàc bòng-bòng, mòng sòc tzòs kòng.	鼉鼓逢逢　矇瞍奏功

The "he" of the first verse was *Mun*. Before *Mun* died he had conquered *Djoung* (see the preceding Ode), and he shifted the *Tiw*-state capital to what had been the capital of *Djoung* state, renaming that town *Phoung* after the local river, a tributary of the Wei. This Ode describes the take-over of this new *Tiw* capital.

It is hard to know how best to translate *rèng*, which I have rendered as "magic". Some have taken it as a conventional name amounting to little more than "royal". But etymologically the word certainly had a supernatural connotation (the lower part of its written graph is the word for a shaman), and other commentators have seen it as having that force here, for instance it explains how a tower could be built overnight. In any case, "royal" and "magic" do not contradict one another. As in mediaeval Europe, early Chinese rulers were held to have what we would regard as supernatural powers.

Bells and drums were mounted on wooden stands, and it is believed that *kha* in verse 3 referred to their uprights and *ngap* to the crossbeams from which the instruments were suspended (though in other contexts the words have unrelated meanings). *Tzong* is said to be a sawtooth decoration applied to this framework—in Ode 280 the word for "tooth" appears explicitly in a similar context. The shape of the graph for *kha* seems to refer to a wild animal, and Legge suggests that the uprights were carved to resemble a mythical beast with the head of a deer and body of a snake.

Later in that verse, *pek* normally denotes a jade emblem of high rank having a particular shape: a disc with a circular central hole. The *Pek Ong* was a hall where the young men of the royal family were given archery training, which was located on a circular island in the middle of a circular (hence *pek*-shaped) moat.

Musicians were commonly blind (*mòng* and *sòc* referred to distinct categories of blindness) because this was one of the few professions for which sight was not essential, and blind people might even have special sensitivity to sounds. (In the West it is sometimes claimed that lords wanted musicians to be blind so that they could have music while they enjoyed their ladies, but I suspect this is a lubricious modern fiction, like the feudal lord's mythical "right of the first night" with village brides.)

243

Following in their Footsteps 下武

Following in their predecessors' footsteps are our *Tiw* dynasty rulers—wise
  leaders in successive generations.
Three sovereigns now live in the sky; our King is their counterpart in the capital.

Gràc mac wi Tiw, lhats wuc trat wang.　　　下武維周　世有哲王
Sùm gòs dzùc thìn; wang phùts wa krang.　　三后在天　王配于京

Our King is their counterpart in the capital, actively cultivating their legacy of
  "virtue".
At all times he is worthy of Sky's mandate; in him the trustworthiness of a king is
  fully developed.

Wang phùts wa krang, lhats tùk tzàk gou. 　　王配于京　世德作求
Wrang ngan phùts mreng; deng wang tu phou. 　永言配命　成王之孚

In him the trustworthiness of a king is fully developed; he is a model for the Earth here below.
At all times he is thoughtful and honours his forebears—in these things he is a standard for the world to follow.

Deng wang tu phou; gràc thàc tu lhuk. 　　　成王之孚　下土之式
Wrank ngan hràws su—hràws su wi tzùk. 　　永言孝思　孝思維則

Lovable is this One Man, and his thoughtful character is responsive to the people's needs.
At all times he is thoughtful and honours his forebears—how gloriously he continues their mission!

Mouys tzu It Nin, ungs gò mlouns tùk. 　　　媚茲一人　應侯順德
Wrank ngan hràws su—tyawc tzù slus buk! 　永言孝思　昭哉嗣服

He has come in glory and been admitted to walk in his forebears' footsteps.
Oh, may the years be countless in which he receives Sky's blessings.

Tyawc tzù rù nghac, mlung gu tzàc mac. 　　昭哉來許　繩其祖武
À, màns se nìn, douc Thìn tu gàc! 　　　　　於萬斯年　受天之祜

He receives Sky's blessings, and the people of the whole world come to praise him.
Oh, may his years be countless; for sure he will never lack for supporters.

Douc Thìn tu gàc, Slits Pang rù gàys. 　　　受天之祜　四方來賀
À, màns se nìn, pu grà wuc tzàys! 　　　　　於萬斯年　不遐有佐

A praise-poem for *Mac*. The "three sovereigns" were *Tànt*, *Kwits*, and *Mun*, rulers of *Tiw* state under the *Un* dynasty and respectively great-grandfather, grandfather, and father of *Mac*. (The succession went in each case to a son other than the eldest; strangely to European ways of thinking, this line of rulers seem to have preferred younger sons as successors.)

In verse 4, *It Nin*, "One Man", is a way of referring to the sovereign. The word "lovable" might sound over-sentimental as applied to a powerful monarch, but the Chinese word *mouys* is written with a "woman" element, so the overtones of the English word may be what the poet intended.

Shaughnessy has recently argued that the second stich of verse 4 should be understood as "The lord of *Ungs* [a small state at Pingdingshan, central Henan] complies in virtue", and that the rest of the poem is about the lord of *Ungs* rather than the king. The argument is interesting, but I have not accepted it; the grammar of *mlouns tùk* would be odd, and the last verse is easier to apply to a king than to a vassal ruler.

244

King *Mun* is Renowned 文王有聲

King *Mun* is renowned; he made a great reputation,
while pursuing his people's tranquillity. He lived to see that achieved.
How splendid was king *Mun*!

Mung wang wuc hyeng; wit tzyouns wuc hyeng,　　文王有聲　遹俊有聲
wit gou kot nèng. Wit kwàn kot deng.　　遹求厥寧　遹觀厥成
Mun wang tung tzù!　　文王烝哉

Sky's mandate was conferred on king *Mun*. He already had military successes behind him
when he conquered *Djoung*, and founded *Phoung* city on the river of that name.
How splendid was king *Mun*!

Mun wang douc mreng. Wuc tsec mac kòng,　　文王受命　有此武功
kuts bat wa Djoung, tzàk up wa Phoung.　　既伐于崇　作邑于豐
Mun wang tung tzù!　　文王烝哉

The city wall he built was moated, and he laid out *Phoung* city within its bounds.
He didn't alter the plans; mindful of his predecessors, he came to sacrifice to the ancestors.
How splendid was the monarch!

Trouk geng i hwit, tzàk Phoung i phit.　　築城伊淢　作豐伊匹
Puyc krùk ku you: wit trouy rù hràws.　　匪革其猶　遹追來孝
Wang gòs tung tzù!　　王后烝哉

The works of the king were resplendent. It was by the walls of *Phoung*
that the people of all the world encountered one another, upheld by the monarch.
How splendid was the monarch!

Wang kòng i dryawk. Wi Phoung tu wan　　王功伊濯　為豐之垣
Slits Pang you dòng, wang gòs wi gàn.　　四方攸同　王后維翰
Wang gòs tung tzù!　　王后烝哉

The waters of the *Phoung* drain eastwards, thanks to the noble work of *Wac*.
This was where the people of all the world encountered one another, with this mighty king as their ruler.
How splendid was the mighty king!

Phoung lhouyc tòng tros, wi Wac tu tzèk.　　豐水東注　維禹之績
Slits Pang you dòng, wàng wang wi pek.　　四方攸同　皇王維辟
Wàng wang tung tzù!　　皇王烝哉

In the capital, *Gàwc*, was the Hall of the Circular Moat. Coming from west and from east,
from south and from north, none thought of failing to acknowledge the king's authority.
How splendid was the mighty king!

Gàwc krang Pek Ong. Dzis sì, dzis tòng,　　鎬京辟廱　自西自東
dzis nùm, dzis pùk, ma su pu buk.　　自南自北　無思不服
Wàng wang tung tzù!　　皇王烝哉

It was the king who, examining the oracle, established his residence at *Gàwc*.
It was a tortoise that determined this, and it was king *Mac* who carried it out.
How splendid was king *Mac*!

Khòuc pòk wi wang, dràk dec Gàwc krang.　　考卜維王　宅是鎬京
Wi kwru tengs tu, Mac wang deng tu.　　維龜正之　武王成之
Mac wang tung tzù!　　武王烝哉

By the river *Phoung* white millet grows. King *Mac* worked—and how!
He passed on his plans to his descendants, to ease the task of his faithful successors.
How splendid was king *Mac*!

Phoung lhouyc wuc khuc. Mac wang khuyc pu shuc!　　豐水有芑　武王豈不仕
Lu kot sòun mu, luc èns yuk tzuc.　　詒厥孫謀　以燕翼子
Mac wang tung tzù!　　武王烝哉

Another praise song about the founders of the *Tiw* dynasty. The phrase "didn't alter the plans" perhaps meant that the groundplan of the city was preserved while the buildings were replaced —the poet clearly felt it important to claim that the *Tiw* régime, though new, could be seen as a continuation of tradition. We saw on p. 7 that *Mun* is commonly called "king" although he was never king in reality; it is not possible to translate this Ode without giving *Mun* that unhistorical title.

In verse 6 the topic quietly switches from *Mun* to his son *Mac*. *Gàwc*, *Mac*'s new capital, faced *Mun*'s capital across the river *Phoung*.

245

Giving Birth to the People　生民

She who first gave birth to the *Tiw* people, this was lady *Ngwan* of the *Kyang* clan.
How did she give birth to the people?
She knew how to offer the various sacrifices to avoid barrenness.
She trod in the big toe of God's footprint, and became elated: she was granted increase and prosperity.
She became pregnant, and promptly; she gave birth, and suckled the baby
—and this was the Millet Lord.

Kot cha sheng min, du wi Kyang Ngwan.　　厥初生民　時維姜嫄
Sheng min na gày?　　生民如何
Khùk in, khùk sluc, luc phut ma tzuc.　　克禋克祀　以拂無子
Ric Tès mac mòc, hum, you krèts, you thruc.　　履帝武拇　歆攸介攸止
Tzùs tuns, tzùs souk; tzùs sheng, tzùs louk:　　載震載夙　載生載育
du wi Gòs Tzuk.　　時維后稷

So, lady *Ngwan* came to her full term, and her first-born emerged.
There was no tearing, no splitting, no ripping, no injury,
showing that this was a miraculous conception. Oh, didn't God on High make things easy for her
—did he not enjoy the sacrifices she had offered! Calmly she gave birth to her son.

Lànt me kot ngwat, sùn sheng na làt.　　誕彌厥月　先生如達
Pu thràk, pu phruk, ma jus, ma gàts,　　不坼不副　無菑無害
luc hràk kot rèng. Dyangs Tès pu nèng!　　以赫厥靈　上帝不寧
Pu khàng in sluc! Kac nan sheng tzuc.　　不康禋祀　居然生子

Then lady *Ngwan* got rid of the baby in a back lane—but cattle and sheep trod close and suckled him.
So she got rid of him in a forested plain—but he was found by the woodcutters of that plain.
So she got rid of him on cold ice—but birds covered and protected him with their wings.
Then the birds went away, and the Millet Lord wailed;
these wails carried far, they were loud—his voice became strong.

Lànt tets tu rrèks gròngs, ngwu yang buy dzus tu.　　誕寘之隘巷　牛羊腓字之
Lànt tets tu breng rum, gòts bat breng rum.　　誕寘之平林　會伐平林
Lànt tets tu gàn prung, tìwc phouks yuk tu.　　誕寘之寒冰　鳥覆翼之
Tìwc nùc khas luc, Gòs Tzuk kwà luc.　　鳥迺去矣　后稷呱矣
Dit lùm, dit hwa; kot hyeng tzùs ràks.　　寔覃寔訏　厥聲載路

And then the Millet Lord crawled, and he learned to get onto his feet, to stand up firmly,
so as to find food for his mouth. He planted large beans in the soil,
and the bean shoots grew long and sinuous. The grain he cultivated produced abundant ears,
the hemp and the wheat grew densely, and the melon vines bore fruit in plenty.

Lànt dit bà-ba, khùk khec, khùk nguk,　　誕實匍匐　克岐克嶷
luc dzous khòc mluk, ngets tu nump nhouk.　　以就口食　蓺之荏菽
Nump nhouk bàts-bàts. Wày wek swits-swits.　　荏菽旆旆　禾役穟穟
Mrày mrùk mònk-mònk; gwàs lìt pònk-pònk.　　麻麥幪幪　瓜瓞唪唪

Now, the Millet Lord's husbandry had the knack of boosting productivity.
He cleared the dense weeds, and sowed the ground with golden beauty.

It grew evenly and densely: he sowed it and it grew tall.
It grew up, flowered and set ears; it became solid and lovely.
The ears were well-shaped and mature. And then the Millet Lord took up residence in the fief of Lù.

Lànt Gòs Tzuk tu shuk, wuc sangs tu lòuc.   誕后稷之穡　有相之道
Put kot phoung tsòuc, tongs tu gwàng mous.   茀厥豐草　種之黃茂
Dit pang, dit pròu; dit tongs, dit yous.   實方實苞　實種實褎
Dit pat, dit siws; dit kìn, dit hòus.   實發實秀　實堅實好
Dit wenk, dit rit. Kuts wuc Lù krà lhit.   實穎實栗　即有邰家室

So the Millet Lord conferred the boon of fine cereal grains on his people: single- and double-kerneled black millet,
red millet and white. He cultivated various grains over a broad area.
He reaped the harvest and stacked it on the land: there were grain stacks wherever you looked.
Then he hefted the harvest and shouldered it, bringing it home to offer sacrifice.

Lànt kròungs krày tonk: wi gac, wi phu,   誕降嘉種　維秬維秠
wi mùn, wi khuc—kùngs tu gac phu.   維穈維芑　恆之秬秠
Dec gwàk, dec mùc: kùngs tu mùn khuc.   是穫是畝　恆之穈芑
Dec num, dec buk, luc kwuy drawc sluc.   是任是負　以歸肇祀

So, how do we make sacrifices?
Now we pound the grain with a pestle, now we scoop it from the mortar; now we winnow it, now we tread it.
We wet it so that it is thoroughly soaked, and we steam it so the vapours rise.
We consult the omens, and we meditate. We gather lad's-love to burn with the fat of the sacrifice.
We take a ram and sacrifice it to the Spirits of the Journey. We roast and we broil, so as to initiate a new farming year.

Lànt ngàyc sluc na gày?   誕我祀如何
Wùk lhong, wùk lou, wùk pàyc, wùk nouc.   或舂或揄　或簸或蹂
Lhak tu shouc-shouc, tung tu bou-bou.   釋之叟叟　烝之浮浮
Tzùs mu, tzùs wi; tsoc sìw tzats ki.   載謀載惟　取蕭祭脂
Tsoc tì luc bàt, tzùs ban, tzùs rat,   取羝以軷　載燔載烈
luc hung slus swats.   以興嗣歲

We ladle the meat out into *dòs* bowls—into *dòs* bowls and *tùng* vessels.
As soon as its fragrance rises, God on High is at ease and delighted.
The pervasive odour is truly right. The Millet Lord instituted these sacrifices, and to this day it seems that no offence or regrets have come about through neglect of them.

Ngàng deng wa dòs—wa dòs, wa tùng.   卬盛于豆　于豆于登
Gu hang lhuc lhung, Dyangs Tès kac hum.   其香始升　上帝居歆

Grà k'hyous tànt du. Gòs Tzuk drawc sluc,　　遐臭亶時　后稷肇祀
lhaks ma dzòuyc mhùs, luc hut wa kum.　　庶無罪悔　以迄于今

The culture-hero *Wac* drained the land and made it fit for agriculture, but it was the Millet Lord, *Gòs Tzuk*, who first planted crops, and who was seen by the *Tiw* kings as their distant ancestor. As an adult, the Millet Lord was said to have been agriculture minister for the legendary emperor *Hwins* and to have been given the fief of *Lù*, mentioned in verse 5—the latter was a real place, in modern Wugong, south-west Shaanxi, so possibly there was some nucleus of truth behind this myth. (We saw in Ode 212 that the creation of agriculture was also attributed to Shen Nong; these two legendary figures appear to stem from separate myth traditions.)

We are not told why the lady *Ngwan* abandoned her baby. The logic of the myth seems to be that this forced the child to invent a novel way of getting food.

According to Legge, the millet varieties listed in verse 6 were specially significant because they were distilled into spirits used for ritual sacrifices. Cooked grain was offered in some sacrifices, but the vapours referred to in verse 7 seem to indicate that this passage describes distillation. For lad's-love see Ode 161.

The beneficiaries of the kind of sacrifice called *bàt* are usually translated as "Spirits of the Road", who would sound out of place in a celebration of the Millet Lord. But one sacrificed to these spirits at the start of a journey. Since the sacrifice here is made to ensure success for the next cycle of sowing and harvest, the agricultural year is treated as a metaphorical journey.

This poem has a rather subtle overall structure, with ten-stich verses alternating regularly with eight-stich verses.

246

Plants by the Roadside　行葦

Those plants by the roadside are making a good show—let's hope sheep and cattle don't trample them.
They're just bushing up and coming into leaf; their leaves are glistening with dew.
How deep the brothers' feelings for one another! None are absent, all are near.
Bamboo mats are unrolled for some to sit on, while others are given stools.

Dòn payc gràng wuyc, ngwu yang mut dzant ric.　　敦彼行葦　牛羊勿踐履
Pang pròu, pang rhìc; wi lap nìc-nìc.　　方苞方體　維葉泥泥
Tsìwk-tsìwk hwrang dìc, màk want, gos nec.　　戚戚兄弟　莫遠具爾
Wùk sits tu lan, wùk dous tu kric.　　或肆之筵　或授之几

A row of attendants are unrolling the mats, laying over-mats on them, and offering stools.
Some guests are proposing toasts, others returning the toasts. Attendants are washing *tzyawk* goblets and setting out *kràc* wine-bowls.
They offer around canapés of salted mince and pickled mince, while meat is roasted and more meat broiled.
There are delicate foodstuffs, tripe and tongue; there is singing and drumming.

Sits lan, nhet slak, dous kric wuc tsup ngas.   肆筵設席　授几有緝御
Wùk nghans, wùk dzàk. Sùnt tzyawk, dìns kràc.   或獻或酢　洗爵奠斝
Thùmp hwùc luc tzùns, wùk ban, wùk tak.   醓醢以薦　或燔或炙
Krày gràw be gak; wùk kày, wùk ngàk.   嘉殽脾臄　或歌或咢

The carved bows are thoroughly sturdy, and the sets of four metal-tipped arrows perfectly matched.
Flights of arrows are released together, with one heat following another in order of competitors' skill.
The four carved bows are bent, the arrows pinched in the archers' fingers
—and then the four arrows stand in the targets as if planted there. Guests vie with one another to avoid disgracing themselves.

Tòuy kwung kuts kìn, slits gòs kuts kwin.   追弓既堅　四鍭既均
Lhac lhic kuts kwin, slac pin luc gìn.   舍矢既均　序賓以賢
Tòuy kwung kuts kò, kuts gèp slits gòs   追弓既句　既挾四鍭
—slits gòs na doc. Slac pin luc pu moc.   四鍭如樹　序賓以不侮

The host is a lineal Descendant. His wine and must are good and strong,
and he serves them out with a generous-sized ladle, making a wish that his guests will live so long that they grow sere and wrinkled
—sere and wrinkled, with backs as round as a pufferfish. This he does to support them, to promote their welfare:
old age is a boon, so he's aiming to increase their great good fortune.

Tzùng sòun wi toc. Tziwc rìc wi noc,   曾孫維主　酒醴維醹
tyawk luc dàts toc, luc guy gwàng kòc   酌以大斗　以祈黃耇
—gwàng kòc, lhù pùks, luc lint, luc yuk.   黃耇台背　以引以翼
Douc khòuc wi gu, luc krèts krank puk.   壽考維祺　以介景福

The opening image here is as opaque as most. *Wuyc* normally translates as "rushes, reeds", but it must refer here to some more interesting plants: reeds have no leaves, and anyway, would anyone care about such humble vegetation getting trampled by animals? The image establishes the season as early spring, but its relevance to the party described in the body of the poem is far to seek.

Some of us today might feel unenthusiastic about the food on offer. But spring was the hungry season in all pre-modern societies.

"Descendant" in the last verse means that the host, a local ruler, descends from the dynasty founders.

247

We are Drunk 既醉

We're drunk with wine; we've stuffed ourselves with the good things your generosity has provided.
May your highness live ten thousand years, and your great prosperity be greater yet.

Kuts tzouts luc tziwc, kuts pròuc luc tùk.　　既醉以酒　既飽以德
Kwun-tzuc màns nìn, krèts nec krank puk.　　君子萬年　介爾景福

We're drunk with wine, and we've been well served with your food.
May your highness live ten thousand years, and your splendour be more splendid yet.

Kuts tzouts luc tziwc, nec gràw kuts tzang.　　既醉以酒　爾殽既將
Kwun-tzuc màns nìn, krèts nec tyaw mrang.　　君子萬年　介爾昭明

May your splendour last a long, long time—may your lofty brilliance lead to a great fulfilment.
That great fulfilment has its beginning now—but the noble Corpse has a happy announcement to make!

Tyaw mrang wuc loung, kàw rànk reng toung.　　昭明有⼺　高朗令終
Reng toung wuc thiwk—klòng Lhi kràɥ kòuk!　　令終有俶　公尸嘉告

What is this announcement? The *pèn* baskets and *dòs* bowls are pure and fine.
We your friends are being served—served with decorum.

Kus kòuk wi gày? Pèn dòs dzenk kràɥ.　　其告維何　籩豆靜嘉
Bùng wuc you nhep—nhep luc ouy-ngay.　　朋友攸攝　攝以威儀

Decorum is right and proper. Your highness has dutiful sons
—dutiful sons will never be lacking, so you shall always receive the privileges of your rank.

Ouy-ngay khònk du. Kwun-tzuc wuc hràws tzuc　　威儀孔時　君子有孝子
—hràws tzuc pu gouts, wrank slèk nec routs.　　孝子不匱　永錫爾類

What are those privileges? The alleys between the many structures of your palace compound
—may your highness live ten thousand years, and may you always be granted the blessings of a legacy.

Kus routs wi gày? Lhit krà tu kwhùnt　　其類維何　室家之壼
—Kwun-tzuc màns nìn, wrank slèk dzàks luns.　　君子萬年　永錫祚胤

What is that legacy? Sky has loaded you with good fortune
(may your highness live ten thousand years): your great Mandate, and your many
    followers.

Kus luns wi gày? Thìn bays nec ròk   其胤維何 天被爾祿
—kwun-tzuc màns nìn—krank Mreng, wuc bòk.   君子萬年 景命有僕

Who are those followers? Sky has bestowed on you the young ladies and young
    gentlemen, your daughters and sons.
Sky has done this, and they will be followed by grandsons and by their sons.

Kus bòk wi gày? Ru nec nrac shuc   其僕維何 釐爾女士
—ru nec nrac shuc, dzong luc sòun tzuc.   釐爾女士 從以孫子

The ruler has feasted his nobles on some ritual occasion, and now receives the praise and good wishes that are his due. It seems odd to identify the ruler's privileges as the alleys between his palace buildings, but I suppose referring to them is one way of expressing the fact that it is a large compound with many buildings.

    Perhaps that is logical, but the poem seems to meander inconsequentially. After the poet interrupts himself and prays silence for the Corpse to make an announcement, one expects something more than an assurance about the purity of the serving dishes. (The language had no word for "close inverted commas", and some have taken the announcement to include everything from that phrase to the end, though this scarcely makes for better logic.) However, the poet did begin by pointing out that he was drunk.

248

Wild Ducks   鳧鷖

Wild ducks are on the *Kèng*. The noble Corpse has joined us, feasting and taking
    his ease.
Your wine is clear, your food smells fragrant.
The noble Corpse is feasting and drinking; may felicity and blessings come and
    make your life perfect.

Bo ì dzùc Kèng. Klòng Lhi rù èns, rù nèng.   鳧鷖在涇 公尸來燕來寧
Nec tziwc kuts tseng, nec gràw kuts hèng.   爾酒既清 爾殽既馨
Klòng Lhi èns um; puk ròk rù deng.   公尸燕飲 福祿來成

Wild ducks are on the sandbar. The noble Corpse has joined us, feasting and
    giving his seal of approval.
Your wine is plentiful, your food is delicious.
The noble Corpse is feasting and drinking; may felicity and blessings come and
    favour you.

Bo ì dzùc shày. Klòng Lhi rù èns, rù ngay.
Nec tziwc kuts tày, nec gràw kuts kràj.
Klòng Lhi èns um; puk ròk rù ways.

鳧鷖在沙　公尸來燕來宜
爾酒既多　爾殽既嘉
公尸燕飲　福祿來為

Wild ducks are on the islets. The noble Corpse has joined us, feasting and relaxing.
Your wine has been strained, and you have biltong for us to eat.
The noble Corpse is feasting and drinking; may felicity and blessings descend upon you.

Bo ì dzùc tac. Klòng Lhi rù èns, rù k'hlac.
Nec tziwc kuts shac, nec gràw i pac.
Klòng Lhi èns um; puk ròk rù gràs.

鳧鷖在渚　公尸來燕來處
爾酒既湑　爾殽伊脯
公尸燕飲　福祿來下

Wild ducks are at the watersmeet. The noble Corpse has joined us, feasting and being honoured by us.
The feast is being held in the ancestral temple, where felicity and blessings descend from above.
The noble Corpse is feasting and drinking; may felicity and blessings pile up upon you.

Bo ì dzùc dzòung. Klòng Lhi rù èns, rù tzòung.
Kuts èns wa tzòung, puk ròk you kròungs.
Klòng Lhi èns um; puk ròk rù djoung.

鳧鷖在潨　公尸來燕來宗
既燕于宗　福祿攸降
公尸燕飲　福祿來崇

Wild ducks are in the gorge. The noble Corpse has joined us, feasting and getting befuddled.
The fine wine is making us merry, and the smells of roasting and broiling are mouth-watering.
The noble Corpse is feasting and drinking, and nobody worries about tomorrow.

Bo ì dzùc mùn. Klòng Lhi rù èns hwun-hwun.
Kic tziwc hun-hun, ban tak phun-phun.
Klòng Lhi èns um; ma wuc ghòc krùn.

鳧鷖在亹　公尸來燕醺醺
旨酒欣欣　燔炙芬芬
公尸燕飲　無有後艱

Bo and *ì* are two kinds of wild duck; *ì* may be the widgeon. For the *Kèng* see Ode 35.

The reference in verse 3 to biltong (dried meat) is odd. It doesn't square with the comments elsewhere about cooking smells, and even in the *Tiw* dynasty it could hardly have been party food. Legge wonders whether the poet was simply hard-pressed to find a rhyme.

249

Great Happiness　假樂

Great happiness may our prince enjoy! His "virtue" is renowned.
He orders well the population, the people. He is blessed by Sky,

which protects him, supports him, and grants his Mandate. It's Sky that maintains him in power.

Kràc ngràwks kwun-tzuc! Hènt-hènt reng tùk.
Ngay min, ngay nin. Douc ròk wa Thìn,
pòuc wus mreng tu. Dzis Thìn lhin tu.

假樂君子　顯顯令德
宜民宜人　受祿于天
保右命之　自天申之

Our prince cultivates decorum as well as every kind of prosperity. He shall have descendants by the thousand, by the hundred thousand.
He is august, majestic, fit to be a ruler—fit to be king.
He doesn't err; nothing slips by him. He follows the ancient model.

Kàn ròk pràk puk. Tzuc sòun tsìn uk.
Mouk-mouk, wàng-wàng, ngay kwun—ngay wang.
Pu khryan, pu mang, shout you gwuc tang.

干祿百福　子孫千億
穆穆皇皇　宜君宜王
不愆不忘　率由舊章

Our prince is dignified and self-controlled. His reputation is unsullied.
He harbours no grudges, no malice; he follows the ideals shared by his peers.
Limitless prosperity is bestowed on him, as governor of the world.

Ouy-ngay its-its, tùk um drit-drit.
Ma ons, ma àks; shout you gwun phit.
Douc puk ma kang, Slits Pang tu kàng.

威儀懿懿　德音秩秩
無怨無惡　率由群匹
受福無疆　四方之綱

Our prince governs the world, he regulates it, enabling those close to him to rest easy.
His vassals and his ministers feel love for Sky's Son.
He never neglects his high office. On him the people rely.

Tu kàng, tu kuc, èns gup bùng wuc.
Pràk pek, khrang shuc, mouys wa Thìn Tzuc.
Pu krès wa wruts. Min tu you huts.

之綱之紀　燕及朋友
百辟卿士　媚于天子
不懈于位　民之攸墍

In the lines spanning verses 3 and 4, the words *kàng* and *kuc* both originally referred to a string or rope which controlled a larger entity—*kàng* was a rope that controlled a net. Here, they are used metaphorically for a ruler regulating a society.

250

Lord *Rou*　公劉

Lord *Rou* was a sound man. He didn't sit still, he didn't relax.
He designated areas to stack vegetables, he put his people to labouring, collecting and storing provisions,
putting up dried meat and grain in bags and sacks.

This accumulation of provisions was on an extensive scale. He distributed bows
    and arrows,
shields, halberds, hatchets, and battle-axes. And then they set off.

Tòuk klòng Rou. Puyc kac, puyc khàng.   篤公劉　匪居匪康
Nùc drang, nùc gank, nùc tzek, nùc tsàng,   迺場迺疆　迺積迺倉
nùc ruc gò rang, wa thàk, wa nàng.   迺裹餱糧　于橐于囊
Sù dzup longs kwàng. Kwung lhic se trang,   思輯用光　弓矢斯張
kàn, kwày, tsìwk, lang. Wan pang khìc gràng.   干戈戚揚　爰方啟行

Lord *Rou* was a sound man. He reached this high plain, and halted.
Finding it fertile, flourishing, and altogether suitable, he proclaimed it to be their
    new home,
and there were no lasting sighs of dissatisfaction. He climbed up to stand on the
    hilltops,
and then went back down to stop on the plain. What did he have at his waist?
He had jade and jasper gems, an ornamented scabbard and a ceremonial knife.

Tòuk klòng Rou. Wa sa se ngwan,   篤公劉　于胥斯原
kuts lhaks, kuts ban, kuts mlouns, nùc swan,   既庶既繁　既順迺宣
nu ma wrank nhàn. Truk tzùk dzùc ngant,   而無永歎　陟則在巘
bouk kròungs dzùc ngwan. Gày luc tiw tu?   復降在原　何以舟之
Wi ngok gup yaw, pènk-pònk, long tàw.   維玉及瑤　鞞琫容刀

Lord *Rou* was a sound man. He arrived at the Hundred Springs,
he gazed over the broad plain, and then he walked up the southern ridge
to survey the site for his citadel—the stretch of country where his citadel would
    rise.
Here he settled, here he fixed his residence.
Here he made speeches, here he took counsel.

Tòuk klòng Rou. Dats payc Pràk Dzwan;   篤公劉　逝彼百泉
tam payc phàc ngwan, nùc truk nùm kàng,   瞻彼溥原　迺陟南岡
nùc kòs wa krang—krang shi tu lac.   乃覯于京　京師之野
Wa du k'hlac-k'hlac, wa du ra-rac.   于時處處　于時廬旅
Wa du ngan-ngan, wa du ngac-ngac.   于時言言　于時語語

Lord *Rou* was a sound man. When he was firmly established in his citadel,
stately and dignified, he had a mat and stool brought.
Stepping onto the mat and leaning on the stool, he sent out his servants
to fetch a pig from its pen. Then, using a gourd to ladle wine,
he gave his henchmen food and drink; he behaved as their ruler, and did them
    honour accordingly.

Tòuk klòng Rou. Wa krang se uy,   篤公劉　于京斯依
tsang-tsang, tzìc-tzìc, pec lan, pec kric.   蹌蹌濟濟　俾筵俾几
Kuts tùng nùc uy, nùc tsòus gu dzòu   既登乃依　乃造其曹
tup lhec wa ròu. Tyawk tu longs bròu,   執豕于牢　酌之用匏
sluks tu, ums tu. Kwun tu, tzòung tu.   食之飲之　君之宗之

Lord *Rou* was a sound man. His new territory was broad west to east, and long north to south.
He charted it by reference to shadows and hill ridges, examining the distribution of sun and shade.
He surveyed the streams and springs. His army comprisesd three divisions.
He measured the wetlands and the dry plain; he fixed taxes on the arable land to provide for public grain stores.
And then he surveyed the land to the west of the hills. The settlements of *Prun* became truly extensive.

Tòuk klòng Rou. Kuts phàc, kuts drang.	篤公劉　既溥既長
Kuts krank nùc kàng, sangs gu um lang,	既景迺岡　相其陰陽
kwàn kus riw dzwan. Gu kwun sùm tàn.	觀其流泉　其軍三單
Dàk gu slup ngwan; thret lìn ways rang.	度其隰邅　徹田為糧
Dàk gu syak lang. Prun kac yount mhàng.	度其夕陽　豳居允荒

Lord *Rou* was a sound man. He resided at *Prun*.
He constructed a ford through the Wei, to get whetstones and hammers.
Once the settlements were founded, their fields were marked out—they were broad, and productive,
stretching up both sides of the *Wàng* gorge, and pushing up the gorge of the *Kòy*.
The settlements were dense, extending to either side of the river bend.

Tòuk klòng Rou. Wa Prun se kòns.	篤公劉　于豳斯館
Dap Wuts way ròns, tsoc rats, tsoc tòns.	涉渭為亂　取厲取鍛
Tuc ku nùc ruc, wan toungs, wan wuc,	止基迺理　爰眾爰有
krèp kus Wàng kràns, sngàks kus Kòy kràns.	夾其皇澗　遡其過澗
Tuc rac nùc mrit, nots kouk tu tzit.	止旅迺密　汭泥之即

Lord *Rou* was an ancestor of the *Tiw* royal line, great-grandson of the Millet Lord whom we met in Ode 245. (Whether we are in the domain of history or myth here is not clear.) I translate the Chinese *klòng* as "lord"; for "Lord *Rou*" the usual Chinese word order would be *Rou klòng* rather than *klòng Rou*, but *Rou* is not the only very early figure whose name is given in the reverse order. (*Gòs Tzuk* for "Millet Lord", and w*ang Kwits* for "king *Kwits*", are other examples.)

After the Millet Lord's death, his family is said to have been forced to flee China for barbarian territory. In this Ode we see his descendant *Rou* re-entering China with his *Tiw* people and founding *Prun* as their new base (see p. 7).

Much is unclear, and has been recognized as such since early times. In the second line I have deviated radically from all earlier versions I have seen, because they make no sense to me: they interpret the first four words as about dividing and subdividing territory. I take this to be a wild guess by an early commentator; it is illogical for land-division to happen immediately before the people emigrate. By treating the second and fourth graphs in the received text as errors for two very similar graphs, I have twisted the line into something that at least fits in with the rest of the verse (though it may be wrong). Then in verses 2 and 3, why the repeated climbs and descents? It makes sense that *Rou* would choose a hilltop as site for his citadel, but too much seems to be made of the hill-climbing—and how does it relate to the accoutrements at his waist?

On the other hand, in verse 4 where Western readers might think that a mat is too humble an object to be celebrated this way, the answer is that in China a mat had considerable symbolic weight. In modern Chinese the word for "chairman", as in Chairman Mao, is 'zhu xi', literally "master of the mat".

In verse 5 we are in the dark again, literally as well as metaphorically. Chinese towns were laid out strictly according to the cardinal directions, and it is reasonable that *Rou* might begin by orienting himself using the shadows cast by the sun, but how do the "ridges" come in? And why does the organization of the army make a sudden appearance? It was very much part of the job of a Chinese ruler to organize stores of grain, to tide their people over years when harvest were poor.

In verse 6, whetstones and iron for hammers are necessities that might well have needed to be got from elsewhere, and both can be found south of the Wei. So far as I know, we cannot now identify the streams called *Wàng* and *Kòy*, or the particular river bend of the last line.

251

Far Away We Dip Water 泂酌

Far away we dip water from that roadside pool: we dip it there, we use it here.
We can use it to steam rice or millet.
Happy be our prince, father and mother of the people!

Gwènk tyawk payc gràng ràwc: up payc, tros tzu. 泂酌彼行潦　挹彼注茲
Khàyc luc pun k'hyuc. 可以餴饎
Khùyc dic kwun-tzuc, min tu bac muc! 豈弟君子　民之父母

Far away we dip water from that roadside pool: we dip it there, we use it here.
We can use it to wash jars.
Happy be our prince, the one to whom the people turn!

Gwènk tyawk payc gràng ràwc: up payc, tros tzu. 泂酌彼行潦　挹彼注茲
Khàyc luc dryawk ròuy. 可以濯罍
Khùyc dic kwun-tzuc, min tu you kwuy! 豈弟君子　民之攸歸

Far away we dip water from that roadside pool: we dip it there, we use it here.
We can use it for washing and cleaning.
Happy be our prince, the one in whom the people find rest!

Gwènk tyawk payc gràng ràwc: up payc, tros tzu. 泂酌彼行潦　挹彼注茲
Khàyc luc dryawk kùts. 可以濯溉
Khùyc dic kwun-tzuc, min tu you huts! 豈弟君子　民之攸墍

An inconsequential little Ode.

252

A Sheltered Slope 卷阿

On a sheltered slope there's a gusty breeze from the south.
Happy be our prince!
Here he comes, singing as he rambles, composing his melodies.

Wuc gon tac ày, pyaw pum dzis nùm.   有卷者阿　飄風自南
Khùyc dìc kwun-tzuc!   豈弟君子
Rù you, rù kày, luc lhic gu um.   來游來歌　以矢其音

May your rambles be relaxing, your leisure be entertaining.
Happy be our prince!
May you live out your full term of years, a life complete as those of your noble forebears.

Phàns-hwàns nec you luc, ou-you nec hou luc.   伴奐爾游矣　優游爾休矣
Khùyc dìc kwun-tzuc!   豈弟君子
Pec nec mec nec sengs, sluc sùn klòng dziw luc.   俾爾彌爾性　似先公酋矣

Your territory is large and splendid, and you are greatly enhancing it.
Happy be our prince!
May you live out your full term of years—the many Spirits make you their host.

Nec thàc wac prànt tang, yak khònk tu gòc luc.   爾土宇昄章　亦孔之厚矣
Khùyc dìc kwun-tzuc!   豈弟君子
Pec nec mec nec sengs, Pràk Mlin nec toc luc.   俾爾彌爾性　百神爾主矣

The Mandate you have been granted is a lasting one; you are blessed with good fortune and high standing.
Happy be our prince!
May you live out your full term of years—may great abundance be a constant for you.

Nec douc Mreng drang luc, phut ròk nec khàng luc.   爾受命長矣　茀祿爾康矣
Khùyc dìc kwun-tzuc!   豈弟君子
Pec nec mec nec sengs, doun kràc nec dyang luc.   俾爾彌爾性　純嘏爾常矣

You have supporters you can rely on, you have a proper attitude towards your ancestors, and you have character;
these things help you and lead you forward.
Happy be our prince! You are a model for the world.

Wuc brung, wuc yuk, wuc hràws, wuc tùk,   有馮有翼　有孝有德
luc lint, luc yuk.   以引以翼
Khùyc dìc kwun-tzuc, Slits Pang way tzùk!   豈弟君子　四方為則

Stately, lofty, like a *kwè* emblem, like a *tang* emblem,
high in reputation, admired by all,
happy be our prince—you who keep the world on track!

Ngong-ngong, ngàng-ngàng, na kwè, na tang, 顒顒卬卬　如圭如璋
reng muns, reng mang, 令聞令望
khùyc dìc kwun-tzuc, Slits Pang way kàng! 豈弟君子　四方為綱

Phoenixes are on the wing—listen to the beating of their wings!
And now they stoop and settle together. You have crowds of splendid officers at your disposal.
Your Majesty assigns their missions; they feel love for you, Sky's Son.

Bums-wàng wa puy, hwàts-hwàts gu wac. 鳳凰于飛　翽翽其羽
Yak dzup wan tuc. Àts-àts wang tày kit shuc. 亦集爰止　藹藹王多吉士
Wi kwun-tzuc shuc, mouys wa Thìn Tzuc. 維君子使　媚于天子

Phoenixes are on the wing—listen to the beating of their wings!
And now they fly right up to the sky. You have crowds of splendid courtiers at your disposal.
Your Majesty assigns their mandates; they feel love for the common people.

Bums-wàng wa puy, hwàts-hwàts gu wac. 鳳凰于飛　翽翽其羽
Yak bas wa thìn. Àts-àts wang tày kit nin. 亦傅于天　藹藹王多吉人
Wi kwun-tzuc mreng, mouys wa lhaks nin. 維君子命　媚于庶人

Phoenixes are calling from that high ridge.
Wutong trees grow on the slope facing the morning sun.
The trees are flourishing, with dense foliage; the birds are singing in harmonious unison.

Bums-wàng mreng luc, wa payc kàw kàng. 鳳凰鳴矣　于彼高岡
Ngà-dòng sheng luc, wa payc traw lang. 梧桐生矣　于彼朝陽
Bònk-bònk, tsì-tsì, ong-ong, krì-krì. 菶菶萋萋　雝雝喈喈

Your Majesty's carriages are many, many.
Your Majesty's horses are well-trained and swift.
I have put these few verses together, so that they'll be sung in times to come.

Kwun-tzuc tu ka, kuts lhaks tsac tày. 君子之車　既庶且多
Kwun-tzuc tu mràc, kuts gràn tsac dray. 君子之馬　既閑且馳
Lhic lhu pu tày, wi luc swits kày. 矢詩不多　維以遂歌

A routine praise-song. The closing line makes explicit a motive which must have underlain many such songs, namely the hope that putting praise into metrical form might enable a ruler's fame to survive his death.

"May the many Spirits make you their host" expressed the wish that the various ritual sacrifices made by the ruler, to obtain good harvests and other desirable things, would succeed —that the spirits would arrive to accept the sacrifices and grant the benefits requested.

For the *kwè* and *tang* of verse 6 see Ode 238. In just what respects the king is said to resemble these things is debatable, though jade was seen as a noble stone.

Verses 7 and 8 contain an interesting chiasm: the phoenixes coming down to perch are linked to the officials' feelings for the king above them, while the former flying up to the sky are linked to the officials' feelings for those below them.

In England the oak is the "tree of trees". In China this place is occupied by the wutong (*Firmiana simplex*, Old Chinese *ngà-dòng*), sometimes called parasol tree in English. It has greenish bark and leaves up to two feet across, and is said to give off an odour mixing lemon and chocolate. In myth, it is the only tree on which a phoenix will perch. In reality, its wood is used for the soundboards of musical instruments.

253

The People are Exhausted 民勞

The people are exhausted; it's time to allow them a little ease.
Be kind to the capital, and thus invigorate the whole kingdom.
Don't go easy on the schemers and the toadies, but make the bad guys watch their step.
Put down the robbers and the bullies who haven't feared the king's majesty.
Be gentle with those far from power and fair with those who are close to it, so as to make our king secure in his position.

Min yak ràw tuc, hut khàyc syawc khàng.	民亦勞止　迄可小康
Wìts tsec troung kwùk, luc snouy Slits Pang.	惠此中國　以綏四方
Ma tzongs kwayc sway, luc kunt ma rang.	無縱詭隨　以謹無良
Lhuk àt khòs ngawk, tsùmp pu ouys mrang.	式遏寇虐　憯不畏明
Nou want nùc nec, luc dèngs ngàyc wang.	柔遠能邇　以定我王

The people are exhausted; it's time to allow them a little relaxation.
Be kind to the capital, to encourage people to mingle in it.
Don't go easy on the schemers and the toadies, but make the rackety types watch their step.
Put down the robbers and the bullies, and avoid letting misery fall on the people.
Don't let up with your efforts, so as to allow the king to relax.

Min yak ràw tuc, hut khàyc syawc hou.	民亦勞止　迄可小休
Wìts tsec troung kwùk, luc way min gou.	惠此中國　以為民逑
Ma tzongs kwayc sway, luc kunt mhùn nràw.	無縱詭隨　以謹惛怓
Lhuk àt khòs ngawk, ma pec min ou.	式遏寇虐　無俾民憂
Ma khits nec ràw, luc way wang hou.	無棄爾勞　以為王休

The people are exhausted; it's time to allow them a little rest.
Be kind to the inhabitants of the royal seat, and thus invigorate the world's states.

Don't go easy on the schemers and the toadies, but make people who lack self-restraint watch their step.
Put down the robbers and the bullies, and don't allow them to behave criminally.
Carefully preserve your dignity, so as to keep the good guys on side.

Min yak ràw tuc, hut khàyc syawc suk.   民亦勞止　迄可小息
Wìts tsec krang shi, luc snouy Slits kwùk.   惠此京師　以綏四國
Ma tzongs kwayc sway, luc kunt mank guk.   無縱詭隨　以謹罔極
Lhuk àt khòs ngawk, ma pec tzàk nhùk.   式遏寇虐　無俾作慝
Krengs dins ouy-ngay, luc guns wuc tùk.   敬慎威儀　以近有德

The people are exhausted; it's time to allow them a little quiet.
Be kind to the capital, and alleviate the people's misery.
Don't go easy on the schemers and the toadies, but make the evil-doers watch their step.
Put down the robbers and the bullies, and don't let upright people be ruined.
You might see yourselves as little more than young boys, yet the task that faces you is a great one.

Min yak ràw tuc, hut khàyc syawc khats.   民亦勞止　迄可小愒
Wìts tsec troung kwùk, pec min ou slat.   惠此中國　俾民憂泄
Ma tzongs kwayc sway, luc kunt k'hyou rats.   無縱詭隨　以謹醜厲
Lhuk àt khòs ngawk, ma pec tengs bràts.   式遏寇虐　無俾正敗
Noung swi syawc tzuc, nu lhuk gwùng dàts.   戎雖小子　而式弘大

The people are exhausted; it's time to allow them a little peace.
Be kind to the capital, and avoid injury to the states.
Don't go easy on the schemers and the toadies, but make the parasitical hangers-on watch their step.
Put down the robbers and the bullies, and don't let upright people be undermined.
The king wants to find you as fine as jade, and that's what leads me to issue this serious lecture.

Min yak ràw tuc, hut khàyc syawc àn.   民亦勞止　迄可小安
Wìts tsec troung kwùk, kwùk ma wuc dzàn.   惠此中國　國無有殘
Ma tzongs kwayc sway, luc kunt khent-kwhant.   無縱詭隨　以謹繾綣
Lhuk àt khòs ngawk, ma pec tengs pant.   式遏寇虐　無俾正反
Wang lok ngok nac, dec longs dàts kràns.   王欲玉汝　是用大諫

A senior minister takes to task those responsible to him. The poem is said to date from the reign of *Rats*, who came to the throne in 859 and was deposed in 841.

We saw in the Introduction that *troung kwùk*, in Mandarin 'zhong guo', is the modern Chinese name for China, and originally meant "the central states". In this Ode, though, *troung kwùk* seems to mean something else again: the centre of the state, the seat of power. If things are as they should be there, the poet assumes, they will be all right throughout the country as a whole.

VOICES FROM EARLY CHINA

254

A Rebuke 板

God on High is great, but the people here below are in dire straits.
You utter remarks which are not in accordance with the facts; you make policies that lack foresight.
You've failed to provide yourself with wise counsellors—you have no solid foundation for your work. You're not wholehearted about being sincere.
The short-sightedness of your policies pushes me into this serious rebuke.

Dyangs Tès prànt-prànt; gràc min tzout tànt. 　上帝昄昄　下民卒瘅
K'hlouts gròts pu nan; way you pu want. 　出話不然　為猶不遠
Mayc lhengs, kwànt-kwànt. Pu mlit a tànt. 　靡聖瘴瘴　不實於亶
You tu muts want, dec long dàts kràns. 　猶之未遠　是用大諫

Don't be so lofty, just when Sky is creating problems.
Don't talk so frivolously, just when Sky is trampling on us.
It's consistency in what we say that makes for concord among the people;
it's mildness in what we say that leads to tranquillity for the people.

Thìn tu pang nàn, ma nan nghan-nghan. 　天之方難　無然憲憲
Thìn tu pang got, ma nan lats-lats. 　天之方蹶　無然泄泄
Slu tu dzup luc, min tu grùp luc. 　辭之輯矣　民之洽矣
Slu tu lak luc, min tu mràk luc. 　辭之懌矣　民之莫矣

I may be in a separate department, but we need to work together.
Yet whenever I come to you to sort out plans, there's arrogance in your attitude.
My remarks are the product of serious thought: don't treat them as jokes.
The ancients had a saying: "Consult even with forage-cutters and fuel-gatherers".

Ngàyc swi luks shuc, gup nec dòng ryàw. 　我雖異事　及爾同僚
Ngàyc tzit nec mu, lhèng ngàyc ngàws-ngàws. 　我即爾謀　聽我嚣嚣
Ngàyc ngan wi buk; mut luc way saws. 　我言維服　勿以為笑
Sùn min wuc ngan: "Swin wa cho ngyaw". 　先民有言　詢于芻蕘

Don't be so flippant, just when Sky is being harsh.
From older men there's an outcry, and the younger generation won't be taught.
My comments are not senile maunderings, yet you turn them into sorry jokes.
If you're just going to come out with a lot of silly blather, you'll be beyond help or cure.

Thìn tu pang ngawk, ma nan nghawk-nghawk. 　天之方虐　無然謔謔
Ròuc pa hwàns-hwàns, syawc tzuc gawk-gawk. 　老夫灌灌　小子蹻蹻
Puyc ngàyc ngan màws: nec long ou nghawk. 　匪我言耄　爾用憂謔
Tày tzang rhàwks-rhàwks, pu khàyc kous yawk. 　多將熇熇　不可救藥

Don't big yourself up, just when Sky is angry with us.
You're completely forfeiting your dignity, and good men are playing the Corpse.
Just when the people are sighing and groaning, there's nobody willing to take me seriously.
There are deaths, riots, and assets are being ruined, yet so far no-one has tried to help our population.

Thìn tu pang dzìs, ma way kwhràt bi.   天之方懠　無為誇毗
Ouy-ngay tzout mì, dant nin tzùs Lhi.   威儀卒迷　善人載尸
Min tu pang tuns huy, tzùk màk ngàyc kàmp gwic.   民之方殿屎　則莫我敢揆
Sàngs, ròns, mèt tzi, dzùng màk wìts ngàyc shi.   喪亂蔑資　曾莫惠我師

The way Sky guides the people is like playing an ocarina or a flute.
It's like displaying a *tang* or *kwè* jade; it's like courting a girl, like leading by the hand
—leading by the hand, and no more than that. Guiding the people is a very gentle thing.
When the people are going badly off the rails, you shouldn't be setting yourself up as a dictator over them.

Thìn tu louc min, na hwan, na dre;   天之誘民　如壎如篪
na tang, na kwè; na tsos, na wè   如璋如圭　如娶如攜
—wè, ma wat ek. Louc min khònk leks.   攜無曰益　誘民孔易
Min tu tày phek, ma dzis rup pek.   民之多僻　無自立辟

The great men of the land are our fence; the multitudes are our bulwark.
The larger states are our protective screen, and the royal dynasty is our support
—their fond regard for us is our peace. The men of the royal family are our defensive wall.
Don't let that wall be ruined. Don't be afraid to be alone in standing up for what's right.

Krèts nin wi pan, dàts shi wi wan.   介人維藩　大師維垣
Dàts pròng wi bèng; dàts tzòung wi gàn   大邦維屏　大宗維翰
—gròuy tùk wi nèng. Tzòung tzuc wi geng.   懷德維寧　宗子維城
Ma pec geng gròuys. Ma dòk se ouys.   無俾城壞　無獨斯畏

Beware of Sky's anger—don't dare joke flippantly.
Beware of Sky changing attitude—don't dare waste your time at the races.
Bright Sky is known for being perceptive: when you are coming and going, Sky is there observing you.
Bright Sky is known for earnestness: when you are frivolous or dissipated, Sky is there watching you.

Krengs Thìn tu nàc—ma kàmp hays las.   敬天之怒　無敢戲豫
Krengs Thìn tu lo—ma kàmp dray kho.   敬天之渝　無敢馳驅
Gòuc Thìn wat mrang; gup nec k'hlout wank.   昊天曰明　及爾出往
Gòuc Thìn wat tàns; gup nec you yant.   昊天曰恒　及爾游衍

One court official tears a strip off another for letting the population down by failing to take his work seriously. But, if this was directed at a specific individual on a particular occasion, how could phrasing the rebuke as a poem and making it public have led to a good outcome? It might perhaps have been written to let off steam privately, but if it was not published, how do we come to be reading it?

In verse 5 the Corpse, the youngster who represented the dead ancestor at a ritual sacrifice, was normally silent, so this line says that subordinates of the rebuked official do not dare speak up about his behaviour.

Verse 6 says that the way to govern is to lead the people in the direction you want them to go, rather than drive them by threatening punishments. The ocarina and flute conjure up a picture akin to the Greek god Pan attracting people to follow his pipe-playing. The *tang* and *kwè* reference, I guess, is like a modern soldier saying that one only needs to let a private see the stripes on one's sleeve to secure obedience. The word I translate as "dictator", *pek*, does not in itself have the negative connotations of that English word, it just means "prince, ruler"; but the point is that the man rebuked is only an official, not a ruler, so he ought not to be so peremptory.

My version of the last stich of verse 7 adds a great deal to the Chinese wording, which is very obscure. And I don't pretend that "waste your time at the races" in verse 8 is likely to be what the poet meant, but here the Chinese is even more obscure—as we saw in Ode 163, both *dray* and *kho* mean "canter", "gallop", or the like; both words are written with a "horse" element. One previous translator has "Dare not race about", as if the man were a schoolchild haring round the playground when he ought to be inside attending to his lessons. My version is at least (slightly) more plausible than that.

255

Woe to Un 荡

Grand is God on High, ruler of the people here below.
Terrible is God on High: his leases of life carry many conditions.
Sky creates numerous people, but his leases of life cannot be relied on:
   we all have a beginning, but rare are those who achieve a fulfilled end.

Lànk-lànk Dyangs Tès, gràc min tu pek.	荡荡上帝　下民之辟
Dzit-ouy Dyangs Tès, gu mreng tày bek.	疾威上帝　其命多辟
Thìn sheng tung min, gu mreng puyc dum.	天生烝民　其命匪谌
Mayc pu wuc cha; sent khùk wuc toung.	靡不有初　鲜克有终

Mun said "Woe! Woe, you dynasty of Un!
These people are violent and oppressive—they're crushing and domineering,
but they hold office, they're in royal service.
It's Sky who gave them reckless personalities, but it's you who've aroused their
   violence."

Mun wang wat "Tzi! Tzi nac Un-Lhang!　文王曰咨　咨汝殷商
Tzùng dec gang ngac—tzùng dec pòc khùk,　曾是彊禦　曾是掊克
tzùng dec dzùc wruts, tzùng dec dzùc buk.　曾是在位　曾是在服
Thìn kròungs lhòu tùk, nac hung dec ruk."　天降慆德　汝興是力

Mun said "Woe! Woe, you dynasty of Un!
You should hold by what's righteous and good. Violence and oppression are creating deep resentment,
but the offenders fob people off with glib words. Robbers and thieves are serving within the government.
They curse and swear—they show no restraint, no self-control."

Mun wang wat "Tzi! Tzi nac Un-Lhang!　文王曰咨　咨汝殷商
Nu prank ngays routs. Gang ngac tày drouts.　而秉義類　彊禦多懟
Riw ngan luc tòuts. Khòs nang lhuk nòuts.　流言以對　寇攘式內
Gò jas, gò touks—mayc krìts, mayc kous."　侯詛侯祝　靡屆靡究

Mun said "Woe! Woe, you dynasty of Un!
You bawl and shout here in the Home States; you see growing resentment as something to be proud of.
It isn't intelligent, your character—you fail to recognize the disloyal and devious for what they are.
Your character, it isn't intelligent—you don't distinguish those people from your supporters and loyal ministers."

Mun wang wat "Tzi! Tzi nac Un-Lhang!　文王曰咨　咨汝殷商
Nac bròu-hòu wa Troung Kwùk; rams ons luc way tùk.　汝炰烋于中國　斂怨以為德
Pu mrang nec tùk—luc mang bùks, mang jek.　不明爾德　以無背無側
Nec tùk pu mrang—luc ma bù, ma khrang."　爾德不明　以無陪無卿

Mun said "Woe! Woe, you dynasty of Un!
It isn't Sky that soaks you in wine—it's wrong for you to give yourself over to drinking.
You have forfeited your dignity—you make no distinction between light and darkness.
Shouting and bellowing, you turn day into night."

Mun wang wat "Tzi! Tzi nac Un-Lhang!　文王曰咨　咨汝殷商
Thìn pu ment nec luc tziwc—pu ngays dzong lhuk.　天不湎爾以酒　不義從式
Kuts khryan nec tuc—mayc mreng, mayc mhùc.　既愆爾止　靡明靡晦
Lhuk ghàw, lhuk hàs, pec trous tzàk yas."　式號式呼　俾晝作夜

Mun said "Woe! Woe, you dynasty of Un!
Your blather is as empty as the shrilling of cicadas, or the bubbling of soup.
Little people and great are close to ruin, yet your men persist in following the same course.

315

They are overbearing here in the Home States, and they're stirring up resentment even in the Region of Devils."

Mun wang wat "Tzi! Tzi nac Un-Lhang!	文王曰咨　咨汝殷商
Na dìw, na làng, na puts, na kràng.	如蜩如螗　如沸如羹
Syawc dàts guns sàngs; nin dangs ghà you gràng.	小大近喪　人尚乎由行
Nòuts brus wa Troung Kwùk, lùm gup Kwuyc Pang."	內奰于中國　覃及鬼方

Mun said "Woe! Woe, you dynasty of *Un*!
It's not God on High who has gone wrong: *Un* has forsaken the old ways.
The perfect men of old may no longer be with us, but we still have laws and conventions;
only you all ignore them. And in consequence, Sky's great Mandate is being overthrown."

Mun wang wat "Tzi! Tzi nac Un-Lhang!	文王曰咨　咨汝殷商
Puyc Dyangs Tès pu du, Un pu longs gwuc.	匪上帝不時　殷不用舊
Swi ma ròuc deng nin, dangs wuc tùnt gèng:	雖無老成人　尚有典刑
tzùng dec màk lhèngs. Dàts Mreng luc kwheng."	曾是莫聽　大命以傾

Mun said "Woe! Woe, you dynasty of *Un*!
People have a saying: 'When a tall tree falls,
the twigs and leaves aren't damaged immediately—it's the roots which are affected first.'
A mirror reflecting what's happening to the *Un* dynasty is not far to seek. We only have to look at the generation of the lords of *Ghàc*."

Mun wang wat "Tzi! Tzi nac Un-Lhang!	文王曰咨　咨汝殷商
Nin yak wuc ngan: 'Tìn pàts tu kat,	人亦有言　顛沛之揭
ke lap muts wuc gàts; pùnt dit sùn pàt.'	枝葉未有害　本寔先撥
Un kràms pu want: dzùc Ghàc gòs tu lhats."	殷鑒不遠　在夏后之世

A poet's reconstruction of *Mun*'s vain attempt to persuade king *Drouc* and his henchmen to mend their ways (see p. 8).

We have often encountered the concept of *Thìn Mreng*, "Sky's Mandate", as the power delegated by Sky to entitle a king or dynasty to rule. But individuals who were not rulers were also seen as living by virtue of a "mandate" issued by Sky; I translate these mandates in verse 1 as "leases of life".

Verses 2 and 3 blame the ills of society on bullies in official positions, perhaps as a safer alternative to starting right in on criticism of the king's own behaviour (though that follows shortly). The wording in verse 5 about light and darkness, day and night, perhaps implies that it was allowable for people in authority to carouse in the evenings, whereas during the day they were expected to discharge their duties soberly.

"Region of Devils" (verse 6) was a name for the land of the *Lèk* tribe to the north of Chinese territory. Non-Chinese were often called *kwuyc*, conventionally translated "devils"—the Mandarin phrase 'yang gui', "foreign devils", has been in standard use into modern times. Although the phrase obviously implies a measure of xenophobia, this is less extreme than it seems: a *kwuyc*/'gui' was not thought of as an agent of Satan, like a European "devil", merely as some kind of frightening spirit—the translation "ghost" might be equally or more suitable.

In the folk-saying of verse 8 the tree stands for society, with the ruling family as its roots and the common people as twigs and leaves; *Mun* implies that when *Un* collapses, the people will survive—but the rulers won't. The last line points out that China had been through dynastic collapse before, when the first, *Ghàc* dynasty ended, and *Un* was heading the same way.

256

Dignified Demeanour 抑

A dignified demeanour is the counterpart of inner character.
People have a saying: "There's no clever man who lacks a foolish side".
The foolishness of an ordinary man is just a nuisance;
but the foolishness of a clever man is really offensive.

Uk-uk ouy-ngay wi tùk tu ngòc.	抑抑威儀　維德之偶
Nin yak wuc ngan: "Mayc trat pu ngo".	人亦有言　靡哲不愚
Lhaks nin tu ngo, yak tuk wi dzit.	庶人之愚　亦職維疾
Trat nin tu ngo, yak wi se rìt.	哲人之愚　亦維斯戾

Is the Sole Man not strong! The whole world is led by him.
His path of virtue is thoroughly straight; every state obeys him.
Through extensive planning he renders Sky's mandate secure; he makes regular announcements about his wide-ranging schemes.
He's careful to safeguard his dignity. For the people he's a model of behaviour.

Ma gung wi nin! Slits Pang kus hwuns tuc.	無競維人　四方其訓止
Wuc kròuk tùk gràng, Slits kwùk mlouns tuc.	有覺德行　四國順止
Hwa màc dèngs Mreng, want you dun kòuk.	訏謨定命　遠猶辰告
Krengs dins ouy-ngay; wi min tu tùk.	敬慎威儀　維民之則

You who live merely for the present, you're creating chaos in government.
You're turning virtue on its head, and steeping yourselves in wine to excess.
You people are just wallowing in self-indulgence, without sparing a thought for your heritage.
You don't devote time to studying our past kings, so you can hold fast their wise laws.

Kus dzùc wa kum, hung mì ròns wa tengs.	其在于今　興迷亂于政
Tìn phouk kot tùk; mhàng tùm wa tziwc.	顛覆厥德　荒湛于酒
Nac wi tùm ngràwks dec dzong, put nìms kot dawc	汝維湛樂是從　弗念厥紹
—mank pha gou sùn wang, khùk konk mrang gèng.	罔敷求先王　克共明刑

Consequently, Almighty Sky doesn't rate you highly. You're like the water falling from that spring:
don't let the lot of you just soak away to nothing, as it does. Get up early in the morning and go to bed at nightfall.

Keep your courtyards sprinkled and swept. Be a pattern to your people.
Keep your chariots and horses, your bows and arrows and other weapons, in good condition
so you'll be ready for military action, and you can resist any incursions from the land of the *Mròn*.

Sits Wàng Thìn put dangs. Na payc dzwan riw: 肆皇天弗尚　如彼泉流
ma roun-sa luc mang. Souk hung yas mits. 無淪胥以亡　夙興夜寐
Shìc sòus lèngs nòuts. Wi min tu tang. 洒掃廷內　維民之章
Siw nec ka mràc, kwung lhic, noung prang, 修爾車馬　弓矢戎兵
longs krùs noung tzàk, longs lhèk Mròn pang. 用戒戎作　用逷蠻方

Show your people your good faith; and be careful to observe the rules laid down by your princes,
so that you'll be ready for the unexpected. Mind what words you utter,
and preserve your dignity. Be mild and decent at all times.
If a tablet of white jade has a flaw, it can always be polished away;
but a flawed choice of words is irretrievable.

Tut nec nin min, kunt nec gò dàks 質爾人民　謹爾侯度
longs krùs pu ngwa. Dins nec k'hlout gròts. 用戒不虞　慎爾出話
Krengs nec ouy-ngay. Ma pu nou kràys. 敬爾威儀　無不柔嘉
Bràk kwè tu tèmp, dangs khàyc mày layc; 白圭之玷　尚可磨也
se ngan tu tèmp, pu khàyc way layc. 斯言之玷　不可為也

Don't let your tongue run away with you. Never say "Too bad,
nobody bridles Our tongue". Words can't just be made to vanish.
There's no speaking which doesn't elicit some response—and no virtue which goes unrewarded.
Be kind to your friends, to the common people, to the young;
then sons and grandsons will follow you in unbroken line, and each of your myriad subjects will revere you.

Ma leks you ngan. Ma wat "Kòc luc, 無易由言　無曰苟矣
màk mùn Drunk mlat". Ngan pu khàyc dats luc. 莫捫朕舌　言不可逝矣
Ma ngan pu dou; ma tùk pu pòus. 無言不讎　無德不報
Wìts wa bùng wuc, lhaks min, syawc tzuc, 惠于朋友　庶民小子
tzuc sòun mlung-mlung, màns min mayc pu dung. 子孫繩繩　萬民靡不承

When you're with your noble allies, keep your countenance peaceful and mild.
It is so easy to go wrong. Monitor your behaviour even in your house,
so you needn't be ashamed if it turns out that bedroom walls have ears.
Don't say "None of the Illustrious Ones can see me here".
There's no calculating the coming and going of the Spirits,
and still less can we afford to ignore them.

Gic nec wuc kwun-tzuc, dzup nou nec ngràn; 視爾友君子　輯柔爾顏
pu grà wuc khryan. Sangs dzùc nec lhit, 不遐有愆　相在爾室
dangs pu kouys wa lhit ròks. 尚不愧于屋漏

Ma wat "Phru hènt, màk lac wun kòs".
Mlin tu kràk su, pu khàyc dàk su,
lhint khàyc lak su.

無曰丕顯　莫予云覯
神之格思　不可度思
矧可射思

Regulate your behaviour by reference to justice, so that it's good and fine.
Be admirable and circumspect in your deportment—don't offend against propriety.
Don't be untruthful; don't harm people; and few will fail to make you their model.
[...]
These boy-men really are rowdy youngsters.

Bek nec ways tùk, pec tzàng, pec kràγ.
Diwk dins nec tuc—pu khryan wa ngay.
Pu tzèms, pu dzùk, sent pu way tzùk.
[...]
Payc dòng nu kròk, dit gòng syawc tzuc.

辟爾為德　俾臧俾嘉
淑慎爾止　不愆于儀
不僭不賊　鮮不為則
...
彼童而角　實虹小子

If a wooden item is delicate and vulnerable, we wrap it in silk.
Gentle, respectful people are the foundation of virtue.
If I teach my lessons to an intelligent man,
he'll follow the path of virtue. On the other hand, if I do the same with someone stupid,
he'll tell me I'm talking rubbish. Everyone has a mind of his own.

Nump-namp nou mòk, ngan moun tu su.
Òun-òun krong nin, wi tùk tu ku.
Gu wi trat nin, kòuk tu gròts ngan,
mlouns tùk tu gràng; gu wi ngo nin,
phouk wuts ngàyc tzèms. Min kàk wuc sum.

荏染柔木　言緡之絲
溫溫恭人　維德之基
其維哲人　告之話言
順德之行　其維愚人
覆謂我僭　民各有心

Oh dear, young people—they don't understand what's right and what's wrong.
I don't just lead them by the hand: I have to demonstrate what needs doing.
I don't just give them instructions face to face: I have to take them by the ear.
They say I don't know what's what—but I held them in my arms as babies.
None of these people are fully mature yet. Who first learns about something in the morning and is a perfect pupil by the evening?

À-ghà, syawc tzuc—muts tre tzàng pruc.
Puyc nhouc wè tu: ngan gis tu shuc.
Puyc mens mreng tu: ngan dè gu nuc.
Tzaks wat muts tre, yak kuts bòuc tzuc.
Min tu mayc leng; douy souk tre nu màks deng?

於乎小子　未知藏否
匪手攜之　言示之事
匪面命之　言提其耳
借曰未知　亦既抱子
民之靡盈　誰夙知而莫成

Bright Sky is very glorious, but my life is no fun.
When I see you so unenlightened, my heart is full of grief.
I teach you again and again, but you take so little notice of me.

You don't take what I say as valuable instruction, but as unwelcome interference.
You say that I don't know what's what, and that I've grown senile.

Gòuc Thìn khònk tyawc, ngàyc sheng mayc ngràwks. 昊天孔昭　我生靡樂
Gic nec mòng-mòng, ngàyc sum tsàwc-tsàwc. 視爾夢夢　我心慘慘
Mhùs nec toun-toun, lhèngs ngàyc myawc-myawc. 誨爾諄諄　聽我藐藐
Puyc longs way kràws, phouk longs way ngawk. 匪用為教　覆用為虐
Tzaks wat muts tre, yak lout kuts màws. 借曰未知　亦聿既耄

Oh dear, you youngsters: I'm telling you about the old ways.
If you'd listen to my advice, you should be able to avoid major regrets.
Sky has got us into a crisis situation just now—we're contemplating the downfall
    of our nation,
and we don't have to look far for a precedent. Bright Sky doesn't make mistakes.
If you let your character go awry now, your people will be heading for great
    distress.

À-ghà, syawc tzuc—kòuk nec gwuc tuc. 於乎小子　告爾舊止
Lhèngs longs ngàyc mu, lhaks ma dàts mhùs. 聽用我謀　庶無大悔
Thìn pang krùn nàns; wat sàngs kot kwùk. 天方艱難　曰喪厥國
Tsoc pheks pu want. Gòuc Thìn pu lhùk. 取譬不遠　昊天不忒
Wùy-wit gu tùk, pec min dàts kuk. 回遹其德　俾民大棘

An elderly tutor to the teenage sons of the royal family laments their resistance to his efforts to fit them for their future role as rulers. "The Sole Man" of verse 2, like "the One Man" of Ode 243, is the king. The "Illustrious Ones" of verse 7 are the ancestral spirits.

I capitalize the "Our" of "Our tongue" in verse 6 to reflect the fact that the original uses the "royal we", *Drunk*: the poet is picturing his pupils when they become arrogant rulers.

An eight-word line in the received text of verse 8 is a close paraphrase of lines in Ode 64: "She threw me a peach; I paid her with a plum". While Ode 64 made good sense, the line makes no sense in the present context, and must be another case of memory confusing two poems.

The immediately following stich, literally "these ones who are horned while calves", is a metaphorical way of saying that the youngsters are mature in body but still have some growing-up left to do in other respects. The "precedent" alluded to in the last verse is the collapse of *Un*.

257

Mulberry Leaves　桑柔

The tender young foliage of this mulberry tree is flourishing; below it there is
    shade everywhere.
But, strip the leaves, and it would die. The people here below are suffering,
and nothing relieves their hearts' grief. Their misery is of long standing.
Bright Sky is mighty—why will it not take pity on us?

Out payc sàng nou, gu gràc gò swin.
Ròt tsùc gu rou. Màk tsec gràc min,
pu dùnt sum ou—changs-hwangs drin ì.
Tràwk payc Gòuc Thìn—nèng pu ngàyc grin?

菀彼桑柔　其下侯旬
捋采其劉　瘼此下民
不殄心憂　倉兄填兮
倬彼昊天　寧不我矜

The teams of war-horses are robust, and falcon flags and turtle-and-snake flags are waving.
Disorder is growing and not being put down: every state is affected.
The people have been decimated, all of them ruined by calamities.
Oh, woe! The nation's path has reached crisis point.

Slits mouc gwruy-gwruy, la drawc wuc phen.
Ròns sheng pu luy, mayc kwùk pu mint.
Min mayc wuc rì, gos gòyc luc dzins.
À-ghà wuc ùy! Kwùk bàs se bin.

四牡騤騤　旟旐有翩
亂生不夷　靡國不泯
民靡有黎　具禍以燼
於乎有哀　國步斯頻

The nation is on a path which is destroying our resources, and Sky isn't supporting us.
We have nowhere to halt and make a stand; we can march, but march where?
A true princely man has a mind which avoids contention.
Who was it who was born an instigator of cruelty, and continues to create misery to this day?

Kwùk bàs mèt tzi; Thìn pu ngàyc tzang.
Mayc shac tuc nguk; wun dzà, gày wank?
Kwun-tzuc dit wi, prank sum ma grangs.
Douy sheng rats krì, tits kum way krànk?

國步蔑資　天不我將
靡所止疑　云徂何往
君子寔維　秉心無競
誰生厲階　至今為梗

My sad heart is grief-stricken as I think of our homeland.
I was born into the wrong age, so that I've encountered the full force of Sky's wrath.
From east to west there's nowhere safe to settle.
So many miseries we've experienced, with our frontiers harassed endlessly.

Ou sum un-un, nìms ngàyc thàc-wac.
Ngàyc sheng pu dun, bong Thìn tànt nàc.
Dzis tòng dzà sì, mayc shac dèngs k'hlac.
Tày ngàyc kòs mhòun, khònk kuk ngàyc ngac.

憂心慇慇　念我土宇
我生不辰　逢天僤怒
自東徂西　靡所定處
多我覯痻　孔棘我圉

Formulate a plan, devise a defensive strategy: if disorder gets any worse it'll tear us to pieces.
I urge you to take this worry seriously—I tell you that you need to organize your noble peers.
Who can grasp something hot? There aren't many who don't use a wet cloth.
If you just say "What's the use?", then we'll all go down together.

Way mu, way pits; ròns hwangs, se syawk.
Kòuk nec ou swit. Mhùs nec slac tzyawk.
Douy nùc tup net? Sent pu longs dryawks.

為謀為毖　亂況斯削
告爾憂恤　誨爾序爵
誰能執熱　鮮不用濯

Gu "Gày nuc diwk?", tzùs sa gup nyàwk.   其何能淑　　載胥及溺

That kind of remark is like a strong wind in the face, which robs people of their breath.
Our people are enterprising at heart, but you're discouraging their initiative.
They love working the land—it puts food in the mouths of a tough people generation after generation.
Sowing and reaping are precious, and for successive generations to be fed is a fine thing.

Na payc sngàks pum, yak khònk tu ùts.   如彼遡風　　亦孔之僾
Min wuc siwk sum, phrèng wun pu lùts.   民有肅心　　荓云不逮
Hòus dec kràs shuk, ruk min lùks mluk.   好是稼穡　　力民代食
Kràs shuk wi pòuc; lùks mluk wi hòuc.   稼穡維寶　　代食維好

Sky is sending down chaos and death; it has destroyed our established king.
Sky has sent this plague of eelworms, so that our agriculture's in dire straits.
Alas for the unhappy Home States: they've become one utter waste land.
We have no strength of our own left, so we can only call on the blue vault of Sky.

Thìn kròungs sàngs ròns; met ngàyc rup wang.   天降喪亂　　滅我立王
Kròungs tsec mou dzùk, kràs shuk tzout yang.   降此蟊賊　　稼穡卒痒
Ùy thòng Troung Kwùk, gos tots tzout mhàng.   哀恫中國　　具贅卒荒
Mayc wuc rac-ruk, luc nhimp kwhung tsàng.   靡有旅力　　以念穹蒼

A good ruler is looked up to by his people.
His mind is furnished with comprehensive plans; he selects his ministers with care.
But the other kind of ruler believes that he alone is competent,
that he alone has guts, and that his people are utter fools.

Wi tsec wìts kwun, min nin shac tam.   維此惠君　　民人所瞻
Prank sum swan you; khòuc dins gu sangs.   秉心宣猶　　考慎其相
Wi payc pu mlouns, dzis dòk pec tzàng,   維彼不順　　自獨俾臧
dzis wuc phats drang, pec min tzout gwang.   自有肺腸　　俾民卒狂

Look into those woods: they're alive with deer.
But among men, we find colleagues briefing against one another rather than striving for mutual welfare.
People have a saying: "Whether things are going your way or not, treat each other well".

Tam payc troung rum: shin-shin gu ròk.   瞻彼中林　　甡甡其鹿
Bùng wuc luc jums, pu sa luc kòk.   朋友已譖　　不胥以穀
Nin yak wuc ngan: "Tzins thòuts wi kòk".   人亦有言　　進退維穀

A wise man looks thirty miles ahead,
whereas a stupid man is happy to be foolish.
The situation isn't hopeless yet, so why let fear stay your hand?

Wi tsec lhengs nin, tam ngan pràk ruc.　　維此聖人　瞻言百里
Wi payc ngo nin, phouk gwang luc huc.　　維彼愚人　覆狂以喜
Puyc ngan pu nùc, gà se ouys gus?　　匪言不能　胡斯畏忌

A decent man isn't greedy for promotion, he doesn't push himself forward,
whereas a self-centred man is now and always looking out for number one.
In their undisciplined self-seeking, people are content to act as bitter poison in the body politic.

Wi tsec rang nin, put gou, put lìwk.　　維此良人　弗求弗迪
Wi payc nunt sum, dec kàs, dec bouk.　　維彼忍心　是顧是復
Nin tu rhùm ròns, nèng way là dòuk.　　民之貪亂　寧為茶毒

A mighty wind sweeps through deep, empty valleys.
A decent man's actions are directed towards the common good,
while the other kind just proceeds as his rotten mind dictates.

Dàts pum wuc swits, wuc khòng dàts klòk.　　大風有隧　有空大谷
Wi tsec rang nin tzàk way lhuk kòk.　　維此良人　作為式穀
Wi payc pu mlouns teng luc troung kòc.　　維彼不順　征以中垢

A mighty wind sweeps past. A greedy man ruins his peers.
If words are obsequious, you respond to them, but you pay no more attention to criticism than if you were drunk.
You don't take what's valuable in my words—on the contrary, you assume I'm just silly.

Dàts pum wuc swits. Rhùm nin pràts routs.　　大風有隧　貪人敗類
Lhèngs ngan tzùk tòuts; slongs ngan na tzouts.　　聽言則對　誦言如醉
Puyc longs gu rang—phouk pec ngàyc bùts.　　匪用其良　覆俾我悖

Alas, my friend, do you imagine I write this without knowing what I'm talking about?
You're like a bird soaring in the air—it too can be brought down by an arrow.
So far I've sheltered you from criticism, but the time has come now when I must rebuke you.

Tzay, nec bùng wuc: lac khuyc pu tre nu tzàk?　　嗟爾朋友　予豈不知而作
Na payc puy droung: du yak luk wàk.　　如彼飛蟲　時亦弋獲
Kuts tu ums nac; pant lac rù hràks.　　既之陰汝　反予來嚇

People have lost all discipline; they're just grabbing what they can get, and encouraging disloyalty.
You do nothing for the people's benefit, as if you had no power to do so.
While people are going astray, you hesitate to enforce the law.

Min tu mank guk: tuk rak dant bùks.　　民之罔極　職掠善背
Ways min pu ris, na wun pu khùk.　　為民不利　如云不克
Min tu wùy-wit, tuk kung longs ruk.　　民之回遹　職競用力

Before people went astray, it was only scoundrels who were robbers.
Now, if I say that plundering is unacceptable, you're rebellious, and sympathize with my detractors.
Say "What, me?" as much as you like: it's you I've written this song about.

Min tu muts rìt, tuk dàws way khòs. 　民之未戾　職盜為寇
Rak wat pu khàyc, phouk bùks dant res. 　掠曰不可　覆背善詈
Swi wat "Puyc lac", kuts tzàk nec kày. 　雖曰匪予　既作爾歌

The poet sees his ruler as "fiddling while Rome burns", and is not afraid to tell him so—though much time is spent on pious platitudes before getting to direct criticism of the ruler. (The pointless remarks in verse 6 about it being a good thing for the population to have food to eat are perhaps a last-ditch attempt to postpone the dangerous moment of serious confrontation.) Traditionally the poem was held to be by a lord of *Nots* and directed against the oppressive king *Rats*, who in 841 was forced from the throne and replaced by regents. As I read the poem, though, the ruler is criticized chiefly for cowardly inaction in the face of internal and external threats to his rule, rather than for active oppression. I wonder whether the man criticized was ruler of a feudal state rather than king of China as a whole. (The question at the end of verse 3 could relate to the king, and verse 7 mentions him explicitly.)

The opening image presumably relates to the fact that mulberries are cultivated in order to feed their leaves to silkworms: this particular tree is not yet mature enough for its leaves to be harvested. A shade-providing tree is often a metaphor for the ruler who looks after the security and welfare of his subjects—does the immature tree stand for a boy-king who has replaced the one who was "destroyed" in verse 7? I take eelworms here (on which see Ode 212) to be intended literally, though in Ode 264 we shall see them used as a metaphor for people who sap the health of the state. The reference to deer in verse 9 is thought to contrast animals which co-exist peacefully in the wild with a human society in which individuals are busy doing one another down. But when it comes to grasping a hot object (verse 5), or the mighty wind (verses 12 and 13), the explanations that have been offered are too far-fetched to take seriously.

The horses and banners of verse 2 are a vivid way of depicting the fact that open war has broken out. In the second line of verse 14, the word *droung* usually refers to insects, but even a skilled *Tiw*-dynasty archer was hardly going to be shooting insects out of the sky: the word can refer to living creatures more generally, so the poet is telling the ruler that he may imagine himself to be safely above the fray but in reality he too is vulnerable.

258

The Milky Way 雲漢

Splendid was the Milky Way, shining as it turned through the sky.
The king spoke as follows: "Alas, what wrong has this generation committed
for Sky to send down destruction and chaos, and famine to arrive again and again?
We've made offerings to every Spirit, and we haven't stinted our sacrificial animals.

We have no more *kwè* or *pek* jades left to sacrifice. So why do none of the Spirits hear us?"

Tràwk payc Wun Hàns, tyaw wùy wa thìn.	倬彼雲漢　昭回于天
Wang wat: "À-ghà, gày kà kum tu nin,	王曰於乎　何辜今之人
Thìn kròungs sàngs ròns, kuy gruns dzùns jin?	天降喪亂　饑饉薦臻
Mayc mlin pu klac; mayc ùts se sheng.	靡神不舉　靡愛斯牲
Kwè pek kuts tzout—nèng màk ngàyc lhèng?"	圭璧既卒　寧莫我聽

"The drought is now extreme. The air is sultry, thunder rumbles, and it's baking hot.
There's been no interruption in our cycle of sacrifices. From the suburb to the citadel,
we've offered sacrifices up to Spirits in the sky, and buried offerings to the Spirits below ground. There are no Spirits we've failed to honour.
Yet the Millet Lord seems powerless, and God on High ignores us,
laying waste and destroying the land here below. Why is he hammering us like this?"

"Gànt kuts thàts dums; ount roung lòung-lòung.	旱既大甚　蘊隆烔烔
Pu dùnt in sluc; dzis kràw dzà koung,	不殄禋祀　自郊徂宮
dyangs gràc dìns èp. Mayc mlin pu tzòung.	上下奠瘞　靡神不宗
Gòs Tzuk pu khùk; Dyangs Tès pu rum,	后稷不克　上帝不臨
mhàws tàks gràc thàc. Nèng tènk ngàyc koung?"	耗斁下土　寧丁我躬

"The drought is now extreme. We can't make it stop.
It's as powerful and terrible as a thunderclap or a lightning bolt.
Not one of the people left in *Tiw* China is whole and healthy.
Bright Sky, God on High, is not allowing us to survive.
How could we not all be frightened? Our ancestral Spirits have taken against us."

"Gànt kuts thàts dums; tzùk pu khàyc thouy.	旱既大甚　則不可推
Gung-gung, ngap-ngap, na lèng, na ròuy.	兢兢業業　如霆如雷
Tiw la rì min mayc wuc kat wi.	周餘黎民　靡有孑遺
Gòuc Thìn, Dyangs Tès, tzùk pu ngàyc wi.	昊天上帝　則不我遺
Gà pu sang ouys? Sùn tzàc wa dzòuy."	胡不相畏　先祖于摧

"The drought is now extreme. We can't end it.
It's fiery, burning—we can't escape it.
The great doom is almost on us, and we have no-one we can look to.
The many princes and rulers of old are offering us no help.
Spirits of our parents and ancestors, how can you be so unfeeling towards us?"

"Gànt kuts thàts dums; tzùk pu khàyc dzac.	旱既大甚　則不可沮
Hràk-hràk, wam-wam, wun ngàyc ma shac.	赫赫炎炎　云我無所
Dàts mreng gunt tuc; mayc tam, mayc kàs.	大命近止　靡瞻靡顧
Gwun klòng sùn teng tzùk pu ngàyc djas.	群公先正　則不我助
Bac muc, sùn tzàc, gà nèng nunt lac?	父母先祖　胡寧忍予

"The drought is now extreme. The hills are devoid of greenery, the rivers are dried up.
The Demon of Drought is behaving cruelly, as one on fire, burning.
Our hearts fear the heat—our grieved hearts feel as though they're sizzling.
The many princes and rulers of old have lost interest in our welfare.
Bright Sky, God on High, why do you make us hide away in fear?"

Gànt kuts thàts dums; lìwk-lìwk shàn k'hloun.   旱既大甚　滌滌山川
Gànt Bàt way ngawk, na làm, na bun.   旱魃為虐　如惔如焚
Ngàyc sum dàns lhac; ou sum na hwun.   我心憚暑　憂心如熏
Gwun klòng sùn teng tzùk pu ngàyc muns.   群公先正　則不我問
Gòuc Thìn, Dyangs Tès, nèng pec ngàyc lòunt?   昊天上帝　寧俾我遯

"The drought is now extreme. We're putting all our energy and emotion into ridding ourselves of it.
Why are we made to suffer this way? We haven't discovered the reason.
We were very prompt in our prayers for the harvest; our prayers to the Four Quarters and to the Spirit of the Soil were never late,
yet Bright Sky, God on High, pays us no heed.
We've been duly reverent to the bright Spirits—they ought not to feel any resentment or anger."

Gànt kuts thàts dums; mrunt-mrant ouys khac.   旱既大甚　蘊勉畏去
Gà nèng tìn ngàyc luc gànt? Tsùmp pu tre gu kàs.   胡寧瘨我以旱　憯不知其故
Guy nìn khònk souk, Pang Dac pu màks.   祈年孔夙　方社不莫
Gòuc Thìn, Dyangs Tès, tzùk pu ngàyc ngwa.   昊天上帝　則我不虞
Krengs krong mrang mlin—ngay ma mhùs nàc.   敬恭明神　宜無悔怒

"The drought is now extreme. The staff of the court have scattered, order and discipline have broken down.
The department heads are at their wits' end, and despair has overcome the chief minister,
the master of horse, the commander of the guard, the controller of the kitchens, and their deputies.
Yet every member of staff is being offered support—nobody needs to leave.
I lift my face towards Bright Sky. How deep my grief is."

Gànt kuts thàts dums; sàns ma wuc kuc.   旱既大甚　散無有紀
Kouk tzù lhaks teng, kwus tzù, tronk tzùc,   鞫哉庶正　疚哉冢宰
tsòc mràc, shi gec, dans pa, tzàyc wuc.   趣馬師氏　膳夫左右
Mayc nin pu tiw—ma pu nùc tuc.   靡人不周　無不能止
Tam ngank Gòuc Thìn; wun na gày ruc.   瞻卬昊天　云如何里

"I lift my face towards Bright Sky. Its stars are so tiny.
You great officers and princes: summon up the enthusiasm to keep on going without giving up.
The great doom is almost on us, but don't abandon your work now.
What do I seek for myself? My prayer is that the department heads' problems can

be solved.
I lift my face towards Bright Sky. When will it be merciful and grant us peace?"

Tam ngank Gòuc Thìn; wuc hwìts gu sèng.	瞻卬昊天　有嘒其星
Dàts-pa, kwun-tzuc, tyaw kràc ma lhèng!	大夫君子　昭假無贏
Dàts mreng gunt tuc; ma khits nec deng.	大命近止　無棄爾成
Gày gou ways ngàyc? Luc rìts lhaks teng.	何求為我　以戾庶正
Tam ngank Gòuc Thìn; gàt wìts gu nèng?	瞻卬昊天　曷惠其寧

In the arid climate of north China, lack of rain to water the crops was a major danger. Each summer the king sacrificed to the Almighty as a plea for rain. At the Odes period, if drought continued, shamans would be required to perform a rain dance, or they might be tied down under the sun until they perished, or they were even burned alive; sometimes people with deformities were used as the victims. (By the end of the dynasty, enlightened opinion turned against human sacrifice.)

The Chinese have various names for the Milky Way, but each name envisages it as a river—here it is called the Cloudy Han River. The word *kràw* in verse 2 means "suburb" in the Roman sense: an area adjacent to but outside the city wall. The significance of "From the suburb …" is that a rite in the southern suburb was the first of the annual cycle of sacrifices.

The term I render "doom" in verses 4 and 8 is *mreng*, which elsewhere I translate as "mandate"—the right to rule granted by Sky to a dynasty, and the lease of life granted to an individual. The implication of the "great doom" being close could be a prediction of dynastic collapse, or simply a statement that everyone is near death. My phrase "don't abandon your work", in the second "great doom" passage, literally says "don't abandon your achievement(s)": the leading officials have made successes of their briefs, but their efforts will have been wasted if they quit their posts now.

My choice of "Bright Sky" to render *Gòuc Thìn* as a name of the supreme god obviously becomes awkward when, as here, the speaker is contemplating the night sky. *Gòuc* could equally well be translated as "splendid"; but Bright Sky is more idiomatic in English, and there are sufficiently many passages where that phrase fits its context that I have preferred to stick with it.

259

The Foundation of *Lhin* and *Pac*　崧高

High is the Holy Peak; its grandeur reaches right up to the sky.
The Holy Peak sent down a Spirit who brought into being the rulers of *Pac* and *Lhin*.
Now *Lhin* and *Pac* became the bulwarks of *Tiw*:
their rulers set out to fence the states safely in, to wall round the whole world.

Soung kàw wi Ngròk, tzyouns guk wa thìn.	崧高維嶽　俊極于天
Wi Ngròk kròungs mlin, sheng Pac gup Lhin.	維嶽降神　生甫及申
Wi Lhin gup Pac, wi Tiw tu gàn:	維申及甫　維周之翰
Slits kwùk wa pan, Slits Pang wa wan.	四國于蕃　四方于垣

VOICES FROM EARLY CHINA

The lord of *Lhin* is an energetic man; the king promoted him into royal service.
He went to establish his seat at *Slaks*. He was a model for the southern states.
The king commanded the lord of *Daws* to establish a residence for the lord of *Lhin*,
who went up to that southern state to assume this meritorious duty on his own and his heirs' behalf.

Muyc-muyc Lhin pràk; wang tzùns tu shuc.	亹亹申伯　王薦之事
Wa up wa Slaks. Nùm kwùk dec lhuk.	于邑于謝　南國是式
Wang mreng Daws pràk, dèngs Lhin pràk tu dràk.	王命召伯　定申伯之宅
Tùng dec nùm pròng, lhats tup kus kòng.	登是南邦　世執其功

The king charged the lord of *Lhin*: "Be a model for the states of the south.
Make use of the men of *Slaks* to build your walls."
And the king charged the lord of *Daws*: "Apportion out the fields of the lord of *Lhin*."
The king commanded the factors to send their ruler's household to join him in *Lhin*.

Wang mreng Lhin pràk: "Lhuk dec nùm pròng.	王命申伯　式是南邦
In dec Slaks nin, luc tzàk nec long."	因是謝人　以作爾墉
Wang mreng Daws pràk: "Thret Lhin pràk thàc lìn."	王命召伯　徹申伯土田
Wang mreng pas-ngas, tsan gu si nin.	王命傅御　遷其私人

The work of the lord of *Lhin* was planned by the lord of *Daws*.
They made a start on building the walls; they completed the ancestral-temple complex
—they completed it, and it was extensive. The king made a gift to the lord of *Lhin*
of four high-stepping stallions, with gleaming hooked breastplates.

Lhin pràk tu kòng, Daws pràk dec weng.	申伯之功　召伯是營
Wuc thyouk gu geng, tsump mraws kuts deng	有俶其城　寢廟既成
—kuts deng mràwk-mràwk. Wang slèk Lhin pràk	既成藐藐　王錫申伯
slits mouc gawk-gawk, kò ung dryawk-dryawk.	四牡蹻蹻　鉤膺濯濯

The king sent the lord of *Lhin* a state carriage, and a team of horses.
"I have organized a residence for you: there is nowhere to beat the south country.
I bestow on you this great jade *kwè*, to be your heirloom.
Go forth, oh royal uncle, and be the guardian of the south lands."

Wang khent Lhin pràk, ràks ka mlungs mràc.	王遣申伯　路車乘馬
"Ngàyc dà nec kac. Màk na nùm thàc.	我圖爾居　莫如南土
Slèk nec krèts kwè, luc tzàk nec pòuc.	錫爾介圭　以作爾寶
Wank kus wang gouc, nùm thàc dec pòuc."	往迓王舅　南土是保

And the lord of *Lhin* did indeed go forth. The king gave him the parting feast at *Mouy*,
and then the lord turned south, and did indeed go to his new home at *Slaks*.

The king charged the lord of *Daws*: "Apportion out the territory of the lord of
   Lhin,
to provide him with an income from taxation." So he hurried on his way.

Lhin pràk sins mràts. Wang dzans wa Mouy.	申伯信邁　王餞于郿
Lhin pràk wèn nùm, Slaks ghà deng kwuy.	申伯還南　謝乎誠歸
Wang mreng Daws pràk: "Thret Lhin pràk thàc kang,	王命召伯　徹申伯土疆
luc druc gu trang." Lhuk don gu gràng.	以峙其粻　式遄其行

The lord of *Lhin* is a warrior.
Once he'd come to *Slaks* the common people and the officials could relax.
Among the states of the *Tiw* kingdom there was general rejoicing—people
   assured him "You shall be well supported."
Highly illustrious is the lord of *Lhin*, the king's mother's eldest brother
and a model for the arts of peacetime and of war.

Lhin pràk pày-pày.	申伯番番
Kuts nup wa Slaks, dà ngas thant-thant.	既入于謝　徒御嘽嘽
Tiw pròng grùm huc: "Noung wuc rang gàn."	周邦咸喜　戎有良翰
Phru hènt Lhin pràk, wang tu ngon gouc,	丕顯申伯　王之元舅
mun mac dec nghans.	文武是憲

The character of the lord of *Lhin* is gentle, kindly, and straightforward.
He makes the states tranquil; his fame extends throughout the world.
I, *Kit*, have made this song, with its stately lyric
and its sweet, informal melody, as a gift for the lord of *Lhin*.

Lhin pràk tu tùk, nou wìts tsac druk.	申伯之德　柔惠且直
Nous tsec màns pròng; muns wa Slits kwùk.	揉此萬邦　聞于四國
Kit-pac tzàk slongs, gu lhu khònk dak,	吉甫作誦　其詩孔碩
gu pum sits hòuc, luc dzùngs Lhin pràk.	其風肆好　以贈申伯

A poem by *Wint Kit-pac*, whom we met in Ode 177 as commander of a military expedition. Here he describes the foundation under king *Swan* of two small adjacent states, *Pac* and *Lhin*, on what early in the *Tiw* dynasty was the southern edge of China—in modern terms, around Xinyang in southern Henan. (The foundation of *Lhin* was also the topic of Ode 227.)

I am not sure why the ruler of another state, *Daws*, figures so largely in these two Odes. Legge believed that the lord of *Daws* was "minister of works", involved *ex officio* in all cases where new territory was brought into the Chinese fold; the verb *thret*, which I translate as "apportion", meant something like compiling a Domesday-style register of landholdings with their respective tax obligations. But even if this was the lord of *Daws*'s job, that scarcely explains why the Ode gives him such star billing, almost as if there was little left for the new ruler of *Lhin* to do himself. We can be sure that there was a political purpose in the writing of a poem like this, and if we knew more about the politics of the time perhaps we would see why *Wint Kit* wanted to stress the lord of *Daws*'s role as "sponsor" of *Lhin*.

Waley believed that the Holy Peak of the opening lines was Mount Song, between Luoyang and Zhengzhou. This was certainly a holy mountain in later ages, for instance the Shaolin Temple, birthplace of Zen Buddhism, is there.

260

Droungs Shàn 烝民

Sky created the many people, with their physical bodies and their moral rules.
The fact that people maintain social norms is due to their love of upright character.
Sky inspected the domain of *Tiw*, and descended in brightness to the earth below.
To protect his Son the king, he created *Droungs Shàn*.

Thìn sheng tung min, wuc mout wuc tzùk.   天生烝民　有物有則
Min tu prank luy, hòus dec its tùk.   民之秉彝　好是懿德
Thìn kràm wuc Tiw, tyaw kràc wa gràc.   天監有周　昭假于下
Pòuc tzu Thìn Tzuc, sheng Droungs Shàn-pac.   保茲天子　生仲山甫

Droungs Shàn's character is mild, kind, and upright.
He has excellent deportment and appearance; he is cautious and respectful.
He models himself on the ancient precepts, and puts effort into behaving with dignity.
Obedient to Sky's Son, he arranges for his bright commands to be promulgated.

Droungs Shàn tu tùk nou kràuy wi tzùk.   仲山之德　柔嘉維則
Reng ngay reng shuk, syawc sum yuk-yuk.   令儀令色　小心翼翼
Kàc hwuns dec lhuk; ouy-ngay dec ruk.   古訓是式　威儀是力
Thìn Tzuc dec nak, mrang mreng shuc pas.   天子是若　明命使賦

The king has commanded *Droungs Shàn*: "Be a model for the many state rulers;
keep up the cult of our ancestors, and protect the person of your king.
Go out and proclaim our royal commands: be the king's throat and tongue.
Take government to the world outside, so that it operates throughout the Four Quarters."

Wang mreng Droungs Shàn: "Lhuk dec pràk pek.   王命仲山　式是百辟
Tzònt noung tzàc khòuc; wang koung dec pòuc.   纘戎祖考　王躬是保
K'hlout nùp wang mreng: wang tu gò mlat.   出納王命　王之喉舌
Pas tengs wa ngwàts, Slits Pang wan pat."   賦政于外　四方爰發

Solemn is the royal command: *Droungs Shàn* undertakes the mission.
Whether states are obedient or not—this he clearly discerns.
Being enlightened and shrewd, he protects the king's person;
he does not slacken day or night in serving the One Man.

Syouk-syouk wang mreng: Droungs Shàn tzang tu.   肅肅王命　仲山將之
Pròng kwùk nak puc, Droungs Shàn mrang tu.   邦國若否　仲山明之
Kuts mrang tsac trat, luc pòuc gu lhin.   既明且哲　以保其身
Souk yas puyc krès luc shuc It Nin.   夙夜匪懈　以事一人

And people have a saying:
"If it's soft, swallow it; if it's hard, spit it out."
But *Droungs Shàn*
doesn't even swallow the soft, still less does he spit out the hard:
he treats widows and orphans with respect, and he doesn't fear hard-boiled opponents.

Nin yak wuc ngan: 　　　　　　　　人亦有言
"Nou tzùk nac tu, kàng tzùk thàc tu." 　柔則茹之　剛則吐之
Wi Droungs Shàn-pac 　　　　　　　維仲山甫
nou yak pu nac, kàng yak pu thàc: 　　柔亦不茹　剛亦不吐
pu moc kwrìn kwràc, pu ouys gang ngac. 不侮矜寡　不畏彊禦

People have another saying:
"Virtue is light as a hair, but few people can lift it."
We just ponder it and roughly estimate it, only *Droungs Shàn* lifts it.
We love him, but nobody is capable of assisting him.
When the royal dragon robe has holes, *Droungs Shàn* alone can mend them.

Nin yak wuc ngan: 　　　　　　　　　人亦有言
"Tùk you na màw, min sent khùk klac tu." 德輶如毛　民鮮克舉之
Ngàyc ngay dà tu, wi Droungs Shàn klac tu. 我儀圖之　維仲山舉之
ùts màk djas tu. 　　　　　　　　　　愛莫助之
Kòunt tuks wuc khot, wi Droungs Shàn pàc tu. 袞織有闕　維仲山補之

Droungs Shàn goes forth and makes the sacrifice for a safe journey.
His four stallions are strong, his troops energetic
—each one keen not to be a laggard.
The four stallions stamp their hooves; their eight harness-bells jingle.
The king has commanded *Droungs Shàn*: "Fortify the eastern region".

Droungs Shàn k'hlout tzàc. 　　　　　仲山出祖
Slits mouc ngap-ngap, teng pa dzap-dzap, 四牡業業　征夫捷捷
mùc gròuy mayc gup. 　　　　　　　每懷靡及
Slits mouc pàng-pàng, prèt ròn tsang-tsang. 四牡彭彭　八鸞鏘鏘
Wang mrang Droungs Shàn: "Geng payc tòng pang." 王命仲山　城彼東方

The four stallions are sturdy; their eight harness bells sound in unison.
Droungs Shàn is on his way to the State of *Dzì*—may he quickly return!
Kit wrote this song, with its stately, pure-sounding melody.
Droungs Shàn has constant worries; with this song I hope to soothe his heart.

Slits mouc gwruy-gwruy, prèt ròn krì-krì. 四牡騤騤　八鸞喈喈
Droungs Shàn dzà Dzì—lhuk don gu kwuy! 仲山徂齊　式遄其歸
Kit-pac tzàk slongs, mouk na tseng pum. 吉甫作誦　穆如清風
Droungs Shàn wrank gròuy; luc outs gu sum. 仲山永懷　以慰其心

Another poem by *Wint Kit*, this time a praise-poem about *Droungs Shàn*, believed to have been king *Swan*'s chief minister, on the occasion of *Shàn* being sent by the king to fortify the State of *Dzì*. (We have seen that "the One Man" is a term for the king.) I discussed on pp. 22–3 the fact that several instances of the honorific *pac* suffixed to *Shàn*'s name seem to be later additions to the text, and I have not translated *pac* even when it appears to be original.

To an English reader, the gross flattery in this Ode might feel distasteful. But such matters are very culture-specific, and in *Tiw* dynasty China you evidently laid it on with a trowel. Doubtless the goodwill of a man in *Droungs Shàn*'s position was valuable to *Wint Kit*.

Chinese has always been given to using metaphors about bodies and bodily functions which look opaque to outsiders. The metaphor of verse 5 about swallowing and spitting out is glossed within the verse itself; but "lifting virtue" in verse 6 is more mysterious. It perhaps means something like "judging precisely what justice requires". Holes in the royal robe obviously stand for defects in the king's manner of ruling.

261

The Greatness of *Gàn* 韓奕

Grand are the *Rang* hills—it was *Wac* who brought them into cultivation. His Way was splendid.
The lord of *Gàn* received his mandate; the king in person charged him: "Keep up the worship of your own ancestors,
but don't neglect Our mandate. Morning and evening, be not remiss.
Have proper respect in the high position we've bestowed on you: Our service is not easy.
Aid your sovereign by keeping in line those vassals who avoid attending court."

Yak-yak Rang shàn, wi Wac lìns tu; wuc tràwk gu lòuc.	奕奕梁山 其道	維禹甸之	有倬
Gàn gò douc mreng. Wang tsin mreng tu: "Tzònt noung tzàc khòuc.	韓侯受命 祖考	王親命之	纘戎
Ma pats Drunk mreng. Souk yas puyc krès.	無廢朕命	夙夜匪懈	
Gan krong nec wouts: Drunk mreng pu leks.	虔恭爾位	朕命不易	
Kàns pu lèng pang, luc tzàys noung pek."	榦不庭方	以佐戎辟	

The four stallions were mighty, very long and broad ...
The lord of *Gàn* entered for an audience, bringing with him his great jade tablet of rank. He entered for an audience with the king.
The king presented to the lord: a fine dragon-banner with tassel ornaments;
a bamboo carriage-cover and patterned carriage-yoke;
a black robe embroidered with dragons; red shoes; for the horses, hooked breastplates, and engraved metal frontlets;
a leather casing for the front carriage-rail, and a short-haired cover for it; metal-tipped reins, and metal yoke-bows.

Slits mouc yak-yak, khònk siw tsac trang.
Gàn gò nup gruns, luc gu krèts kwè. Nup gruns wa wang.
Wang slèk Gàn gò: diwk guy nouy tang;
lìmp put tsàk gràng;
gwìn kòunt khlak sak; kò ung, ròs lang;
kwhàk kwhùng, tsent mèk, lìw rùk, kum èk.

四牡奕奕　孔脩且張
韓侯入覲　以其介圭　入覲于王
王錫韓侯　淑旂綏章
簟茀錯衡
玄袞赤舄　鉤膺鏤錫
鞹鞃淺幭　鞗革金厄

The lord of Gàn departed, making the appropriate sacrifice beside the road for a safe journey; he departed, and stayed the first night at Dà.
Hènt-pac gave the farewell feast for him, with a hundred gà pots of clear wine.
How was the food he provided? There was roast turtle and rare fish.
What about the vegetables? There was everything from bamboo shoots to bà.
And how about the farewell gifts? A team of four horses, and a large carriage.
The pèn fruit-baskets and dòs food-bowls were numerous, and the lord's party feasted far into the night.

Gàn gò k'hlout tzàc, k'hlout souk wa Dà.
Hènt-pac dzans tu, tseng tziwc pràk gà.
Gu gràw wi gày? Bròu pet, sent nga.
Gu sòk wi gày? Wi swint gup bà.
Gu dzùngs wi gày? Mlungs mràc ràks ka.
Pèn dòs wuc tza. Gò gec èns sa.

韓侯出祖　出宿于屠
顯父餞之　清酒百壺
其殽維何　炰鱉鮮魚
其蔌維何　維筍及蒲
其贈維何　乘馬路車
籩豆有且　侯氏燕胥

Then the lord of Gàn took a wife, niece of the Bun king and daughter of Gots-pac.
The lord went to meet his bride at Gots's village.
His hundred carriages rumbled over the cobbles, bang bang; the eight bells on each horse-harness tinkled, tsang-tsang.
His splendour was very bright.
The "younger sisters" followed the bride, massed like clouds;
the lord turned to survey them, as they filled the gateway in their radiance.

Gàn gò tsos tsùy, Bun wang tu sheng, Gots-pac tu tzuc.
Gàn gò ngrang tu, wa Gots tu ruc.
Pràk rangs pàng-pàng, prèt ròn tsang-tsang.
Phru hènt gu kwàng.
Ta dìs dzong tu, gri-gri na wun.
Gàn gò kàs tu, ràns gu leng mùn.

韓侯娶妻　汾王之甥　蹶父之子
韓侯迎之　于蹶之里
百兩彭彭　八鸞鏘鏘
丕顯其光
諸娣從之　祁祁如雲
韓侯顧之　爛其盈門

Gots-pac was a mighty warrior, and there was no state he hadn't visited.
He had looked for a suitable place for his daughter Grit, and nowhere pleased him as well as Gàn.
The land of Gàn was truly enjoyable, with many streams and pools
full of large bream and tench, and does and stags were abundant.
There were black bears and brown-and-white bears, wild-cats and tigers.
Gots-pac was so pleased with Gàn that he instructed his daughter to marry there, and the lady Grit feasted and rejoiced.

Gots-pac khònk mac, mayc kwùk pu tàws.　蹶父孔武　靡國不到
Ways Gàn Grit sangs you, màk na Gàn ngràwks.　為韓姞相攸　莫如韓樂
Khònk ngràwks Gàn thàc, k'hloun drak hwa-hwa,　孔樂韓土　川澤訏訏
bang slac pac-pac, ou ròk ngwac-ngwac.　魴鱮甫甫　麀鹿噳噳
Wuc wum wuc pay, wuc maw wuc hlàc.　有熊有羆　有貓有虎
Khrangs kuts reng kas, Gàn Grit èns las.　慶既令居　韓姞燕譽

Great is the city wall of *Gàn*, which was built by the men of *Èn*.
Because his forefathers had received Sky's mandate, the lord moved on to the many *Mròn* peoples:
the king gave him possession of the *Trouy* and *Mràk* tribes.
He received full possession of these northern nations, and went on to rule them as their lord
—that is to say, he walled and moated their settlements, allocated landholdings, and compiled land-tax registers.
He presented the king with panther skins, ruddy leopardskins, and brown bearskins.

Phàc payc Gàn geng, Èn shi shac gòn.　溥彼韓城　燕師所完
Luc sùn tzàc douc mreng, in duc pràk Mròn.　以先祖受命　因時百蠻
Wang slèk Gàn gò kus Trouy, kus Mràk　王錫韓侯　其追其貊
amp douc pùk kwùk, in luc gu pràk:　奄受北國　因以其伯
dit long dit hàk, dit mùc dit dzak.　寔墉寔壑　寔畝寔籍
Nghans gu bi bay, khlak pràwks, gwàng pay.　獻其貔皮　赤豹黃羆

This Ode, said to date from about 800, celebrates the life of a marquis of *Gàn*—a place-name which applied at different early periods to larger or smaller territories in modern Shaanxi.

On *Wac*, see p. 8. "*Rang* hills" probably refers to a range still called by that name (modern Liang) north-west of present-day Hancheng, Shaanxi; the reason for beginning the poem by naming it is that the range was regarded as the "guardian" of *Gàn*. (Hancheng is the modern pronunciation of *Gàn geng*, mentioned in the last verse—the "city of *Gàn*".)

Karlgren takes the word *lòuc* to refer literally to roads built by *Wac*, and that is possible; but *lòuc* is often used figuratively, and I take it to be so here.

In the first two verses, his father having died, the new marquis travels to the *Tiw* royal court for the king to confirm him in his title and duties. In verse three we read about the marquis's return journey after receiving his mandate at court. It was etiquette for a visitor to be escorted homewards; in this case the king has evidently delegated a minister, *Hènt*, to go a full day's journey with the marquis, and organize a farewell feast at the first overnight stop.

The graph which I have spelled *sent* and translated as "rare" can alternatively represent a word pronounced slightly differently and meaning "fresh"; and some commentators have taken the phrase to mean "fresh fish". But to say that the fish served at a feast honouring a nobleman was fresh would be damning with faint praise. On the other hand, we know from James Davidson's *Courtesans and Fishcakes* that the Ancient Greeks saw unusual fish as the height of gourmet luxury, and perhaps it was the same in China. As for the *bà* vegetable, all the reference books translate this word as "rushes, reeds", and one commentator asserts that when young these are edible. I wonder whether, several thousand years ago, *bà* did not refer to some more appetizing food.

VOICES FROM EARLY CHINA

The four horses which the lord received as his farewell gift are presumably the ones which the poet began to reminisce about at the beginning of the second verse, before abruptly changing the subject.

It was normal for a nobleman to marry as soon as he was accepted by the king as succeeding to his father's position, hence verse 4 follows naturally on from verse 3. The "*Bun* king" was *Rats*, who was deposed and exiled to the river *Bun*, with the government carried on by co-regents while *Rats* lived.

The Chinese text repeatedly refers to *Gots*'s daughter as "*Grit* of *Gàn*", but that was what she became after she married. (And *Grit* was her clan name, not her individual name.) *Gots*'s instruction to his daughter, if one translates the Chinese word for word, was to reside in *Gàn*. But this clearly did not mean she was to go and live there independently; the marquis must have suggested the marriage, and her father agreed.

The last verse describes the marquis's role in the colonization of China. The Chinese categorized the surrounding tribal groups in different ways, but, confusingly, using the same words. When the classification was geographic, the *Mròn* were those to the south; but that cannot be what is meant here, since the poem is about people to the north of China proper. The alternative was classification by cultural level, in which case the *Mròn* were the most wild and woolly tribesmen (the word *mròn* meant "savage, uncivilized").

Èn was a state far to the north, around the area of modern Peking: at this period *Èn* was probably at best only semi-Chinese. Evidently the *Tiw* king had given the marquis's line a mandate to rule not only the central state of *Gàn* but also other areas to the north: earlier members of the family had brought *Èn* into the Chinese fold and used its workforce to fortify their seat of government, and now this lord moved on to some of the tribes even further from the Chinese heartland.

The last line could be taken as the tribesmen presenting furs to their new overlord; but probably it was the lord presenting them to the king, and I have translated it so. Winters in North China are fierce, so fur coats would have been a valuable export from an area not likely to have had many sophisticated goods to offer.

262

The Yangtze and the Han 江漢

The Yangtze and Han were in spate, and warriors were streaming through.
There was no time for rest or leisure: we were hunting down the *Wì*-river tribes.
We had brought out our waggons and raised our falcon flags.
There was no time for rest or relaxation: we were out to harass the *Wì*-river tribes.

Kròng Hàns lhòu-lhòu; mac-pa bou-bou.	江漢滔滔　武夫浮浮
Puyc àn, puyc you: Wì Luy rù gou.	匪安匪遊　淮夷來求
Kuts k'hlouts ngàyc ka, kuts nhet ngàyc la.	既出我車　既設我旂
Puyc àn, puyc lha: Wì Luy rù pha.	匪安匪舒　淮夷來鋪

The Yangtze and Han were in full flood, and warriors formed a turbulent torrent.
After our troops had reduced the world to good order, we reported success to the king.
Once the world was calm, the king's states were pretty well settled.
There was no fighting now, so the king's heart was at peace.

Kròng Hàns lhang-lhang; mac-pa kwàng-kwàng.	江漢湯湯　武夫洸洸
Kèng-weng Slits Pang, kòuk deng wa wang.	經營四方　告成于王
Slits Pang kuts breng, wang kwùk lhaks dèngs.	四方既平　王國庶定
Duc mayc wuc jèng. Wang sum tzùs nèng.	時靡有爭　王心載寧

On the banks of Yangtze and Han the king commanded *Hlàc* of *Daws*:
"Open the Four Quarters up: compile a tax register of my territories.
Don't be harsh or oppressive, but go through my domains thoroughly,
establishing boundaries and field divisions, all the way to the Southern Sea."

Kròng Hàns tu nghàc, wang mreng Daws Hlàc:	江漢之滸　王命召虎
"*Lhuk bek Slits Pang, thret ngàyc kang thàc.*	式闢四方　徹我疆土
Puyc kwus, puyc kuk; wang kwùk rù guk,	匪疚匪棘　王國來極
wa kang, wa ruc, tits wa Nùm Mhùc."	于疆于理　至于南海

And the king commanded *Hlàc* of *Daws*: "Go everywhere, be thorough.
When Sky's mandate was conferred on *Mun* and *Mac*, the Duke of *Daws* was their support.
Don't say 'I'm just a boy'—the Duke of *Daws* could have said the same.
If you go about this task energetically, I shall richly reward you."

Wang mreng Daws Hlàc: "Rù swin, rù swan.	王命昭虎　來旬來宣
Mun Mac douc mreng, Daws klòng wi gàn.	文武受命　召公維翰
Ma wat 'Lac syawc tzuc': Daws klòng dec sluc.	無曰予小子　召公是似
Drawc-mawc noung kòng, longs slèk nec thruc."	肇敏戎功　用錫爾祉

"I shall give you a libation-ladle with *kwè*-jade handle, and a *youc* pot of sweet-scented black-millet wine,
for when you report to your ancestors. I shall give you hills, land, and fields.
You have received your mandate from *Tiw*: let it be the successor to the mandate which your *Daws* forebear received."
Hlàc bowed his head low in homage, saying "Long live Sky's Son".

"*Ru nec kwè dzànt, gac thrangs it youc,*	釐爾圭瓚　秬鬯一卣
kòuk wa mun nin. Slèk shàn thàc lìn.	告于文人　錫山土田
Wa Tiw douc mreng, dzis Daws tzàc mreng."	于周受命　自召祖命
Hlàc prèts khìc lhouc: "Thìn Tzuc màns nìn".	虎拜稽首　天子萬年

Hlàc bowed his head low in homage, and responded by extolling the king's grace.
He brought the deeds of the Duke of *Daws* to fulfilment. May Sky's Son live for ever!

Sky's Son shines brightly; his fine reputation never fades.
He disseminates his ethos of civility, and brings the states of the world together in unity.

Hlàc prèts khìc lhouc, tòuts lang wang hou. 虎拜稽首　對揚王休
Tzàk Daws klòng khòuc. Thìn Tzuc màns douc! 作召公考　天子萬壽
Mrang-mrang Thìn Tzuc, reng muns pu luc. 明明天子　令聞不已
Lhic gu mun tùk, grùp tsec Slits kwùk. 矢其文德　洽此四國

This Ode is about a campaign in 822, under king *Swan*, against some of the *Luy* tribes. (*Luy* was a generic term for tribal societies to the east of China.) *Hlàc*, "Tiger", was the lord of *Daws* who appeared in Ode 259; the Duke of *Daws*, on the other hand, was the royal henchman who had helped establish the *Tiw* dynasty two centuries earlier. The Han and Yangtze rivers meet at what is now the city of Wuhan, but that would be very far south to be relevant to an expedition to the *Wì*-river *Luy*, around modern Jiangsu province, so I wonder whether the name *Kròng* was here used for some river other than the Yangtze.

After *Luy* territory was brought under king *Swan*'s control, in verse 3 and following he ordered his new domains to be surveyed for taxation in very much the same way that, after the Norman Conquest, William I had Domesday Book compiled. *Nùm Mhùc*, "southern sea", sounds as though it ought to mean the South China Sea, but that is implausible at this early date; perhaps it meant the Yellow Sea, south of the Shandong peninsula.

263

Unrest in *Sla*　常武

The king, in his majesty and brightness, charged his minister Second-Son *Nùm* in the temple of his great ancestors,
and charged sire *Wàng*, commander in chief of the army, as follows:
"Get my six regiments onto a war footing, by preparing my weaponry.
Having given this due care and attention, go and relieve the southern states."

Hràk-hràk, mrang-mrang, wang mreng khrang shuc 赫赫明明　王命卿士
Nùm Droungs thàts tzàc, thàts-shi Wàng-pac: 南仲大祖　大師皇父
"Tenk ngàyc rouk shi, luc siw ngàyc noung. 整我六師　以修我戎
Kuts krengs, kuts krùs, wìts tsec nùm kwùk". 既敬既戒　惠此南國

And the king said to sire *Wint*: "Tell *Hou*, count of *Dreng*
to assist in the task of forming up the ranks, and give my regiments and brigades a pep talk.
Follow the banks of the river *Wì* and inspect the *Sla* country.
Don't linger, don't delay, you three officers: get to work!"

Wang wuts Wint-gec: "Mreng Dreng pràk Hou-pac 王謂尹氏　命程伯休父
tzàys-wùs drin gàng, krùs ngàyc shi rac. 左右陳行　戒我師旅
Shout payc Wì phàc, senk tsec Sla thàc. 率彼淮浦　省此徐土
Pu rou, pu k'hlac, sùm shuc dzous slac!" 不留不處　三事就緒

Awe-inspiring and majestic, Sky's Son was grave.
The king acted with deliberation and circumspectly, and he didn't slacken or lose sight of his goal.
Unrest was widespread in the *Sla* region. He shook *Sla* and frightened it,
like a peal of thunder, a thunderclap: yes, the *Sla* region was shaken and frightened.

Ngap-ngap, hràk-hràk, wuc ngam Thìn Tzuc.	赫赫業業　有嚴天子
Wang lha pòuc tzàk, puyc thaw, puyc you.	王舒保作　匪紹匪遊
Sla pang lak sòu: tuns kreng Sla pang,	徐方繹騷　震驚徐方
na ròuy, na lèng—payc pang tuns kreng.	如雷如霆　徐方震驚

The king roused his martial spirit, like one fired up and angry.
He sent his special forces forward, roaring like enraged tigers.
He massed his troops on a broad front along the *Wì*. Again and again they took numbers of prisoners,
and they brought order to the banks of *Wì*, wherever the royal army went.

Wang puns kot mac, na tuns, na nàc.	王奮厥武　如震如怒
Tzins kot hlàc gin, hrùmp na hòu hlàc.	進厥虎臣　闞如虓虎
Pha tòun Wì bun. Nung tup k'hyou ràc.	敷敦淮濆　仍執醜虜
Dzèt payc Wì phàc, wang shi tu shac.	截彼淮浦　王師之所

The king's troops were numberless, mobile as if winged, as if they were flying,
pouring through the land like the Yangtze or Han rivers, massed together like mountains,
flowing like rivers in long, disciplined files,
uncountable, invincible, smartly-turned-out, they marched against the *Sla* nation.

Wang rac thàn-thàn, na puy, na gàn,	王旅嘽嘽　如飛如翰
na Kròng, na Hàns, na shàn tu bawc,	如江如漢　如山之苞
na k'hloun tu riw, ment-ment, yuk-yuk,	如川之流　緜緜翼翼
pu chuk, pu khùk, dryawk teng Sla kwùk.	不測不克　濯征徐國

The king's policy was principled. The *Sla* country surrendered
and accepted annexation. This was the achievement of Sky's Son.
Once the world was calm again, the leaders of the *Sla* country paid their duty visit to court,
and that region no longer wavered in fealty. The king said "We can go home now".

Wang you yount sùk. Sla pang kuts rù,	王猶允塞　徐方既來
Sla pang kuts dòng. Thìn Tzuc tu kòng.	徐方既同　天子之功
Slits Pang kuts breng, Sla pang rù lèng.	四方既平　徐方來庭
Sla pang pu wùy. Wang wat "Swen kwuy".	徐方不回　王曰還歸

The king here is again believed to be *Swan*, and *Wint-gec* (meaning the head of the *Wint* clan) is supposed to be the same man as *Wint Kit* who figured in Ode 177. Here he is functioning as the king's chief of staff to pass on orders to count *Hou*, who will be second in command to *Wàng*. (*Hou*'s state *Dreng* lay within the modern boundaries of Luoyang city.) The fact that the king gave *Hou* his orders indirectly was normal; an official who was granted an audience did not approach the king closely enough for conversation, the royal words were passed on by an intermediary.

Sla was an area of northern Anhui province, lying at this time on the southern edge of Chinese territory. Particularly in view of the word *dòng* in the second line of verse 6, I believe the campaign described was not against a rebellion by a fully Chinese state, but a chapter in the process of turning tribesmen on the Chinese periphery, who recognized no allegiance to the Chinese king and doubtless saw China as a valuable source of plunder, into well-behaved Chinese states. However, this distinction would have been less clear to a *Tiw* Chinese than it seems to us today. The Chinese of course saw a difference between themselves and wild tribesmen who didn't understand the role of the Chinese king, but they had no concept that China could be just one among a number of independent countries. This concept remained lacking into modern times—hence the famous occasion in 1793 when George III sent George Macartney as a first British ambassador to the Chinese court, where he was required to kowtow before the emperor as a sign of obeisance. Macartney declined, as representative of a brother sovereign; but to the Chinese this was absurdly gauche, since the whole point of sending people to court was to demonstrate loyalty to the universal empire—as Ode 205 says, "Under Sky's vast expanse, there's no land which is not the king's". The emperor wrote to king George, ending with an admonition to "tremblingly obey and show no negligence".

Before a campaign it was usual for troops to be given a speech encouraging them to fight well and threatening them with punishment in case of failure. I can find no apter English term for this than the slangy "pep talk", but the Chinese term *krùs*, "warning", suggests that threats were at least as prominent as encouragement.

Calling a punitive expedition an "inspection" was a standard euphemism. In verse 4, *hlàc gin* are literally "tiger-officers"; the nearest English equivalent might be "special forces" like the SAS.

In the first line of verse 6, *yount* and *sùk* both literally mean "sincere". The idea here was that the king was not having his army beat up the inhabitants of *Sla* just to throw his weight around, but for their own ultimate good.

264

We Raise Our Eyes 瞻卬

We raise our eyes to Bright Sky, but it shows us no mercy.
For a very long time there has been no peace, with these great evils descending on us.
The state is at sixes and sevens: how officials and the common people are suffering!
Eelworms are gnawing away and undermining the body politic; there's no peace, no moderation.
Offenders are not being dealt with; there's no peace, and no prospect of cure.

Tam ngank Gòuc Thìn, tzùk pu ngàyc wìts.
Khònk drin pu nèng, kròungs tsec dàts rats.
Pròng mayc wuc dèngs—shuc min gu jèts!
Mou dzùk, mou dzit, mayc wuc luy krìts.
Dzòuyc kà pu hyou; mayc wuc luy rhiw.

瞻卬昊天　則不我惠
孔填不寧　降此大厲
邦靡有定　士民其瘵
蟊賊蟊疾　靡有夷屆
罪辜不收　靡有夷瘳

People own land and fields, but you come along and commandeer them.
People own their serfs, but you come along and snatch them for yourself.
Some people by rights are innocent, yet you have them arrested,
while other people by rights count as wrongdoers, yet you let them off.

Nin wuc thàc lìn, nac pant wuc tu.
Nin wuc min nin, nac phouk lòt tu.
Tsec ngay ma dzòuyc, nac pant hyou tu.
Payc ngay wuc dzòuyc, nac phouk lhòt tu.

人有土田　汝反有之
人有民人　汝覆奪之
此宜無罪　汝反收之
彼宜有罪　汝覆脫之

An able man builds up a city wall, but if a woman has ability, she overthrows the wall.
Your Majesty's lady is beautiful as well as intelligent—but she is a *hou*-bird, an owl.
Women have long tongues. It's they who instigate evil.
Strife isn't something Sky imposes on us: it's womenfolk who create it.
Unteachable, untrainable, that's women and eunuchs for you.

Trat pa deng geng; trat buc kwheng geng.
Its kot trat buc; way hou, way thi.
Buc wuc drang mlat, wi rats tu krì.
Ròns puyc kròungs dzis Thìn: sheng dzis buc nin.
Puyc kràws, puyc mhùs, dit wi buc slus.

哲夫成城　哲婦傾城
懿厥哲婦　為梟為鴟
婦有長舌　維厲之階
亂匪降自天　生自婦人
匪教匪誨　寔維婦寺

True, when they target someone with their malice and deceit, at first their troublemaking may be entirely rejected.
But how can you say "They're of no account, what harm can they really do"?
They do a roaring trade in their gossip. Gentlemen understand that,
which is why ladies are given no public roles, and stick to rearing silkworms and weaving.

Kouk nin kes lhùk, jums lhuc krangs bùks.
Khuyc wat "pu guk, i gà way nhùk"?
Na kàc sùm bùc. Kwun-tzuc dec lhuk,
buc ma kòng shuc, hou gu dzùm tuk.

鞫人忮忒　譖始竟背
豈曰不極　伊胡為慝
如賈三倍　君子是識
婦無公事　休其蠶織

What has Sky got against us? Why are the Spirits dissatisfied?
You're ignoring your serious responsibilities, in favour of stirring up dissension among us.
You have no consideration for distress, you don't encourage optimism, and your behaviour is unworthy of your position.
If people are fleeing the country, the nation will founder.

Thìn gày luc tseks? Gày mlin pu puks?   天何以刺　何神不富
Lhac nec krèts lhèk, wi lac sa gus.   舍爾介狄　維予胥忌
Pu dyàwk, pu syang, ouy-ngay pu routs.   不弔不祥　威儀不類
Nin tu wun mang, pròng kwùk dùnt dzouts.   人之云亡　邦國殄瘁

When Sky sends down disorder, how widely it spreads!
When people flee the country, it's a grief to the heart.
When Sky sends down disorder, how close we are to the brink!
When people flee the country, it's misery in the heart.

Thìn tu kròungs mank, wi gu ou luc!   天之降罔　維其優儀
Nin tu wun mang, sum tu ou luc.   人之云亡　心之憂矣
Thìn tu kròungs mank, wi gu kuy luc!   天之降罔　維其幾矣
Nin tu wun mang, sum tu pruy luc.   人之云亡　心之悲矣

The spring gushes forth noisily—how deep it is!
My heart is grief-stricken. Why did all this have to happen now?
Why couldn't it have happened before my time, or after I'm gone?
— But no-one is beyond the help of distant Bright Sky.
Don't disgrace your glorious ancestors, and you may yet save yourself.

Pit-put gàmp dzwan, wi gu nhum luc!   觱沸檻泉　維其深矣
Sum tu ou luc. Nèng dzis kum luc,   心之憂矣　寧自今矣
pu dzis ngàyc sùn, pu dzis ngàyc ghòc?   不自我先　不自我後
Mràwk-mràwk Gòuc Thìn: ma pu khùk konk.   邈邈昊天　無不克鞏
Ma lhèmp wàng tzàc, lhuk kous nec koung.   無忝皇祖　式救爾躬

This poem was composed as the Western *Tiw* dynasty was collapsing as a consequence of king *Iw*'s infatuation with *Bòu Sluc*. It was natural to blame the disaster on that lady, but the poet generalizes this into a remarkable diatribe against the entire female sex. Present-day readers will see this as inexcusable, which it doubtless is. On the other hand it is not unexplainable. A standing problem about the Chinese system of government throughout history was that there was no rigid rule of succession to the throne, as we have in Britain; when that was allied to polygamy, so that kings and later emperors had many wives who could all scheme to get their own sons onto the throne, it is easy to see that someone at the heart of government whose main concern was the welfare of the state might well develop a jaundiced view of the role of women. (The women's quarters at the palace were supervised by a corps of eunuchs, who inevitably got drawn into the women's scheming.) In verse 3, the "city wall" is a metaphor for any complex achievement of a society: the poet is saying that men use ability in order to build things up, women use it to undermine them.

In this and the next Ode, eelworms (see Ode 212) are a metaphor for delinquent officials, royal wives, or both.

I take "you" in the poem to be king *Iw* himself—which does not imply that the poet necessarily intended the king actually to see what he had written.

The last word in the received version of this Ode is not *koung* but *ghòc*, meaning that *Iw* is being offered the possibility of saving not his own position but that of his successors. Karlgren argues that this is likely to be a corruption of the original text; the arguments seem finely balanced, but I have accepted his emendation.

265

Raining Down Death 召旻

Sky is terrible in its severity, raining down death and destruction on a large scale,
putting us through the misery of famine. And our population is slipping away abroad,
so our settlements and border areas are all reverting to wasteland.

Mrun Thìn dzit-ouy; Thìn tòuk kròungs sangs,   旻天疾威　天篤降喪
tìn ngàyc kuy-gruns. Min tzout riw mang,   瘨我饑饉　民卒流亡
ngàyc kac ngac tzout mhàng.   我居圉卒荒

Sky is planting crime and guilt among us. Eelworms are sapping the integrity of government,
and the eunuchs have grown insubordinate.
Turbulent, wrongheaded, these are the people who are expected to keep peace in our land!

Thìn kròungs dzòuyc kà. Mou dzùk nòuts gòng,   天降罪罟　蟊賊內訌
mhùn-tròk mayc krong.   昏椓靡共
Gwùts-gwùts, wùy-wit, dit dzenk luy ngàyc pròng!   潰潰回遹　實靖夷我邦

Sunk in laziness and backbiting, they have no awareness of their own faults.
Things are fearsome, they are dreadful.
For a very long time there's been no peace, and our authority has been greatly reduced.

Kòu-kòu, tzec-tzec, tzùng pu tre gu tèmp.   皋皋訿訿　曾不知其玷
Kung-kung, ngap-ngap.   兢兢業業
Khònk drin pu nèng; ngàyc wruts khònk pramp.   孔填不寧　我位孔貶

Things are like a drought year, with crop plants scanty and not growing properly,
so that they resemble the dry stems in birds' nests.
I look at this nation, and see only turbulence.

Na payc swats gànt, tsòuc pu wuts mous,   如彼歲旱　草不潰茂
na payc sì tsa.   如彼棲苴
Ngàyc sangs tsec pròng, ma pu gwùts tuc.   我相此邦　無不潰止

The prosperity of the old days, now: what wasn't that like!
And the misery of the present: what isn't this like!
Then, people were satisfied with coarse food—now, they must have the finest. Why don't they just retire?
But far from it, they prolong this situation.

Wi sak tu puks: pu na du!   維昔之富　不如時
Wi kum tu dzit: pu na tzu!   維今之疚　不如茲
Payc sha, se brès. Gà pu dzis thìs?   彼疏斯粺　胡不自替
Tuk-hwangs se lint.   職況斯引

If a pool dries up, isn't that because nothing is flowing in from its banks?
If a spring dries up, isn't it because of a failure within it?
Well, this damage to the body politic is just getting worse:
won't it lead to calamity for us personally?

Dray tu gat luc, pu wun dzis bin?   池之竭矣　不云自頻
Dzwan tu gat luc, pu wun dzis troung?   泉之竭矣　不云自中
Bàk se gàts luc, tuk-hwangs se gwùng: 溥斯害矣　職況斯弘
pu tzù ngàyc koung?   不烖我躬

In the old days, when Sky conferred its mandate to rule on our past kings, they
    had men like the Duke of *Daws* to rely on.
He would extend the bounds of the state a hundred li in a day.
But now, the state contracts by a hundred li a day.
Alas and alack!
The men of today: would I not rather have those of yesteryear!

Sak sùn wang douc mreng, wuc na Daws klòng,   昔先王受命　有如召公
nit bek kwùk pràk ruc.   日闢國百里
Kum layc, nit tziwk kwùk pràk ruc.   今也日蹙國百里
À-ghà, ùy-tzù!   於乎哀哉
Wi kum tu nin: pu dangs wuc gwuc!   維今之人　不尚有舊

An Ode very similar in tone to the previous one, leading some to suggest that it was by the same poet at the same period; though here the criticisms are levelled not at the king but only at the courtiers serving him. The pool and the spring in verse 6 seem to stand for the fact that the state is being ruined both by depopulation of outlying areas (entailing loss of tax revenue) and also by misbehaviour at the heart of government.

The Eulogies

Eulogies of *Tiw*

266

The Pure Temple 清廟

Ah, how splendid is the pure temple! Its distinguished priests harmonize in solemn chorus.
August are the many officiants, holding fast by the "virtue" of *Mun*.
Antiphonally they celebrate those who dwell in the Sky; quickly they bustle about in the temple.
You highly illustrious, highly honoured ones, don't lose patience with us mortals!

À mouk tseng mraws, siwk ong hènt sangs.   於穆清廟　肅雝顯相
Tzìc-tzìc tày shuc, prank Mun tu tùk.   濟濟多士　秉文之德
Tòuts wat dzùc Thìn; tzyoungs pùn tzòc dzùc mraws.   對越在天　駿奔走在廟
Phru hènt, phru dung, ma lak wa nin se.   丕顯丕承　無射於人斯

As mentioned in the Introduction, many poems in the "Eulogies" section make little use of rhyme, and they contain many metrical irregularities.

267

Sky's Mandate 維天之命

Now, Sky's Mandate—ah, its glory never ceases.
Wahey, *Mun*, the supremely illustrious one: how great is his "virtue"!

Wi Thìn tu mreng, à mouk pu luc.   維天之命　於穆不已
À-ghà phru hènt, Mun Wang tu tùk tu doun.   於乎丕顯　文王之德之純

He loads us to overflowing with good fortune, and we reap the benefit.
Our *Mun*'s rule is secure, and his fame will be enhanced by even our remote descendants.

Kràc luc uk ngàyc, ngàyc kus hyou tu.   叚以溢我　我其收之
Tzyouns trits ngàyc Mun Wang, tzùng sòun tòuk tu.   駿惠我文王　曾孫篤之

268

Clear 維清

Clear, and continuously splendid, is the law code of *Mun*.
He instituted the sacrifices,
and through them we have achieved the fulfilment: the exaltation of *Tiw*.

Wi tseng tsup hu Mun Wang tu tùnt. 　　維清緝熙　文王之典
Drawc in, 　　肇禋
hut longs wuc deng: wi Tiw tu treng. 　　迄用有成　維周之禎

269

Brilliant and Accomplished 烈文

You brilliant and accomplished past rulers of *Tiw*, you've bestowed on us
　　blessings and prosperity.
Boundlessly you've favoured us; may your descendants maintain this heritage!

Rat mun pek klòng, slèk tzu thruc puk. 　　烈文辟公　錫茲祉福
Wìts ngàyc ma kang. Tzuc sòun pòuc tu. 　　惠我無疆　子孫保之

There is no fief but what belongs to your domain: it is the king who grants them.
We remember your achievements, and unceasingly we revere them.

Ma pong mayc wa nec pròng: wi wang gu djoung tu. 　　無封靡于爾邦　維王其崇之
Nìms tzu noung kòng, kès slac gu wàng tu. 　　念茲戎功　繼序其皇之

Is the Sole Man not strong! The whole world obeys him.
Is his character not illustrious! The vassal rulers all model themselves on him.
Ah, our former kings will never be forgotten.

Ma gung Wi Nin! Slits Pang gu hwuns tu. 　　無競維人　四方其訓之
Pu hènt wi tùk! Pràk pek gu gèng tu. 　　不顯維德　百辟其刑之
À-ghà, dzèn wang pu mang. 　　於乎前王不忘

For "the Sole Man", compare Ode 256.

270

Sky Made a Hill 天作

Sky made a high hill, and *Tànt* found that area spacious.
He felled the woods.
Mun found the site pleasing.
He cleared the ground.
Now the mount *Ge* area has good roads.
May the descendants preserve them!

Thìn tzàk kàw shàn, Thàts wang mhàng tu.	天作高山　太王荒之
Payc jàk luc.	彼柞矣
Mun wang khàng tu.	文王康之
Payc djac luc.	彼徂矣
Ge wuc luy tu gràng.	岐有夷之行
Tzuc sòun pòuc tu!	子孫保之

For *Tànt*, alias *Thàts wang*, see pp. 7–8.

271

The First Three Kings 昊天有成命

Bright Sky had a well-defined Mandate, which was received by the Two Sovereigns.
King *Deng* didn't presume to relax:
morning and evening he laid the foundations of the Mandate—large-minded yet unassertive, oh, his splendour was continuous.
He had a generous heart, and so he brought about peace.

Gòuc Thìn wuc deng mreng, Nits Gòs douc tu.	昊天有成命　二后受之
Deng wang pu kàmp khàng:	成王不敢康
souk yas ku mreng, wus mrit à tsup hu.	夙夜基命　宥密於緝熙
Tàn kot sum, sits kus dzenk tu.	單厥心　肆其靖之

The "Two Sovereigns" were *Mun* and *Mac*. *Deng* was *Mac*'s son and successor.

272

We Present Our Offerings 我將

We present our sacrificial offerings—a ram and a bull.
May Sky value them!

Ngàyc tzang ngàyc hang, wi yang wi ngwu. 我將我享　維羊維牛
Wi Thìn gu wus tu! 維天其右之

It is proper that we follow the rites of *Mun*, so as daily to ensure peace throughout the world.
The great *Mun* has valued and enjoyed our offerings.

Ngay lhuk gèng Mun wang tu tùnt, nit dzenk Slits Pang. 儀式形文王之典　日靖四方
I kràc Mun wang, kuts wus hang tu. 伊嘏文王　既右享之

May we, night and day, be awed by the majesty of Sky,
and constantly secure its favours.

Ngàyc gu souk yas ouys Thìn tu ouy, 我其夙夜　畏天之威
wa duc pòuc tu. 于時保之

Sung at the royal court during the annual ritual marking the return of winter.

273

The Tour of Inspection 時邁

He is making his regular tour of inspection through his fiefs—may Bright Sky cherish him as its son!
Sky has truly supported and bestowed the succession on the House of *Tiw*
—indeed, if the king has to call them to order, not one of his vassals fails to quake with fear.
He looks after the many Spirits and leads them to be gentle with us, even those of the Yellow River and the Holy Peak.
The king is sovereign indeed.
Bright and glorious, the House of *Tiw* has succeeded to the throne.
And so now we collect up shields and halberds, and we return bows and arrows to their cases.
We seek out solid virtue, in order to spread it throughout these Home States.
We can rely on the king to protect us.

Duc mràts gu pròng—Gòuc Thìn gu tzuc tu!　　時邁其邦　昊天其子之
Dit wus slac Wuc Tiw　　寔右序有周
—bàk-ngan tuns tu, màk pu tuns lèp.　　薄言震之　莫不震疊
Gròuy nou pràk mlin, gup Gày Gaw Ngròk.　　懷柔百神　及河喬嶽
Yount wang wi gòs.　　允王維后
Mrang tyawc Wuc Tiw lhuk slac dzùc wruts.　　明昭有周　式序在位
Tzùs jup kàn kwày, tzùs kòu kwung lhic.　　載戢干戈　載櫜弓矢
Ngàyc gou its tùk, sits wa du Ghàc.　　我求懿德　肆于時夏
Yount wang pòuc tu.　　允王保之

274

Awesome and Mighty　執競

Awesome and mighty was king *Mac*—was his energy not mighty!
Very illustrious were *Deng* and *Khàng*—God on High made them kingly.

Tep gung Mac wang—ma gung wi rat!　　憼競武王　無競維烈
Phru hènt Deng Khàng—Dyangs Tès dec wàng.　　丕顯成康　上帝是皇

From the time of those kings *Deng* and *Khàng*, our rule has spread throughout the world.
Their intelligence was clear-sighted.

Dzis payc Deng Khàng, amp wuc Slits Pang;　　自彼成康　奄有四方
kuns-kuns gu mrang.　　斤斤其明

Bells and drums boom, flutes and musical stones shrill out.
Blessings in full measure are bestowed on us.

Tong kàc hwàng-hwàng, khèngs kònt tsang-tsang.　　鐘鼓喤喤　磬筦將將
Kròungs puk nank-nank.　　降福穰穰

Blessings of great magnitude are bestowed on us; our dignity is pre-eminent.
And now we are sozzled with drink and stuffed with food. May blessings and prosperity come to us ever and again!

Kròungs puk krènt-krènt; ouy-ngay prànt-prànt.　　降福簡簡　威儀反反
Kuts tzouts, kuts pròuc. Puk ròk rù pant.　　既醉既飽　福祿來反

Deng and *Khàng* were the second and third *Tiw* kings, reigning respectively from 1037 to 1006 and 1005 to 978.

Many of us today might see verse 4 as contradictory, with its references to great dignity paired with carousing. But I think our Viking forebears of a thousand years ago might have seen no contradiction, and they perhaps offer a better analogy than the sober 21st century for the society of the early *Tiw*.

VOICES FROM EARLY CHINA

275

The Millet Lord 思文

Oh, you accomplished Millet Lord, you are worthy of your place alongside Sky itself.
You provided our multitudes with the staff of life—all that is your achievement.
You have given us wheat and barley.
God ordained that all should be nourished,
irrespective of boundaries and narrow frontiers such as this:
the way of life you initiated has been spread throughout these Home States.

Su mun Gòs Tzuk, khùk phùts payc Thìn.	思文后稷　克配彼天
Rup ngàyc tung min, màk puyc nec guk.	粒我烝民　莫匪爾極
Lu ngàyc mrùk mou.	貽我麥麰
Tès mreng shout louk,	帝命率育
ma tsec kang nec krèts:	無此疆邇界
drin dyang wa du Ghàc.	陳常于時夏

One of the royal rituals was a sacrifice at the border of *Tiw* to the Millet Lord; this poem was probably recited as part of that ritual. The point of the closing lines is to assert the legitimacy of *Tiw* rule over the vassal states.

276

Ministers and Officials 臣工

Now, you ministers and officials, be attentive while you are at court.
The king's assigning your tasks: come and discuss them, come and plan.
Now, you assistants, it's late spring,
so what are you waiting for? How are the new fields and the established fields looking?
"Oh, the wheat and barley plants are in fine shape—we can look forward to reaping their golden bounty."
God on High is bright;
we've reached a year that's going to give us the benefit of an abundant harvest, so pass the word to our serfs:
"Get to work with your hoes now, so in due course we see sickles reaping everywhere".

Tzay-tzay gin kòng, krengs nec dzùc klòng.	嗟嗟臣工　敬爾在公
Wang ru nec deng; rù tzi, rù nas.	王釐爾成　來咨來茹
Tzay-tzay pòuc krèts, wi thoun tu màks,	嗟嗟保介　維春之莫
yak wus gày gou? Na gày sin la?	亦又何求　如何新畬
À, wàng mrùk mou—tzang douc kot mrang.	於皇麥车　將受厥明

349

VOICES FROM EARLY CHINA

Mrang tyaw Dyangs Tès;
hut longs khàng nìn, mreng ngàyc toungs nin:
"Dru nùc tzant pàk, amp kwàn trit ngàts".

明昭上帝
迄用康年　命我眾人
持乃錢鎛　奄觀銍刈

I have ventured to amend the received text at two points. In the last line, where my text has *dru*, "to grasp", the received text has *druc*, written similarly in Chinese, which means "to prepare" or "to store"—but hoes scarcely need to be prepared before use, and storing them away is the opposite of what is needed in late spring. For that matter, although line 3 is accepted as referring to late spring, and *thoun tu màks*, "spring's evening", might be a reasonable way to express that, the received text has the phrase the other way round —"evening's spring"—which makes no obvious sense. I guess that the words somehow got switched; switching them back makes *màks* a near-rhyme to *nas* in the line above, and to *ngàts* in the last line.

277

Woo-hoo!　噫嘻

Woo-hoo, king *Deng*! He's come among us in glory,
leading our farmers in sowing their many kinds of grain.
Be quick to turn the first sod of your private fields, throughout our thirty li!
Be magnificent in putting your hands to the plough! May each pair of ploughmen
　　reap a hundredfold harvest!

U-hu Deng wang! Kuts kyawc kràc nec,
shout du nòung pa, pàys kot pràk kòk.
Tzyouns pat nec si, toung sùm gip ruc!
Yak buk nec krèng, gip tsìn wi ngòc!

噫嘻成王　既昭假邇
率時農夫　播厥百穀
駿發爾私　終三十里
奕服爾耕　十千維耦

The ruler was held to have responsibility and power over the harvest.

Gip tsìn, "ten thousand", in the last line does not mean the number 10,000—Chinese had (and has) a single word for that. It means "may the ratio of harvested grain to seed sown be a hundredfold" (let ten be a thousand). The thirty li (about ten miles) is presumably the size of whatever community this poem sprang from.

278

A Flock of Herons　振鷺

A majestic flock of herons is on the wing over the western town moat.
Our guests have arrived, resembling the birds in appearance.

Tun ràks wa puy wa payc sì ong.
Ngàyc khràk rìts tuc, yak wuc se long.

振鷺于飛　于彼西邕
我客戾止　亦有斯容

Wherever you look, there's nothing for the ancestors to dislike, for them to find unappealing.
May we be on hand morning and night, so their praise is maintained perpetually.

Dzùc payc ma àks; dzùc tsec ma lak.
Lhaks-kuy souk yas, luc wrank toung las.

在彼無惡　在此無斁
庶幾夙夜　以永終譽

The poem is set in a temple where a ritual sacrifice is about to take place—the third line is saying that the offerings will be perfectly acceptable to the ancestors. The comparison between human guests and birds is intended as flattering: the heron in question is the Eastern great egret, *Ardea alba modesta*, renowned for pure white plumage and elegant movement.

279

A Bumper Harvest 豐年

It's a bumper harvest, with abundant millet and rice,
and we have full granaries, holding tens of thousands, hundreds of thousands, indeed, millions of measures of grain.
We make wine and must to offer to the male and female ancestors,
so as to fulfil the many requirements of ritual. Very full blessings are bestowed on us.

Phoung nìn, tày nhac, tày làc,
yak wuc kàw rump: màns, uk, gup tzic.
Way tziwc, way rìc, tung pits tzàc pis,
luc grùp pràk rìc. Kròungs puk khònk krìc.

豐年多黍多稌
亦有高廩　萬億及秭
為酒為醴　烝畀祖妣
以洽百禮　降福孔皆

280

Blind Musicians 有瞽

There are blind men, blind musicians, at the *Tiw* court.
They've installed the posts and crosspieces of the bell-frames, complete with their dogtooth finials and upright plumes.
They've set up the drums—the small introducing and answering drums, the large suspended drums, and the hand drums—the musical stones, the rattles, and the tiger-shaped clappers.
Now all is ready, and the music starts.

Flutes and pan-pipes are raised to the musicians' lips and shrill out
—solemnly and harmoniously they blend their notes. The Ancestors are listening with us.
Our guests have arrived and settled down, and they watch the musicians' performance to the end.

Wuc kàc, wuc kàc, dzùc Tiw tu lèng. 有瞽有瞽　在周之庭
Nhet ngap, nhet gac, djoung ngrà, dos wac, 設業設虡　崇牙樹羽
ungs, lins, gwèn kàc, làw, khèngs, thouk, ngac. 應田縣鼓　鞉磬柷敔
Kuts bruks nùc tzòs. 既備迺奏
Sìw kònt bruks klac, hwàng-hwàng kot hyeng; 簫管備舉　喤喤厥聲
siwk ong wày mreng. Sùn tzàc dec lhèngs. 肅雝和鳴　先祖是聽
Ngàyc khràk rìt tuc; wrank kwàn kot deng. 我客戾止　永觀厥成

As noted with Ode 242, musicians were traditionally blind men. *Gac* were the uprights (called *kha* in that Ode) supporting the horizontal *ngap* or *swint* from which bells and drums were hung, and these frames were decorated somehow with dogtooth shapes, *djoung ngrà*, and *dos wac*—"tree feathers", upright plumes.

281

In the Depths 潛

Ah, the depths of the *Tsit* and the *Tzas* are teeming with fish.
There are sturgeon, there are switchtails, there are chub, catfish, and carp.
We offer them as sacrifices to the Spirits, and thus our great good fortune increases.

Ay, la Tsit Tzas, dzem wuc tày nga. 猗與漆沮　潛有多魚
Wuc tran, wuc wruc, lìw, dyang, ant, ruc. 有鱣有鮪　鰷鱨鰋鯉
Luc hang, luc sluc, luc krèts krank puk. 以享以祀　以介景福

On the rivers named, see Ode 180.

282

My Godlike Father 雝

People are coming, in fellowship; they arrive and assemble, solemnly.
Rulers and princes are in attendance; Sky's Son is august, saying:

Wuc rù ong-ong; tits tuc siwk-siwk. 有來雝雝　至止肅肅
Sangs wi pek klòng; Thìn Tzùc mouk-mouk. 相維辟公　天子穆穆

"Now, we are offering up a fat bull—help me to set out the sacrificial offerings.
Great, indeed, was my godlike father. He inspires me, his dutiful son."

"A, tzùns kwànk mouc—sangs lac sits sluc. 　　於薦廣牡　相予肆祀
Kràc tzù wàng khòuc. Snouy lac, hràws tzuc." 　假哉皇考　綏予孝子

"He was a man of all-embracing wisdom. In peace and in war he was every inch a sovereign.
He pleased even divine Sky; and he will be able to bestow prosperity on his descendants."

"Swan trat wi nin; mun mac wi gòs. 　　　　宣哲維人　文武維后
Èns gup wàng Thìn, khùk k'hlang kot ghòc." 　燕及皇天　克昌厥後

"He cheers me with a vigorous old age, and bestows blessings on me in abundance.
And so I am here to invite my brilliant late father, and my refined mother, to partake of these sacrificial offerings."

"Snouy ngàyc muyc douc, kràts luc ban thruc. 　綏我眉壽　介以繁祉
Kuts wus rat khòuc, yak wus mun muc." 　　　既右烈考　亦右文母

The funeral eulogy for *Mun*. By the time of Confucius in the decades around 500, when the vassal states were moving towards independence from *Tiw* rule, in Confucius's home state of *Ràc* one self-important clan was using this Ode in its own rituals, which disgusted the sage: " 'Rulers and princes are in attendance; Sky's Son is august'—how can that apply in *their* family temple?"

283

Appearing Before the Rulers　載見

They appear before the rulers and the kings, looking to be granted their insignia of rank.
Dragon flags gleam in the sunshine; bells on the carriages and flagpoles tinkle.
Metal-studded reins jingle loudly. The bright splendour is wonderful to behold.

Tzùs gèns pek wang, wat gou kot tang. 　　載見辟王　曰求厥章
Rong guy lang-lang; wày rèng rrang-rrang. 　龍旂陽陽　和鈴央央
Lìw rùk wuc tsang. Hou wuc rat kwàng. 　　鞗勒有鶬　休有烈光

They are led before the forefather of the even row, in order to demonstrate filial respect and make sacrifice-offerings,
and so that vigorous old age might be bestowed on them. Long may they preserve that vigour.

Magnificent are the many favours they receive. The brilliant and refined ancestral rulers and princes
hearten them with many blessings, so they're continually bright in their great felicity.

Shout gèns dyaw khòuc, luc hràws, luc hang,   率見昭考 以孝以享
luc krèts muyc douc. Wrank ngan tu pòuc.   以介釁壽 永言之保
Su wàng tày gàc. Rat mun pek klòng   思皇多祜 烈文辟公
snouy luc tày puk, pec tsup hu wa doun kràc.   綏以多福 俾緝熙于純嘏

Vassal rulers attend the *Tiw* ancestral temple to pay their respects to the ancestors of the royal family, who included both recent ancestors who were *wang*, kings, and earlier ancestors who were *pek*, rulers of states but not kings of China. The tablets representing successive *Tiw* rulers were arranged in two rows in the temple, called *dyaw* and *mouk* and comprising respectively even-numbered and odd-numbered descendants of the ultimate ancestor, the Millet Lord. The "forefather of the even row" here was king *Mac*: counting the Millet Lord as 1, *Mac* was sixteenth in line of succession. The vassal rulers will in many cases have been descendants of *Mac* or of his clan, hence owed him not just the respect due to a past king but also *hràws*, filial piety.

In the second line of verse 2, the received text ends with the words *pòuc tu*, but I suspect these words originally occurred in the reverse order as I show them, which gives better rhyming as well as good Old Chinese grammar.

284

I Have a Guest 有客

I have a guest, I have a guest, and his horses are greys.
The men of his retinue are numerous, they are many, and their features look carved, look engraved.

Wuc khràk, wuc khràk, yak bràk gu mràc.   有客有客 亦白其馬
Wuc tsì, wuc tza, tòuy tròk gu rac.   有萋有且 敦琢其旅

I have a guest who stays one night, he stays another night.
I give him ropes to hobble his horses.

Wuc khràk souk-souk; wuc khràk sins-sins.   有客宿宿 有客信信
Ngan dous tu trup, luc trup gu mràc.   言授之縶 以縶其馬

And now I escort him further on his journey, attending to his needs and keeping him merry.
He's a man of immense dignity. May Sky bestow good fortune and great peace on him.

Bàk-ngan trouy tu, tzàys wus snouy tu.   薄言追之 左右綏之
Kuts wuc lum ouy. Kròungs puk khònk luy.   既有淫威 降福孔夷

VOICES FROM EARLY CHINA

There is a traditional interpretation of this poem which purports to use the colour of the horses as a clue to the identity of the guest; and that interpretation might explain why the poem has been placed in this section of the *Odes*, where it does not obviously fit. But we should probably accept the wording for what it is and no more.

The "carved" features are a Chinese simile for a refined appearance—as handsome men's features are described in English as "chiselled".

285

King *Mac* 武

Ah, *Mac*, how godlike you are—your brilliance, is it not powerful!
And *Mun* was as accomplished as his name implies: he succeeded in opening the path for you, his successor.
As *Mun*'s heir you, *Mac*, received Sky's mandate; you conquered *Un* and ended its murderous cruelty.
Our stable régime was your achievement.

À, wàng Mac wang—ma gung wi rat! 　　於皇武王　無兢維烈
Yount mun Mun wang: khùk khùy kot ghòc. 　　允文文王　克開厥後
Slus Mac douc tu: lhungs Un àt rou. 　　嗣武受之　勝殷遏劉
Kic dèngs nec kòng. 　　耆定爾功

286

Have Pity for Me, a Small Boy 閔予小子

Have pity for me, a small boy; to me has come a house incompletely built.
I'm helpless, alone, and in distress.
Ah me, my august late father: generation after generation of descendants will rightly revere you.

Mrunt lac syawc tzuc; tzòu krà pu dzòuc. 　　閔予小子　遭家不造
Gweng-gweng dzùc kwus. 　　嬛嬛在疚
À-ghà, wàng khòuc: wrank lhats khùk hràws. 　　於乎皇考　永世克孝

I think of our august ancestors, who ascend and descend to the court.
I, a small boy, will revere them morning and night.

Nìms tzu wàng tzàc, truk kròungs lèng tuc. 　　念茲皇祖　陟降庭止
Wi lac syawc tzuc souk yas krengs tuc. 　　維予小子　夙夜敬止

Ah me, august king: you will ever be remembered and never forgotten.

À-ghà, wàng wang: kès slac su pu mang. 　　於乎皇王　繼序思不忘

The poet puts these words into the mouth of the boy-king *Deng* (see p. 8). It was only through his uncle's efforts that the *Tiw* dynasty became firmly established, hence the "incomplete house".

The spirit of a dead king ascended to live in (or with) Sky, but descended to earth to supervise his descendants and receive their sacrificial offerings.

287

My Late Father 訪落

I study the example of my late father: I model myself on that excellent occupant of the even row.
Ah me, how distressed I am; so far I've not seen order in the land.
If in time I do come that far, I shan't be a responsible grown-up even then.
I'm just a small boy, not yet equal to the many problems besetting our family.
—But then, at court the Spirits continue to rise and descend, going up to Sky and down to visit their House.
Rest in peace, my august late father—may he protect my body and enlighten my mind.

Phangs lac ràk tuc: shout du dyaw khòuc. 　訪予落止　率時昭考
À-ghà, ou tzù; Drunk muts wuc ngats. 　於乎憂哉　朕未有乂
Tzang lac dzous tu, kès you phàns-hwàns. 　將予就之　繼猶判渙
Wi lac syawc tzuc, muts khùm krà tày nàns. 　維予小子　未堪家多難
—Dawc lèng dyank gràs, truk kròungs kot krà. 　紹庭上下　陟降厥家
Hou luc wàng khòuc—luc pòuc mrang gu lhin. 　休矣皇考　以保明其身

Again written in the persona of *Deng*. This poet makes it very explicit that a boy king is speaking about another king: in the first line he uses the word *ràk*, which originally referred to leaves falling from a tree in autumn but came to be used for the death of kings, and in the second line for "I, me" he uses the word *Drunk*, the "royal we" which only rulers used. For the "even-numbered row" see Ode 283.

288

Be Reverent 敬之

Be reverent, be reverent: Sky is bright
—though oh, its Mandate is not easy. Don't say "But Sky is far away up there";
Sky's business brings it down as well as up, every day Sky inspects us down here.
I'm just a small boy, neither clever nor well-behaved,

but each day I make progress, each month I advance; I learn from those who are enlightened.
Great is this burden on my shoulder, but Sky shows me the bright path of virtue.

Krengs tuc, krengs tuc: Thìn wi hènt su   敬止敬止 天維顯思
—mreng pu leks tzù. Ma wat "Kàw-kàw dzùc dyangs";   命不易哉 無曰高高在上
truk kròungs kot shuc, nit kràm dzùc tzu.   陟降厥事 日監在茲
Wi lac syawc tzuc, pu tsòng krengs tuc,   維予小子 不聰敬止
nit dzous, ngwat tzang; gròuk wa kwàng mrang.   日就月將 學于光明
But du tzu kèn, gis ngàyc hènt tùk gràng.   佛時仔肩 示我顯德行

We saw on p. 20 that "bright" is a key idea in the *Odes*, hard to translate. In the first line here the poet is saying much more than "it's a sunny day"—that is an outward token of the fact that the Almighty is splendid and deserves reverence.

The received text of this poem has some large deviations from the usual four-word metre. The fourth and tenth stichs are respectively six and seven words long, and the closing stich has five words. There is no obvious explanation in terms of unstressed words. It seems understandable for the last stich to be special, but in the other cases I suspect the text may have been corrupted at some stage. In the tenth stich the received text does not even look grammatical, and I have ventured to omit three words which seem redundant, but I have not been bold enough to do anything similar with the fourth stich.

289

Nobody Made Me Do It 小毖

After punishment like that, I need to guard against further disasters.
Nobody made me get stung: I sought that bitter pain out all by myself.
Those wrens are nimble indeed, they fly up and wheel around, being birds.
But I'm not yet equal to the many problems besetting our family, and I'm left down here sitting amid the arse-smart.

Lac kus drung, nu pits ghòc gròns.   予其懲 而毖後患
Màk lac phrèng phong: dzis gou sin lhak.   莫予荓蜂 自求辛螫
Drawc yount payc làw droung, phan puy wi tìw.   肇允彼桃蟲 翻飛維鳥
Muts khùm krà tày nàns, lac wus dzup wa rìwc.   未堪家多難 予又集于蓼

We know nothing about what lies behind this little poem. The stich about "problems besetting our family" suggests some connexion with Ode 287 where the identical words occur, and traditionally it was taken that the "I" of this Ode is again the boy king.

Arse-smart is another name for the water-pepper plant, *Persicaria hydropiper*: it was laid in beds to kill fleas, but it stings bare skin.

290

When We Come to Plough 載芟

First we scythe down the grass and clear away the shrubs and trees, and then the plough lays open the soil, furrow after furrow.
A thousand [... ... ...], working down to the edges of the wetlands and the raised field-paths.
All are here: heads of families, eldest sons, younger sons, and the rest of their menfolk,
volunteers and hirelings. An endless stream of women carry lunch bowls out to us.
Lovely are the women, sturdy are the men,
and sharp are the ploughshares. We begin with the southern acres.
We sow the many kinds of grain—seeds that contain life within them.
The shoots break through the soil in abundance: each stem is healthy
—indeed all the sprouts are in fine shape. Men with hoes weed them, strung out across the field, one to each row of plants.
Then a crowd of reapers harvest the crop, heaping the grain up in rich stacks.
Tens of thousands of measures, hundreds of thousands, become millions. It will be turned into wine and must
to offer to our forefathers and foremothers, so as to fulfil the many requirements of ritual.
Its odour is very sweet, the glory of our state and dynasty.
Its fragrance is like the pepper plant, and it offers peace to those who've reached extreme old age.
All these activities are not something we do for the moment, temporarily—it isn't that we do them just now, for the time being:
from ancient times, things have always been so.

Tzùs shàm, tzùs jàk; gu krèng lhak-lhak.
Tsìn ngòc gu wun, dzà slup, dzà tunt.
Gò toc, gò pràk, gò rràks, gò rac,
gò gang, gò luc. Wuc rhùmp kus wap.
Su mouys kus buc; wuc uy kus shuc;
wuc rak kus sluc. Thiwk tzùs nùm mùc.
Pàys kot pràk kòk, dit gùm se gwàt.
Lak-lak kus dàt, wuc ems gu gat.
Ems-ems gu maw. Ment-ment kus paw.
Tzùs gwàk tzìc-tzìc, wuc mlit gu tzeks.
Màns, uk gup tzic. Way tziwc, way rìc,
tung pits tzàc pis, luc grùp pràk rìc.
Wuc bìt gu hang, pròng krà tu kwàng.
Wuc tziw gu hèng; grà khòuc tu nèng.
Puyc tsac wuc tsac, puyc kum se kum:
tuns kàc na tzu.

載芟載柞　其耕澤澤
千耦其耘　徂隰徂畛
侯主侯伯　侯亞侯旅
侯彊侯以　有嗿其饁
思媚其婦　有依其士
有略其耜　俶載南畝
播厥百穀　實函斯活
驛驛其達　有厭其傑
厭厭其苗　綿綿其穗
載穫濟濟　有實其積
萬億及秭　為酒為醴
烝畀祖妣　以洽百禮
有飶其香　邦家之光
有椒其馨　胡考之寧
匪且有且　匪今斯今
振古如茲

I have left some words in the second line untranslated: assuming that they are original rather than a scribal corruption, I don't know what they mean and it seems to me that no-one else knows. *Ngòc* normally means a two-man ploughing team, but ploughs are expensive pieces of capital equipment, and it is unimaginable that hundreds of them could be in the field together. The dictionaries give *wun* as "to weed", but weeding between ploughing and sowing makes no sense; and, while a primitive plough might take two men to operate, there is no reason to team people together for weeding. Perhaps a thousand men might use rakes for a crude form of harrowing—but again why in pairs?

In line 4 *gang* is literally "strong", and the commentators say that it refers to men who had sufficient energy to help out with agriculture on top of their own jobs—"volunteers" as contrasted with hirelings.

Three lines from the end, I am not sure whether peace for the elderly means that they can relax, knowing that their society is provided for (since presumably much of the grain will be eaten, even though the poem focuses on its use to make wine), or whether pensioners were perhaps expected to spend their declining years quietly sozzled.

291

Sharp are our Ploughshares 良耜

Good and sharp are our ploughshares, as we begin ploughing the southern acres.
We sow the many kinds of grain—seeds that contain life within them.
Someone comes to see you, carrying basket and flute
—the basket has millet for lunch. How lovely she is in her bamboo hat!
Our hoes cut through the soil, clearing away the weeds.
The weeds are left to rot, while the millet flourishes.
Now the sickles are reaping, stroke upon stroke; and the sheaves are stored in
    dense stacks,
lofty as a wall, and tight-packed like the teeth of a comb.
And so the clan households are opened to receive the threshed grain.
Now the clan households are full, and wives and children can relax.
We slaughter this giant bull (his horns are very long and curved),
so as to imitate and continue—continue the life of the men of old.

Chuk-chuk rang sluc, thiwk tzùs nùm mùc.
Pàys kot pràk kòk—dit gùm se gwàt.
Wùk rù tam nac, tzùs kwhang gup kònt.
Gu nhank i nhac. Gu rup i gawc!
Gu pàk se dyàwc, luc hòu là rìwc.
Là rìwc houc tuc, nhac tzuk mous tuc.
Gwàk tu trit-trit, tzeks tu rit-rit,
gu djoung na long, gu bis na jit.
Luc khùy pràk lhit.
Pràk lhit leng tuc, buc tzuc nèng tuc.
Shàt du noun mouc, wuc gou gu kròk,
luc sluc, luc slok—slok kàc tu nin.

畟畟良耜　俶載南畝
播厥百穀　實函斯活
或來瞻汝　載筐及筥
其饟伊黍　其笠伊糾
其鎛斯趙　以薅荼蓼
荼蓼朽止　黍稷茂止
穫之挃挃　積之栗栗
其崇如墉　其比如櫛
以開百室
百室盈止　婦子寧止
殺時犉牡　有捄其角
以似以續　續古之人

So much here is word for word identical to passages in the previous Ode that wording must have been copied, whether by the original author or when memory was cudgelled to reconstruct the poems. *Pràk lhit*, literally "the hundred houses", is said by one commentator to refer to the households of a clan, who lived in a single moated compound and undertook agricultural work communally.

292

His Silken Robe 絲衣

How immaculate his silken robe; his cap is jewelled.
From the hall he goes to the ground floor of the gatehouse, from the mutton to the beef.
He inspects the cauldrons and the tripods, large and small—how long and curved is the wild-buffalo drinking horn!
The fine wine is soft on the tongue.
There are no raised voices, no clamour: just the calm of extreme old age.

Su uy gu phu; tzùs brans gwu-gwu.	絲衣其紑　載弁俅俅
Dzis dàng dzà ku, dzis yang dzà ngwu.	自堂徂基　自羊徂牛
Nùs tènk gup tzu—syuyc kwràng gu giw!	鼐鼎及鼒　兕觥其觩
Kic tziwc su nou.	旨酒思柔
Pu ngwà, pu ngàw: grà khòuc tu hou.	不吳不敖　遐考之休

"He" may have been an official connected with the organization of some feast or ritual sacrifice. What I translate as mutton and beef could have been the live animals waiting for slaughter.

293

Your Majesty's Army 酌

Oh, your majesty's army is splendid.
Over the time you developed it, it began as an obscure organization, but grew to be brilliant indeed,
so that now it's an outstanding force, which we regard with affection.
Your majesty has been warlike in your deeds, and hence they have endured.
Thanks to you this is a real army.

À, hyawk wang shi.	於鑠王師
Tzoun yank duc mhùc, duc doun hu luc,	遵養時晦　時純熙矣
dec longs dàts krèts. Ngàyc rhonk douc tu.	是用大介　我寵受之
Kawc-kawc wang tu dzòuc, tzùs longs wuc slus.	蹻蹻王之造　載用有嗣
Dit wi nec kòng yount shi.	寔維爾功允師

VOICES FROM EARLY CHINA

Ode 293 and the following three Odes (and also Ode 285) are thought to have belonged to an all-day balletic ritual celebrating *Mac*'s overthrow of *Un*; the ritual has been reconstructed in detail by Wang Guowei in an article I have not seen. One clue to this is that these Odes all have single-word traditional titles which (except in the case of Ode 285) seem unrelated to the poem content—respectively *tyawk* "ladle out wine", *wàn* "turn back", *rùks* "bestow a gift", and *bàn* "turn round", which could well label episodes in a ballet.

294

Every Inch a Warrior 桓

He brought peace to the many states, and provided a succession of bumper harvests.
He never treated Sky's mandate lightly.
King *Mac* was every inch a warrior. He protected and supported his officers.
He came to hold sway over the world, and successfully established his dynasty.
Oh, he was bright in the eyes of Sky, and majestically he succeeded to the throne.

Snouy màns pròng, ros phoung nìn.   綏萬邦　婁豐年
Thìn mreng puyc krès.   天命匪懈
Wàn-wàn Mac wang. Pòuc wus kot shuc.   桓桓武王　保右厥士
Wa luc Slits Pang, khùk dèngs kot krà.   于以四方　克定厥家
À, tyaw wa Thìn, wàng luc krèns tu.   於昭于天　皇以閒之

295

Abundance 賚

Mun exerted himself, and we receive the benefit.
He spread this abundance everywhere,
and now we go and seek to establish firmly this mandate of Sky's in favour of *Tiw*.
Oh, the abundance!

Mun wang kuts gun tuc, ngàyc ung douc tu.   文王既勤止　我膺受之
Pha du lak su,   敷時繹思
ngàyc dzà wi gou dèngs du Tiw tu mreng.   我徂維求定　時周之命
À, lak su.   於繹思

"Abundance" evidently means the preconditions for material welfare, namely peace and good government. *Mac*'s father *Mun* is seen as having created a potential for these things, which it is now for the generations after *Mac*'s conquest to make real and consolidate.

296

The Destiny of *Tiw* 般

Oh, this dynasty of *Tiw* is majestic! Climb that high mountain,
see the long ridges and lofty peaks; follow the rushing, roaring Yellow River:
the whole expanse spread out below the sky—for all of this, the dynasty is responsible.
This is the destiny of *Tiw*.

À, wàng du Tiw! Truk kus kàw shàn,
lòyc shàn gaw ngròk; yount you hup Gày:
pha thìn tu gràc—bòu du tu tòuts.
Du Tiw tu mreng.

於皇時周　陟其高山
隋山喬嶽　允由瀘河
敷天之下　裒時之對
時周之命

VOICES FROM EARLY CHINA

Eulogies of Ràc

Ràc was one of the easternmost states, based on modern Qufu, Shandong.

297

Sturdy are the Stallions 駉

Sturdy are the stallions out here in the wilds.
And these sturdy beasts include leopard-spotted horses and skewbalds, pure blacks and bays.
Between the shafts their feet pound the ground unceasingly.
These are fine horses.

Kwèng-kwèng mouc mràc dzùc kwèng tu lac.　　駉駉牡馬　在坰之野
Bàk-ngan kwèng tac: wuc wit, wuc wàng, wuc rè,　　薄言駉者　有驈有皇　有驪
　wuc gwàng.　　　　　　　　　　　　　　　　　　　　有黃
Luc ka pàng-pàng, su ma kang.　　　　　　　　　　以車彭彭　思無疆
Su mràc se tzàng.　　　　　　　　　　　　　　　　思馬斯臧

Sturdy are the stallions out here in the wilds.
And these sturdy beasts include grey-and-white horses, yellow-and-white, chestnuts and dappled greys.
Between the shafts they pull strongly for any length of time.
These are horses of quality.

Kwèng-kwèng mouc mràc dzùc kwèng tu lac.　　駉駉牡馬　在坰之野
Bàk-ngan kwèng tac: wuc touy, wuc phru, wuc seng,　薄言駉者　有騅有駓　有骍
　wuc gu.　　　　　　　　　　　　　　　　　　　　　有騏
Luc ka phru-phru, su ma gu.　　　　　　　　　　　以車伾伾　思無期
Su mràc se dzù.　　　　　　　　　　　　　　　　思馬斯才

Sturdy are the stallions out here in the wilds.
And these sturdy beasts include blue-black horses, white-spotted, and black-maned horses, both greys and bays.
Between the shafts they canter freely and untiringly.
These are powerful horses.

Kwèng-kwèng mouc mràc dzùc kwèng tu lac.　　駉駉牡馬　在坰之野
Bàk-ngan kwèng tac: wuc tèn, wuc ràk, wuc rou,　薄言駉者　有驒有駱　有騮
　wuc ràk.　　　　　　　　　　　　　　　　　　　　有駱
Luc ka lak-lak, su ma lak.　　　　　　　　　　　以車繹繹　思無斁
Su mràc se tzàk.　　　　　　　　　　　　　　　　思馬斯作

Sturdy are the stallions out here in the wilds.
And these sturdy beasts include piebalds and roans, horses with hairy legs and horses with fish-eyes.
Between the shafts they are strong, never swerving from their course.
These horses travel.

Kwèng-kwèng mouc mràc dzùc kwèng tu lac.   駉駉牡馬　在坰之野
Bàk-ngan kwèng tac: wuc in, wuc grà, wuc lèmp, wuc nga.   薄言駉者　有駰有騢　有驔有魚
Luc ka kha-kha, su ma sya.   以車祛祛　思無邪
Su mràc se dzà.   思馬斯徂

As we saw with Ode 128, we cannot be sure about the traditional glosses for the many Odes horse terms. *Nga*, "fish", is said by some to refer to coats which somehow resembled fish-scales, by others to mean some quality of the horses' eyes. In verse 3 we find *ràk*, defined as a white horse with a black mane, listed twice, which must suggest that something has gone amiss somewhere. (The received text avoids repetition by changing one of the graphs to another word also pronounced *ràk* but meaning some kind of bird: that must be wrong.) I have fitted the Chinese definitions onto English horse terms as best I can.

298

Solid and Strong   有駜

Very solid and strong—the team of bays is very solid and strong.
Morning and evening, courtiers attend the palace—they shine at the palace.
Herons are flocking: they fly down to the ground.
Intoxicated with the drumbeat, the courtiers dance, to the blended notes of music.

Wuc bit, wuc bit—bit payc mlungs gwàng.   有駜有駜　駜彼乘黃
Souk yas dzùc klòng—dzùc klòng mrang-mrang.   夙夜在公　在公明明
Tun-tun ràks: ràks wa gràc.   振振鷺　鷺于下
Kàc wwìn-wwìn, tzouts ngan mac, wa sa ngràwk ì.   鼓咽咽　醉言舞　于胥樂兮

Very solid and strong—the team of stallions is very solid and strong.
Morning and evening, courtiers attend the palace—they drink wine at the palace.
Herons are flocking: they're on the wing.
Stupefied by drums and drink, the courtiers stumble bedwards, to the blended notes of music.

Wuc bit, wuc bit—bit payc mlungs mouc.   有駜有駜　駜彼乘牡
Souk yas dzùc klòng—dzùc klòng um tziwc.   夙夜在公　在公飲酒
Tun-tun ràks: ràks wa puy.   振振鷺　鷺于飛
Kàc wwìn-wwìn, tzouts ngan kwuy, wa sa ngràwk ì.   鼓咽咽　醉言歸　于胥樂兮

Very solid and strong—the team of blue-black horses is very solid and strong.
Morning and evening, courtiers attend the palace—they feast at the palace.
From this time forth, how good the harvests are going to be!
Our prince is favoured by fortune, and transmits good fortune to his successors,
    to the blended notes of music.

Wuc bit, wuc bit—bit payc mlungs hwèns.　　有駜有駜　駜彼乘黃
Souk yas dzùc klòng—dzùc klòng tzùs èns.　　夙夜在公　在公載燕
Dzis kum luc lhuc, swats gu wuc!　　自今以始　歲其有
Kwun-tzuc wuc kòk, lu sòun tzuc, wa sa ngràwk ì.　　君子有穀　詒孫子　于胥樂
　　　　　　　　　　　　　　　　　　　　　　兮

The horses seem to be opening images detached from the rest of their verses, but the brilliant white herons are perhaps a metaphor for the flock of courtiers, "shining" in the sense discussed on p. 20.

299

The Half Moon Pool　泮水

Oh, the Half Moon Pool is pleasant; we gather watercress there.
The lord of *Ràc* is here. I see his dragon banners
—the banners are fluttering, and his harness-bells are jingling.
Great men and small all mingling together, we follow our ruler as he proceeds on
    his way.

Su ngràwks Phàns Lhouyc; bàk tsùc gu gun.　　思樂泮水　薄采其芹
Ràc gò rìts tuc. Ngan kwàn gu guy　　魯侯戾止　言觀其旂
—gu guy bàts-bàts, ròn hyeng hwàts-hwàts.　　其旂筏筏　鸞聲噦噦
Ma syauc ma dàts, dzong klòng wa mràts.　　無小無大　從公于邁

Oh, the Half Moon Pool is pleasant; we gather *tzàwc*-fern there.
The lord of *Ràc* is here. His horses are high-steppers.
His horses are high-steppers, and his renown is glorious.
Letting himself be seen and laughing, he gives us our orders in a cordial tone.

Su ngràwks Phàns Lhouyc; bàk tsùc gu tzàwc.　　思樂泮水　薄采其藻
Ràc gò rìts tuc. Gu mràc gawk-gawk.　　魯侯戾止　其馬蹻蹻
Gu mràc gawk-gawk, gu um tyawc-tyawc.　　其馬蹻蹻　其音昭昭
Tzùs shuk, tzùs saws, puyc nàc i kràws.　　載色載笑　匪怒伊教

Oh, the Half Moon Pool is pleasant; we gather water-shield there.
The lord of *Ràc* is here. By the Half Moon Pool he's drinking wine.
Thanks to the fine wine he has drunk, he'll enjoy a rare old age far into the
    future.
He took the distant road and subdued the tribal rabble.

Su ngràwks Phàns Lhouyc; bàk tsùc gu mròuc. 思樂泮水　薄采其茆
Ràc gò rìts tuc. Dzùc Phàns um tziwc. 魯侯戾止　在泮飲酒
Kuts um kic tziwc, wrank slèk nàn ròuc. 既飲旨酒　永錫難老
Mlouns payc drang lòuc, khout tsec gwun k'hyou. 順彼長道　屈此群醜

The lord of *Ràc* is splendid. He takes pains to polish his "virtue",
and to maintain his dignity. He's a model for his people to follow.
He's truly well-versed in the arts both of peace and of war, and in brightness he maintains the cult of his illustrious ancestors.
He omits his duties to none of them, and he asks their blessings on himself.

Mouk-mouk Ràc gò. Krengs mrang gu tùk, 穆穆魯侯　敬明其德
krengs dins ouy-ngay; wi min tu tzùk. 敬慎威儀　維民之則
Yount mun, yount mac. Tyaw kràc rat tzàc, 允文允武　昭假烈祖
mayc wuc pu hràws. Dzis gou i gàc. 靡有不孝　自求伊祐

The lord of *Ràc* is bright, and he has the ability to make his "virtue" bright.
He has built the Hall of the Half Moon Pool, where the *Wì*-river tribesmen come to make their obeisance.
His special forces were fierce: at the Half Moon Pool they presented him with his enemies' chopped heads.
His inquisitors were as skilled in interrogation as *Kòu Law*; at the Half Moon Pool they handed their prisoners over to him.

Mrang-mrang Ràc gò; khùk mrang gu tùk. 明明魯侯　克明其德
Kuts tzàk Phàns Koung, Wì Luy you buk. 既作泮宮　淮夷攸服
Kawc-kawc hlàc gin: dzùc Phàns nghans kwrùk. 蹻蹻虎臣　在泮獻馘
Diwk muns na Kòu Law: dzùc Phàns nghans syou. 淑問如皋陶　在泮獻囚

The corps of officials are impressive, knowing how to disseminate "virtuous" attitudes.
They mount expeditions to make the south-eastern tribes keep their distance.
Illustrious they are, and august. They never shout or raise their voices,
they don't brief against one another; at the Half Moon Pool they report their achievements.

Tzìc-tzìc tày shuc: khùk kwànk tùk sum. 濟濟多士　克廣德心
Wàn-wàn wa teng, lhèk payc tòng nùm. 桓桓于征　狄彼東南
Tung-tung, wàng-wàng. Pu ngwà, pu lang. 烝烝皇皇　不吳不揚
Pu kòuk wa hong; dzùc Phàns nghans kòng. 不告于訩　在泮獻功

How long and curved were the bows with their fittings of horn, how many the sheaves of arrows!
The war-chariots were imposing, the foot-soldiers and charioteers were tireless.
The *Wì*-river tribes have now been dealt with. They're wholly submissive, with no inclination to rebel.

Your tactics were resolute, Sire, and you vanquished the *Wì*-river tribes once and for all.

Kròk kwung kus giw, lhok lhic gu shou!　　角弓其觩　束矢其搜
Noung ka khònk pàk, dzongs ngas ma lak.　　戎車孔博　徒御無斁
Kuts khùk Wì Luy. Khònk diwk, pu ngrak.　　既克淮夷　孔淑不逆
Lhuk kàks nec you, Wì Luy tzout wàk.　　式固爾猶　淮夷卒獲

The owls' wings flutter overhead as they settle into the copse by the Half Moon Pool.
They eat our mulberries, but their lovely calls are a comfort to us.
From afar those *Wì*-river tribesmen arrive to hand over valuables as tribute:
giant tortoises, tusks of ivory; they surrender quantities of southern gold.

Phen payc puy waw, dzup wa Phàns rum.　　翩彼飛鴞　集于泮林
Mluk ngàyc sàng dump, gròuy ngàyc hòuc um.　　食我桑黮　懷我好音
Kwrank payc Wì Luy rù nghans gu nhrum　　憬彼淮夷　來獻其琛
—ngon kwru, syank k'hyuc; dàts ràks nùm kum.　　元龜象齒　大賂南金

The plants gathered in verses 1 to 3 are all aquatic, and the ones we can identify are edible; doubtless *tzàwc* was edible too, but we don't know exactly what this was (it is thought to have been some cryptogam). "Water-shield" is the English name for *Brasenia schreberi*, a plant with floating leaves rather like water-lilies.

In verse 5, for "special forces" see Ode 263. *Kòu Law* was appointed by the legendary predynastic emperor *Hwins* as Minister of Crime to deal with barbarian tribesmen, rebels, and so forth by administering the Five Punishments, which were branding, cutting off the nose, cutting off the feet, castration, and death.

The last word of the Ode, *kum*, could mean bronze, or "metals" generally, rather than gold.

300

The Temple of the Mysteries　閟宮

The temple of the Mysteries is wholly quiet now, solidly rebuilt, board upon board.
—Lady *Ngwan* of the *Kyang* clan was majestic, her character constant.
God on High made her fruitful.
With no accidents or injuries, completing her term and not overdue,
she gave birth to the Millet Lord. And he has bestowed a hundred blessings on us:
foxtail and broomcorn millet, slow-ripening and fast-ripening cereals, early-sown and late-sown grain, beans and wheat.
Far and wide he took command of the countries here below, and led their people to sow and to reap:
there were rich harvests of foxtail and broomcorn millet, of rice and of black

millet.

Far and wide he took command of the land here below, and built on the achievements of *Wac*.

Pits koung wuc hwuks, mlit-mlit, mùy-mùy.	閟宮有侐　實實枚枚
Hràk-hràk Kyang Ngwan; gu tùk pu wùy.	赫赫姜嫄　其德不回
Dyangs Tès dec uy.	上帝是依
Ma tzù, ma gàts, me ngwat pu dri.	無災無害　彌月不遲
Dec sheng Gòs Tzuk. Kròungs tu pràk puk:	是生后稷　降之百福
nhac, tzuk, dreng, rouk; truk, dris, nhouk, mrùk.	黍稷重穋　植稺菽麥
Amp wuc gràc kwùk, pec min kràs shuk.	奄有下國　俾民稼穡
Wuc tzuk, wuc nhac, wuc lòuc, wuc gac.	有稷有黍　有稻有秬
Amp wuc gràc thàc, tzònt Wac tu slac.	奄有下土　纘禹之緒

Tànt was a descendant of the Millet Lord,

and settled on the southern slopes of mount *Ge*. He it was who began the task of cutting *Un* down to size.

Then later, *Mun* and *Mac* took *Tànt*'s work further.

On Herdsman's Heath *Mac* put into effect the expiry of Sky's mandate.

(Don't lose faith, don't be anxious: God on High is watching over you.)

Mac rounded up the troops of *Un*,

and made a complete success of the mission he'd undertaken. And in due course his successor, king *Deng*, said "Uncle,

I'm setting up your eldest son as marquis in *Ràc*.

I'm conferring extensive territory on you, so you can be a bulwark to the house of *Tiw*."

Gòs Tzuk tu sòun, dit wi Thàts wang,	后稷之孫　寔維太王
kac Ge tu lang. Dit lhuc tzent Lhang.	居岐之陽　寔始翦商
Tits wa Mun Mac tzònt Thàts wang tu slac.	至于文武　纘太王之緒
Trits Thìn tu krìts wa Muk tu lac.	致天之居　于牧之野
(Ma nits, ma ngwa: Dyangs Tès rum nac.)	無貳無虞　上帝臨汝
Tòun Lhang tu rac,	敦商之旅
khùk grùm kots kòng. Wang wat "Nhouk bac,	克咸厥功　王曰叔父
kans nec ngon tzuc, pec gò wa Ràc.	建爾元子　俾侯于魯
Dàts khìc nec wac, way Tiw lhit bac."	大啟爾宇　為周室輔

And so *Deng* appointed the lord of *Ràc* to rule the East.

Deng bestowed on him hills and rivers, countryside and fields, with the serfs attached to them.

And now lord *Hu*, descendant of the Duke of *Tiw* and son of lord *Jang*,

arrives with dragon banners to offer sacrifice. His six reins are strong as sinews.

At spring and autumn rites he's never remiss, making the offerings faultlessly.

To Almighty God in his great glory, and to the glorious ancestor, the Millet Lord,

he sacrifices pure red animals. The Spirits enjoy the sacrifices, they approve them.

You have already received from them blessings in goodly number,

and your glorious ancestor, the Duke of *Tiw*, he too will bestow blessings on you.

Nùc mreng Ràc klòng pec gò wa tòng.	乃命魯公　　俾侯于東
Slèk tu shàn, k'hloun, thàc, lìn, bos long.	錫之山川　　土田附庸
Tiw klòng tu sòun, Jang klòng tu tzuc,	周公之孫　　莊公之子
rong guy dung sluc. Rouk prus nus-nus.	龍旂承祀　　六轡耳耳
Thoun tsiw puyc krès, hang sluc pu lhùk.	春秋匪懈　　享祀不忒
Wàng-wàng gòs Tès, wàng tzàc Gòs Tzuk,	皇皇后帝　　皇祖后稷
hang luc seng nghay. Dec hang, dec ngay.	享以騂犧　　是饗是宜
Kròungs puk kuts tày;	降福既多
Tiw klòng wàng tzàc yak gu puk nac.	周公皇祖　　亦其福汝

In autumn we carry out the "tasting" sacrifice, having in summer fixed guard-bars
to the horns of the white bull and the red bull. The sacrificial *tzòun* vase is imposing.
There are a hog roast, minced meats, and broth, served in *pèn* baskets and *dòs* bowls and on the great carcass-stand.
The scorpion dance is magnificent, filling the ancestor-respecting *Hu* with joy.
May you flourish in glory and live long and well,
guarding the East. Your state of *Ràc* will last for ever,
not suffering harm, not collapsing—never shaken, never conquered.
And you will be a counterpart of those who lived three lifetimes, enduring like the mountain ridges, like the peaks.

Tsiw nu tzùs dyang; gràs nu pruk-gràng	秋而載嘗　　夏而楅衡
pràk mouc, seng kàng. Nghay tzòun tzang-tzang.	白牡騂犅　　犧尊將將
Màw bròu, jus, kràng; pèn, dòs, dàts bang.	毛炰胾羹　　籩豆大房
Màns mac yang-yang, hràws sòun wuc khrang,	萬舞洋洋　　孝孫有慶
pec nec thuks nu k'hlang, pec nec douc nu tzàng,	俾爾熾而昌　　俾爾壽而臧
pòuc payc tòng pang. Ràc pròng dec dyang:	保彼東方　　魯邦是常
pu kwhay, pu pùng, pu tuns, pu lùng.	不虧不崩　　不震不騰
Sùm douc tzàk bùng—na kàng, na rung.	三壽作朋　　如岡如陵

My lord's chariots number a thousand,
each with two red-ornamented lances, and two green-banded bows.
My lord's foot-soldiers number thirty thousand, in their red-threaded cowrie helmets
—so numerous are his foot-soldiers. You lords of *Ràc* held firm against attacks by the *Noung* and *Lèk* tribes,
and brought the *Kreng* and *Lha* tribes to heel, so now none dare face us in battle.
The ancestors will ensure that you flourish in glory, living long and happily,
until your hair is grey and your back is bowed as round as a pufferfish. You and your successors will vie with one another in length of life.
The ancestors will ensure that you flourish in greatness, and grow so old that your hair will be quite white.
You will live ten thousand years and then thousands more, enjoying vigorous, unimpaired old age.

Klòng ka tsin mlungs:
to rrang, rok lùng, nits mou, drong kwung.
Klòng dà sùm màns, pàts driws to sam.
Tung dà tzùng-tzùng. Noung, Lèk, dec ung,
Kreng, Lha, dec drung, tzùk màk ngàyc kàmp dung.
Pec nec k'hlang nu thuks, pec nec douc nu puk,
gwàng pat lhù pùks; douc sa lac lhuks.
Pec nec k'hlang nu dàts, pec nec gri nu ngats,
màns wuc tsìn swats, muyc douc ma wuc gàts.

公車千乘
朱英綠縢　二矛重弓
公徒三萬　貝冑朱綅
烝徒增增　戎狄是膺
荊舒是懲　則莫我敢承
俾爾昌而熾　俾爾壽而富
黃髮鮐背　壽胥與試
俾爾昌而大　俾爾耆而艾
萬有千歲　眉壽無有害

Ràc state looks up to the lofty mount Tai.
You thoroughly mastered the area of mounts *Kwru* and *Mòng*, and then extended your rule over the wide East,
all the way to the seaboard. The *Wì*-river *Luy* willingly joined with us
—none among them are unsubmissive. All this is the achievement of you lords of *Ràc*.

Thàts shàn ngràm-ngràm, Ràc pròng shac tam.
Amp wuc Kwru Mòng, swits mhàng dàts tòng,
tits wa mhùc pròng. Wì Luy rù dòng,
màk pu shout dzong. Ràc gò tu kòng.

泰山巖巖　魯邦所瞻
奄有龜蒙　遂荒大東
至于海邦　淮夷來同
莫不率從　魯侯之功

Once mounts *Bo* and *Lak* were under your sway, you went on to annex the *Sla* area,
again getting as far as the seaboard. The *Wì*-river *Luy*, the *Mròn* and the *Mràk*,
and down as far as the Southern *Luy*, all now obey you
—none dare say you nay. Their fealty is to you, oh lord of *Ràc*.

Pòuc wuc Bo Lak, swits mhàng Sla dràk,
tits wa mhùc pròng. Wì Luy, Mròn, Mràk,
gup payc Nùm Luy, màk pu shout dzong
—màk kàmp pu nàk. Ràc gò dec nak.

保有鳧嶧　遂荒徐宅
至于海邦　淮夷蠻貊
及彼南夷　莫不率從
莫敢不諾　魯侯是若

Sky bestows great abundance on our ruler, who keeps *Ràc* secure in his vigorous old age.
He spends time in *Dyang* and *Nghac*, and restores the domain of the Duke of *Tiw*.
The lord of *Ràc* feasts and makes merry. A good wife, a mother surviving into old age,
able officials, great and small, the state—the nation: all these he possesses.
He has been granted so many blessings; though his hair is grey, he still has a young man's teeth.

Thìn slèk klòng doun kràc; muyc douc pòuc Ràc.
Kac Dyang lac Nghac, bouk Tiw klòng tu wac.
Ràc gò èns huc. Reng tsùy, douc muc,
ngay dàts-pa, lhaks shuc, pròng kwùk: dec wuc.
Kuts tày douc thruc; gwàng pat, nge k'hyuc.

天錫公純嘏　眉壽保魯
居常與許　復周公之宇
魯侯燕喜　令妻壽母
宜大夫庶士　邦國是有
既多受祉　黃髮兒齒

The pines of *Dzà-rù* and the cypresses of *Sin-pac*
were felled and measured by the *slum* and by the *thak*.
The pine rafters are stout, and the principal temple chamber is spacious.
The new temple is grand. *Gè Se* built it.
It is very long and wide, fitting for our large population.

Dzà-rù tu slong, Sin-pac tu pràk,	徂來之松　新甫之柏
dec tònt, dec dàk, dec slum, dec thak.	是斷是度　是尋是尺
Slong kròk wuc sak, ràks tsump khònk dak.	松桷有舄　路寢孔碩
Sin mraws yak-yak, Gè Se shac tzàk.	新廟奕奕　奚斯所作
Khònk mans tsac dak; màns min dec nak.	孔曼且碩　萬民是若

This Ode was composed on the occasion of the reconstruction of a dynastically-important temple in *Ràc*, now quiet after the racket of sawing and hammering. (Because even important buildings were made of wood rather than stone or brick, inevitably they had to be rebuilt periodically.) After introducing this theme in the first line, the bulk of the poem celebrates the current ruler of *Ràc* and his ancestors, returning to the rebuilding in the last verse.

We don't know how *Tànt* (on whom see pp. 7-8) began "cutting down" the *Un* dynasty. As we see in verses 2-3, *Deng* rewarded the Duke of *Tiw* for his work as regent during *Deng*'s childhood by conferring the fief of *Ràc* on the duke's heir (according to one version, the original intention was for the duke to rule *Ràc* himself, but his court duties made that impractical so he accepted the fief for his son). By the time of the Ode, the current lord of *Ràc* was *Hu*, who died in 626. (His name does not appear in the poem, but we know what it was and it serves in my translation to help keep the *dramatis personae* straight.)

Verse 4 begins with a description of the *dyang* or "tasting sacrifice", an autumn ritual. Sacrificial animals were expected to be "pure", that is, of a uniform colour. The usual colour was red, but to mark the special status of the Duke of *Tiw* a white bull is sacrificed to him. When bulls were selected for sacrifice, wooden bars were fixed across their horns to prevent them goring anyone, since doing that would make them inauspicious. An interesting issue arises with the phrase *nghay tzòun* in the second line. A *tzòun* was a vase-like vessel, here perhaps used to hold liquor for pouring out as a libation, and *nghay* was the word for an animal to be ritually sacrificed (as in verse 3). Some have taken it that the *nghay tzòun* was made in the shape of a bull. But Karlgren argues that the original meaning of *nghay* may have been "happy, sportive". Readers of Mary Renault's novels reconstructing the world of the Greek myths will remember that for the Ancient Greeks it was important that sacrificial "victims" consented to their fate—the animals' movements at the moment of being killed were interpreted as showing this. Karlgren evidently believed that the Chinese had a similar idea, and so the sacrificial animal was called "the happy one".

The later part of verse 4 is clearly a wish or prophecy about the future. (We don't understand the phrase I translate as "lived three lifetimes", but it is obviously a way of saying "Long live (the ruler)".) Corresponding to this future orientation, Legge takes the material about eastward and southward expansion of *Ràc* state, in verses 5 to 7, to represent hopes for the future—"Such shall be the achievements of the lord of [*Ràc*]". He points out that some of the mentions of tribes subdued go far beyond anything that *Ràc* ever achieved in reality. But Old Chinese has no tenses, and I take the passage to be a hyperbolic account of the past deeds of the marquis and his predecessors.

The commentary tradition claims that "cowrie helmets" had cowrie-shells dangling from them on red strings, like corks dangling from Australian bush hats. I wonder. Might it alternatively be that the helmets themselves were ribbed like cowrie shells, or something of that sort?

The *Noung* and *Lèk* tribes lived respectively to the west and the north of the Chinese culture area. The *Kreng*, already encountered in Ode 178, were to the south (they later became the Chinese state of *Chac*, see Ode 305), and the *Lha* were a smaller group to the east of the *Kreng*, around modern Lujiang, Anhui.

In China, where black hair is universal, old people's hair was described as "yellow"; for a Western readership, many of whom are blond, that doesn't work and I substitute "grey".

Mount Tai is the great 5000-foot mountain of eastern China; *Kwru* and *Mòng* are ranges in the southern part of the Shandong mountains, and *Bo* and *Lak* are further south, near the present border of Shandong with Jiangsu and Anhui. For *Sla* see Ode 263. *Mròn* and *Mràk* are commonly used as names of northern tribes, but here they must refer to tribes in the south—we saw in Ode 261 that *Mròn* was sometimes applied to particularly uncivilized peoples irrespective of geography, and perhaps the same was true of *Mràk*.

In verse 8, *Dyang* and *Nghac* were cities near the western and southern borders respectively of *Ràc* state, which had been retrieved for *Ràc* rule after being annexed by its neighbours; lord *Hu* is described as regaining the entire patrimony originally conferred by king *Deng* on the Duke of *Tiw* (or more precisely on his son). In verse 9, *Dzà-rù* ("Going and coming") and *Sin-pac* were mountains near Mount Tai. *Slum* and *thak* were units of length: a *thak* was about fourteen inches, and a *slum* was eight *thak*, which would make it something over nine feet.

The penultimate line seems at first sight to end with a question: "what kind of man could have built this (marvel)?" However, the commentary tradition says that *Gè Se* was the name of the *Ràc* ruler's brother. A name that translates as "What This?" seems surprising, and I wonder whether the tradition is reliable knowledge, or an ancient guess that has been rendered authoritative through centuries of repetition. Not knowing the answer to that question, I do not press my scepticism.

VOICES FROM EARLY CHINA

Eulogies of Un

301

Splendid 那

Oh, how splendid! We set out our drums, little and great;
we play them with a fine loud sound, we celebrate our illustrious ancestors.

Ay la, này la! Truks ngàyc làw kàc, 　　猗與那與　置我靴鼓
tzòs kàc krènt-krènt, khàns ngàyc rat tzàc.　奏鼓簡簡　衎我烈祖

In a rush, *Lhàng*'s Descendant arrives, to complete our happy occasion.
Deep are the drumbeats, while the flutes play a shrill tune.
Everything is in harmony and balance, taking its time from our musical stones.
Ah, how majestic is *Lhàng*'s Descendant; statesmanlike is his reputation.

Lhàng sòun tzòs kràc, snouy ngàyc su deng.　湯孫奏假　綏我思成
Làw kàc wwìn-wwìn, hwìts-hwìts kònt hyeng.　靴鼓淵淵　嘒嘒管聲
Kuts wày tsac breng, uy ngàyc khèngs hyeng.　既和且平　依我磬聲
à hràk Lhàng sòun, mouk-mouk kot hyeng.　於赫湯孫　穆穆厥聲

Truly full-bodied is the sound of the great bells and drums; the scorpion dance is danced grandly.
We have an illustrious guest: isn't everything as it should be and just perfect!

Long kàc wuc làks, màns mac wuc yak.　鏞鼓有斁　萬舞有奕
Ngàyc wuc kràyc khràk, yak pu luy lak!　我有嘉客　亦不夷懌

From the beginning, in olden days, our ancestors initiated this sacrificial service.
With worshipful fervour, morning and evening, they organized it in due reverence.

Dzis kàc dzùc sak, sùn min wuc tzàk.　自古在昔　先民有作
Òun krong traw syak, tup shuc wuc khàk.　溫恭朝夕　執事有恪

May they now look favourably on our own seasonal sacrifices, offered today by *Lhàng*'s Descendant.

Kàs lac tung dyang, Lhàng sòun tu tzang.　顧予烝嘗　湯孫之將

Lhàng was the founder of the *Un* dynasty.

302

Illustrious Ancestors 烈祖

Sing hey for our illustrious Ancestors, and the blessings they regularly confer on us!
They repeatedly bestow bounty on us without end: it reaches all of you, wherever you live.

Tzay-tzay rat tzàc, wuc drit se gàc.　　嗟嗟烈祖　有秩斯祜
Lhin slèk ma kang, gup nec se shac.　　申錫無疆　及爾斯所

We've poured out the clear new wine for them, and in return they make our welfare complete.
We also have well-seasoned broth. We've been attentive, and quiet.
We come forward and take our places without speaking—there's no dissension among us now.
The Ancestors will reward us with a vigorous old age—we shall go on for ever, though sere and wrinkled.

Kuts tzùs tseng gàc, rùks ngàyc su deng.　　既載清酤　賚我思成
Yak wuk wày kràng. Kuts krùs, kuts breng.　　亦有和羹　既戒既平
Tzòng kràc ma ngan, duc mayc wuc jèng.　　鬷假無言　時靡有爭
Snouy ngàyc muyc douc, gwàng kòc ma kang.　　綏我眉壽　黃耇無疆

[...] to come forward and present our sacrificial offerings. We've received a powerful Mandate.
Sky has sent down prosperity, bumper years of abundant grain harvests.
We come forward, we approach and present our sacrificial offerings. May good fortune endlessly continue to be sent down.
May Sky look favourably on our seasonal sacrifices, offered today by *Lhàng*'s Descendant.

[...]
luc kràc, luc hang. Ngàyc douc mreng phàc tzang.　　以假以享　我受命溥將
Dzis Thìn kròungs khàng, phoung nìn nank-nank.　　自天降康　豐年穰穰
Rù kràc, rù hang. Kròungs puk ma kang.　　來假來饗　降福無疆
Kàs lac tung dyang, Lhàng sòun tu tzang.　　顧予烝嘗　湯孫之將

In the received text, the first line of verse 3 is word for word identical to a passage in Ode 178, where it fits in; here, it is out of context, so I omit it as another case where a poem was imperfectly remembered. The last line of the poem is identical to the last line of the preceding Ode, and perhaps did not originally belong there.

303

The Dark Bird 玄鳥

Sky commanded the Dark Bird to descend and give birth to *Khèts*, who settled in the vast territory of *Un*.
Long ago God commanded the warlike *Lhàng* to fix boundaries within the Four Quarters.

Thìn mreng gwìn tìwc, kròungs nu sheng Lhang, dràk Un thàc màng-màng.
Kàc Tès mreng mac Lhàng, tengs wuk payc Slits Pang.

天命玄鳥　降而生商
宅殷土芒芒
古帝命武湯　正域彼四方

Then he commanded the *Un* sovereign to take comprehensive possession of the Nine Domains.
That first *Un* sovereign received Sky's unchallengeable Mandate,
and it remained with that warrior-king's descendants.

Pang mreng kot gòs, amp wuc Kouc Wuc.
Lhang tu sùn gòs, douc mreng pu lùc,
dzùc mac wang sòun tzuc.

方命厥后　奄有九有
商之先后　受命不殆
在武王孫子

Mac Tèng, descendant of the warrior-king, never lost a battle.
With dragon banners flying from his ten chariots, he performed the great ritual sacrifice of cooked millet.

Mac wang sòun tzuc, Mac Tèng mayc pu lhungs.
Rong guy gip mlungs, dàts k'hyuc dec dung.

武王孫子　武丁靡不勝
龍旂十乘　大糦是承

The Royal Domain was a thousand li wide, and that is where our people settled
—but he also fixed the boundaries of all the states within the Four Seas.

Pròng guy tsìn ruc, wi min shac tuc
—drawc wuk payc Slits Mhùc.

邦畿千里　維民所止
肇域彼四海

People came to pay him homage from everywhere within the Four Seas; they came in great numbers.
Their great encircling boundary was the Yellow River.
For *Un* to have received Sky's mandate was utterly right, and every dignity was conferred on our dynasty.

Slits Mhùc rù kràc, rù kràc gri-gri.
Krank wen wi Gày.
Un douc mreng grùm ngay, pràk ròk dec gàyc.

四海來假　來假祁祁
景員維河
殷受命咸宜　百祿是何

A summary of the foundation myth of the *Un* dynasty. The founder was *Lhàng*, whose ultimate ancestor was *Khèts*, said to have been minister to the legendary emperor *Hwins*. (Translated literally, the opening line says that the Dark Bird gave birth to the dynasty, but this is a way of saying that it was responsible for the birth of *Khèts*.) There are different versions of the myth linking the birth of *Khèts* to a dark bird. (*Gwìn* means "black", but this was not the species called in English "blackbird", which is not native to China; it is said to have been a swallow.) According to one version, his mother *Krànt Lèk* was bathing in the open air when a dark bird appeared and dropped an egg which *Krànt Lèk* swallowed, leading to the birth of *Khèts*.

Lhàng was ruler of a vassal state in Henan, who overthrew the *Ghàc* dynasty and ruled all China from 1554 to his death in 1543. (While there is disagreement between sources about *Un*-dynasty dates, there is no particular reason to think them unreasonable. It is not a case like the Book of Genesis, where we find Methuselah living for hundreds of years: successive *Un* kings are assigned credible reign-lengths.) The *Un* king *Mac Tèng* reigned from 1250 to 1189 (which was a longer reign than average, though not as long as that of our own current Queen), and he was regarded as the last capable ruler of that dynasty (see Ode 305), which then decayed until it was conquered by *Mac* of *Tiw*.

(*Mac*, "brave, warlike", was a common name, and, confusingly, in this and the next Ode *Lhàng* is described as *mac wang*, "the warrior king". To add to the potential confusion, the dynasty which my translation consistently calls *Un* is referred to in the early verses of this Ode by its alternative name, *Lhang*—in Chinese a quite different name from that of its founder *Lhàng*.)

"Fixing the boundaries" means that although the *Un* king directly ruled only a domain a few hundred miles wide, he was feudal overlord over a much larger area, and defined the respective territories of his vassal kings. (The "Four Seas" are a way of referring to the supposed edges of the world.) For the Nine Domains, see the notes for the next Ode.

304

The Roots of Un　長發

Deep and subtle are the roots of the *Un* dynasty; ever and again it is favoured with auspicious omens.
Floodwaters roiled far and wide, until *Wac* tamed them and laid down land boundaries.
He demarcated the great outer states: the wide circumference encircling them all was long.
The state of *Snoung* was becoming influential at that time, and God appointed its son to found the line of *Un*.

Syouns trat wi Lhang, drang pat gu syang.　濬哲維商　長發其祥
Gòng lhouyc màng-màng, Wac pha gràs thàc pang.　洪水芒芒　禹敷下土方
Ngwàts dàts kwùk dec kang; puk wen kuts drang.　外大國是疆　幅圓既長
Wuc Snoung pang tzang, Tès rup tzuc sheng Lhang.　有娀方將　帝立子生商

This Black King was forcible in imposing order.
When he acquired a small state, it prospered; and when he acquired a large state, it prospered.

He trod his path without turning aside, and then checked to see his instructions had been followed.
His grandson *Sangs Thàc* was also illustrious, and even beyond the seas there was order.

Gwìn Wang wàn pàt. 　　　　　　　　　玄王桓撥
Douc syawc kwùc dec dàt, douc dàts kwùc dec dàt. 　受小國是達　受大國是達
Shout ric pu wat, swits gic kuts pat. 　　　　率履不越　遂視既發
Sangs Thàc rat-rat, mhùc ngwàts wuc dzèt. 　　相土烈烈　海外有截

God's commands were never disobeyed—this was the same right down to *Lhàng*'s time.
Lhàng came down into the world when the world needed him.
He grew in wisdom and piety day by day; slowly and steadily his glory developed.
God on High was his all in all, and God commanded him to be a model to the Nine Circuits.

Tès mreng pu wuy, tits wa Lhàng dzì. 　　帝命不違　至于湯齊
Lhàng kròungs pu dri. 　　　　　　　　　湯降不遲
Lhengs krengs nit tzì; tyawc kràc dri-dri. 　　聖敬日躋　昭假遲遲
Dyangs Tès dec ke; Tès mreng lhuk wa Kouc Wuy. 　上帝是祇　帝命式于九圍

He received the lesser *gou* jade and the greater *gou* jade, as symbols of the fealty of the states below him.
He carried Sky's blessing.
He wasn't overbearing, nor impatient; he wasn't over-hard, nor over-soft.
He spread his governance with a light hand, and assembled all the elements of prosperity.

Douc syawc gou dàts gou, way gràc kwùk trots rou. 　受小球大球　為下國綴旒
Gàyc Thìn tu hou. 　　　　　　　　　　　何天之休
Pu grangs, pu gou, pu kàng, pu nou. 　　　不競不絿　不剛不柔
Pha tengs ou-ou; pràk ròk dec dziw. 　　敷政優優　百祿是遒

He received the lesser *konk-pek* jade and the greater *konk-pek* jade, and thus was made mighty by the states below him.
He carried Sky's favour. He pressed forward courageously on many fronts,
not shaken, imperturbable, showing no kind of fear.
He gathered together all the elements of prosperity.

Douc syawc konk dàts konk, way gràc kwùk tzyoungs mròng. 　受小珙大珙　為下國俊厖
Gàyc Thìn tu rhonk. Pha tzòs gu lonk. 　何天之寵　敷奏其勇
Pu tuns, pu dònk, pu nant, pu sonk, 　　不振不動　不戁不竦
pràk ròk dec tzònk. 　　　　　　　　百祿是總

Then this warrior-king set out, grasping his battle-axe and bent on killing.
He blazed like fire, so that none dared stand up to us.
The stump of *Ghàc* had thrown up three lively new suckers of resistance, but

> none made headway, none got anywhere.
> Throughout the Nine Domains there was order.
> After smiting the lords of *Wuy* and *Kàs*, he dealt with the lord of *Kòun-ngà*, and finally with *Gat*, last king of *Ghàc*.

Mac wang tzùs pat, wuc gan prank wat.	武王載發　有虔秉鉞
Na mhùyc rat-rat, tzùk màk ngàyc kàmp àt.	如火烈烈　則莫我敢遏
Pròu wuc sùm ngat: màk swits, màk dàt.	苞有三櫱　莫遂莫達
Kouc Wuc wuc dzèt.	九有有截
Wuy, Kàs kuts bat, Kòun-ngà, Ghàc Gat.	韋顧既伐　昆吾夏桀

> In times past, in the middle age, this was one who was majestic, awe-inspiring,
> truly Sky's Son. And a minister was sent down to him,
> namely *Ày Gràng*—the left- and right-hand man of the king of *Un*.

Sak dzùc troung lap, wuc tuns tsac ngap.	昔在中葉　有震且業
Yount layc Thìn Tzuc. Kròungs wa khrang shuc,	允也天子　降予卿士
dit wi Ày Gràng—dit tzàys-wus Lhang wang.	寔維阿衡　寔佐佑商王

Wac was the 20th-century B.C. culture hero who is said to have created the conditions for successful agriculture by controlling the Yellow River floods, and he had divided China (as it then was) into nine provinces, here called "circuits" or "domains". (The phrase "great outer states" is probably anachronistic; later, when there were far more than nine states, the central, thoroughly-Chinese states tended to be smaller than the outer, semi-barbarian states, but that pattern did not apply to *Wac*'s Nine Circuits as traditionally mapped.) *Wac* was regarded as the founder of the *Ghàc* dynasty. The "son of the state of *Snoung*" was *Khèts* (see Ode 303); his mother *Krànt Lèk* was from the *Snoung* ruling family (descendants of a 21st-century royal concubine). The phrase "Black King" in verse 2 refers to *Khèts*, here called king by courtesy after his descendants had become kings; the epithet "Black" perhaps refers to his father being a black bird.

The idea that any Chinese ruler's influence extended "beyond the seas" as early as the second millennium B.C. seems fanciful.

Gou and *konk-pek* jades were symbols of authority, like a European monarch's sceptre. Feudal states evidently handed them over to *Lhàng* in acknowledgement of his supremacy. We have seen that a *pek* (in modern Chinese, 'bi') was a disc with a hole in the middle, though the precise nature of *konk-pek* is not known. *Gou* is now the word for "sphere" ('qiu' in modern pronunciation), so perhaps that was its shape.

The "three suckers" from the stump of *Ghàc* are evidently a metaphor for the lords of three states which the poet lists as attacked before *Lhàng* eventually extinguished *Ghàc*. The "middle age" seems to refer, from the point of view of a poet writing later in the *Un* or *Tiw* periods, to the time between *Khèts* and the beginning of *Un* kingship.

After many verses praising *Lhàng* in extravagant terms, the closing lines of verse 7, dealing with his minister *Ày Gràng*, might give an impression of bathos. But *Ày Gràng* is more central to the topic of this poem than first appears. Without him there would have been no *Un* dynasty. He became *Lhàng*'s chief minister when *Lhàng* was a *Ghàc* vassal. (According to one story, it was *Ày Gràng*'s prowess as a cook that first recommended him to *Lhàng*.) At that time, the *Ghàc* king was a thoroughly dissolute monarch named *Gat*. (Obviously, if what we have can be regarded as "history" at all, it is victors' history.) *Gat* was so strong that he twisted bars of iron as if they were ropes. He exhausted his people through endless wars, and then he became so infatuated with a beautiful new wife that he ignored his duties as ruler. *Lhàng* sent *Ày Gràng* to *Gat* to try to persuade the latter to mend his ways. But *Ày Gràng* found *Gat* incorrigible, so saw it as his duty to convince *Lhàng* to rebel and seize the throne, after which *Ày Gràng* became the "power behind the throne", outliving *Lhàng*.

305

Mac Tèng of Un 殷武

Mac Tèng of *Un* was an energetic king. He hastened to war with the *Kreng-Chac*.
Leading his men into the depths of their difficult terrain, he rounded up the
    Kreng troops,
and thoroughly pacified their population centres. This was the achievement of
    Lhàng's descendant *Mac Tèng*, who spoke as follows:

Thàt payc Un Mac, puns bat Kreng-Chac.	撻彼殷武　奮伐荊楚
Me nup gu jac, bòu Kreng tu rac;	采入其阻　裒荊之旅
wuc dzèt gu shac. Lhàng sòun tu slac.	有截其所　湯孫之緒

"You people of the *Kreng-Chac*, you are now living in the southern region of our
    nation.
In ancient days there was *Lhàng* the Peacemaker: among all the *Tì* and *Khang*
    peoples,
none dared fail to come and make sacrificial offerings, none dared fail to
    demonstrate fealty to him by appearing at court,
because the *Un* dynasty is for ever."

"*Wi nac Kreng-Chac, kas kwùk nùm hang.*	維汝荊楚　居國南鄉
Sak wuc Deng Lhàng. Dzis payc Tì-Khang,	昔有成湯　自彼氐羌
màk kàmp pu rù hang, màk kàmp pu rù wang,	莫敢不來享　莫敢不來王
wat Lhang dec dyang."	曰商是常

"Sky commanded the many princes to follow in the steps of *Wac* in setting up
    their capitals.
As an annual duty they came to audience with their ruler,
begging 'Don't punish us for failings: in sowing and in reaping we have never
    been remiss'."

"*Thìn mreng tày pek, nhet tà wa Wac tu tzek.*	天命多辟　設都于禹之蹟
Swats shuc rù pek,	歲事來辟
'*Mut lac gòyc trèk, kràs shuk puyc krès.*' "	勿予禍適　稼穡匪懈

"Sky charged the king to inspect his subjects. The common people were well-
    disciplined,
with no wrongdoing, no excesses; none who dared to be idle.

Sky charged the king to divide the land on Earth into fiefs, and thus provide for its welfare."

Thìn mreng kròungs kràm. Gràc min wuc ngam, 天命降監 下民有嚴
pu tzèms, pu ràms, pu kàmp lùc wàng. 不僭不濫 不敢怠遑
Mreng wa gràc kwùk, pong kans kot puk. 命于下國 封建厥福

Un City is systematically laid out; it is the cynosure of the whole world.
Majestic is its fame; its spiritual sway is refulgent.
With its immemorial age and its peace, it continues to safeguard us of later generations.

Lhang up yuk-yuk, Slits Pang tu guk. 商邑翼翼 四方之極
Hràk-hràk kot hyeng, dryawk-dryawk kot rèng. 赫赫厥聲 濯濯厥靈
Douc khòuc tsac nèng, luc pòuc ngàyc ghòc sheng. 壽考且寧 以保我後生

Climbing the slopes of Mount *Krank*, pines and cypresses stood like lofty sentinels.
We felled them and transported them, we dressed them square and planed them into shape.
The trees were turned into long purlins and numerous pillars, good and stout.
With the temple hall completed, there fell a great peace.

Trùk payc Krank Shàn, slong pràk wàn-wàn. 陟彼景山 松柏桓桓
Dec tònt dec tsan, pang tròk dec gan. 是斷是遷 方斲是虔
Slong kròk wuc rhan, rac leng wuc gràn. 松桷有梴 旅楹有閑
Tsump deng khònk àn. 寢成孔安

A celebration of *Mac Tèng* (reigned 1250–1189), who, as said with Ode 203, was seen as the last "good" *Un* king. The Ode is thought to have been written to commemorate the building of a temple to him, separate from that of his *Un* ancestors, perhaps in the eleventh century—this is what the last verse is said to be about. Some commentators believed the poem was written at that time. But the reference in the first line to the *Kreng-Chac* tribe makes that doubtful. This is a combined name for a tribe in and around the area of modern Hubei, originally called *Kreng* (we met them in Odes 178 and 300) but which later evolved into the large Chinese state of *Chac* (both names mean "thorns"). It is believed that the *Chac* name only came into use in the seventh century, implying that since this poet knew it, his poem must be not one of the earliest Odes but one of the latest.

The second-person pronoun at the beginning of verse 2 shows that someone is being quoted, but it is a matter of inference that the speaker is *Mac Tèng*; nothing in the Chinese tells us that, and nor does it tell us where the quotation ends. I take it to cover all of verses 2 to 4, in which the king is haranguing his new subjects about what is expected of populations brought under Chinese rule. (The *Tì* and *Khang* were tribes in the Gansu area.) Then verses 5 and 6 would be written as if by someone involved in the later temple building.

Mac Tèng's capital was at or near modern Yanshi, downriver from Luoyang, and Mount *Krank* is south of that.

Glossary

The words "a" and "to" are used to distinguish noun from verb senses, e.g. "a crow", "to crow".
For the symbol ○ see p. 42.

a	in, at, on, with 於		*bac*	1. protect, help 輔
à	a crow 烏			2. father 父
à, à-ghà	oh! 於, 於乎			3. cooking pot 釜
àk	bad 惡			4. detachable sides to wagon 輔
àks	to hate 惡		*bàk*	to press; thin 薄
amp	1. to cover, spreading over; *Amp Suk* (Yan Xi), a nobleman of *Dzin* 奄; 奄息		*bàk, bàk-ngan*	initial particle: well now, ... 薄, 薄言
	2. thickening, gathering (clouds) 渰		*bam*	every 凡
an	1. thereat; *X an*, when X 焉		*ban*	1. abundant 繁
	2. how? 焉			2. burn, roast 燔
	3. a syllable inserted for rhythm 焉			3. fence, hedge 樊
àn	1. how, where, what? 安			4. uncoloured garment 袢
	2. peace, peaceful, solemn 安			5. hoary mugwort 蘩
ang	1. middle; end 央		*bàn*	1. turn round 般
	2. deep and strongly flowing 泱			2. joy 槃
ank-thank	disconcerted 怏怏		*bang*	1. withstand, be a match for; dyke, embankment 防
àns	repress 按			2. bream 魴
ant	1. lie down 偃			3. room, esp. side-room 房
	2. silurid catfish 鰋		*bàng*	1. side 旁
àt	stop, repress 遏			2. forceful 彭
àts	ample, rich (of clouds); numerous 藹		*bàns-wans*	relaxed, undisciplined 畔援
aw, aw-dawc	delicately lovely 夭, 夭紹		*bas*	attach; reach to 傅
awc	kill, destroy 夭		*bàs*	a course, career 步
àwk	1. moisten, hence glossy; *Àwk* (Wo), a place-name 沃		*bat*	1. to attack, hit; to cut 伐
	2. silver-washed 鋈			2. a shield 伐
ay	1. ah!; *ay-tzay*, whoopee! 猗; 猗嗟		*bàt*	1. trudge, trample; *bàt-dap*, "trudge and wade": travel across country 跋; 跋涉
	2. igiri tree, *Idesia polycarpa* 椅			2. halt in the open 茇
ày	1. a slope 阿			3. end of an arrow 拔
	2. pillar, beam; *Ày Gràng* (A Heng), kingmaker to first *Un* king 阿; 阿衡			4. sacrifice to the Spirits of the Road 軷
ayc	lean on, pull aside 倚		*Bàt*	Bo, the Demon of Drought 魃
àyc, àyc-nàyc	luxuriant 猗, 猗儺		*bats*	to bark 吠
			bàts	1. flutter; a streamer 旆
				2. thin out 拔
bà	rushes, reeds 蒲		*bawc*	compact, dense 苞
bà-ba	crawl 匍匐		*bàwks*	violent; use strength to overcome 暴
ba-sngà	rose mallow 扶蘇		*bay*	skin 皮

bày-sày	a ritual dance, see Ode 137 婆娑		bongs	seam 縫
bays	to cover, be covered; a head-dress 被		bos	be added to, stick to 附
be	1. accumulate 垺		bou	1. strong and numerous 浮
	2. tripe 脾			2. float 浮
bek	1. a law; lawful 辟		bòu	1. collect, assemble; come together; all 裒
	2. to open 闢			2. a long coat, esp. quilted 袍
	3. beat the breast 擗			3. a wide-skirted robe; *Bòu* (Bao), a place-name; *Bòu Sluc* (Bao Si), concubine of king Iw 褒; 褒姒
bèk	tile 甓			
beks	avoid, move away 避			
ben	glib; insincere words 諞		bou-you	mayfly 蜉蝣
bèng	1. jug 缾		bouc	large and fat; a large mound; abundant; *bouc-toung*, grasshopper 阜; 阜螽
	2. screen, protecting wall 屏			
bènk	side by side, together 並		bòuc	carry in the arms 抱
bès	netsuke; to wear hanging from girdle 佩		bouk	return, restore 復
bets	worn-out 敝		bràk	white 白
bi	1. abundant, large; enlarge 肥		Bràng	Peng, a place in *Drengs* 彭
	2. make ample, strengthen; big oneself up 毗		brans	cap, specifically the cap of manhood 弁
			brànt	slope 阪
	3. panther 貔		bràts	be ruined 敗
bin	1. urgent, pressing 頻		bren	punctilious 采
	2. become wife to 嬪		breng	1. level, to be just; to settle; peaceful; *Breng* (Ping), name of first Eastern *Tiw* king (p. 9) 平
	3. a water plant, probably water clover 蘋			
bint	female animal 牝			2. lad's-love (see Ode 161) 苹
bis	1. assemble, unite, combine; be concordant 比		brès	fine grain 粺
			bric	be separated 化
	2. braid 紕		bròu	1. bake, roast 炰
bit	1. nonchalant, offhand 伾			2. gourd 匏
	2. fat and robust (of a horse) 駓			3. kitchen, butchery 庖
bìt	fragrant 苾, 飶		bròu-hòu	shout and bawl 咆虓
biw	flow; *Biw-dray* (Biaochi), a stream in Xi'an 滮; 滮池		bruks	prepare, provide, ready, complete 備
			brun	poor, poverty 貧
bo	wild duck; *Bo* (Fu), a mountain in southern Shandong 鳧		brung	1. full, solid 馮
				2. stand on, rely on 馮
bòk	driver, servant 僕			3. wade across a river 馮
bong	1. meet 逢		brus	overbearing 奰
	2. sew 縫		bù	accompany, associate, support 陪
bòng	1. luxuriant foliage 蓬		bu-luc	plantain 芣苢
	2. a plant, possibly hairy fleabane 蓬		buc	1. lady, wife 婦
	3. boom! 韸			2. carry on the back 負
	4. disorderly 蓬			

bùc	double 倍		chày	choose 差
buc-sang	carriage-box, carriage 服箱		chay-dray	uneven, long and short mixed 差池
buk	1. serve, service 服		cho	1. grass used for fodder or fuel 芻
	2. to wear; clothes 服			2. hurry, run to; *cho-tsang*, to step in an agile, well-balanced manner, as in sport, ritual, or dance 趨; 趨蹌
	3. lie down 伏			
	4. train and use an animal 服		chòng	wagon 蔥
	5. submit, be dominated 服		chots	robe with figured top and embroidered skirt 黼
	6. a quiver 服			
	7. inner horses of a team 服		chuk	1. sharp 戚
	8. intense thought 服			2. to measure depth 測
bùks	turn the back on, be disloyal, rebel 背		chum	gallop 驟
Bùks	Bei, a place-name (see p. 66) 邶		chum-chay	uneven 參差
bum	float about 汎		chup	flap the ears 濕
bùm	bushy 芃			
bums-wàng	phoenix 鳳凰		dà	1. the common people; foot soldier, follower 徒
bun	1. river bank, embankment 濆, 墳			2. to butcher; *Dà* (Tu), a place-name 屠
	2. a type of elm 枌			3. fatigue, suffering; disabled 瘏
	3. great 賁, 頒			4. consider, plan, calculate 圖
	4. well-set (of fruit) 賁		dac	1. altar to Spirit of Soil; sacrifice to that spirit 社
	5. burn, destroy 焚			
Bun	Fen, a river of Shanxi 汾			2. field hut 野
bùng	1. a match, equal; a friend 朋		dàc	1. roots 土
	2. string of cowrie shells 朋			2. Chinese pear-tree, *Pyrus pyrifolia*; *Dàc* (Du), a river of Shaanxi 杜
bunt	swell up 墳		dak	1. stone, rock 石
but	1. great 佛			2. stately, great 碩
	2. oppose, offend 咈		dàk	to measure, calculate, consider 度
bùts	disordered, silly 悖		dàks	a measure, rule 度
buy	1. follow on foot 腓		dàn	sandalwood tree 檀
	2. fat 肥		dang	1. splendid, ample 裳
	3. sick 痱			2. garment covering lower part of body 裳
byawc	to drop 摽			
cha	begin 初		dàng	1. hall 堂
chac	1. bushy, luxuriant, rich; numerically complete, ample; *Chac* (Chu), a southern state 楚			2. pear tree 棠
			dangs	1. wish, would that 尚
				2. add to 尚
	2. thorns, thorny tree 楚			3. still, yet 尚
changs-hwangs	grief, distress 愴怳			4. high; consider high; *Dangs* (Shang), a Tiw general 尚

dans	cooked food 膳		*dìs*	younger sister, secondary wife 娣
dàns	to fear 憚		*dit*	true, really; that is to say; this, that 寔
dant	1. good; approve 善		*dìt*	1. laugh scornfully 咥
	2. area of levelled ground for sacrifices 墠			2. old age 耋
				3. anthill, mound 垤
dànt-slèk	naked torso 禮裼		*dìw*	1. to adjust, to tune 調
dap	wade across a stream 涉			2. a kind of cicada 蜩
dàt	come forward, become prominent, prosper; for a plant to break through the soil 達		*diwk*	lithe, beautiful; good 淑
			dìwk	level and easy (road) 踧
dats	1. reach, get to, go to, go away 逝		*djac*	hoe 鉏
	2. swear, promise 誓		*djàm*	1. crafty 毚
	3. tell the future using yarrow stalks, see Ode 58 筮			2. high and craggy 漸
			djàms	slander 讒
dàts	big; *dàts-bang*, large framework supporting a hog-roast; *dàts-pa*, dignitary, courtier 大; 大房; 大夫		*djang*	bed 牀, 床
			djànt	carriage box made of interwoven laths 棧
dawc	continue, transmit 紹		*djas*	to help 助
dàwks	sad 悼		*djos*	running fast (of a horse) 驟
Daws	Shao, a place-name, see p. 56 召		*djoung*	1. pile up, accumulate; to exalt, honour; high; *Djoung* (Chong), a state; *djoung ngrà*, dogtooth decoration for bell stand 崇; 崇牙
dàws	robber, scoundrel 盜			
dày	alligator 鼉			
de	to flock to the roost 提			2. end; all, whole of 崇
dè	1. tranquil 提		*djù*	wolf 豺
	2. lift 提		*do*	1. strongly, very 殳
dec	this; be like this, be correct 是			2. a kind of lance; baton 殳
deng	1. sincere; truly 誠		*dò*	throw to, to present; throw out 投
	2. to complete, achieve; peacemaking; *Deng* (Cheng), second *Tiw*-dynasty king (p. 8) 成		*doc*	to plant, establish 樹
			dok	1. apply; applied to 屬
				2. caterpillar 蠋
	3. put into a receptacle 盛		*dòk*	alone 獨
dèngs	fix, settle 定		*don*	hasten; rapid 遄
dès	look at 題		*dòn*	1. grieved 惇
dèts	a solitary tree 杕			2. rich, plentiful (dew) 溥
dì	1. cormorant 鷉			3. numerous 敦
	2. a sprout, shoot 荑			4. eagle 鵰
dìc	1. younger brother 弟		*dòng*	1. bushy, ample 童
	2. pleased 弟			2. young person; lamb, calf 童
dìn	sound of drum 闐			3. tung tree 桐
dins	careful, circumspect 慎			4. join; sort into categories, match; same,
dìns	to set out, present offerings 奠			

	shared; together; a hunt meet 同		3. arena, threshing floor; yard used for growing vegetables in spring and storing them in autumn 場
donk	swollen, inflated, conceited 腫	drang-chac	starfruit tree, carambola 萇楚
dònk	to move 動	dras	pass away 殂
dos	tree 樹	draw	audience; morning reception of visitors; court 朝
dòs	a 'dou' food bowl 豆	drawc	1. to initiate, institute; active, nimble; *drawc-mawc*, active 肇; 肇敏
dou	1. reject, be hostile to 讎		2. a flag showing tortoise and snake 旐
	2. enemy 讎	draws	to summon 召
	3. repay, recompense, answer 讎	dray	1. canter (see Ode 163) 馳
	4. to toast someone, take wine with them, return a toast 酬, 醻		2. a pool 池
dòu	stick with feathers attached 翿		3. a leat 沱
douc	receive 受	drayc	cleave wood along the grain 柂
douc, douc-khòuc	long life; *Douc* (Shou), a personal name 壽, 壽考	drays	earth, ground 地
dòuk	1. poison 毒	dre	a kind of flute 篪
	2. a kind of creeper ○	dre-dro	walk haltingly 踟躕
doun	1. great 純	dreng	norm, rule; *Dreng* (Cheng), a state 程
	2. a quail 鶉	Drengs	Zheng, a state 鄭
dòun	tie together 純	dret	clear, limpid 澈
dòuns	blunted; *Dòuns* (Dun), a hill 頓	drets	discard; left over 滯
dous	1. give, issue 授	dri	1. whetstone 砥
	2. sell, esp. sell slaves 售		2. islet 坻
douy	who? 誰		3. tarry, be late; walk slowly; slow, long 遲
dòuy	1. collapse, fall down 隤	dric	pheasant 雉
	2. tornado 頽	drin	1. old, of long standing; for a long time 塡
dòuyc	cap on butt end of weapon 鐏		2. old grain 陳
doy	hang 垂		3. display, set out, arrange, diffuse; *Drin* (Chen), a state 陳
dra	1. eliminate, remove 除		4. path from gate to Great Hall 陳
	2. collect, store, heap up 儲	dris	1. young, childish 稚
drac	1. stand in attendance 佇		2. sow or plant late 穉
	2. lamb 羜	drit	order, regulate, orderly, pure 秩
	3. ramie (see Ode 139) 紵	driw	1. dense, thick 綢
	4. a shuttle 杼		2. nightdress 裯
drak	1. choose 擇	driw-miws	to bind round 綢繆
	2. marsh, pool 澤	driwk	axle; *Driwk* (Zhou), a place in *Drengs* 軸
dràk	residence, to inhabit 宅	driws	helmet 胄
dran	the landholding of one farmer 廛		
drang	1. long, tall; a long time; always 長		
	2. intestines 腸		

dròk	muddy, muddled 濁		2. level 殖	
drong	1. slow-ripening grain 重		3. limpid 湜	
	2. double; *Drong-nuc* (Chong-er), heir to the dukedom of *Tzins* who deposed a pretender in 636, see Ode 134 重; 重耳	dùk	1. upright, straight 特	
			2. one of a pair, mate; a match for; an only one 特	
drong-gaw	see *gaw*		3. a three-year-old animal 特	
dronk	heavy 重	dum	1. reliable, trustworthy; to trust, rely on 忱, 諶	
drouc	crupper; *Drouc* (Zhou), last *Un* king (see p. 8) 紂		2. small stove 煁	
drouk	cylinder 柚	dump	mulberry fruit 葚	
droung	1. metallic sound, tinkle 沖	dùmp	hang down (hair) 髧	
	2. insect; a living creature generally 蟲	dums	excessively, very 甚	
droungs	a second son; *Droungs* (Zhong), a clan name 仲	dun	1. time; timely 辰	
			2. doe 麎	
drouts	cause resentment 懟	dung	1. lift up, present, honour, celebrate; receive, hence meet in battle 承	
dru	1. grasp, hold 持			
	2. regulate, arrange, work with, manipulate 治		2. continue 承	
		dùnt	cause to cease; extinguish, ruin, destroy 殄	
druc	1. provide, collect 峙			
	2. stand, stand still, stop 時	dyang	1. standard, normal, constant; *Dyang* (Chang), a city in the west of *Ràc* 常	
druk	straight; right; extensive 直			
druks	hold upright 植		2. to taste; the "tasting", hence the autumn sacrifice 嘗	
drum	submerged; to sink 沉			
drùmp	soaking (in dew), deep 湛		3. bagrid catfish 鱨	
drun	dust 塵	dyang, dyang-lìts	cherry tree 常, 常棣	
drung	1. to correct, chastise 懲			
	2. suppress 懲	dyangs	above, up, on 上	
drunk	I, said by king; the "royal we" 朕	dyank	go up 上	
drup	to cluster like insects 螽	dyaw	tablets of even-numbered ancestors in temple 昭	
dryawk	sleek, brilliant, glossy; to wash 濯			
		dyàw	1. Chinese trumpet vine, *Campsis grandiflora* 苕	
dryawks	wash clothes 濯			
du	1. this, a certain 時		2. a type of pea 苕	
	2. correct, good 時	dyàwc	pierce, cut 趙	
	3. fowl-hole in wall 塒	dyàwk	to condole, pity; grieved 弔	
dù	1. a tower 臺	dyawk-yawk	peony 勺藥	
	2. sedge used to make rainwear 臺			
duc	1. time; then, now; season, seasonable; at all times, constantly 時	dzà	advance, go to, pass; *Dzà-rù* (Culai), a mountain near Mount Tai 徂; 徂來	
		dzac	stop, prevent 沮	
	2. rely on, depend on 恃	dzak	register of field revenues 籍	
	3. market 市	dzàk	1. return a toast, reward 酢	
duk	1. namely 寔		2. oak 柞	

387

dzàks	blessing, prosperity, dignity 祚		dzit	sickness, pain, injure; urgent, energetic; *dzit-ouy*, terrifying 疾; 疾威
dzàn	damage, injury; cruel 殘		dzìt	crestlike 節
dzang	1. injure 戕		dziw	1. collect, bring together 揫
	2. wall 牆			2. to achieve, to end 酋
dzàng	to store, hoard, treasure up 藏		dziw-dzì	larva of a kind of beetle 蝤蠐
dzans	gift of food; to give a farewell feast 餞		dzòk	clan 族
dzant	1. tread, trample 踐		dzong	follow, pursue, attend to business 從
	2. shallow; armoured with thin mail 俴		dzongs	follower, attendant 從
dzànt	a ladle for pouring a libation 瓚		dzot	1. exceed; extremely 絕
dzap	1. break off hastily 萻			2. extinguish 絕
	2. victory; nimble 捷		dzòu	servant, set of servants; *Dzòu* (Cao), a small state 曹
dzaw	1. collect firewood 樵			
	2. worn 譙		Dzòu	Cao, a city of *Wets*, briefly its capital 漕
dzàwk	to bore, chisel out 鑿		dzòuc	1. make, do; achieve 造
dzày	disease 瘥			2. unripe (grain) 阜
dzem	to lie at the bottom of water; wade 潛		dzòung	junction of two rivers 潨
dzèn	before, precede, former 前		dzòunt	cherry salmon 鱒
dzeng	1. for sky to clear 星		dzous	come to, attain 就
	2. affection 情		dzout	high-pointed 崒
dzenk	quiet, pure; to make tranquil, to be quiet, acquiesce 靖, 靜		dzouts	1. collect, assemble 萃
				2. fatigue, distress 瘁
dzes	accumulate; a heap 柴		dzòuy	1. repress 摧
dzèt	cut, trim, hence restrain, govern 截			2. break; hence, cut fodder 摧
dzi	1. thatch; to pile up 茨		dzòuy, dzòuy-ngòuy	craggy 崔, 崔嵬
	2. puncture-vine 茨			
dzì	1. equal, uniform; reverent; *Dzì* (Qi), a state 齊		dzòuyc	offence, crime 罪
			dzòyc	sit 坐
	2. quick-witted 齊		dzòys	a seat 坐
dzìc	shepherd's-purse 薺		dzù	well-endowed, able, strong 才
dzin	1. luxuriant, growing profusely 蓁		dzùc	at; exist, live 在
	2. cicada 螓		dzùk	injure 賊
Dzin	Qin, a state, later the first imperial dynasty 秦		dzùm	silkworm 蠶
			dzùn	to dwell at 存
dzins	1. promoted, prominent 藎		dzùng	1. hate 憎
	2. ashes; burned 燼			2. marker of perfect tense 曾
dzint	exhaust, entirely 盡		dzùngs	give; a gift 贈
dzis	1. follow, associate with; from 自		dzùns	repeatedly 薦
	2. oneself 自		dzup	1. harmonious 輯
dzìs	1. angry 懠			
	2. sheaf, bundle 穧			

	2. collect, bring together, hold together 輯	gàk	a badger 貉
		gàmp	rumbling of a carriage 檻
	3. come together and settle, as birds; accomplish 集	gan	1. reverent 虔
dzùp	mixed, variegated 雜		2. cut, kill 虔
dzus	to breed, nurture, love, fondle 字	gàn	1. cold 寒
dzùs	1. to load 載		2. prop up, support; wing, to fly 翰
	2. to erect shuttering for building walls 栽	Gàn	Han, a place-name 韓
		gang	strong, violent 疆
dzwan	a spring 泉	gàng	1. travel by water 杭
ek	increase 益		2. for a bird to stretch its neck 頏
èk	part of a yoke 厄		3. a row, rank 行
em	contented, tranquil 厭	gàngs	strong, vigorous 行
emp	a kind of wild mulberry tree 檿	gank	make an effort; compel 疆
ems	satiate; abundant, fine 厭	gàns	guard, protect, ward off 扞
Èn	Yan, a state 燕	gànt	dry, drought; Gànt (Han), a mountain 旱
èns	take pleasure, be at ease; to feast; a feast 燕, 宴	gat	1. to exhaust 竭
èns-èns	a swallow (bird) 燕燕		2. surpassing, outstanding; hero; single 傑
èns-ont	beautiful 嬿婉		3. perch (for birds); Gat (Jie), last king of Ghàc dynasty, see Ode 304 桀
èp	bury 瘞		
ep-up	moist 厭浥		4. lift on shoulder; high 揭
ga	vast, spacious 渠	gàt	1. what, where, when, how, why? 曷
gà	1. how, why, what? 胡		2. rough haircloth 褐
	2. dewlap 胡	gàts	to hurt, be hurt; damage, harm 害
	3. calabash; a 'hu' vase 壺	gaw	high 喬
ga-dra	rough bamboo mat 籧篨	gaw, drong-gaw	a long-tailed species of pheasant 鷮, 重鷮
gac	1. oppose, resist 距		
	2. black millet 秬	gawc	elegant, beautiful 糾
	3. upright posts of drum or bell stand 虡	Gàwc	Hao, Western Tiw capital (p. 8) 鎬
gàc	1. rely on, depend on 怙	gawk	high-stepping, robust-looking; conceited 蹻
	2. blessings 祜	gàwk	a crane 鶴
	3. door, house 戶	gay	chisel 錡
	4. wooded hill 岵	gày	1. what, how, why? 何
	5. unknown tree species 楛		2. lotus 荷
	6. must (scarcely-fermented wine, see Ode 165) 酤	Gày	Yellow River 河
		gayc	cooking pot 錡
gak	tongue 臄	gàyc	carry 何
		gàys	congratulate 賀
		ge	1. illness; suffer 疧

	2. wheel hub 軝		(Tang), an antiquarian name for *Tzins* state 唐; 唐棣
Ge	Qishan, a mountain 岐		
gè	why, what, where? *Gè Se* (Qi Si), brother of a lord of *Ràc* 奚; 奚斯		2. dodder (a parasitic weed) 唐
			3. path to temple door 唐
gec	a clan; suffix to a name indicating a lady, or the clan leader 氏	go	toil 劬
		gò	1. a particle, often introductory: "Now, …", or equivalent to *wi*, q.v. 侯
geng	city wall, esp. inner wall; city; to fortify 城		
gèng	1. punish; law 刑		2. marquis, noble in general; princely 侯
	2. a model; imitate 形		3. target 侯
Gèng	Xing, a state 邢		4. throat 喉
gèns	appear 見		5. dried food, provisions 餱
gènt-gwrànt	beautiful 睍睆	gòc	thick, ample, generous 厚
		gok	bend the body, curl up 局
gèp	grasp; hold between fingers, pinch; hold on to; embrace 挾	gon	1. a bend; curved; handsome 卷
			2. fist; force, strength 拳
ghà	a verbal question mark or exclamation mark 乎	gòn	to build, to complete; *Gòn* (Wan), son of *Jang Kyang*, see Ode 26 完
ghà	at; X *ghà*, at X 乎	gon-la	to sprout; beginning of anything 權輿
ghàc	great; *Ghàc* (Xia), the first Chinese dynasty, later used for the culturally-Chinese states as opposed to the tribal periphery 夏	gong	1. distressed 邛
			2. mound 邛
		gòng	1. flood 洪
Ghàc Kyu, Ghàc Nùm	Xia Ji, Xia Nam: a mother and son of *Drin* 夏姬, 夏南		2. disorder, trouble 訌
			3. wild goose 鴻
			4. toad 鴻
ghàw	cry out 號	gongs	together 共
ghòc	after 後	gos	all, together, complete 具
ghòs	go behind, support 後	gòs	1. to escort, wait on 候
gic	regard 視		2. sovereign, lord; *Gòs Tzuk* (Hou Ji), the Millet Lord, first cereal grower and ultimate ancestor of the *Tiw* kings, see Ode 245 后; 后稷
gin	slave, servant 臣		
gìn	wise, worthy 賢		
gip	1. ten 十		
	2. archer's armlet 拾		3. arrow with metal tip 鍭
gis	1. to show 示	got	stumble, trample 蹶
	2. enjoy 嗜	gots	1. agile; alert; *Gots* (Gui), a personal name 蹶
git	straight 佶		
gìt	1. tuck flaps of skirt under girdle to make a carrying-pocket 襭		2. small sacrificial table 巖
		gòts	unite, assemble, collect, encounter; *gòts brans*, a skullcap (which gathers the hair together) 會; 會弁
	2. for a bird to straighten its neck 頏		
giw	long and curved like a horn 觩	gou	1. urgent 絿
glang	1. great; *glang-lìts*, a type of cherry, probably great white cherry; *Glang*		2. long and curved like a horn 捄

	3. seek, beg for 求
	4. meet, assemble 逑
	5. mate, companion; antagonist 仇
	6. a ritual jade object 球
	7. chisel 銶
gouc	1. mother's brother 舅
	2. fault, blame, inauspicious 咎
gòuc	1. bright, splendid; *Gòuc Thìn*, "Bright Sky": a name for the supreme god 昊; 昊天
	2. vast, great 浩
gòuk	a bird, perhaps crane; *Gòuk* (Hu), a place-name 鵠
goung	poverty, destitution 窮
gount	distress; embarrassed 窘
gouts	1. fail; defective 匱
	2. food; a gift of food 饋
gòuyc-dòuy	exhausted, ill 瘣隤
gòyc	calamity; chastise 禍
grà	1. what, how? 遐
	2. far, far from, far-reaching; *pu grà X*, X is very probable, there is sure to be X 遐; 不遐 X
	3. flaw, blemish 瑕
	4. horse of mixed red and white colour 騢
gràc	down, below 下
gràm	to carry in the mouth 銜
gràmp	jet of water 檻
gràms	mirror 鑒
gràn	1. large, ample 閑
	2. to train; well-trained 閑
	3. see *grèn*
gràng	1. walk, a road; act, practise 行
	2. yoke of carriage, crossbeam 衡
grangs	quarrel, quarrelsome 競
gràngs	go round, inspect 行
grànk	floating-hearts, see Ode 1 荇
gràs	1. go down, send down 下
	2. summer 夏

	3. leisure, respite 暇
gràt	hub of axle and linchpin 轄
gràw	eat; food 殽
gràws	imitate 傚
gre	run sure-footedly 伎
grèn, gràn	move leisurely 閑
grènt	refined 嫻
grès-gròs	happy and carefree 邂逅
gri	1. old 耆
	2. great, numerous 祁
grì	cold 湝
grin	1. vigorous 矜
	2. pitiable, to pity 矜
Grit	Ji, a clan name 姞
groc	straitened, in want 窶
gròngs	alley, lane, street 巷
grònk	neck, to stretch the neck 項
gròns	calamity 患
gròts	word, speak 話
grou	road junction, crossroads 逵
gròuk	learn 學
gròung	submit 降
gròuy	bosom; to cherish, be anxious about, hope for, long for 懷
gròuys	ruin, ruined 壞
grùk	1. kernel; stone fruit 核
	2. wing 翃
grùm	all; complete; to unite 咸
gruns	1. to plaster, bury 墐
	2. have an audience with a superior 覲
	3. famine 饉
Grùp	a town or river in *Nots* state 郃
grùp	assemble; accomplish; to accord with, concordant 洽
grùs	weapon, tool 械
gu	1. his, her, its, their; (occasionally) your, my, our; *A gu B*, how B A is! 其
	2. to wish that; auxiliary expressing future or wish 其
	3. dappled grey 騏, 綦

	4. prosperity; fortunate 祺		gwàs	melon, gourd 瓜
	5. a fixed time, date 期		gwàt	1. alive; keep someone alive 活
Gu	Qi, a river of Henan, see Ode 48 淇			2. join 佸
gu-rin, rin	unicorn, see Ode 11 麒麟, 麟		gwèn	suspend 縣
guk	extreme point; a limit; attain; arrive at extreme 極		gweng	1. scared, alone and helpless 惸, 㷀, 嬛
gum	1. reeds 芩			2. precious; precious stone 瓊
	2. a Chinese lute 琴		gwènk	distant 泂
gùm	contain 函		gwènt	pure (of jade) 鞙
gùmp-lùmp	lotus blossom 菡萏		gwi	mallow 葵
			gwic	measure, estimate, examine, manage 揆
gums	sash 衿		gwìn	black 玄
gun	1. toil, diligent, devoted 勤		gwits	a shaking movement 悸
	2. watercress 芹		gwràng	to plough crosswise 衡
gung	strong, terrible 兢		gwrànt	brilliant (of stars) 睆
gùng	constant 恆		gwren	handsome 婘
guns	be near to, keep close to 近		gwruy	sturdy 騤
gunt	near 近		gwu	1. fur garment 裘
gup	come to, attain, go as far as; and, together with 及			2. adorned with jewels 俅
				3. triangular blade 厹
gùp	join, unite; harmony; complete; a mate 合			4. remote wilderness 芁
			gwuc	ancient 舊
gus	dread; hate; cautious 忌		gwun	a flock, class; all 群, 羣
guy	1. tall 頎		gwùng	vast, to enlarge 弘
	2. pray, beg, announce 祈		gwùts	violent, energetic; for a river to break its banks 潰
	3. doorway, threshold 畿			
	4. royal domain; guy-pac, minister of war 畿, 圻; 圻父		gyaw	1. piled up, high, dangerous 翹
				2. mallow 荍
	5. dragon banner 旂			
gwà	fox 狐		ha	modest 虛
gwàk	1. boil 濩		hàc	whack! 許
	2. reap, cut; Gwàk (Huo), a place-name 穫		hàk	moat 壑
			Hamp-sòn	Xianyun, a northern tribe, see Ode 167 玁狁
gwaks	fear 懼			
gwàn	rush, sedge 萑, 莞		hang	1. fragrant, perfume 香
gwang	mad, foolish 狂			2. region, tract 鄉
gwàng	1. yellow; gwàng tìwc, "yellow bird": black-naped oriole 黃; 黃鳥			3. a feast; enjoy a feast; provide food and drink for a feast or sacrifice 享, 饗
	2. reed organ, or tongue of wind instrument 簧		hangs	1. turn towards, face towards; facing; south (i.e. facing the sun) 鄉
gwank	deceive 迋			2. north-facing window 向
gwànt	wash 澣			

VOICES FROM EARLY CHINA

Hàns	Han River 漢	
hànt	scorch 暵	
hap	sides of body 脅	
hàs	call out, shout 呼	
hat-haw	type of dog 獦獢	
hàw	1. clamour, noise 囂	
	2. wormwood 蒿	
hays	to joke, sport 戲	
hèng	fragrance 馨	
hènt	bright, illustrious; *Hènt* (Xian), a personal name 顯	
hi	yarrow 蓍	
hlàc	tiger; *Hlàc* (Hu), a personal name; *hlàc gin*, "tiger officers": special forces 虎; 虎臣	
hok	urge, stimulate 勖	
hong	1. unlucky, bad; contrary to natural order 凶	
	2. discord; to litigate 訩	
hòng	burn 烘	
hos	warm; heat 煦	
hou	1. to rest; ease, rest; benefit, blessing, happy; grace 休	
	2. kind of bird—owl? 梟	
hòu	1. to clear away, to weed 薅	
	2. a tiger's roar 虖	
houc	to rot, decay 朽	
hòuc	good, beautiful 好	
houk	cherish 慉	
hòus	to love 好	
hràk	1. majestic 赫	
	2. fire-red 赫	
	3. to manifest 赫	
hràks	scold, rebuke 嚇	
hràwk	rich white colour (of birds) 翯	
hràws	filial piety 孝	
hriwk	Japanese dock 蓫	
hrùmp	roaring, enraged (as a tiger) 闞	
hu	brightness, splendour 熙	
Hu	Xi, a marquis of *Ràc*, see Ode 300 僖	
huc	joy, rejoice 喜	
huk	red 奭	
hum	enjoy; elated 歆	
hun	rejoice; delicious 欣	
hung	raise, rise, prosper 興	
hup	1. united, harmonious; to draw in 翕	
	2. to stretch 翕	
	3. roar of rushing water 潝	
hut	come to, reach 迄	
huts	to collect, to rest 墍	
huy	1. groan 屎	
	2. first light of the sun; to dry 晞	
hwa	1. oh!, alas!; pained; *hwa-tzay*, exclamation of excitement or grief 吁; 吁嗟	
	2. great 訏	
hwac	1. cork-oak, see Ode 121 栩	
	2. a ceremonial cap 冔	
hwàk	sprouting leaves of bean plants 藿	
hwan	1. forget 諼	
	2. ocarina 塤	
hwàn	a badger 貆	
hwàng	loud sound of crying or bell 喤	
hwangs	1. give, confer on 貺	
	2. increase 況	
hwank	distressed, disappointed, confused 怳	
hwàns	1. ample 渙	
	2. cry out, clamour 嚾	
hwant	brilliant, illustrious, conspicuous 恒, 咺	
hwàt	sound of splash 濊	
hwàts	1. ample, deep 㦛	
	2. tinkle 㦛	
	3. sound of wings 翽	
hwe	marlinspike 觿	
hwen	smart, nimble 儇	
hwèns	bluish-black horse 駽	
hwìn	far away 泂	
hwins	hibiscus; *Hwins* (Shun), a legendary emperor 舜	
hwìt	water channel, moat 洫	
hwìt	blood 血	

393

hwìts	small; to make a shrill sound 嘒	its	1. excellent, beautiful; deep 懿
hwrang	elder brother 兄		2. repress; repressed, dignified 懿
hwùc	dried, minced, and pickled meat 醢	ìts	1. overcast, windblown sky 曀
hwuk	bundle of threads 緎		2. kill; a fallen dead tree 殪
hwuks	still, quiet 侐	iw	1. dark; *Iw* (You), last king of Western *Tiw* 幽
hwun	1. befuddled 醺		2. the call of a deer 呦
	2. to smoke, steam 熏	ìwc-kiwc	elegant, beautiful 窈嬌
hwuns	instruct, explain; obey 訓	ìwc-lìwc	alluring 窈窕
hwuy	1. flame, brightness 輝		
	2. a kind of pheasant 翬	ja	to pickle 葅
hwuyc	1. sound of thunder 虺	jac	1. precipitous, dangerous, impenetrable 阻
	2. the young of snakes, brood of snakes 虺		2. small sacrificial table 俎
hwuys	vegetation 卉	jàk	clear away trees and bushes 柞
hyàw	alarm call 嘵	jàmp	to cut off, cut down 斬
hyawc	few 少	Jang	Zhuang, name of various nobles; *Jang Kyang* (Zhuang Jiang), a noblewoman of *Wets*, see Ode 26 莊; 莊姜
hyawk	beautiful, fine 鑠		
hyeng	sound, voice, fame 聲		
hyos	guard a border 戍	jangs	strong, robust, great 壯
hyou	receive, harvest; front-to-back dimension of a vehicle 收	jas	to curse; an oath 詛
		jàw	nest 巢
hyouc	1. to keep, guard 守	jek	oblique, slanting 仄
	2. to hunt 狩	jèk	mat 簀
hyous	an animal; to hunt 獸	jèng	strife, contend with one another; *jèng X*, fight about X 爭
		jèts	suffer; distress 瘵
i	this; is; a grammar word; equivalent to *wi* 維, q.v. 伊	jì	purify oneself; purified 齋
ì	1. a wild duck, perhaps widgeon 鷖	jin	1. numerous, prolific 溱
	2. a syllable inserted for rhythm 兮		2. arrive, reach 臻
i-ouy	woodlouse 伊威		3. hazel 榛
in	1. continue 因	Jin	Zhen, a river of Henan 溱
	2. rely on, trusting, devoted 因	jit	a comb 櫛
	3. marriage; an in-law 姻	jo	a groom 騶
	4. sacrifice 禋	jot	to sprout 茁
	5. piebald horse 駰	Jou	Zou, a personal and place name 聚
	6. mat 茵	jòuc	claw 爪
in-tà	double gate in an outer town wall 闉闍	jous	crinkle 縐
it	one; *it X*, all X, the whole of X; *It Nin*, "the One Man": the king 一, 壹; 一人	ju	1. black 緇
			2. newly cultivated field 菑
ìt	choke 噎	juk	side; turn on its side 側

jums	to bad-mouth, accuse 譖			(Gan), a place name 干
jup	1. cluster together, swarm 揖	kang	1. limit, frontier 疆
	2. collect, store; fold up (wings) 戢		2. ? fierce, or ? uxorious, see Ode 49 疆
	3. crowded together 濈	kàng	1. hard 剛
jus	1. cleave apart 菹		2. controlling rope of a net; regulator, to regulate 綱
	2. minced meat 菹		3. hill, ridge 岡
	3. standing dead tree 菑	kans	set up, establish 建
ka	1. grasp 据	kàns	to correct, keep in line 幹
	2. netsuke gem 琚	kas	1. arrogant 倨
	3. vehicle 車		2. depend on 據
	4. a grammar word 居		3. "walking-stick tree", see Ode 241 椐
kà	1. now, for the moment 姑		4. see kac, kas
	2. guilt, crime 辜	kàs	1. old, long acquaintance 故
	3. father's sister 姑		2. turn one's head and look; look with favour on; Kàs (Gu), a state 顧
kac	1. in the end 居		3. cause, reason 故
	2. round basket 筥	kat	1. rising straight and slender, as a lance 孑
kac, kas	dwell; sit down, repose; a position; tranquil 居		2. raise; high, tall 揭
Kac	Ju, a place name 莒		3. whole, integral 孑
kàc	1. ancient 古	kàt	lablab bean and related vines (see Ode 2) 葛
	2. blind 瞽		
	3. slack, remiss, defective 監	kàts	namely; yes indeed; and so; because 蓋
	4. drum; to play a percussion instrument 鼓	kaw	1. elegant, beautiful 嬌
	5. merchant 賈		2. high; proud, arrogant 驕
	6. net 罟	kàw	1. high 高
	7. ram (male sheep) 羖		2. lamb 羔
	8. thigh 股	kawc	strong, warlike 蹻
kàk	1. each 各	kàwc	white or undyed silk 縞
	2. shelf; kàk-kàk, one above another like shelves 閣; 閣閣	kàws	grease, ointment; moisten, enrich 膏
kàks	strong, firm 固	kày	1. all right 哿
kàm	sweet; kàm dàng, birchleaf pear 甘; 甘棠		2. sing; song 歌
kàmp	dare 敢		3. axe-handle 柯
kàn	1. seek, get 干	kayc	pull aside 掎
	2. dry 乾	ke	1. only 祇
	3. rod, pole 竿		2. branch 支, 枝
	4. a shield 干	kè	chicken 雞
	5. river bank; stream in a ravine; Kàn	kec	a grammar word; may it be so!; verbal exclamation mark 只
		kèk	beat a drum 擊

395

kèm-krà	rushes, sedge 蒹葭	*khens*	reprimand 譴
kèn	1. shoulder 肩	*khèns*	be visible, be like 倪
	2. mature pig 豜	*khent*	send 遣
Kèng	Jing, a river of Shaanxi 涇	*khent-kwhant*	cling to; attached closely 繾綣
kèng	to plan; a norm; *kèng-weng*, regulate 經; 經營	*khes*	slanting ○
kèns	to see 見	*khèt-khòt*	separated, far apart 契闊
kes	wicked, malign 忮	*khèts*	1. to notch a tortoise shell for divination 契
kès	continue, connect 繼		2. distressed; *Khèts* (Qi), ancestor of the *Un* dynasty, see Ode 303 契
kèt	pure 潔		
kets	to tailor clothes 制		3. separated, distanced 契
kha	1. strong, robust 祛	*khìc*	1. to open, lead the way 啟
	2. sleeve 袪		2. bow head to ground 稽
	3. mound, ruins, abandoned city 虛		3. kneel; *khìc-kac*, *khìc-k'hlac*, to rest, take a break 啟; 啟居, 啟處
	4. uprights of a musical-instrument stand 虛		
khac	put away, eliminate 去	*khìn*	lead a beast 牽
khàc	bitter; sowthistle 苦	*khits*	throw away, abandon 棄
khak	coarse cloth 綌	*khlac*	large; large-mouthed 哆
khàk	respect; reverent 恪	*k'hlac*	stay, dwell; to place, stay still; be tranquil 處
Khang	Qiang, a western group of tribes 羌		
khàng	prosperous; at ease; joyful; *Khàng* (Kang), name of the third *Tiw*-dynasty king, and of a lord of *Dzin* 康	*khlak*	red 赤
		k'hlang	splendid, bright; to flourish 昌
		k'hlangs	to lead singing, intone 倡
khàngs	1. high 伉	*khlayc*	enlarge 侈
	2. to set up 抗	*khlong*	even, just 傭
khàns	rejoice 忻	*k'hloun*	stream, river 川
khas	go away 去	*k'hlout*	go out, bring out, send out 出
khat	1. go away 揭	*k'hlouts*	bring out, take out 出
	2. martial-looking 揭	*k'hlung*	lift up 稱
khàt	thirst, thirsty 渴	*k'hlungs*	estimate, appreciate; equal to, corresponding to 稱
khats	1. to rest 愒, 憩		
	2. lift one's clothes 揭	*kho*	drive forward; trot (see Ode 163) 驅
khaw	vigorous, robust 驕	*khòc*	mouth 口
khàyc	be able to; *khàyc Verb*, Verbable, worth Verbing; *khàyc luc*, can use X to do, (or just) can, be able 可; 可以	*khok*	a bend; bent; *khok-gok*, tangled 曲; 曲局
		khòng	hollow, empty 空
khec	stand on tiptoe 跂	*khòngs*	1. to exhaust 空
khèngs	1. empty; exhaustively 磬, 罄		2. pull up a horse; throw; throw oneself on, hence rush to 控
	2. musical stone 磬	*khonk*	fear 恐
khènk	be willing 肯	*khònk*	very, greatly 孔

khòs	robber 寇		*khùyc*	happy, joyous, pleasant 豈, 凱
khot	1. gap, defect 闋		*k'hyou*	1. ugly, wicked, ominous 醜
	2. watchtower over gateway 闕			2. multitude 醜
khòuc	1. old; deceased father 考		*k'hyous*	strong smell 臭
	2. achieve, complete (a feast) 考		*k'hyuc*	1. teeth 齒
	3. examine 考			2. cooked millet, or to cook millet, esp. for a sacrifice 饎, 糦
	4. to beat 考		*ki*	fat, grease 脂
	5. a tree species, perhaps *Ailanthus fordii* 栲		*kì*	hairpin 笄
khoun	granary 囷		*kic*	1. delicious 旨
khoung	house, palace, temple 宮			2. to point 指
khout	subdue 屈			3. bring about, settle 耆
khòut	dig out 掘		*kim*	needle; *Kim Hlàc* (Zhen Hu), a nobleman of *Dzin* 鍼; 鍼虎
khòy	beautiful ○			
khràk	guest, visitor, stranger 客		*kimp*	pillow 枕
khran	to tuck up one's skirt 褰		*kìn*	hard, strong, solid 堅
khrang	a minister 卿		*kit*	1. lucky, auspicious; *Kit* (Ji), a personal name 吉
khrangs	happiness, rejoice 慶			2. grasp 拮
khròts	comfortable 噲		*kìt*	to tie, a knot 結
khròus	artful, skilful 巧		*kiw*	down-curving (branch) 樛
khrup	weep silently 泣		*kiwc*	twist 糾
khryan	err, exceed 愆		*kìws*	call out, shout 叫
khu	like a demon mask 傀		*klac*	lift, present offerings 舉
khuc	1. rise 起		*klòk*	valley 谷
	2. matrimony-vine or boxthorn 杞		*klòng*	duke, prince; palace 公
	3. a high-quality white millet 芑		*ko*	colt 駒
	4. bare hillside 屺		*kò*	1. curved 句
khùk	1. self-controlled 克			2. hook 鉤
	2. can, be able to 克		*koc*	oriental raisin-tree 枸
	3. crush, dominate 克		*kòc*	1. if only; truly 苟
khum	1. intense; solemn 欽			2. old; old and wrinkled face 耇
	2. coverlet 衾			3. fish trap 笱
khùm	able to bear, equal to 堪			4. filth 垢
khùmp	thump 坎			5. doesn't matter 苟
khup	dry, scorched 燺		*kòk*	1. treat well; luck 穀
khùts	1. sad 愾			2. grain; salary 穀
	2. to sigh 愾			3. paper mulberry, *Broussonetia papyrifera* 穀
khùy	to open 開			
khuyc	how? 豈			4. wheel hub 轂

kòn	1. cap 冠			3. nourish 鞠
	2. a groom, servant 倌			4. to address, inform 鞠
kong	provide, serve 供			5. exhaust, go to extreme; destitute 鞠
kòng	1. public, impartial 公			6. handful 匊
	2. officiate; officer 工			7. outside of river bend 沅
	3. effort, achievement, merit 功		kòuk	announce, report 告
konk	1. strengthen 鞏		koun	fallow deer 麕
	2. join hands; Konk (Gong), a state 共		Kòun	a branch of the Luy tribes 混
konk, konk-pek	ritual jade disc (see pek) 珙, 珙璧		kòun	elder brother; Kòun-ngà (Kunwu), a state 昆; 昆吾
kons	look on with affection 眷, 睠		koung	1. body, person 躬
kòns	1. lodge; lodging-house 館			2. palace, citadel; temple 宮
	2. pour a sacrificial libation 祼		kòung	to work at; well-worked, solid 攻
	3. perforate; fuck; serve 貫		kòunt	1. cord 緄
kont	to roll; kont-nuc, mouse-ear chickweed 卷; 卷耳			2. royal robe embroidered with dragons 袞
kònt	tube, flute 管, 筦		kous	1. rescue, help 救
kòs	1. come across, meet 覯			2. go to extremes; extravagant 究
	2. come/bring into conflict with, plot against 構			3. scrutinize 究
	3. favour 媾			4. a stable 廐
	4. lattice 冓		kòuy	a kind of gemstone 瑰
	5. pheasant's call 雊		kouys	ashamed 愧
kot	1. his, her, its, their 厥		kòy	pass by; Kòy (Guo), a stream 過
	2. "turtle-foot" fern, see Ode 14 蕨		kòyc-ròyc	1. potter wasp, Eumenes pomiformis 蜾蠃
kòt	Chinese juniper; Kòt (Gui), a state 檜			2. plant related to cucumber, see Ode 156 果臝
kòts	to mince 膾		krà	1. house, family; Krà (Jia), a personal name 家
kou	1. collect 捄			
	2. pearl-necked dove 鳩			2. rush, sedge 葭
kòu	1. large drum 鼖		kràc	1. great; abundance, felicity 嘏, 假
	2. bow-case, quiver; put in bow-case 櫜			2. go to, esp. go to an ancestor's temple to worship him 假
	3. lazy, incompetent; Kòu Law (Gao Yao), Minister of Crime for the legendary emperor Hwins 皋, 臯; 臯陶			3. borrow; kràc mits, "borrow sleep": to have a nap without undressing 假; 假寐
kòu mùn	outer gate of citadel 皋門			4. a three-legged 'jia' wine bowl 斝
kouc	1. nine 九		krak	a kind of lance or sword 戟
	2. onion, leek, garlic 韭		kràk	arrive, spread out, extend to 格
kòuc	pure, bright 皓, 杲		kràm	look at, inspect 監
kouk	1. full, ample 鞠		kràms	mirror 鑒
	2. entirely 鞠		kràn	red-grass, see Ode 139 菅
			krang	mound, hill; great; capital city 京

kràng	soup 羹	
kràng-ngàc	seventh in the 60-day cycle 庚午	
krangs	to the end, entirely 竟	
kràngs	continue 賡	
krank	1. great 景	
	2. shadow; *Krank* (Jing), a hill in Henan 景	
krànk	suffering, distress 梗	
kràns	1. remonstrate, admonish 諫	
	2. stream in a ravine 澗	
Krànt Lèk	Jian Di, mother of *Khèts*, q.v. 簡狄	
kràp	1. familiar, be familiar with 狎	
	2. shell, leather body-armour 甲	
kràs	1. grain; to sow 稼	
	2. for a woman to marry 嫁	
kràw	area outside city wall 郊	
kràwc	1. artful, crafty 狡	
	2. beautiful 佼	
	3. rude 絞	
kràwk	chariot sidebars, used as elbow-rests 較	
kràws	teach; instruction 教	
kràh	1. obtain, hit 加	
	2. excellent, delicious, happy; to approve; *kràh-nga*, barbel 嘉; 嘉魚	
	3. a hairpin jewel 珈	
kràys	a yoke, to yoke 駕	
krèn	1. orchid 蘭	
	2. intervening space, middle, among, in; insert 間	
kreng	1. attentive; afraid 驚	
	2. bramble, thorny; *Kreng* (Jing), a southern tribe later absorbed into China as *Chac*, q.v. 荊	
krèng	to plough 耕	
krengs	respectful, careful 敬	
krènk	wide awake 耿	
krèns	replace 間	
krènt	1. loud, great 簡	
	2. nonchalant 簡	
	3. bamboo writing-slip 簡	

krèp	be on both sides of 夾	
krès	idle, careless, remiss 懈	
krèts	1. increase, enlarge; great 介	
	2. fishscale 介	
	3. boundary 界	
kri	a fast, hunger 飢	
krì	1. cold 喈	
	2. in unison 喈	
	3. stair, (hence) promoter 階	
krì, krìc	all; in accord; together, to coincide; complete; plentiful; *krìc ròuc*, "grow old together": (be one's) spouse 皆, 偕; 偕老	
kric	a stool, small table; *kric-kric*, decorated with studs 几; 几几	
krìt	hold up flaps of skirt to make a carrying-pocket 袺	
krìts	reach to; a limit; to moderate oneself 居	
krìw	1. glue; to fasten together 膠	
	2. sound of cock crow 膠	
kròk	1. horn, (or by extension) beak 角	
	2. rafter, horizontal branch 桷	
kròn	bar, barrier; also used for *kòns*, perforate, q.v. 關	
krong	reverent, respectful, sincere 恭	
Kròng	the Yangtze (though see pp. 6–7) 江	
kròns	1. custom, usage 串	
	2. child's hair bunches 丱	
kros	sandal, shoe 屨	
krouc	1. wheel-hub 軌	
	2. a wide 'gui' food bowl 簋	
kròuc	disturb 攪	
kròuk	1. straight 覺	
	2. wake up 覺	
kròungs	descend, send down 降	
kròy	bay horse with black mouth 騢	
krùk	1. change 愅	
	2. animal hide 革	
krùmp	abridge, moderate 減	
krun	headcloth 巾	
krùn	distress, difficulty; difficult 艱	

krùs	1. guard against, warn; careful; be ready for 戒		kwàn	look, look at, see 觀
	2. press, harass 恆		kwàng	1. broad, extensive 光
kryan	faulty, fault 騫			2. brightness 光
kryàw	to cross; across one another 交			3. rushing water; fierce 洸
ku	1. foundation, to found 基		kwànk	wide 廣
	2. winnowing-basket 箕		kwàns	1. heron 鸛
	3. a question particle 其			2. dense growth 灌
kuc	leading thread; regulate; rule, norm 紀		kwànt	fatigue; exhausted, helpless, lacking anything to rely on 瘝
kùc	change 改		kwàt	1. bring together, bind 括
kuk	1. hurry; urgently; rapid 亟			2. to purl (flowing water) 活
	2. harassing 棘		kwày	halberd, see Ode 151 戈
	3. thorns; jujube tree 棘		kwayc	1. dilapidated 塊
	4. collar 襋			2. perverse, wily 詭
kum	1. now 今		kwè	jade tablet of rank, see Ode 238 圭
	2. gold, bronze, metal generally 金		kwèn	purify; pure 蠲
	3. collar 衿		kwèng	1. sturdy (horse) 駉
kump	brocade, patterned silk 錦			2. outlying area far from the capital 駉
kùmp	touch, budge 感		kwènk	light of fire 熲
kung	cautious, fear 兢		kwèt	1. a buckle 觿
kùngs	spread out, everywhere 恆			2. archer's thimble, see Ode 60 決
kuns	perspicuous 斤		kwhàk	1. wide, ample 廓
kunt	1. cautious 謹			2. leather 鞹
	2. (probably) violet-cress 菫		kwhàn	wide; open-hearted 寬
kup	urgent; Kup (Ji), a personal name 急		kwhang	1. succour, assist, regulate 匡
kùp	knee-cover 韐			2. square basket 筐
kus	1. this, that 其		kwhàngs	desolate, waste 曠
	2. a closing grammar word 忌, 迋		kwhàt	separated, far apart 闊
kuts	marker of perfect tense; entirely, all; since, when 既		kwhay	damage, injure, destroy 虧
kùts	wash, throw water on 溉		kwhec	split bands, see Ode 217 頍
kuy	1. near, imminent 幾		kwheng	1. slanting; kwheng-kwhang, a basket with slanting sides for gathering crops 頃; 頃筐
	2. famine 饑			2. turn over, overthrow 傾
kuyc	a few; how many? 幾		kwhènk	an unlined hempen garment 褧
kwà	1. wail 呱		kwhet	to break, splinter 缺
	2. a net 罟		kwhìnt	a dog 犬
Kwac	Ju, a clan name 橘		kwhìt	to be at rest 関
kwac	solitary 踽		kwhràt	big oneself up, boast 誇
kwaks	anxious; flurried 瞿		kwhu	hill 丘

kwhung	hole, hollow 穹			2. rich, abundant 與
kwhùng	leather-covered leaning-board of carriage 靷			3. upward-curling 旟
kwhùnt	alley between buildings in a palace compound 壺			4. surplus, remains 餘
				5. falcon flag 旟
kwin	even, equal, adjusted 均			6. field which was already cultivated in the previous season 畬
kwits	1. young; youngest son; *Kwits* (Ji), grandfather of king *Mac* 季			7. a closing grammar-word 與
			là	1. mud; plaster, to plaster 塗
	2. autumn 季			2. bitter; dandelion, sowthistle (see Ode 237) 荼
kwrà	melon 瓜			
kwràc	solitary, widow; *kwràc tsùy*, "sole wife": principal wife, consort 寡; 寡妻		lac	1. and, with; help, associate with 與
				2. I, me 予
kwràng	drinking-horn 觥			3. give 與, 予
kwrank	far away 憬			4. wild country 野
kwrìn	widow 矜		làc	glutinous rice 稌
kwru	tortoise; *Kwru* (Gui), a mountain range in southern Shandong 龜		lak	1. great, ample, amply-growing, abundant 繹
kwruc	spring gushing from a rock wall 氿			2. pleased; pleasant, mild 懌
kwrùk	behead 馘			3. fed up with; dislike 射, 斁
kwrùn	widower; "widower-fish", see Ode 104 鰥		Lak	Yi, a mountain in southern Shandong 嶧
kwuc	1. long time 久		làk	underclothes 襗
	2. a precious stone, perhaps obsidian 玖		làks	sounding full-bodied (music) 斁
kwùk	a country, state 國		lam	attract with a bait, provoke 餤
kwun	1. prince; *kwun-tzuc*, "princely man", see p. 15 君; 君子		làm	1. aflame 惔
				2. speak, chat 談
	2. army 軍		lan	bamboo mat 筵
kwung	bow (for shooting) 弓		lang	1. sunny; elated; the "Yang" of Yin v. Yang; the southerly side of a hill or northerly side of a valley; the tenth moon 陽
kwùng	arm, upper arm 肱			
kwus	suffering, distress 疚			
kwuy	go home, go where one belongs; for a bride to go to her new home 歸			2. to lift, stir, raise, winnow 揚
kwuyc	devil, ghost 鬼			3. poplar 楊
Kyang	Jiang, a clan name; *Kyang Ngwan* (Jiang Yuan), mother of the Millet Lord, see Ode 245 姜; 姜嫄			4. forehead 揚
				5. battle-axe 揚
				6. sparrowhawk 揚
kyaw	bright, illustrious 昭			7. metal frontlet for horse 鍚
kyawc	glorious 昭		làng	a kind of cicada 螗
kyàwc	bright 皦, 皎		lànk	1. immense, grand; smooth 蕩
Kyu	Ji, a clan name 姬			2. carefree, extravagant 惕
la	1. I, we 余		lànt	1. disorderly 誕

	2. an opening particle 誕		2. summer heat 暑
lap	1. leaf 葉	lhak	1. put away 釋
	2. generation, epoch 葉		2. wash rice 釋
las	1. joy, amusement, recreation; praise, renown 譽, 豫		3. to sting 螫
			4. lay open 澤
	2. some black bird, perhaps raven 鸒	lhàk	dead leaves 蘀
lat	toil, fatigue, suffering 勩	lhaks	all, numerous, abundant; the crowd, the people; probably, possibly, would that ...; *lhaks-kuy*, more or less, possibly, it is to be hoped 庶; 庶幾
lats	1. to drag, trail; dragging, slow-moving 曳, 泄		
	2. be dispersed; relieved; leisurely, comfortable 渫, 泄	lhàmp	young silvergrass 炎
		lhang	1. flowing abundantly 湯
	3. babble; garrulous 詍		2. to wound, afflict 傷
law	pleased with oneself 陶	Lhang	original name (Shang) of the *Un* dynasty 商
làw	1. abscond, avoid 逃		
	2. peach tree; *làw droung*, "peach insect": wren 桃; 桃蟲	lhàng	hot liquid, soup; *Lhàng* (Tang), the first *Un* dynasty king 湯
	3. small hand drum 鞀	lhas	halt, stay overnight 舍
lay	compliant, conceited, pretentious 訑	lhàs	hare, rabbit; *lhàs-tza*, net for trapping rabbits 兔; 兔罝
lày	1. flow 沱		
	2. tress of several threads 紽	lhats	generation; from generation to generation 世
layc	terminates an assertion; *A B layc*, A is B 也		
		lhàw	restless 挑
lek	1. lizard 蜴	lhay	set a net, spread out 施
	2. raised border dividing fields 場	lhày	other 它, 他
Lèk	Di, tribes of the north, including the *Hamp-sòn*, q.v. 狄	lhàyc	lay burden on 佗
		lhays	bestow, give; spread out, extend 施
leks	easy; well-cultivated 易	lhec	pig 豕
lemp	pointed, sharp 覃	lhek	proceed to, to suit, to like, to fall in with 適
lèmp	horse with hairy legs 驔		
leng	1. fill; full 盈	lhèk	1. distant; keep at a distance, remove 逷, 逖
	2. pillar 楹		
lèng	1. straight, upright 庭		2. anxious; anxiety 愁
	2. court; attend court 庭		3. grieved 惕
	3. thunderclap 霆		4. to cut 剔
lèngs	palace courtyard 廷	lhèks	swaddling clothes, wrapper 裼
lèp	fear 疊	lhèmp	to disgrace 忝
lèt	black horse 驖	lhèng	1. slow, slack 縵
lha	1. relax; at leisure; *Lha* (Shu), a small tribe near Lujiang, Anhui 舒		
			2. hear; sound 聽
	2. writing, document 書	lhengs	wise, a sage 聖
lhac	1. put aside, let go, let off 舍	lhèngs	to listen to someone, obey 聽
		lhep	archer's thimble 韘

lhi	1. to set something out, preside 尸		2. measure of capacity, about a quart 升
	2. corpse; *Lhi*, living representative of ancestor receiving a sacrifice 尸	lhungs	conquer 勝
		lhyàw	mean, ungenerous 佻
lhi-kou	cuckoo 鳲鳩	lhyàwk	jump 躍, 趯
lhic	1. to display, marshal, extend, spread out; swear, make a solemn declaration 矢	li	a plant, perhaps *Orontium aquaticum* 梀
		lìmp	bamboo mat 簟
	2. arrow 矢	lìn	field, cultivated land; to "take the field", i.e. hunt 田
lhin	1. extend; repeat; *Lhin* (Shen), a state 申, 伸		
		lins	1. trace (linking draught horse to vehicle) 靷
	2. body; *wuc lhin*, "have body": be pregnant 身; 有身		
			2. small "introducer" drum 棟
lhint	how much more, *a fortiori* 矧	lìns	1. bring into cultivation, put in order 田, 甸
lhit	1. lose, fail 失		
			2. lightning 電
	2. room; house 室	lint	to lead, prolong 引
lhìw	gather mulberry leaves for silkworms 條	lit	be at ease 逸
		lìt	1. alternate 迭
lho	tilt, overturn 輸		
lhok	bind; a bundle 束		2. stem of melon or gourd 胅
lhong	thresh grain with pestle and mortar 舂	lits	1. remnant; a remaining branch 肆
lhot	to speak, to excuse 說		2. toil 肆
lhòt	peel off, take away; escape, disappear 脫	lìts	cherry tree 棣
		lìw	1. long, drawn-out 條
lhots	halt, make overnight stop 說		2. metal-ornamented 鋚
lhòts	1. easy, leisurely 脫		3. pale chub, *Zacco platypus* 鰷
	2. withdraw, flee 駾		4. branch 條
lhòu	1. voluminous flow, overflowing; reckless 滔		5. rowan 條
		lìwk	1. advance; promote 迪
	2. go away, pass on 慆		2. cleanse; cleansed, denuded, dried up 滌
lhouc	head; used for counting animals, cf. "three *head* of cattle" 首		
		lo	1. enjoy; enjoyable 愉
lhouyc	water; river 水		2. pass or jump over 踰
lhu	poetry 詩		3. change 渝
lhù	pufferfish 鮐		4. David elm, *Ulmus davidiana* 榆
lhuc	begin 始	loc	1. to increase 愈
lhuk	1. know 識		
	2. adorn; ornament 飾		2. sickness, suffering 瘉
	3. to use; *lhuk muy*, it's no use 式; 式微	lok	to wish 欲
		lòk	recite, read 讀
	4. a model; follow a model 式	loks	liberal, indulgent 裕
	5. equivalent to *nu*, q.v. 式	long	1. use; be busy; *Long* (Yong), a clan name 庸
lhùk	make a mistake; deceitful 忒		
lhuks	to apply; to test, (hence) to vie with 試		2. contain, hold, admit 容
lhung	1. go up 升		

	3. a wall, to wall 墉		assertion; a syllable inserted for rhythm; oh! 矣
	4. appearance 容	lùc	1. idle, negligent 怠
	5. large bell 鏞		2. come to; when 迨
	6. ceremonial knife 容		3. danger, dangerous; (hence) possibly, perhaps 殆
Long	Yong, a place-name (see p. 83) 廊	luk	shoot arrow with string attached; Luk (Yi), a clan name 弋
longs	to use; by means of; X longs, because of X 用	luks	different, strange, rare 異
lonk	1. brave 勇	lùks	generation; from generation to generation 代
	2. jump 踊	lum	great 淫
lot	1. pleased, glad 悅	lùm	1. spread, extend 覃
	2. hole, burrow 閱		2. speak; Lùm (Tan), a state 譚
lòt	snatch, rob 奪	lung	a fly 蠅
lòts	open a way through 兌	lùng	1. rise 騰
lou	scoop grain from a mortar 舀		2. tie, band 縢
lòu	1. rope 綯	luns	descendants, posterity 胤
	2. pottery, to mould; a potter; a kiln 陶	lùp	babble; garrulity 沓
louc	1. to lead, entice 誘	lùts	1. in the extreme 棣
	2. window 牖		2. come to, come forward 逮
lòuc	1. way, road 道	luy	1. level, even, peaceful; Luy (Yi), tribes of the east 夷
	2. rice paddy (the crop before threshing) 稻		2. custom, institution 夷
louk	to rear, breed, nourish 育		3. rule, law, norm; regular 彝
loung	extensive, protracted 久		4. sister-in-law 姨
lòung	1. red 彤	lyàw	come, go 佻
	2. hot vapour 烔	lyawk	tapering 篍
lòunt	withdraw, skulk, escape; evasive 遯, 遁	lyàwk	pheasant feather 翟
lòus	1. mobile, shifting, inconstant 蹈	lyawks	gleam, shine; brightness 燿, 曜
	2. show the way, explain, speak 道		
	3. gallop 陶		
lout	thereupon 聿		
lòyc	long and narrow mountain 隋	ma	1. there is not, not have, don't! Ma X, is X not so? 無
lu	1. give 詒, 貽		2. deceive 無
	2. sweet rice cakes 飴	ma X, ma Y	fail to distinguish X from Y 無 X 無 Y
Lù	Tai, a small state in Shaanxi 邰	mac	1. military, warlike; Mac (Wu), first Tiw-dynasty king; mac-pa, warrior; Mac Tèng (Wu Ding), the last able Un king 武; 武夫; 武丁
luc	1. to use, employ, treat; with, by means of; A luc, with A, thanks to A, because of A; luc A way B, to consider A as B, treat A as B 以; 以 A 為 B		2. big, important 膴
	2. to stop, end 已		3. dance 舞
	3. a word making the preceding words an		4. footprint 武

màc	to plan, counsel 謨			2. extensively 采
màk	1. not have, there is no-one who ... 莫	mec	1. finish, stop, cease 弭
	2. to plan, deliberate, settle 莫		2. strong flow in river 瀰
	3. suffering, distress 瘼		3. a bow (for shooting) having ends capped with bone 弭
	4. luxuriant plant growth 莫	mèk	cover of elbow-rest at front of carriage 幭
màks	1. evening, late 莫		
	2. a grave 墓	meng	name; fame 名
	3. a plant, probably sorrel 蓂	mèng-lùk	a caterpillar destructive to crops 螟螣
mang	1. disappear, exile, there isn't; mang X, mang Y, same as ma X, ma Y, q.v. 亡	mèng-rèng	cotton bollworm, *Heliothis armigera* 螟蛉
		mènk	dark, darkness 冥
	2. forget 忘	mens	face 面
	3. look towards, admire 望	ment	1. in a continuous row; long and thin, long drawn-out; tiny, delicate; *ment-mròn*, delicate 綿, 縣; 綿蠻
màng	extensive 芒		
mank	1. be without, lack 罔		
	2. deceive; be deceived, confused 罔		2. flowing heavily 沔
	3. net 網		4. *ment X*, sink something in X 湎
mans	1. extended, long 曼	met	extinguish 滅
	2. creeper; creep, spread over 蔓	mèt	destroy 蔑
màns	1. ten thousand 萬	mhàng	cover, extend, enlarge; extensive, regard as extensive; excess; weed-covered, waste 荒
	2. scorpion 萬		
màt	feed grain to horses 秣		
maw	1. wild-cat 貓	mhàws	diminish, waste 耗
	2. a sprout 苗	mhay	to signal 麾
	3. a hunt, esp. one held in summer 苗	mhayc	1. demolish 毀
màw	1. eminent, fine 髦		2. blazing fire; *Mhayc* (Hui), a ruler 燬
	2. hair; *màw-bròu*, pig roasted after hair removed by scalding 毛; 毛炰	mhet	destroy, extinguish 威
		mhòun	suffering, distress 瘖
	3. long hair, mane; *Màw* (Mao), a tribe 髦	mhùc	1. obscure; darkness 晦
			2. sea 海
	4. ox-tail pennon 旄		3. property, valuables 賄
	5. backward-sloping; *Màw*, a hill 旄	mhùk	black 黑
màws	1. very old, senile 耄	mhùn	1. disorderly 惛
	2. gather 芼		2. dusk; dark (literally or psychologically) 昏
mày	grind, polish 磨		
mayc	1. not, there is not 靡		3. marriage; wife; relative by marriage; *mhùn in*, marriage 昏; 昏姻
	2. slowly 靡		
mdoun	river bank, esp. overhanging lip 湄	mhùn-tròk	eunuch 昏椓
mdun	morning; *mdun-pum*, "morning breeze": falcon 晨; 晨風	mhùng	numerous 甍
		mhùs	1. instruct 誨
			2. regret 悔
me	1. complete 彌	mhùt	destroy 忽

mhuy	good, admirable 徽	
mhùyc	fire 火	
mì	to go astray 迷	
min	people 民	
mint	to ruin, destroy; troubled, disorderly 泯	
mits	fall asleep 寐	
mla	remiss 紓	
mlak	hit with arrow 射	
mlaks	shoot 射	
mlat	tongue 舌	
mlay	snake 蛇	
mlin	a spirit 神	
mlit	1. fill, stop up; full; solid 實	
	2. fruit 實	
mlok	redeem 贖	
mlouns	follow, accord with; submissive 順	
mlount	shield 盾	
mlout	follow the right path 述	
mluk	eat 食	
mlung	1. continue; in a continuing line 繩	
	2. to mount, ride, drive 乘	
	3. string, cord 繩	
mlungs	chariot; team of four horses 乘	
moc	despise, insult 侮	
mòc	thumb, big toe 拇	
mòk	1. wash one's hair 沐	
	2. tree; *mòk gwàs*, "tree melon": Chinese quince, *Pseudocydonia sinensis* 木; 木瓜	
	3. ornamental leather band round carriage pole 鞣	
mòng	1. full 懜	
	2. darkened, blind 夢, 朦	
	3. to cover; *Mòng shàn* (Meng Shan), a mountain range in southern Shandong 蒙; 蒙山	
	4. sky dark with rain 濛	
mònk	dense, luxuriant 懞	
mou	1. lance 矛	
	2. insects, esp. eelworm 蟊	
	3. barley 麰	
	4. long tufts of hair worn uncut by children 〇	
mouc	a stallion, or other male quadruped 牡	
mouk	1. stately, splendid; *Mouk* (Mu), a personal name 穆	
	2. eye 目	
moun	cord; wrap round, envelop 縕	
mous	1. flourishing, beautiful 茂	
	2. 5th, 15th, 25th etc. in the 60-day cycle 戊	
mòus	1. make an effort, enforce 懋	
	2. look down on 冒	
	3. to trade 貿	
mout	object, thing; quality; to sort by quality 物	
mòut	to exhaust 沒	
mouy	1. margin of river 湄	
	2. eyebrow 眉	
Mouy	Mei, a place name 郿	
mouyc	beautiful 美	
mouys	love; lovable 媚	
mràc	horse 馬	
Mràk	Mo, a northern tribe 貊	
mràk	settle, still, silent; calm and respectful 嘆	
mrang	1. bright; *Mrang Sèng*, "bright star": the Morning Star 明; 明星	
	2. covenant, treaty 盟	
mràng	snake's-head lily 莔	
mràngs	firstborn; eldest brother; *Mràngs* (Meng), a personal name 孟	
mràns	slow 慢	
mrant	make an effort; vigorous 勉	
mràs	sacrifice made in camp to the Spirits of the Soil 禡	
mràts	1. displeased; dislike 邁	
	2. proceed, march 邁	
mràwk	distant, far-reaching, extensive 邈	
mraws	temple for the dawn sacrifice 廟	
mrày	hemp 麻	
mrèk-mròk	drizzle 霢霂	
mreng	1. to command, a mandate; one's destiny,	

	one's life 命		3.	river gorge 亹
	2. bird or animal call; *mreng-kou*, turtle-dove 鳴; 鳴鳩		4.	red millet 穈
		mung	dream 夢	
mrit	silent, quiet, secret; dense; *Mrit* (Mi), a tribe 密	muns	1.	ask, enquire; ask after, hence care about 問
mròn	savage; *Mròn* (Man), a category of tribal people, see Ode 261 蠻		2.	be heard; fame 聞
		Muns	Wen, a river of Shandong 汶	
mròng	1. great, ample 厖	mùs	pain, distress 痗	
	2. shaggy dog; *mròng-nong*, shaggy 龙; 龙茸	mut	don't! 勿	
		muts	not yet 未	
mròu	cogon grass (see p. 64) 茅	mùts	1.	younger sister 妹
Mròuc	the Pleiades 昴		2.	dyed with madder 靺
mròuc	water-shield (see p. 367) 茆		3.	dusk, dark 昧
mrù	wind whirling up dust 霾	Mùts	Wei, a town in Henan 沫	
mrùk	wheat 麥	muy	1.	reduced, hidden, eclipsed; *muy X*, it isn't that X 微
mrun	severe, austere 旻			
mrùng	the population 氓		2.	royal fern 薇
mrunt	pity, pitiable; *Mrunt*, a ruler of *Wets* 閔	mùy	branch, twig; a gag; a board 枚	
mrunt-mrant	toil heavily 黽勉	muyc	1.	cute 媺
			2.	vigorous 亹
mu	1. don't! 毋		3.	tail 尾
	2. to plan, scheme; to consult 謀	mùyc	smooth-flowing 浼	
mù	1. flourishing, abundant, rich 脵	myawc	small; regard as small 藐	
	2. plum tree 梅			
	3. a go-between (to arrange marriages) 媒	na	1.	as, like (*pu na*, "not like": not as good as); as if; if; *X na tu gày*, *X na gày*: what about X? how is X? *Na X na Y*: like X Y, like the Y of X 如 (不如); X 如(之)何; 如 X 如 Y
	4. type of large dog collar 鍪			
muc	mother 母			
mùc	1. each 每			
	2. diligent, active 敏		2.	go to, proceed to 如
	3. measure of land, about a seventh of an acre 畝		3.	equivalent to *nu* or *nan*, qq.v.
muk	to herd; a herdsman; pasture; *Muk Lac* (Muye), Herdsman's Heath, site of *Tiw* conquest of *Un* 牧; 牧野	nà	wife and children 孥	
		na-ra	madder plant 茹藘	
		nac	1.	you 汝
			2.	to swallow, eat 茹
mun	1. hear 聞	Nac	Ru, a river of Henan 汝	
	2. design; ornate, striped; accomplished; civil rather than military; *Mun* (Wen), father of *Mac*; *Mun Kyang* (Wen Jiang), sister of a *Dzì* ruler, see Ode 104; *mun nin*, "cultured people": one's forebears 文; 文姜; 文人	nàc	angry 怒	
		nak	agree, be concordant to; like, as; a grammar word 若	
		nàk	agree, say yes 諾	
mùn	1. lay hand on, hold 捫	nan	-ly (suffix forming adverbs); so, thus;	
	2. gate, door 門			

	approve, affirm 然		4. a grammar word, or syllable inserted for rhythm; X *ngan*, when X 言
nàn	difficult; difficult to obtain 難		
nang	1. heavy with dew 瀼	ngàng	1. I, we 卬
	2. steal 攘		2. high 卬
	3. push aside, pull treetrunks away 攘	ngank	look up to 卬, 仰
nàng	a sack 囊	ngans	adornment; talented 彥
nangs	yield 讓	ngàns	1. high river-bank 岸
nank	grain growing abundantly 穰		2. prison 犴
nàns	difficulty, calamity 難	ngant	hilltop 巘
nant	to fear 戁	ngap	1. strong; terrible 業
nas	calculate, examine 茹		2. crossbeam of musical-instrument stand 業
này	much, ample; beautiful 那	ngas	1. set forth, present 御
nàyc	rich, fine 儺		2. tell 語
nec	1. you, your 爾		3. charioteer; officer, attendant; to direct, drive, manage 御
	2. near; *nec ngan*, "near words": shallow words 邇; 邇言	ngàs	1. wake; awake 寤
nèc	1. numerous 瀰		2. meet; face to face 晤
	2. flowering, luxuriant 薾	ngat	1. calamity 孽
Nèc	Ni, a place-name 禰		2. sucker, shoot from base of tree 櫱
nèng	1. why, how? 寧		3. a high-piled hairstyle 孽
	2. would that; rather 寧	ngats	1. white-haired 艾
	3. peace; tranquil 寧		2. govern, regulate; hence, make stable 乂
nèns	sunlight, heat 晛		3. mow, hence cut off, end 刈
net	hot 熱	ngàts	mugwort, or some other artemisia species 艾
nga	fish 魚	ngàw	1. tall; *Ngàw* (Ao), a hill in Henan 敖
ngà-dòng	wutong tree (see p. 310) 梧桐		2. amuse oneself, stroll about; a pleasure-ground 敖
ngac	1. speech, speak 語		3. distress call of birds; clamouring voices 嗷, 囂
	2. border, frontier 圉	ngawk	cruel; oppress, maltreat 虐
	3. opponent; refractory; oppose, withstand 禦	ngàws	proud, arrogant 傲
	4. tiger-shaped clapper for music 敔	ngay	1. to estimate 儀
ngàc	five 五		2. dignity; decorum; a ceremony, rule; right, proper, to approve; to set in order; liable 宜, 儀
ngàk	1. suddenly 鄂	ngày	1. high 宜
	2. beat drums, make a loud noise 咢		2. slanting 俄
ngam	orderly, well-trained; stern, majestic 嚴		3. mugwort 莪
ngamp	dignified 儼	ngayc	silkworm moth 蛾
ngan	1. I, we 言		
	2. high and large; *Ngan* (Yan), a place-name 言		
	3. speech, to speak 言		

ngàyc	I, me 我		*ngrang*	meet 迎
ngays	1. righteous 義		*ngrangs*	go to meet, receive 迎
	2. plan for, discuss, criticize 議		*ngrans*	console, condole 唁
nge	baby, child 兒		*ngràns*	wild goose 雁, 鴈
ngèk	"pheasant plant", see Ode 142 鶪		*ngràs*	meet 御
ngets	to sow, to plant 藝		*ngràwk*	music 樂
nghac	approve, allow, admit; *Nghac* (Xu), name of a city or state 許		*ngràwks*	joy, rejoice 樂
			ngrins	to be willing 憖
nghàc	river bank 滸		*ngròk*	a mountain, peak, esp. a holy mountain 嶽
nghan	high-rising 軒			
nghans	1. offer, present, make a gift; show, display 獻		*ngròyc*	tile 瓦
			nguc	luxuriant growth of grain 薿
	2. a model 憲		*nguk*	stop, settle, stand still, stand up straight and firm 疑
nghànt	rare 罕			
nghawk	to ridicule, joke 謔		*ngung*	freeze, coagulate 凝
nghay	a beast used as sacrificial offering, see Ode 300 犧		*ngut*	great 仡
			ngwa	1. consider, think anxiously about, foresee; *Ngwa* (Yu), a small state, also another name for *Hwins*, q.v. 虞
nghèk	wrangle 鬩			
nghramp	precipitous; a precipitous track 險			
ngo	1. ignorant, stupid 愚			2. rejoice 娛
	2. corner 隅			3. gamekeeper 虞
ngòc	1. a pair 偶		*ngwà*	shout 吴
	2. two ploughmen working as a team 耦		*ngwac*	great, tall; numerous, in crowds 俣, 虞, 嘆
ngok	1. jade 玉		*ngwan*	1. a high plain 邍
	2. trial at law 獄			2. a spring 原, 源
ngon	principal, eldest; great 元			3. red horse with white belly (?) 騵
ngong	great, dignified 顒		*ngwat*	moon 月
ngons	wish, long for 願		*ngwàts*	outside 外
ngos	happen to meet 遇		*ngways*	deceitful, false 偽
ngòu-syang	go to and fro 翱翔		*ngwu*	cow 牛
			ngwuy	high; *Ngwuy* (Wei), a state 魏
ngòut	shake 扤		*ngyaw*	plants used for fuel 蕘
ngòy	1. false 訛		*nhac*	1. mouse, rat 鼠
	2. move, change 訛, 吪			2. foxtail millet, *Setaria italica* 黍
ngrà	tooth 牙			3. suffering, grief 瘋
ngràc	a musical instrument; a ritual dance; correct, proper; see p. 18 雅			
			nhàn	sigh 欸, 嘆
ngrak	rebellious 逆		*nhank*	bring food to workers in field 饟
ngràm	rocky, lofty 巖		*nhans*	to blaze 煽
ngràn	face, complexion, colour 顏		*nhep*	hand things to, assist, encourage to eat and drink 攝

nhet	establish	設
nhimp	to report, remonstrate	諗
nhouc	hand	手
nhouk	1. gather, harvest	叔
	2. beans, pulses	菽
	3. third son; *Nhouk* (Shu), a personal name	叔
nhòyc	tranquil, relaxed	妥
nhrum	a precious object	琛
nhùk	evil, wrong	慝
nhum	deep	深
nì	mud	泥
nìc	wet with dew; luxuriant	泥
nìms	think of, remember	念
nin	1. good, benevolent	仁
	2. man, person	人
nìn	harvest; year	年
nit	sun, a day	日
nits	two; *nits, nits sùm*: double-hearted, changeable, unreliable	二, 貳; 二三
nìwk	hungry for; hungrily; dissatisfied	怒
no	moisten; wet, glossy	濡
noc	strong (drink)	醹
nok	disgrace	辱
nong	great, ample, rich	禯
nòng	thick, heavy (dew)	濃
nos	child; mild, gentle	孺
Nots	Rui, a state	芮
nots	inside of river bend	汭
nou	soft, gentle; a pliable shoot	柔
nòu	monkey	猱
nouc	tread, trample	蹂
noun	a large variety of ox	犉
noung	1. you, your	戎
	2. great	戎
	3. help	戎
	4. weapon; war chariot; *Noung* (Rong), tribes of the west	戎
nòung	agriculture	農
nous	make pliable, tranquillize	揉
nòuts	inside	內
nouy	tassel, pennon	緌
nrac	girl, woman; (hence) smaller	女
nrac-ràу	dodder (a parasitic weed)	女蘿
nràw	1. disorderly	㤳
	2. clamour	呶
Nràw	Nao, a hill in Shandong	猺
nrouc	1. practise, repeat	狃
	2. a tree species, related to cherry	杻
nruk	near; be familiar with	暱
nu	1. subordinates preceding clause to what follows	而
	2. equivalent to *nan*, q.v.	而
	3. you	而
nuc	ear	耳
nùc	1. you	乃
	2. then, thereupon; but then	迺
	3. can, be able to; endure	能
	4. treat well	能
num	1. great	壬
	2. to carry, to load; support, sustain, endure; strong; *Num* (Ren), mother of *Mun*	任
nùm	1. male	男
	2. south	南
	3. a ritual dance	南
nump	a type of large bean	荏
nump-namp	soft, flexible	荏染
nung	1. in a long row	陾
	2. repeat; accumulated	仍
nuns	full	牣
nunt	endure; cruel	忍
nup	to enter	入
nùp	1. convey	納
	2. fixed rein, see Ode 128	靹
nus	sinew	胹
nùs	large tripod	鼐
nyàwk	to sink	溺
nyot	to sow, plant	藝

		oy	wither 萎	
ò	thorn-elm, *Hemiptelea davidii* 樞	oy-lay	1. compliant, complaisant 委蛇, 委佗	
òk	house, roof 屋		2. serpentine, long and winding 逶迤	
on-ang	mandarin duck 鴛鴦			
ong	1. harmonious 雝	pa	man, fellow 夫	
	2. cooked rice, prepared food 饔	pac	1. great; *Pac* (Fu), a state 甫	
	3. ceremonial hall 廱		2. axe 斧	
	4. city moat 邕		3. embroidered with axe motifs 黼	
onk	to cover 雖		4. biltong 脯	
ons	resent, resentment 怨		5. an honorific suffix: *A-pac*, Master A 父, 甫	
ont	1. beautiful, gentle 婉			
	2. obliging, polite 宛	pàc	mend 補	
	3. small; *Ont* (Wan), a hill in *Drin* 宛	pàk	1. wide, ample 博	
	4. elude 宛		2. hoe 鎛	
os	one's fill of food or drink 饇	pan	hedge, fence 藩	
òs	soak 漚	pang	1. just then, just now; by the side of 方	
òts	to screen 薈		2. take a place, occupy 方	
ou	1. grief, grieved 憂		3. begin 方	
	2. mild, generous, ample; *ou-you*, relaxed, indulgent, mild 優, 優游		4. square, cardinal direction, region; regular, norm, pattern; *Pang* (Fang), a personal and place name 方	
	3. doe 麀		5. raft 方	
ouc-douc	tranquil 慢受	pàng	bang! 彭, 旁	
ouk	1. warm, genial 奧, 燠	pant	to turn, reverse; contrary, on the contrary; *pant-juk*, fidget 反; 反側	
	2. richly growing crop 彧			
	3. a cove 奧	pas	1. give, distribute; tax 賦	
	4. *Vitis bryoniifolia* 薁		2. assist; *pas-ngas*, manager, steward 傅; 傅御	
òun	warm, gentle 溫			
ouns	hate, anger 慍	pàs	1. cloth 布	
ount	accumulate, block up; sultry 蘊		2. a park; vegetable plot 圃	
out	1. pent-up feeling; oppressed 菀	pat	1. great, greatly 廢	
	2. wither 苑		2. shoot; to start, to open; go away; set going, implement a practice; rapid, rushing 發	
	3. luxuriant growth 菀			
	4. Oriental bush cherry 鬱		3. hair of head 髮	
outs	1. to comfort, be quiet 慰	pàt	1. establish order, arrange 撥	
	2. to screen 蔚		2. sound of splash 發	
	3. *Artemisia japonica* 蔚	pats	fail; cast aside 廢	
ouy	terrified, overawed, to terrify; dignity; *ouy-ngay*, dignity 威; 威儀	pàts	1. uprooted 沛	
			2. cowrie shell 貝	
ouys	to fear 畏	paw	1. ample 濾	

	2. run 儦		2. shore 泮
	3. to weed 穮		3. semicircular pool 泮
	4. horse's bit 鑣	phàns-hwàns	undisciplined, unbridled, relaxed 伴奐, 判渙
pàwk	embroidered coat collar 襮	phats	lung 肺
pay	1. river bank 陂	phàts	dense 肺
	2. brown and white bear 羆	phàys	break 破
pày	1. warlike 番	phek	depraved, perverse 僻
	2. a wave 波	pheks	compare; example 譬
payc	that, the 彼	phen	1. oblique, inclined to one side 偏
pàyc, pàyc-lang	winnow 簸, 簸揚		2. fly to and fro, flutter 翩
pàys	to sow 播	phengs	enquire 聘
pe	low 卑	phit	one of a pair; correspond to; peer 匹
pec	1. to cause; so that 俾	phìts	in crowds; to float, as a banner or a boat 淠
	2. consider 俾	phoc	to lay the hand on, to comfort 拊
pek	1. ruler, prince 辟	phong	1. beautiful 丰
	2. jade emblem of rank, disc-shaped with a central hole 璧		2. turnip 葑
pèn	fruit basket 籩		3. bee, wasp; a sting 蜂
peng	all together 并	phonk	to present, receive 奉
penk	remove 屏	phou	1. confidence; sincere; trust 孚
pènk-pònk	scabbard ornament (see Ode 213) 鞞琫		2. kind of bird-net 罦
pèns	all round, universally 徧	phouk	turn over, overthrow; on the contrary 覆
pent	narrow 褊	phouks	to overspread, cover, protect; a cover 覆
pènt	thin and flat 扁		
pet	turtle 鱉	phoung	abundant (harvest); Phoung (Feng), a river at Xi'an 豐
pets-puts	shady, luxuriant 蔽芾	phràng	boil 烹
pha	extend, spread out; extensively 敷, 鋪	phrèng	to cause, make 并
phà	suffering, exhausted, disabled 痡	phrìns	black and white of eyes contrasting 盼
phàc	1. great, vast 溥	phru	1. great, overbearing; very; ample 丕
	2. river bank 浦		2. robust 伾
phàk	sound of rapid chariots 薄		3. horse of mixed yellow and white colour 駓
phan	1. to wave, flutter; fickle, frivolous 幡	phruk	cleave apart 副
	2. spread the wings, fly, fly about 翻	phu	1. clean and bright (of clothes) 秠
	3. a turn; Phan (Fan), a personal name 番		2. double-kerneled black millet 秠
phang	heavy snowfall 雱	phuk	turn over, revert 覆
phàng	heavy flow 滂	phuks	a type of headdress 副
phangs	enquire, scrutinize 訪	phun	1. ample 紛
phàns	1. melt 泮		

	2. fragrant 芬	pouc	pottery, a pot 缶
	3. decorative plaque attached to horse's bit 幩	pòuc	1. protect; *pòuc krèts*, assistant 保; 保介
phut	1. brush off, eliminate 拂		2. treasure, precious 寶
	2. purify, expel noxious fumes; (hence) happy 祓		3. a (black and white) bustard; hence, piebald horse 鴇
phùts	counterpart 配	pouk	belly; embrace 腹
phuy	1. for a horse to run without let-up 騑	pòus	1. repay 報
	2. heavy fall of snow 霏		2. to plait 報
phuyc	1. ornate 斐	pra	1. fine, admirable 膚
	2. radish 菲		2. skin 膚
phyaw	1. blow down 飄	prà	sow, pig 豝
	2. make a rushing noise, as a carriage 嘌	pràk	1. hundred 百
phyàw	strike down, crush 摽		2. eldest, eldest brother; lord; *Pràk* (Bo), a personal name 伯
pic	1. compare 比		3. cypress 柏
	2. spoon 匕	pramp	diminish, reduce 貶
pin	1. guest 賓	prang	weapon 兵
	2. river bank, shore 濱	pràng	side of temple gate 枋
pins	set out, arrange 儐	prangs	1. grieved 怲
pis	deceased mother 妣		2. a handle 柄
pit	1. must 必	prank	grasp 秉
	2. all, entirely 畢	prànt	1. great 販
	3. sparkling 玭		2. plank 板
	4. fork 畢	pràts	to ruin 敗
	5. knee-cover 韠	pràwk	mixed-colour, roan 駁
	6. strong wind; spring welling up; *pit-pat*, gale; *pit-put*, gush forth 滭; 滭發; 滭沸	pràwks	leopard 豹
		prèt	eight 八
	7. hand-net (for catching birds) 畢	prèts	to bow, bend a branch 拜
pits	1. give 畀	prit	lath tied to unstrung bow to prevent warping 柲
	2. to close 閟	pròk	cut, flay, peel, pluck 剝
	3. caution; guard against 毖	pròng	a state 邦
	4. mystery, secret 祕	pròu	1. bushy, dense, massive 苞
	5. bubble up from a spring 毖, 泌		2. wrap 包
pòc	knock down, crush 捊	pròuc	full of food, make full of food 飽
pòk	tell the future, esp. from cracks in shells or bones 卜	pruc	bad 否
pòk, pòk-sòk	undergrowth, low shrubby trees 樸, 樸樕	pruk	puttee 幅
		pruk-gràng	protective wooden bar on bull's horns (p. 371) 楅衡
pong	fief 封	Prun	Bin, early *Tiw* homeland, see pp. 7–8 豳
pònk	numerous (of fruit) 唪		

prung	1. ice 冰
	2. quiver-cover 掤
prus	reins 轡
pruy	grieve; sad 悲
pu	not 不
puc	1. not; or not 否
	2. soar 不
puk	1. wide 幅
	2. good fortune, happiness 福
	3. spoke of wheel 輻
	4. pokeweed 蔔
pùk	north 北
puks	rich; self-important 富
pùks	the back 背
pum	wind; a (musical) air 風
pums	criticize 諷
pun	to steam rice 饙
pùn	1. ? ardent, brave (or) uxorious (see Ode 49) 賁
	2. run, elope 奔
pùng	1. for a mountain to collapse 崩
	2. epidemic in a herd 崩
puns	spread one's wings, fly up, make an effort; energetic 奮
pùnt	root 本
put	1. not, not able to, not willing to 弗
	2. large 芾
	3. adorned with emblems 黻
	4. gush forth 沸
	5. clear away dense vegetation 茀
	6. knee-cover 市
	7. rope 紼
	8. gust 弗
	9. hanging at carriage entrance 第, 茀
puts	to bubble 沸
puy	1. is not; wrong 非
	2. to fly 飛
puyc	not; it is not that ... 匪
pyaw	whirlwind 飄

ra	hut; ra-rac, lodging 廬; 廬旅
rà	a hound 獹
rac	troops, multitude 旅
ràc	captive 虜
Ràc	Lu, a state 魯
rac-ruk	spine and sinews 脊力
rak	1. sharp 略
	2. plunder, rob 掠
ràk	1. fall; die (said of kings) 落
	2. white horse with black mane 駱
Ràk	Luo, a river, and Eastern Tiw capital 洛
ràks	1. great 路
	2. contribute, present 賂
	3. road 路
	4. large carriage; charioteer 輅
	5. dew 露
	6. Eastern great egret 鷺
ram	a type of dog 獫
ràm	indigo 藍
ramp	Chinese snake gourd, Trichosanthes kirilowii, and related plants 蕨
rams	gather, accumulate 斂
ràms	go to excess 濫
ran	1. wavy 漣
	2. connect, in a row, consecutively 連
rang	1. good, excellent 良
	2. chilly, cold 涼
	3. pole, bridge, dam; Rang (Liang), a place-name 梁
	4. millet, sorghum, grain generally, provisions 粱, 糧
ràng	1. darnel 稂
	2. wolf 狼
rangs	1. bright 亮
	2. sincere; to trust; truly 諒
	3. chariot 兩
ràngs	reckless 浪
rank	two, a pair 兩
rànk	bright 朗

ràns	brilliant 爛	rhenk	drive fast 騁
rant	two-man handcart 輂	rhìc	form, shape; limb 體
rap	to hunt 獵	rhiw	1. pull out, take out 抽
ras	think of, foresee 慮		2. be cured, recover 瘳
rat	1. cold 冽	rhonk	favour, affection 寵
	2. blaze, blazing; brilliant; broil; famous, meritorious 烈	rhouk	nourish, cherish 畜
		rhouks	collect; a store 蓄
	3. rank, degree 列	rhuc	shame 恥
rats	1. cruel, oppressive, evil; *Rats* (Li), a 9th century king 厲	rhuk	1. arrange 敕
			2. make ready 飭
	2. a ford; wet the clothes 厲	rhùm	covet 貪
	3. dangling ends of a sash 厲	rhùmp	numerous 噆
	4. whetstone 厲	rì	numerous, all 黎
ràw	hard work, trouble 勞	ric	1. tread; a path 履
ràwc	puddle, pool 潦		2. dignity 履
ràws	encourage, recompense 勞	rìc	1. propriety, ritual 禮
ray	1. leave, be dispersed 離		2. a fish, perhaps blenny 鱧
	2. traverse, hang down; fall into; fasten, fastened to 離		3. must, sweet wine 醴
		rin	1. neighbour 鄰
	3. to drag into; trouble, sorrow 罹		2. small bell, or the sound it makes 令
	4. apron 縭		3. sound of rumbling carriage 鄰
ràyˊ	kind of bird-net 羅		4. see *gu-rin*, and *reng*
re	rope 纚	rìn	1. fall in drops, drizzle 零
rè	black horse 驪		2. cocklebur 苓
rèn	lotus fruit 蓮	rins	worn thin, fretted 磷
reng	good 令	ris	profit; profitable, favourable 利
rèng	1. magic, divine, lucky; *Rèng* (Ling), a lord of *Drin* 靈	rit	1. solid, full; *rit-rat*, very cold 栗; 栗烈
			2. fear; tremble 慄
	2. bell attached to flag 鈴		3. chestnut tree 栗
reng, rin	to command 令	rìt	transgress; offence 戾
renk	neck 領	rìts	come to; settle 戾
res	revile, defame 詈	riw	1. flow, drift down 流
rès	1. fasten to, be attached to 麗		2. catch 流
	2. a number 麗	rìw	for a while; a little; may it be that ..., it will happen that ...; a grammar word 聊
rets	sapling 栵		
rhan	long, of a beam 梴	riw-ray	a bird—owl? 流離
rhàts	scorpion 蠆	rìwc	water pepper 蓼
rhàwks	shout, bawl, clamour 謞	riwk	tall-growing, of a plant 蓼
rheng	1. dead drunk 酲	ro	heap up 摟
	2. tamarisk 檉		

rò	1. empty, worthless 婁		roung	thunder 隆
	2. unknown tree species 蔞		rout	a row, tier 律
rok	1. green 綠		routs	1. a class, hence high-class, good in general 類
	2. a food plant, perhaps lentil 菉			2. (offer) a sacrifice to God 類
ròk	1. deer 鹿		rouy	rope, bonds 纍
	2. wooded mountain slope 麓		ròuy	1. thunder 靁, 雷
	3. blessing, prosperity, dignity 祿			2. large 'lei' jar 罍
ròks	to leak 漏		rouyc	liana, creeper 藟
ròn	1. emaciated 臠		rràks	1. second, next in sequence 亞
	2. bell on horse harness 䜌, 鑾			2. brother-in-law 亞
rong	dragon 龍		rrang	1. brilliant 央, 英
ròng	well fed (horse) 龐			2. a blossom; a kind of gem; an ornament 英
ròngs	manipulate, play with 弄			3. tinkling bell 央
ròns	1. to cross; crossing-place 亂		rràns	bright, pleasant 晏
	2. disorder, rebellion 亂		rrèks	narrow; a defile 隘
ront	beautiful 孌		rrèng	1. contrasting colours in plumage 鶯
ros	repeat; frequently 屢			2. bird call 嚶
ròs	carve, engrave 鏤		rròk	1. moisten, smear 渥
ròt	gather, pluck 捋			2. grasp, handful 握
rou	1. detain; remain 留		ru	1. give 釐
	2. kill, butcher, mutilate; Rou (Liu), a Tiw ruler 劉			2. regulate 釐
	3. pale, black-maned horse 騮, 駠			3. wildcat 狸
	4. pendant of banner 旒		rù	1. come 來
ròu	pen for animals 牢			2. a horse more than a certain height 騋
rouc	1. fine, stately 懰			3. goosefoot 萊
	2. deep and clear (water) 瀏		ruc	1. grieved 里
	3. willow 柳			2. mark out fields 理
	4. fish trap 罶			3. village; homestead; a li (about a third of a mile) 里
ròuc	old 老			4. a carp 鯉
rouk	1. six; rouk-pràwk, "six colours": a tree, perhaps yellow catalpa 六; 六駁			5. plum tree 李
	2. fast-ripening grain 穋			6. inside; lining 裏
	3. a level height 陸		ruk	strong, strength, effort; to force 力
roun	1. ripple 淪		rùk	reins 勒
	2. twist a cord 綸		rùks	give 賚
	3. principle 倫		rum	1. look down at, oversee 臨
	4. wheel 輪			2. approach; a siege engine 臨
roun, roun-sa	all together, indiscriminately 淪, 淪胥			3. a wood, forest; numerous (like trees of

		a forest) 林	sày-sày	imitating drunken dancing 傞傞
rump	granary 廩		se	1. this 斯
rung	1. ice 凌			2. a final particle 斯
	2. high mound, hill, height 陵		sèk	1. white 皙
rup	1. to stand, set up 立			2. split, cleave 析
	2. to live on grain 粒		sen	fresh, good 鮮
	3. peasant's hat made of split lengths of bamboo 笠		seng	1. for different materials to fit together well 鮮
rùs	stimulate 勑			2. sacrificial animal, red horse 騂
ruts	come 迨		sèng	star 星
ryàw	body fat 膌		sengs	1. nature, disposition; life 性
ryàwc	1. fine, good, lovely 僚			2. surname; family 姓
	2. office 僚		senk	observe 省
ryàwk	oak tree 櫟		sèns	sleet 霰
ryawks	cure ○		sent	rare, solitary 鮮
ryaws	torch; flame; brilliant; to burn; burnt-offering 燎		sèp	march 燮
			ses	completely 斯
sa	1. together, mutually 胥		sha	1. distant 疏
	2. linger 胥			2. coarse grain 疏
sac	unburden 寫		shac	1. mutually 湑
sak	1. great 舃			2. flourishing, luxuriant, abundant 湑
	2. former 昔			3. to strain liquor; heavy dew 湑
	3. slipper, shoe 舃			4. the place where; X shac Verb, that which X Verbs 所
sàk	twist rope 索		shàm	mow 芟
sam	thread 縿		shàn	hill, mountain 山
san	caper about 僊		shang	frost 霜
sang	1. mutually 相		shank	go astray; defective 爽
	2. boil 湘		shàns	wicker fish-trap 汕
	3. box of carriage 箱		shànt	tears flowing 潸
sàng	1. burial, mourning 喪		shàt	kill 殺
	2. mulberry; sàng-gàc, Japanese grosbeak, Eophona personata 桑; 桑扈		shày	1. sand 沙
				2. yellowfin goby 鯊
sangs	look at, look to, hence assist; appearance, quality; Sangs Thàc (Xiang Tu), grandson of Khèts, q.v. 相; 相土		shày-kè	katydid (Tettigoniidae spp.) 莎雞
			she	to strain wine 釃
sàngs	lose; destroy 喪		sheng	1. give birth to, be born, live 生
sàns	scatter; undisciplined 散			2. child of one's sister 甥
sàs	white, colourless 素			3. sacrificial animal 牲
saws	laugh 笑			4. reed organ 笙

shi	1. master; *shi gec*, mistress of a household 師; 師氏	sin-mròuc	28th day of the 60-day cycle 辛卯
	2. population of a district; multitude; troops, regiment, army 師	sins	1. believe, trust; true, sincere 信
			2. interrogate 訊
shìc	sprinkle 洒		3. stay two nights in one place 信
shin	1. long, prolonged; *Shin*, a state and clan name (Shen) 莘	sit	all, completely 悉
		sits	1. then, thereupon 肆
	2. large crowd, flock 甡		2. lax 肆
shit-shout	a cricket 蟋蟀		3. unrestrained, violent 肆
shoc	to count 數		4. kill 肆
shok	first day of a moon; *Shok* (Shuo), a personal and place name 朔		5. spread out, display; extensive 肆
			6. snot, snivel 泗
shòng	a pair 雙	siw	1. long 脩
shou	numerous 搜		2. dry 脩
shouc	moisten, soak 溲		3. arrange, repair, cultivate 修
shouk	to bind 縮	sìw	1. cold, chilly 蕭
shout	1. all 率		2. lad's-love (see p. 182) 蕭
	2. follow, go along; lead 率		3. pan-pipes 簫
shuc	1. to cause 使	siwk	1. solemn, reverent 肅
	2. to work, serve; service; an office, occupation, business; an officer, gentleman 士, 仕, 事		2. quick, eager 肅
			3. shrivel 肅
			4. hit 擆
	3. wait; move on 俟	siwks	embroider 繡
	4. scribe, recorder 史	siws	1. to flower and set seed 秀
	5. river bank 涘		2. some kind of precious stone 琇
shuk	1. reap, harvest; husbandry 穡	sìws	1. wail 歗
	2. looks, countenance; to show off 色		2. make sound with pursed lips; sing without fixed tune, croon 嘯
Shum	Orion's Belt 參	sla	slow; *Sla* (Xu), a state in northern Anhui 徐
shùm	tender, delicate 摻		
shùmp	grasp 摻	slac	1. fine-tasting (wine) 醑
shun	numerous 詵, 駪		2. continue, succeed; arrange in order 序
si	1. private 私		
	2. brother in law 私		3. work, achievement 緒
sì	1. west 西		4. tench 鱮
	2. to roost, rest; bird's nest 棲	slak	1. large, loose-fitting 蓆
sic	die; dead 死		2. mat 席
sìc	washed clean 洒	Slaks	Xie, capital of *Lhin* 謝
sin	1. new; *Sin-pac* (Xinfu), a mountain near Mount Tai 新; 新甫	slans	desire; a surplus; affluence 羨
		slat	leak, reduce; *Slat Lac* (Xie Ye), a minister of *Drin* 泄, 洩; 泄冶
	2. bitter, pungent, painful 辛		
	3. firewood 薪		

slek	wig, hairpiece 鬄	snouy	1. walk slowly and cautiously; solemn 夊
slèk	1. give 錫		2. to comfort, give rest 綏
	2. tin 錫	sòc	1. blind 瞍
slit	pure; consider pure; stoop to 屑		2. marshland full of game 藪
slits	1. four; *Slits Pang*, "the Four Quarters": the whole world; *Slits kwùk*: the states of the "Four Quarters" 四; 四方; 四國	sok	grain 粟
		sòk	1. rapid; urge on; invite 速
	2. team of four horses 駟		2. worthless, mean 蔌
slok	1. continue 續		3. vegetables 蔌
	2. water-plantain 藚	sòngs	to escort, esp. on first part of a journey; follow 送
slong	1. litigate 訟		
	2. pine-tree 松	sonk	fear 悚
slongs	1. admonish; recite; a song 誦	sont	choose; find the faults 選
	2. eulogy 頌	sònt	to count, measure, keep in time with music 選
slu	1. words, speech 辭		
	2. the spring sacrifice 祠	sot	snow 雪
sluc	1. resemble 似	sou	scratch 搔
	2. sacrifice 祀	sòu	move, disturb, set in motion 騷
	3. plough 耜	sòuc	anxious 慅
	4. sidestream 汜	souk	1. stay overnight 宿
	5. wife of elder brother; *Sluc* (Si), a clan name 姒		2. early morning; early 夙
		sòun	1. grandson; *Sòun Tzuc-droungs* (Sun Zizhong), a military commander of *Wets* 孫; 孫子仲
sluks	food; feed 食		
slum	1. large boiling-pan 鬵		2. cooked grain 飧
	2. a measure of length, eight *thak*, about nine feet 尋	soung	high 崧
		Sòungs	Song, a state 宋
slup	1. flap the wings, flutter 習	sòus	sweep 掃, 埽
	2. wet ground, low ground, riverside (see Ode 38) 隰	souts	reprimand 誶
		sòuts	break 碎
slus	1. continue, succeed, inherit 嗣	sòy	peasant's raincoat made of straw, rushes, etc. 蓑
	2. eunuch 寺		
smàngs	destroy 喪	sòyc	small, a fragment 瑣
snang	rise, rear up, remove 攘	sprit	1. pure, fresh-looking, bright 瑟
snet	1. familiar 暬		2. an ancient zither-like instrument 瑟
	2. garments worn next to body 褻	su	1. think 思
sngàks	1. go upward against; adverse 遡		2. regulate; *su-dà*, Master of Labour; *su-khòng*, Master of Works 司; 司徒; 司空
	2. inform; complain 愬		
sno	wait; *Sno* (Xu), a place-name 須		3. silk 絲
Snoung	Song, a royal concubine in the 21st c. B.C. 娀		4. a grammar word 思
snount	a bird of prey 隼	sù	bearded 思

419

suk	to repose 息			goer": firefly 宵; 宵行
sùk	1. sincere 塞		syaw-yaw	be at ease, saunter 逍遙
	2. to block, stop up 塞		syawc	small; *syawc sum*, "small heart": care, cautious 小; 小心
sum	heart 心			
sùm	three 三		syawk	scrape, cut; destroy 削
sùn	before; past 先		syou	prisoner 囚
sùns	go in front, lead 先		syòu-shyàw	spider 蠨蛸
sùnt	wash 洗			
sus	think about, brood 思		syouns	1. deep 濬, 浚
swan	1. boastful 宣			2. lofty 崚
	2. proclaim 宣		Syouns	Xun, a town in *Wets* 浚
	3. to spread; all-embracing; *Swan* (Xuan), a personal name, in particular name of a *Tiw* king; *Swan Kyang* (Xuan Jiang), concubine of a lord of *Wets* 宣; 宣姜		syous	sleeve 褎
			syouts	1. a tree, perhaps birchleaf pear 檖
				2. a jade insignium carried at the belt 璲
	4. unit of length, on the order of a yard 宣		syuyc	wild water-buffalo 兕
swats	harvest; year 歲		ta	a grammar word; *ta A*, the As, all the As 諸
sway	conform to; obsequious 隨			
swen	turn round; agile; promptly 還,旋		tà	1. elegant 都
swi, switzùk	although 雖, 雖則			2. outer city wall; capital city 都
			tac	1. *X tac*: X-er, he/she/they who X; as for X, ... 者
swin	1. truly, really 恂			
	2. everywhere, all round, equally distributed, equal 旬			2. islet 渚
				3. red paint 赭
	3. to plan, consult 詢		tàc	a set length of wall, perhaps about 80 feet 堵
Swin	Xun, a state 郇			
swint	bamboo shoots 筍		tak	roast, broil 炙
swìt	care about; solicitude, anxiety, sorrow 恤		taks	kind of mulberry tree 柘
			tàks	destroy, destruction 殬
swits	1. then, thereupon 遂		tam	see, look at 瞻
	2. progress, achieve 遂		tan	him, her, it 旃
	3. ear of grain 穗, 穟		tàn	1. ample, generous 亶
sya	oblique, perverse 邪			2. unit 亶
syak	evening 夕			3. vermilion 丹
syang	1. auspicious, good omen, lucky day 祥		tang	1. a pattern, ornament, décor, emblem; rule, statute; refined 章
	2. examine fully, explain details 詳			
syank	elephant, ivory; hence carved, patterned 象			2. a jade emblem, see Ode 238 璋
			tans	fear 戰
syaw	1. melt, dissolve, annihilate; *Syaw* (Xiao), a place in *Drengs* 消		tàns, tàt	1. painful, grieved, earnest 怛
				2. dawn 旦
	2. evening, night; *syaw-gràng*, "night-			

tànt	1. ample 僀			2. earth, ground; *thàc-wac*, territory 土; 土宇
	2. sincere, truly; *Tànt*, grandfather of *Mun* (pp. 7–8) 亶		thak	a measure of length, about fourteen inches 尺
	3. disease, suffering, distress 癉		thàk	1. bag 橐
tàt	see *tàns*			2. thumping sound 橐
tats	bright 晣, 晢		tham	apron 襜
tàts	girdle, sash 帶		thàn	1. numerous 嘽
taw	beckon 招			2. exhausted 嘽
tàw	1. grieved 忉		thàng	sound of drum 鏜
	2. knife 刀		thant	slow, easy-going, long-drawn-out 嘽
	3. canoe ("knife boat") 舠		thàt	1. rapid, brisk 撻
tawc	pool, pond 沼			2. go to and fro 達
tàwc	overturn 倒			3. door, room 闥
tàws	arrive 到		thàts	great, greatly; too; *Thàts Pràk*, uncle of *Mun*; *Thàts shàn*, Mount Tai; *thàts shi*, commander-in-chief of army; *Thàts Wang*, alternative name for *Tànt*, q.v. 太, 泰; 泰伯; 泰山; 太師; 泰王
tày	many 多			
tàys	exhausted 憚			
tèk	1. son of principal wife 嫡			
	2. hoof 蹄		thaw	an unbent bow 弨
tem	tell the future 占		thàwk	indulgent, gentle 綽
tèmp	flaw in a gemstone 玷		thènt	face 靦
tèn	bluish-black horse with white spots 驔		thènt-thònt	trampled ground 町畽
teng	1. go on a military expedition against, attack, punish; go 征		thès	comb-pin 搔
			thi	owl; *thi-waw*, tu-whoo 鴟; 鴟鴞
	2. first; centre of target 正		thìc	weep; tears 涕
	3. a kind of bell 鉦		thìn	sky; *Thìn*, Sky, the supreme god; *thìn gràc*, "below the sky": the whole world; *Thìn Tzuc*, "Sky's Son": the king, later the emperor 天; 天下; 天子
tèng	1. hammering sound 丁			
	2. forehead; *Tèng* (Ding), a constellation (see Ode 50) 定			
tengs	1. to regulate, to correct; correct; a ruler 正		thìns	jade ear-stopper, see p. 26 瑱
			thìs	take away, discontinue, dismiss 替
	2. govern 政		thiwk	begin 俶
tenk	arrange, dispose 整		t'hliw	agitated, anxious 妯
tènk	1. hit, sound of hitting 打		tho	lovely, fine; agreeable, compliant 姝
	2. cauldron 鼎		thon	bore through 穿
tep	fear; be scared stiff 慹		thong	1. to rush, knock; a battering-ram 衝
tès	God, emperor 帝			2. kind of bird-net 罿
tet	break 折		thòng	pained, grieved 恫
tets	to place, set aside 寘		thots	pant 喙
tèts-tòng	rainbow 螮蝀		thouk	a rattle 柷
thàc	1. spit out 吐		thoun	spring (season) 春

thòun	1. ample, complete 焞			3. illness, suffering 瘨
	2. groan 啍		tint	black hair 鬒
thoung	full; to fill; *thoung-nuc*, ear-stopper, see p. 26 充; 充耳		tìt	stop up 窒
			tits	come to, arrive; highest point 至
thount	wriggle 蠢		tiw	1. give; succour 賙
thòut	burst forth 突			2. circle, bend; everywhere; surround; *Tiw* (Zhou), the Odes dynasty 周
thòuts	withdraw 退			
thouy	push, push away 推		tìwc	bird 鳥
thòuy	motherwort 蓷		tiws	mistletoe 蔦
thoy	to blow 吹		to	red 朱
thoys	musical concert 吹		toc	1. master, lord, host 主
thra	Tree of Heaven 樗			2. ladle 斗
thràk	split, be torn 坼		tok	joined, attached to 屬
thrangs	1. long 暢		tòks	beak 咮
	2. aromatic spirits 鬯		tong	bell 鍾, 鐘
	3. bow-case, put bow in case 韔		tòng	east 東
			tongs	to sow 種
threng	red 赬		tonk	seed 種
thret	1. remove 撤		tòns	a hammer 鍛
	2. penetrate, understand 徹		tònt	cut off 斷
	3. to tax arable land by acreage 徹		tos	a kind of horse, see Ode 128 騅
thrits	chagrined, angry 懥, 懫		tòt	pick, gather 掇
throung	agitated, grieved 忡		tots	unite; together 贅
thruc	happiness, prosperity 祉		tòts	a baton 祋
thruns	suffer, fever 疢, 疢		tou	1. boat 舟
thruy	fine cloth 絺			2. islet 洲
thu	jesting, jolly; *thu-thu*, a jokester 蟲; 蟲蟲		Tou-hwa	Zhou Xu, would-be usurper of the rulership of *Wets*, see Ode 26 州吁
thuks	blaze, to heat; glorious 熾		tòuc	pray 禱
thùmp	minced meat pickled in brine 醓		touk	1. pray, prayer 祝
thùnt	good 腆			2. bind 祝
tì	1. illness; suffer 疧		tòuk	firm, solid, to make solid 篤
	2. a ram (male sheep) 羝		touks	to curse 祝
Tì	Di, a western group of tribes 氐		toun	inculcate, repeat 諄
tic	1. come to 底		tòun	thick; make thick, assemble 敦
	2. settle, determine 厎		toung	1. end; everlasting; in the last analysis; definitely; *toung A tsac B*, there has occurred both A and B 終; 終A且B
tìc	foundation, base 氐			
tin	true 眞			
tìn	1. top of head, forehead; fall headlong, be overthrown 顚			2. locust, grasshopper 螽
	2. top of a mountain 巔		tòung	winter 冬

toungs	multitude, numerous, all 眾		tronk	mound, peak; great 冢
tòuts	respond to, correspond to; counterpart 對		tront	turn 轉
touy	1. wood-pigeon 鵻		tros	flow to; make flow to; apply 注
	2. horse of mixed grey and white colour 騅		trot	1. grieved 惄
tòuy	carve, engrave 追			2. gulp 啜
toys	anxious 懠		trots	sew, stitch, badge 綴
traks	area between gateway and screening wall 著		trou	1. cheat, impose on 侜
tran	Sakhalin sturgeon 鱣			2. carriage pole 輈
trang	1. to stretch; broad; *Trang* (Zhang), a personal name 張		tròuc	pain in guts 疛
	2. provisions 粻		trouk	1. pound earth, build 築
trank	grow; senior; to preside 長			2. bamboo 竹
trans	ritual robe 襢		troung	middle, inside; *troung-kwun*, army commander 中; 中軍
trant	truly 展		trous	daybreak, daytime 晝
trat	wise, perspicacious 哲		trouy	pursue; *Trouy* (Zhui), a northern tribe 追
traw	morning 朝		truk	1. ascend 陟
tràwk	splendid, great 倬			2. sow or plant early 稙
tràwks	basket for catching fish, see Ode 171 罩		truks	to place, arrange 置
tre	know; someone you know well, intimate friend 知		trup	to hobble a quadruped 縶
trèk	blame, punish 謫		tsa	1. straw 苴
trem	moisten, soak through 霑			2. rocky hill 岨
treng	1. auspicious 禎			3. shrike, butcher bird 鵙
	2. verticals of scaffolding used in making earth walls; supports 楨		tsa-kou	fish-hawk (see p. 29) 雎鳩
trent-tront	toss and turn 輾轉		tsac	and, moreover, again; temporarily 且
trit	1. to beat; a stroke 挃		tsak	1. reverent demeanour 踖
	2. sickle 銍			2. magpie 鵲
trits	1. weighed down heavily 輊		tsàk	ornamented; crossing each other; whetstone 錯
	2. bring forward, convey 致		tsan	transfer, remove 遷
	3. to slip, trip 躓		tsàn	eat; food 餐
	4. secure 寘		tsang	1. beg, request 將
tro	tree-stump; *Tro Rum* (Zhu Lin), "Stump Wood", seat of the *Ghàc* family 株; 株林			2. move in a stately way 蹌
				3. ? a saw (see Ode 154) 斨
tròk	1. hew, carve 斲, 琢			4. tinkling sound 鏘, 瑲, 鶬
	2. peck up 啄		tsàng	1. blue or green; *tsàng lung*, bluebottle 蒼; 蒼蠅
	3. strike 椓			2. granary 倉
tron	turn round, remove 轉		tsàng-kràng	oriole, *Oriolus chinensis* 倉庚
			tsàns	bright, splendid; fine food; a set of three

423

	beautiful things or women 粲	tsòt	small cap 撮
tsàwc	grief, grieved 慅	tsots	kerchief 帨
tsày	to file, polish stone 磋	tsòuc	1. rough, coarse; troubled 草
tsàyc	shining white 瑳		2. grass, small plants 草
tse	female bird 雌	tsoun	make a dance move 蹲
tsec	1. this, the 此	tsòunt	measure, consider 忖
	2. petty 佌	tsòus	go to, send out 造
tsèc	bright, lustrous 玼, 泚	tsouyc	run about 趡
tsek	prod, stab 刺	tsòuyc	deep 漼
tseks	criticize, reprove 刺	tsù	forceful, strong 偲
tseng	clear, pure; Tseng (Qing), a city in Drengs state 清	tsùc	1. colour, colourful 綷
			2. pluck, gather 采
tsèng	blue or green 青	tsum	invade, encroach 侵
tsent	shallow 淺	tsùm	the outside horses in a team 驂
tsì	1. chilly, cold 淒	tsump	1. lie down to sleep 寢
	2. dense; luxuriant foliage 萋		2. part of an ancestral temple 寢
tsin	oneself 親	tsùmp	1. grieved, afflicted 慘, 憯
tsìn	thousand 千		2. marker of perfect tense 憯
tsìns	pink 綪	tsup	1. babble; gossip 咠
tsis	1. arrange in order; next in order 次		2. to hem; a connected row; continuous 緝
	2. assist, back up 佽	tsùs	vegetable, edible plant 菜
tsit	1. seven 七	tsùy	wife 妻
	2. lacquer tree, *Toxicodendron vernicifluum* 漆	tsyawc	anxious, grieved 悄
		tu	1. this 之
Tsit	Qi, a river of Shaanxi 漆		2. go to 之
tsìt	cut 切		3. genitive particle: A tu B, A's B, the B of A 之
tsiw	1. autumn 秋		
	2. stork 鶖		4. all-purpose object pronoun: him, her, it, them; occasionally me, us, you 之
tsìwk	1. intense feelings, affection; grieved; loved ones, relatives 戚		
		tuc	1. stop, settle; *tuc ku*, settlement 止; 止基
	2. hatchet 戚		
tsìwk-lhay	toad 戚施		2. deportment, behaviour, dignity; courteous 止
tsoc	take 取		
tsòc	a groom; *tsòc mràc*, Master of Horse 趣; 趣馬		3. heel 趾
			4. islet 沚
tsong	sawtooth ornamentation 樅		5. a final particle 止
tsòng	hear well; intelligent 聰	tuk	1. simply, only, merely; *tuk-hwangs*, but what's more ... 職; 職況
tsòns	furnace; to heat, cook 爨		
tsos	1. hasten to 趣		2. weave 織
	2. take a wife 娶	tùk	1. get 得

	2. character, "virtue" (see pp. 19–20) 德	tzà	straw bedding, packing 葅
tuks	1. remember 識	tzàc	1. ancestor 祖
	2. coloured silk fabric 織		2. roadside sacrifice before a journey 祖
tùm	soak; soaked in (esp. pleasure); indulge oneself, rejoice 湛, 耽		3. cord 組
		tzàk	1. rise 作
tun	majestic; numerous 振		2. work, exercise one's function, make; active 作
tung	1. numerous 烝		
	2. splendid 烝	tzaks	borrow, claim 借
	3. offer gifts; the winter sacrifice 烝	tzam	1. moisten 渐
	4. to advance 烝		2. destroy 殲
	5. kindling wood 蒸	tzang	1. great; enlarge 將
tùng	1. go up 登		2. take, undertake, attend to, bring, advance, (hence) course of a river; future marker 將
	2. a 'deng' vessel 登		
tuns	1. protect 殿		3. to nurse, support 將
	2. sigh 殿		4. congee 漿
	3. shake, vibrate; marshal troops; fear 振	tzàng	1. good 臧
			2. luxuriant (foliage) 牂
	4. thunderclap; majestic 震		3. ewe 牂
	5. from 振	tzant	hoe 錢
tunt	raised path between fields 畛	tzap	oar 楫
tùnt	statute, law code 典	Tzas	Ju, a river of Shaanxi 沮
tup	seize, grasp 執	tzas-nas	marshy ground 沮洳
tùp	respond, reply 答	tzats	sacrifice 祭
Tùs Kway	Dai Gui, a lady of Wets 戴媯	tzaw	roast; Tzaw (Jiao), a place-name 焦
tut	substance, natural qualities; natural, simple, honest; good faith; give pledge 質	tzàwc	"ditch grass" (see Ode 15); algae 藻
		tzàwk	fine, brilliant 鑿
Tuts	Zhi, a place in the Un royal domain 摯	tzay	alas!; now then! 嗟
		tzàyc	left (hand); tzàyc-wuc, assistant 左; 左右
tuts	pledge of good faith; hostage 質		
tyaw	1. bright 昭	tzàys	assist; tzàys-wus, to "left and right" someone, serve as their assistant 佐; 佐佑
	2. shine, shine on, enlighten 照		
tyawc	glorious 昭	tzec	defame, slander 訿
tyawk	1. brilliant 灼	tzek	1. collect, accumulate 積
	2. pour wine into cup 酌		2. footprint; follow the track; go the right way; walk with small steps 蹟
tyàwk	1. to pity, condole 弔		
	2. bullseye in a target 的		3. spine 脊
tyàwks	to fish 釣	tzèk	1. twist, spin 績
tza	1. plenty, many 且		2. achieve merit; meritorious deed 績
	2. dull, slow, unskilful 怚	tzek-reng, tzek-rèng	a bird, perhaps pied wagtail 脊令, 鶺鴒
	3. a closing particle, verbal exclamation mark 且		

tzeks	to stack or store 積			2. jujube 棗
tzèms	err, error; falsehood; disorder 僭		tzoun	follow a route 遵
tzeng	pennon, banner, feather flag 旌		tzòun	a vase-like 'zun' wine vessel 尊
tzèng	luxuriant, bushy 菁		tzòung	clan, ancestral temple; to honour ancestors, as in the temple 宗
tzent	to clip 翦		tzòunt	chat 噂
tzi	1. alas! 咨		tzout	finish; utterly 卒
	2. consult 咨		tzouts	drunk 醉
	3. resources, supplies 資		tzu	1. this 茲
	4. sacrificial grain ○			2. diligent 孜
tzì	1. ascend; steep 躋			3. burden 仔
	2. rainbow; rising vapour 隮			4. small tripod 鼒
tzic	1. million 秭		tzù	1. begin 哉
	2. elder sister 姊			2. disaster 災, 烖
tzìc	1. numerous 濟			3. verbal exclamation mark 哉
	2. fine-looking, dignified 濟		tzuc	1. son, young man; young lady; a polite "you"; (occasionally) I, me; N tzuc, Sir N; Tzuc, Tzuc-ka, clan names (Zi, Ziche) 子; 子車
Tzìc	Ji, one of the four former great rivers of China 濟			
Tzins	Jin, a state 晉			2. hoe earth round plants 秄
tzins	approach, enter, send forward 進			3. Chinese catalpa 梓
tzint	cut off 戩		tzùc	attendant, steward, minister 宰
tzìs	ford; cross a stream 濟		tzuk	broomcorn millet, *Panicum miliaceum* 稷
tzit	go to 即		tzùk	1. *A tzùk B*: if/when A then B 則
tzìt	joint in bamboo and other plants 節			2. a rule, pattern; follow a pattern 則
tziw	fragrant; *tziw, tziw-rìw*, pepper plant 椒; 椒聊		tzums	overflow 浸
tziwc	wine, or other alcoholic drink 酒		tzùng	1. increase, numerous 增
tziwk	to press, harass; reduced to extremes 蹙			2. add; late, remote; *tzùng sòun*, "remote grandson": descendant 曾; 曾孫
tzo	enquire, consult 諏			3. hate 憎
tzòc	run, hurry 走			4. a grammar word introducing a clause or equivalent to *tzùk*, q.v. 曾
tzok	1. enough 足			
	2. foot 足		tzùns	set forth, present 薦
tzong	longways 從		tzup	growing plants 蓺
tzòng	1. come, come forward, arrive 倓		tzùs	1. to start; after this; consequently 載
	2. piglet 豵			2. carry; convey or be conveyed on wheels; fill; achieve 載
tzongs	let loose, indulge; admittedly 縱			
tzònk	bind together 總			3. an item; *tzùs A, tzùs B*, on one hand A, on the other B 載
tzònt	continue, succeed to 纘			
tzòs	perform; display, press forward 奏		tzyawk	1. nobility, dignity, rank 爵
tzòu	meet with 遭			2. a three-legged 'jue' goblet 爵
tzòuc	1. early in the day 蚤			

	3. sparrow 雀	ùy	lament; *ùy, ùy-tzù*, woe! 哀; 哀哉
tzyouns	1. eminent, talented, great; make great; prolong 俊	uys	wear 衣
	2. quickly 駿	wa	at; go to 于
	3. overseer, inspector of fields; to rule 畯	wà	flower 華
		wac	1. rain 雨
u-hu	shout of joy or fear 嗚		2. feathers, wing 羽
uk	1. oh!; an opening particle; but 抑		3. eaves, or area below eaves; hence cover, protect; territory 宇
	2. full, overflowing 溢	Wac	Yu, mythical founder of the first Chinese dynasty 禹
	3. increase 益	wàk	succeed, catch, hit the mark 獲
	4. repress; careful, attentive 抑	wam	blaze, blazing 炎
	5. 100,000; a very large number 億	wan	1. there, then; go there; a grammar word 爰
uks	think; idea 意		2. dragging slowly 爰
um	1. drink 飲		3. raise; ladder 援
	2. sound, music, message, reputation 音		4. wall 垣
	3. shady; the Yin of Yin v. Yang 陰		5. garden 園
ums	1. to shelter 陰	wàn	pillar; warlike in appearance 桓
	2. give to drink 飲	wàn-ràn	rough-potato plant (see Ode 60) 芄蘭
un	1. grieved 慇	wang	king; to have audience with the king 王
	2. great, many; *Un*, the dynasty which preceded *Tiw* 殷	wàng	1. almighty, splendid; regard as splendid, revere; later used for "emperor"; *Wàng*, a stream; *Wàng-pac* (Huang-fu), a chief minister 皇; 皇父
ùn	kindness, favour, love 恩		2. brilliant 煌
ung	1. receive 膺		3. to correct, regulate 皇
	2. breast; breastplate; "to breast", i.e. withstand 膺		4. skewbald 皇
	3. eagle 鷹		5. leisure 遑
ungs	answer, respond; small "answering" drum; *Ungs* (Ying), a state; *ungs mùn*, inner gate to palace 應; 應門	wank	go towards 往
unt	1. conceal 隱	wans	keep far from, leave 遠
	2. thunder 殷	want	far 遠
up	1. ladle out 挹	wap	1. shine, gleam 煇
	2. to bow, salute 揖		2. carry food out to workers 饁
	3. city, town 邑	was	to rain 雨
ùts	to love; to grudge 愛	wat	1. verbal "open inverted commas" 曰
uy	1. luxuriant, ample; to make ample 依		2. because; what about? 曰
	2. lean on, accord with; firmly settled 依		3. transgress, deviate; take beyond; proclaim 越
	3. garment; *uy-buk, uy-dang*, clothes 衣; 衣服, 衣裳		4. type of axe 鉞

wat, wat-luc	and; a grammar word 越, 越以		wrank	eternal 永
waw	a small bird, possibly owl 鴞		wreng	a kind of gemstone 瑩
way	do, make, act as, be; there is, there are 為		wri	curtain 帷
			Wruc	Wei, a river of Henan 洧
wày	1. harmony, harmonious, peaceful; blend, make proportions correct 和		wruc	switchtail 鮪
	2. bell attached to carriage 和		wrunt	fall down, drop, throw down 隕
	3. growing grain 禾		wruts	place of honour 位
ways	on behalf of, for 為		wu	fault, blame, excess 尤, 訧
wàys	respond in singing, attune 和		wuc	1. have, there is/are; rich; *wuc X*, very X; *Wuc N*, the Domain of N, Lord of N, House of N; *wuc na X*, (I swear) by X! 有; 有如 X
wè	take by the hand 攜			
wek	work, serve; military service 役			2. right (hand) 右
wen	round, a circle 員, 圓			3. friend 友
wèn	1. turn round, return 還		wuc-wic	call of hen pheasant 有鷕
	2. a ring 環		wuk	1. boundary; graveyard 域
weng	1. to plan, demarcate 營			2. fishing net 罭
	2. buzz about 營			3. water-demon 蜮
wenk	point of ear of grain 穎			4. oak 棫
wens	1. a belle 媛		wùk	someone, something, perhaps 或
	2. courtyard wall; *Wens* (Yuan), a state 阮		wuks	park, garden 囿
			wum	black bear 熊
went	to crawl, as an insect 蜎		wun	1. numerous, much 云
wets	to guard; *Wets* (Wei), a state 衛			2. say; oracle 云
wi	1. is 維			3. to weed 耘
	2. only, is only 唯, 維			4. cloud; *Wun Hàns*, "Han River in the clouds": the Milky Way 雲; 雲漢
	3. think 惟			
	4. reject, leave behind, leave over, remain 遺			5. a grammar word 云, 員
			wung	male animal or (particularly) bird 雄
	5. tie, bind together 維		wuns	1. rich, ample (of flowers) 芸
Wì	Huai, a river of eastern China 淮			2. brightness 煇
win	clear land for cultivation 昀		wunt	richly ornamented 苑
wint	straight, true, regular; *Wint* (Yin), a clan name 尹		wup	gleaming 熠
			wus	1. also; repeat 又
wit	1. then, thereupon; a grammar word 迺			2. large-minded 宥
	2. black horse with white legs (?) 驈		wus X	to "right-hand" X: to help X, esteem X, encourage X to drink 右, 佑, 侑
	3. rapid flight 欥			
wìt	hole, pit 穴		wuts	1. numerous 彙
wìts	kindly; obedient 惠			2. say 謂
wrangs	1. wade 泳		Wuts	the river Wei, which meets the Yellow River at its eastward bend 渭
	2. long-drawn-out chant 詠			

wuy	1. go away, go against, deviate from 違	yon	black kite 鳶
	2. go opposite ways; *Wuy* (Wei), a state 韋	you	1. as, like; still, yet 猶
	3. encircle, a circuit 圍		2. light (in weight); a light carriage 輶
wùy	1. revolve, deviate; *wùy-wit*, awry, perverse 回; 回遹		3. proceed from; follow; from 由
	2. go against the current 洄		4. to long for; long-brooding; long-trailing; far away 悠
wuyc	1. blaze; bright 煒		5. flow 滺
	2. brilliant, of flowers 韡		6. float, swim; wander about, ramble; an amusement, leisure; *you rong*, "floating dragon": *Persicaria amphibia* 游, 遊; 游龍
	3. reed 葦		
wwà	dirty; untidy; to soak 汙, 污		7. plan 猶, 猷
wwen	dissatisfied, grieved 悁		8. a place; the place where; passive marker: *you* Verb, that which is Verbed 攸
wweng	to wind, twine round 縈		
wwìn	1. abyss, deep; deep note 淵	youc	1. a 'you' wine pot 卣
	2. drumbeat 咽		2. weeds, useless, damaging 莠
		yount	to trust, sincere, truly; *Yount* (Yun), a personal name 允
ya	awry, deflected, depraved 邪	yous	1. tall (of cereal plants) 褎
yak	1. also; and yet; but; a grammar word 亦		2. to store firewood 槱
	2. great 奕		3. full dress, with long sleeves 褎
yams	lovely 豔	yuk	1. respectful, reverent; orderly, well-trained 翼
yang	1. vast, voluminous flow of water 洋		
	2. sheep, goat 羊		2. wing, hence shelter; to assist 翼
	3. disease 痒	yyaw	1. waist, waistband 要
yangs	1. long 羕		2. milkwort 葽
	2. suffering; grieved 恙		3. sound made by insects 喓
Yangs	Yang, a place name 向	yyawk	bind 約
yank	nourish, rear 養		
yant	overflow; abundant; go to excess, be extravagant 衍		
yas	night 夜		
yaw	1. meet; a rendezvous 要		
	2. sing 謠		
	3. shake, be shaken, agitated 搖		
	4. a precious stone, perhaps jasper 瑤		
yawk	1. medicine; to cure 藥		
	2. the summer sacrifice 禴		
	3. flute, pan-pipes 籥		
yoc	1. a catalpa species, perhaps Manchurian catalpa 楰		
	2. open-air stack of grain 庚		